The Tender Passion

Books by Peter Gay

Freud for Historians (1985)

The Bourgeois Experience: Victoria to Freud
Volume I   The Education of the Senses (1984)

Freud, Jews and Other Germans:
Masters and Victims in Modernist Culture (1978)

Art and Act: On Causes in History—Manet, Gropius, Mondrian (1976)

Style in History (1974)

Modern Europe (1973), with R. K. Webb

The Bridge of Criticism: Dialogues on the Enlightenment (1970)

The Enlightenment: An Interpretation, volume II,
The Science of Freedom (1969)

Weimar Culture: The Outsider as Insider (1968)

A Loss of Mastery: Puritan Historians in Colonial America (1966)

The Enlightenment: An Interpretation, volume I,
The Rise of Modern Paganism (1966)

The Party of Humanity: Essays in the French Enlightenment (1964)

Voltaire's Politics: The Poet as Realist (1959)

The Dilemma of Democratic Socialism:
Eduard Bernstein's Challenge to Marx (1952)

The Bourgeois Experience

VICTORIA TO FREUD

VOLUME II

The Tender Passion

PETER GAY

New York   OXFORD UNIVERSITY PRESS   Oxford
1986

Oxford University Press

Oxford   New York   Toronto
Delhi   Bombay   Calcutta   Madras   Karachi
Petaling Jaya   Singapore   Hong Kong   Tokyo
Nairobi   Dar es Salaam   Cape Town
Melbourne   Auckland

and associated companies in
Beirut   Berlin   Ibadan   Nicosia

Copyright © 1986 by Peter Gay

Published by Oxford University Press, Inc.,
200 Madison Avenue, New York, New York 10016

Oxford is a registered trademark of Oxford University Press

Library of Congress Cataloging-in-Publication Data
(Revised for vol. 2)
Gay, Peter, 1923–
The Bourgeois experience.
Includes bibliographies and indexes.
Contents: v. 1. Education of the senses—
v. 2. The tender passion.
1. Middle classes—Europe—History—19th century.
2. Middle classes—United States—History—19th century.
3. Sex customs—Europe—History—19th century.
4. Sex customs—United States—History—19th century.
5. Sex (Psychology)   6. Love.   7. Psychoanalysis and
culture.   I. Title.
HT690.E73G39   1984   306.7'094   83-8187
ISBN 0-19-503352-3 (v. 1)
ISBN 0-19-503741-3 (v. 2)

Printing (last digit): 9 8 7 6 5 4 3 2 1

Printed in the United States of America
on acid free paper

TO
JULIE BOLTIN
WITH LOVE

Contents

The illustrations will be found after pp. 172 and 332.

It is awful work, this love. . . .
Byron to Thomas Moore, 1821

Love—maternal or sexual, it's all the same. . . .
Tchaikovsky to
Vladimir Vasilievich Stasov, 1877

Je voudrais enfin qu'en hermaphrodite nouveau tu me donnasses avec ton corps toutes les joies de la chair et avec ton esprit toutes celles de l'âme.
Flaubert to Louise Colet,
September 28, 1846

Abbreviations

BL	British Library
DPT	David Peck Todd Papers
FB	Family Beneke
G.W.	Sigmund Freud, *Gesammelte Werke*, ed. Anna Freud et al., 18 vols. (1940–68)
Int. J. Psycho-Anal.	*International Journal of Psycho-Analysis*
J. Amer. Psychoanal. Assn.	*Journal of the American Psychoanalytic Association*
MLT	Mabel Loomis Todd Papers
PQ	*Psychoanalytic Quarterly*
PSC	*Psychoanalytic Study of the Child*
S.E.	Sigmund Freud, *Standard Edition of the Complete Psychological Works*, tr. and ed. James Strachey et al., 24 vols. (1953–74)
St. A.	Sigmund Freud, *Studienausgabe*, ed. Alexander Mitscherlich et al., 11 vols. (1969–75)
Stabi	Staatsbibliothek
Y-MA	Yale University Library, Manuscript and Archives

The Tender Passion

BOURGEOIS EXPERIENCES, II

⬚

Counterpoint

The nineteenth-century bourgeois experience of love was both stylized and spontaneous. Efficient middle-class institutions all the way from the adroitly orchestrated dinner party to the cool treaty between mercantile clans fostered suitable unions. They could not keep the impressionable from falling in love, but they could make sure that young men and women encountered few except eligible partners. If one refused to marry for money or good family, it became proverbial that one might be persuaded to go where money or good family could be predicted. Acceptable paths to love were plainly marked and heavily guarded; the penalties annexed to misalliances threatened or consummated—social ostracism, transfer to remote posts, legacies withheld—were extremely harsh. But their very severity speaks to the urgency of the temptations. The clashes of social styles, pressures of temperament, neurotic inhibitions or proclivities, the anarchic charm of infatuation, made for variety in patterns of respectable love, sometimes for surprises. They provided generous space for amorous motives less calculating than material advantage or social ascent. Impulse increasingly won out over defense.

The eternal, interminable contest between freedom and control is the critical issue in all civilization, not least in love. In the age of Victoria perhaps more than any other, the boundaries between erotic expressiveness and reserve were shifting, problematic, almost impossible to map with any sense of finality. The old paternalistic order was crumbling, most visibly among the middling classes in Western Europe and the United States, while the reign of the young had not yet dawned. In this increasingly opaque, anxiety-provoking situation, it was only rational for

3

the bourgeoisie to develop an almost desperate commitment to privacy and to mount a largely sincere, only partly conscious search for refined variants of earthy desires. This gives psychoanalysis its opportunity to assist the historian intent on discovering the farther reaches of love behind the smoke screens thrown up by purposeful propriety, diligent self-censorship, and tense moral preoccupations. It is a central point of this volume, as it was of its predecessor, that it would be a gross misreading of the bourgeois experience to think that nineteenth-century bourgeois did not know, or did not practice, or did not enjoy what they did not discuss. What holds true for sexuality holds true all the more for the love of one adult for another which is, whatever else it might be, something more than mere lust.

While aggressive anti-Victorians have tried to make the world believe the opposite, much middle-class love was out in the open, in fervent letters and heedless actions. But far more of it requires the programmatic suspicion of manifest surfaces that lies at the heart of Freud's investigative technique. Nineteenth-century bourgeois love all too often paraded in genteel artistic or literary disguises, in incomprehensible dreams and unintended confessions—all of which cry out for the kind of deep archeological reading psychoanalysis specializes in. This is not to deny that psychoanalysis is primarily the psychology of the individual. It has social dimensions, generally underrated and far from wholly explored. But its proper object of study—of its systematic voyeurism—is the single, unduplicable person. We all know that a historical epoch, like a historical event, is a set of possibilities realized in the expanse of space and the flux of time, and that every actor—and actress—in the human drama, whether principal performer or simple spear carrier, is prompted to read assigned parts through the haze of character, economic fortunes, and regional or social identifications. Yet, since everyone belongs to a class with certain predictable styles of thought and conduct, and shares with all humans essential passions and defenses, the portraits that the psychoanalytically informed historian may draw of individuals can throw welcome new light on their class and their time.

These were my thoughts as I wrote the two true love stories that serve as the overture to this volume. Each of these lovers, Walter Bagehot and Otto Beneke, was unique. But each, like the rest of the species, had to contend with the unconscious domains of his mind, underwent the developmental stages of the sexual drive beginning in infancy and marked forever by the oedipal experience, sensed anxiety as a signal of danger from the self or the world, and constructed a panoply of adaptive devices. Hence, though in different ways, Bagehot and Beneke are representative men. They remain individuals, and the individual, as one cannot insist too much, is the sole center of experience. But together, they dramatize some of the careers in love open to the middle class in the decades of Victoria and beyond.

1. The Real Thing

Around the first of November, 1841, Otto Beneke met Marietta Banks at her parents' house. He was twenty-nine, an educated and eligible bachelor with a law degree, and employed in the public archives of Hamburg, his native city-state; she was, at eighteen, just entering society, which is to say the marriage market, the charming, shy, and sensible offspring of a distinguished local family. Hers was a patrician house, with English roots and Italian connections. Two or three days later, Beneke happened across Marietta Banks again on the Jungfernstieg, that lovely promenade fronting on the Alster inlet, designed for strolling and shopping and much favored by Hamburg's *Bürger* as a setting for innocent flirtations. Her friendly greeting, "by no means so terribly proud, severe, cold, icy as recently in her father's house," gave him unsuspected pleasure. A day or two after that, Otto Beneke began to compile a meticulous record of his meetings with Marietta Banks; he noted down her conversation, her gestures, her look, her tone of voice and her silences, and explored the meaning of her responses to his words, his letters, his presents. I know of no document that can rival this journal for morbid minuteness in tracing the vicissitudes of nineteenth-century bourgeois love from its very inception. For beyond a doubt, from his first meeting with Marietta Banks, Otto Beneke was irrevocably in love; this, he knew, was the real thing. His erotic Odyssey was over, his erotic aim determined—though far from reached.

Other girls were suddenly as nothing to him. "God knows what is the matter with me"—these are the words with which he opens his accounting which would, in the course of four years, fill two substantial little boxes. "My thoughts, which at other times fly to Susette whenever they are unencumbered, steadily lose their way to her and always end up with Mariette, feeling themselves magnetically attracted." Beneke could not recall the moment when her magnetism had begun to work. "Either M. has enchanted me or I was before, bewitched by Susette, under Susette's charm." This vocabulary, borrowed from the domain of the uncanny, permitted him to present himself as a passive plaything of forces he could not control, not even fathom. "Now, suddenly," so he dismissed Susette, "her magic is feebly failing." The journal he would keep from then on, probing and self-lacerating, circled entirely around Marietta Banks; it is just another illustration of Shakespeare's observation, trite by Otto Beneke's time, that the course of true love never did run smooth.[1]

But there were those for whom it did—more or less. On January 24, 1857, Walter Bagehot met Eliza Wilson. The parallels between his amorous experience and that of Otto Beneke are striking, until they diverge to make a vivid and instructive counterpoint. Like Beneke, Bagehot was no longer in his first youth: he was thirty-one when he went to visit James Wilson, editor of the *Economist*, to discuss some possible contributions to his periodical. Thus, like Beneke, Bagehot found his future wife in her father's house. Like Beneke again, Bagehot conducted himself impeccably, in irreproachable bourgeois fashion: whatever his desires conscious or unconscious, he made no attempt on the virtue of Eliza Wilson any more than Beneke did on that of Marietta Banks. Finally, precisely like Otto Beneke, Walter Bagehot sensed his destiny without delay. Whatever his youthful flings, this was different. In an early literary essay, on Hartley Coleridge, which has striking autobiographical touches, he records that Coleridge's "love-affairs were hopeless."[2] Eliza Wilson represented hope to him. "It was Eliza's fate to be taken to dinner by Walter," her youngest sister, Emilie, would remember more than seven decades later. "If it was not love at first sight, it was distinctly a keen interest at first sight,"[3] a foundation of mutual attraction on which love could build. But for a single looming threat that in the end quickly evaporated, Walter Bagehot and Eliza Wilson encountered no encumbrances on their quest for consummation. Their experience in love, though it signally fails to fit the popular stereotypes of romantic travail on the one hand, or of commercial calculation on the other, proved as realistic a road to marriage in the nineteenth century as the turmoil that marked the courtship of Otto Beneke and Marietta Banks at every stage.

Otto Beneke's torments were wholly self-inflicted, but that made them no less troubling and all the more interesting. For a month or two, his campaign of conquest proceeded at the snail's pace he thought fitting to his strategy. This military language is his own; he liked to see himself as

1. Otto Beneke, November 7, 1841, Marietta Diary, F6, Family Beneke [FB], St. Ar. Hamburg. On January 20, 1858, Walter Bagehot actually quotes this all-too-familiar line from *A Midsummer Night's Dream* in a letter to his fiancée, Eliza Wilson. *The Love-Letters of Walter Bagehot and Eliza Wilson written from 10 November 1857 to 23 April 1858*, ed. Mrs. Russell Barrington (1933), 126.

2. "Hartley Coleridge" (1852), *The Collected Works of Walter Bagehot*, ed. Norman St. John-Stevas, 9 vols. so far (1965–   ), I, 170.

3. *Love-Letters*, "Introduction," 14.

a combatant crossing the treacherous mine field of love. He would speak of "skirmishes" and "advanced posts in action"—of *Plänkeleien* and *Vorpostengefechten*. Even when he does not resort to this martial vocabulary, his reports read like bulletins from general headquarters, enumerating feints employed, positions invested, and casualties suffered. Pacific as Marietta Banks was by temperament, Otto Beneke took her very attractions for him as an incitement to combat.[4]

The social style of the leading Hamburg families—bankers, merchants, prosperous attorneys—provided opportunities for tentative erotic rehearsals, and Beneke took them eagerly, at rounds of dinner dances or chamber music concerts in the spacious villas of affluent and settled families. They proved good occasions on which to snub Susette and to cultivate Marietta. Less than two weeks after he had first met "Mariette," he saw her again at a ball and maneuvered himself to secure the last dance before supper that he might take her in to table. He spoke to her a few times, but "principally I observed her." He would do much close observing in the months and years to come. The very next evening he noted that he had seen her once more at a recital, as usual in a private house. While he thought her looking "quite charming," he found the event laden with "impediments to the forwarding of my affair." An assertive lieutenant had kept Marietta "blockaded," and besides, the quartet music had exacted a most unproductive silence.[5]

From the beginning, the subtlety of Beneke's anxious voyeurism was projective far more than perceptive. In early November of 1841, he found that Marietta looked "really pretty, blooming, and sprightly," yet was "apparently constrained with me, though she concealed it very well and gracefully." Again, late that month, after he had taken her little brother to an equestrian show and was invited to stop by her house, he saw "Mariettinola" in the midst of her "highly eminent" family sewing, saying little, and blushing often. He fastened on her expressive coloration: "This tender blushing is one of her most charming characteristics; not merely does it look delightfully girlish, but it is also a tinted proof of the agitation of her soul, since she often blushes wholly without external cause."[6] Acting as many lovers will, he could not acknowledge, in his consistently self-denigrating mood, that *he* might be the external cause of her blushes. Placing every merit in Marietta Banks, he left none for himself. The psychological analysis he intensely pursued aided him not

4. See Otto Beneke, January 6, February 27, 1842, Marietta Diary.
5. November 12, 13, 1841, ibid.
6. November 12, 22, 1841, ibid.; see also December 19, 1841, and February 6, 1842.

to reach clarity about his situation but to deepen his sense of discourage-
ment. Beneke's style of courting leaves a distinct flavor of pervasive,
barely contained depression.

Plainly, Otto Beneke was obsessed with Marietta Banks. He would
ruminate about her at night, unable to sleep, devising plan after plan of
campaign. He would exquisitely torture her—and himself—with reproaches for her indifference, her mute reserve. Encountering both his
old flame and the new at a dance in December, he pointedly ignored
Susette, only dancing with her twice, for discretion's sake. "In contrast,
my inclination for Mariettinola blossomed more and more! And she was
really charming. God knows where my eyes have been all this while!"
He angrily taxed himself with having wasted his time and somberly
reflected that Marietta would not begin to trust him as long as Susette
maliciously gossiped to her. Recalling the evening, he listed eleven little
incidents and fleeting impressions just how his strategy was working. It
was, he was only too sure, working badly.[7]

Otto Beneke converted everything into stuff for interpretation. Later
that month, at yet another ball, Beneke extracted her birthdate—it was
November 7—and took the opportunity to scold Marietta Banks for her
apparent distrust: "that she so often did not know what to reply, I interpreted either as intention, mask—or as preoccupation, embarrassment,
particularly in my presence, since she knows I am observing her." She
was "so visibly constrained and embarrassed"—no wonder, the historian
might interject—that she could "barely bring out" any answers at all.
With a lover's masochism he entreated her to tell him what she disliked
about him, and after persistent nagging she obliged by gently objecting
to his "*Tourmacherei*," his willingness to appear captivated by several
girls at once. He thanked her, without conscious irony, for throwing him
these crumbs of confidence, apparently oblivious to the meaning of the
criticism he had extorted from her: it was a delicate invitation to be
captivated by one girl alone.[8]

Beneke's unrelieved pessimism appears as a psychological tactic only
justified by conflicts beyond the reach of his consciousness. At the beginning of 1842, an outspoken friend boldly encouraged him to marry
Marietta Banks. "The girl is devilishly fond of you, a blind man can see
that." In fact, the friend added, "promising, amiable fellow that you are,"
her parents would certainly welcome him. But Beneke chose to discount
this heartening slap on the back as a joke. To accuse Marietta Banks of

7. December 10, 15, 1841, ibid.
8. December 19, 1841, ibid.

perfidy, as he did more than once to her face, was to round out this pattern of persecution, for, objectively, his charges were ludicrous. But he pursued his policy, though it bewildered and dismayed her, regularly embroidered his grievances in his journal, and went on interpreting. In February 1842, Marietta Banks sent him a set of "prognostications" in English, an innocent though far from meaningless social game in which the participants made rhymes on their partner's future. As usual, Beneke examined every word with a magnifying glass, turning it over and over in search of disheartening clues. "And be not downcast, love shall favor thee," her prognostication concluded, "Heed not the rest et suis ta destinée!" Why lapse into French at the end? Beneke asked. What if, instead of writing the noncommittal "et," she had written the promising "je"?[9] He would not see that she was offering herself as his destiny, shyly as became a well-brought-up girl, but transparently to anyone but him.

When he was not tossing on his bed, brooding about her, Otto Beneke would dream of his Mariettinola. After a mere two weeks of acquaintance, he noted that he dreamt of her "very charmingly." A month later he recorded in more poignant language: "Again and again she stirs me inwardly to the very depths! Daily my thought, nightly my dream! In the daytime my thoughts fly to her, as iron to the magnet—at night I cannot sleep before the mass of images in which she appears as a queen"; when he did manage to drop off, he dreamt of her slender form walking with him on some romantic forest path. Two months after that he asked himself, after noting that he was dreaming of Marietta almost every night, whether she perhaps had ever dreamt of him.[10] The gloomy negative answer was implied in his question.

Even palpable gains did not appease him. Late in February 1842, just after he had speculated whether she ever dreamt of him, he recorded that "the word 'friendship' has now been found for us." But his wishes had outrun his successes. "A poor, patient word!" he commented and added, scarcely aware of what he was saying: "first virginal love" is as pure as "alpine air," so spiritual, so soulful that it "excludes everything terrestrial." Unconsciously, so exigent that in part they became conscious, Beneke's terrestrial passions were pushing him toward desires that virginal love could never gratify. In a diary he kept separately from the one devoted to Marietta Banks, he had already wondered the previous December: "What has been agitating me for some time now? An in-

9. January 2, February 6, 1842, ibid.
10. November 16, December 15, 1841, February 25, 1842, ibid.

expressibly ardent wish, an unspeakably deep longing—which I can scarcely confess to myself, since its aim is as unattainable as the stars, and which barely finds utterance in dreams every night." He added his characteristic ominous note, the ground tone of his wooing: "Like a man I struggle against it.—May God send me strength to renounce, since renunciation is necessary once again." Two months later he was at once more explicit and more discreet, unable to entrust his longing to his most private record: "Internally indescribably agitated—by the most extreme motives! But one predominates — — — — —."[11] Nothing could be more eloquent than those dashes.

It is easy to see what urge stirred him, and to name the young woman in whom he had concentrated it. Beneke's sensual frustration erupted into activity; all his "suppressed passionateness" found energetic sublimation in his dancing. He would run through the wildest tarantella until his "delicate, exhausted" partners were compelled to stop; one of them told him, with a shudder, that she felt "such a terrible passion streaming from you!" He half liked this tribute, half disowned it. After all, the "principal motive" that made him dance with such terrifying abandon was "so lovely, so rich, so magnificent," it made him so blissful, that he found it all the more painful to know that his ship must founder in very sight of the harbor.[12]

His unconscious was playing games with Otto Beneke, extorting avowals he did not recognize. Certainly their recipient was too well bred to appreciate their full gravity. As his campaign progressed, Beneke fell into the habit of sending Marietta Banks selected books—carefully noting in his journal all their titles and her reception of them. Early in 1842, he composed for her a detailed exegesis of *The Chessplayer*, an etching by the then well-known illustrator Moritz Retzsch. It depicts a thoughtful young man in a Gothic setting, head resting on his hand, playing chess with the devil. His satanic majesty is decked out in cap and feather and staring balefully at his appealing human opponent, while a sad-faced angel looks on. Satan's chessmen are little dragons, devils, seductive Eves, while white has chaste, cross-bearing figurines. In his wordy commentary, Beneke notes that the devil has the upper hand in the game, and then proceeds to interpret the scene, and its symbols, to "the thoughtful young spectator, be she," he adds coyly, "who she may, but I will assume she is one of those delicate, *noli-me-tangere* girlish souls of Hamburg, who

11. February 27, 1842, ibid.; December 20, 1841, February 20–28, 1842, Diary 1840–42, F6, FB; St. Ar. Hamburg.
12. February 20–28, 1842, Diary 1840–42.

withdraw shyly and timidly into themselves and into deep silence before every spiritual approach and the intrusion of strangers." The "thoughtful spectator" will see that the devil incorporates pleasure in wickedness, his king representing him at work, while his queen is "mankind's most powerful, most general motive for evil, the devil's most successful instrument of seduction: *sensual lust*, a beautiful, alluring, seductive female figure proffering the bowl of intoxication." Then Beneke ventures to improve on the original by giving the young man a chessman whom Retzsch has "irresponsibly overlooked: *honor*." And the watching guardian angel is *"Love*. Hence he must win!" For where *"honor* is on guard," and *"love* flutters around him," man is bound to emerge triumphant over the most satanic seductions.[13]

The moral of this fable is anodyne enough. Nor must one press it too hard, since Beneke's laborious presentation was nothing more than a suitor's attempt to ingratiate himself with a sensitive and sheltered young woman whom he thought skittish, inaccessible, fleeing from any hint of an advance. Moreover, his interpretation of Retzsch's set piece has a certain plausibility; to associate the devil with lust is anything but an original discovery with Beneke. But, even though his manifest lesson is that love is equivalent to self-restraint, his preoccupation with sensuality subverts this unexceptionable conclusion. Beneke "corrected" the *Schachspieler* by having purity win out over wickedness, but his deeper unacknowledged sympathies were with the devil; his ruminations run on that "most powerful, most general motive for evil," the libidinal desire for sexual gratification.

Beneke's conflicts had neurotic roots but cultural implications. The proper nineteenth-century bourgeois in search of a wife had first to establish himself in a profession or a trade before he could venture to propose marriage. "Chemistry," Freud wrote to his fiancée from his laboratory, "consists two thirds of waiting, life probably just as much." That was in the summer of 1882; a year later in their long engagement, he commented with mixed pride and regret on the "habit of continuous suppression of natural drives" characteristic of the educated middle classes.[14] Freud tasted the miseries of self-imposed sexual frustration, about which he was to theorize so authoritatively later, in his own faultlessly bourgeois life. So did Otto Beneke and thousands of other young men

13. His handwritten commentary bears the title "Schachspieler/ gezeichnet und radirt/ von/ Moritz Retzsch/ erläutert/ (nach Karl Borromäus von Miltitz)/ von/ Otto Beneke/ 1842/ für/ Fräulein Marietta Banks." F6, FB, St. Ar. Hamburg.

14. Freud to Martha Bernays, June 27, 1882, August 29, 1883, *Briefe 1873–1939*, ed. Ernst L. Freud (1960), 13, 49.

making their way in the world and following prescribed paths to the establishment of a household that would embody and perpetuate bourgeois values.

Yet with Beneke, this sexual impasse took particularly poignant forms. Most men in his position, including Walter Bagehot, chafed under their frustrations and acted as vigorously as they could to alleviate them. In the nineteenth century, the period of engagement was an intermediate stage that made certain familiarities permissible; this transitional phase in the education of the senses was far more pleasing though, at the same time, still more tormenting than the time of early amorous approaches.[15] But Otto Beneke seemed eager to fail rather than to secure his prize. Even in his dreams, he continued to address Marietta Banks in the formal mode, calling her *"Sie"* instead of the intimate and confident *"du."* Then in June 1842, he suffered the defeat he had unconsciously been waiting for: after Leonclair Gossler was named to the Hamburg senate, Otto Beneke's friends proposed him as Gossler's secretary, a post that would have put him into the inner circle of Hamburg's governing class. Gossler was a household name in Hamburg; officials, senators, *Bürgermeister* had been drawn from the family for generations and Beneke reluctantly agreed to apply, only to lose out against an older candidate by twelve votes to nine.

This, as he read the event, meant the end of his hopes. *"Mariette's possession,"* he noted in a moment of defiance, *"now or never!"* But he was all too certain that it would be never. For the next months, his journal swarms with outbursts of almost suicidal gloom. He describes himself as being "in the most desperate mood." In his thirtieth year, he has "missed" his way, "gambled away" his happiness. Now " 'agony,' 'torment' "—*Pein, Qual*—are words he has a right to employ in all seriousness. By mid-July he has concluded it to be his honorable duty "to renounce Mariette." He will not desert her abruptly, will not wound her by revealing his real reasons, but will hint at his predicament and gradually withdraw from her cherished presence. He cannot quite bring himself to give her up: "O! I believe if I opened my arms and said, 'Come, Mariette!' she would be mine in life and death," but then quickly rejects such fantasies: "Dreams of a fool!" Through the whole summer, he continues to rehearse these themes, alternately flagellating himself with the pathos of his resignation and congratulating himself on his capacity for self-denial.[16]

15. See Peter Gay, *The Bourgeois Experience: Victoria to Freud*, vol. I, *Education of the Senses* (1984), 80–81.

16. Otto Beneke, June 1–24, June 29, July 16, 1842, Marietta Diary.

The calculated coolness he felt obliged to affect was a mystery and a trial for Marietta Banks, who only wanted him to propose to her. In October 1842, after she had watched his self-display for some months with increasing agitation, she sent him a little note. "I ask you urgently for an explanation of your puzzling behavior, which has become perfectly inexplicable to me in the last few days." Her plea, far from delighting Otto Beneke or resolving his doubts, only became another incident in need of analysis. What could "the poor girl" mean? In any event, he remained convinced that to give her up was his only honorable course. He continued to dream of her, of his "golden child," his "poor girl," but persuaded that any thought of possessing her is nothing less than a "crime."[17] So he continued to see her, to send her books, only reducing the temperature of his wooing to freezing point.

In December 1843, as Beneke lost the next opportunity to be named "extraordinary Secretary to the Senate," he found his sad resolve strengthened. "Rejected for a second time, refused, rebuffed, whatever you want to call it," Beneke read this second failure as the finger of God sternly counseling renunciation. But a sensible and pleading letter from his Mariettinola puts a different light on his despair. She told him that she had discussed the matter with her father who believed, as she did, that he should not take this setback so tragically. A year more or less hardly matters in the life of a capable man like him, a man who is bound to make his way! Kindly, worldly-wise, greatly attached to his daughter, Edward Banks invited Otto Beneke to a little chat and asked him bluntly whether he loved Marietta. The conference somehow did not please Beneke, and no wonder: Marietta's father was threatening to deprive him of his only excuse for not marrying the girl he professed to love and dreamt of practically every night. But Beneke was not so easily caught. Had he got the post, he told his putative father-in-law, he would have asked for Marietta's hand. As it was, he could promise nothing. Yet Marietta would not let him go. Early in January 1844, during these agitated weeks, he had met her at a private concert and told her, tactlessly: "Really, this seeing one another is now more painful than not to see one another at all," but she demurred: "Oh no! just seeing is something—and better something than nothing." Then she added, and he faithfully recorded it, "suddenly, in the most imploring of tones, 'O please, please don't let it be all over.'" That very night, he dreamt of her in "the most vivid" way, of things he had never seen in his fantasies, "secret, sweet

17. Marietta Banks to Otto Beneke, October 10, 1842, F6, FB, St. Ar. Hamburg; Otto Beneke, January 1, 1843, Marietta Diary.

pictures of wooing," and awoke from his "blissful shudders of the wedding night."[18] Otto Beneke had no intention of terminating the affair—and no intention of consummating it. The pleasure he got from his pain was too great.

In reality, his situation was auspicious. He claimed to be clear in his mind about his desires; the girl he loved wanted nothing more than to be married to him. Although he had failed, in his early thirties, to obtain some prized patronage, his professional status was secure and his prospects for eventual promotion in the Hamburg archives bright. In May 1842—a signal catastrophe for which he found no room in his Marietta journal though it made an epoch in the city's history—a great fire devastated whole districts of Hamburg, inflicting grievous losses. The dismayed citizenry had witnessed ineffective fire-fighting, widespread panic, and ugly incidences of looting, and Hamburg's archives suffered severe damage in the conflagration. Beneke, though he modestly did not say so, had heroically labored to rescue what could be rescued and restore what must be restored; and his activity beyond the call of duty could not have escaped the attention of his future father-in-law, who, as an influential Syndic, prominently superintended the recovery of his city after the fire. Nor did differences in rank or family lineage offer the slightest impediments to his aspiring to the hand of Marietta Beata Banks: the most acute of snobs must have found Dr. Otto Beneke eminently suitable. Beneke, after all, came from a solidly respected family: his father, like Otto Beneke a lawyer who did not practice, had married into a distinguished Hamburg family and spent his mature years in the public service on powerful government committees, exercising his notable tact to reconcile the claims of rivalrous public bodies almost bound to clash in Hamburg's complicated constitution. In fact, after two years of self-sabotaging courtship, Otto Beneke began to suspect that he was largely responsible for his misery: he confided to his journal that he must have wanted this "non-election, for otherwise I would have been elected."[19] It dawned on him that the fault was in himself, not in the stars he liked to accuse, that he was still an underling—and a bachelor.

Walter Bagehot, too, had a secret fault, or thought he did, that might keep him from marrying. Born in 1826 at Langport in Somerset, the son of a prosperous and intelligent banker who loved and pushed his son, he proved to be a clever, somewhat precocious boy whose record at school,

18. December 22, 27, 1843, January 6, 10, 1844, ibid.
19. December 27, 1843, ibid.

t Bristol College, and, later, at University College, London, gave promise
f a brilliant future. But in 1852 he abandoned London and the prospects
f a legal career for Langport, where he joined his father's bank. He was
eginning to acquire a reputation as an original, controversial political
ublicist and as an expansive, thoughtful literary reviewer for the journals.
'et, while he enjoyed a wide acquaintance among talented contempo-
aries, his reserve was impenetrable. Some seven years before he left
London, Richard Holt Hutton, his closest friend, later to become a
rominent editor and journalist, gently reproached Bagehot for drawing
he circle of his affections so tightly about himself. "I wish you had more
nterests around you, not merely of intellect but of feeling, which are
vith you too much limited to the exclusive interests of home." Hutton
;ladly acknowledged that Bagehot was capable of friendship; certainly
Walter Bagehot was good company, high-spirited much of the time,
vitty always. But this, Hutton shrewdly perceived, was only Bagehot's
ocial surface. "I wish you had not simply more friends but more attach-
nents." Bagehot knew this only too well; he knew that his mordant and
urprising wit was not just a bubbling up of vitality but also a defense.
"Sauciness is my particular line," he would write to Eliza Wilson later. "I
m always rude to everybody I respect."[20]

As his biographers have noted, Walter Bagehot had several good reasons
or quitting the bar, but his principal impulsion was his mother, amusing,
:nergetic, loving, and intermittently psychotic. It was her episodes of
nsanity, more than anything else, that made for her son's reserve and
he barely suppressed isolating melancholy that Hutton had so regretted.
"Every trouble in life," Bagehot once said, "is a joke compared to mad-
1ess." Having watched it, sympathetically and at close range, he knew
vhat he was saying. When his mother was in one of her manic fits, he,
1er treasured, only surviving son, was singularly able to soothe her. He
1ad learned the rhythms of her attacks.[21] We can only conjecture how
nuch it cost Walter Bagehot to master the calm and clinical tone he
1sed to describe her condition.

Doubtless, Mrs. Bagehot found the hovering devotion of her son one of
he rewards of her madness. She gently prodded him to appreciate the
:harms of her husband's banking business to get him to come home, and
einforced her claims on his affectionate attention by her sprightly, un-

---

20. Hutton to Bagehot, December 10, 1845, Mrs. Russell Barrington, *The Life of
Walter Bagehot* (1914), 67–68, and see St. John-Stevas, "Walter Bagehot: A Short
Biography," Bagehot, *Works*, I, 36; Bagehot to Eliza Wilson, November 22, 1857,
Love-Letters, 35. See below, p. 33.
21. Barrington, *Life*, 66; *Love-Letters*, 75.

predictable turn of phrase, her disinterested desire to see him married
and her manifest concern for his career. No wonder he could not find
anything but boredom in the "stupid" local balls he attended and among
"all the little blue and pink girls, so like each other." The hold of an
original, vivacious, pretty, and pathetically needy mother was hard to
break. It was, in fact, even harder to break than Bagehot wholly recognized. His sentiments of pity and tenderness, his feeling indispensable and
very much loved, were somewhat pathetic pleasures. But, beyond that
Bagehot was bound to his mother by the largely unconscious conviction
common among children of suffering parents, that he bore some responsibility for her harrowing episodes.

> The highest spirits deepest sorrows claim,
>   The noblest destinies are tinged with fear;

he wrote in an early sonnet disagreeing with his friend Hutton's postulating a "causeless melancholy":

> No pain is causeless; o'er God's mightiest
>   sons
> Two angels Grief and Guilt divide their
>   sway.

His grief, his capacity to empathize with his mother kept Bagehot's sense
of guilt from paralyzing him with the burden of his unmitigated wickedness; his guilt complicated his outpouring of sympathy. "The most terrible
punishment of sin which God has inscribed on our nature," he wrote in
his first published essay, sounding like a man speaking from personal
experience, is "in the sin itself." Penance brings no relief, remorse no
comfort, for punishment is internal. "The first of sinners is the overseer of
their prison house." One of his much-quoted epigrams suggests that at
times he rebelled against his fate as his mother's favorite, and then converted his rebellion into wit. One day, when his mother once again im-
portuned him to get married, he evaded her benevolent meddling by
telling her, "A man's mother is his misfortune, but his wife is his fault."
Bagehot lacked the technical vocabulary to give a psychological account
of his fundamental ambivalence, but had the perceptiveness to express it
obliquely in poetry and apophthegm. Its unresolved subterranean exist-

22. "Blue and pink girls": Alastair Buchan, *The Spare Chancellor: The Life of
Walter Bagehot* (1959), 93; "The highest spirits": St. John-Stevas, "Short Biography,"
Bagehot, *Works*, I, 49n; "The most terrible punishment": "Festus" (1847), ibid.,
117–18; "A man's mother," ibid., 82.

ice imposed on him that latent depression and that self-protective dis-
ince from others which Hutton had observed and deplored.

Yet, like his mother, Walter Bagehot found some indirect, sometimes
istressing dividends in her travail. Her episodes of elation, dejection,
id delusion honed his sensitivity to human irrationality, to the devious
ictics of the unacknowledged motive. Rationalists, he came to believe,
iiss the "unconscious exuberance of inexplicable and unforeseen beauties,"
id the ultimate meaning of religion, which "has its essence in awe, its
harms in infinity, its sanction in dread." In self-proclaimed contrast to
iese thinkers, who are tone-deaf to the music of the universe, Bagehot
iought he had an *"ear* for much of religion," and was determined to face
ie beauty and the terror of unreason. The literary and biographical essays
e wrote during the mid-1850s, when he lived at home and worked as a
ountry banker, repeatedly and delicately skirt the hidden theme that
arkened his life. He wrote with imaginative fellow-feeling about William
owper, the poet of homely English country life who had endured long
retches of insanity; he sprinkled reflections on the mysteries of mind
irough his writings. There were, he noted, "clear, precise, discriminat-
ig" intellects who shrank "at once from the symbolic, the unbounded,
ie indefinite." But "the misfortune is that mysticism is true." Drawing
ie thinnest possible veil over his personal interest in the matter, he
orried in print about the possible dangers that his mother's condition
iight pose to his own sanity. In his essay on Hartley Coleridge, Samuel
aylor Coleridge's gifted and unworldly son, Bagehot wondered whether
ie younger Coleridge's "weakness" and susceptibility to "vice" might
ave been hereditary. He sensibly observed that one did not know enough
oout the father to speculate fruitfully about the son. But then he sternly
ided, as if to goad and to encourage himself, "though it be false and
iischievous to speak of hereditary vice, it is most true and wise to observe
ie mysterious fact of hereditary temptation."[23]

This is a remarkable statement, attesting to Bagehot's struggle between
ourage and fear. He lived in an age thoroughly persuaded that heredity
'as a significant, probably the most widespread, cause of insanity, and
e had a feebleminded half-brother, his mother's child from a previous
iarriage, to remind him of this medical commonplace. The eminent Dr.
ames Cowles Prichard, who was Bagehot's relative by marriage and
'hom he knew well, had insisted, in his famous *Treatise on Insanity*, that

23. "The First Edinburgh Reviewers" (1855), ibid., I, 319, 340, 339, 330; "Hartley
oleridge," ibid., 154.

"a certain peculiarity of natural temperament or habit of body is a nece
sary condition for the development of insanity." While this peculiarit
might be unique to the sufferer, it "is a fact too well established to adm
of doubt," that "the predisposition to insanity, when it has once arisen,
frequently transmitted." Bagehot was not disposed to push denial to th
point of disputing this established truth of modern science. After all, th
great Etienne Esquirol, to whom Prichard had dedicated his textboo
thought "heredity the predominant cause of madness." So did oth
experts of the day. "The fact is clear," Bagehot commented. "Tendenci
and temptations are transmitted even to the fourth generation both fo
good and for evil, both in those who serve God and in those who ser
Him not."[24] He left himself a margin for hope; a tendency was not
certainty.

Bagehot's controlled but persistent anxiety over madness was on
exacerbated by his sensual needs. These, too, emerge in his essays und
the legible guise of general comments on human nature. Hartley Coleridg
in whose constricted life he read aspects of his own, was required to "li
in an atmosphere of respect and affection," but with "the waywardne
of childhood without the innocency of its impulse," and, worst of a
"with the passions of manhood without the repressive vigour of a mar
will." It is plain that Walter Bagehot enlisted that repressive will in his ow
service. Love, after all, as he once defined it, is "the most pure and eag
of human passions." That was a prudent, somewhat self-deceptive way o
putting it. Certainly, love was the most eager of the passions, but he kne
that it was not always pure. "Temptation," he acknowledged in his essa
on Shelley, "is the mark of our life." Beyond a doubt, that temptatio
was sensuality. "Discipline," he thought, is "the order-book of the pa
sions," and he was visibly concerned whether he possessed enough disc
pline of his own to guide him through the swamps of sexual inducemen
Some years earlier, in a cryptic discussion with his friend Hutton o
celibacy, he had argued the "important principle" that "no man shou
begin to put down the disinterested part of his original nature, unle
he has thoroughly put down the selfish and the unnatural." He found
awful to contemplate, but thought it frequent that men, "after conquerir

24. Prichard: A Treatise on Insanity and Other Disorders Affecting the Mi
(1835), 157–58; Esquirol: Des Maladies mentales considerées sous les rapports médic
hygiénique et médico-légal, 2 vols. (1838), I, 64; Bagehot: "Hartley Coleridge," Wor
I, 154. In Esquirol's own establishment, 150 out of 264 mental patients suffered fro
hereditary insanity and, in the Salpêtrière, this cause was also by far the largest, 1
out of 466. Des maladies mentales, ibid.

the affections" only "succumb to the appetites." The "affections," he
added, "are the best aids in what may be called the inevitable sphere of
human action." Naturally, that sphere included marriage.[25] Until he was
over thirty, Bagehot was by no means sure that this union of affection
and appetite would ever be in his grasp.

Eliza Wilson was Bagehot's supreme opportunity. She was intelligent,
handsome, an impassioned and ambitious reader, an accomplished linguist,
thought just slightly frail and wholly unspoiled—a prize. Her German,
to judge from casual entries in her diary, was letter perfect and her
French fluent. To keep up with recent literature, she faithfully perused
the reviews in the *Spectator*. This was, in part, work, for she, like her
younger sister Julia, wrote reviews for her fathers' journal, *The Economist*.
Her household, complete with doting father, sociable mother, and five
agreeable younger sisters, abounded in good talk, informal picnics, and
lively dinner parties. The Wilsons, it seemed, met everybody: on a visit
to France in the winter of 1855, they encountered the "de Tourgenoffs,"
to say nothing of "Mr. Browning, the poet"; they visited Rosa Bonheur
and Ary Scheffer in their studios; they knew Dickens; they gave dinner
parties in which they included prominent politicians and novelists like
Bulwer-Lytton and Lady Eastlake.[26] Eliza's father was an interesting
personage: publisher, editor, member of Parliament, treasury official, an
enterprising man of business and a rewarding companion. The atmosphere
in his house made Eliza Wilson, if anything, more desirable still to Walter
Bagehot, who was used to affectionate, but far leaner domestic fare and
starved for companionship, playfulness, and sheer exuberance.

The Wilsons were not untouched by that modern disease, neurasthenia.
Mrs. Wilson often took to her room with violent headaches, sometimes
keeping herself invisible for two or three days. Her eldest daughter had
her own repeated attacks of headaches and eye-strain, and they recurred
in a suggestive pattern—normally just after her mother had gone to bed
with one of her painful episodes. It seemed as though the daughter was
competing for the attention of the father by adopting her mother's
symptoms.[27] On her father's fiftieth birthday—Eliza gave him a pair of

25. "Hartley Coleridge," *Works*, I, 153; "Percy Bysshe Shelley" (1856), ibid., 435,
446; Bagehot to Hutton, September 20, 1847, Barrington, *Life*, 168.
26. See Eliza Wilson, diary, December 28, 1855, January 16, 30, June 14, 1856. In
the possession of Norman St. John-Stevas.
27. As her terse notes show, at times Eliza Wilson succeeded with the opposite
tactic; when, on the day of a dinner party, her mother was incapacitated, she would
preside at table.

braided slippers that she and her sister Julia had worked for him—she
"did not go to church having a bad headache. Mama in bed all day." Yet
none of this kept her from gaiety and energetic party-going. "We were
very merry," reads one diary entry from Paris in the fall of 1855; "danced
all night," and "very merry all night" read two others.[28] Sometimes she
would stay in bed all day cosseting her headache only to emerge for a
dance in the evening and to come home after three in the morning.
Walter Bagehot enjoyed her liveliness and was not put off by her occasional ailments; he, too, had intermittent crippling headaches and accepted
her psychosomatic symptoms, like his own, as most nineteenth-century
bourgeois accepted them: with resignation, practically as a matter of
course.

Bagehot proved an instant success with all the Wilson family, more
even than Beneke had proved with the Bankses, and he went to see them
often, in their country house at Claverton near Bath, and at their place in
London. "My mother had told Walter," Eliza's youngest sister remembered many years later, "that when he came to London she would be glad
if he would pay us a call. He soon was in London—and he called: he was
asked to dinner—and he dined—eagerly snatching every opportunity of
again personally coming under the spell." He talked well, and not merely
to Mr. Wilson; from policy and for pleasure he democratically included
the whole household in his benevolent and amusing attention. He paid
long visits to the Wilson family, and at dinners, on weekends, during
expeditions to notable sights in the neighborhood pursued his goal. Unlike
Otto Beneke, he had no hesitations, or just one: his mother and the possible
threat of her madness to his own stability.

Yet, though purposeful, Walter Bagehot was not precipitous. He had
first met Eliza Wilson in late January 1857, but it was not, her sister
reports, "till the autumn" that "real love-making began," love-making of
the decorous Victorian kind: "walks on the terrace by moonlight, readings tête-à-tête of Walter's specially favourite poems, and close attendance
on Eliza and her donkey during those walks on the downs—the downs
where Gainsborough painted—Eliza not being strong enough to go far
on foot. On these occasions we would cannily watch Walter kicking
the donkey in order to secure Eliza alone." His pace, at least in the judgment of Eliza's youngest sisters, who watched the affair with approval
and fascination, was only too deliberate. There were resemblances, as I
have noted, between his and Otto Beneke's campaign: Walter Bagehot,

28. See ibid., November 29, 30, 1856, June 3, October 26, November 3, 4, 1855.

hough he knew what he wanted, was not wholly certain that he deserved
t. In contrast to Beneke, though, Bagehot was too confident to torment
imself for years. "Sept. 27," Eliza Wilson wrote in her diary for 1857.
'Sat in the conservatory where Mr. Bagehot told me his mother was
nad." It was a difficult moment for them both, but especially for "Mr.
Bagehot." Recalling this critical conversation two months later, he told
ner that "since the day in the conservatory, the feeling has been too eager
not to have a good deal of pain in it, and the tension of mind has really
been very great at times." Tactfully, Bagehot gave Eliza Wilson time to
digest the grave intelligence he had confided to her; it was only on
November 4, after earnest discussions with Eliza's father that he formally
proposed. She was deeply stirred, but hardly ambivalent. "Talked over
ny proposed marriage with mamma," she noted on November 5, "and
vent to bed at 9, but did not sleep till 3." The foregone conclusion came
wo days later: "Nov. 7th. Mr. Bagehot came at 10 for my answer. I was
n the dining room and engaged myself to him then and there."[29] The
ime had come for Mr. Bagehot to become Walter.

2. New Objects for Old

Love must come to terms with memories, mainly unconscious memories.
Childish attachments continue to assert their claims in the young adult as
ome favored intruder, some attractive stranger, seeks to supplant early
choices. "Papa quite ill," Eliza Wilson told her diary after James Wilson
nad to acknowledge that he must surrender his first daughter to another.
t is impossible for anyone to disregard this parental pressure, however
gentle. The finding of a love object, as Freud would put it succinctly in
905, is always a refinding. There are those who never undergo the great
experience of loving anyone other than mother or father; in the nine-
eenth century, this was the fate of some notable men and women, a fate
often masquerading as filial duty. Indeed, among those who venture into
he world to gratify their erotic needs, many discover that their loves
uncannily resemble the parent they thought they had outgrown. "A man
hall leave his father and his mother—according to the Biblical precept—
and cleave to his wife," Freud wrote in 1912. "Tenderness and sensuality
are then united." But that, as he knew better than anyone, was the ideal.
'A husband is, so to speak, never anything but a proxy, never the right
man," he noted rather sardonically some six years later, "another man has

29. *Love-Letters*, "Introduction," 16; Buchan, *Spare Chancellor*, 100–01.

the first claim to a woman's capacity for love, in typical cases the father he, at best, the second."[30] And what holds true for the husband, though Freud does not say so here, holds true for the wife. She, too, is partly substitute. In fact, those who intently, angrily choose a partner the dia metric opposite of their first love and first disappointment only display in their flight from home, its persistent claim on their emotions. The pull of early incestuous attachments is invisible, unacknowledged, and tenacious.

In his wrestling match with compulsive repetition in love, Walter Bagehot's seems at first glance far more difficult than the one Otto Beneke had to face. But, while Bagehot pushed briskly on, Beneke nearly succumbed. His mother's loving, perennially dutiful son, he was powerfully attached to her; among the three dates he would piously commemorate all his life was the day of his mother's death. Significantly, as he approached the climax of his strange quest for Marietta Banks, with nothing settled but the outcome virtually inescapable, he broke off his exhaustive record of his encounters, his dreams, and ruminations; his diary ends abruptly, without warning, in early April 1845, three and half years after Beneke had first met and quickly come to love his Mariettinola. It is as though he could not bear to witness his own success He had seen Marietta at a dance the day before, as so often, and hurt her feelings once again with his deliberate distance, and then instantly regretted his brutality: "If I only knew," he asked himself for the hundredth time, "what I should or should not do!" There is in the Beneke papers a poignant document showing what in fact he did. It is signed "Marietta," now Marietta Beneke long since. Her husband Otto had been physically, though not mentally, paralyzed by a stroke four years before and she had come upon his journal. "That love," she commented, "of which these pages report, has stood the test in good days and bad through forty years." She thought of burning them, "for the day is far spent, and soon there will be no one who will care to read them. And yet"—the historian is grateful—"the hand refuses to burn them. May others do it." But *should* anyone read them, let him know what happened after Otto Beneke had stopped writing. Late in April 1845, he had decided to go

30. "Papa quite ill": Eliza Wilson, Diary, November 2, 1857, ibid., 100; "Finding of an object": Freud, *Drei Abhandlungen zur Sexualtheorie*, St.A., V. 126, *Three Essays on the Theory of Sexuality*, S.E., VII, 222; "A man shall leave his father" Freud, "Über die allgemeinste Erniedrigung des Liebeslebens," St.A., V, 201, "On the Universal Tendency to Debasement in the Sphere of Love," S.E., XI, 181; "A husband is a proxy": Freud, "Das Tabu der Virginität," St.A., V, 223, "The Taboo of Virginity," S.E. XI, 203.

and see her adored father, "and take counsel with him what next." The engagement promptly followed, and the pair were married that October.[31]

In a second commentary on Otto Beneke's journal written fifteen years later, in 1900, nine years after her husband's death, Marietta Beneke ascribed the happy ending to both unconscious and conscious forces. "*Consciously*, my dear father recognized Otto's wish, and led Otto out of his bitterness with a soft, firm hand." If he had had other plans for Marietta, he dropped them as he witnessed her love for Otto, and came to value Otto Beneke more and more. And "*unconsciously*, it was my firm love for him, which did not allow itself to be shaken, that became the foundation of our life's happiness."[32] The combination was one that Otto Beneke, try as he might, could not resist.

Interesting, if rather predictable, as this denouement may have been, Marietta Beneke's appraisal of her husband's character is more interesting still. "While these papers contain truths," she commented, "still, a stranger must get a completely wrong impression of us both, since Otto persistently emphasized his intention to renounce me, an intention he had in his heart especially when, sitting at his desk, he would ponder the many obstacles obstructing his wishes. But it did not monopolize his dealings with me; it was neutralized by a love that could not deny itself"—a revealing formulation. Her own character, "since I was then a very young, quiet, shy and modest girl," seemed to her distorted in his account, as did that of others, whom Otto Beneke then saw through "misanthropic spectacles," giving every act, every word, the "worst, the blackest" interpretation. Often, reading his journal, Marietta Beneke would "think, smiling, 'Is that you? Was Otto like that?'" She fervently believed that their marriage had made their happiness, "a happiness for which we have always thanked God. But we did not perhaps always sense how sad our life would otherwise have been." She attributed to that marriage "the greatest transformation in Otto." In the years just preceding it, he was sometimes tempted, "by various tormenting worries," to "fall victim to bitterness," and to "lose his true nature," a nature she describes—a little astonishingly in view of what we have just read in Otto Beneke's private confessions—as "cheerful, gay, free of care." Once he was married, he found himself again, "and the gruff aspects of his temperament, his passionateness, melted away in our sunny, cheerful, quiet life."[33]

31. Otto Beneke, April 7, 1845, Marietta Journal; Marietta Beneke, commentary of April 12, 1885, enclosed with Marietta Journal.
32. Marietta Beneke, commentary of August 1900, enclosed with Marietta Journal.
33. Marietta Beneke, commentary of April 12, 1885.

Unquestionably, Otto Beneke's professional career prospered. He continued his steady pace in the Hamburg archives; in 1863, when Johann Martin Lappenberg, his distinguished chief, retired, Otto Beneke became his successor, and something of a force in Hamburg's political life. Even before, he had come to permit himself some ambitious plans. In the 1850s, delighted with the "old, venerable town" of Lübeck, with its clean streets and medieval houses, he cultivated a fantasy of becoming the archivist in charge of all the archives preserved in the Hansa cities of north Germany —"Gesamtarchivar"—and living somewhere near the Lübeck cathedral. Moreover, his domestic routine, to judge from his later, far less introspective diaries and annual celebrations of his wedding day, was relatively settled and peaceful. It was not without its obscure and ambivalent desires: early in 1849, after more than three years of a marriage that was to remain childless, he dreamt that he had "a charming little daughter," about two years old, sitting in her mother's lap and singing beautifully, a "musical prodigy" from birth. Later that year, he took the matter of generation into his own hands in an "absurd" dream, in which he found himself pregnant.[34] He ascribed both these dreams to physical impulses entirely: the first to the singing of his tame finch, the second to a full stomach. We may add unsatisfied wishes complicated by residual confusions about sexual identity. But these are the human lot; his wife was right to describe their married life as happy. Yet if, in her affectionate retrospect, Marietta Beneke gave proper weight to the beneficial impact of his marriage on his state of mind, she misread the nature of the problems that had kept Otto Beneke in suspense so long. Beneke's professional setbacks were not the cause of his depressed mood of resignation, but an excuse for his resistance to marriage.

Otto Beneke's dreams suggestively hint at his malaise, his difficulties in giving up his first love for a new one. He dreamt, as he noted with some astonishment, about Marietta Banks night after night, and such recurrent dreams are generally a sign of unfinished business, a reiterated effort to settle a persistent conflict; they exhibit the work still to be done and the resolution so ardently wished. Otto Beneke's dreams are of that type: they tell of encounters with a woman, are filled with desire, and exquisitely erotic in their symbolic machinery, yet they hint as much at the wish to fail as at the wish to succeed. In one of these, which he reports in the minutest detail, Beneke found himself on an excursion to a neighboring

---

34. See Renate Hauschild-Thiessen's note in *Zeitschrift des Vereins für Hamburgische Geschichte*, LX (1974), 239; Otto Beneke, January 28, March 16, 1849, Marietta Journal.

spot, realistically represented. Marietta Banks was there, with many others, and avoided being alone with him, clinging to her girl friends instead. Then nature intervened: a powerful and interminable downpour (which Beneke interpreted, in his dream, as a happy portent) scattered the company, and quite "unintentionally" Marietta Banks and Otto Beneke were thrown together, climbing a hill and finding shelter from the rain, pressed close, and silent. Neither of them wanted to begin speaking, and he felt "a great moment, that of decision, drawing near, and shrank from it." For, he comments, "love is timorous, shy, faint-hearted, cowardly." Self-confidence, to say nothing of arrogance, are wholly out of place at such a moment. But, reserved and fearful as they were, the pair were proud, too. "Neither wanted to confess to the other, 'I love you, I want to be yours, I cannot be without you, ever—I am *nothing* without you, my All!'" As evening fell, the two continued to stand together, in silence, pressed so closely that each could hear the other's heart beating. Finally, attempting to find their way home in the dark, but only getting more and more lost in the landscape, they came to a brook, with a small boat inviting them. He said to her, while the "double meaning" of his words chilled him all through, "'Will you follow me? Make your lot depend on mine? Will you step into the frail boat of my life?'" Without a word, she assented; he began to row and then let the boat drift down the swollen brook, as the rain kept dripping into the waters, making a "strange, sweetly deafening rushing noise." Water nymphs watched them and said, "Grasp your happiness." She remained sitting silently, with folded hands, and the boat shot forward "with the speed of an arrow." Suddenly, he looked up to find that they were speeding, not toward the familiar mill he had expected to see, but a gigantic and ominous machinery of gears and wheels; thirty wheels equipped with enormous shovels were turning rapidly and threatening to dash the couple to pieces. Desperately he tried to work his little boat out of the undertow, but in vain. She too looked up and comprehended her imminent demise; her look meant to say, "'Life would be so beautiful still!'" Now, as the thundering roar of the wheels stifled their words, he rose, "opened my arms to her, in silence,—she flew into them rejoicing, to my heart." To forget their mortal peril, to die together, "dissolved lovingly into one," gave death "a wonderful blissfulness." He pressed her firmly to his heart and found it an inexpressible joy to die in her embrace. From somewhere the words came, "'now comes death,'" the portentous meaning of the words underscored by a series of dashes—and he awoke. So powerful was the impress of his dream that for a moment Beneke thought he had died in *her* embrace until he became aware "that I was alone, that a phantom had rested in my arms, that now

bitter wakefulness followed the blissful dream."[35] The little death of
simultaneous orgasm after long, thrilling, and dangerous intercourse—the
beating hearts, the rushing rain, the accelerating boat, the devouring
machine, the tremendous climax, the mortal outcome—has never been
dreamt more vividly than this.

Another dream, which Otto Beneke recorded six weeks later, essentially
turned on the same theme: love desired and threatened. He was once again
in Wohldorf, that place for excursions and picnics, and Marietta was
there, too, this time with her Italian relatives. There was much cheerful
bustle, which left Beneke feeling very lonely. Among the crowd was "a
handsome Italian cousin, slender, tall, dark-eyed, with brown locks,
chivalrous, adroit, cheerful"—all the seductive qualities, we may conjecture, that Beneke thought he lacked and envied. This Italian rival "paid
much attention to his blond, slender cousin Marietta." She enjoyed
listening to him, and in the end preferred his company to that of all the
others, so that "outwardly, too, I was quite lonely." But he, Beneke,
continued to say not a word. He wore a white lily in his buttonhole, a
silent reproach to Marietta; she came to him and asked the meaning of
the flower. "I remained silent and only looked at her sharply." Then she
tore the flower from him, threw it into the water, and told him that from
then on, he must wear colored flowers. "After that, I wore a dark red
one,—and again she asked me: 'Now, what does *this* one mean?' Then
I said, 'It is the white flower which has grown so red in my heart's
blood!' "[36] These last few words, Beneke concludes, he said in his dream;
they woke him up and he heard them, as he spoke them, clearly and
slowly.

In the absence of Beneke's associations, these dreams will forever guard
some of their secrets. Moreover, some of his reporting is suspect: the
elevated diction in some passages suggests a certain literary bent that
belongs less to his dreams than to the aspirations of Beneke, the author.
Similarly his sententious comments—love is timorous, his double-edged
words to Marietta—may be elements in the dream, the neatening up of
the involved dream-story that Freud called secondary revision, or even a
later exegesis. But Beneke's vivid, enormously detailed dreams display some
salient features that provide access to his mind. They were, after all,
repetitive rehearsals of overwhelmingly important and hitherto unresolved

35. Otto Beneke, February 25, 1842, ibid.
36. Otto Beneke, April 5, 1842, ibid. For the "language of flowers," see Freud, *The Interpretation of Dreams, S.E.*, IV, 319–25.

reoccupations. Nor are the day's residues, the events and thoughts of
1e previous day that triggered his dreams of Marietta, particularly eso-
:ric: Wohldorf was a place that Beneke had often visited, and in her
ompany; he certainly saw her several times a week and thought of her,
bsessively, when he was alone. Marietta Banks was the instigator of his
reams, but she does not exhaust their meaning.

Some of that meaning, I have no doubt, enshrined desperately pressing
eeds and no less desperate inner discord. The sexual symbolism of the
rst dream is blatant; it exhibits a desire for physical consummation to
vhich a frustrated bachelor might well give expression in his night life.
`he erotic implications of the second dream are only marginally less
bvious. Beneke, jealous and depressed, wears a white lily, that universal
ymbol for purity, in his buttonhole "as a silent reproach"—a reproach
or her insistent virginity. It is Marietta herself who tears it from him
nd extorts from him the recognition of her as a woman of flesh and,
terally, of blood. We know that Beneke brought Marietta Banks flowers
nd then calibrated her responses in his diary. Her unassailable innocence
hallenged him to doubt whether he was indeed the man to deprive her of
. Yet here she was in his dreams, inviting him to do so, though, in her shy,
vell-brought-up way, by using the language of flowers—speaking *durch
ie Blume*, as the Germans say when they want to characterize an elliptical,
uphemistic, shamefaced communication.

The speeches in these dreams buttress this interpretation. Freud dis-
overed spoken words in dreams to be quotations from real speeches, or,
1 exceptional cases, from obsessional thoughts. Beneke had many times
vanted to tell Marietta that he loved her and had doubtless often rehearsed
he manner of his proposal if only he could find his voice. The eloquent
lences in his dreams—it is noteworthy how emphatic he is about her
ersistent refusal to speak—only underscore his despair at his indecisive-
ess and her timidity. Those impassioned words, "I love you, I want to
e yours, I cannot be without you, ever—I am *nothing* without you, my
All!" read like contributions from his daydreams.

As Otto Beneke's inconclusive courtship lumbered on, occasionally
liciting heartrending appeals from Marietta Banks, so did his dreams. In
ne of them, of February 1844, he was in a large company with Marietta
nd, after some rather tart exchanges, became engaged to her. A vicious
mp first insulted and later attacked him, leaving him with a painful
vound. While Marietta seemed only too pleased to nurse him, a physi-
ian declared the wound beyond cure. It was as if his bold approach to
natrimony, so desirable and so perilous, had put his very manhood at

risk. Two weeks later he gave his vacillation about marriage even mor
explicit symbolic form: he dreamt that he felt an oddly formed gold ring
on his finger, a ring which, having nothing to do with him, he would
take off over and over as it persisted in reappearing on his finger. At last
he threw it out of the window only to discover that Marietta, who was
present during the whole strange scene, was behind it all. He then fever
ishly searched for the ring everywhere and woke up, wondering if he
would ever find it again, consistent only in his inconsistency.[37]

In the course of 1844, Beneke's dreams became more and more candidl
carnal, the pressures of his amorous fantasies so keen as to mobilize all th
resources of the distorting dream work. In June, he dreamt he was in
church he did not know, with Marietta, listening to the sermon. Sh
would look at him "to see if he was still there, and what he might b
thinking." After the sermon, in the sacristy, as the pastor prepared t
examine him on the discourse he had just heard, Marietta whispered t
Beneke to remain unperturbed: she had listened carefully and woul
prompt him well. Her anxiety about his continued presence and abou
his private thoughts beautifully reflect his apparently incurable hesitancy
her offer to prompt him, her pleas not to torment the two of them an
further and to give in to his love. Afterwards, the couple walked in th
church yard where it was so windy that "a rose-colored little neckerchie
that she was wearing around her neck and her white throat" was blow
away. Blushing, she covered her nakedness with her "little hands," and h
gallantly picked up the bit of cloth, then silently, not looking at her, pu
it around her "without wounding her girlish delicacy"; it earned him
grateful and loving look.[38] Beneke's imperious desire to take Mariett
precisely wounding her girlish delicacy, and to make a woman of her
here reversed into fraternal solicitude, just as he reversed her unmistakabl
wish to have him go beyond words into gratitude for his restraint.

For, around this time, Marietta Banks was increasingly prepared to ad
a physical touch to their inconclusive amorous sparring match. Late i
September 1844, Beneke kissed her for the first time, not without he
tender and timid provocation. The two had been at a large party in th
countryside and, after dinner, they took a stroll in a park familiar to hir
from his childhood days. "As it got dark, our hands found one anothe
she placed my hand (under her mantilla) on her beating heart,—so w

37. Otto Beneke, February 29, March 12, 1844, Marietta Journal. The repeate
gesture may also allude to nocturnal masturbation with Marietta Banks in his fantasi
—she is behind it all!
38. Otto Beneke, June 25, 1844, ibid.

walked for a while, sometimes bright stars sparkled into her clear, countenance shining with love." Making an extreme effort, the two managed to talk trivia, lest those about them become suspicious at their silence. On the walk back, "this sweet enlacement began once more, ever more intimately. Again she put my hand on her little heart, close to her golden, virginal bosom, and she pressed both her little hands on my hand." They would look at one another once in a while, "smiling blissfully." He finally embraced her and ran down a slope with her into a dark hut; and "here—a shy, silent, and yet so eloquent embrace—my mouth touched her cheek with a kiss, she had turned her little head sideways." It gave him much to think about: his happiness in the great moment largely obscured his long-buried memories of the spot and was, at the same time, enhanced by them. The others around them were "close to us, invisible,—a quick, once again an intimate embrace,—silent, not a word, not a sound,—a kiss," covered by conversation, in which she astutely assisted. Once back with the company in a brightly lit room, Marietta Banks avoided Otto Beneke's eyes and, "in the liveliest manner possible, sat down next to her *mother*." Recalling the event in his diary that night, he found it all "so characteristic of her.—The artlessness of her love in the way she placed my hand on her heart—the virginal shyness as the first kiss nears." Yet, not even this, as his dreams, like his conduct, reveal, was enough to drag him to the altar. In October, he dreamt that Marietta had come to him in his room and, as he embraced and kissed her, he noticed that it "was another being in her form," and thought this "an ambiguous, very thought-provoking dream,—as though it was meant as a warning, an admonition."[39] There was clearly much in his waking life to feed his dreams.

But this cannot be all. Powerful as Beneke's desire for Marietta was, more than that must have instigated his nightly encounters with her. She was, as figures can be in dreams, both herself and a stand-in for someone else. Freud insists that "*a wish which is represented in a dream must be an infantile one*,"[40] and this invites a deep reading. Otto Beneke's dreams about Marietta Banks underscore their infantile origins in palpable ways. We know that the dreaming Beneke addressed his beloved Marietta with the formal *Sie*, as he did in real life; and those excursions into the country side, those church services, and those Italian relatives were not an invention of Otto Beneke's dream work. There is necessarily some distortion

39. Otto Beneke, September 30, October 26, 1844, ibid.
40. Freud, *Traumdeutung*, St.A., II, 528; *The Interpretation of Dreams*, S.E., V, 553.

in his dreams, but their realistic settings, their perfectly logical if rather
adventurous plots, make them akin to the dreams of children, in which
wish-fulfillment is undisguised. I suggest, then, that Beneke's dreams
represent both the wish to remain a child, lovingly united with his mother,
and the incompatible wish for lifelong erotic union with Marietta, further
complicated by his anxiety over the moment of sexual performance. It
seems that he at once wanted to free himself from his first loves and
remain faithful to them: in May 1844, he dreamt that he was being married in some remote village church to a bride who was not Marietta but
looked like his sister Ida, who had died eleven years earlier.[41] Marietta
Banks was Otto Beneke's escape route to maturity. In the end, with her
father's help, she compelled him to take it. Her observation that Otto
Beneke's harsh moods cleared up and his bitterness vanished once he was
married are doubtless accurate enough. As much as was in his power, he
had finally, better than many others, resolved his oedipal struggles and
left them behind.

Walter Bagehot for his part kept the amorous initiative very much in
his hands. Protective, even possessive as he was about his mother, he was
fairly confident that if Eliza Wilson would only have him, he could
gain a new love without simply aping or basely betraying the old. He
left no circumstantial record of his mental state as he came to know his
future wife better and better in the course of 1857. But as luck would
have it, just after he became engaged, Eliza's headaches and eye-strain
made resort to a distant healer in Edinburgh advisable so that, with brief
interludes, for nearly half a year the couple wrote one another affectionate
and exploratory letters, sharing their feelings, confessing their defects, and
celebrating their newfound happiness. "I am not used to this sort of feeling
and it is dreadfully exciting," Walter Bagehot told Eliza Wilson late in
November 1857 and she responded in kind three days later: "Affection
like ours *is* awful and gives such new significance to life—at least to me
it does." Plainly, he had not experienced this sort of love before. "I have
a vague notion," he told her, "that there used to be a great blank and a
dreary sense of feelings for which there was no object and seemed likely
to be none." How exhilarating it was to have found such an object! She
agreed wholeheartedly. "I am conscious of a feeling akin to what you
describe, of a consciousness then of depths in my heart that had not been
reached, of a power of affection which had as yet lain dormant, but I
dared not dwell upon it for fear it were not fated I should meet the soul

41. Otto Beneke, May 14, 1844, Marietta Journal.

that could take possession of those depths."[42] In all candor, they acknowledged that even writing such letters was an experiment for them; it seems that neither of them had seen, or written, such letters before.

Even stronger than the feelings of exuberance and awe were those of relief and closure. "I have a repose of affection quite new to me," he told her three days after she had engaged herself to him, "and such a rest from the burning pain of a man's love." He had "never felt before any happiness which was so intense and soothing," and thought of her "*nicely and mildly.*" Yet he honestly added that he found love strenuous: "The affections are always *fatiguing.*" Once again she was wholly in tune with him, and admitted that now things were settled, she no longer felt "the weight on my heart that was there a month ago." In her serenity, she thought she could contribute to his own peace of mind. "It is delicious to think I *can* do anything to calm and soothe you."[43]

That redolent word "delicious" became the signature of this correspondence, a private password serving to describe all sorts of mental pleasures, and supplying these tender, decent, wholly proper if profoundly agitated letters with a carnal energy all their own. Of the two, Walter Bagehot was more ready to acknowledge the claims of the body than she. He had from the outset of their acquaintance enjoyed their intellectual conversations, their taste for the romantic poets, but he admitted that he liked nothing better than a good meal; when the two began to discuss wedding arrangements, he was anxious lest they fail to include a satisfying collation. He acknowledged, too, that he had felt attracted to her looks as much as to her mind: "Young ladies should not let their hair fly in the wind—that was the original beginning." Then, immediately, he took it back: "Seriously, it is not right to talk so." Confession and disavowal together disclose the state of his mind—and hers as well. This is what the word "delicious" encapsulated for them both: a civilized, restrained, but openly avowed passionateness. She thinks it delicious that he has given her a mission in life, lets her mind "float in delicious fancies" circling about him, and finds it "delicious to fancy" that she will be a "prop" to her husband. He in turn finds her letters "too *delicious* to dwell on in public and business places," and "delicious to hear your name mentioned." She, too, thinks his letters delicious, especially when there are two of

42. Walter Bagehot to Eliza Wilson, November 29, 1857; Eliza Wilson to Walter Bagehot, December 1, 1857; Walter Bagehot to Eliza Wilson, December 31, 1857; Eliza Wilson to Walter Bagehot, January 1, 1858, Barrington, *Love-Letters*, 47, 49, 74, 76.

43. Walter Bagehot to Eliza Wilson, November 10, 18, 1857; Eliza Wilson to Walter Bagehot, November 23, 20, 1857, ibid., 23, 26, 38, 28.

them. But theirs was a rather placid, or, better, controlled sensuality. The "*gratitude*" he feels for her affection is, he tells her, "one of the most calm, gentle and delicious feelings which I have ever experienced."[44]

Their serenity, though, was scarcely unbroken. Another word that punctuates this correspondence, second only to "delicious," is "nervous." Though prone to vanity now, Walter Bagehot tells Eliza Wilson, "I assure you I am quite nervous at other times at the confidence you give me and the awful trust your happiness is." She for her part is nervous that he might find her letters disappointing, or her mind inadequate to his. But he can play the same lovers' game: each invests the other with perfections while questioning his own worth. "I am very nervous at times," he writes, "about your overrating me intellectually, but I get over it."[45] He saw the matter correctly. Nervousness was an accompaniment, not the dominant melody, of their love. What these letters disclose is a growing confidence in themselves and one another, a gradual relaxation of caution and defensiveness. They begin—as they almost had to, since the correspondence did not start until they had become engaged—mezzo forte and rise to a fortissimo as comfortable as it is rousing. The epithet "dearest," which reads at the outset almost as a mechanical endearment, gains in solidity as the letters piled up.

It was this mixture of trust and exhilaration that enabled Walter Bagehot, banker, economist, literary critic, political observer, to write one of the truly charming love letters of the nineteenth century. Thanking Eliza Wilson in November 1857 for her "most kind and "*delicious* letter," he tells her that he has "now read yours over and over more times than I should like to admit," and that her letter "has given me more pleasure than I thought it possible I could receive from one." Part of that pleasure stemmed from his feeling that she was now writing him affectionately without visible strain. "Yet it tells me things which with your deep and reserved nature it must have cost you much to put on paper." Lapsing into momentary self-denigration, he wishes "indeed I could feel worthy of your affection." But Bagehot recovers quickly, happy to receive what he does not quite deserve: "My delight is at times intense." His delight has

44. Walter Bagehot to Eliza Wilson, January 17, 1858, December 4, 1857; Eliza Wilson to Walter Bagehot, December 4, 1857; Walter Bagehot to Eliza Wilson, December 1, November 29, 1857; Eliza Wilson to Walter Bagehot, January 20, February 3, 1858; Walter Bagehot to Eliza Wilson, December 31, 1857, ibid., 119, 58, 60, 55, 46, 121, 167, 73.
45. Walter Bagehot to Eliza Wilson, November 25, 1857; Eliza Wilson to Walter Bagehot, December 7, 1857, January 10, 1858; Walter Bagehot to Eliza Wilson [January 11, 1858], ibid., 42, 67, 93, 98.

not been uninterrupted or unalloyed. He has, he tells Eliza, at times felt "wild, burning pain," but his love for her, he adds, deftly taking out the sting, has never been "mere suffering. Even at the worst there was a wild, delicious excitement which I would not have lost for the world." The calm affection investing their early acquaintance and their earnest conversations had been "simple pleasure"; but then, "since the day in the conservatory," the day he had told her of his mother's madness, his feeling "has been too eager not to have a good deal of pain in it, and the tension of mind has really been very great at times." Judiciously, Bagehot adds, not to disguise but to clarify his feelings: "still the time I have known and loved you is immensely the happiest I have ever known." He had experienced fantasies of her refusing him, and these fantasies, though now overtaken by events, had continued to oppress him: "I had a vision of the thing which I keep by me." He recognizes that writing about himself at such length is "egotistical," but he is not, or only a touch, apologetic about his self-centeredness: "I am not sure that egotism is bad in letters, and if I write to you I *must* write about what I feel for you."

As observant of himself as he was of the English scene, Bagehot repeated that declaring his love for her had been a strain, precipitating hysterical side effects: "No one can tell the effort it was to me to tell you I loved you—why I do not know, but it made me gasp for breath, and now it is absolutely pleasure to me to tell it to you and bore you with it in every form, and I should like to write it in big letters I LOVE YOU all across the page by way of emphasis." He recognized the infantile origins of his feelings, but stood by them: "I know you will think me very childish and be shaken in your early notion that I am intellectual, but I cannot help it. This is my state of mind." It is a state he finds impossible to contain; he must act out his excitement and manage it by the partial denial of humor: having read her letter once more, he tells her, "I go about murmuring, 'I have made that dignified girl *commit* herself, I have, I have,' and then I vault over the sofa with exultation. Those are the feelings of the person you have connected yourself with. *Please* don't be offended at my rubbish"—a plea for reassurance beyond objective need, for there was no reason why she should have been offended, and good evidence that she was not. "I could write you of the deep and serious feelings which I hope you believe really are in my heart, but my pen jests of itself and always will." But his subscription leaves jesting aside. "Yours with the fondest and deepest love, Walter Bagehot."[46]

---

46. Walter Bagehot to Eliza Wilson, November 22, 1857, ibid., 32–37. We may take his "vaulting" over the sofa literally; he was inclined to such physical expressiveness.

It was only appropriate that the wedding, on April 21, 1858, should go off without a hitch and with little nervousness—"a day full of sunshine," her youngest sister would remember many years later. One person was in no state to be present, Walter Bagehot's mother, and he thought of her immediately after the wedding, sending her a hasty little note from the carriage, that all had gone well. Then, two days later, he wrote her in more detail, and his wife added a little postscript: "I am your affectionate daughter, ELIZA BAGEHOT. This is the *first* time I have signed my *new* name." For nineteen years, until it was fatally disrupted by his premature death in 1877, the marriage of Walter and Eliza Bagehot seems to have been rich in affection, if punctuated by headaches. During their engagement, Eliza Wilson had already signalized what was to come with her declaration, at once passionate and decorous: "It is so pleasant to love and be loved."[47]

3. Love and Work

The energies that fuel the pleasures of love and its pains reach far beyond the domain normally assigned to it. Thus, Walter Bagehot's erotic style, and, for that matter, Otto Beneke's and nearly everyone else's, left its recognizable mark on his work. To be sure, the claim that work is largely a battery of sublimations of instinctual needs, though reasonable enough, cannot make reductionism attractive, let alone acceptable. Men and women construct their sublimations from materials they find ready-made around them; they are richly layered compromises between conflicting internal urges and far from obvious external possibilities. Still, Bagehot's and Beneke's writings and their public performance exhibited a certain emotional ground tone testifying to the imperialistic ventures of libido in unsuspected places.

Otto Beneke's characteristic style of loving was almost pathetically defensive. His investments of affection, once he had sorted them out, display a stubborn fidelity, but he was more likely to respond to events than to dominate them, and to seek out grounds for gloom and resignation. Even those first kisses he implanted on Marietta Banks's cheek and lips that September evening of 1844 were invited, subtly provoked, by the blushing Marietta pressing his hand against her beating heart. The path out of the jungle of self-hatred and vacillation that he had planted himself was hacked out for him by Marietta Banks's father. Walter Bagehot,

---

47. Eliza Bagehot to Edith Bagehot, April 23, 1858; Eliza Wilson to Walter Bagehot, November 23, 1857, ibid., 204, 41.

ve know, was different. Once he had identified the object of his love,
e moved toward it with all the deliberate speed that his culture would
llow him. In his detailed exposition of Clough's fine long poem, *Amours
e Voyage*, he discusses with marked derision its protagonist, a "hesitat-
ng young gentleman," who cannot make up his mind about anything,
east of all about a girl with whom he may or may not be in love. By this
ime married for over four years, Bagehot could look back at his own
ourtship days with the complacent conviction that when it counted he,
t least, had not hesitated at all. Bagehot quotes at some length the more
grating verses displaying the hero's incurable ambivalence and concludes
with the sardonic hope that the girl in question went on to find "a more
atisfactory lover and husband."[48] If Walter Bagehot had been courting
Marietta Banks, he would probably have married her within the year. He
would have built on each successive encounter at dances and concerts
and family gatherings, to urge his merits and consummate his desires. If
Otto Beneke had been courting Eliza Wilson, with her father so reluctant
to give her up, she might have died an old maid. He would have silently
resented the presence of her family on their spirited excursions, with
Eliza jogging along on her donkey, and read their intrusiveness as a stern
hint from Providence that the auguries for his amorous prospects were
inauspicious. But Walter Bagehot kicked Eliza Wilson's donkey to be
alone with her.

In tune with these traits, Bagehot tried to master his destiny in the
world: he gave up a promising career in law that was making him uncomfortable for a spell as a successful country banker which he enjoyed;
he made his name with provocative political and literary essays whose
originality and assurance offended some readers and attracted many more;
he stood, unsuccessfully, for Parliament more than once, facing down his
liabilities as a political candidate—probity, candor, and a poor speaking
voice—because he thought such service important as well as gratifying;
he proved himself, in his long essays, and above all in his classic, *The
English Constitution*, a clear-eyed political observer and a penetrating
social psychologist unafraid to criticize and genially lampoon the institutions he loved. Beneke, for his part, was something of a pedant: an
assiduous student of the fine details of genealogical tables, a prolific
biographer of local worthies and no less prolific retailer of local historical
anecdotes, and a lifelong public servant who spent more than four decades
in one office, the Hamburg Archives.

But Otto Beneke was no mere plodding and submissive bureaucrat. He

48. "Mr. Clough's Poems" (1862), Bagehot, *Works*, II, 250–56.

never overcame moments of self-consciousness and self-doubt, when his
ant-like diligence troubled him. One day in 1869, looking at his files, he
mused that much of the stuff he had amassed should be thrown away
"How much have I brought together, endlessly, in part written myself
and preserved, convinced that there is much of value in all this! The
older I grow, the more worthless it all appears to me!" What is more, his
biographer took the occasion to note his learning, his humor, and the
"lively temperament in his youth."[49] Those tender young dance partners
whom he exhausted and terrified with his wild, tormented tarantellas,
would have been able to lend life to this appraisal. He wrote one book
that departed some distance from his monotonous excursions into the past
glories of Hamburg and of its eminent burghers, a book that reads almost
like a timid declaration of independence from the drudgery of parochial
celebration: it is a study of "dishonest folk," of wandering minstrels,
strolling actors, town criers, executioners, barber-surgeons, and other
unrespectable types—mainly in Hamburg, of course—whom cultural historians were just beginning to discover.

Beneke's finest opportunity to distance himself from conformity came
with the Franco-Prussian War of 1870 and the establishment of the
Second Reich the following January. With unexpected vehemence, Beneke
moved against the grain of German society. More precisely, he did not
move: it was his country and many of his Hamburg compatriots who
moved while he stood still. Beneke detested the war and blessed the fate
that had spared one of his close French friends, recently dead, the sight of
France's humiliation. His contempt for those cheering Prussian military
bulletins was unmeasured. After Bismarck's Reich was proclaimed, his
rage, if anything, reached for new intensity. He would put words like
"Reich" or "German Emperor" into derisive quotation marks, and denigrated Wilhelm I as an emperor created by success alone—"*Erfolgskaiser*,"
he called him. As enthusiastic or servile Hamburgers saluted each new
triumph—the victory at Sedan, the proclamation of the Empire, the
surrender of Paris—with celebratory cannon salvos, divine services of
thanksgiving, fireworks, and displays of flags, he glumly stood aside.
Sourly observing the festive mood of the city, Beneke confided sarcastic
comments to his journal as his fellow citizens sent fulsome addresses of
congratulation to the new *Kaiser*, renamed streets and shops after him,

49. Otto Beneke, Tagebuch, October 12, 1869, F8, FB, St. Ar. Hamburg; A. Hage-
dorn, "Beneke, Otto Adalbert," *Allgemeine Deutsche Biographie*, XXXXVI (1902),
357.

and produced his likeness (as one historian has noted) "in chocolate, in marzipan, in wax, in soap, in wood and metal."[50]

Unquestionably the war against France and the unification of Germany were immensely popular in Hamburg with the general populace and only less so with the political elite. It took a solid dose of civic courage to stand up against this avalanche of patriotic sentiment: in mid-August of 1870, two weeks before Prussia's decisive victory in the field, Beneke noted that anyone in Hamburg who "dared to utter a word" against "Prussia and Prussia's heroes, the lieutenants," would be stoned to death. He had long resented Hamburg's powerful, power-hungry neighbor, and now his unreconstructed local patriotism made him a man of the opposition, a small and shrinking minority. Some old-timers could hear in his grumbling the accents of his father, whose devotion to the former Free City of Hamburg had been proverbial. Otto Beneke, we know, had been his mother's attached son; now he became, more overtly than ever, his father's political heir. As Bismarck's Reich went on its way, Beneke in his last years acquired the reputation of a stubborn and isolated particularist, an opinionated, almost cranky, champion of his city-state's fading privileges. The more he venerated the past, the more he despised the present. When he died in early February 1891, expansive and respectful obituaries could not avoid commenting on his rigidity. His father, the *Hamburger Nachrichten* wrote, had left him a legacy of piety, historical sense, love for Hamburg, "and an unshakeable attachment to antique, inherited constitutional forms which, in changing times, in many ways failed to correspond to the desires of more impetuous youth."[51] It was a gentle way of calling Beneke a reactionary.

Beneke, in short, never enlarged the strait circle of his affections. He loved his parents, he loved his wife, he loved his city. The large step he took (or, better, was pushed into taking) after he was thirty, when he married Marietta Banks, was a step he never repeated in the worlds of work and politics. Satisfaction lay, for him, in the familiar, in objects awakening resonant echoes from days long vanished. This is not a criticism. Petty, even vindictive as Beneke's disaffection with the German Reich might appear to his detractors, it was not wholly unperceptive. Nor was it mere resentment; Beneke opposed to Bismarck's mixture of

---

50. See Otto Beneke, Tagebuch, September 1, 30, 1870; January 22, 25, 30, 1871; Renate Hauschild-Thiessen, "Hamburg im Kriege 1870/71," *Zeitschrift des Vereins für Hamburgische Geschichte*, LVII (1971), 34.

51. Otto Beneke, Tagebuch, August 15, 1870; *Hamburger Nachrichten*, February 13, 1891, F63, FB, St. Ar. Hamburg.

opportunistic and authoritarian politics an old-fashioned liberalism of his own. It is characteristic of his political stance that when, in June 1888, Emperor Frederick III died after his tragically brief reign, Beneke lamented the disappearance of this hope for liberal Germans with a mournful entry in his diary: "A painful loss. He would have done many good things! Great in small things."[52]

This appraisal would not be inappropriate for its author. Beneke was great in small things, with his scores of biographies and local histories and his no less copious collections of local folk tales standing as the public counterpart of his filial piety and his hard-won domestic felicity. In his diary, he would faithfully recall, in addition to his mother's death, his wife's birthday and his wedding day. These were the cardinal dates in his emotional calendar. Once, early on, in 1844, when the issue of his campaign to win Marietta Banks was still very much in doubt, he had dreamt that she had come to see him and he had wanted to tell her something; when he awoke, he recalled that what he had tried to say to her in vain in his dream was to wish her a happy birthday. During their long and unclouded years together, he would make up for that inhibition with thoughtful presents, little verses, and devout exclamations: *"Marietta's birthday! God be, and remain, with her!"* he exclaimed in 1849, in red ink, only to add the mundane detail so much at home in diaries: "(Rainy weather.)" He appended the list of presents that Marietta had received and a draft of the poem he had written for the occasion, which "proclaims my sentiments, basically: Thanks be to God for giving her to us, thanks be to her for all her love and fidelity!" The recurrence of his wedding day moved Beneke no less; every year he would voice his gratitude to God for the "inexhaustible treasure of love and domestic happiness that He has bestowed on us in Mariette!" In 1890, he celebrated the last wedding anniversary he would live to see with all the old exuberant way of earlier years: *"Our blessed 45th Wedding Day, God be Thanked and Praised* for the Grand Prize of Happiness allotted to me!"[53] The language is worn and trite, the feelings are fresh and authentic. Beneke's distaste for Bismarck and all his works was only the shadow side of his

52. Otto Beneke, Tagebuch, June 15, 1888, F8, FB, St. Ar. Hamburg. His liberation had emerged earlier, in his book on "dishonest folk," where he had praised Hamburg's relative freedom from prejudice against the outcasts of earlier times. See *Von unehrlichen Leuten. Cultur-historische Studien und Geschichten aus vergangenen Tagen deutscher Gewerbe und Dienste, mit besonderer Rücksicht auf Hamburg* (1863), esp. p. 80.
53. November 7, 1844, November 7, 1849, October 19, 1869, October 19, 1890. Marietta Tagebuch.

loyalty to individuals and institutions he felt only too privileged to serve; the energy that allowed him to hate emerged from the energy that fueled his love.

Bagehot is harder to capture. His published work is both substantial and varied: a stream of journalistic pieces on economics and politics, essays on poets and novelists, extended studies of the Bank of England, the perils of parliamentary reform, the application of recent psychological and biological ideas to social theory, and the anatomy of the English constitution. He wrote quickly and well; it is striking to see his best phrases and most pointed epigrams, which have entered the language of political discourse, freely quoted by his exegetes—including this one. Bagehot thought in essays, in the kind of pensive and leisurely exploration for which the august English reviews of his day and their cultivated readers had an insatiable appetite. All of his books, except one, *Lombard Street*, on the money market, were first serialized. "The modern man must be told what to think,—shortly, no doubt,—but he *must* be told it," Bagehot wrote in 1855. "The essay-like criticism of modern times is about the length which he likes."[54] It was also his favorite length. His dominant tone was one of genial irony, the tone of a gentleman who experiences his culture with the sovereign assurance available to a man with a good education, a good mind, and a good social position.[55] Bagehot was surely no democrat; he wanted governance to be left in the hands of a political elite that would govern its deferential inferiors firmly but humanely, in their best interest. The Reform Act of 1867, which enfranchised the urban working man, deeply worried him. But while policies and strategies obviously mattered to him—his papers on English politics are a running commentary on both—his governing intellectual passion was the search for political substance behind legal form. Bagehot's brilliant *English Constitution*, a book that, more than a century after its publication, remains the most stimulating of texts, is as much about feelings as it is about institutions; with its famous distinction between the "efficient" and the "dignified" elements of the largely unwritten rules by which England is governed, Bagehot's masterpiece reads like a long

54. "The First Edinburgh Reviewers," Bagehot, *Works*, I, 313.
55. This tone deserted him, if I read him aright, only once, when his humane anger was aroused by Thomas Carlyle's obtuse and callous defense of the bloodthirsty Edward Eyre, Governor of Jamaica, who, after putting down a native rebellion, had a black member of the legislature executed and then launched a vengeful bloodbath that took more than six hundred lives. See "Mr. Carlyle on Mr. Eyre" (1866), ibid., III, 563–65.

review of political theatre in which what people think they see and feel they believe matters as much as what the laws prescribe. Bagehot had a keen nose for those elusive forces that move men in ways they dare not acknowledge and rarely understand.

It seems not surprising, then, that students of Bagehot's ideas have failed to place him precisely in the political spectrum. They have ranked him with conservatives and with liberals or, admitting defeat, made do with such helpless labels as liberal conservative or conservative liberal. This failure is instructive: Bagehot's thought circles about the unresolvable tension between change and continuity. Change, he was certain, was the supreme fact of his time. "One peculiarity of this age is the sudden acquisition of much physical knowledge." These are the opening words of an essay he first published in 1867. I have quoted them at the beginning of *Education of the Senses* among other evidence to suggest that Bagehot was right to consider the pervasive experience of change as the organizing theme of the age, mingling confidence and anxiety in unique ways. "There is scarcely a department of science or art," he continued, "which is the same, or at all the same, as it was fifty years ago. A new world of inventions—of railways and of telegraphs—has grown up around us which we cannot help seeing; a new world of ideas is in the air and affects us, though we do not see it." It was a view he held early and late. The century, he had conjectured in the mid-1850s, is a time of "inextricable confusion," an "age of confusion and tumult, when old habits are shaken, old views are overthrown, ancient assumptions rudely questioned, ancient inferences utterly denied, when each man has a different view from his neighbor, when an intellectual change has set father and son at variance, when a man's own household are the special foes of his favourite and self-adopted creed."[56] When change invades the family, setting generations at odds and spawning self-adopted creeds, the appropriate rational response is bound to be hard to discover.

In such a heady and unstable age, which no amount of wishing can transform into some placid, imaginary Old Regime, two postures, Bagehot thought, are bound to be destructive of the common good: a blind worship of the past producing reactionary adherence to outworn solutions, and a no less blind infatuation with radical, rationalistic utopias. He distrusted fanatics of all persuasions: "The wish to call down fire from heaven," he wrote in unequivocal distaste, "is rarely absent in pure zeal for a pure cause." Politics, he was convinced, is neither archaeology nor

56. *Physics and Politics* (1872; ed. 1873), 1, see *Education of the Senses*, 52–53; "The First Edinburgh Reviewers," Bagehot, *Works*, I, 321, 317.

geometry: Bagehot was a receptive reader of Edmund Burke though, more like Tocqueville in this than Burke, he could reconcile himself to change and was not inclined to quarrel with the inevitable. "One of the greatest pains to human nature," he thought, "is the pain of a new idea,"[57] but it is one that men must learn to endure, even welcome.

This stance—superb, tough-minded, and demanding, at once embroiled in party politics and floating above it—informs Bagehot's ambivalence about stupidity, which was one of his favorite and most characteristic diagnostic terms. The Tory reactionary who wants to repeal history, who does not have "an experiencing nature," is stupid in the ordinary sense of the word: he cannot learn from experience, does not think he needs to learn anything from it, and is therefore unfit to govern. For governing means coping with realities, no matter how unpalatable. If the Reform Act of 1867 had, perhaps rashly, expanded the English political public to social strata hitherto thought beneath rational electoral decisions, the need was not to lament but to teach: "The cry should now be, 'Educate! Educate! Educate!' " The great lesson that Burke had taught, "politics are made of time and place," must be read in two contrasting ways: to manufacture solutions designed on speculative principles is frivolous; to resist, or sabotage, innovation from panic-stricken fear of the unknown is folly.[58]

This meant that Bagehot had isolated another kind of stupidity, a positive, stabilizing force. Shakespeare, he thought, had been right to believe that "for most of the purposes of human life stupidity is a most valuable element." It is the tenacity of the common man reluctant to experiment though open to experience, of the solid citizen too fond of his accustomed ways to abandon them at the call of some persuasive demagogue. "The first duty of society is the preservation of society," he wrote in his "Letters on the French *coup d'état*" from Paris in early 1852, "By the sound work of old-fashioned generations—by the singular pains-taking of the slumberers in churchyards—by dull care—by stupid industry, a certain social fabric somehow exists," and manages worthily to survive. This, of course, was one of Bagehot's youthful magisterial pronouncements embedded in a brash political commentary on French affairs, designed to startle, even to shock, his English readers. But Bagehot's affection for productive stupidity never waned; he gave it credit for what he loyally valued as the supreme English talent for politics. But there was

57. Ibid., 326; *Physics and Politics*, 163.
58. "Experiencing nature": "Shakespeare—The Man" (1853), Bagehot, *Works*, I, 174; "Educate! Educate!": St. John-Stevas, "Short Biography," ibid., 71; "Politics are made of time and place": "Letters on the French *Coup d'Etat*" (1852), Letter III, ibid., IV, 48.

nothing automatic about the virtue of stupidity. The phenomenon required a penetrating appraisal of circumstances that would respect the
working of political symbols in men's minds and the grasp of habits on
character. The study of politics became, for Bagehot, without much
fanfare but with impressive results, parasitical on the study of psychology.

This is the point where Bagehot's style of loving and style of thinking
merge, both on the level of conscious reflection and on that of emotional
coherence. In poetry, in economics, and in politics, Bagehot detected the
very forces at work that shape man's intimate life in moments of infatuation, in mundane conjugal transactions, in bed. It is revealing that he
should have defined "political life" as a "vast accumulation of ideas and
sentiments and hopes, of love and hatred." More lucidly than anyone else
in his day, he appreciated the play of private passions on the public stage.
"By nature we shrink from contemplating ourselves," he observed in
his first, precocious, published essay dating from 1847, when he was
twenty-one.[59] It was a hint of his lifelong fascination with the powers
that men naturally refuse to recognize: their real reasons. That is why
he made it his principal rule for interpreting the work of poets and
statesmen that a man's character pervades that work. Shakespeare had
written his masterpieces out of an "experiencing nature"; some of the
"peculiarities" of Shelley's works and life may be traced to the "peculiarity of his nature." The work of Adam Smith, he thought, "can hardly be
understood without having some notion what manner of man he was."[60]
Bagehot was no vulgar reductionist, but, rather, supremely attuned to
the inexplicable in things, to the range of responses that experience may
evoke, to the choices that talent can enforce, to the sheer unpredictability
of genius. But it seemed obvious to him that character and work are in
uninterrupted commerce, mutually define one another, and thus enable
the commentator moving between the two to illuminate them both.

Bagehot exhibited this subtle and complex dialectic in his own life.
His love for Eliza Wilson was his way of taking his chances and trusting
his feelings, of exploring uncharted terrain with bracing confidence in
the outcome. The traits he prized as the cardinal civic virtues—an ability
to live with uncertainty and confusion, yield to facts, and accept am-
biguity—were precisely the traits he cultivated, buffeted as he was by the
temptations of London, the unsatisfactory society at Langport, the con-

59. "Shakespeare—The Man," ibid., I, 189; "Letters on the *Coup d'Etat*," Letter II,
ibid., IV, 36; "Festus," ibid., I, 132.
60. "The Practical Operation of the American Constitution at the Present Extreme
Crisis" (1861), ibid., IV, 289; "Shakespeare—The Man," ibid., I, 174; "Percy Bysshe
Shelley" (1856), ibid., 476; "Adam Smith as a Person" (1876), ibid., III, 85.

flicting urgencies of spectatorship and action, and his beloved mother's madness. He was free to express impatience but could tolerate delay. "My dearest Eliza," he would scold her when she was out of reach in distant Edinburgh, "do not write to me by that wretched second post," which deprived him of news from her for a day. All this signaled a good augury for his life with Eliza Wilson, and she fully sensed this. She had been thinking, she told her "dearest Walter," of acquaintances who, after twenty years, were as close as they had been on the first day of their life together, and applied their felicity to her own future. Her optimism was obviously not the result of a disinterested scientific survey; there was much tremulous wishing in it. Surely, the case books of psychiatrists, the tearful confessions poured out to pastors and priests, the sordid testimony on which gossip writers and divorce courts lived, plainly suggest that unhappy marital partnerships were far from unknown among the respectable in the nineteenth century. "How many love-marriages carry on well to the last—?" Thackeray bitterly asked in *Pendennis*, "and how many sentimental firms do not finish in bankruptcy?—and how many heroic passions don't dwindle down into despicable indifference, or end in shameful defeat?"[61] Thackeray was, a little self-indulgently, translating his own sad personal history into a sour appraisal of life; still, he could have easily found abundant support for his cynical case. But Eliza Wilson postulating widespread marital happiness was not simply imagining things. "It is just as it should be no doubt," she mused, "in well-assorted unions. I think about these things now and am delighted to find how many I know. Happy marriages are not uncommon." Had she lived to write the history of nineteenth-century middle-class love, she would not have been compelled to change her mind.

61. "Do not write to me": Walter Bagehot to Eliza Wilson, November 28 [1857], Byrnmore Jones Library, Hull University; William Makepeace Thackeray, *The History of Pendennis: His Fortunes and Misfortunes, His Friends and His Greatest Enemy* (1849–50), The Centenary Biographical Edition of the Works of William Makepeace Thackeray, ed. Lady Ritchie, 26 vols. (1910–1911), III, 279–80 [vol. II, ch. 21]; "Happy marriages are not uncommon": Eliza Wilson to Walter Bagehot, January 10, 1858, *Love-Letters*, 91.

❧ ONE ❧

Two Currents of Love

THE VOLUMINOUS theorizing on love, so characteristic for the nineteenth century, adds up to a rich and fascinating library of cultural documents. The work of novelists, philosophers, and psychologists who for the most part did not crave—and for decades did not secure—popular approval, it was far less a pointer to pleasure than a literature of reproach. Too sophisticated or too austere to regulate the erotic life of the average bourgeois undiluted, it came eventually to find readers and to make its mark. Paradoxically, the very distance of these aphorisms, essays, and monographs from ordinary middle-class lives and loves secures their relevance to them. With their outspoken, experimental, often mutually contradictory diagnoses, they made themselves not merely a distinct presence in an agitated time, but a symptom of that agitation. They read like disenchanted reports from the cultural front, amusing, acerbic, often devastating bulletins detailing middle-class disasters in love. This literature was better equipped to record bourgeois failures than their undoubted but unheralded successes. It was partisan and unjust, but, given the critical intentions of its authors, it could hardly be anything else. It conveniently condensed middle-class anxieties that most bourgeois lovers could not articulate or had wholly repressed. Ruthlessly, it uncovered unconscious conflicts that exigent middle-class morality sternly imposed and just as sternly compelled its devotees to conceal.

With its urbane condescension or its esoteric erudition, nineteenth-century writing on love supplies clues to the culture of that century in still a larger way. It provides forceful evidence for the cruel civil war that would tear bourgeois culture apart, that irrepressible conflict between the artistic, intellectual, and political avant garde and what it was pleased to call the materialistic, reactionary, callous philistine. Bourgeois bungling in love, as their critics perceived it, was only a particular symptom of greater failures—failures in aesthetic discrimination and moral perceptions, failure above all in the supreme domain of the finer feelings.[1]

Yet, however distant or disdainful, nineteenth-century thinkers about love were not simply adversaries but also ingredients in bourgeois culture. They projected and organized bourgeois wishes no less than bourgeois fears, gave voice to unspoken or clumsily formulated fantasies of desire. There was in fact one essential principle on which cynics, metaphysicians, researchers, and ordinary bourgeois could cheerfully unite: true love is the conjunction of concupiscence with affection. Freud was only summing up the accepted wisdom when he observed that "a completely normal attitude in love" requires the uniting of "two currents," the *tender* and the *sensual.*" The failure of such a fortunate confluence was a neurotic symptom, most devastating among men suffering from psychological impotence: "Where they love they do not desire, and where they desire they cannot love."[2]

This ideal of joining attachment to lust was as old as the scriptures, had been preached by Greeks and Romans, and transmitted to modern culture through such imperishable classics as Plutarch. It was accepted with little debate in the nineteenth century. "The great and wonderful work of generation," Plutarch had told posterity, "is properly the work of Venus, where Love is an assistant when present with Venus; but his absence renders the act altogether irksome, dishonorable, harsh and ungrateful." After all, "the conjunction of man and woman without true affection, like hunger and thirst, terminates with satiety, and produces nothing truly noble or commendable." That is what Emerson read in his Plutarch, and he, like almost everyone else, had no reason to dispute Plutarch's formulation. One could find it everywhere, trite and uncontroversial. Writers on women's clothes repeated it and so did fashionable novelists. The "highest" beauty, we read in a book on dress published in 1892, is "spiritual, intellectual, and moral excellence"; a "perfect body" reflects a "noble soul." Again Henry Sienkiewicz observed, "Man is neither a beast nor a celestial

1. I plan to devote a separate volume to this cultural civil war.
2. "Über die allgemeinste Erniedrigung des Liebeslebens" (1910), *St.A.*, V, 200, 202; "On the Universal Tendency to Debasement in the Sphere of Love," *S.E.*, XI, 180, 181.

being, but a compound."[3] The question that remained was whether middle-class lovers, supremely rule-bound and conventional as they appeared to their critics, could ever attain this exalted ideal, the perfect compound. This was to become a pervasive theme in cultural criticism from Stendhal and Coleridge to Freud.

1. Conflicting Legacies

In thinking about love, the nineteenth century was the heir of the ages. Like the definition of love as a synthesis of earthy and elevated passions, the very perception of love as a madness and the supreme subverter of rules, so romantic in sound, goes back to the ancients. There is something appropriate about Freud's throwing a bridge to the distant past in claiming that the libido of psychoanalytic theory coincided largely with "the *Eros* of the divine Plato."[4] But, though endowed with a respectable past, theorists on love continued to debate its nature, as they had for centuries. Some, as nineteenth-century readers did not fail to note, had discovered the origins of love in man's yearning for higher spheres, others in his capacity for self-delusion, still others in his animal instincts. Most segregated sacred from profane love; a few held this to be an untenable distinction. Love appeared as a divine blessing, a potent energy, an infectious disease, a slow poison. Dante had concluded his *Divine Comedy* with a moving invocation to "the love that moves the sun and the other stars"; Pascal, in a long-lost "discourse" rediscovered for the nineteenth century by Victor Cousin in 1842, had seen love as the confluence of aesthetic and carnal elements. In the early nineteenth century, Lord Byron, the arch-Romantic, restated for this repertory the gloomy insight that love and hatred were really inseparable: "Lovers may—and indeed generally are—enemies," he wrote in 1822, "but they never can be friends." Not without bravado, he was moved to confess, "I rather look upon love altogether as a sort of hostile transaction."[5] It was a view that arch-anti-

3. *Plutarch's Morals*, ed. William Goodwin (1874), IV, 274, in Gay Wilson Allen, *Waldo Emerson* (1981), 121; Frances Mary Steele and Elizabeth Livingston Steele Adams, *Beauty of Form and Grace of Vesture* (1892), 49, 53. I owe this reference to Valerie Steele. F. E. Worland, *Love: Sacred and Profane* (1908), 110. In *Emma* (1816; ed. Ronald Blythe, 1966), Jane Austen's heroine, Emma Woodhouse, describes her friend Harriet Smith as being "exactly what every man delights in—what at once bewitches his senses and satisfies his judgment" [ch. 8], p. 90.

4. *Drei Abhandlungen zur Sexualtheorie* (1905), *St.A.*, V, 46; *Three Essays on the Theory of Sexuality*, S.E., VII, 134.

5. Pascal: Sully Prudhomme, "Examen du Discours sur les passions de l'amour," *Revue des Deux Mondes* (1890), 318–36. Byron to [Lady Hardy, October 10, 1822]. *Byron's Letters and Journals*, ed. Leslie A. Marchand, 10 vols. (1973–1980), X, 50.

Romantics like Ivan Turgenev and George Bernard Shaw would reiterate later in the century. All could agree that the poets were justified in singing love's infinite variety.

Some ideas on love, then, survived the most harrowing emotional earthquakes, merely altered in expressive detail. There were eloquent dissenters clustering at each end of the spectrum of opinion, but they *were* dissenters. Diderot's cool definition of love as "the voluptuous rubbing of two intestines"[6] stood at one extreme; the ascetics for whom true love was a celestial emotion purged of sensual admixtures stood at the other. But, as I have noted, a broad center party holding a solid majority united on the proposition that the mutual libidinal attraction of two adult beings must include large doses of esteem, admiration, tenderness, to qualify as love at all.

This solid consensus, reinforced by its extended and impressive past, did not prevent anguished self-searching among nineteenth-century bourgeois, a self-searching that reflected the perennial tension between those who celebrated, and those who denigrated, the sensual element. It was one thing to define love as a necessary mingling of eroticism with affection, it was quite another to assign each its proper place. Despite all the appeal of the mainstream of opinion about love, two conflicting legacies were at work, exemplified in the nineteenth century by two timeless types: Hebrews and Hellenes. Drawing on the highly selective classical humanism of Winckelmann and Goethe, Heinrich Heine, that witty and angry poet and polemicist, developed this typology into a weapon of attack more than an instrument of understanding. Then, with a measure of detachment, serving his own cultural needs as he saw them, Matthew Arnold naturalized Hebraism and Hellenism in England and introduced them to the general educated public in his *Culture and Anarchy*. Arnold was scarcely a sensualist; for him, the confrontation of Hebraism and Hellenism was one between two irreconcilable roads to human perfection: the first a programmatic, often wild-eyed rejection of the world; the second, a tough-minded acceptance of human nature and its rich possibilities.[7] The issue raged across many domains of thought and action: ethics, esthetics, politics. But it was also, and significantly, a conflict over the meaning of love. Behind Arnold's idealizing perception of two views of human

6. Diderot to Sophie Volland (August 29, 1762), *Correspondance*, ed. Georges Roth, 16 vols. (1955–1970), IV, 120; a month earlier, he had spoken of intercourse as "the voluptuous loss of a few drops of fluid," ibid., 84.

7. *Culture and Anarchy* (1869; 2nd ed. 1875), ch. IV. These formulations are indebted to Lionel Trilling, *Matthew Arnold* (1939; 2nd ed. 1949). I will discuss the partisan, debased use of "Hellenism" as a defense of homosexuality below.

nature, there stood, barely concealed by the decency of his diction, the hoary debate over Eros and his true nature.

Arnold, like Heine before him, acknowledged that the ascetic Hebraic mode had on occasion played a beneficent, even an indispensable role on the stage of culture. Heine, self-appointed public defender of the flesh who excoriated "unnatural" Christianity for inventing both sin and hypocrisy, thought that in its beginnings the "Christian-Catholic world view" had been "necessary as a salutary reaction against the horrifying colossal materialism that had developed in the Roman Empire and threatened to destroy all of man's spiritual splendor." Asceticism had been the appropriate antidote to unchecked erotic self-indulgence. "Flesh had become so impudent in that Roman world that it may have required Christian discipline to tame it." After Trimalchio's dinner, that splendid and horrifying orgy that is the centerpiece of Petronius's *Satyricon*, men needed a "starvation diet like Christianity."[8]

This, if rather slapdash, is a brilliant intuition. The attitude of Christianity toward sex, after all, was not without its own ambivalent history; some theologians, at least, had defined sensuality, prudently circumscribed, as the impulsion to innocent and even praiseworthy activities. Principled advocates of sacerdotal celibacy set the clerical elite who followed the call to self-denial apart from the faithful whose place was in the world, to beget more good Christians. Many chose to remember St. Paul's saying that it is better to marry than to burn; ascetics who thought it better to burn than to marry always remained in a minority. St. Jerome, to be sure, had denounced as an adulterer the husband who has passionate loving intercourse with his wife, and his ferocious pursuit of lust into the very lair of lawful marriage found disciples through the ages. But there is little evidence that it made much difference in the sexual practices of sound Christians. That churches of most denominations reprobated sensuality, even married sensuality, cannot be dismissed as a malicious slander spread by disrespectful unbelievers. But thousands of pious men and women seem to have found it possible to combine the most unquestioning submission to religious doctrine with a considerable measure of erotic satisfaction.

This matters to any analysis of nineteenth-century love, for Christian values continued to dominate the lives of millions of nineteenth-century bourgeois. Certainly Christianity found many ways of adapting its ascetic ideals to the exigencies of human nature. The old Roman Catholic belief

8. Heine, *Die Romantische Schule*, in *Heinrich Heines sämtliche Werke*, ed. Oskar Walzel et al., 10 vols. (1910–1915), VII, 8–9.

of Mary's immaculate conception, significantly raised to dogmatic status by Pope Pius IX in 1854, is a historic piece of denial. It freed at least one woman from the burden of original sin, even though her parents, St. Joachim and St. Anne, had conceived her in the ordinary human manner. Coupled with the dogma that Jesus's mother remained a virgin and that his father was God, these legends clustering around Mary must be the boldest, most picturesque family romance ever concocted. They embody, and deftly elaborate, children's typical refusal to believe that their parents engage in sexual intercourse and their favorite secret fiction that, in any event, their parentage is supremely exalted. Yet secular literature written in the Catholic centuries was often an energetic, sometimes coarse tribute to the pleasures of sexuality. Andreas Capellanus's much-quoted treatise, *De amore*, which sums up chivalric notions of love, flatly describes the erotic emotions as a physical passion, a keen suffering, generated by looking and thinking about the body of a person of the other sex; Capellanus insists that only those "capable of doing the work of Venus" are fit for love. This was one view, a secular view, characteristic of the French court circles late in the twelfth century; around the same time, Peter Lombard, the celebrated Italian theologian, could voice distaste for all, even for married, sensuality by echoing the stringent words of St. Jerome: "All ardent love for one's own wife is adultery." Christian reflections on love moved between these two poles, though there was, in the prescriptive literature, unremitting emphasis on the sinfulness of sex. Hence sexuality remained, even for the devout, something of a problem. Centuries before Andreas Capellanus and Peter Lombard, St. Augustine, whom no one would accuse of relaxed morals after his conversion, had argued that sexual intercourse itself had once been innocuous enough, in the Garden of Eden. It was only after Eve's disobedience, with the Fall, that lust came into the world; before that, Adam and Eve had copulated without sin, without any admixture of concupiscence.[9]

Protestants would make their own accommodations. The Puritans, for all their reputation of dour prudery (a misreading that went unquestioned in the nineteenth century) did not frown on married joys; they were not puritanical in their view of love. "The Use of the Marriage Bed," wrote one early Massachusetts divine, Edward Taylor, is "founded in mans Nature"; others, like John Cotton, enthusiastically seconding Taylor, ridiculed the Catholic cult of virginity, and quoted the "Holy Spirit" as

9. Andreas Capellanus: *The Art of Courtly Love*, tr. and ed. John Jay Parry (1941), 33; C. S. Lewis: *The Allegory of Love: A Study in Medieval Tradition* (1936), 15; St. Augustine: *The City of God*, Book XIV, chapters 18–24. See Peter Gay, *The Enlightenment*, II, *The Science of Freedom* (1969), 196n.

reminding erring humans that "it is not good that man should be alone."
They thought highly of marriage, so highly that they legislated against
adultery and fornication with draconic severity. But they did not seri
ously expect their laws to be invariably obeyed. "The Protestant ethic,"
Oskar Pfister, Swiss pastor and highly effective lay analyst, wrote to
his friend Sigmund Freud in 1909, "removed the odium of impurity from
sexual intercourse. Indeed," he speculated, "the Reformation is funda
mentally nothing other than an analysis of Catholic sexual repression"—
though, he immediately conceded, "unfortunately a very inadequate
one."[10] Nineteenth-century Protestants, wrestling with their demanding
superegos as they pondered their contraceptive devices, were not quite so
confident; their lives exhibited how inadequate the Reformation's work
had been in liberating men from guilt over sexual pleasure. But Pfister's
sweeping generalizations, like those of Heine, hint at the complexity of
religious attitudes toward sexuality, a complexity that anti-Christian
polemicists did not have the grace to acknowledge.

Still, when all allowances have been made for the capacity of Christian
casuistry to accommodate carnal human nature, the Catholic cult of
virginity and praise of monasticism, the Protestant constriction of love
to the sober performance of lawful procreative tasks, and the insistence
of both that lust is a sin, left deposits of guilt and depression on many
nineteenth-century minds. There was a general sense that respectable
love is the very antithesis of libertine, and no hesitation in affirming that
Christian civilization had tamed Eros. For nineteenth-century bourgeois
the consequences of religious doctrines were all too plain: they sub
ordinated concupiscence to affection in lawful, lifelong marriage, and
laid it down, once more, that erotic desire is permissible only as it is
directed to the procreation of offspring. This Christian perspective re
mained, for most bourgeois, a regulative if not always an attainable ideal

But it was not without its critics. The dominant religious definitions
of love were under attack from two quarters, the Enlightenment tradi
tions and the romantic movement. It is customary, and appropriate, to
set these two great waves of philosophical inquiry, political polemics, and
literary production into opposition to one another; certainly, many of
the romantics, in country after country, thought of the philosophes as
the enemy—or, rather, as one enemy. A number of romantics, after all
never left, or returned to, the Christian faith of their fathers. But in their

10. Taylor: "Commonplace Book"; Cotton: *A Meet Help* (1699), 16, Edmund S
Morgan: "The Puritans and Sex," *The New England Quarterly*, XV, 4 (1942), 592
Pfister to Freud: February 18, 1909, *Sigmund Freud-Oskar Pfister, Briefe, 1909–1939*
ed. Ernst L. Freud and Heinrich Meng (1963), 14.

challenge to accepted views on love, the Enlightenment and Romanticism found themselves intermittent, somewhat improbable, allies. Both affronted respectable middle-class prescriptions on eroticism at their most tender points.

For the men of the Enlightenment, all Christianity was the sworn enemy of reason and passion alike, Protestantism only slightly less so than Catholicism. It was, in their eyes, addicted to superstition and myth-making, preferring fairy tales to scientific explanations—so vehemently that it had always persecuted scientists and philosophers as viciously as lay in its power. These charges were epitomized, wittily or ponderously, in the tendentious dissections of Christian doctrine and practice that the eighteenth-century deists and their atheistic successors conducted across Europe. Indeed, the pitiless unmasking of the Christian war on reason became the supreme mission of Voltaire's later years, and Voltaire had active and talented supporters in his acts of intellectual aggression.

This anti-religious crusade is familiar. What is less well known is that the Enlightenment also assailed the Christian dispensation for its hostility to the passions. Religion, the philosophes charged, made room for man's emotions, but principally to lament his incurable hankering for sin, which is to say that it grievously slandered human nature. The philosophes, in company on this point with educated and disciplined Christians, disdained shameless emotional displays as the preserve of religious enthusiasts. These outbursts of credulous, often fanatical effervescence were obviously not the passions the Enlightenment found praiseworthy; they were a primitive, highly dangerous excitement in the service of superstition, mainly endemic among the lower orders. Besides, the Christian urge to annihilate the devotees of reason, or of competing superstitions, struck the philosophes as the natural and necessary by-product of Christian arrogance. In fostering enthusiasm and intolerance, Christians gave play to man's least creditable passions. In depressing contrast, they failed to value those passions that characterize human nature at its best: pride, the confident sense of one's worth, and sensuality, that pleasurable and valuable family of sensations.

The philosophes' praise of erotic passion, then, was embodied in their general view of the world and a chapter in their critique of Christianity. "Our passions," wrote David Hume, "are the only causes of our labour," a proposition that his fellow philosophes had no difficulty endorsing. Denis Diderot, less inhibited than his friends, would translate this appreciation of the elemental passions into a lyrical hymn to sexuality. He recognized that sensual excitement, exigent and monopolistic, had its dangers; it distorted judgment as it subverted reason. Still, he could celebrate erotic ardor as the magnificent, ubiquitous spring of action. "There is a bit of testicle," he wrote with vulgar and unmatched economy, "at the bottom of our most sublime sentiments and most refined tenderness."[11] Freud might have quoted this aphorism as an early, rather crude, comment on the work of sublimation. He knew, as Diderot had known before him, that the most exquisite flower of love grows from the soil of erotic urges.

Freud in fact quoted more than once, and with evident pleasure, another sentence of Diderot's, from *Le neveu de Rameau*. "If the little savage were left to himself," Diderot has his spokesman say about Rameau's nephew's little boy, "keeping all his childish simplicity and joining the bit of rationality of the infant in the cradle to the violent passions of the man of thirty, he would strangle his father and sleep with his mother."[12] We have come to understand that the particular family triangle Diderot has sketched is only one form, and that the simplest, of the Oedipus complex. But this intrusive discovery—never elaborated, never followed up— was an epoch-making contribution to man's reflections on love; a perception, however intuitive and incomplete, of the hidden but critically important work that sexual and aggressive drives perform in all human beings. It would take more than a century before psychoanalysis could systematize the share of the Oedipus complex in man's erotic history.

Diderot, making the philosophes' case most amusingly and persuasively, took the logic of the Enlightenment to its utmost limits. His lubricious aphorisms and unbuttoned analyses of sexuality pervade all his writings, his letters as much as his essays and his fictions, and they all make the same aggressive point. They were weapons in the great polemic against Christianity in which he, and his associates, were so passionately engaged. Philosophes other than Diderot—Hume and Holbach and the pioneer,

11. "Of Commerce," *The Philosophical Works of David Hume*, ed. T. H. Green and T. H. Grose, 4 vols (1882 ed.), III, 293; Diderot to Damilaville (November 3, 1760), *Correspondance*, III, 216. Significantly, Diderot did not claim this idea as his own, and quoted Madame d'Aine, Holbach's mother-in-law, as saying that "it is impossible to analyze the most delicate of feelings without discovering a bit of filth in them." To Sophie Volland [November 2 to 6 or 8, 1760], ibid., 236. The idea was familiar to advanced circles at mid-eighteenth-century. Thus the marquis de Vauvenargues, an aphorist and minor thinker whom Voltaire took under his protection, wrote: "The great thoughts come from the heart," and "Reason misleads us more often than nature." "Réflexions et maximes," in *Maximes et réflexions*, ed. Lucien Meunier (1945), 43, 44.
12. *Le neveu de Rameau*, ed. Jean Fabre (1963), 95. Freud found occasion to quote this observation in his *Introductory Lectures on Psychoanalysis* (1917), *S.E.*, XVI, 337–38; "The Expert Opinion in the Halsmann Case" (1931), *S.E.*, XXI, 251; and the posthumous *Outline of Psychoanalysis* (1940), *S.E.*, XXIII, 192.

Montesquieu, before them—also put the validity of Christian attitudes about love on trial, calling them depressing, mendacious, and hypocritical. They were impressed by the variety of moral customs and codes across the world and throughout history, and far from persuaded that the erotic impulse is somehow sinful. Hume conjectured that incest might be pernicious in all societies, but less certain that lifelong monogamy is everywhere the appropriate institution to reconcile individual desires with social needs. Christian asceticism struck Hume and his allies as an absurdity, probably more pernicious than incest could ever be. Invoking their vision of a human nature freed from all admixtures of original sin, the philosophes worked out a radical alternative to Christian doctrines of love. They opened vistas that the nineteenth-century bourgeois found most disquieting, vistas he might encounter in his occasional shamefaced resort to libertine literature but in general would refuse to explore.

Compared with the philosophes' subversions of Christian prescriptions for love, romantic alternatives proved comparatively tame. While only a few bourgeois would find the romantics' ideas appropriate guides to their own conduct, these ideas would generate fantasies and suggest actions that the more venturesome among middle-class lovers could at least imagine as realistic. The very retreat of romanticism from the unapologetic, scientific carnality of the Enlightenment made romantic erotic speculations appear as interesting invitations or deserved reproaches to bourgeois who thought themselves unimaginative, downright timid, in the domain of love.

Needless to say, the romantics did not perceive their ideas about love as a retreat. Those among them who chose to comment on the history of ideas—Blake, for one, or the Schlegel brothers—would criticize the philosophes for shallowness, for their one-sided passion for physiology; to them, Enlightenment writings on love reduced the most exalted of emotions into a mere play of glands. It is true enough that the Age of Enlightenment did not develop a distinctive philosophy of love, though Richardson's *Clarissa* or Rousseau's *La nouvelle Héloïse* and its other novels found much to say about it. In their reading, their private lives, and more permanently, their essays and treatises, the philosophes had shown a far more intense interest in sex than in love. Their achievement was impressive; they pursued the erotic to its roots in desire and liberated it from facile moralizing. But the romantics were inclined to discount this achievement, and, until Freud was to return to it around 1900, the Enlightenment's work on love seemed written in water. Moralizing, shallow or profound, returned to invade the nineteenth-century debate on love. Many of the romantics conducted their lives in ways no more respectable

than had the philosophes. But their pronouncements on love read like a
reply to what was, to their minds, the debased sensuality of the Enlightenment.

Precisely like the philosophes, the romantics embedded their reflections
on love in whatever general view of life they could muster. But they were
more united on what they opposed—low-minded philosophes on one side
and philistine bourgeois on the other—than on what they advocated: the
romantics did not form a school of thought. Some liked to stress the
excruciating difficulties, others the unearthly consummations attending
erotic life. Not surprisingly, their readers found themselves troubled and
enchanted by both. The moderate position, later expressed by Freud, that
"an obstacle is required to drive libido to its height,"[13] had less appeal
than the masochistic or orgiastic extravagance that romantic notions
seductively invited. They gave rise to nostalgic fantasies, to regressive
longings for union with infantile objects.

This romantic celebration of love, a somewhat narcissistic overvaluation
not so much of the loved object as of love itself, gave romanticism (as
commonly understood) its lasting vogue. "Eternal love," as Valentin,
Musset's youthful hero in *Il ne faut jurer de rien*, calls it, was the watchword of the romantics' fictions and, among the more philosophical of the
tribe, their thinking. It was, as the English travel writer and popular
biographer Francis Gribble put the consensus in 1910, not so much that
"the Romantics invented, or even discovered, love. Love, we may take it,
is a great deal older than literature; many men and women had loved and
written of love before the turn of the Romantics came." But, Gribble
thought, they were the first "who put love, so to say, on the programme,
took it seriously as an experience and as a pageant, and regarded it as an
integral part of the liberal education of a man and woman of letters."[14]

The popular perception of "romantic love" which conjures up yearning
heroes, pale heroines, exotic scenery, stormy nature, cruel obstacles, and

13. "Über die allgemeinste Erniedrigung des Liebeslebens," *St.A.*, V, 207; "On the
Universal Tendency in Love," *S.E.*, XI, 187.
14. *The Passions of the French Romantics* (1910), 2–3. Opening a rambling essay,
mainly devoted to demonstrating the pernicious influence of women over politics,
Ralph Nevill, a prolific English amateur, author of books on fashion, travel, and art,
wrote in 1912, in a characteristic declamation: "Of all the passions which have dominated humanity and eternally excited its interest, love alone still asserts that supremacy
assumed when the first man folded the first woman in his ardent embrace. Empires
have fallen, entire races have disappeared; but the primeval affection of our first
parents, which Nature has dignified above all other passions, remains stable in a world
of perpetual change." The title of the book that this passage opens is, fittingly, *The
Romantic Past* (1912), 1.

deeply satisfying deaths is, though debased, in a rough and ready way a fair condensation of romantic preoccupations and romantic settings. The intimate, sultry association of love with death, above all, was a seductive romantic theme that enjoyed an enormous and tenacious popularity, appealing to a widespread latent need for regression to early undifferentiated joys in nineteenth-century readers. By the time that Wagner's Tristan and Isolde went to their love deaths, it was an old story. But while this little catalogue—yearning heroes, pale heroines, dying lovers and the rest—summarizes the intrigues of romantic poems and novels accurately enough, it slights the metaphysical, often religious claims that romantics liked to stake out for the highest of all emotions and grandest of all destinies. More: it wholly neglects what would emerge as the central tenet of all branches of romanticism, the creative energy of the imagination. No matter how carnal the romantic in his inclinations or his expression, he trusted his imagination to purify his sensuality. He saw its work as something better than the mere elaboration of ready-made materials, as, rather, an autonomous shaping force, "a dim analogue," as Coleridge put it, "of creation."[15] That is why poetry proved to be the preferred romantic vehicle, why romantics found myths so attractive and interpreted nature as a vast system of symbols.

Romantic love naturally participates in this enthusiastic vision, at once a foundation and demonstration of its force. "Love," wrote Novalis, "is the final purpose of world history—the amen of the universe." For him, at least, human love is nothing less than applied religion. "Adoration," that word much abused as a picturesque synonym for the passionate overvaluation of the loved object was, in the romantic era, seriously canvassed as an apt characterization of real feelings. Love, after all, was, for them, applied religion. The imagination even transfigures physical appearance: the lover finds the beloved beautiful no matter what her actual appearance; he may adore even a woman he has never seen. Philosophes might have agreed, coolly, that infatuation is a species of willful blindness, but they would have assigned physiological and psychological causes to conduct for which the romantics found less earthy explanations. "The universe is and remains my watchword," Friedrich Schlegel wrote to his beloved Dorothea. "Do you really love if you do not find the world in your beloved?"[16] It was a rhetorical question.

15. René Wellek, "The Concept of Romanticism in Literary History" (1949), in Concepts of Criticism, ed. Stephen G. Nichols, Jr. (1963), 180–81.
16. Ricarda Huch, Die Romantik: Blütezeit, Ausbreitung und Verfall (2 vols., 1908, 1911; ed. 1951), 227, 234.

But most romantics found adoration to be highly problematic. They proclaimed erotic gratification to be a beautiful and necessary ingredient in love, and in their lives they tried to honor their proclamation. Some elevated sexual intercourse into a symbol of that uniting and universal force, Eros, which holds the organic universe together. "Perhaps," Novalis speculated, "sensual ecstasy belongs to love as sleep does to life. It is not the noblest part, and the robust person will always rather be awake than asleep." Yet sleep he must, regularly and deeply. This puts the romantic doctrine on love with fair precision, and not the German version alone. Carnal and spiritual elements are, in true love, intertwined, but of the two, the spiritual is the nobler. "A marriage," to quote Novalis once more, "should really be a slow, continuous embrace, generation, nutrition, formation of a common harmonic being."[17]

This was a strenuous ideal. It also sounded like a subversive ideal. Much followed from it, far more destructive of accepted ways than fashionable romantic rhetoric, with its often evasive elevation, would lead one to suspect. The romantic ideal implied a new appreciation of woman's nature and woman's place. But here, too, the romantics did not present a united front. It was Byron, after all, a great romantic, who wrote those much-quoted lines in Don Juan, setting it down that

> Man's love is of man's life a thing apart,
> 'Tis woman's whole existence.

Conventional bourgeois subscribed to this doctrine without hesitation, for it corresponded perfectly with the dominant middle-class ideal of domesticity. Man stands in the grinding, ugly world of business and politics; gratifying ambitions and searching out profits are as imperative for him as satisfying the tender passion. Woman, for her part, guardian of the hearth and of familial purity, has the time, the duty, nothing less than the sacred mission to put love first. Love, that belated romantic, Jules Michelet, insisted is woman's destiny.[18] This sexual separation was neither simple nor complete: the romantics were not alone in pointing out that men often sought power or made money to win love. And this rather shopworn romantic notion of modern man as the chivalrous knight in a black coat conquering the world that he might conquer his woman was a practical ideal for the time: respectable bourgeois, after all, could not marry until the prospective husband had a secure position and an adequate bank account.

At the same time, romantics offered women other, less constricted

17. Ibid., 244–45.
18. Byron: Don Juan, canto I, cxciv; Michelet: L'Amour (1858; 4th ed., 1859), 65.

vistas. If true love presupposes mutuality, if that slow continuous embrace that Novalis saw as the ideal marriage is to aim higher than merely at frequent love-making, woman must be granted the untrammeled unfolding of her capacities. Much happiness in romantic love, the romantics thought, issued from intelligent, wide-ranging conversation, from the play of wit, from companionable activities that an ignorant, unschooled woman, no matter how natively gifted, could never sustain. Moreover, the romantic ideal implied the need for experimentation in the world. First love, or love at first sight, were not prominent elements in the romantic program. Some thinkers, like Kierkegaard, defined romantic love precisely as "immediate: to see her was to love her."[19] But for most romantics, in contrast, love was a joint and extended expedition, calling for skill and maturity and the kind of experience that only years of loving, and loving more than one partner, could provide. Eternal love was transferable. While, for the romantics, dreams generated true visions, and the imagination created its own beauty, this did not imply monasticism, or commend the substituting of fantasies for realities. In fact, their celebration of experience and experimentation called marriage, especially lifelong marriage, into question. It even raised difficulties, though quite delicately and only under the pens of a handful of exalted spirits, about the proper limits of love. At this risky point, where the very validity of the incest taboo was in doubt, Shelley, to say nothing of Byron, joined hands with Diderot.

These radical explorations, however exceptional and, as it were, unpolitical, only sharpened the seductive romantic reproach to bourgeois morality. A few romantics, notably William Wordsworth, celebrated the conjugal state in verse and in life. The impassioned love letters that he and his wife Mary exchanged after ten years of marriage and five children —"how profoundly in body & soul we love each other"—are tributes to the persistence of love and its possibilities. Wordsworth, as Coleridge noted, unable to repress a sneer, was "tenderly attached" to his wife and would "ridicule the existence of any other passion, than a compound of Lust with Esteem & Friendship, & confined to one Object." But that, Coleridge thought, only showed Wordsworth to be thoroughly conventional and "by nature incapable of love."[20]

19. Søren Kierkegaard, *Either/Or* (1843), tr. Walter Lowrie, rev. Howard A. Johnson (1959), 2 vols., II, 20.
20. William Wordsworth to Mary Wordsworth, June 3–4, 1812, *The Love Letters of William and Mary Wordsworth*, ed. Beth Darlington (1981), 229; Coleridge to Henry Crabb Robinson, March 12, 1811. *Collected Letters of Samuel Taylor Coleridge*, ed. Earl Leslie Griggs, 6 vols. (1956–1971), III, 305.

This was an ungenerous reading, and an involuntary tribute to at least one loving married couple, but Coleridge's point was plain: bourgeois, among whom he included Wordsworth, were incapable of the kind of exalted union to which the romantics aspired. Their marriages were mere shams or, at best, inferior unions. "What people call a happy marriage," Friedrich Schlegel wrote, "stands to love as a correct poem stands to an improvised song." As he formulated the position in one of his most uncompromising fragments, "most marriages are mere concubinage, morganatic marriages, or rather provisional attempts and remote approximations to a real marriage." In bourgeois marriage, he charged in his early novel, *Lucinde*, an explicit, rather disheveled manifesto on romantic love, "the husband loves in his wife only her gender, the wife in her husband only the degree of his natural qualities and of his civic existence, and both in their property."[21] This was the utmost to which ordinary mortals could aspire, and it was not enough. With its tepid feelings, boring conversations, constrained friendships, and assiduous efforts to please others, middle-class marriage did not embody love but institutionalized indifference. *Lucinde* is an early exemplar of what I have called the literature of reproach.

The bourgeois struck back. When *Lucinde* was first published in 1799, its readers saw only what they derided as its sensuality and its obscenity, and took care to overlook its implicit program. In pointed allegories, inserted vignettes, lush detail, and willful asides, *Lucinde* depicts a love affair as a happy blending of physical and spiritual qualities, and woman as something better than an erotic toy, submissive wife, and angelic mother. Schlegel presented his short experimental novel as a "hieroglyph" of "eternal love." But his readers preferred to concentrate on the abandon with which Julius and Lucinde scatter their clothes about them, the suggestive dialogue of the naked lovers, the earthy representations of what Schlegel was pleased to call the "sacred fire," the "fresh charm of her breasts" revealed in "love's combat," the hints at the erotic nature of children and the childish roots of eroticism: "Surely! It is an essential element in the nature of man that he wants to eat everything he loves." This was doctrine heady enough to make bourgeois uncomfortable. Schlegel's own mother, already worried to learn that her son was living in Berlin with a Jewess, found *Lucinde* sad proof that her Friedrich had

21. Fragment 268. Friedrich Schlegel, *Seine prosaischen Jugendschriften*, ed. J. Minor, 2 vols. (1882), II, 247; Fragment 34, ibid., 208; *Lucinde* (1799; ed. n.d.), Postscript Jürgen Sang, 51.

"neither religion nor sound principles."[22] The respectable could do nothing with such writing except to shake their heads.

They could do little more with the writings, or the lives, of romantics elsewhere. Shelley, in his short, concentrated, fierce existence, formed and defiantly enjoyed the most unconventional domestic arrangements, and trumpeted the doctrine that love is always primary and marriage, at least bourgeois marriage, always slavery: "Love withers under constraint; its very essence is liberty." A little later, in France, Alfred de Musset experimented with loves in which one element or the other—the sentimental, the carnal, the intellectual—predominated. And in Shelley's own time, Byron, accompanied by scandal, followed by rumors, pilloried by pamphlets, cut his sexual swath across England and the Continent, amassing scores of mistresses in a display of frantic sexual athleticism. In January 1819, stung by a report that Lord Lauderdale had been gossiping about him and about some "piece" he had had, Byron was reduced to boasting to his friends John Cam Hobhouse and Douglas Kinnaird by cataloguing his recent conquests as though he were adding the role of Leporello to that of Don Giovanni: "Which 'piece' does he mean?—Since last year I have run the Gauntlet; it is the Tarruscelli—the Da Mosti— the Spineda—the Lotti—the Rizzato—the Eleanora—the Carlotta—the Giuletta—the Alvisi—the Zambieri—the Eleanora da Bezzi—(who was the King of Naples' Gioaschino's mistress—at least one of them)—the Theresina of Mazzurati—the Glettenheimer—& her sister—the Luigia & her mother—the Fornaretta—the Santa—the Caligari—the Portiera—the Bolognese figurante—the Tentora and her sister—cum multis aliis—some of them are Countesses—& some of them are Cobblers' wives—some noble —some middling—some low—& all whores—which does the damned old 'Ladro & porco fotutto' mean?—I have had them all & thrice as many to boot since 1817."[23] The hints at homosexual pleasure in Shelley's poems and the more obscure among Byron's erotic expeditions did not make the romantic pace any more eligible as a guide to middle-class ways of loving. A rather vulgarized, desiccated notion of romantic love, imprecise but immensely suggestive, hinting at ineffable experiences, at extraordinary longings and consummations, retained its popularity long after the waves of romanticism in music, painting, and literature had exhausted them-

22. Ibid., 83–84, 20; Ernst Behler, *Friedrich Schlegel in Selbstzeugnissen und Bild-dokumenten* (1966), 16.

23. Shelley: from his essay on free love, an appendix to Note 9 of *Queen Mab*, in *Shelley on Love, An Anthology*, ed. Richard Holmes (1980), 45; Byron: January 19, 1819. *Byron's Letters and Journals*, VI, 92.

selves. The conduct of the more notorious among the romantics, whether Friedrich Schlegel or Percy Bysshe Shelley, Alfred de Musset or Lord Byron, might be taken, as I have suggested, as a reproach to bourgeois too timid to follow such strenuous performers. For the most part, though, it was a scandal that good bourgeois could only deplore, and in their most candid moments, envy.

2. Cynics and Enthusiasts

In his life and his ideas, the most rewarding theorist of love in the early nineteenth century combined and intermingled the intellectual legacies on love that made ordinary bourgeois so uneasy. Henri Beyle, the man of many pseudonyms best known as Stendhal, was a romantic by profession and a philosophe by inclination. His life was a persistent, intelligent, witty, sometimes rather forlorn exploration of love and of its often devious by-ways: intimations of impotence, hints at homosexual moments, desires for incest richly complicate the already rich amalgam of amorous adventure and sexual arousal that pervade his novels. His thinking about love proved so rewarding because, in addition to enacting a variety of erotic possibilities in his love affairs and reporting on them in his novels, he published a brilliant, highly personal essay, De l'Amour, which he advertised as a "Physiology of love."

The study of love has sturdily resisted becoming a science, but there were, throughout the nineteenth century, intrepid spirits who tried to make it so. I am speaking not of recipes for seduction; those belong to the domain of art, or better, of craft. I am speaking of efforts to classify types of love, to describe its symptoms, diagnose its cause, chart its course, and document its exhaustion. The most penetrating, if by no means complete or wholly satisfactory, contribution to this genre came after 1900, with the work of Freud. But among its predecessors, Stendhal's De l'Amour stands supreme, original for all its shameless borrowings, a disarming, irresistible mixture of poignant confession and technical treatise, a monograph in the science of love.

It was rather odd science that Stendhal was doing; the romantic, the novelist, and above all, the distraught lover shoulder aside the competent investigator on page after page. Stendhal was an impassioned and, more often than not, an unfortunate lover of women. His first defeat came at the hands of fate, with the tragic end to his oedipal engagement with his mother, prolonged far beyond the usual time. "My mother," he wrote in his unfinished autobiography, La vie de Henry Brulard, "was a charming woman, and I was in love with my mother." He could never forget her plumpness, her fresh prettiness, and his childish lust for her. He remembered that he wanted her to be naked, and to cover her with kisses, especially on her breasts. He found it gratifying to recall that his mother had loved him extravagantly in return and had often kissed him; he would respond to "her kisses with such ardor she was often obliged to leave." Young Stendhal's paradise was complete with snake: "I abhorred my father when he came and interrupted our kisses." But paternal rivalry was not the worst calamity the young lover must face: "Deign to remember that I lost her through childbed, when I was barely seven years old."[24] It was after that, he comments subtly and sagely, that his moral life began. The idealized females he would love in later years, sometimes in vain, were woven of solid physical reality and touching cherished memories.

When Stendhal began drafting De l'Amour late in 1819 he was, once again, in the grip of an unrequited passion. Mathilde Viscontini Dembowski must have been an extraordinary woman. Energetic, clever, self-confident, she was the mother of two sons, and committed to the patriotic underground movement for Italian independence, the Carbonari; separated from her husband, she was not at all in love with her importunate suitor. De l'Amour remains the record of an experience, if scarcely a conventional experience. If the book deserves the name of science, it is experimental science, with its author using himself as a guinea pig. Stendhal, in short, was as much the student of mind as he was the teller of tales and the lover of women. He aspired to the detachment of the diagnostician, and aimed to give an "exact and scientific description" rather than a novel of love. His ambition, he recognized, was almost beyond him; the short, much quoted ninth chapter of De l'Amour dramatizes his straining for clarity and objectivity, and his unconquerable loyalty to the veracity of his feelings: "I am making every possible effort to be dry. I want to impose silence on my heart which believes it has a great deal to say. I am always trembling that I may have only written a sigh when I think I

24. Stendhal, Oeuvres intimes, ed. Henri Martineau (1955), 60. The psychoanalyst Edmund Bergler, commenting on this famous passage, has rightly wondered why Stendhal did not repress this early passion, as is the normal fate of oedipal wishes, and speculates that this insistence on his oedipal love covers, in complicated ways, powerful unconscious homosexual feelings. Certainly, Stendhal had occasional conscious glimpses of homosexual attractions—and recorded them candidly. Bergler, Talleyrand, Napoleon, Stendhal, Grabbe: Psychoanalytisch-Biographische Essays (1935), 78–87.

have stated a truth."[25] *De l'Amour* was perhaps a failure, in part, but it was a glorious failure. It is an improvisation of genius.

As an aristocrat of experience, with his lofty contempt for the mediocre multitude, Stendhal was plainly not writing for the average bourgeois of his day. It is notorious that he defined his public as "The Happy Few," and basked in an imagined posthumous triumph fifty or perhaps a hundred years later. Like other romantics, he had revelled in the heady excitement of the Napoleonic days and diagnosed the years of the Restoration as the reign of boredom. The perception that *ennui* is the abominable signature of his time informs Stendhal's two masterly novels, *Le rouge et le noir* and the *Chartreuse de Parme*, and it flavors his diagnosis of the age in *De l'Amour* where he deplores "our present boredom" and the deadly conventionality that governs all. Love, he writes, is "a kind of madness very rare in France." Indeed, he explicitly doubts that money-grubbing bourgeois would ever understand him: while he had made sincere efforts to be "clear and lucid," he feared that men with money and of coarse tastes, men who had made a hundred thousand francs the year before they opened his treatise, especially "bankers, manufacturers, respectable industrialists," were probably beyond his reach. "I cannot work miracles." Rather, his book would be more intelligible to those "who have made a great deal of money on the stock exchange or the lottery," that is, to the adventurers, the conquistadors, among the bourgeoisie; their way of getting rich was, after all, compatible with day dreaming, with allowing oneself to be stirred by the paintings of Prudhon, by a passage from Mozart, and by the glances of a woman one desires. In depressing contrast, the archetypal bourgeois is sadly lacking in imagination: "This is not how people who pay two thousand workers at the end of the week *waste their time*; their minds are always on the useful and the positive." Such typical bourgeois traits as the fear of ridicule and the appetite for social climbing are love's nemesis.[26]

This is why Stendhal chose to single out the United States where, he thought, the rule of the bourgeoisie was most secure. Americans are supreme rationalists, hence love is not at home there. "Nothing is quite so anti-imagination as the government of the United States of America." In his chapter on love in the United States, significantly the shortest in his comparative survey, he notes, almost with a movement of sympathy: "It is as if the sources of sensibility have dried up among these people. They

25. *De l'Amour* (1822; ed. Henri Martineau, 1938), 21, 57.
26. Ibid., 36, 21–27.

are just, they are rational, and they are not happy at all."[27] Like others in the nineteenth century pursuing that favorite intellectual pastime, the study of national character, Stendhal did not allow ignorance to slow him down; he had been in the United States only in his mind, and his reading about the country was skimpy. But that mattered little: the Americans were, for Stendhal, the quintessential bourgeois, and it followed, by definition, that their hope for experiencing real love was exceedingly slim.

But De l'Amour, though a splendid model for the literature of reproach, is not just another derisive dissection of the materialistic bourgeoisie. It is, somewhat surprisingly, a reformist tract. Stendhal's chapters on the education of women are early forceful statements of a position that feminists would make their own several decades later. Like much of the rest of De l'Amour, these chapters draw heavily on the work of others, notably on that of the psychologist Destutt de Tracy, whom Stendhal greatly admired and cheerfully pillaged, but they bear the imprint of Stendhal's wit, his irresistible verve. The foolishness, timidity, empty-headedness of most modern women was, Stendhal argues, entirely the product of oppressive social arrangements: "Present-day education of young girls is the fruit of chance and of the most absurd pride." It "leaves idle the most brilliant faculties in them," much to their sorrow and, ironically, to that of men as well. For while prudent men may insist on finding a wife who is gentle and retiring, they will pay for it once they have married one of that type, when both will be mortally bored.[28]

Stendhal had no patience with arguments from appearance: women are what men have made them. "People concede that a little girl of ten has twenty times the cleverness of a young rascal of the same age. Why is she, at twenty, a great idiot, awkward, timid, and afraid of spiders, while the rascal is a man of wit and intelligence?" The question was rhetorical, since the answer was obvious: men are, and have for untold centuries been despots. They have degraded women into household drudges, into slaves to their children, into sick nurses; they have kept women ignorant lest, literate and eager for more education, they neglect the tasks to which masculine selfishness has condemned them. But this traditional way with women is not only unjust and cruel, it is also self-defeating: unlike the stupid wax doll whom modern man seems to like, a bright and educated

27. Ibid., 52, 197. And he says: "Young American girls in the United States are so imbued with, and secure in, rational ideas that love, that flower of life, has deserted the youth there. In Boston one can leave a young girl alone with a handsome stranger, certain that she will be thinking only of the marriage portion of her future husband." Ibid., 276.

28. De l'Amour, 220.

woman will not need to step outside her home for love, even physical love, to enjoy a little pathetic happiness. "I maintain," Stendhal proposed tersely, "that a woman should spend every day three or four hours at leisure, just as men of sense spend their leisure hours." The woman emancipated from her enslavement to ignorance and ascribed domestic duties will not lose her femininity in the process: "The graces of women are in no way linked to ignorance." On the contrary, free spirits will produce happier marriages.[29]

For Stendhal was not a critic of marriage as such. Like other physiologists of love, he strongly urged the proposition that love joins affection to passion. In his first classification of love—passion-love, stylized love (*l'amour goût*), physical love, and love-from-vanity—he already laid it down that sheer lust, physical love, is not the kind of love that matters most or that he proposes to analyze. And he notes that among civilized peoples, "an affectionate woman reaches the point of finding physical pleasure only with the man she loves." No admirer of the noble savage, Stendhal proclaimed love to be "the miracle of civilization. Among savage or barbarian peoples one finds only physical and the coarsest love." He subscribed to the dictum in the medieval code of courtly love that "it is improper to love her whom one would be ashamed to desire in marriage."[30]

On this point, Stendhal's reformist impulses merge with his exalted definition of love. Love requires esteem, and esteem is possible only after woman is allowed to exercise her gifts to the full. In fact, only a marriage incorporating all these qualities, he insists, has the right to that name: "Woman's fidelity in a marriage in which there is no love is probably against nature." This is strong talk, and its implied defense of a right to free divorce must have seemed daring to the few good bourgeois who happened upon Stendhal's treatise. "It offends modesty far more to go to bed with a man one has seen only twice, after pronouncing three Latin words in church, than to surrender, in spite of oneself, to a man one has adored for two years."[31] This was no less daring, and not only to those *bien-pensant* rich bourgeois families who continued to believe, throughout the nineteenth century, that arranged marriages were best.

Like a true romantic, Stendhal had serious doubts whether bourgeois could ever rise to the imaginative heights he thought essential to love, whether in marriage or out. Men of imagination were exposed to grievous risks, notably to that of the "fiasco"—impotence, in other words—to

29. Ibid., 223.
30. Ibid., 39–41, 43–44, 93, 343.
31. Ibid., 238, 80.

which Stendhal devotes a terse, partly autobiographical chapter and, indeed, later, a whole novel, *Armance*. But without the risk of fiasco, no hope for love: this was the ambiguous share of the imagination in man's erotic economy.

Stendhal's treatment of the imagination is the most enduring contribution of *De l'Amour* to nineteenth-century thinking about love. The idea that the imagination is indispensable to lovers is, of course, as old as Plato. The troubadours had explored its artful devices. Stendhal's beloved Shakespeare had said it for all time, deftly joining love to poetry and madness:

> The lunatic, the lover, and the poet,
> Are of imagination all compact.

It remained to reduce the work of the imagination in the erotic sphere to rule, or to find a telling metaphor that would persuasively condense its share in that poetic lunacy called love. Stendhal proposed to do so with his felicitous invention, "crystallization." He is his own best expositor: "Leave a lover alone with himself for twenty-four hours, and this is what you will find: At the salt mines of Salzburg, they throw the bough of a tree defoliated by the winter into the depths of the mine that have been abandoned; two or three months after, they haul it out covered with brilliant crystallizations: the smallest twigs, those no larger that a chickadee's claw, are adorned with an infinite number of diamonds, changeable and dazzling; the original branch is no longer recognizable. What I am calling crystallization is the work of the mind, which draws from everything that happens the discovery that the beloved object possesses new perfections."[32] It is not that all beautiful creatures are loved, but that all loved creatures are beautiful.

This imaginative overvaluation does not erupt with the beginning of love. In the timetable of love's course that Stendhal devises, it emerges at a fairly late stage. Love begins with admiration; then fantasy enters with the thought that it would be most pleasurable to kiss the girl. Hope arises and desire makes itself visible. Then, only then, comes real love, the wish to see and touch the lovable object: a century before Freud would do so, Stendhal associated these two senses in erotic activity. It is only after this that "the first crystallization begins." The lover, as the psychoanalysts would later say, empties out his ego and invests his libido in his chosen object: "He underrates his own good qualities and overrates the smallest favors his beloved bestows." But crystallization comes in more than one

---

32. Ibid., 42. Jean Stewart and B. C. J. G. Knight have also noted these lines from *A Midsummer Night's Dream*, "Introduction," Stendhal, *Love* (1975), 19.

wave. After the lover is beset by doubts, after the woman has tried to cool his sanguine fantasies, he finds himself prey to a second repetition, to the scintillating idea, "she loves me." Crystallization, then, has a life of its own: the lover's recognition that he has been mistaken about the target of his love, his need to discard his false hopes and to start again, will produce "doubts about crystallization as such."[33] Yet, however volatile, however often it needs renewal, this imaginative transformation must always come to the lover's aid.

It is arguable, and has been argued, that this analysis is neither very profound nor very original, but only a fanciful way of saying that in love the wish is father to the thought. Stendhal does, after all, say explicitly, that "From the moment he loves, the wisest of men no longer sees any object *as it is*." In all the other passions, "desires must accommodate themselves to cold realities. But here realities ardently model themselves upon desires." Still, crystallization is more than a simple restatement of the old saw that love is blind. It is, to begin with, not a condition but a process, far less a kind of blindness that an adaptive misperception serving the pleasure principle. "Nature commands us to have pleasure," Stendhal notes, and "pleasure augments with the perfections of the loved object."[34] In love, the ego temporarily suspends some of its operations, notably that of reality testing, to secure its desire—a desire that may turn out, even after crystallization has faded, to be really desirable. To associate this process with love is to understand that love contains an admixture of revived memories, old fantasies, perennial needs. It need not be self-destructive: to supply in fantasy what reality embodies only imperfectly, if at all, is to generate pleasure and to sustain morale. A kind of self-fulfilling prophecy, distant ancestor to William James's will to believe, it lends the lover audacity. Finally, crystallization is also, unlike blindness, susceptible of radical revision; it is open to self-criticism, sometimes even to correction.

Certainly, Stendhal had distinguished ancestors in his patient exploration of amorous self-deception. What rescues his treatment from derivativeness—I shall not say, banality, for Stendhal is never banal—is the evocative precision of his metaphor and the brilliant specificity of his instances. The way to reach a new truth, he told his sister Pauline as early as 1804, in one of the didactic letters he liked to send her, was through "many examples." For, the more one took distance from facts, the more "one falls into systems, one starts dreaming, and those listening to you will

33. *De l'Amour*, 42, 63, 46.
34. Ibid., 62–63, 43.

ıake fun of you." His thirst for empiricism was insatiable: while Montes-
uieu, Buffon, and Rousseau, in many respects his masters, had departed
rom the ideal, he for his part had "need of examples, of many, many
acts." Appropriately, then, Stendhal's De l'Amour is a treasure house of
xamples. In the scientific study of love, no less than in its passionate
ursuit, the significant detail can encapsulate the whole course of an affair,
he smallest incident may signify the most decisive erotic event. "In love,"
;tendhal writes in De l'Amour, "everything is a sign." And he lends this
erse assertion, too, as is his habit, concrete form. "The greatest happiness
ove can offer," he notes, "is the first pressure of the hand by the woman
ne loves."³⁵ As a provident, economical writer, Stendhal would later
:mbody this very moment, the lover secretly taking the hand of his be-
oved as the first step in an inexorable, fatal love affair, in his great Le
ouge et le noir.

In short, memories evoked by a flower, a patch of silk, a distant land-
cape, a duet by Rossini, can stimulate the work of crystallization more
ɔotently than the physical presence of the beloved. Stendhal provides
;atisfying material to support Freud's proposition, already quoted, that
finding a love object is always a refinding. With his willful lists and
:onfident aphorisms, his dazzling classifications and illuminating anecdotes,
his rapid tour from lovers to lovers in country after country and suggestive comparison between the erotic styles of Don Juan and of Werther,
Stendhal adumbrates in De l'Amour not merely the analytic flights of
Sigmund Freud but also the melancholy explorations of Marcel Proust, as
scientific in their way as any psychoanalytic study. What is most astonishing about De l'Amour is not its ancestors but its descendants.

Stendhal had called his De l'Amour a physiology. This name, and the
genre he explored so memorably, retained their grip on the nineteenth-
century imagination. Honoré de Balzac published a Physiologie du mariage
in 1829, and Paul Bourget, deftly blending these two titles, a Physiologie
de l'amour moderne, in 1891. It is symptomatic that when Stendhal's De
l'Amour was first translated into German in 1888, it should bear the title,
Physiologie der Liebe.³⁶ The characterization seemed to imply that theo-

35. [August 1804]. Correspondance de Stendhal, ed. Henri Martineau and V. del
Lillo, 3 vols. (1962–1968), I, 143–44; De l'Amour, 158, 122.
36. Translated by Bernhard Saint-Denis. In 1903, the second German translation,
by Arthur Schuring, bore the literal title Ueber die Liebe. Other French physiologies
include Catulle Mendès, L'Art d'aimer (1894) [see below, p. 79], and Rémy de
Gourmont, Physique de l'amour (1903). And see the prolific Italian author Paolo
Mantegazza's enormously popular book of the 1870s, Fisiologia dell' Amore.

rists of love were principally interested in the physical component o
erotic life, and in the strategies leading to sexual conquest.

This impression, though not without substance, is incomplete. To ca
these treatises physiologies was to place them among those irresistibl
popular books of advice, of "codes" and "arts," that publishers coul
count on selling to a sizable, appreciative public.[37] Moreover, it evoke
the materialistic psychology dominant in the century; intent on tracin
mental states back to bodily impulsions, psychologists were inclined t
diagnose the fevers of love as a physical ailment, as a special case o
insanity. Perhaps more significant still was the implicit demand for seriou
scientific consideration that such titles put forward. Jean-Anthelme
Brillat-Savarin, humane magistrate, passable violinist, and immortal gour
met, who dignified his "gastronomical meditations" with the name, L
physiologie du goût, set the tone; endowing the art of cooking with the
polish and prestige of cultivated conversation and philosophical reflection
he encouraged theorists of love to advance similarly exalted claims fo
their work. Indeed, Bourget, in a rather coy self-criticism, noted in the
Preface to his Physiologie that the word (to which, of course, he wa
giving prominence) was merely the sign of a "naive literary snobbery"
that would remind readers of an "old, outmoded genre."[38]

For all these artful pretensions, nineteenth-century physiologists of lov
and marriage were, grave asides apart, worldly, light-hearted, almost
self-consciously frivolous—at least on the surface. Accepting the legacy
of the eighteenth century to the nineteenth, they celebrated the excitement of the chase and insinuated the ecstasies of consummation. They were
guides to the pleasures, complete with astute warnings against the pitfalls,
of sexual adventures, rehearsing once more the cynical geography of love
so memorably laid out in Mozart's and Da Ponte's Così fan tutte. The
energy and authentic feeling that had animated Stendhal's poetic, pseudo-
scientific analysis of love did not wholly die out in the writers who
borrowed his ideas and, sometimes, his language. But enthusiasm came
increasingly to be laced with cynicism, even despair. Metaphors drawn
from the art of war, originally employed to convey a certain hostile
strength, were debased into rhetorical commonplaces. The physiologies
became reports of military campaigns mounted to secure mistresses and to
insure their fidelity, treatises on beds and honeymoons, anatomies of ob-

37. See Herbert J. Hunt, Honoré de Balzac, A Biography (1957), 15; "Préface"
by Maurice Regard, to Balzac, Physiologie du mariage (1829; ed. 1968), 14.
38. Paul Bourget, Physiologie de l'amour moderne (1891), iii.

essive jealousy and the ambiguous joys of adultery, prescriptions for the
malady of infatuation. Hence they had little to say to the average men and
women of the middle class, torn between their pressing feelings and their
exacting consciences, and skeptical of the kind of aristocratic libertinism
that produced such books. Virginity, monogamy, purity—these bourgeois
ideals made only rare appearances in such nineteenth-century works of
strategy and consolation. Rather, the physiologists explicitly addressed
themselves to the topmost strata of the bourgeoisie, to millionaire bankers
and merchants, successful speculators and fashionable writers, to cynics
like the Goncourts, through whose journals the most brutal misogyny runs
much like a compulsive refrain. They sought their readers among those
rich, cultivated, or at least socially ambitious enough to conduct salons and
establish the erotic atmosphere in which, according to Balzac, love alone
can flourish. Balzac, in fact, flatly maintained that if the beloved woman
is a bourgeoise, the lover will blush to acknowledge it; a working girl, to
say nothing of a dancer, would be far more creditable in his set.[39]

In fact, Balzac found most middle-class women, like most middle-class
men, unsuitable for love in any event. Love, he insists, is expensive, a
pursuit for the happy few. In one statistical calculation, he reserves the
honorific rank of "woman" to less than a million of "white sheep" inhabiting "a privileged sheep fold that the wolves seek to enter"; elsewhere,
he finds even this number excessive, and reduces to four hundred thousand in all of France the women whose possession "could provide
fastidious men with the exquisite and refined pleasures" they seek. "Love"
is the "religion" of such women, and their faith requires all the accoutre-
ments of luxury and idleness. In his cynical set of aphorisms about what
constitutes the "femme honnête," Balzac underscores, once again, the
place of adultery and the power of money in love: "A virtuous woman
is necessarily a married woman"—she alone is a worthy object of the
lover's pursuit. "A married woman whose favors are *paid for* is not a
virtuous woman"—a *femme honnête* is, of course, never a prostitute. But,
then, she will not need the money: "A woman who does her own cooking
at home is not a virtuous woman," but, in forceful contrast, "A married
woman who has her own carriage is a virtuous woman."[40] This sort of
thing was sharply seasoned, costly food for libertine high society alone.

Yet all is not satire or cynicism in Balzac's vademecum to love. His
Physiologie du mariage in its final form of 1829 is measurably different

39. *Physiologie du mariage*, 61.
40. Ibid., 58.

from its primitive version dating from three years earlier: Balzac was, with all his loose talk about sexual warfare, on his way from being an entertainer to being something of a moralist. The neglected child of an eccentric old father and a lovely young mother, he came to develop a taste for older women and, with his first affairs, a certain expertise in the writing of love letters and the making of declarations. When he insisted that love is "the first of the passions," he was talking from experience. But love, he also insisted, must never be confounded with sheer lust. "Physical love is a need similar to hunger," but love itself is more refined, more varied, even more violent than hunger, that most importunate of bodily appetites. To apply the word "love" to the "reproduction of the species," to reduce it, in other words, to sexual intercourse, is "the most odious blasphemy" that modern society can utter. After all, nature has raised the human species, with its "divine gift of thought," above the beasts, and has "made us capable of experiencing sensations and senti- ments, needs and passions." Love therefore is "the accord of need and sentiment." At once erotic and affectionate, it is "the poetry of the senses."[41]

Balzac stayed to ask whether this poetry can survive in so forbidding an institution as marriage. And at this critical point his ambivalence, his inability to make a clear choice between the incompatible stances of the suave man of the world and the indignant critic of society, claims con- sistency for its victim. On the first page of his *Physiologie*, he describes marriage as "contrary to the laws of nature," though necessary to "the maintenance of society," and argues that in this clash between the de- mands of nature and the needs of culture, love must perish. Is it not the aim of physiology to demonstrate that "life is in passion, and that no passion can resist marriage?" But later, in one of his bouquets of aphorisms, Balzac proposes radically opposed conclusions. "To be passionate is always to desire. Can one," he asks rhetorically, "always desire one's wife?" and replies, sturdily, that one can. "It is as absurd to claim that one cannot love the same woman always as it is to say that a famous artist needs several violins to play a piece of music or to invent an enchanting melody." No doubt a marriage that is at once passionate and tender calls for tact, patience, forebearance, delicacy, but then it is at least one purpose of Balzac's *Physiologie* to instill, or enhance, such qualities. "Never begin

41. *Physiologie du mariage*, 64, 75, 84-85. "His many love-affairs always started with the declaration: 'I never had a mother. I never knew a mother's love,'" V.S. Pritchett, *Balzac* (1973), 25. The unpublished version of 1826, edited in 1940 by Maurice Bardèche under the title *La Physiologie du mariage pré-originale*, is an im- portant text, establishing the rapid evolution of Balzac's ideas.

a marriage with a rape," he warns and, again, "The fate of a household depends on the first night."[42]

Following the line laid down by Stendhal, the disciple of Destutt de Tracy, Balzac called marriage "a science." It is up to the husband, normally somewhat older and more experienced than his young wife, to seize its principles and preside over its application. "The husband's self-interest, at least as much as his honor, prescribes that he never permit himself a pleasure which he has not the talent to make his wife desire." Plainly, Balzac sees woman as a sensual being, quite as sensual as man, but modern society keeps her ignorant of the promise that erotic passion holds for her. "The chastest married woman," he observes, "can also be the most voluptuous." It is the husband's assignment to arouse that voluptuousness and to keep it alive during the long years of marriage. That devouring monster, habit, which must be battled unceasingly, is a most formidable adversary.

Aphorisms like these, and Balzac's *Physiologie* as a whole, reflect the social realities or, rather, the social ideals, of his day. His book is addressed to men who are, in marital love above all, the active partner. "The married woman is a slave whom one must know how to put on a throne." People generally think of man as someone "charged with chipping, polishing, cutting, and mounting the diamond that will be passed from hand to hand and will one day be admired all round." The work of woman, that rough diamond, is, in contrast, one of passive expectation; at best she can interpose obstacles to the man's advances, for the more effectively she can resist him, the more valuable possessing her will be. Balzac here merely echoes common opinion. The man is in charge, responsible for creating woman. "A wife is to her husband what her husband has made her."[43]

All this superb posturing, relentlessly masculine, seems conventional enough, unimaginative in the extreme. At times, indeed, Balzac abuses his imagination to descend into sheer absurdity. "A man cannot marry without having studied anatomy and dissected at least one woman." He embeds these self-satisfied pronouncements into a potpourri of anecdotes, conversational set pieces, and little treatises on coquetry, on lovers—"a lover has all the qualities and all the defects a husband has not"—and, foremost, on matrimonial warfare: on the choice of weapons, the value of surprise, the enlisting of allies, the suing for peace. His book spoke a language that fashionable Parisian society could understand. Even its

42. Ibid., 45, 83–86.
43. Ibid., 86–88, 114–15, 106, 200.

praise of marriage hit the right note: it could hint at the excitement of the forbidden without arousing fantasies that made readers excessively nervous.

Yet Balzac's *Physiologie du mariage*, with all this froth, all its sly suggestiveness, sometimes sounds themes at once critical and uneasy. Balzac proclaimed current social arrangements to be sadly in need of repair, particularly the futile education of girls, and the financial considerations controlling marital arrangements. "Hypocrisy is gaining ground among us, and keeps us from laughing as our fathers laughed." And low calculation is gaining ground right along: "Do not most men marry precisely the way they buy a parcel of shares at the stock exchange?" In this society, modern woman is a mere "salon ornament, a mannequin of fashion." The way that girls are prepared for the world is nothing less than a scandal: it leaves them ignorant, vain, insecure, only too impatient to taste the promised glories of luxury. "A girl may emerge from her boarding school a virgin; chaste? no."[44] She is ready for adultery before she is even married.

Here Balzac hints at more solemn preoccupations. Beneath his flippancy and the rather casual reach of his *Physiologie* for more serious ideas, he scatters intimations of anxiety. Like other physiologies, Balzac's *Physiologie du mariage* offers prescriptions to counteract, perhaps master, the conflicts and anxieties—fear of rejection, of impotence or loss—that the pursuit of love entails. The men in his treatise are strikingly defensive, nervous lest the supreme ignominy of them all, cuckoldry, befall them. Balzac foresees a moment in the happiest of marital unions when it dawns on the wife that the honeymoon is over. The observant husband will notice the squalls to come, the almost imperceptible cooling of the marital temperature, through a sequence of subtle clues. But, then, very few husbands are observant. Most of them need drastic reminders. At the beginning, the wife, gently, ostensibly acting in her husband's interest, will find him just a shade imperfect, whether in his manner of stating his opinions or of girding on his sword. Or she will neglect to provide the company or the comforts that the husband, in the glow of a new marriage, had come to expect as a matter of course. Balzac devotes a whole meditation to these "first symptoms" and proffers one of his tersest aphorisms on this gravest of matters: *"Plus on juge, moins on aime."* Criticism is the death of love or, more precisely, the most unmistakable symptom of its waning. And love will wane, for wives long before husbands. Led to expect perfection, unprepared for reality, longing for an aura of unbroken erotic bliss, a kind of perpetual regressive honeymoon,

44. Ibid., 86, 206, 112, 96, 131, 94.

the young married woman gradually comes to see her husband as he is, flawed, mediocre, if not worse. The imaginative crystallization that has protected him, first as a suitor and then as a husband, now melts away. "One fine Spring morning, the morning after a ball, or the day before a party in the country," the scattered hints of wifely disillusionment will coalesce into an unspoken, still inchoate program for infidelity. "Your wife is bored and legitimate pleasure no longer attracts her. Her senses, her imagination, perhaps the caprice of nature call out for a lover."[45] She is not likely to embark on an affair immediately; her husband continues to have some merit in her eyes and the risks of illicit involvement are great. But the wife's imagination has been piqued precisely because her illusions have left her. Adultery now is only a matter of time and opportunity. All it needs is an alert and hungry bachelor who knows from experience how to read the signs of conjugal trouble.

To avert this fate and defend the man, his honor, his self-esteem—in short the integrity of his masculine powers—Balzac scatters sage advice. Cuckoldry is for him, as I have said, the supreme disgrace, a kind of castration. So Balzac composes a "treatise" on "marital policy," pages on how to scrutinize visitors, even how to lay out and furnish one's apartment for security. "A married man should make a profound study of his wife's face." For, deep and subtle as woman may be, her real feelings break through to the surface; confessions, as Freud once said, burst out through every pore. The twitch of a woman's eyelid, the almost imperceptibly changing tints in her pupils, the slightest movement of her lips, speak to her husband, eloquently, of her adulterous desires, or actions. She will be, or has been, "indiscreet," which is to say unfaithful, yet more discreet than ever in her social conduct and her private conversation. In a meditation offering a "theory of the bed," Balzac insists that the very choice of sleeping arrangements will help determine the prospects of fidelity or infidelity. Separate bedrooms are unthinkable, and twin beds unsatisfactory. Only the double bed is appropriate for a married couple. Yet Balzac's reason is not so much the charming and tender thought that physical intimacy will foster lasting affection, but the almost paranoid suggestion that it will facilitate effective surveillance. The double bed helps the wife to keep her love at an excited pitch, but, more that that, it faithfully transmits her feelings, makes her, as it were, a spy upon herself, enabling the husband to listen to her even while she is asleep.[46] Balzac is ready to endorse the respectable middle-class view that love is more than

45. Ibid., 114–24.
46. Ibid., 171, 200.

lust. But, as he ruefully puts it, love is, *hélas*, a rare and tender plant, only too susceptible to all the blights in which a cruel world abounds.

The pathetic possibilities that lend Balzac's sprightly and entertaining collection of recipes and warnings its dark hues emerge as the leading, practically the only, theme of Paul Bourget's *Physiologie de l'amour moderne*. The book is an obsessive, almost voluptuous investigation of failure. Bourget portrays his protagonist, his imaginary friend Claude Larcher, whose surviving posthumous papers he professes to have collected and edited, as a spectacular victim of love. In the end, deserted by Colette, his enchanting and cruel mistress, Larcher dies of his melancholy—but not before he has written down what he has learned about love from meditating on his own experiences, and from conversations with his friends. His fate, which the reader, of course, always has in his mind, sabotages whatever hint of optimism about Eros one or the other of Larcher's interlocutors might muster.

Bourget's *Physiologie de l'amour moderne* is, for all its strenuous distancing devices, the most subjective of books. Its pathos is the self-pity of Bourget, the psychological orphan. A wicked reviewer, a notoriously ambitious man of letters, a great snob cheerfully dissecting snobs, he seemed to be taking revenge on the world for an incurable slight. Bourget early experienced, and forever nourished, a deep loss. When he was little more than five, his mother died of tuberculosis, and later (sounding much like Balzac, whose loss had been rather different) he would defend his notorious coldness by blaming his irreparable deprivation: "He who has not had a mother knows neither how to love nor how to be loved."[47] The tenor of his book on love is precisely what one might expect of such a man, especially if he travelled in the sophisticated circles among which Bourget made his home.

His physiology is more remarkable for its timing than for its ideas. First issued, beginning late in 1888, in *La vie Parisienne*,[48] it had obviously been germinating in his mind at the time he was completing *Le disciple*, published in 1889, the most influential of his many novels. The two books serve as commentaries on one another: The protagonist of *Le disciple*, the dogmatic, unworldly philosopher Adrien Sixte, appears in a chapter of his physiology of modern love. *Le disciple*, a thinly disguised pamphlet,

47. Michel Mansuy, *Un Moderne. Paul Bourget de l'enfance au 'Disciple'* (1960; 2nd. ed. 1968), 15.
48. Bourget archly characterized this periodical as "that adorable journal of observation and banter." "Préface," *Physiologie de l'amour moderne* (1891), i.

olemicizes against the pernicious consequences of "the religion of science." It is a study in the death-grip of system-making, the inhumanity f godless positivism and, with that, a conspicuous voice amid the rising lamor among French publicists against the ravages of the intellect and in ehalf of a return to Catholic Christianity. A student of medicine and hilosophy, a novelist and essayist who specialized in psychological dis-ctions of considerable, somewhat self-indulgent finesse, Bourget was, 1 the 1880s, slowly but inexorably making a place for himself on the 'rench Right. In *Le disciple*, Bourget mercilessly caricatures a character-stic folk hero of the French Left, the irreligious intellectual, in the figure f Adrien Sixte, in whom more than one French positivist thought he ecognized himself. Sixte's doctrines move one of his young disciples to est out his master's theories by heartlessly seducing a girl who eventually ommits suicide. It is significant that Bourget should choose, to make his >oint, an experiment in love—the very emotion, he implies, least sus-eptible to scientific inquiry. The principal lesson Bourget meant to im->art, beyond exposing the essential brutality of atheistic metaphysics and he blasphemous pride of science, was that men are responsible for their deas. The added lesson he suggests is that sympathetic goodness is infinitely nore valuable that dry-as-dust knowledge. Bourget even offers, at the :onclusion, a glint of hope. The crime that Sixte has unwittingly caused 1as brought him, the philosophical unbeliever, to acknowledge the futility of his arrogant pursuit of certainty, and may lead him back into the wel-:oming arms of mother Church.

Speculative and insubstantial, the ending of *Le disciple* holds more optimism than Bourget admits to the whole of his *Physiologie de l'amour moderne*. In that book, all is bleakness, perhaps nowhere more oppressive :han in the chapter that Bourget devotes to Sixte's "therapeutics of love." Seeking to persuade an incredulous, secretly amused Claude Larcher, the professor spells out his "system" by resorting to ridiculous algebraic formulas and childish definitions. Upon questioning, he concedes that he has never been in love: "I haven't had the time. But," he triumphantly concludes, "I have a theory that one understands all the better the passions one has experienced the least."[49] This is ludicrous, and intended to appear ludicrous: mathematical rationalism, Bourget hints rather broadly, as he was already hinting in *Le disciple*, is the worst possible guide through the maze of love. This had been a commonplace since the romantics: passion cannot survive the cool stare of research; we murder to dissect.

49. Ibid., 379.

Bourget's *Physiologie* is a heavily derivative book in more ways than this. In its very form, with its numbered aphorisms and axioms, and its chapter headings all called "Meditations," it demonstrates its unabashed dependence on earlier physiologies, whose intentions were certainly different from Bourget's own. His notions about love are no more original. Bourget deftly conceals the thin texture of his invention behind those informal, elegant dramatizations that were a French specialty. But his grip on satire is not firm enough to permit the modern reader to conclude whether the absence of a certain energy is designed to pillory the failures of modern love, or unintentionally exhibits the poverty of Bourget's own thoughts on the subject. His *Physiologie* is a confession of bankruptcy, and it is not clear whose bankruptcy it is confessing.

Professing to be alarmed at modern decadence, Bourget takes aim at the degenerate, effeminate fashion for *fin de siècle* love, but his own work seems not an anatomy so much as a specimen of that decadence. The antihero of the *Physiologie* is a weak-willed, passive, maundering aesthete who cannot survive rejection; Bourget displays him pursuing egotistical ruminations, overhearing confessional dialogues, and recording little encounters between subtle, normally unhappy lovers. Gallants parade through these pages, and mistresses, rehearsing fine discriminations of feelings, at moments worthy of Bourget's friend Henry James. But love, even modern love, somehow escapes. Bourget defines love, as others had defined it before him, as something that transcends mere self-regard or downright "bestiality."[50] But there is very little in the book to indicate that such love existed in his day, or had ever existed.

Still, read as a compendium of "advanced" modern attitudes toward love, Bourget's *Physiologie* has considerable evidential value. Bourget was, after all, a sensitive and intelligent man. His classifications testify to the general rage for science, rampant even, it would seem, among professed critics of scientism. His exploration of suffering and of the intimate traffic between love and hate have, in addition, a measure of clinical interest. Abandoned and betrayed by his Colette, Larcher yields to his rage by indulging his most sadistic sensuality: "I closed my eyes. I saw before me the body every line of which I knew, these shoulders at once full and slender, that pliant bosom, those slim hips, all her nudity, and me, with a knife, ripping up that flesh, covering those limbs with blood, and their shudder under the sharp end of the steel—and *her pain*. . . ." But he immediately takes it all back: "No, action shall never be the sister of

50. Ibid., 165.

desire." But, while he will not act out his rage, he will think and define: "Love," he reflects bitterly, is "a ferocious hatred between two couplings." He recognizes that his love has been a "cruel" affair, "mingled with hate."[51] But, driven to madness by his misery, he takes some consolation from his discovery that other men, too, have suffered like him.

He tries other, more conventional kinds of consolation: he spends a night in the arms of a lady of pleasure. He talks about love, and, eventually writes it all down. He makes compulsive lists: there are eight types of persons excluded from love; there are three reasons for women to take lovers; there are perhaps three kinds of therapies. He absorbs stories from his friends; he listens and yet does not listen. One of his more virile, vital acquaintances insists that reasoning it out and writing it down will not assuage the suffering inherent in love's disappointments. " 'You are comforting yourself by smudging your paper, and you'll always find a dozen or so readers who resemble you and who will be comforted by reading you. That's a sort of result. . . . But you would have done better for your cure by writing neither a *physiologie*, nor a *psychologie*, nor anything in *ogie*, and by seeing your mistress morning, noon, evening, and night, and possessing her as much as you could. . . .' "[52] But Larcher goes on probing his wound.

He discovers ever new reasons for despair: there are all too many cocottes whose real aim in life is to make others suffer; there are, he finds, vaguely echoing Balzac, few "virtuous women"; love (and here is Balzac again) is a species of warfare; women are, he notes (repeating what men had said for centuries) unfathomable: "is there ever a why and wherefore for woman's conduct? They are charades without words." If there is any happiness to be found in love it must come to the man who does not love and who, in cold blood, betrays his mistress. Worst of all, even knowledge is pernicious: "To learn to know women," so runs one of Larcher's— Bourget's—most disenchanted aphorisms, "*is to learn to know in advance what wrong they will do you, without any way of protecting you from it. This kind of science consists of augmenting the misery of love by the lucid prevision of that misery.*"[53] Briefly, very briefly, Bourget is here traveling in the land of Proust, with far less authority than his much-admired Stendhal, who had been there before him.

51. Ibid., 3, 9.
52. Ibid., 17, 392, 156–57, 98.
53. Ibid., 148, 187, 305, 169.

3. From Physiology to Psychology

Foreigners liked to say that the French had a monopoly on devising theories about love, especially worldly love, and thrived in conducting its business. Failing to observe the anxiety barely concealed by the cynicism, they would denigrate them as heartless sensualists. In 1856, in one of its numerous head-shaking articles on French literature and French culture, the *Saturday Review* called a compendium, *La Femme jugée par l'Homme*, to the attention of its readers, and quoted some choice epigrams: "If, in France," one D. Caron had said, "marriage is so much to women's taste, that is because for them it is a cage whose door is open." And Etienne de Neufville was responsible for this gem, scarcely less nervous: "Has she pretty feet? She will cross amd uncross them unceasingly; has she a pretty profile? You will never see her full face." What struck the *Saturday Review* as characteristic was not that most French women were like that, but that many French men seemed only too willing to speak of them in this scandalous fashion. This was the culture that produced a Balzac or a Baudelaire, or for that matter, a George Sand, that uninhibited—and appealing—theorist and practitioner of modern love. As he told Turgenev, Tolstoy thought Paris quite simply Sodom and Gomorrah. Toward the end of the century, when Germany's Chancellor Caprivi proposed to Wilhelm II that Berlin should sponsor a world exhibition just as Paris had recently done, the Emperor demurred at imitating such a model: "Paris is, after all," he wrote Caprivi, "what Berlin, I hope, will never become—the great whore-house of the world."[54]

What these self-satisfied and self-righteous critics failed to acknowledge was that many Frenchmen freely shared this censorious view. Everyone agreed, Dumas fils wrote in 1864, that "French literature" was "the most immoral in the world."[55] It is easy to see how this impression arose. The Goncourt brothers' icy aphorisms on women as the stupid, greedy, insatiable suppliers and consumers of sexual pleasure; Jules Michelet's somber physiological obsession with woman, at once the sickly menstruating animal and the powerful nurturing mother; Emile Zola's emphatic

54. "Qu'est-ce que la Femme?" *Saturday Review*, V (June 26, 1858), 662–63; V. S. Pritchett, *The Gentle Barbarian: The Life and Work of Turgenev* (1977), 107; Hans Herzfeld, "Berlin als Kaiserstadt und Reichshauptstadt, 1871–1945" (1952), *Ausgewählte Aufsätze* (1962), 311.
55. Preface to *L'ami des femmes*, in Klaus Heitmann, *Der Immoralismus-Prozess gegen die französische Literatur im 19. Jahrhundert* (1970), 42.

explorations, in his letters and his novels, of love as necessary and fatal at once: for all the drastic differences among these writers, their English or American or German readers saw them as typically French, all of them proving that their nation was a family of experts on love respectable or otherwise—mainly otherwise.

French authors on love doubtless specialized in productions like Adolphe Retté's salacious brief dialogue, *Paradoxe sur l'Amour*, of 1893, which argues—if so serious a term is appropriate here—that only cold and mercenary women are suitable for love. Doubtless to enhance its appeal to collectors, the little book was decorated with an etched frontispiece by Emile-H. Meyer depicting a nubile young girl, still flat-chested but with her genitals prominently exposed, tied to a tree with her hands bound above her head and her bloody feet spread apart, nailed to the trunk. Doubtless there were customers who found such blasphemy, especially of this pictorial bluntness, a kind of sacred sadism, highly arousing. There were tamer French productions as well, like Catulle Mendès's cynical *L'Art d'aimer*, addressed to young men ready to plunge into the world of amorous intrigue. Mendès counseled his readers—male, of course—to practice insincerity and other ingenious tricks in the pursuit of the "adorable enemy, woman," so that, in the end, "you will wholly dominate the one to whom you are subject; you will know, in the humility of slavery, the triumphant joys of tyranny."[56] Then there was, on a far higher level, Marcel Proust, engaged from 1909 in composing his oceanic masterpiece, *A la recherche du temps perdu*, that cycle of seven novels devoted, among its other grave topics, to the minute dissection of love. Proust sought to establish and to document, meticulously, the disheartened proposition that love is always yoked to jealousy and that it can never bring happiness. For love must feed precisely on absences, on misunderstandings, on the indifference of the other, even on disdain; and it will rapidly and irreparably cool when it is reciprocated. The process of crystallization that Stendhal had urged as the essential ingredient in love is for Proust a desperate and tragic fraud. By no means all French writings on love were obscene, or even suggestive. Some promised only misery.

Nor were the French alone in the great nineteenth-century search for the essence and the meaning of love. The Germans in particular developed a metaphysics of love that built it into man's very nature, made it into the fuel of life. The German romantics had already nominated love as an

56. *L'Art d'aimer*, 10, 236.

emblem, an expression, possibly the very heart of religion. In the hands of more secular spirits, this biological, philosophical perception of love became the hallmark of a whole school of thought. Its master and prophet was Arthur Schopenhauer.

No matter how abstract or apparently rational their system, philosophers of love inevitably import their own erotic history into their theorizing. Stendhal had done so, as had Balzac and Bourget. Schopenhauer was no exception. It is only his pervasive influence, slow to ripen but, once established, irresistible, that permits the historian to treat his ideas as in any way representative of the nineteenth-century cultural experience. What makes the bonds between Schopenhauer's private life and published philosophy all the more tantalizing is that his thought was, as it were, a photographic negative of his life, supplying what he lacked. The most famous pessimist of the nineteenth century, Schopenhauer was, in his eccentric way, an exuberant lover of life. He taught Oriental apathy but indulged his tastes for art, music, and the theatre and all the other good things that his money could buy; he preached philosophical indifference in the midst of attacks of anxiety he could not master; most significant for our purposes, he was an outspoken, often brutal misogynist who enjoyed women and sought out sexual adventures.[57] As so often in the century, so with Schopenhauer, his personal needs diverged markedly from his public demeanor, not from hypocrisy but because he felt compelled to find a way of managing his imperious impulses.

Schopenhauer's need to conceal even from himself what these impulses urged upon him began in his childhood. The son of a restless, temperamental merchant and a self-willed, undemonstrative mother, Arthur Schopenhauer grew up in a household as frigid in its affectionate atmosphere as it was abundant in intellectual stimulation. Heinrich Schopenhauer read intelligently in philosophy, knew English and French, and had a compulsive fondness for travel which his financial circumstances allowed him to indulge to the full; Johanna Schopenhauer, who shared her husband's ambulatory tastes, wrote popular novels and pressed her son to amount to something more than a flighty *bel esprit*. An obedient son, he set his wishes aside for the mercantile career that his father had per-

---

57. As the German psychologist Julius Moebius put it: Schopenhauer was not suited to the kind of Western marriage in which a man hands himself over to a woman. "He could have concluded a marriage that would have been suitable for him only in the Orient, here there was nothing for it but an occasional socalled illicit affair." *Ueber Schopenhauer* (1899), 38, 71. In this paragraph, I am much indebted to Patrick Gardiner, *Schopenhauer* (1967), 16–17.

emptorily chosen for him. But shortly after beginning his hated apprenticeship, his father died in a fall from an attic window, almost certainly a suicide.

It seems only too likely that Heinrich Schopenhauer's son, for all his unfeigned and lifelong admiration, desired this dismal death in his turbulent unconscious. It is no wonder that, afflicted with attacks of melancholy and oppressed by guilt feelings, he remained in his apprenticeship for two years after his father's death, as though Heinrich Schopenhauer were still there to direct his life. While Arthur Schopenhauer's love for his father probably concealed a measure of anger, his notoriously bad relations with his mother speak of desperate wishes, of longing turned into hatred. Mother and son squabbled persistently, over money, over literature, over his career. She showed contempt for his abstruse dissertation; he countered by disparaging her novels. Worse, the two fell out over the men in her life. The breach came in 1813, in Weimar, when Schopenhauer was twenty-five. His mother, then forty-seven, had a much younger man living in her house, whether as friend or lover remains unclear. Arthur Schopenhauer demanded that she discard this intruder who, as he put it rather grandly, dishonored his father. She refused, and they parted enemies. In the same year, as he was working in solitude on his masterpiece, *Die Welt als Wille und Vorstellung*, he made himself, metaphorically, into a loving pregnant woman. "The work grows," he noted, "concretizes gradually and slowly, like the child in its mother's body."[58] In a parody of his own genesis, Schopenhauer was supplying himself with the affectionate care he had not had from his mother.

Schopenhauer's almost proverbial misogyny fed on many sources, among them balked desire; certainly to call him a hater of women is to simplify a labyrinth of needs and defenses. There was a conventional male in Schopenhauer, driven on by spleen, bearing all the marks of an almost consciously cultivated bearishness, and endowed—unfortunately—with the gift of pungent, memorable expression. "In our monogamous part of the world," he said in his notorious essay on woman, "to marry means to halve your rights and double your duties." He acknowledged that woman is a help to children, a pleasure to man in middle life, a consolation to the old. But he ungraciously added that a mere look at woman's body reveals that she is "intended for neither great mental nor physical work. She bears the burden of life not by action, but through suffering." The lesser sex, she has no use for art or for thought. She is fit to nurse and educate

58. Moebius, *Ueber Schopenhauer*, 20.

young children, precisely because "she is herself childish, silly, and short-sighted, in *one* word, a big child all her life."[59]

Schopenhauer did not need to be an original philosopher to air such bits of homely wisdom. He could have heard them in men's clubs, read them in antifeminist editorials, copied them from Michelet's egregious pronouncements on woman as the walking wounded. But Schopenhauer also developed another view of woman, less condescending if less explicit; he saw her as the bearer of the fundamental and irrational force of life. This view subsists on a wholly different level of discourse; significantly, Schopenhauer concentrates it in the chapter of his great treatise that he entitled "Metaphysics of Sexual Love." It is an extraordinary performance, and was to become the source of much excited philosophizing on female nature. Ann Whitfield, the determined young woman who snares that reluctant modern Don Juan, John Tanner, in Shaw's *Man and Superman*, speaks Schopenhauer's lines and aims to fulfill Schopenhauer's program.

Schopenhauer begins by observing that sexual love is usually the province of imaginative writers, of lyric poets, playwrights, novelists, all over the world. But their favorite theme, fateful sexual attraction, is by no means reserved to their luxuriant imagination. Newspapers reporting crimes of passion, suicides, or lovers going mad, confirm how very active the force of love can be. Hence, Schopenhauer invites himself, as a philosopher, into the ongoing debate on sexual love. He was far from claiming to be the first thinker who had taken that kind of love seriously. On the contrary: he cites Plato, Spinoza, Rousseau, and Kant, but only to deride them. Their work on love has been uninformed, superficial, naive, generally wrong. "I therefore have no need either of using predecessors or refuting them." Yet his own ideas, he predicts, will not be popular; particularly individuals governed by the passion of love and accustomed to paint it in "the most sublime and ethereal" fashion will find "my view too physical, too material, though it is, at bottom, metaphysical, indeed transcendental."[60]

Schopenhauer was right to think that his ideas on sexual love were radical, wrong to anticipate that they would be unpopular. During the decades of silence, the public, learned or lay, disregarded them as it disregarded everything else he had written. But once Schopenhauer became

59. "Über die Weiber," *Parerga und Paralipomena*, ch. 27. *Arthur Schopenhauer, Sämtliche Werke*, ed. Wolfgang Freiherr von Löhneysen, 5 vols. (1960–1965), V, 730, 719–20.
60. "Metaphysik der Geschlechtsliebe," *Die Welt als Wille und Vorstellung, Sämtliche Werke*, II, 680–81.

fashionable in the 1850s, his ideas on love came to command a sizable and enthusiastic following. They seemed to fit into that widespread fear of women that literature and the arts were exemplifying and spreading, in their own way, late in the nineteenth century. More, they seemed to satisfy some philosophical need that other thinkers failed to address. Schopenhauer was, one might say, a metaphysical Diderot. As we know, Denis Diderot had professed to detect a bit of testicle in men's most exalted ideas. Arthur Schopenhauer argued that "all infatuation, however ethereal its deportment may be, is rooted in the sexual drive alone." It shows itself in the world "next to the love of life, as the strongest, most active, of all impulsions." In several passages, indeed, much like Freud some decades later, Schopenhauer economically combines these two drives, the love of life and the love of love, into one; he takes the sexual urge to be the device by which nature sees to the renewal of the human species. Sexual love, tearing sacred bonds, subverting cherished ideals, confusing sober thinkers, distressing diplomats and scholars alike, conducts itself almost like "a hostile demon, intent on turning everything upside down, on confounding and overthrowing everything."[61] Lovers, drawn to one another sexually, see only their partner and live in the moment. But wise nature, which has implanted this irresistible urge in men and women, cares neither for the individual nor for the present; it looks to the collectivity and to the future. The sexual act, Schopenhauer adds, bluntly and consistently, is the way in which the will affirms itself. The life of man, with all its endless troubles and sufferings, is nothing more than the "explication and paraphrase of the act of procreation."[62] Schopenhauer tied this affirmation of life to an affirmation of death: his unrelieved pessimism followed his celebration of the irrational power of Eros like a shadow and lent it a certain poignancy and seductiveness. But pessimism was not essential to the metaphysics of love, as emerges from the ideas of Nietzsche, who used the philosophy of Schopenhauer as a ladder to reach his own. For Schopenhauer himself, though, in tune with some of the writers on love whom he ignored, the temper of his thinking on sexuality resembles the fabled moment of depression after coitus: it made him sad.

61. Ibid., II, 682.
62. "Von der Bejahung des Willens zum Leben," ibid., II, 730. Byron had seen the matter very much the same way. In the letter to Lady Hardy in which he had called love a hostile transaction (see above, p. 46), he went on to say, hostile but "very necessary to make—or to break—matches and keep the world a-going—but by no means a sinecure for the parties concerned." December 10, 1822. *Byron's Letters and Journals*, X, 50. And so, later, would Strindberg see the matter.

Friedrich Nietzsche, Arthur Schopenhauer's most independent and most imaginative reader, adopted Schopenhauer's fundamental principle: the will driving the universe is erotic in its essence. But he treated this proposition with unabashed exuberance, as the champion rather than the nemesis of the passions. His originality has been somewhat obscured by his appalling epigrams against women, in which he sounded much like all the misogynists of his day, only more intemperate. He was so malicious on the subject—no less so than Schopenhauer, who was malicious enough— that even the admiring commentators he began to attract in the last decade of his life sought for some untoward biographical constellation to explain his irrational anti-feminism. Thus in 1901, the year after Nietzsche's death, Dr. Julius Reiner published a brief epitome of Nietzsche's thought "for cultivated laymen" characteristic of this rapidly growing literature. He recited some of Nietzsche's more offensive sentences on women and noted the "remarkable and mysterious phenomenon" of a penetrating thinker (who had, after all, known some of the "most cultivated and learned" women of his day) persisting in treating the female sex as grossly inferior to the male. He concluded that there must be "some personal motives" to account for his "hostile, indeed often extremely spiteful and boorish attitude."[63]

The little band of psychoanalysts who met at Freud's house every Wednesday from 1902 on could only agree. They found Nietzsche an intriguing figure, with his uncanny psychological intuitions, his brilliant and strange career, his impulsive proposals of marriage and his madness, a mixture of megalomania and silence that cut him off from the world for the last eleven years of his life. Freud and his followers canvassed the causes of Nietzsche's paralysis, speculated that it might be the result of a syphilitic infection, debated whether he could properly be called a neurotic, and detected strong hints of repressed homosexuality. The group devoted two full evenings to Nietzsche's late writings, while Dr. Eduard Hitschmann, one of Freud's earliest and most loyal supporters, quoted a Nietzschean aphorism that the group was well equipped to understand if not to accept: "When a woman displays scientific interests, then there is something out of order in her sexuality."[64]

Nietzsche said much more to the same effect. He called women pedantic, superficial, petty, arrogant, immodest beasts of prey who had

63. *Friedrich Nietzsche für gebildete Laien* (1901), 64–65.
64. November 9, 1910. *Protokolle der Wiener Psychoanalytischen Vereinigung*, ed. Hermann Nunberg and Ernst Federn, 4 vols. (1976–1981), III, 57.

so far been barely kept in check by sheer fear of the male. "Woe if one day the 'Eternally-Boring in woman'—she is richly endowed with it!— dares to show itself." Emancipated woman, he thought, was a grave symptom of modern decay: "There is a *stupidity* in that movement, an almost masculine stupidity." Nothing is more damaging, more destructive, than well-meaning modern attempts to propel women into literature, the arts, let alone politics, attempts of which any true woman, who is clever in her own way, would be fearfully ashamed.[65]

Nor was Nietzsche unwilling to dredge up that hoary maxim about woman the puzzle and to offer a solution both condescending and commonplace. "Everything about woman," he wrote in *Also Sprach Zarathustra*, "is a riddle, and everything about woman has *one* solution: its name is pregnancy." Here sound the accents of anxiety, personal malaise disguised as cultural concern. Woman is a "dangerous and beautiful cat"; her nature inculcates "respect and, often enough, fear," for she is " 'more natural' " than the male, with her "cunning suppleness," her "tiger's claw within the glove," her naive egotism, her uneducability and savagery, her incomprehensible appetites and virtues. The most notorious of Nietzsche's pronouncements from *Also Sprach Zarathustra*—"You go to women? Don't forget the whip!"—is, in its brutality, a panic-stricken call to self-defense.[66] It is anti-feminism, literally, with a vengeance.

Among these savage pronouncements, however, there are a few that propel Nietzsche's misogyny into a large context. "Woman has always conspired with the very type of the *décadent*, the priest, against the 'powerful,' the 'strong,' against *men*," he wrote in the 1880s in notes he intended to weave into a book, *The Will to Power*. Nietzsche's attack on woman is many things, not least, to be sure, a strategy dictated by breathless fear. But it was also a defense of the passions against those who would enfeeble or wholly extirpate them. He had his ancestors in this line of reasoning, as in his nasty remarks on modern woman. Voltaire's battle cry, *Ecrasez l'infâme!*, echoes in Nietzsche on the passions; as a latter-day philosophe, he sees religion, most infamously Christianity, as their implacable adversary. To be woman and to be Christian is, for Nietzsche, practically the same thing. Woman, physically feeble, needs a "religion of weakness,

65. *Jenseits von Gut und Böse*, No. 239, Friedrich Nietzsche, *Werke*, 5 vols., ed. Karl Schlechta (1972), III, 148.
66. *Also Sprach Zarathustra*, "Von alten und jungen Weiblein," *Werke*, II, 602; *Jenseits von Gut und Böse*, No. 239, ibid., III, 149; *Also Sprach Zarathustra*, "Von alten und jungen Weiblein," ibid., II, 604.

which she glorifies as divine," in order to be *"weak*, to love, to be humble" or better still (if she can only manage to enfeeble the strong) in order to rule.[67]

In an important chapter of *Götzen-Dämmerung*, Nietzsche sets out this argument in some detail. "All passions," he declares, "have a time when they are only fatal, when they drag down their victim with the weight of stupidity—and a later one, very much later, when they marry the spirit, 'spiritualize' themselves." At one time, men "waged war against passion itself: there was a conspiracy to annihilate it; all the moral-monsters of antiquity were unanimous—*'il faut tuer les passions.'* " Christianity has driven this malevolent crusade to terrifying extremes. "The Church combats passion with excision in every sense: its practice, its 'cure,' is *castratism*." Men, Nietzsche observes with a singularly apt metaphor, no longer admire dentists who yank out teeth to keep them from aching. Granted, the early church had no way of spiritualizing the passions intelligently; still, it has kept up its ancient practice of seeking to stifle them all—pride, ambition, greed, sensuality. "But to attack the passions at their roots is to attack life at its root: the practice of the Church is *hostile to life*."[68]

The inexhaustible source, then, from which life draws its energy, is passion, foremost the passion of sexuality. The cure for its stupidity—for every passion is natively stupid—is not to annihilate or to geld but to cultivate it. And that is what love, in Nietzsche's thought, is supremely equipped to do. "The spiritualization of sensuality is called *love*: it is a great triumph over Christianity." Love is sexual passion sublimated. "All virtues are really refined *passions*" so that "compassion and love of mankind" are "developments of the sexual drive" just as the thirst for justice is a "development of the drive for revenge."[69] Nietzsche, the aristocratic radical, liked to ridicule the self-serving morality of the chicken telling the fox it is wrong to raid the hen house. Reaction formations like philanthropy and pacifism roused his deepest suspicions; as he argued in *The Genealogy of Morals*, one of his most coherent books, the modern ethics of pity for the weak, at once bourgeois and Christian, was nothing more than the ethics that slaves had cleverly imposed on their masters. His celebration of war, however metaphorical in intent, displays unmastered bits of sadism in him. But within defined limits, freely given from a feeling

67. "Aus dem Nachlass der achtziger Jahre," ibid. IV, 300; *Götzen-Dämmerung*, "Wie die 'Wahre Welt' endlich zur Fabel wurde," ibid., III, 409; "Aus dem Nachlass," ibid., IV, 299–300.
68. *Götzen-Dämmerung*, "Moral als Widernatur," ibid., III, 411–12.
69. Ibid., 412; "Aus dem Nachlass," ibid., IV, 505.

of overflowing strength, kindness and generosity are the disguised and beneficent offspring of the passions.

That is why Nietzsche could celebrate the uninhibited outpouring of passion in *Rausch*—the state of ecstasy or intoxication. How much it could do, *Rausch*, being at once love and more than love! It is love that shows how effectively *Rausch* transfigures the human animal. That, too, is why Nietzsche could vehemently, excitedly, say yes to life in the manner of the ancient Greeks as he chose to read them; he called for "the religious affirmation of life, of the whole life, not of denied or halved life." He added, elliptically but pregnantly: "typical—that the sexual act arouses profundity, mystery, awe." That, finally, is why he could denounce the "fear of the senses, of the appetites, when that fear goes far enough to counsel against them," for then it is only "a symptom of *weakness*. Extreme methods," he concluded, sounding for all the world like a psychoanalyst before psychoanalysis, "always characterize abnormal conditions."[70]

For Nietzsche, then, love, rising on the foundations "of a heated sensuality," commendably displays "warmth of passion." This celebration linked Nietzsche to other critics of nineteenth-century bourgeois ways of loving: he thought it only too obvious that the middling orders of his day wanted none of the kind of love he saw as life-giving. "In marriages in the *bourgeois* sense of the word," he wrote, "understand me: in the most honorable sense of the word 'marriage,' it is by no means a question of love." It is, rather, "society's permission granted to two persons for sexual gratification, naturally observing certain conditions, particularly those that keep the *interest of society* in mind."[71] The sentence is a little involuted, but its import is unmistakable: middle-class marriage is manifestly an unloving, crass affair. Yet quite unwittingly it performs the task for which nature has appointed it: to perpetuate the race. On this vital issue, Nietzsche, who had rejected so much of Schopenhauer, returned to the great teacher of his early years. Like Schopenhauer, he added some telling pages to the literature of reproach.

From the perspective of these theories about love, Freud's thoughts on the subject, unsystematically but copiously scattered through many of his writings, appear at first as little more than a brilliant condensation of German ideas laced with French admixtures. Certainly Schopenhauer had explored, in his racy way, many of the propositions associated with the psychoanalytic theory of the libido. He had not only pleaded "for the

70. Ibid., 433, 344, 365, 316.
71. Ibid., 162, 514.

primacy of the emotions," as Freud summarized Schopenhauer's thought later, "and the overwhelming significance of sexuality," but had recognized, in addition, "the mechanism of repression." Yet Freud explicitly adds, "I read Schopenhauer very late in life"; he wanted to keep his mind uncluttered, his intuitive freedom—his *Unbefangenheit*—intact. The same held true for Nietzsche. Freud appreciated that master psychologist's aphoristic way with men's minds. But he deliberately stayed away from his writings; he was never able to study Nietzsche, "partly because of the similarity of his intuitive insights with our laborious investigations," and partly because he felt overwhelmed by the profusion and the immense suggestiveness of Nietzsche's ideas. Freud was far less concerned with "priority" than with maintaining his distance, his room for maneuver.[72]

Freud's conscious resistance to these persuasive amateur psychologists was a sensible defense of science against poetry. Nietzsche in particular was an almost irresistible ancestor; without the aid of research, he had flatly asserted that dreams are meaningful, that the drives are ringed round with defenses, that religion is a neurosis, that civilization exacts sacrifices, that, in a word, the sublimation of instincts does the work of culture—all adumbrations of psychoanalytic theories. And Freud—he could not have said it any better—quoted more than once Nietzsche's trenchant pronouncement on the power of passion over judgment: " 'I did this,' says my memory. 'I cannot have done this,' says my pride and remains inexorable. In the end—memory yields."[73] Still, we have good reason to trust Freud's version of his scientific development; though the most ambitious of innovators, he rarely hesitated to give others credit for anticipating his ideas or stimulating his imagination. He acknowledged the powers of perceptive dilettantes, particularly those of the poets. "Everything has already been said," he thought, "certainly in the domain of love,"[74] and he derived intellectual sustenance from the burgeoning

72. "Selbstdarstellung" (1925), *G.W.*, XIV, 86; "An Autobiographical Study," *S.E.*, XX, 59–60; October 28, 1908, *Protokolle*, II, 28; see also Freud, "On the History of the Psycho-Analytic Movement," *S.E.*, XIV, 15–16. I shall return to Freud on love below, pp. 349–52, when I discuss his views on modern nervousness.

73. Nietzsche, *Jenseits von Gut und Böse*, No. 68, *Werke*, III, 71; quoted by Freud in *The Psychopathology of Everyday Life*, *S.E.*, VI, 147n, and *Notes upon a Case of Obsessional Neurosis*, ibid., V, 184.

74. "Angst und Triebleben," *Neue Folge der Vorlesungen zur Einführung in die Psychoanalyse*, *St.A.*, I, 540; "Anxiety and Instinctual Life," *New Introductory Lectures*, *S.E.*, XXII, 107. The first chapter of his *Interpretation of Dreams* is a thorough, by no means ungenerous, survey of earlier writings on the subject; and on the opening page of his book on jokes he pays tribute to the novelist Jean Paul, and the philosophers Theodor Vischer, Kuno Fischer, and, above all, Theodor Lipps, without whom, he writes, he could not have done this book at all (*S.E.*, VIII, 9.)

professional interest in sexuality that marked the late bourgeois century. But he transformed, ingenious alchemist that he was, conventional materials into the precious substance of theory by discovering dynamic conjunctions for phenomena that others had merely observed. He put the study of Eros to uses that would have dazzled even Plato's expansive imagination.

Moreover, Freud had impulsions other than Schopenhauer's or Nietzsche's ideas to direct his attention to the centrality of the sexual drives in human life, notably the celebrated French neurologist Jean-Martin Charcot. It is a fair guess that when the historian must choose between a philosopher and a physician as an intellectual ancestor for Freud, the historian is well advised to take the physician. In the winter of 1885, spending some intensely productive months in Paris studying with Charcot, Freud enjoyed several evenings at the master's house. Forty years later, he recalled one particular reception, when he had overheard his host discussing the arresting case of a young couple, the husband possibly impotent, the wife presenting severe, presumably neurasthenic symptoms. Suddenly, Freud heard Charcot breaking out with his characteristic animation: *"Mais, dans des cas pareils c'est toujours la chose génitale, toujours—toujours—toujours."* This was heady intelligence for Freud and for a moment, he remembered, he fell into "an almost paralyzing astonishment," and said to himself: "Yes, but if he knows that, why does he never say so?" This authoritative tribute to the power of "the genital thing" seemed, to this eager and inexperienced neurologist, an astonishing diagnostic generalization. Astonishing and perhaps not so far-reaching after all, since he soon forgot—later, Freud would have said, repressed—the episode: "brain anatomy and the experimental induction of hysterical paralyses had absorbed all my interest."[75] Only gradually, piecemeal, in the practice that Freud opened in Vienna after his return, did the truth of Charcot's casual, emphatic observation, and its gravity, come to possess him.

Freud's way of discovering psychological causes and of gathering disparate observations into organic patterns is most striking in his handling of that commonplace, very ancient perception of love as the synthesis

75: "Zur Geschichte der psychoanalytischen Bewegung" (1914), *G.W.*, X, 53; "On the History of the Psychoanalytic Movement," *S.E.*, XIV, 14. On April 1, 1908, Freud told his Wednesday group that he had "a peculiar relationship to philosophy," whose "abstract character" he found so uncongenial that he had in the end given up studying it. Hence Nietzsche's ideas had had no influence on him. As an instance of the complex filiation of ideas, he mentioned that he had, after first rejecting it, come to adopt the sexual origins of neurosis by hearing three eminent physicians speak of it, "Breuer, Charcot, and Chrobak." *Protokolle*, I, 338.

of desire and affection. "A completely normal attitude in love," to quote him once again, requires the uniting of "two currents," the *tender and the sensual.*" Those who do not, however impressive their sexual record, are failures in love: Don Juan, that widely envied machine of conquest, must have been battling some deep-seated neurotic malaise, whether disappointment with the reality of woman, homosexual panic, or fear of fiasco. The facility with which such an unstable, helplessly restless lover crystallizes woman after woman and lives in a continuous fever of ever-changing illusions betrays his need for a self-deception far more treacherous than the occasional idealization of the loved object that accompanies the normal madness that is love. The mature lover—on this conclusion Freud and the most conventional bourgeois would have agreed—is less adventurous, and paradoxically less unhappy, than this.

Triumphantly, Freud's theorizing incorporated love into an over-arching developmental scheme that he designed to hold valid, with inescapable cultural and personal variations, for all of humanity. That scheme tied love to the body but did not leave it there: love (like hate) is born early and progresses through the succession and interplay of erogenous zones, culminating in the genitals as the principal region for the concentration of erotic pleasure as the exciting companion of "aim-inhibited" affection. Freud, like Diderot and Schopenhauer before him, elevated human erotic energies into essential vital forces, engaged in a prolonged history of differentiation and an unending contest with their immortal adversary, the power of destruction and death. That is how Freud threw his bridge between physiology and psychology: the libido is a biological endowment which finds expression and defines its shape in feelings no less than in acts and which eventuates in experiences that are more than the sheer gratification of appetite. Freud was not using idle rhetoric when he likened sexuality in his view of man to the Eros of the divine Plato.

Freud, then, plotted the affectionate and passionate currents of love onto his timetable of human maturation. But he left some illegible and contradictory directions for his successors to unriddle. His writings on sexuality strongly invite the inference that the libidinal drives are at first a wholly indiscriminate collocation of emotional needs, wishes, and outbursts, insinuating and exigent, touching and cruel, wholly self-centered, partially sublimated later in life into a thoughtful, caring investment of feelings in others. But in venturing one of his rare accounts of how love actually grows, Freud in fact argued that of its two strands, the affectionate one is the older. Tenderness, he wrote, "springs from the earliest years of childhood." These "tender fixations of the child are continued through childhood, again and again taking eroticism along, but un-deflected from their sexual aims." Then, with puberty, the time of physical changes and mental turmoil, there enters a "powerful 'sensual' current, which no longer fails to recognize its aim." This sensuality had always been there, latent, masked, powerless to translate wish into action. Its underground vegetation, from which adolescence so dramatically liberates it, explains why virtually all physicians and other observers had put the birth of sexuality at puberty—until Freud compelled the world to revise its notions and accept the shocking fact of infantile sexuality.

Pursuing this developmental history, Freud saw the young adult, forced by the incest barrier to give up early erotic desires, transferring attention "from these really unsuitable objects as soon as possible" to "other, un-familiar objects, with whom a real sexual life can be carried on." True, these new objects "are still chosen after the model" of the "infantile ones." The past retains some of its authority: the adult lives out the "conditions for loving" laid down in childhood. These adult objects will in time "attach to themselves the tenderness once anchored" in the early "imago" of mother or father. In such an ideal evolution, by no means common, "the highest measure of sensual infatuation will bring with it the highest mental valuation";[76] the normal lover will yoke happy erotic memories to the physical and mental possibilities that only adulthood can provide. It is no accident that Freud should have devoted such ample space to love in his classic papers on psychoanalytic technique which deal so largely with transference. He never tired of insisting that love draws at least some of its energy and formulates most of its needs—always more than lovers know—from the transfer of early experiences to later amorous encounters.

The discovery that unconscious memories play an incalculable, often dominant role in the course of love is probably Freud's most original contribution to nineteenth-century thinking on the subject. That love is irrational is, certainly, not a new insight. Stendhal had memorably imaged that old truth in his master metaphor of crystallization; Balzac had stated it tersely when he said that "the more one judges, the less one loves"; Wilkie Collins had put it melodramatically in his novel *Basil* when he has his unfortunate hero muse, after he has fallen in love for the first time, at first sight, "Prudence, duty, memories and prejudices of home, were all absorbed and forgotten in love." But Freud reversed

76. "Erniedrigung des Liebeslebens," *St.A.*, V, 200–202; "On the Universal Tendency to Debasement in the Sphere of Love," *S.E.*, XI, 180–81. For another exploration of Freud's contribution to an understanding of culture, see *Education of the Senses* (1984), ch. I.

Collins's depiction of what Basil called this "giant sensation": it did not eclipse, but, rather, it employed memories and prejudices of home. They, indeed, were powerful motives for this irrational passion; ghosts from what Freud called "the forgotten past"[77] presiding over the tragicomedy of love in which the principals were at once directors, spectators, leading actors—and dramatists unwittingly plagiarizing scripts they had repressed.

That love is governed by memories beyond the reach of awareness held, in Freud's mind, as forcefully for being loved as for bestowing love on others. The adults' sense of themselves as lovable, both in healthy self-esteem and in brute self-infatuation, draws heavily on a pervasive sense of having been cherished early, dependably, unconditionally. For it is possible to give love only after one has received it, and knows it. Early childhood provides the particular setting; it even offers rehearsals for later fidelity: the acquisition of object constancy, the capacity of the child to recall its parents even during their absence, and their love even during their anger, is the primitive prototype of the adult's constancy, which makes of love something better than the sheer discharge of sexual tension. Freud had all of this in mind when he called love the great educator.

But education in love, as for anything else, was in Freud's pessimistic anthropology an education through loss. As civilization compels children to postpone gratifications, to curb pressing appetites and give up cherished wishes, it proceeds to set limits to the permissible in the erotic sphere. And it reinforces its lessons by threats, notably the threat that love will be withdrawn. For the adult, therefore, to fall in love is an act at once courageous and inescapable, an experience pregnant with conflicting possibilities. It is a defense against the intolerable fear of losing love, an unconscious reenactment of early amorous entanglements, an assumption of risks. Lovers' accesses of jealousy and pathetic demands for reassurance, their possessiveness and anxiety in the midst of bliss, all testify to the precariousness that is lovers' lot.

Freud's pessimism was not capricious; it followed from the difficult course he charted for the maturation of the drives and the inescapable clashes of drives with defenses. The likelihood of failure was built into Freud's theory of development. That theory envisioned the libido not as a single, fixed endowment but as the convergence of component drives ideally intended but rarely destined to concentrate wholly on appro-

---

77. "Jenseits das Lustprinzips," *St.A.*, III, 229; "Beyond the Pleasure Principle," *S.E.*, XVIII, 19.

priate aims and eligible objects. Heterosexual genital primacy securely in
tandem with stable affection was, in Freud's gloomy estimation, far
from a matter of course, but an impressive, fragile, rather uncommon
achievement. Since all humanity is in some way or other tainted by
neurosis, Freud thought it only too probable that the amalgamation of the
component libidinal drives, much like the amalgamation of the tender
and the passionate strands of love, would be imperfect. Their cohesion
would be sadly incomplete, their cooperation only intermittent, their
development highly uneven. It was the general fixation on early erotic
objects, whether moderate or crippling, that accounted for the be-
wildering varieties of sexual tastes in humans—for the perversions, for
fetishism, impotence, frigidity, for the thousand erotic shocks that the
flesh is heir to. Freud went so far as to conjecture that there is something in the very nature of the sexual drives hostile to their complete
gratification.[78]

He gave way to this gloom in analyzing the suffering that so many
lovers, especially men, seem to take upon themselves voluntarily, almost
gladly, when they abase themselves before the object of their adoration.
To invent, exaggerate, or obsessively advertise the perfections of the
beloved seemed, Freud thought, to leave little room for one's own good
qualities. The man's "sexual overvaluation" of the woman, Freud wrote in
1914, "doubtless springs from the original narcissism of the child and
thus corresponds to its transference to the sexual object. This sexual
overvaluation permits the rise of that peculiar condition of being in love,
reminiscent of a neurotic compulsion."[79] Women, too, can deplete their
ego in aggrandizing the object of their erotic choice.

Unsympathetic or amused observers have often lampooned this need
for self-denigration. Certainly in the nineteenth century, there were
countless jokes and fictional representations of the type. Charles Dickens's
David Copperfield makes a proper fool of himself over the women he
loves, and Copperfield is a fairly typical young hero in the nineteenth-
century novel. Certainly reality rivaled fiction in faintly poignant, sometimes fairly pathetic scenes. Otto Beneke proclaimed himself unworthy
of Marietta Banks; Walter Bagehot was far from sure that he really
deserved Eliza Wilson. And when Effie Gray sat down to reply to an

78. "Erniedrigung des Liebeslebens," *St.A.*, V, 208; "Tendency to Debasement,"
S.E., XI, 188–89.
79. "Zur Einführung des Narzissmus" (1914), *St.A.*, 55; "Narcissism, An Introduction," *S.E.*, XIV, 88.

extravagant love letter from John Ruskin, she could, though generally a
sturdy and sensible young woman, hardly contain her feeling of in-
feriority: "My dearest John," she began. "I do not know how I can
sufficiently thank you for your inestimable letter this morning so full
of tenderness and affection almost too kind and good, you will quite
spoil me, my love, it almost made me weep with joy to think myself so
beloved, not but what I was fully impressed with that before, but this
morning's letter almost made me rejoice too much in thinking that so
much happiness was permitted to me who am so unworthy of it."[80] It
may have been the longest sentence she ever wrote, and, it turned out, in
a lost cause.

Significantly, Freud has very little to say about the more pleasant forms
that erotic idealization can take. The amorous overvaluation of the other
need not, after all, result in the masochistic undervaluation of the self.
On the contrary, it often encourages a kind of reflexive crystallization;
to fantasize the perfections of the beloved can generate fantasies about
one's own. The intoxicated lover then looks at his chosen as into a mirror,
astonished and exhilarated to think that, since some magnificent being
has consented to love him, he must embody some admirable characteristics himself. But Freud was inclined to ascribe such elevated self-esteem
to an inappropriate survival of narcissistic preoccupations. As far as we
can determine, Freud's life as lover and husband was less conflict-ridden
than his theory of love would have allowed for. It was almost as though
he was revenging himself, in sketching the history of grim-faced Eros, on
a culture that had condemned him to wait, through years of impatient
sexual frustration, before he could consummate his love with his fiancée.
Yet, while Freud's pessimism outran his evidence and his experience, the
explanatory range of his thinking about libido was enormously impressive.
Freud was in agreement with other psychologists with his belief in the
genetic chain of causality, but he took it more seriously than his colleagues did. He saw it as far longer, infinitely more tangled and twisted,
than they. The career of libido, as Freud mapped it out, did more than
explain the origins of neuroses, of perversions, and of normal erotic
gratification. It also explained ways of feeling and modes of acting that
had hitherto seemed quite remote from sexuality: the child's rage at its
newborn sibling, the adolescent's volatile friendships, the spinster's unappeasable fear of sexual assault, the pacifist's bellicose love of peace, the
fanatic's foaming proselytizing, the fat man's uncontrollable overeating.

80. February 10, 1848. Mary Lutyens, *The Ruskins and the Grays* (1972), 88.

Beyond that, it could illuminate inquiries and activities, like folklore and history, art and politics, presumably innocent of erotic urges. Psychoanalysis first made it possible to think systematically about so comprehensive, complex and elusive a world of experience as bourgeois love, about the paths, and obstructions, to the confluence of its two currents.

∛ TWO ∜

Experience: The Best Teacher

I<small>N</small> 1872, speaking for a sizeable clan of well-informed publicists, the eminent French economist and moral philosopher Henri Baudrillart noted: "It is the destiny of our time to put everything into question once again."[1] His observation was trite, but that made it no less true—nor less significant, for his essay was a contribution to the already vast literature on women's rights and, with that, another drop in the ocean of nineteenth-century writing about love and its currents. It was a literature easily produced and eagerly read, by women as much as by men. Women, after all, if not its most original authors, were its privileged subject, and they would respond to it freely, since it ranged from the most ferocious misogyny to the most Utopian feminism. Thus it gave its feminine consumers abundant materials to resist or, for that matter, to applaud and utilize in their halting march toward equality. Still, for all this influential outpouring in print, both scholarly and popular, books and articles enjoyed less authority as guides to conduct than the world. In general, bourgeois principally learned about love from parents and siblings, from cherished domestics and a handful of friends or casual encounters. Experience, "the best of

1. "L'Agitation pour l'émancipation des femmes," *Revue des deux mondes* (1872), vol. 5, 651. From the 1850s on, *bien-pensant* periodicals like the *Revue des deux mondes* in France, and its counterparts in other countries, were inundated with thoughtful, often very troubled, essays on the education, the status, the aspiration of women, and nearly all of them would advert to the state of flux threatening the stability of manners and morals in the Victorian decades.

:achers,"[2] efficiently performed its pedagogic assignment in the sphere f love as it did everywhere else.

This made for repetitions. The bourgeois experience of love was filtered hrough custom, that cultural memory: by and large, middle-class men nd women would take Eros as they found him. Their parents' precepts nd practices remained more or less authoritative for them. They might ear of imaginative radical proposals—by the Saint Simonians, or by Charles Fourier—on how to take experimental notions about love and overs out of books into life. But these projects, though at times suggestive nd appealing, struck most of them as unrealistic; in fact they were rarely out into practice. Most bourgeois would accept the respectable com-promises between sexual drives and cultural defenses as good enough. They could hardly afford to overlook some sober realities, notably money, power, and women's aspirations.

1. Sober Realities

Love was strong but not without its rivals. Nineteenth-century bourgeois thought they knew, as people had thought since Virgil, that love conquers all; they liked to believe that love moves mountains, leaps barriers, laughs at locksmiths. Love, they might say with Stendhal, is "a tender passion,"[3] but its soft, melting ways notoriously masks a will of steel. An unhappy suitor smarting under an unrequited infatuation could cite proverbs docu-menting his slavery; cynics might argue that it was money, not love, that conquers all. But common wisdom saw love as a ladder to freedom enabling lovers to surmount the obstacles—differences in status, religion, or regional loyalties—that convention would throw into their path. For good or ill, love, that primordial energy, seemed the universal solvent, the triumphant nemesis of social and cultural rigidities. So, at least, popular poets, essayists, and novelists would depict it.

Experience enforced a more differentiated and less theatrical lesson. Nineteenth-century bourgeois only rediscovered what other classes, and

---

2. Eliza Wilson to Walter Bagehot, January 27, 1858. *The Love-Letters of Walter Bagehot and Eliza Wilson*, ed. Mrs. Russell Barrington (1933), 148. "The most valu-able capital, or culture, or education usable in the building of novels," Mark Twain wrote in 1890, "is personal experience." Obviously, this dictum held all the more in love. Walter Blair and Hamlin Hill, *America's Humor: From Poor Richard to Doonesbury* (1978), 303.

3. Stendhal (22 pluviôse XIII, February 11, 1805), *Journal, Oeuvres intimes*, III (1955), 624.

other times, had already discovered, often centuries before them. Th
passage to marriage, which was for all but bohemians and impeniter
romantics the ultimate purpose of love, was not a straight highway, eithe
of rational calculation or heedless passion. It was, rather, a battlefield o
competing and conflicting emotions, many of them unconscious. Parent
preoccupation with monetary security or social ascent could clash wit
their children's imperious desire for emotional fulfillment, and in the tangl
of family affections and tensions, the outcome was far from settled i
advance. Indulgent parents might graciously overlook the social blemishe
of unsuitable partners for their sons and daughters to escape squabbles
scenes, and tears, or, more positively, let the younger generation fin
its own way to happiness. But the opposite was no less true, and probabl
more frequent: many a young man and woman, trained to obedience an
unused to questioning domestic decrees, would mutely bow to parenta
commands and fail to avail himself—or, more likely, herself—of th
protection against forced marriages enshrined in the country's legal code
That is why the laws governing the rights of parents and the obligation
of their offspring were unreliable guides to the conduct of any family
One truth was beyond dispute, for the nineteenth-century middle classe
as for others: an emotional entanglement with a prospective life's partne
able to pass the most rigorous muster was the safest. Well-regulated
romantic attachments formed within one's own circle, or aiming only
marginally above it, faced the smallest prospects of stern vetoes from the
family.

The particular mixture of rationality and emotion governing parents'
decision to impose a spouse on their children, or simply to ratify their
personal choices, differed from family to family, within each family, and
at times from infatuation to infatuation. Those passionate undercurrents
complicating family relationships subtly colored the demands that parents
would make on their marriageable offspring and, no less subtly, that
offspring's idiosyncratic manner of falling in love. As we know, the
intimate early experiences that constitute the search for objects cast their
shadow over the adult's apparently most unhampered erotic choices. The
repressed love that a young woman might bear her father, or a young
man his mother, could override the love for suitors of one's own age, or
dictate the kind of suitor deemed worthy. There were numerous reasons
why nineteenth-century bourgeois might remain unmarried; the marked
surplus of women in England or Germany was one of them. But there
were respectable lifelong bachelors and spinsters whose deepest reasons
would have astonished them.

The real motives of parents and children at work in the delicate transaction of making a marriage were often concealed behind the social conventions they refused to flout. But this conventionality was not simply an alibi. What I have called the mixture of rationality and emotion in that transaction was subject to prevailing cultural styles tied to country, status, and time. The historian in search of fine distinctions within the nineteenth-century middle classes of Europe and the United States will find a feast of discriminations here. Contemporary cultural critics and traveling journalists certainly discovered abundant material for moralizing comment comparing the social habits of their own country and those of others, sometimes in disdainful superiority, sometimes in open envy. Count de Gasparin's popular book of 1865 on the modern family is a representative instance of this literature. "In France," he wrote, "stupid custom, very little to the credit of our morality, prevents the future husband and wife from becoming really acquainted before marriage. They may have met at a ball; the question of money will have been arranged by the lawyers; the proposal will then have been made and agreed to; and then, all having been duly decided upon, some insignificant interviews will have taken place." In refreshing contrast, "in England, in Germany, in the United States, and in Switzerland, things are not conducted this way. Great liberty of intercourse is authorized between young men and young women. They have met, they will have discoursed of all honourable things, and their consent to marry is anything but a vain formality." De Gasparin readily acknowledged that "doubtless all is not perfect in these countries; the independence of young people is carried too far in America; betrothal is prolonged to an excess in Germany." Still, the French had much to learn from those countries. "Liberty of choice is at least maintained; inclination preserves its legitimate place; serious and spontaneous attachment precedes the vow to love for ever; marriage does not supervene like a coarse fact, without preface of any sort; they do not pass in one hour from the most distant and ceremonious relations to all the intimacy of married life." He lamented that love, even in marriage, was in France "not in good odor."[4]

Other publicists took the same sort of observation to reach diametrically opposed sociological conclusions. The clamor of the 1860s and later, calling for couples to marry for love alone, struck conservative and censorious moralists as a deplorable sign that the peculiarly modern disease, the movement for woman's emancipation, was getting out of control. Love defined itself by free choice, and this, in turn, seemed nothing less than a plank in the subversive feminist platform; the chaos

4. Count Agénor de Gasparin, *The Family. Duties, Joys, and Sorrows* (1865; tr. 1867), 16–17. The sixth printing of this highly characteristic production was published in 1869.

it threatened to unloose was most visible in the land of the future, the
United States, with its "rage for equality." Irresponsbile reformers of
marital morals who idealize love matches, then, are self-absorbed dreamers
who, as Henri Baudrillart indignantly charged, "always talk of rights,
never of duties."[5]

Such free-swinging verdicts, like the unequivocal generalizations about
social relations on which they are based, are of questionable validity.
Nineteenth-century middle-class culture swarms with exceptions. Even in
France, which among Western countries controlled the marital choices
of the young, especially of young women, most tightly, there were
parents who consulted their sons' and daughters' wishes, respected their
hesitations, and sympathized with their disgust at the prospect of some
elderly, unappealing husband imposed solely for his good name or tempting fortune.[6] Still, speaking broadly, middle-class English and, even more,
American girls were far less inhibited from selecting their husbands, or
cajoling their parents, than their German or French, let alone their
Russian counterparts. Moreover, the uppermost or most tradition-bound
within the bourgeoisie—old commercial clans, rich and anxious parvenus,
patrician Catholics, orthodox Jews—were more likely than their less
proud or prosperous fellow-bourgeois to treat marriage negotiations as
affairs of state rather than as affairs of the heart. Finally, with the domestication of romantic notions about love as personal destiny and the mounting
pressure of young women for higher education and access to professional
careers, as the range of possibilities for free attachments widened, the hold
of parental authority weakened. The bourgeois girl of the 1820s had
passively obeyed dictates that her granddaughter would have indignantly,
and often successfully, resisted. Yet even toward the end of the nineteenth
century, reason entered, and often dominated, the selection of a marital
partner in the middle classes. "It is better . . . to face reality," a German-
Jewish governess, who had married an elderly widower, pronounced with

5. "Equality": M.B., "L'éducation ailleurs que chez nous," *Journal des demoiselles*,
IIL (1880), 119; "rights": Baudrillart, "L'Agitation pour l'émancipation des femmes,"
677.
6. "Mon Dieu! What indecision! What perplexity! What to do?" exclaimed
Stephanie Jullien, then twenty-one, to her brother Auguste, in conflict about a
suitor. "I almost wish not to be so free, that one would compel me, give me orders;
then I would not have the responsibility for my future misery or happiness." Jullien
Family Papers, 39 AP 4, Archives National, Paris. I owe this passage to Barbara
Corrado Pope, University of Oregon. For passages from Jullien's letters, see Erna
Olafson Hellerstein, Leslie Parker Hume, and Karen M. Offen, eds., *Victorian
Women: A Documentary Account of Women's Lives in Nineteenth-Century
England, France, and the United States* (1981), 144–49.

, certain quiet decisiveness in the early 1890s. She was fortunate; the husband and the children she acquired appear to have made her happy. Still, she concluded, with iron logic, "Ideals don't bring much."[7]

In the early decades of the century, far more than later, love was for many well-brought-up young women a rare emotional luxury. They could imagine it through novels they surreptitiously read, by identifying with the heroines. They could wallow in crushes on tutors. They could harbor grand, largely theoretical passions for handsome visitors to the house. But over and over, the force of family pressure won out. "We do not marry, but we are given in marriage," says Olga, the heroine of Goncharov's mid-century novel *Oblomov*; she spoke for thousands of her sisters, and not in Russia alone. Love was prescribed in paternal injunctions, marriage manuals, even in codes of law: "The woman must obey her husband, reside with him in love, respect and unlimited obedience," ran the Russian code of 1836, "and offer him every pleasantness and affection as the ruler of the household."[8] Love, for the young woman subject to such a regimen, was not an irresistible impulse but a domestic accomplishment, to be learned as she had learned to play the piano or to speak a foreign language.

To soften the harsh contours of reality, parents would persuade their daughters to enter a marriage of prudence with the enticing promise that love would grow with the passage of years. They sold it as a cultivated virtue. This is the line of attack with which Frau Konsul Buddenbrook lures her daughter Tony into accepting the unctuous, unprepossessing Herr Grünlich, whose ostentatious financial solidity makes him an eligible son-in-law at a time of reverses for the Buddenbrook firm: "Look, I assume that you still have no decided feelings for Herr Grünlich, but, I assure you, that will come, that comes with time." For Tony, her mother's reasoning carries conviction, coupled as it is with her father's earnest, unconsciously seductive, reminder what her duties are to the House of Buddenbrook. After the wedding is over, and the couple are about to depart on their wedding trip, Tony, now Tony Grünlich, leaps out of the coach to embrace her father passionately once more, and whispers very softly, "Are you satisfied with me?" He is, at great cost to his daughter.[9] Another disastrous practical bourgeois marriage has been

7. Marion A. Kaplan, "For Love or Money: The Marriage Strategies of Jews in Imperial Germany," Leo Baeck Institute, *Year Book XXVIII* (1983), 263–300; quotation at 281.

8. Richard Stites, *The Women's Liberation Movement in Russia: Feminism, Nihilism, and Bolshevism 1860–1930* (1978), 6–7.

9. Mann, *Buddenbrooks* (1900; ed. n.d.), Part III, ch. 2, p. 100; Part III, ch. 14, p. 159.

launched. Mann's *Buddenbrooks* was fiction, but it faithfully evoked familiar realities of the nineteenth century.

Negotiations over the dowry spread the frigid air of business dealings over marriage preliminaries, even when the prospective spouses were already in love with one another. "Convenience, policy, friendship, position, influence, money—all these are given as motives for matrimony," the Boston physician H. S. Pomeroy observed in the late 1880s in a book on marriage,[10] and the haggling over the bride's dowry graphically exhibits these motives in play. The nineteenth-century institution of having the bride's family endow her with worldly goods—cash, silver, jewelry, furniture, linens—was almost universal among those who could afford it, and pathetically desired among those who could not. It looked back on a long history, at least to the high Middle Ages. But in the Victorian age, the dowry, and its natural companion, the trousseau, experienced radical if erratic evolutions, reenacting the tensions of the time. The trousseau had once been, and in some circles remained, an intensely personal expression, an orderly pile of table linens and bed clothes, handkerchiefs and dresses, laboriously worked by maturing girls and put away in hope chests—significant name!—against the glorious day of the wedding, to be at once useful and ornamental. Late in the nineteenth century, though, it became increasingly the domain of specialty shops and, with that, far more expensive, less a testimony to a girl's skill in needlepoint and embroidery than a tribute to her parents' affluence. The traditional dowry, too, though it retained a tenacious hold right into the twentieth century, came under sustained attack. It continued to have its attractions for aspiring grooms—the fledgling physician or attorney setting up his practice and facing heavy expenses, the ambitious bureaucrat eking out a modest living on his salary and aching for a few luxuries, the energetic businessman in search of venture capital. It was telling that in advertisements seeking wives, the dowry was nearly always a prominent ingredient. Indeed, there were those bachelors who, quite candidly, sought to marry a store or a practice—what the Germans called "Einheirat" was precisely this—with the bride an unavoidable appendage.[11]

There was nothing cynical or clandestine about this kind of naked practicality. Men pursued the settlements they thought they deserved; in turn, the bride's family, once it trusted the future son-in-law's resources and prospects, had no objections to a frank canvass of financial arrangements. Quite the contrary, parents would derive genuine satis-

10. Pomeroy, *The Ethics of Marriage* (1888), 46.
11. See Kaplan, "For Love or Money," 266–67, 276.

ction (and welcome prestige) from the consciousness of leaving a
ughter financially secure in her married state. After mid-century,
lough, even conventional bourgeois could be heard to denounce this
aterialistic hunt as unworthy of an idealized union which should be a
ending of hearts rather than a transfer of funds. The poets and phi-
sophers of love were finding heartening and surprising echoes in middle-
ass families, especially in those whose daughters were not obstructed in
eir heroic efforts to educate themselves and enter a wider world. In
880, an English divine, George St. Clair, maintained flatly that "A young
oman now is free to accept or reject any offer which is made to her."[12]
le was speaking about his own country: matters were by no means so
ear-cut on the Continent. But even in more conservative societies mar-
ages for love alone were becoming a familiar sight and found fluent and
rceful celebrants.

It is unwise to see the triumph of love as total. In the heady flush of
omantic infatuation, under the spell of sentimental fiction, most lovers
etained their heads. Motives remained mixed. The most fundamental
amilial habits were in transition and, not unnaturally, the "new ideas"
ncountered the most determined resistance. That traditional maxim,
Don't marry for money, but go where the money is, kept alive by
Tennyson, Trollope, Meredith and others, awakened the disapproval of
omantic and principled minds. But many obeyed it, with a kind of
nnocent impudence, throughout the century. As late as 1893, Isidor
Hirschfeld and his brother Joseph founded a successful clothing store
n Hamburg and decided, the following year, that they should visit spas
o make themselves usefully visible: "Perhaps a girl with money will fall
n love with us."[13] Anti-Semites liked to suspect a typical Jewish trait in
uch calculating courtships. In fact, while arranged and planned marriages
emained in vogue among observant Jews longer than among most other
ethnic and religious communities, the Hirschfeld brothers looking for
well-to-do brides were in large Christian company and had Jewish as
much as gentile critics. In a world very much in flux, contrary convictions
could live side by side in the same family, sometimes in the same mind.

The autobiography of a pioneering German woman physician, Rahel
Straus, records these strains with artless exactitude. Speaking of her
mother's engagement some time late in the 1870s, she observes that it was

12. St. Clair, *Early Marriage and Home Life* (1880), 10.

13. Isidor Hirschfeld (1868–1937), diary, undated, Leo Baeck Institute, in Monika
Richarz, ed., *Jüdisches Leben in Deutschland*, vol. *II, Selbstzeugnisse zur Sozial-
geschichte im Kaiserreich* (1979), 243–50, quotation at 248. Note the comment by
Kaplan, "For Love or Money," 271.

not a romantic accident: "rather, father came directly to Posen to look at mother. In Jewish households it was then, and later, too, very much the custom that parents, relatives, friends of the family, or professional marriage brokers would come to propose this or that man for this or that young woman. Then, if external conditions—family, profession, fortune, health—were appropriate, the girl's parents would give their permission to have the young man 'take a look.' It was rare that the young man would leave without being engaged—this was seen as a powerful insult for, after all, one married 'into a family,' not the individual girl. Custom and tradition would take care that the two afterwards suited one another." In sharp contrast, Rahel Straus's grandfather, "a rare exception" in his day, "could not comprehend why his daughters did not fall in love and find a man of their choice." Her sister was still married in the time-honored way: a young rabbi had heard many good things about Trude from a cousin and asked to be allowed to visit. "To me the way in which my sister Trude found her husband," Rahel Straus later noted, "was wholly incomprehensible, although I saw how rapidly she gained confidence in him and felt love"; ungrudgingly, she admitted in retrospect that her sister was to live "in happy marriage with the man who had chosen her according to ancient Jewish tradition."[14] But for her own part, fulfilling her grandfather's program, she herself married for love, her first love, even though her pious father-in-law, strictly orthodox and wholly committed to the old dispensation, had no use for his son's modern ways. Unquestioning respect for paternal authority, the solid support of the dowry, the continued observance of archaic cultural habits—these were anxious defenses against the corrosive action of liberal culture, against the opening wedges for the sheer unpredictability of love.

It was no secret, even to the defenders of tradition, that the dowry system was open to abuse. That is why families did not scruple to conduct confidential inquiries, inspect bank balances, employ marriage brokers and even detective agencies to discover whether a reputed heiress really enjoyed as great expectations as rumored, or whether the suitor's business was as sound as he gave it out to be. Before Konsul Buddenbrook pressed Grünlich on his daughter Tony, he had conscientiously investigated his prospective son-in-law, but that suave confidence man had managed to

---

14. Straus, *Wir lebten in Deutschland: Erinnerungen einer deutschen Jüdin 1880–1933*, ed. Max Kreutzberger (1961), 19–20, 81–83, 104–107. The idea that one married a family, not an individual, was by no means confined to German Jews. Alexandre Dumas fils reached the mature conclusion that marriage is "not only the union of two people but the alliance of two families." Theodore Zeldin, *France 1848–1915*, vol. I, *Ambition, Love and Politics* (1973), 289.

:ceive the closest observers with his self-assured bearing and his pathetic
:otestations. Grünlich was a portrait from life, a common plague. Still,
ie gathering protest against mercenary or materialistic marriages was
med far less against the raids of fortune hunters than against the com-
lex of tacit convictions underlying the very idea of the dowry itself.

Bluntly, the institution symbolized woman's dependence on the re-
iurces of others, her passive role as a bit of booty carried off by the
iumphant warrior male.[15] It was part and parcel of a system of power,
oncretely the power of men over women. A man acquiring a wife in
ie traditional manner married a visible financial guarantee, whether
isinterestedly cherished or not, a private fountain of cash and connec-
ons. But by definition romantic love excludes all thoughts of acquisi-
veness and inequality; it celebrates, in its very nature, the absence of
ower. Dr. Pomeroy, spokesman for many of his contemporaries in the
ite nineteenth century, explicitly contrasted the motives for marriage,
f convenience, position, money and the rest, with "the ideal marriage of
omance—for love," an ideal that gave no room to considerations of
olicy or displays of superiority. "True marriage," he insisted, "is the
fe union of one man and one woman who are in suitable conditions of
ealth in mind and body, of age, of temperament, of convictions, and of
astes to enable them to live together in harmony and happiness." Marriage,
he prolific French writer on the subject, Emile Acollas, had put it flatly
1 1868, in the same vein, though in less medical language, "is the associa-
ion of man and woman founded on the moral sentiment of love, and
ubject to the double law of equality and liberty." This was a terse
ormulation of a spreading idea. Thackeray in his somewhat forced
:heeriness, had summed it up before: "if Fun is good, Truth is still better,
nd Love is best of all."[16] Such uncomplicated aphorisms denied the
:onflicts troubling respectable minds, but they exhibit the growing pros-
)erity of the love ideology from mid-nineteenth century onward.

There was in fact nothing very novel in such views. The romantics
iad played imaginative variations on them and had, with their respect
'or woman's talents, sought to bring social realities, or at least their
)rivate lives, into tune with their erotic ideals. In fact, long before the
'omantics, in the much-maligned "rationalistic" eighteenth century, poets
ind novelists had sharply segregated the desire to amass wealth and

---

15. See the shrewd summary in Kaplan, "For Love or Money," 266.
16. Pomeroy: *Ethics of Marriage*, 46; Acollas: in the anthology by John Grand-
Carteret, *Mariage, Collage, Chiennerie. Les trois formes de l'union sexuelle à travers
les âges* (n.d.), 214; Thackeray: *Works*, ed. Saintsbury, IX, 493.

influence through love from true love itself. That minor English poe
Anna Laetitia Barbauld,[17] spoke for this opinion in the 1770s:

> The world has little to bestow,
> When two fond hearts in equal love are joined.

It was precisely the faded repetitiousness of such sentiments by 1850 tha
demonstrates how available they had become to middle-class circle
struggling with inherited cultural habits.

Beyond doubt what passes for love in the decades of Victoria conceale
ingredients of power protected by defensive, usefully self-deceptiv
stratagems. The most affectionate and benevolent parents exercised powe
over their children, husbands over their wives, masters over their servant
—always for their good, usually in their name. Such authoritative conduc
often enough amounted to little more than a self-indulgent resort t
superior legal privileges, emotional resources, or physical strength. In
situation in which customs and the laws made man the master, libidina
expressiveness was rarely untainted by aggression, exhibiting an urge t
wound or control, dominate or destroy, or just to show one's strength
thus exorcising the fear of one's weakness. Significantly, when, in 1905
Freud asserted that sexuality shows "an admixture of *aggressiveness*,"
desire to subjugate the sexual object, he attributed this inclination t
"most men."[18]

But while these deadly serious amorous contests were usually quit
unequal, they were by no means wholly one-sided. The weaker vesse
could mobilize some power of her own by resisting advances or with
holding affection; she might, by accesses of shyness, displays of indecision
and sheer teasing, enhance her value to the man who desired her. "T
many women affection is sweet," Charlotte Brontë wrote to Elizabet
Gaskell at mid-century, "and power conquered indifferent—though w
all like influence won."[19] Men, feeling beset in a world no longer occupie
by adoring, docile, wholly domestic wives and faced with the need t
reappraise their comfortable sense of supremacy, were inclined to se
their manly sanctuary invaded by conspirators. There were uncounted
numbers of women, just as uneasy at the prospect of change, to applaud
them. While these women would have resented, and effectively resisted,

---

17. *Delia. An Elegy* (1773), in *The Works of Anna Laetitia Barbauld*, ed. with a
Memoir by Lucy Aikin, 2 vols. (1825), I, 92.

18. Freud, *Drei Abhandlungen zur Sexualtheorie* (1905), St.A., V, 67; *Three Essays
on the Theory of Sexuality*, S.E., VII, 157.

19. Brontë to Gaskell, September 20, 1851, Elizabeth Gaskell, *The Life of Charlotte
Brontë* (1857; ed. 1919), 402 [ch. 24].

ny parental attempts to manipulate, let alone dictate, their choices of a
usband, they continued to mouth the time-honored commonplaces about
male supremacy. Identifying with the aggressor, adopting his language
nd argumentation, they solemnly demonstrated why women needed no
igher education or legal autonomy, let alone the vote, since they had,
fter all, at their disposal the unfailing arts of tenderness, flattery, and
ears. "I have never met a man, however inferior," Beatrice Potter once
rovocatively exclaimed at a suffragist luncheon, "whom I do not con-
ider to be my superior." She was young then, had been irritated by
what she thought wearisome chatter about women's rights, and was
being perverse.[20] But intelligent and independent-minded women said the
ame thing quite sincerely. The logic of unforced, unmercenary, wholly
equal mutual love, of love without power, was the outermost limit to
which few nineteenth-century men, and fewer nineteenth-century women,
aspired.

It would take generations of feminists, female and male, notorious or
obscure, and some social changes too far-reaching to be denied, to offer
the old ideology some effective competition. The beneficiaries themselves experienced their agonizingly slow conquests as painful in the
extreme, partly because they discovered to their dismay that the love
that offered itself to them was inseparable from power—male power.
There were exceptions: some of the most active feminists like Elizabeth
Cady Stanton in the United States and Millicent Garrett Fawcett in
England were married to men capable of appreciating their wives' preoccupations and of tolerating their long absences on business. But many
women, late in the nineteenth and early in the twentieth century, found
it necessary, often after bitter reflection, to renounce love altogether and
to choose work over marriage. That such a decision was, in those decades
of transition, widely condemned as unnatural, did not make it any easier.
But these social workers, political activists, and physicians could not be
satisfied to flee from the cage of the dowry system to the illusory freedom
of a love match that threatened to confine them to the circumscribed
sphere of house-keeping, child-raising, and husband-pleasing. Contemporary anti-feminists, preachers and editorial writers and social phi-

20. Beatrice Webb, *My Apprenticeship* (1926; ed. 1971), 354. This was in 1889,
shortly before she met Sidney Webb. In the same year, she "took what afterwards
seemed to me a false step in joining with others in signing the then notorious manifesto, drafted by Mrs Humphry Ward and some other distinguished ladies, against
the political enfranchisement of women" (ibid., 353). But Beatrice Webb quickly
and shrewdly analyzed this step, recognized its defects, and changed her mind. Many
other women never did.

losophers, liked to insinuate that these voluntary spinsters were motivated
by unsavory, unprintable erotic appetites.[21] Doubtless, there were advanced women so deeply entangled emotionally with other women—
whether they acted on their homoerotic inclinations or not—that they
were unsuited for a conventional household. But whatever their sexual
tastes, they did not subvert their cause, for they were in league with
the future.

Almost without exception introspective and articulate, those nineteenth-
century women who refused to marry even for love if it meant compromising their vocation, left records—diaries, journals, autobiographies
—of their embattled progress toward clarity about their unconventional
priorities. Perhaps the most rewarding of these forays into self-exploration
is the diary that Beatrice Webb started in 1873 at fifteen, when she was
still Beatrice Potter. She was, for all her intermittent melancholy, a fortunate creature, endowed with all the advantages: her family was rich,
liberal, civilized, and sociable. Beatrice Webb's parents, very much like
Eliza Bagehot's, knew everybody. They were also persuaded that women
have minds. Beatrice Webb would celebrate her father as "the only man
I ever knew, who genuinely believed that women were superior to men,
and acted as if he did. . . . He always talked to us as equals." The confidence of Richard Potter, "capitalist at large," in the female sex was so
pronounced that, according to her own account, his most brilliant daughter
later reacted against his "over-appreciation" of women.[22] All her life
Beatrice Webb would be saddled with the uneasy suspicion that traditional notions about men's superior intellect and strength of character
were really true.

The eighth of nine sisters, most of them apt to bring promising young
men into the house, Beatrice Potter lived among serious books, animated
conversation, and a refreshing array of interesting visitors. Handsome,
obviously clever, with an insatiable appetite for knowledge and a rather
brooding hankering for self-improvement, she noted down her passionate
interests, her low moods, her sallies into society, learning, and love with
a mixture of copious description, literary felicity, and unsparing severity
that make her diaries an inexhaustible resource. With no professional
instruments at her command—she sometimes regretted her ignorance of
psychology—her self-analysis was extraordinarily perceptive. She failed
to recognize that her intermittent bouts of depression (rather like Eliza

21. I have studied some of these charges, and their psychological origins in male
anxieties, in *Education of the Senses*, ch. II.
22. Webb, *My Apprenticeship*, 35–36.

Vilson's headaches) were not just consequences, but also imitations, of ther mother's emotional episodes. But she was sensitive enough to register, omberly, her mother's distance from her, a distance that left her, amid a tevy of lively sisters, lonely and starved for affection. She could not ccount for her own fluctuating appraisal of her talents as an intellectual vorker, oddly paired as it was with a proper appreciation of her handome appearance. But she found room for it in her diaries with a poignant vealth of detail. She was, in a way she never fully understood, at once earful and desirous of rejection, imagining, soliciting, almost forcing it, compelling reality to conform to her dismal sense of herself as an unovable child. But, again, she preserved in her diary the raw evidence tecessary to put her child-like self-punishment into perspective.[23] In her etters, her journals, her formal writings, she was a trustworthy and penetrating autobiographer inviting, and enabling, her historian to explore further.

Beatrice Webb, the famous Socialist, would present herself to the vorld as supremely self-possessed, well-informed, and single-minded, to Ill appearances an awesome, not wholly lovable, thinking machine. When ther mother died in 1882 and her married older sisters were setting up heir own households, she ably presided over her aging father's table, poth in London and in the country. Then, after her marriage to Sidney Webb in 1892, she acquired a reputation as a formidable hostess, student of society, prolific historian, and political broker. But, as she confessed to her prized intimate, her diary, in entry after entry, she was, and never wholly ceased to be, the battlefield of tormenting conflicts. She had moments, in her early years, when she playfully rehearsed the role of a Society Woman, but she quickly sensed that a fashionable marriage would only doom her to boredom. At the same time, while she intensely wished to do her duty as an independent professional woman, she was beset by nagging doubts about her capacity for the grind of humble empirical social inquiry and for sustained researches into the arid expanses

23. This must remain speculation, but I am persuaded that one source of Beatrice Potter's oppressive guilt feelings was the early death of her only brother at the age of two. "Dicky" was the Potters' only son and, among her ten children, Mrs. Potter's most passionately beloved. Faced with so engrossing a rival at the age of four, it would have been only human if Beatrice Potter would, at least sometimes, have wished him ill; his early death, a fulfillment of her wishes, is bound to have appalled her as evidence of her wickedness. As for her indebtedness to her mother—she had some inkling of that. "I never knew how much she had done for me," she noted on August 13, 1882, not long after her mother's death, "how many of my best habits I had taken from her, how strong would be the influence of her personality when pressure had gone." My Apprenticeship, 41.

of political economy. These vivid, conscious dilemmas over her career and her gifts barely covered over well-concealed clashes between the elemental passions she could never quite repress and the controlled rationality to which she clung as her best hope of sanity. When she was only sixteen, she noted with pathetic precocity that she must resist making a fool of herself over men. "And now, my dear friend," she apostrophized herself in her diary, "I want to tell you something seriously, because nobody else will have the chance of telling it you. You are really getting into a nasty and what I should call an indecent way of thinking of men, and love, and unless you take care you will lose all your purity of thought, and become a silly vain self-conscious little goose." Earnestly she instructed herself "to think purely and seriously about Love." Her fervent wish underscores her helplessness: "Oh, that I had thorough command over you." This search for a reasonable love, far from the kind of "feverish, almost lustful passion" she found so disagreeable in *Jane Eyre*,[24] made her Odyssey very trying, for she was too honest to deny that she was regularly prey to that indecent way of thinking of men and love.

Her conflicts reached a traumatic climax in her mid-twenties, when she fell passionately in love with Joseph Chamberlain, and told him so. She was torn between her unconquerable attraction to Chamberlain and her equally unconquerable, eminently sensible, fear of him, between the push of her professional aspirations and the pull of submissive domesticity. She nearly broke down several times and wished for death; more than once during these years, outwardly brimming with youthful vitality, she made her will. The crisis stretched her emotional and intellectual resilience to the utmost.

Tall, austere, and magnetic, a rich man of business and, since 1873, the controversial, immensely popular radical mayor of Birmingham, Joseph Chamberlain was a supremely suitable catch for someone as attractive, well-to-do, and socially prominent as Beatrice Potter. Twice widowed, with six children in his care, Chamberlain grimly hid his private wounds behind a mask of superb pride and a passion for politics. In an age just beginning to experiment with mass meetings and poised on the verge of far-reaching social legislation, he was a portent of the future: the demagogue with ideas who seduces his constituency. Beatrice Potter, shrewdly anticipating psychoanalytic diagnoses, observed Chamberlain at a political meeting in Birmingham doing precisely that: "At the first sound of his

---

24. Diary, March 13 (1874), July 11 (1875). Norman and Jeanne MacKenzie, eds. *The Diary of Beatrice Webb*, vol. I, *1873–1892, Glitter Around and Darkness Within* (1982), 17, 21.

voice they became as one man. Into the tones of his voice he threw the warmth of feeling which was lacking in his words, and every thought, every feeling, the slightest intonation of irony and contempt was reflected on the faces of the crowd. It might have been a woman listening to the words of her lover! Perfect response, unquestioning receptivity. Who *reasons* with his mistress?" The future of this democratic politician, "the master and darling of his town," seemed dazzling—people were speaking of him as a possible prime minister—and he dazzled Beatrice Potter almost from their first meeting. "Met sundry distinguished men," she noted in her diary on June 3, 1883, "among others Joseph Chamberlain. I do, and I don't, like him. Talking to 'clever men' in society is a snare and delusion as regards interest. Much better read their books." But three weeks later, she was already caught on the hook of his fascination: "Mr. Chamberlain joined us in the evening and I had much conversation with him. His personality interested me." He interested her all the more as other men fatigued her. "How I should like to study that man!" she wrote in July.[25]

Chamberlain proved a dangerous study, but Beatrice Potter pursued it, with mounting excitement and trepidation. Her diary entries, even those ostensibly not about him, disclose the drift of her ruminations: "*If* I remain free (which alas is a big if) I see pretty clearly where the work is which I *would* do." Even in the first flush of her passion, she linked the thought of marriage to Chamberlain with the thought of slavery, of pain, of being almost literally swallowed up. There were times when she would flog herself to think better of her prospects; "in this phase of my work," she wrote hopefully in November 1883, "my duties as an ordinary woman are not interfered with by the pursuit of my private ends." But at heart she knew that these were fond fantasies. "One thing I will *not* do," she wrote, firmly and a little ominously in the following month. "I will not give way to a feeling, however strong, which is not sanctioned by my better self. I will not desert a life in which there are manifold opportunities for good for a life in which my nature is at war with itself."[26] With pitiless lucidity, which corroded even if it could not resolve her illusions, she recognized Joseph Chamberlain as the deadly adversary of her life's plan, of her very chance to breathe.

These were not abstract speculations. During the late months of 1883, the time of her indecisive inner debate, Beatrice Potter had every cause to expect a proposal of marriage from Joseph Chamberlain. "My tortured

25. Journal, March 16 (1884), June 3, 27, July 15 (1883), ibid., 107–108, 88, 89, 91.
26. Diary, November 5, December 7 (1883), ibid., 95, 100.

state," she noted just after Christmas in a characteristic entry, "cannot long endure. The 'to be or not to be' will soon be settled." She was facing a "horrible dilemma" between "principle and feeling."[27] The principle was her autonomy, the feeling was a compound of erotic desire and submissiveness.

In a long atmospheric entry dated early the following year, Beatrice Potter reported what had happened. Chamberlain had come to visit the Potters and there had been continuous, strong, unreserved talk. A "dispute over state education" had broken "the charm" of casual dinner conversation. " 'It pains me to hear any of my views controverted,' " Chamberlain had told his astonished listener, and then laid out his own views in detail. What he needed was " 'intelligent sympathy' " from women, a requirement that Beatrice Potter, not unreasonably, translated into "servility." Chamberlain would refute any divergent view she ventured to offer "by re-asserting his convictions passionately, his expression becoming every minute more gloomy and determined." That his authoritative demeanor might be wounding seemed not to trouble him at all. "Not a suspicion of feeling did he show towards me." While he was intolerant of any dissent whatever, he found it particularly exasperating coming from women. " 'My sister and daughter are bitten with the women's rights mania,' " he informed Beatrice Potter. " 'I don't allow any action on the subject.' 'You don't allow division of opinion in your household, Mr. Chamberlain?' 'I can't help people *thinking* different from me.' 'But you don't allow the expression of the difference?' 'No.' And that little word ended our intercourse."[28]

In the privacy of her journal recording these exchanges, Beatrice Potter anatomized Chamberlain's character with a mordant exactitude justifying her conclusion: "It is all over." Chamberlain, she thought, "is neither a reasoner nor an observer in the scientific sense." The "political creed is the whole man; the outcome of his peculiar physical and mental temperament played upon by the experiences of his life." His intuition of what his countrymen want is uncannily accurate, and his charm rests on that. But "by nature he is an enthusiast and a despot"; he "hates the moderate man." In short, "enthusiasm and self-will are the dominant forces in Chamberlain's mind." No question, "it is all over."[29]

But it was not all over. Chamberlain continued to seek out Beatrice

27. Diary, December 27 (1883), ibid.
28. Diary, January 12 (1884), ibid., 102–103.
29. Diary, same day, ibid., 104.

Potter, and she continued to be infatuated with him. They corresponded, they met, they kept up indirectly. She broke with him definitively more than once, bidding farewell to her love often and poignantly. Her addiction was classical in its simplicity: she would mournfully celebrate anniversaries of memorable moments with Chamberlain. "Shall always consider this day as sacred," she noted in the summer of 1889, two years after his last visit; it was six years since they had first met. "A sacrament of pain fitting me for a life of loneliness and work, a memory of deep humiliation, and a spur to unremitting effort to gain for others the peaceful joy which I have lost myself."[30] In November of the previous year, as Chamberlain was marrying again, she prayed for the happiness of the couple, composed an "epitaph" to him for her journal, and yielded to her depression. The result, "A week of utter nervous collapse." "It is strange," she mused, "that a being who will henceforth be an utter stranger to my life should be able to inflict such intense pain."[31] Her occasional, noncommittal regression to a religious faith she had long ago intellectually abjured, taking communion or saying a prayer, had given at best temporary relief. Work alone proved efficacious as a healer for her devastating erotic injury.

Work—and Sidney Webb. In her end, as in her beginnings, Beatrice Potter was fortunate. In March 1889, she confessed to her journal that she longed "every day more for the restfulness of an abiding love." But she had no intention of sacrificing "work for which all the horrible suffering of six years has fitted me." As often before, she lectured herself to take courage. "I must not let myself get morbid over it. I must check those feelings which are the expression of physical instinct craving for satisfaction; but," she acknowledged, "God knows celibacy is as painful to a woman (even from the physical standpoint) as it is to a man. It could not be more painful than it is to a woman."[32] She could check the physical instinct alive in her, but she could not, and would not, eradicate it.

Sidney Webb was a supremely improbable life's partner for her. Even after she had reluctantly decided to marry him, after months of fighting down her doubts, she could not bring herself to impart the news to her dying father and worried over the response of her family and close friends. They had warned her against Chamberlain, fearing his narcissism; to marry him, her cousin and intimate Mary Booth had told her, "would be

30. Diary, July 29 (1889), ibid., 288. The editors comment that the next eight pages were torn out, so that her final verdict on Chamberlain will never be known. His ascendancy over her imagination after all this time remains astonishing.
31. Diary, November 18 (1888), ibid., 266–67.
32. Diary, March 7 (1889), ibid., 275.

a tragedy—a murder of your independent nature."[33] But Sidney Webb only threw Joseph Chamberlain's spectacular qualities into bold relief—Webb was ugly, he was poor, he was uncouth. A hard-working minor civil servant from an impecunious lower-middle-class family, he had had none of the advantages that a classical education was thought to impart; his manners were inelegant, his appearance less than pleasing, his cockney speech a little embarrassing to fastidious ears. But he was utterly brilliant, a committed Socialist busy converting anyone willing to understand the urgent need for reconstituting English society on a more just and more rational basis. His command of economic and political realities was uncanny, his memory almost proverbial, his capacity for work superior to Beatrice Potter's. He was, in George Bernard Shaw's view, "the ablest man in England."[34] He had met Beatrice Potter in January 1890, when she sought him out as an expert on the early days of English cooperatives, on which she was beginning to write a book—her first. Not unnaturally, he had fallen in love with her quickly, but Beatrice Potter, though impressed by Sidney Webb's mental agility and purity of social purpose, was not drawn to him physically and was, in any event, wary of any man seeking to ensnare her. She came to value, to esteem, and after a time, to love him; but for a time they lived uneasily within the highly artificial, self-conscious boundaries of the working friendship she had decreed for them. With obsessive care, she drew up elaborate treaties of conduct laying down rules he was to violate at peril of eternal banishment. The tone of these diplomatic documents was cool and controlled; the secret temperature of their association, though fluctuating, was high and gradually rose to the climax that Sidney Webb had anticipated. "You understand," she had written to him early on, "you promise me to realise that the chances are 100 to 1 that nothing follows but friendship."[35] Patiently and persistently, not always tactfully, Sidney Webb labored to reverse those proportions.

The history of their odd romance was marked with intimate scenes that might have been lifted from Stendhal—there was that decisive moment when Sidney Webb took Beatrice Potter's hand and she did not pull it away—and the kind of subdued drama at home in the novels of Henry James. She was not swept away by erotic longing as she had been for Joseph Chamberlain, but she came to prize her ugly little Socialist more and more, with a love that had something of the maternal warmth

33. See Jeanne MacKenzie, *A Victorian Courtship: The Story of Beatrice Potter and Sidney Webb* (1979), 31. Her sisters felt the same way.
34. See editors' comment, *Beatrice Webb's Diary*, 317.
35. MacKenzie, *Victorian Courtship*, 76.

hat she had never enjoyed and always sorely missed.[36] Beatrice Potter, playing mother to Sidney Webb, could at once repair a fateful neglect, doing unto another what had not been done for her, and, perhaps, taking the role of her mother, establish a fantasied bond with her cherished father. These are deep waters, and their exploration does not, in any event, tell the whole story. For Sidney Webb was not just a son to Beatrice Potter; he was her liberator. She gratefully recognized his role in freeing her from the baleful enchantment that had made her miserable for more years than she cared to recall. Happening to travel on the same train as her old love late in 1891, already secretly engaged to Sidney Webb, she "shuddered" as she "imagined the life I had missed," and reflected once again just how unsuited she would have been "for the great role of 'walking gentlewoman' to the play of *Chamberlain*." Well before they were married, the pair established an intense and orderly working routine. But all was not dry labor on interviews, reports, and books. As they met on their way to conferences and congresses at railroad hotels, they would take a break from copying documents or extracting useful passages with "a few brief intervals" of what Sidney Webb, delirious with delight, called " 'human nature.' "[37] The patronizing assessment, popular in their later years, of their lifelong partnership as two typewriters that clicked as one misses not merely the feelings of the two for one another, but their undisguised pleasure in physical intimacy. In 1897, Shaw, who came to know the Webbs intimately, observed them on a shared holiday: everyone talked endlessly about politics, wrote busily, ate simply but well, went cycling, and there were the Webbs, with their "incorrigible spooning

---

36. "At times I am afraid, and disconsolately ask myself whether from my own point of view I have been wise," she wrote as she thought over her engagement. "But the need for a warmer and more responsible relationship with another human being has made it seem the best even for me. The world will wonder. On the face of it, it seems an extraordinary end to the once brilliant Beatrice Potter . . . to marry an ugly little man with no social position and less means, whose only recommendation, so some may say, is a certain pushing ability. And I am not 'in love,' not as I was. But I see something else in him (the world would say that was proof of my love)— a fine intellect and a warm-heartedness, a power of self-subordination and self-devotion for the 'common good.' And our marriage will be based on fellowship, a common faith and a common work. His feeling is the passionate love of an emotional man, mine the growing tenderness of the mother touched with the dependence of the woman on the help of a strong love, and in the background there is the affectionate *camaraderie*, the 'fun,' the strenuous helpfulness of two young workers in the same cause." Diary, June 20 (1891), *Beatrice Webb's Diary*, 356–57. There is, one might think, a touch of willed optimism in this pensive entry, but since it all came true, as predicted, one must add that Beatrice Potter was listening here not just to her wishes but to her deepest feelings as well.

37. Diary, October 21, 10 (1891), 364, 363.

over their industrial and political science." Half a century of marriage did not permanently cure Beatrice Webb's moments of depression, but it brought her what she had almost despaired of ever obtaining. From their working honeymoon in Dublin, Sidney Webb wrote a letter to Graham Wallas, Fabian Socialist and social psychologist—his best man—and left room for a heartfelt postscript by his new wife. "We are very very happy," she wrote, "far too happy to be reasonable."[38]

No one could call Beatrice Webb typical of anything; she was too remarkable to be representative. But her predicament, more keenly felt and more subtly analyzed than that of others, throws light on the dilemmas, and possible resolutions, facing less exceptional bourgeois mortals in search of love without power. Woman's craving for work which organized Beatrice Webb's emotional economy from her adolescence onward, had diverse causes. For her, it was a defensive operation, a palliative that soothed her misery by hiding it from her, a form of restitution that assuaged her sense of her unworthiness, and the gratification of what her contemporaries would have called, rather unperceptively and condescendingly, her masculine side. For other women, no doubt, the need to become something more than a wife and a mother had similar multiple origins. But, whatever its sources in unconscious and non-rational emotions, it was in tune with the drift of the times. What Beatrice Webb discerned as "a new consciousness of sin among men of intellect and men of property," a sense that was to fuel social inquiry and social reform, offered a constructive outlet, a firm direction, to hidden and complex needs. Beatrice Potter's successful struggle to make her own way, her sturdy refusal to yield her independence to the most seductive erotic temptations, hold a still more heartening lesson, a lesson that Sidney Webb taught her: love need not usurp a woman's place in the world. Even better, love and work, which Beatrice Potter, for one, had thought impossible to reconcile, could be profitably joined. Still, it is significant for her priorities, and for the urgency of her struggle, that when she reflected on this junction, she reversed their conventional order: she had not dreamt, she wrote in May 1891, "that those years of dull misery, with flashes of veritable agony, would end in Work and Love."[39] The confluence of the two currents of love, affectionate and passionate, which all agreed was the only true ideal, might be hard to achieve. But it was not a Utopia.

38. George Bernard Shaw to Ellen Terry, May 28, 1897, Christopher St. John, ed., *Ellen Terry and Bernard Shaw: A Correspondence* (1932), 154.

39. Beatrice Webb, *My Apprenticeship*, 191; Diary, May 31 (1891), *Beatrice Webb's Diary*, 356.

2. Desire, Holy and Pure

The feminist campaigns to burst the bonds of sweet domesticity and compliance complicated women's experience of love. But it did not lessen the general appetite to find instruction, whether through intimate involvements, confidential conversation, or, most safely, through print. Reading, I have suggested, was only one possible road to experience, especially technical reading in philosophers or psychologists, no matter how lucid. Still, bourgeois read about love, constantly. The outpouring of pious tracts on conjugal joys and duties, news reports about glittering marriages or (in the later decades of the century) sensational divorces, and sentimental novels serialized in family periodicals attests to that.[40] So do those idealized, sometimes faintly scandalous biographies of great lovers that inundated the nineteenth-century market for books. In 1858, Lola Montez, that sensual and impudent dancer who had been the spectacular mistress of King Ludwig I of Bavaria, lent her name to a miserable compendium of hastily gathered *Anecdotes of Love*. The collection purported to be, as its subtitle advertised it, "A True Account of the Most Remarkable Events Connected with the History of Love, In All Ages and Among All Nations." This gathering of sometimes tantalizing and often boring snippets begins with Alexander the Great, includes stories about the loves of Henri IV, Mary Queen of Scots, Napoleon, and other historic figures, and ends with an innocuous account of a visit to a harem. Such typical confections were sure of devoted and numerous readers.

These volumes, often elaborately decorated and tastefully bound, suitable as a gift and for the guest's bedside table, survived into the late nineteenth century and beyond. T. F. Thiselton-Dyer published *The Loves and Marriages of Some Eminent Persons* in 1890, requiring two volumes for his collection. A little more sober than most of his fellows, and more ambitious, he divided his biographies into such chapters as "Married Happiness" or "Marriage Romance." Not all was happiness or romance for Thiselton-Dyer; some of his pages explore marital discord

---

40. In 1864, the *Saturday Review*, a stern guardian of literary quality and British morals, attacked the "attractive and lucrative indecency of *The Times*." The journal severely called for "a Moral Sewers Commission. To purify the Thames is something, but to purify *The Times* would be a greater boon to society. . . . The unsavory reports of the Divorce Courts, the disgusting details of the harlotry and vice, the filthy nauseous annals of the brothel, the prurient letters of adulterers and adulteresses, the modes in which intrigues may be carried out, the diaries and meditations of married sinners, these are now part of our domestic life." Harold Perkin, "The Origins of the Popular Press" (1957), in *The Structured Crowd* (1981), 52.

and separation. But the miasma of good cheer overhung the work as a whole; Thiselton-Dyer sought out ideal marriages in eighteenth- and nineteenth-century England, like that of Dr. Arnold, to elevate his readers while he amused them. Many of these resolute and handsome trivia—and there *were* many, in many languages—specialized in the lives and loves of poets and painters; they kept alive, often adopting a breathless, rather vulgar tone, the old romantic notion that artists and writers enjoyed thrilling emotional lives. The implicit intention of these books, though, was didactic. Beyond providing material for a kind of literary voyeurism, they conveyed the welcome news that love is available, should be exciting, and might even survive the disciplined rigors and unvarying routine of marriage.

A far less sanguine view of nineteenth-century middle-class erotic life, of its ideal and its practice, has long been plausible and popular.[41] In fact, there is no shortage of material lending a measure of credibility to this critical perception. There were, after all, those medical specialists who asserted that normal women are fortunately free from clamorous sexual desires; those preachers and philosophers who frowned on marital erotic pleasure unaccompanied by the intention to generate offspring; those parents who irresponsibly sent the young to their wedding night wholly unprepared for the traumas of sexual initiation; those novelists who invented disembodied, asexual heroines, either silly, immature dolls one could patronize or long-suffering paragons one must worship. "So pure and bloodless in their love passages"—thus George Meredith pilloried the writings of a hypocritically pious poet and his adoring readers—"and at the same time so biting in their moral tone, that his reputation was

41. Let one biting satire on the bourgeois as lover stand as an exemplar for almost innumerable instances invented (or observed) in the nineteenth century: the smug trader who is a protagonist in *Max Havelaar*, a novel by the Dutch essayist and novelist Eduard Dowes Dekker, who long enjoyed an international reputation under his pseudonym Multatuli. "My maxims are, and will always be, Truth and Common-sense," this sensible hero confesses, "making, of course, an exception for the Holy Scriptures." Novels and children's stories and all the talk about romantic love are lies. "Love is a bliss; you fly with some dear object or other to the end of the earth. The earth has no end, and such love is all nonsense. Nobody can say that I do not live on good terms with my wife,—she is a daughter of Last and Co., coffee-brokers,—nobody can find fault with our marriage. I am a member of the fashionable 'Artis' club, and she has an Indian shawl which cost £7, 13s, 4d., but yet we never indulged in such foolish love as would have urged us to fly to the extremities of the earth. We married, we made an excursion to the Hague. She there bought some flannel, of which I still wear shirts; and further our love has never driven us. So, I say, it is all nonsense and lies!" The anti-poetic, anti-romantic animus could not go further than this. *Max Havelaar, or the Coffee Auctions of the Dutch Trading Company* (1859; tr. Baron Alphonse Natuys, 1868), 2–4.

great among the virtuous, who form the larger portion of the English book-buying public."[42] There is no denying that nineteenth-century bourgeois culture swarmed with profound and unresolved ambivalences toward love, and with an often unpleasant timidity. Still, rather more than sardonic observers like George Meredith, with their glib caricatures seemed to recognize, these *were* symptoms, not the rule. Strident cultural critics mistook bourgeois pathology for the ideal itself, ungenerously treating the spectacle of middle-class marital felicity as a triumphant instance of hypocrisy.

Unfortunately but not unexpectedly, the pathology has proved easier to document than the felicity. In the nineteenth century, as we have good reason to know, loving couples kept their private lives concealed behind an almost impenetrable curtain of discretion. Reticence was their signature. One sister might tell another delicate details of her erotic life— pregnancies, miscarriages, ways of finding an abortionist; one brother might ask another for help in procuring pornographic books or effective contraceptives. But both would solemnly entreat their correspondent to destroy the evidence, and it would often be destroyed. Unlike most of the poor, middle-class couples had a bedroom door to close, and they closed it, firmly. There is much we shall never know, more we can only conjecture. Couples who kept intimate diaries and wrote each other intimate letters frequently kept the matters that touched them most from the written record. The Bagehots, for one, present something of a puzzle. Their tender devotion to one another seems beyond question. Richard Holt Hutton, Walter Bagehot's closest friend, said in his memoir that his "marriage gave Bagehot nineteen years of undisturbed happiness."[43] Even though this assertion was in chaste print, written under the widow's eye, there is good reason to believe that it has much of the truth in it. But Eliza Bagehot's frequent headaches, to say nothing of her husband's, hint at some unresolved neurotic business which may, just may, have inhibited the sensual side of their love. The Bagehots had their headaches to share in addition to the passions of the intellect; whether they enjoyed one another's bodies as they enjoyed one another's minds must remain a question.

The Benekes were no less uninformative about their life together, though their closeness and relaxed union breathes from page after page of his diaries; Otto Beneke, as we may read in Marietta Beneke's affec-

---

42. Meredith, *The Ordeal of Richard Feverel* (1859; rev. ed., 1869), 2.
43. Richard Holt Hutton, "Memoir" (1877), in Walter Bagehot, *Literary Studies* (*Miscellaneous Essays*), ed. Hutton, 3 vols. (1895; ed. 1910), I. 1.

tionate retrospect, overcame his depressive moods and his self-doubts
once he had married the girl he had claimed to love so passionately and
done so little to win. His wife is, to be sure, scarcely a disinterested
witness, but Otto Beneke left at least one intimation, beyond the formulaic
exclamations of fond gratitude on his wedding anniversaries, that supports
his wife's smiling recollections of their intimate life. Concluding a true
"Love Story" which he had reconstructed from the documents in the
Hamburg archive, Beneke demurred from the common view that enthusiastic loves forecast failed marriages. His story dates from mid-
eighteenth century: the daughter of a prosperous Hamburg merchant and
a young Prussian baron had fallen in love, only to be frustrated by his
father's determined refusal to give his consent. After long, infuriating
delays and some melodramatic incidents, the couple were united at last,
giving Beneke the opening for his gloss: "If the reader has taken some
interest in the baron and his Elisabeth, he will surely be pleased to hear
only good things about what became of them. People are readily given to
the suspicion that uncommonly strong love, animated by the breath of
poetry, will lead to an unsatisfactory marriage. This view is refuted by
our couple, which were granted an undisturbed happy life's idyll as just
compensation for the sufferings they had undergone in their romantic
schooling." At last, "after so many storms, the lovers had touched the
longed-for harbor of peace." They lived together for forty years, building
their "earthly paradise" in which "there was no serpent, no flaming
sword."[44] Serenity after trials, love rising to new heights in marriage: it
sounds like a slightly idealized version of Beneke's own life.

There was always room for skepticism whether this experience was
really very widespread. Even relatively mild critics of modern marriage
wondered whether the bourgeois was not perhaps given to a one-sided
union, though they could never agree whether he sinned by giving undue
prominence to sexless adoration or to lustful sensuality. In 1892, speaking
coyly with the voice of "Amor," Julia Duhring, an American essayist on
literature and manners, complained that "many so-called intelligent people" actually "and sincerely believe that only one side of love—sentiment
—is good, while the other side—passion—is so bad that it ought not even
to be named." Taking the opposite side in this debate, her countryman,
the journalist and travel writer Junius Henri Browne argued that in
modern marriage, love is "likely to be confounded with sensuous passions," an error that, to his mind, produced much mischief. "Evidently,

44. Beneke, "Eine Liebesgeschichte (1768–1772)," *Hamburgische Geschichten und
Denkwürdigkeiten*, 2 vols. (1856; 2nd and 3rd ed. 1890), II, 378–408.

there can be no love without passion; but there is an incalculable sum of passion without love."[45] Whichever side was right, each was in accord with the other that love should happily combine its two strands.

Most novelists, of all persuasions, heartily endorsed this doctrine. Denise, the heroine of Zola's *Au bonheur des dames*, with whom her author plainly sympathizes, is characteristic: she rejects the well-meant but indelicate suggestion of a young woman friend, like her a clerk in a department store, that she "give herself" to some young man in return for financial security. "First of all," Denise objects, her cheeks flushed, "one must have *amitié* for someone"—true sexual love commands affectionate feelings. In 1913, the minor popular Austrian philosopher Emil Lucka said the same thing, using more elevated language, in his book on the "three levels of eroticism": the lowest level is the sexual drive, the second, higher level is occupied by love; and the third, the highest, constitutes the synthesis of sexuality and love.[46]

Those who did not yet enjoy this highest love ardently desired and deliberately cultivated their character to achieve it. "I must never allow myself any preferences or antipathies which are not approved of by my conscience and reason," the young Louisa de Rothschild severely reminded herself during her engagement to her cousin Anthony de Rothschild. "I must never permit myself to have any affections unfounded on esteem, and must never, either from self interest, caprice or thoughtlessness demonstrate more affection than I really feel." Her pressing need to curb her amorous impetuosity offers suggestive evidence for its concentrated, partly unconscious strength.[47] Love in the nineteenth century made severe demands on lovers, but it also offered gratifying rewards. The synthesis between the tender and passionate currents of love was, for nineteenth-century bourgeois, a matter not only of hope but of experience.

In fact, the failure to achieve this synthesis, whether from policy or incapacity, brought sardonic comment, troubled self-examination, or exquisite despair. When Sydney Smith's father complained about his son's choice of a wife, that great English wit, journalist, and cleric replied, "I know you think Miss Pybus's person very disagreeable, but this consideration is so entirely confined to opinion, and the evil (if it exists) is so

45. Duhring: *Amor in Society: A Study from Life* (1892), 13, 32; Browne: "To Marry or Not to Marry," *Forum* (December 1888), 435.

46. Zola: *Au bonheur des dames*, ch. 5 (1883; ed. 1971), 161; Lucka: *Die drei Stufen der Erotik* (1913; 12th to 15th ed., 1920).

47. [May 1839?], *Lady de Rothschild and her Daughters, 1821–1931*, ed. Lucy Cohen (1935), 9.

exclusively my own, that I am sure you will not give unprovoked pain by commenting on the subject." He added, for good measure, "Her fortune is, I beleive, £8,000 Sterling."[48] For his part, Henri-Frédéric Amiel, that probing Swiss self-tormentor, essayist, and diarist, yearned for a love that would be at once spiritual and sensual; he repeatedly lamented, in his private journal, his inability to combine them. One night, alarmed at an "abundant pollution" on his reclining chair, he noted, pathetically, "So I have an imagination (nocturnal) quite unworthy of me." He was appalled by the way that his senses took the initiative, and wished for nothing more than an "unstained love," a love he would never soil. But his body, he feared, was at war with his heart, for in that heart he had preserved the virginal purity of his longing. Later he complains, no less pathetically, that he cannot break with a girl he loves, for all her laziness and malice: "*I worship or I detest*," he comments, and professes satisfaction that he has "done wisely to close the door on my passions, lest I be devoured by them. All or nothing; alas, that is my sentence. O Epictetus! Where is your calm?"

Amiel would never achieve either the stoical detachment or the loving union he thought he wanted so badly. Brooding on marriage in his later years, he catechized himself, mixing economic and social considerations with thoughts of affection and passion: "Before dreaming of a wife, reply to the following questions: 1. Can you support her and the children you may have, even if you are ruined and lose your post? 2. Can you commit yourself to an affection that is not returned? 3. Can you, in your position, marry a girl without dowry, that is to say, depend on your post, consequently on caprice and chance?" This most unworldly of bachelors could not evade thoughts about the palpable reality of a dowry. Much like Amiel, the German dramatist and actor Karl von Holtei often mused on the fate that compelled him to sever strands of love that he knew belonged together, and wondered whether "among young men of my age, the decisive separation of feelings, which has made me into a double human being, has also taken place—in the degree true of me, and, above all, lasting so long, beyond the years of mature youth?" It was a tortuous and tortured question. Taking his accustomed lonely walks on which he would make his "comparative-anatomical studies of souls and hearts," he would pose that question over and over again. "I grew up; wishes, impulses, tender dreams, human appetites grew with me," but he never found his "earthy intentions" combined with "heavenly, sentimental adoration for one and the same object." When he did love, he would see

---

48. Sydney Smith to Robert Smith, 1798. Alan Bell, *Sydney Smith* (1980), 23.

n his love only "the unattainable, the inaccessible, the pure," and, in fact, "*wanted* to see nothing else in her." What he called with unself-conscious pomposity "the angel in me" only "sought another angel," while "the animal demanded its like." He was afraid that this might be his private misfortune and aware that it *was* a misfortune: "In his relationship with the female sex, a man, it seems to me, becomes a complete human being only when the angel and the animal blend into each other."[49] No psychologist could have stated the ideal, and its difficulties, more plainly and more poignantly than this.

The desire to marry physical to mental love was so insistent in the Victorian decades that at times it would haunt men's dreams. Writing to his wife Harriet in early 1857, John Stuart Mill recorded that he had, at York, "slept little & dreamt much—among the rest a long dream of some speculation on animal nature." It was an ambiguous formulation, clarified only by "a still droller dream" dreamt the same night, and, in the manner of successive dreams, a commentary on the first. "I was seated at a table like a table d'hote, with a woman at my left hand & a young man opposite—the young man said, quoting somebody for the saying, 'there are two excellent & rare things to find in a woman, a sincere friend & a sincere Magdalen.' I answered 'the best would be to find both in one'—on which the woman said 'no, that would be too vain' —whereupon I broke out 'do you suppose when one speaks of what is good in itself, one must be thinking of one's own paltry self-interest? no, I spoke of what is abstractly good & admirable." Mill found it "queer," he told his wife, "to dream stupid mock mots, & of a kind totally unlike one's own ways or character." He acknowledged "the usual oddity of dreams," for he had been sure in the dream that the man had misquoted the phrase, and that "the right words were 'an innocent Magdalen,' not perceiving the contradiction." Then Mill speculated that it might have been "reading that Frenchman's book" that had suggested the dream. He concluded, a little lamely, with a slightly pathetic appeal to his wife's good opinion: "These are ridiculous things to put in a letter, but perhaps they may amuse my darling."[50]

Mill's associations are tantalizing rather than revealing—who *was* that Frenchman he had been reading? But while a full interpretation of his dreams would be rash, their general import appears unmistakable. The "animal nature" of that first dream, though it is there associated with a

49. Amiel: June 24, 1841, June 2, 1849, April 7, 1850, *Journal intime*, ed. Bernard Gagnebin and Philippe M. Monnier, 6 vols. so far (1976–   ), I, 196–97, 466, 690; Karl von Holtei: *Vierzig Jahre*, vol. I (1843), 318–19.
50. *John Stuart Mill and Harriet Taylor*, ed. F. A. Hayek (1951), 253–54.

cow, almost certainly refers, as the second dream explicates it, to man's
animal nature, his sensuality. Seated between a man and a woman, John
Stuart Mill may have found the precise nature of that sensuality something of a problem. His marriage to Harriet Taylor, built on unrelieved
mutual admiration, strenuous intellectual companionship, and the husband's abject worship of his wife's gifts, was in all probability the chaste
cohabitation of two invalid companions. Much earlier, not long after
the two had discovered their love for one another while she was still
married to John Taylor, they had endorsed a rather broader view of
the matter; they had explicitly and approvingly cited Robert Owen's
summary definition of *"Chastity"* as "sexual intercourse *with* affection,"
counterposed to *"Prostitution,"* which was "sexual intercourse *without*
affection." But now, it seems, the state of their health, both physical and
mental, imposed on them a third posture: affection without sexual intercourse. In the early 1830s, seeking to differentiate between Harriet
Taylor's feelings for her husband and for him, John Stuart Mill had
called her love for John Taylor "affection, not *passion*," and saw as the
"justification of passion" at its best that it kept alive all those other sentiments that deserve to exist on their own.[51]

For many years, then, consciously and unconsciously, Mill had thought
it best to find both loves in one—to have a partner with whom one
could both talk and sin. The boldness of his desire, even though driven
back into the reaches of the repressed, evidently frightened him, married though he was. Charged by the woman with vanity—the voice,
surely, of his own superego or of the walking conscience he married—
Mill retreats from expressing any wishes of his own: was it not considerations of abstract good rather than paltry self-interest that had made him
speak out? If such "stupid mock mots" were, as he thought, out of
character, they were so only as far as he was aware. He could not speak
for his unconscious, except to call it names. Just below the threshold of
the accessible, though, there lay Mill's sensuality, unappeased, in his sad,
loving, anxious, not wholly realized marriage. To put such "ridiculous
things" into a letter to "amuse" his darling seems not merely a mild plea
for gratitude, but, in addition, a no less mild act of aggression, of rare
self-assertion; it reads like the pathetic protest of a male feminist against
a love that gave Eros too little room for play. It suggests a desire on
Mill's part, just as pathetic, to be ordinary for once, to enjoy the kind

51. Manuscript essay on marriage and divorce, ca. 1832; John Stuart Mill to W. J.
Fox, November 5 or 6, 1833, *J. S. Mill and Harriet Taylor*, 74 and 291n, 52.

of love that many other married men—and women—simply took for granted.

Marriage did not mean the end of such love for good bourgeois. It was widely thought that the romantic occupations of an infatuated respectable couple—their coy looks, intimate talks, innocent presents, chaste kisses, and incomplete invitations collectively known as "making love"—would cease once the woman had secured her prey with the saying of the vows. "It was a strange condition of things," David Copperfield muses in Dickens's great autobiographical novel, "the honeymoon being over, and the bridesmaids gone home, when I found myself sitting down in my small house with Dora; quite thrown out of employment, as I may say, in respect of the delicious old occupation of making love."[52] But there were masses of clandestine romantics who in the seclusion of their private lives kept up such delicious occupations, early and late into marriage. When he was still a young historian, away on his research trips, Jules Michelet would write home the letters of a lonely lover to his wife Pauline: "Adieu, my good and dear wife; thoughts of you charm and torment me so." And in the summer of 1907, Paul Güssfeldt, a prominent German mountain climber and scientific traveler, returned from a North Sea voyage with high military and diplomatic officials to be greeted by his wife, Helene. He was then sixty-seven, having married late, just a dozen years earlier. But his journal captures his youthful fervor: "Reunion with Helene, more beautiful than a beautiful dream." Charles Kingsley spoke for them all when he exclaimed to a friend after five years of marriage: "People talk of love ending at the altar. Fools!"[53]

Many irreproachable middle-class husbands and wives were, at least in this respect, no fools. Many of them, in fact, self-critical as they were inclined to be, were pleased to think that they had not fallen short of the exacting ideal that the doctrine of the two currents imposed. They found that ideal so realistic, in fact, that they rejoiced without any show of surprise when they approached it, and felt cheated when they fell short. Mabel Loomis Todd, that splendid American diarist, lecturer, and unabashed adulteress, was at the same time proper and passionate, neither promiscuous nor frigid. Her need for sexual gratification, whether with her husband or her lover, was pressing, her pleasure in it wholehearted,

52. Dickens, *David Copperfield*, opening of ch. 44.
53. Michelet: August 28, 1828, *Journal, texte intégral*, ed. Paul Viallaneix, 4 vols. (1959–1976), I, 705, 812; Güssfeldt: Notebook K I 1. Güssfeldt Nachlass Berlin Stabi; Kingsley: to J. M. Ludlow, August 17, 1849. *Charles Kingsley: His letters and Memories of His Life*, ed. by his wife, 2 vols. (1876; ed. 1879), I. 172. See below, p. 301.

her response to it unapologetic. But she would not have known how to segregate affection from passion. "His love for me," she noted with satisfaction about her husband David in 1879, in the first year of their marriage, "is so passionate, & yet so pure." In the same way, she dignified the great adulterous escapade of her life, which made her, in fact if not in law, a bigamist, as a transcendent, almost a sacred love. With the verve that she mobilized so readily, she loved those she slept with and, perhaps a little less consistently, slept with those she loved.

Lester Ward and "the girl" who would become his wife were little different. Their first venture into sexual intercourse, though it antedates their marriage by almost ten months, was, in their own eyes, pure and clean, hallowed by their unequivocal monogamous intentions, a teasing, accelerating surrender to an impulse in which tenderness and sensuality were inseparable, indeed indistinguishable, and in which the couple collaborated step by step. In the same fashion, the educated American women who responded to Dr. Clelia Mosher's questionnaire on their sexual habits could, most of them, envision intercourse quite independent of the wish for children, but not of mutual married devotion. Intercourse, said No. 12 of her informants, was "not sensual pleasure, but the pleasure of love"; it was, No. 22 agreed, "the expression of love between man and woman," and "simply the extreme caress of love's passion." For these women, sex was never raw sensuality but the physical expression of a spiritual union—as another put it, "a very beautiful thing." It was just as beautiful for the imaginary couple of Gustave Droz's light-hearted history of a bachelor and his marriage, *Monsieur, madame, et bébé*: once the blushing bride had shed her ignorance, she could smile at her awkward timidity in bed on her first night, an amusement in which her husband joined.[54] Whether frankly sentimental or faintly embarrassed, many bourgeois perceived loving feelings as the bridge between the body and the mind. "Dearest beloved," Karl Koch, a young German botanist, on his way to a scientific expedition in the Caucasus, wrote from St. Petersburg in April 1838 to the girl he would later marry: "When these lines have reached you, give your longing free rein and yield wholly to the sweet hope that you may soon clasp me in your loving arms." Some years later, married by now and the father of two children, he wrote to his wife, as he prepared to go on a second expedition, in almost the same accents: "My dearest, my All!" He recalled his first long absence: "It was, after all, a very different farewell seven years ago, when we loved one another so fervently, but our present feeling is truly unutterable and boundless;

54. See *Education of the Senses*, 71–108, 127–44, 149.

t has seized the most earnest and deepest life of our souls." Embraces of the most respectable bourgeois lovers at best joined desire with affection. In May 1844, after half a year of courting his "dear cousin," Ludwig Bamberger, prominent German businessman and liberal politician, closed a love letter "with all ardor, your Louis embraces & kisses you, and calls you his dear sweet Anna."[55] Walter and Eliza Bagehot, Otto and Marietta Banks and others demonstrate that Bamberger's feelings and his way of sharing them were anything but eccentric or extravagant. Eliza Wilson, gently brought up and not given to effusions, hailed her engagement to Walter Bagehot as "the *great fact*," while the recognition of that great fact made her fiancé vault over his sofa in sheer exuberance.

None of these instances, even all of them together, would entitle anyone to wax dogmatic about the bourgeois experience in love. Still, middle-class lovers made enough of an explicit record to permit some fairly confident conclusions. The emotional energies pulsating through the lives of ordinary couples were, as we have discovered, often formidable. Consider, as final testimony, the love of the Roes. Early in 1860, Alfred Roe began to court Emma Wickham only a few months after he had lost his first wife in childbirth. Roe's twelve-year marriage had, especially toward its end, become stormy, marred by his wife's moodiness and addiction to stimulants. Recalling those days for Emma Wickham in the summer of 1860, Alfred Roe spoke ruefully of "that (to me) fearful summer of 1858." He had, he protested, "loved my Dear departed one," but that had been a "love of earnest yearning compassion over what was almost an erring wayward but afterwards repentant and thank God restored child."[56] His love for Emma Wickham, he assured her—and himself—would be different, closer to the ideal to which they both subscribed.

Born in New York City in 1823, the son of a grocer who later took up farming in rural New York, Alfred Roe had studied theology but, after graduating from New York University, had opened an engineering school. It was never particularly profitable, and eventually forced to close with the outbreak of the Civil War. Roe's prospects were not exactly promising, and his domestic imbroglios had left a deposit of gloom on his mind, relieved only by his new love. He was thirty-seven, responsible for three surviving small children, and in debt. "Upon my present footing," he told Emma Wickham in August 1860, "even, if I

55. Koch: April 22, 1838. Karl Heinrich Emil Koch Nachlass, box 1; May 17, 1843, ibid., box 2; Bamberger: May 4, 1844. Bamberger Nachlass. Both Stabi Berlin.
56. Arthur Roe to Emma Wickham, July 14, March 31, 1860, Roe Family Papers, Y-MA.

should do no better, I can stand and be able with your help to pay off though slowly my liabilities." His was an ordinary bourgeois story in many ways, marked by long spells of impecuniousness and at least one bankruptcy. But with the ease characteristic of mobile America in his time, Roe shifted careers and places of employment to battle on for solvency. In 1863, he was ordained a Presbyterian minister, served from January 1864 as a military chaplain, and, after the Civil War, between 1867 and 1877, ran through no fewer than four ministerial appointments. His short tenure at Lowell, Massachusetts, the mill town where he seems to have offended the owners with unwelcome radical observations, suggests that he was, aside from being improvident, far from politic.

But in his courtship of Emma Wickham, Roe's impetuosity served him well. His "Dear Friend" in early spring became, rapidly, his "Darling Birdie," and when he married her in the fall of 1860, he had good reason to believe that this was as intelligent a move as he ever made. He would describe his love for her, and hers for him, as sacred and secular together. Had he not "traced so plainly," he told her, "Gods hand in all our intercourse"? Was he not humbly absorbing the lessons that Providence was teaching him? Emma Wickham took good care to help him keep these lessons firmly in mind. "Mrs. Roe," he wrote, "during our long engagement used to allow me considerable freedom in handling her person & I thought it all right. I see now how much more right you were & I not only respect you more but you have lifted *me* above my former self." She was evidently telling him to keep his hands to himself, and he bowed to her moral authority without protest, even with some solemn pleasure: "I feel even now that I am learning much, much from you. I am stronger, wiser, better for your influence over me. There is that in you which calls me out, makes me more of a man & urges me on to reach out ever more from day to day to-wards the pattern of the standard man in Christ Jesus."[57]

Still, Alfred Roe did not yield up his masculinity to the woman he loved. On the contrary, she made him, as he told her, more of a man. As a good Presbyterian, schooled in the faith, he had the name of God and the image of Christ in his mind, and under his pen, at every opportunity. But while his faith and his love urged him, as he would have said, steadily upward to the thin, clean air of Christian attachments, this did not imply an anemic affection. His wife, little less devout than he, and nine years younger, was only too happy to adopt the erotic course

57. Arthur Roe to Emma Wickham, August 2, 1860.

e set for them both. The Roes had two children in rapid succession—
ne in 1861, the next in 1863—only to be parted for long stretches, as he
ent off to war with the New York Volunteers. And this compelled
em to pursue that course largely on paper.

Indeed, far from inhibiting them, their separation gave the couple's
morous imagination unsuspected space for play, and they explored it
ith abandon. Mutual seduction by mail was, they agreed, a poor substi-
te for the real thing, and in many ways a dangerous expedient; it
irred them beyond bearing without a suitable opportunity to discharge
eir importunate desires. Yet their fantasies would not leave them alone,
nd each would not, could not, keep them from the other. Their cor-
espondence was so passionate that it made him nervous, and induced
im to implore her—in vain—to learn enough shorthand to let them
ommunicate in complete confidentiality. "These letters much as I loved
hem from you & loved to send them to you always worried me lest they
hould get under other eyes." He told her that he wanted "to say things
ften that I cannot if I think others may see or wh. might excite wonder
f you decline to let them see & read." Yet he did not want to resist his
mpulse to make their letters as erotic as their conversations: "I miss the
ittle notes we used to send to & fro & though I do not think it perhaps
vise to write quite in the same way we did *very often* I want the privilege
f writing something in the way we would talk when we lay so happily
ogether with your head resting on my shoulder & my arms about your
dear person & hands on your sweet breasts."[58] They had been married for
more than four years, but she seemed as fresh to him as on the first day.

To judge from her letters to him, it was the husband who took the
lead in stimulating the wife's fantasies. It troubled her a little, but not
much. "I was never in my life in so excitable a condition—," she wrote
him in August 1864. She anxiously wondered: "Ought we to write again
reserved as of old. Would it not be wiser." Yet she immediately yielded
to the seductiveness of her sensual needs, relying on pious sophistries:
"Yet perhaps there is no harm I know there is no sin in it—but Gods
dear word permits and encourages our love." She was so aquiver with
sensual appetite that even her nursing baby called up her husband canvassing her body: "I had little Mamie most weaned," she wrote in
October 1864, "but now she nurses day & night a great deal—As I lie
awake with her at my breast I think of you. Sometimes if I remember
the exciting letters you have lately written—or imagine what our

58. Arthur Roe to Emma Roe, February 22, 1865.

pleasure shall be when side by side again I get so excited that I sometim
fear lest it unfavorably affect Mamie."[59] Yet her fear was easily eclipse
by her passion.

There were times when she had to reassure her husband that their co
respondence was acceptable in her eyes and not offensive to God. '
did mean Alfred not to allude again to the matter of our future sexu
relations," she wrote him in early October 1864, "but since you say s
much and hope you are not 'too free' in doing so, let me assure you tha
you can not give me more pleasure until you can come vour very ow
dear self to my arms—than by writing *just what* you did." What gav
their future sexual relations a little spice of uncertainty was the questio
whether they should have another child. This led to what she called "ov
disputes" which, she confidently added, the two would not have "muc
trouble in amicably & pleasurably settling" in bed. But whatever the
might decide, she had no intention of denying him her person: "I a
perfectly and forever content to do what despite *all men* can *invent* t
say—I *know God allows. You are right*—*all* right and *never* shall I ca
on your forbearance to practice that severe self denial that is rathe
sinful than pleasing to him who united us and made us '*one flesh*' n
more *twain*." Again she reassured him: "I *love* to look forward to bein
pregnant again—It seems as if your presence and love would mak
sweetness of every trial even that we may share *together* those littl
insect cares and worries that used to annoy me so. Yes I think we shal
lie many a night in sweeter intimacy than we ever yet have known bod
& soul knit in former bonds." She added, sounding very much as Mabe
Loomis Todd was to sound in appraising her happy early married year
with David Todd: "No *bride* adorning for her husband—can burn wit
a passion so *pure* and so *ardent—to be pleasing and attractive—to th
man she* loves." Far from a rebellious feminist, Emma Roe yielded do
mestic supremacy to her husband. She was no Beatrice Potter. "May
the *bearing matron* be as precious in your eyes as ever a virgin to he
first possessor. *All my desire* is to my *Husband*—and I can not think o
greater worldly pleasure than to have him joy over me. Yes and rule
over me—so God ordains & not less for *my* pleasure than *yours*."[60] Wha
husband could resist such sweet terms of surrender?

59. Emma Roe to Arthur Roe, October 14, 16 (1864).
60. Emma Roe to Arthur Roe, October 5, September 28, October 5, 1864. There is
a curious slip in the last letter, suggesting at least a touch of ambivalence about his
supremacy. She wrote: "*All my desire* is to my *Husband*—and I can not not think o
greater worldly pleasure than to have him joy over me. Yes and rule over me. . . ."
But then, the second "not" occurs at the top of a new page, and may therefore mear
relatively little.

Alfred Roe did not resist. As the Civil War wore on and he remained with the Union troops, he let his fantasies roam over his favorite theme and hastened to sketch it out for her. "I often lay in the morning & think of all the sweet times we had together. I do not deem it wrong"—which is to say, he could not help wondering whether it was wrong and plunged headlong into a breathless sentence—"to allow my thoughts to dwell thus on all our intercourse to its minutest circumstances as all though so pleasant then & exciting to think of even now only seems to draw *you* closer to my soul to make you unlike every one else & in very fact make my mind recoil from every low thought. With you sexual intercourse & desire is holy & pure. I look in imagination on your dear naked form & lean up on the sweet fragrant resting place I have so often rested my weary face upon your soft breast & feel I have the right to do so." This was in late February 1865; three weeks later, he insatiably revived the same images and the same arguments, with his characteristic slightly apologetic tone. What purified his love, he hoped, was the cohabitation in his mind of tenderness with passion, which had found concrete embodiment in his marriage. He remembered his wife's "dear breast so white & fair & tempting," but quickly assured her that it "covered a true heart & when I nestled down there the heart of her husband *trusted* in her." He sturdily told her, unable to suppress that timbre of doubt in his voice, "there can be no harm in my recalling to mind how sweet & fair your dear person appeared to me those nights when you came entirely naked to my arms. How fair & soft your breasts were & how sweetly one restless & weary reposed his cheek there & felt truly *at home*. How pleasant to feel your arms around & dear limbs pressed against mine. How sweet & how precious a thing is true & pure wedded love."[61]

This, of course, was always the saving point: "However pleasant conjugal delights & intercourse may be, even in the physical sense it is this perfect trust & perfect love that is their chief charm." The question of another child was much on his mind, and he advised her that it would be best not to wait until they were out of debt. That would take too long and would "I think be tempting Providence." Besides, he added, settling down to a little lecture on comparative physiology, "to speak truth, too, Darling, a man of strong passionate nature is ever in a false position in such circumstances. I would not myself be otherwise for the lower part of the brain gives force & momentum to the higher. But at the present it is a constant fight with me against nature. A pure minded woman, as you know before your marriage, seldom gets excited. There

61. Arthur Roe to Emma Roe, February 22, March 14, 1865.

is no annoying exciting cause wh needs to be got rid of. No man of strong passions is really in his normal state, able to do his best, except as a pure, chaste, yet *married* man." Here ended the lesson, at least for this time. The Roes lived on together, companionably it seems, for nearly another four decades, until his death in 1901, seeing three more children into the world. Apparently they continued to enjoy what Emma Roe called their "*soul* communings," interpreting their pure, chaste, and married love in their own, somewhat self-serving way.[62]

The discourse the Roes left behind was explicit and copious. But there is much they left opaque, not by adopting a shorthand code, but by indulging in those tantalizing ellipses so characteristic of the communications of close partners. Alfred Roe's insistence on his impatient virility, his "strong passionate nature," coupled with Emma Roe's reassurance that she would never condemn him to marital celibacy, and with their slightly tense discussions of birth control, suggests that they employed coitus interruptus as their contraceptive technique of choice and were in consequence not exactly serene. The almost ostentatious way in which Emma Roe welcomed the prospect of another pregnancy almost incidentally articulates her fervent wish for sexual intercourse complete and uninhibited, uncompromised by prudential calculations. Her association of sex with children and with the steady improvement in their love-making makes this conjecture all the more plausible: in September 1864, when she praised to her husband their "*soul* communions," she suggested that they had only "*comparatively*" tasted them in the past, "for when together we did not love as now, though we thought then we could love no more. It will be like getting married again but I think *far far* better." She added, without any transition, as if she were reporting a free association: "You will too enjoy the children so."[63] Alfred Roe's own perception of sexual pleasure was not untouched by archaic admixtures, traceable to his earliest years: while she was nursing their child, she thought of him, and while he was picturing intercourse, he yearned to nestle on her bosom. The Roes, like everyone else, imported some long-cherished, largely unconscious memories into their married love-making.

The Roes' rhetoric makes them sound impervious to the accidents that so often compromise the fusion of the tender and the passionate strands

---

62. Arthur Roe to Emma Roe, March 14, 1865; Emma Roe to Arthur Roe, September 28, 1864.

63. Emma Roe to Arthur Roe, September 28, 1864.

of love. *Their* love was at once pure and ardent, *their* sexual congress a celebration of mutual trust. But such flawless embodiment of the tender passion is rarely given to mere humans, and the Roes, too, did not fully realize the ideal to which they aspired in company with their fellow-bourgeois. The most spectacular victims of psychological dilemmas were doubtless those cripples of love who somehow could not reconcile their lust for purchased orgasms with their adoration of chaste women, but less eloquent, and better adjusted men and women were also susceptible to them. Alfred Roe's insistence that there is nothing wrong about sharing his erotic fantasies with his wife, or hers that his suggestive letters are welcome and proper, eventually emerge as a somewhat nervous campaign to still nagging doubts over their lustful imaginings. But it is precisely these gropings that make the Roes such good witnesses. So do the clichés with which their correspondence abounds: woman is the moral arbiter, male desire is superior in strength to that of the female, married love is literally sacred, Providence works its visible ways in disaster as much as in happiness—all these were staples of middle-class thinking in the Age of Victoria, employing a common language for individual feelings.

The Roes' medical beliefs, too, like Alfred Roe's sense that the lower, physical energies feed the higher, spiritual ones, fit smoothly into their time. Certainly when it came to "self-pollution," the couple were comfortable with dominant persuasions. Susan, one of Alfred Roe's children from his first marriage, was a visibly troubled girl and an inveterate masturbator. "Unchecked as she grows older," he wrote his wife in 1865, "nymphomania idiotism & the peculiar consumption that marks the secret vice will follow & end the scene."[64] The Roes innocently traded these commonplaces as though they were supplying Gustave Flaubert with material for his *Dictionnaire des idées reçues*. Yet this very ordinariness, their failure to step outside the well-defined domain of received opinion, makes their sexual candor all the more telling, for it suggests that similar exchanges about the pleasures of intercourse cannot have been as exceptional as critics of "Victorianism" have been saying for a hundred years. It leads the historian, at least this historian, to suspect that the accessible record of the bourgeois experience in love is far different, in fact, far more tepid, than that experience itself. How many letters like the Roes' lie buried in attics and archives, or were destroyed by shocked and protective heirs? Questions like this impel the inquirer to seek out less

64. Arthur Roe to Emma Roe, May 25, 1865.

direct evidence about love, harder to read perhaps, but also harder to destroy—evidence like cultural institutions, sublimated expressions of erotic desire, and fictional precipitates like the novel, that supreme middle-class art form that explored the tender passion in all—well, nearly all—its guises.

≥ THREE ≤

The Work of Fiction

NINETEENTH-CENTURY novelists explored all the themes that mattered: money, class, politics. They studied the maneuvers of social climbers and the adventures of tropical travelers, the seductions of power and the consolations of religion. Notebook in hand, they strolled through the new worlds of sports, the railroad, the industrial slum. They anatomized the cultural texture in which they were embedded and discriminated among the finer shadings of rank and manners. In the service of their craft, they became experts in parliamentary procedure, the implications of political economy, the grievances of strikers, the rituals of dinner parties, the etiquette of morning calls and of duels. They made theirs the age of the society novel. But their governing preoccupation always remained with love. Try as they might, they could not escape it. Even Bazarov, the difficult and doomed hero of Turgenev's *Fathers and Sons*, a fanatical devotee of an unemotional, scientific, materialistic world view, falls victim, much to his astonishment, to love's sting. A novelist like Gogol who, from desperate psychological conflicts of his own, sought to excise any intimations of deep erotic involvements in his fictions, paid indirect tribute to love by his energetic exertions to evade it.[1]

As with theorizing, so with fiction, some thought that only the French, or Frenchified writers like Turgenev, gave love such prominence. In 1833, the reviewer of George Sand's *Indiana* in the *Athenaeum* wondered

---

1. I should perhaps note that I am, in this chapter, writing neither literary criticism nor literary history, neither appraising style nor assigning merit. Taking my evidence from across the century and from any novel that may serve my purposes, I am solely concerned here with the portrayal of love in nineteenth-century fiction.

at the way French readers could take pleasure in novels that are "lov
from beginning to end." He was certain that "in England, they woul.
not be tolerated, not only on account of their immoral tendency an.
licentious descriptions" but also because, "really, two volumes of all lov
and nothing but love, would be palling to English tastes." But the soli.
popularity of George Sand among English writers for half a century
proves this commentator's obtuseness: love dominated the fiction o
civilized countries, including England. Anthony Trollope wrote *Mis*
Mackenzie, he reports in his autobiography with amused resignation, "t.
prove that a novel may be produced without any love; but even in thi
attempt it breaks down before the conclusion." Steeling himself for th.
task, Trollope had made his heroine into "a very unattractive old maid
who was overwhelmed by money troubles; but even she was in lov.
before the end of the book, and made a romantic marriage with an ol.
man."[2] If a novelist should dare to experiment with a tale free from
amorous concerns, his characters would briskly compel him to return
to his true business.

Trollope, the most professional of craftsmen, drew the conclusion fo
the trade: "There must be love in a novel," he wrote. Recalling one o
his favorites, *Framley Parsonage*, published in 1861, he took some prid.
in the way he had presented "downright honest love,—in which there wa
no pretence on the part of the lady that she was too ethereal to be fon.
of a man, no half-and-half inclination on the part of the man to pay a
certain price and no more for a pretty toy. Each of them longed for the
other, and they were not ashamed to say so."[3] And when they were
ashamed to say so, love—or its regretted absence—still shaped the lives of
fictional characters. Dorothea Brooke of *Middlemarch* is, as George
Eliot frequently reminds her readers, an "ardent" young woman, and
the Homeric epithet characterizes more than Dorothea's passion to do
some good in the world. It subtly draws attention to her alert, though
long unawakened sensuality and her irremediable discontent with her
disastrous first husband, the sterile pedant Casaubon, who seems to have
been quite as impotent in bed as he was at his desk.

2. *Athenaeum*: March 1833, p. 163. Patricia Thomson: *George Sand and the
Victorians* (1977), 12; Trollope: *An Autobiography* (1883; ed. 1953), 162.
3. Ibid., 123–24. In his admiring lectures on Thomas Hardy, David Cecil argues
that "all Hardy's novels are love stories. Love is the predominating motive actuating
his characters. Once or twice he presents us with a hero moved by other desires:
Jude longs for learning; Swithin's story soon becomes a love story; and before we
are a third through Jude's history he has forgotten his intellectual ambitions and is
absorbed solely in his passion for Sue." *Hardy the Novelist: An Essay in Criticism*
(1943), 29–30.

Even when the tale was ostensibly about something else, love pulled
ae strings behind the scenes. Serious nineteenth-century fiction, as dis-
nct from its slick or trivial incarnations, undertook critical, pointed
vestigations of society. "The supreme virtue of a novel," Henry James
sserted in a famous essay of 1884, is its "air of reality (solidity of spe-
ification)." Still, love was always a principal ingredient in that reality—
 James's own fictions as in those of others. French novels as disparate as
Ionoré de Balzac's *Eugénie Grandet*, Emile Zola's *Pot Bouille*, and Guy
e Maupassant's *Bel Ami* attest that the quest for money and power was
ntangled with the quest for love, but the French were not alone to
ecognize this. Henry James's *Wings of the Dove* and Trollope's *Phineas
inn* shows love-making to be essentially a political game and, conversely,
olitics often an erotic sport—for high stakes. Love was ubiquitous. In
ça de Queiros's *The City and the Mountain* the hero's inability to love
vorks as an appropirate symbol for worldliness and decadence; in Eliza-
eth Gaskell's *North and South*, class differences prove an incitement no
ess than an obstruction to desire. Delicately, indirectly, almost uncon-
ciously, some novelists explored more problematic attachments: Herman
1elville's *Moby-Dick* and Mark Twain's *Huckleberry Finn* invite the
eader into worlds of love to which women gain no entrance. It is signifi-
ant that when, in 1867, the French critic Charles de Mazade listed the
quipment a novelist needed for his work, he was not satisfied with merely
finesse of analysis" and "penetrating grace of observation," the "gift of
entiment and emotion" and close acquaintance with "all social nuances."
 real "intimacy with the passions of the heart" was essential. Since he
vas attempting to account for the fact that the modern novel seemed to
e "the privileged domain of women,"[4] a close acquaintance with the
assions of the heart necessarily ranked high in any catalogue of the
ovelist's essential talents.

Committed to contemporary realities, the modern novel could scarcely
verlook the bourgeois and his loves. In 1870, Perez Galdós, just begin-
ing to make a name for himself as a writer, faulted his Spanish fellow
ovelists for neglecting the middle classes, "the supreme model, the
nexhaustible source." With their "sense of initiative and their intelli-
ence," he thought, bourgeois were "taking over the leadership of
ociety"; it was among them that one found "nineteenth-century man,
vith his virtues and vices, his noble and tireless ambitions, his reforming

    4. James: "The Art of the Novel," *Henry James, The Future of the Novel: Essays
n the Art of Fiction*, ed. Leon Edel (1956), 14; Mazade: "Revue littéraire. Un
oman d'une femme du monde," *Revue des deux mondes*, LXVIII (1867), 526.

zeal, his extraordinary energy."[5] That was in Spain, still mired in pre
industrial modes of thinking; elsewhere, the middling orders, with thei
virtues and vices, had long conquered the center of novelists' attentio
While Galdós did not mention love among the bourgeoisie's traits, he lef
no doubt in his own novels that it was as fateful to the middle classes a
to any romantic aristocrat.

Predictably, the *bildungsroman*, that fictional record of a young man'
education through life, a great favorite among striving, ambitious middle
class readers, made love into the supreme educator. To be sure, in tha
genre, Eros often proved himself an ambiguous or treacherous Cicerone
in Gottfried Keller's *Der grüne Heinrich*, the women Hermann Le
loves teach him decisive but contradictory lessons; in Gustave Flaubert'
Education sentimentale, which reads like a sour parody of Goethe'
Wilhelm Meisters Lehrjahre, an unattainable married woman and an al
too attainable cocotte perform the same service for Frédéric Moreau. Bu
whether the source of misery or felicity, love was the nineteenth-century
novel's least dispensable, the novelist's most saleable ware.

The pressures of libido determined the reception of novels no less than
their making. "One is used to seeing the writer," Schopenhauer noted
"principally occupied with depictions of sexual love." He was sure tha
love was everywhere and had for centuries supplied principal themes fo
drama and poetry and, above all, for those "high piles of novels which
in every civilized country in Europe, every year produces as regularly
as the fruits of the soil." For centuries: Schopenhauer was right. As early
as 1670, in his famous essay on the origins of the novel, Bishop Huet had
defined the modern novel—quite distinct from earlier fictions on love
which had been written in verse—as a tale in prose specializing in
"amorous adventures." Eighteenth-century novelists, from LeSage to
Richardson and Rousseau, had borne him out.

Nineteenth-century writers would reiterate this old assertion, more
frequently and more emphatically than before. Stendhal laid it down in
De l'Amour that "from the first novel a woman surreptitiously opens at
fifteen, she secretly awaits the arrival of passion-love." In the 1890s, the
essayist Julia Duhring would again voice the palpitating expectations of
innumerable readers when she confessed that she looked "for but one
special feature in novels—the love story."[6] The love story was of absorb-

5. J. D. Rutherford and F.W.J. Hemmings, "Realism in Spain and Portugal," *The
Age of Realism*, ed. Hemmings (1974), 275.
6. Schopenhauer: *Die Welt als Wille und Vorstellung, Sömtliche Werke*, II, 678;
Stendhal: *De l'Amour* (1822; ed. Henri Martineau, 1949), 322; Duhring: *Amor in
Society: A Study from Life* (1892), 232.

ng interest to everyone, for it was everyone's story, whether exciting or
humdrum, real or imagined, an invitation to experiment or a drug for
anxiety.

1. A Community of Fantasies

Just before 1900, in a historic reading of *Oedipus Rex*, Freud provided a
dynamic explanation for the way that fictional love works within its
readers. In his *Interpretation of Dreams*, he attributes the astonishing
persistent power of Sophocles's tragedy to the echoes it awakens in the
unconscious minds of its audiences. Sheer intellectual pleasure or pure
aesthetic appreciation could never wholly explain its hold on the educated
world more than two millennia after it had first been performed: "There
must be a voice within us, ready to acknowledge the compelling force of
destiny in *Oedipus*." In short, the fate of Oedipus the king moves us only
because it might have been our own.[7] The fantasy that had animated
Sophocles gathered up unconscious longings and unconscious conflicts
that all men harbor and greet, when they encounter its representation,
with a shock of recognition. The erotic triangle, first experienced in early
childhood and reenacted in adult life, is immortal.

But Freud, sensitive to the historical dimensions of mind, also knew
that, though immortal, the triangle of love draws the most varied shapes
from its culture. If some fictions are for all time, each bears the impress of
its own age. The oedipal entanglements of Hamlet are no longer precisely
those of Oedipus. Hence the "fantasies, castles in the air, and day dreams"
that inform the work of the imaginative writer are by no means "rigid or
unalterable. Rather, they cling to life's shifting impressions of existence,
change with every variation in the human situation." Like the child, the
writer creates "a world of his own, or rather, rearranges the things of
his world in a new order, pleasing to him"—pleasing to him and to others.[8]

Fantasies are scenarios of desire. They are in touch with the deepest
motions of the mind, principally its unmet needs. "We may say," in
Freud's words, "the happy man never fantasizes." The "motive forces of
fantasies are unsatisfied wishes, and every single fantasy is the fulfillment
of a wish, a correction of unsatisfying reality." Fantasies reshape memories
and rehearse portentous encounters; they picture the daydreamer earning
flattering applause, making witty and devastating rejoinders, performing

7. *Traumdeutung* (1900), *St.A.*, II, 266–67; *Interpretation of Dreams*, *S.E.*, IV, 262.
See *Education of the Senses*, 48.

8. "Der Dichter und das Phantasieren" (1908), *St. A.*, X, 173–74; "Creative Writers
and Day-Dreaming," *S.E.*, IX, 146.

noteworthy sexual feats. "In Fiction," George Henry Lewes noted in his journal, "readers love to see a reflection of their own egotism. They like to fancy themselves doing and feeling what the heroes and heroines do and feel."[9] One did not need to be a psychoanalyst to see fiction at work.

At their most palpable, fantasies parade as vivid daydreams in which impermissible and implausible schemes find their magical realization. Their unconscious counterparts, which underlie these daylight reveries of glory and conquest, are at once more difficult to detect and more rewarding to analyze. They rise to awareness heavily censored, as dreams, slips, symptoms and, artistically formed, cunningly stylized, as paintings or poems or novels. Heavily overdetermined, they may serve as handbooks to prudent or to rash action, induce orgasmic excitement or quietist nostalgia.

Whatever they are, and whatever they do, conscious or unconscious, fantasies stand at the boundary, and serve as a bridge, between the personal and the collective imagination. This is most strikingly true of fictions, which are fantasies disciplined, organized, embellished. Like all acts of the mind, the making of fictions is the privilege of an individual. But to the degree that a novel enjoys cultural circulation, securing satisfactory sales, stirring up impassioned debate or probing repressed feelings, it may illuminate that segment of culture from which it springs and to which it speaks. Any group that has a solid grip, and can therefore make a strong claim, on its members—a religious sect, a social class—attempts to perpetuate itself by imposing styles of feeling and expression. It forces appetites into what it considers proper channels and organizes communities of fantasies that will appear in the attitudes they foster, actions they deprecate, conflicts they exhibit or provoke. While the individual's drives and anxieties provide the energy, culture supplies the materials for fantasies and aesthetic requirements act as their architect. Fantasies are such rich historical material in large part because they are not simply fantastic.

Nineteenth-century novelists and literary critics had intimations of all this. Freud's psychological and cultural reading of *Oedipus Rex* and of *Hamlet*, his insight into the power and realistic relevance of fantasies, and his theory of dreams were at once original and in the intellectual mold of his time. Decades before his discovery that dreams are condensed and distorted scripts conflating recent events and infantile wishes, conveying cryptic messages from the unconscious, Turgenev and Dickens, Thackeray and Flaubert, Wilkie Collins, Charlotte Brontë, and Guy de

9. Freud: ibid., 174, 171; 147, 145; Lewes: journal, February 9, 1859, in Gordon S. Haight, *George Eliot: A Biography* (1968), 273.

Maupassant had their characters recount dreams and would, in their pre-
psychoanalytic way, analyze them as disguised offspring of reality, pregnant with meaning. Early in the century Stendhal had defined the novel
as a mirror traveling along a highway—an efficient metaphor that implied
what was to become a commonplace in the age of Victoria: a fiction is
not simply an autonomous text or a wholly private rumination but, rather,
a reflection of its society.

Around 1800, the romantics had developed a persuasive psychology of
aesthetics that had sought the source of literary creativity in unconscious
conflicts, in that rare and precious eccentricity they called genius, in
buried troubles to be denied or buried deficits to be made good. But the
sociological countertheory, to which some romantics also subscribed,
followed the psychological theory with little delay: Madame de Staël
and William Hazlitt gave currency to the proposition that society and
the novel mirror one another; restated and modernized at mid-century
by deterministic theorists of literature like Hippolyte Taine, it came to
acquire the unassailable status of a truism. A mounting uneasiness with
historical novels as escape literature only reinforced this rather facile
sociological interpretation of fiction. Theodor Fontane was attesting to
this uneasiness when he argued, in a thoughtful review of Gustav Freytag's
Die Ahnen, that the modern novel "should be a picture of the time to
which we ourselves belong" and a faithful picture, nothing less.[10]

We are now inclined to see the mirror of fiction traveling along the
highway of nineteenth-century society as often curiously devised, badly
discolored, sometimes cracked. The writer's needs and rages and particular
talents, and the demands that his craft made on him, were potent ingredients in the making of his work no less than his social status, religious
convictions, or political loyalties. Only the most sensitive readers in the
nineteenth century, Sainte-Beuve at his best or Henry James, did justice to
these conflicting claims. Certainly Taine's memorable, much criticized
formula, "*race, milieu, moment*," a brave but rather primitive effort at
specifying the weight of the world on its artists, including its novelists,
was blind to such pressures. In ways that few then understood, the writer
listens, and in a sense speaks, as much to other writers as he does to the
buying public. His professional superego is exacting and importunate.
It sets the tone for bellicose literary manifestos and quarrelsome literary
coteries. In the nineteenth century, style battled and succeeded style;
realists, as the textbooks have it, followed romantics, to be followed in

---

10. "Gustav Freytag. *Die Ahnen*, Band I–III" (1875). Theodor Fontane, *Werke*, ed.
Kurt Schreinert, 3 vols. (1968), III, 861–62.

turn by naturalists and symbolists. But these epithets were more usefu
for combat than they are for diagnosis: there were always countercurrent
at work—romantics in the age of realism, realists in the age of symbolism
Besides, the most distinguished of nineteenth-century writers—Flaubert
Dickens, or Tolstoy—defied these imprecise and convenient labels t(
forge for themselves a style not quite fitting any of them. In that century of realism, which its most determined adversaries could not wholl)
ignore, there was much dependable social reportage in fiction: ever
Dostoevsky, that compelling fantast, took pride in his assiduous reading
of the daily newspapers to gather material for his work. But what make:
the nineteenth-century novel such an informative, if rather temperamental, witness is far less its journalistic precision than its capacity fo1
analyzing, representing, and in significant ways distorting the erotic
experience of contemporary culture.

Fixated on love, novels responded to personal and cultural needs o1
many levels. No matter how trashy, they could count on a kindly reception from someone. Late in 1849, Jane Welsh Carlyle thanked her frienc
John Forster for sending her "Mulock's" novel which, she told him, "]
read with immense interest." She can only have meant The Ogilvies, a1
appalling potpourri of declamatory speeches, theatrical gestures, wilc
misunderstandings, sudden and opportune deaths, and, of course, unsurpassed and undying love. The whole novel is a parade of exclamatior
points. "It is long since I fell in with a novel of this sort, all about love
and nothing else whatever," Jane Carlyle told Forster. "It quite remind:
one of one's own love's young dream. I like it, and I like the poor gir
who can still believe, or even 'believe that she believes,' all that. God helr
her! She will sing to another tune if she goes on living and writing fo1
twenty years."[11] But Mrs. Craik, living and writing for more than twenty
years after, kept singing the same tune. An irreproachable celebrant ol
the bourgeois virtues, she found an enthusiastic readership for her primitive fictions, clumsily knocked together from borrowed and shoddy
lumber.

Still Jane Carlyle, a woman of intelligence, wit, and taste, liked The
Ogilvies, and she knew precisely why. It provided her with some pleasing
regressive moments, took her back to daydreams she thought harsh
experience had forced her to outgrow. These moments were further
sweetened by her somewhat complacent sense of superiority over ob-

11. Jane Carlyle to John Forster, December 1849, Letters and Memorials of Jane
Welsh Carlyle, prepared for publication by Thomas Carlyle, ed. James Anthony
Froude, 3 vols. (1883), II, 94; Dinah Maria Mulock, later Mrs. Craik, wrote some
children's books long popular and one famous novel, John Halifax, Gentleman (1856)

viously naive purveyors of nostalgia. Her pleasure is more than an idiosyncratic lapse in taste or polite response to a thoughtful gift. Jane Carlyle's gracious and self-aware acknowledgment strongly intimates how effectively the nineteenth-century novel, whether sheer entertainment, earnest uplift, or discriminating literary exercise, preserved and expressed erotic fantasies universal in their import yet characteristic in their expression.

Lovers contemplating a literature they must regard, in their condition, as supremely interesting, found much in it to gratify but also much to disconcert them. Nineteenth-century fictions nourished the appetites of respectable bourgeois no less than those of jaded worldlings. The novel of courtship, ranging from outright pornography or gushy sentimental romance to astringent social comedy, could serve as a cheering echo to the adept, informal guide to the inexperienced, and bracing counselor to the panic-stricken. The young men and women whose emotional encounters most fictions charted could navigate the perilous seas of love only to steer at length into the safe harbor of marriage, blessed with unconditional parental approval and the promise of unvaried felicity. As distinguished and scrupulous a writer as George Eliot could entitle a concluding chapter of *Adam Bede*, "Marriage Bells." Most readers expected, and normally got, nothing less.

Often they got more: many of the entertainments running serially in the family periodicals of the time would spell out fantasies in which the triumph of love brought social advancement in its train. Traversing predictable adventures told at satisfying length, low-born maidens would secure aristocratic husbands, poor but sturdy and self-reliant young men, highly eligible beauties. This was the merchandise that the inimitable Marlitt hawked through the pages of Germany's *Die Gartenlaube*, making her own, and the magazine's, fortune in the process. More slippery texts would permit their consumers to imagine and in some measure share heroic sexual triumphs and explosive sexual satisfaction by inviting them to act out their urgent desires in solitary self-gratification or with prostitutes.

The more ambitious, less compliant fiction of the nineteenth century was more gloomy, or at least more sober, than this. In his *Basil*, Wilkie Collins's eponymous hero is only one among many fictional characters to discover that love could be a destructive madness. In most of the novels making up Zola's Rougon-Macquart cycle, amorous passions provide spasmodic joy but serve, far more generally, as agents of misery and doom; they incite to brutality and murder. In Theodor Fontane's most famous novel, *Effi Briest*, love clashes with a rigid, anachronistic code of honor and propels the protagonist into disgrace and an early death. The hero of Machado de Assis's *Dom Casmurro*, hounded by the jealous conviction—the reader will never know whether justified or delusional—that his wife has betrayed him with his best friend, repudiates the love of his life and drives her into shameful, permanent exile. True, in *Adam Bede*, Eliot conjures good from evil: Bede, who had loved a narcissistic shallow beauty, Hetty, loyally and in vain, eventually marries a saintly Methodist, and can look forward to a lifetime of quiet happiness. But the evil that serves this satisfying consummation is very terrible—Hetty murders her illegitimate baby. "Love," says a character in Turgenev's play, *A Month in the Country*, "whether happy or unhappy, is a real calamity if you give yourself up wholly to it," and many of his fictions read like commentaries on this text. For Marcel Proust, love and misery are practically synonyms. And Eugène Fromentin's exercise in mordant recall, *Dominique*, is representative of many novels in which great love ends in great loss. Authors could not always produce the happy ending for which so many readers so fervently pleaded.

But the pressure for such an ending was unremitting: Charles Dickens was even induced to rewrite the last page of *Great Expectations* by his friend and fellow-novelist Bulwer Lytton, to hint at the possible marriage of Pip to Estella. Not without a twinge of his artistic conscience: the new ending, highly implausible and poorly motivated, would, Dickens hoped, make the novel "more acceptable."[12] A writer who catered to a large middle-class public had his obligations. Cruel as some novelists apparently liked to be to their audience, pushing its face into the harsh realities of unhappy love, most of them made concessions to the pleasure principle.

With its self-imposed, self-protective prevarications and compromises, the nineteenth-century novel went from triumph to triumph, both as entertainment and as literature: a genre "flexible, varied, mobile," as the French critic Armand de Pontmartin characterized it in 1861. He noted its successes with some lingering astonishment: "We are seeing a rather remarkable phenomenon in literature: poetry is weakening and the novel persists." But, then, it could hardly be otherwise. The novel, after all, "draws on the diverse elements that society and life offer it."[13] It was

12. John Forster, *The Life of Charles Dickens* (1872–74; ed. Andrew Lang, 2 vols. n.d.), II, 361.

13. Pontmartin: "Le roman et les romanciers de 1861," *Revue des deux mondes* (1861), 701–702.

true: novelists developed an enormous repertory of plots and techniques and gratifications. They needed to do so, for there were many in the age who would not, or could not, read sustained or subtle fictions, and consumed only its most primitive versions. With the democratization of pedagogy both formal and informal and the growing need, in industrial civilization, for literate working hands, a previously untapped, virtually inexhaustible reservoir of common readers at once enlarged and complicated the tasks of writers, publishers, and reviewers. But even the narrower audience, that extended family of middling men and women from impecunious clerks and overworked housewives to cultivated professional men and influential bankers, never coalesced into a single identifiable reading public, never gave its writers unequivocal instructions. Middle-class taste ranged as widely as middle-class income and education.

Much of that taste wanted only simple pleasures. Lending libraries, railway stalls, readers' circles, and book clubs, the stable suppliers of the bourgeois appetite for novels, specialized in predictable romances and melodramas. All aimed at the happy ending and were systematically committed to trivializing the instability and disenchantment that bedevil real love. "How many pretentious love-stories are published annually," one English critic, Alexander Shand, complained in the 1880s, stories "showing neither the slightest acquaintance with actual life nor any instinct for the appreciation of unfamiliar human nature." Most nineteenth-century bourgeois readers, in short, wanted no part of fictions that would explore psychological conflicts or refract the dismaying vicissitudes of their emotional world. Like earlier readers in earlier times, they craved escape, primitive identifications with spotless heroes and heroines, and had no stamina for the austere and ambitious novelistic program that the Goncourt brothers laid down for themselves: "to do, after nature, the three great acts of life, CHILD-BED, COITUS, and DEATH." At best, in their youth, they might mix frivolous diversion with serious reading, and, rarely, graduate from the first to the second. Mabel Loomis Todd, an avid reader in her school days and later something of a writer herself, listed in her youthful journal dozens of engrossing tales of very varied literary quality, from *Story of a Bad Boy*, by J. B. Aldrich ("real nice") to *Little Women* by Louisa May Alcott ("very Beautiful"); from *The Cousin from India*, by Georgiana M. Craik ("perfectly beautiful") to *The Last of the Mohicans* by James Fenimore Cooper ("just splendid"). Her eclecticism was characteristic of her class and time; her self-critical aspirations were rather less so. "Sometimes," she commented as she surveyed her recent reading, "I hope to have an entirely different style of books to put down."[14] Most of her fellow-bourgeois never graduated to that different, more difficult style. Some literature of the nineteenth century was critical and demanding, but most of it was conformist and easy. While the most distinguished exemplars, the novels that have survived into the history of culture, served in the main to make the comfortable uncomfortable, they were accompanied at every point, and often overwhelmed, by entertainments designed to make the uncomfortable comfortable. From all this palatable, eminently digestible fare, the historian can glean mainly what squeamish and anxious readers wanted to avoid or, to put it more precisely, in what soothing guise they could tolerate encountering their passions in the public print.

There were times when the best educated and most discriminating middle-class readers sought the solace of trivial and optimistic fiction to numb them against overpowering realities. Mary Chesnut, that civilized and energetic American diarist, suffering through the Civil War from her vantage point in South Carolina, had kept up with the best of novels, both in English and French, since her earliest youth. "How much I owe of the pleasure of my life," she noted after reading Trollope's *Framley Parsonage*, "to these much reviled writers of fiction." But that had been early in 1861. By March 1864, in anguish over appalling news from the front and grievous personal losses, she looked only for diversion and reassurance. Hawthorne's *Blithedale Romance*, she confessed, "leaves such an unpleasant impression. I like pleasant, kindly stories now. We are so harrowed by real life. Tragedy is for hours of ease."[15]

More typical middle-class consumers of fiction, though far less beset than Mary Chesnut, were no less eager for pleasant, kindly stories. They had never developed a taste for tragedy. In 1915, looking back on a century in which novels had become the favorite bourgeois fare, the American classicist and critic Grant Showerman recalled the ways that generations of readers had used the novel not as a mirror but as a narcotic. The "old-fashioned woman of a generation ago" was always "looking for that isle of safety in the perilous thoroughfare of current fiction which she called the 'sweet pretty story.'" A generation before her, "her mother had escaped to it from unpleasant writers like Thackeray and George Eliot." As for herself, she "sought refuge there from the deeper

14. Alex. Innes Shand: *Half a Century, Or Changes in Men and Manners* (1888), 241; Goncourts: August 1858, Edmond and Jules de Goncourt, *Journal: mémoires de la vie littéraire 1851–1896*, ed. Robert Ricatte, 22 vols. (1956–58), III, 41; Todd: Journal I, 1871–1875, MLT, box 45. Y-MA.
15. February 25, 1861; March 11, 1864, *Mary Chesnut's Civil War*, ed. C. Vann Woodward (1981), 10, 581.

distresses of Thomas Hardy, the shocking young cynicism of Kipling, and those new importations from France and Russia of the strange thing called realism." And even as he was writing, Showerman imagined young women fleeing "the novels of sex, of crime, of sophistication," by seeking out "the white-and-gold volume with the red-haired girl on the cover." They might be a little embarrassed by their innocence, but they were continuing to consume what they like to call " 'just a nice story.' "[16]

It was true that modern masters had a habit of being unpleasant. Though often eccentric to their culture, they perceived its features more subtly, probed them more sensitively, and rendered them more precisely than the manufacturers of best sellers ever could. Seeing more, these difficult writers also gave more—to contemporaries prepared to do the strenuous if rewarding work of reading them, and to historians in quest of penetrating analyses. Paradoxically, though the masters commanded an imagination less stereotyped and more fertile than that available to confectioners of popular fiction, the characters they constructed were more solidly grounded in psychological and social realities than those invented (or copied) by their lesser colleagues. They forced access to the very conflicts, particularly the conflicts of love, that their culture was doing its best to drive from the stage of awareness.

This does not mean that the demanding writers of the century consistently disdained the devices with which the literary hack pandered to his insatiable customers; they, too, could fashion heroes and villains of straw, compose sentimental love scenes, call upon implausible coincidences, and stage rescues that would have pleased the innocents who went to the theatre to hiss the villain. Zola brims over with excessive animation and so fastidious a writer as Fontane descends to the accidental discovery of some love letters to prepare the tragic climax of *Effi Briest*. Perhaps the most naked melodramatic moment in a serious nineteenth-century novel, perceived even in its day as an unwarranted lapse of taste, is the climactic scene in *Adam Bede*. Hetty is in the cart near the scaffold to be hanged for child-murder; but she is saved (the chapter title explicitly notes, at the last moment) as her seducer, Arthur Donnithorne, urges his sweating horse through the crowd come to watch the execution, holding aloft the royal reprieve that will convert her death sentence to transportation.[17] But, of course, neither George Eliot nor Theodor Fontane nor Emile Zola lived by these tricks of their trade. They all aimed at, and in their best

16. " 'Just a Nice Story,' " *The Dial*, LIX, No. 706 (November 25, 1915), 471.
17. "I think I was *good*," William Lucas Collins, after reviewing *Adam Bede* for *Blackwood's* (the magazine of Eliot's publisher), wrote to John Blackwood, "not to mention Donnithorne galloping up with the reprieve." Haight, *George Eliot*, 278.

work reached, the riven heart of their culture and the nature of man, the conflict-ridden amorous animal.

2. Hearts, Undisciplined and Others

Subtle or not, novelists found love a serious business. Hence, with the thoughtful epigrams, small sermons, and philosophical asides they would insert into their writings, nineteenth-century makers of fiction regularly performed as moralists. Their excursions into portentousness and exhortation did not strike them, or their readers, as intrusive; the very stories they told, after all, often bore heavy burdens of missionary uplift. And no one shouldered that burden more bravely, made it easier to carry, than Charles Dickens. He is of peculiar interest to the historian of nineteenth-century bourgeois culture because he was one of its most inspired spokesmen. His middle-class public claimed him in his lifetime, and Matthew Arnold confirmed the claim in 1881 when Dickens had become a historical figure. *David Copperfield*, Dickens's most personal creation and his "favourite child," was, Arnold thought, "charming and instructive," an "all-containing treasure house" that revealed both the severe and the light side of "English middle-class civilisation."[18] Dickens bestrode the English literary scene like no one else, beloved by the masses of ordinary and the elite of cultivated readers alike, intriguing to the most demanding literary critics, a source of honest admiration and barely concealed envy to his competitors. When he died in 1870, the throne of national novelist remained empty.

Among the diverse sources of Dickens's unrivaled appeal, his consistent moralizing was by no means the least attractive. His villains end up in prison, wallow in drunken beggary, hang themselves, or burn themselves to a cinder through spontaneous combustion; his virtuous, modest young heroes and heroines happily marry one another. And there is a scene in *David Copperfield* that brilliantly condenses the moral preoccupations, literary tactics, and psychological dividends of the novels in Dickens's decades. He stages it in the study of Dr. Strong, the elderly, gentle, unworldly scholar who had been David Copperfield's kindly teacher and is now his valued friend. Dr. Strong's young wife Annie, beautiful, reserved, and somewhat mysterious, has for some years labored under a gathering cloud of suspicion; her best friends fear that she is harboring an illicit inclination for her handsome but egotistical and unprincipled

18. Dickens: Preface to *David Copperfield*, edition of 1869; Arnold: "The Incompatibles," *Nineteenth Century*, IX (June 1881), 1035–39 passmi.

cousin Jack Maldon. Dickens, indeed, has taken good care to scatter suggestive hints to make such suspicions eminently plausible. David Copperfield himself, though free of guile and reluctant to believe evil of anyone, uneasily wonders whether Annie has not forgotten her sacred wifely duty. Only Dr. Strong, who had been Annie's fatherly friend before he became her fatherly husband, refuses to see anything amiss. Now, in one of those operatic ensembles that Dickens found so irresistible, Annie Strong sets all doubts to rest. In the presence of her garrulous, mischief-making mother, of David Copperfield, and of other principals, the whole a grand sextet, she declares to her husband on her knees that while she and her cousin "had been little lovers once," she had never seriously loved Jack Maldon; had she persuaded herself that she did, and married him, she would have been "most wretched." For, she comments a little sententiously, "There can be no disparity in marriage like unsuitability of mind and purpose." Innocence, sorely tempted and long in question, has been triumphantly vindicated.

David Copperfield, listening intently, finds Annie's words oddly meaningful. He himself has made a thoughtless marriage, choosing a delightful, good-hearted, but incurably childlike girl, Dora Spenlow, and he now senses that Annie Strong's apophthegm has some "strange application" that he cannot quite divine. Annie delivers other pronouncements for him to ponder. In a long, impassioned apostrophe to Dr. Strong—"Oh, my husband and father"—she proclaims her love for him to be pure; it had always been pure: "Oh, take me to your heart, my husband, for my love was founded on a rock, and it endures!" She is grateful to him for much, including his saving her from Maldon, "from the first mistaken impulse of my undisciplined heart."

In the days and weeks that follow, David Copperfield obsessively returns to this formulation. The obscure application of Anne Strong's sentences is obscure no longer. In marrying Dora he had listened to his infatuated inclinations alone—he had been swept away by her beauty, her voice, her charming little habits, her very defects. Esteem for solid qualities, thoughts on a long future together, the sober anticipation of the mature affection that shared experience alone can bring—he has failed to consult them all, paid no heed to the reality principle. His love, unlike Annie Strong's, had not been founded on a rock; his marriage had been the first mistaken impulse of an undisciplined heart.[19]

Dickens makes sure that David Copperfield does extravagant penance

19. *The Personal History of David Copperfield* (1850; ed. Trevor Blount, 1966), 716–33 [ch. 45].

for his rashness. He must endure, in affectionate resignation, his wife's pouting impracticality, her stubborn incompetence in household matters, and, worse, her touching but futile attempts to understand the literary work in which he has begun to make a reputation: in short, her pathetic, almost programmatic refusal to grow up. When she dies a soft, lingering death following a miscarriage, David Copperfield is free to mourn at length and to marry Agnes Wickfield, his "sister," whom he has known since his childhood, and who embodies all the perfections that a husband in Victorian fiction could ask for in a wife; quiet beauty, inexhaustible generosity, a gift for domesticity and maternity.

Dickens was writing novels, not moral tracts. But *David Copperfield* is, among other things, a morality tale contrasting the penalties attached to following the promptings of an undisciplined heart with the rewards awaiting those willing to discipline it. The wishes that the undisciplined heart aches to see realized are for the immediate gratification of desires aroused by a prepossessing figure or a magnetic presence, by unrealistic, insatiable longings for rank or wealth—social success. Nineteenth-century fiction is crowded with these immature and irresponsible victims of desire: Hetty Sorrel in *Adam Bede*, to say nothing of Effi Briest, Emma Bovary, and Anna Karenina in the novels that bear their names, and many others like them, yield to amorous impulses that their station in life, their religious obligations, and the rules of their society have declared out of bounds. Adultery provided tantalizing glimpses of the undisciplined heart in full career.

Dickens, circumspect as he was, did not hesitate to toy with this dubious and omnipresent theme. But unlike other novelists, mainly French, for whom adultery was a favorite ingredient in their plots, Dickens only teased his readers with the appearance of infidelity without compelling them to face its consequences. In *Bleak House*, he lends adultery some ludicrous touches, as Mrs. Snagsby comes to labor under the conviction that her tender-hearted, mild-mannered husband is betraying her with a succession of highly implausible rivals. Again in *Dombey and Son*, painting with the most somber hues on his palette, Dickens has the villainous Carker run off to the Continent with Edith Dombey, Mr. Dombey's wife, under exceedingly compromising circumstances. But, as in *David Copperfield* and *Bleak House*, Dickens again reassures his readers after he has aroused their suspicions and whetted their appetites. Annie Strong, we know, rehabilitates herself to the satisfaction of all. Mrs. Snagsby is enlightened about her delusions by the sensible police inspector Mr. Bucket, who advises her to read *Othello*. And Edith Dombey, raised to be a beautiful, heartless object for sale to the highest bidder, retains enough moral fiber to refuse herself to her would-be seducer in a melodramatic confrontation. Certainly, without intimations of immorality, the nineteenth-century novel would have been insufferably anodyne. But many novelists in most countries found it advisable to show these intimations to have been unjustified. Some exceedingly proper nineteenth-century novels turn on erotic provocations that remain unrealized.

Readers derived a double profit from such tantalizing performances. They could let themselves feel venturesome as they closed in on lurid sexual experiences far beyond their ordinary reach and then enjoy the relief that came with the revelation of innocence preserved. Only someone addicted to acting out the fantasies that reading generates would be disappointed by such tactics. Most others, fanatics for purity excepted, found hints at adulterous passions, at promiscuity, even at incest, particularly welcome when these turned out to be mistaken, though carefully cultivated impressions. It was like anticipating the uncertain prospects of a safari into a hazardous, unexplored jungle and discovering it to be nothing more than a trip to one's favorite zoo.

For all its flirting with illicit experiences, much nineteenth-century fiction functioned as a prudent warning against the perils of precipitous infatuations, unsuitable alliances, marital irregularities. Some among the most celebrated novels of the age—Tolstoy's *Anna Karenina*, Eliot's *Middlemarch*, Thackeray's *Vanity Fair*—follow the contrasting fates of two pairs of lovers, with one destined to suffer shipwreck and the other to be suitably mated by the end, or with both to be unhappy in their own way. The interest that the travail of one couple arouses is more than doubled by that of the second, as the novelist rehearses the possibilities of love among his protagonists; each is a reminder to the other of what might have been.[20]

Quite as often, as in *David Copperfield*, the novelist had his protagonist undergo the hard school of two, perhaps of more loves, the first grievously misguided, the last supremely right. In Trollope's *Three Clerks*, which economically condenses the varieties of proper amorousness through the story of three sisters and their three suitors, one of them, Harry, begins by loving the glamorous Gertrude only to marry the self-effacing Linda.

20. Reviewing *Middlemarch*, Henry James singled out for special praise "the balanced contrast between the two histories of Lydgate and Dorothea. Each," he noted, "is a tale of matrimonial infelicity, but the conditions in each are so different and the circumstances so broadly opposed that the mind passes from one to the other with that supreme sense of the vastness and variety of human life, under aspects apparently similar, which it belongs only to the greatest novels to produce." "George Eliot's 'Middlemarch'" (1873), *The Future of the Novel*, 86.

In *Democracy*, Henry Adams has a witty and affluent young widow move from New York to Washington where she is almost swept off her feet by a magnetic, ruthless Senator on his way to the White House, but is saved by her good sense and by the devotion and probity of another man whom, the ending implies, she will end up marrying. Friedrich Spielhagen, Germany's best-known serious—or at least most ambitious—novelist of the 1860s and 1870s, has the protagonist of *Hammer und Amboss* settle on the admirable Paula, who has been his good friend all his life, only on practically the last page, after he has taken some spectacular missteps in infatuation.

While in most nineteenth-century fiction erotic impetuosity proves a source of disaster, the capacity to postpone gratifications, to wish only what a decent and responsible bourgeois should wish for, generally brings lasting happiness. It is striking how many novelists distinguish and reward their heroines for their angelic patience. In general Dickens's good women, with the uncertain exception of Bella Wilfer in *Our Mutual Friend*, are experts in serene waiting. Agnes Wickfield, near the conclusion of *David Copperfield*, when all has become clear and David is a free man, confesses to him that she has loved him all her life—and not just as a sister. And Spielhagen's Paula had been a sister to the hero-narrator of *Hammer und Amboss* just as Agnes Wickfield had been, uncomplaining and supportive and selfless, for nearly six hundred pages. Linda, too, in Trollope's *Three Clerks*, has schooled herself to endurance until Harry discovers her quiet charms. Dobbin, who nobly loves Amelia for many years until she finally recognizes his worth and solicits his affection, reverses the traditional sexual roles—in *Vanity Fair*, it is the man who serves and waits, not the woman. But the lesson is the same, the fundamental moral of the novel in the bourgeois century: civilization extracts sacrifices, and whoever refuses to make them must pay for his failure to discipline his erotic urges.

A subject as heavily charged and ferociously disputed as the right place of morality in fiction could hardly produce a consensus among nineteenth-century novelists or their audiences, let alone the practitioners of that new, impressive growth industry, literary reviewing. The doctrine of literature for literature's own sake won converts with every passing decade. Théophile Gautier and Charles Baudelaire in France, Edgar Allen Poe and Ralph Waldo Emerson in the United States, Heinrich Heine and Friedrich Theodor Vischer in Germany, restated and varied Alexander Pushkin's famous terse formula: "The aim of poetry is poetry." Grandiose romantic claims for the artist's exemplary stature in society, claims that expanded even as romanticism waned, raised unresolved questions about the writer as pedagogue. As the unacknowledged legislator of mankind, the imaginative writer might be expected to assert moral leadership; but as the pure artist dwelling in realms remote from the mundane preoccupations of the philistine, he might well be dispensed from preaching virtue and denouncing vice.

Incoherence and inconsistency on the issue abounded and persisted. At the beginning of his literary career, Thackeray rejected the idea that the novelist should write sermons in disguise and refused to ambush the unsuspecting reader with portentous announcements about the sickness of contemporary society. But then tragic reverses in his family life and earnest reflections on the art of fiction induced him to change his mind. He came to join, he told a friend, the "Satirical-Moralists" and announced rather grandly that his "profession seems to me to be as serious as the Parson's own." But preachment did not always perfectly match practice: Anthony Trollope, finely attuned to the needs of the market, was not inclined to be solemn in his novels, but he sounded positively funereal in his autobiography. He argued there that while many, whether cynics or purists, "would laugh at the idea of a novelist teaching either virtue or nobility," he for his part did not think of novelists as a tribe pandering "to the wicked pleasures of a wicked world." Quite the contrary: "I have ever thought of myself as a preacher of sermons," and he professed to take pride in the fact that "no girl has risen from the reading of my pages less modest than she was before." In fact, he hoped, "some may have learned from them that modesty is a charm well worth preserving."[21] While no one would have accused Trollope of being salacious in his treatments of love, few would have believed, reading his well-wrought inventions, that he had had so grave a purpose in view as mounting the pulpit to deliver sermons on morality.

The confusion was by the nature of things incurable. Disagreeable writers—satirists like George Meredith and Theodor Fontane or frowning judges of the human condition like Thomas Hardy or Emile Zola—thought themselves purifiers, scourges of hypocrisy: to strike through the mask of defensive evasions and genteel euphemisms in the erotic domain was in itself to perform a moral act. After all, as contemporary

21. Thackeray: Gordon N. Ray, "*Vanity Fair*: One Version of the Novelist's Responsibility," *Essays by Divers Hands: Being the Transactions of The Royal Society of Literature of the United Kingdom*, n.s. XXV (1950) 90–91; Trollope: *Autobiography*, 126.

critics and later historians of Victorian culture would not fail to observe, much of what went for sound morals in its fiction was only decorum. To compound this confusion further, it was often a matter of envenomed controversy precisely what lessons a novelist wished to impart, just who were the targets of his irony or his derision. Fontane has the young Effi Briest fade and die not long after her husband has discovered her brief adultery and has shot her one-time lover to death in a duel. But it remains a question whether Fontane is here sermonizing against her momentary lapse from fidelity or against the conventions that induced her stiff and humorless husband to commit a tolerated murder in the name of his anachronistic aristocratic code. Nor is it easy to decide whether Gautier's *Mademoiselle de Maupin*—a novel to which I will turn presently—was a glittering tribute to beauty thrown in the face of low-minded, utilitarian bourgeois or the invention of a sly pornographer.

Such questions go to the heart of the issue that morality in fiction posed for the Victorian age. The social satirist was compelled to depict, crudely or suavely, at least some of the details of the immorality he was scourging. Hercules could not cleanse the Augean stables without wading in filth. This, of course, had been the lame and transparent excuse of traders in smutty merchandise before the courts. But while their insincerity was blatant enough, sometimes a fine sense of discrimination was required to distinguish the fearless critic of his corrupt time from the unprincipled profiteer in vicious tastes.

Many nineteenth-century novelists setting themselves up as moral preachers struck portions of their public as supremely distasteful and at times as downright indecent. One reader's satirist was another reader's seducer. Thackeray, precisely because he was so successful, evoked such contradictory judgments perhaps more than anyone else in the age. Mary Chesnut, not a notably squeamish reader, greatly admired Thackeray for the very texts that made so many among his audience exceedingly uneasy. She was, she recalled, "wild" for *Vanity Fair*, while others denounced its author as "a coarse, dull, sneering writer" who "stripped human nature bare, made it repulsive &c&c&c." She remembered "the most devoted, unremitting reader of fiction I ever knew—everything French or English that came to hand—would not tolerate Thackeray. 'He. is a very uncomfortable, disagreeable creature.'" But, Chesnut philosophized, "poor humanity morally stripped makes us shiver." That is what made Thackeray uncomfortable and disagreeable; he did not shrink from "laying bare the seamy side—going behind the pretty curtain of propriety we hold up." But even Mary Chesnut's tolerance for sexual

affairs in print had its limits: "Read a book," she noted, "utterly abominable, there is no gainsaying that—Balzac's *Cousine Bette*."[22]

The struggle between the aesthetic and the ethical domains was, in the
nineteenth century, nothing if not complicated, though some professed
to find it simple. Saint-Marc Girardin, an influential lecturer on literature
at the Sorbonne and no less influential as a publicist and politician, flatly
identified moral goodness with literary greatness, commended the virtues
of chastity and domestic happiness, and damned the fiction of his time as
the supreme corrupter of its susceptible audiences. Girardin denounced
the contemporary novel as a major cause of misery and suicide. Some
decades later, Leo Tolstoy polemicized against the pessimistic teachings
and the sexual preoccupations of modern literature and called for an art
that would be didactic, comprehensible to everyone, as elevated as religion. While literary pundits and prophets like John Ruskin and Matthew
Arnold could be quoted on all sides in this controversy, their idealization
of literature permitted their pronouncements to be enlisted by the unre-
pentant moralists who wanted fictions to dramatize the triumph of good
and the defeat of evil—and in decent language.[23]

While there was no perfect correspondence between attitudes toward
the moral mission of literature and toward its treatment of love, those
who called for aesthetic autonomy easily translated their demands into a
plea for frankness about sensual life and for freedom from the inhibiting
blue pencil of ethical and religious censors. With equal logic, the guardians
of nineteenth-century bourgeois morality, whether prosecuting attorneys,
owners of lending libraries, or activists in societies for the suppression of
vice, tended to equate what they thought the social obligation of the
writer with an insistence on his restraint in amorous matters and his
enforcement of moral lessons. Thomas Hardy, more explicit about physical appetites than most novelists in the later days of Victoria, was only
the most conspicuous sufferer at the heavy hand of easily offended
readers and desperately prudent editors. What Henry James "roughly
(and we trust without offense)" called "the sexual point of view," was
at the mercy of this alliance.[24] In a late story, "John Delavoy," James
immortalized one of the leading villains, to his mind, in this conspiracy

22. January 21, 1864, March 12, 1865, February 13, 1862, *Mary Chesnut's Civil War*,
546, 762, 288.
23. I have heavily leaned, in this paragraph, on René Wellek, *A History of Modern
Criticism, 1750–1950*, 4 vols. so far (1955–   ), III, 15–19; IV, 155–80.
24. "Eliot's 'Middlemarch'" (1873), *The Future of the Novel*, 85. For Thomas
Hardy, see *Education of the Senses*, 412–13.

against candor, by inventing the editor of *The Cynosure*, a periodical
enjoying a massive readership. James makes that editor into the kind of
literary arbiter who cares only about circulation, and who would do
nothing to assist a Flaubert or Zola, Ibsen or Hardy, and let them fall
victims to harassment, slander, and legal persecution.

While James sets this story in London, the notoriously tender English
conscience had no monopoly on interfering with the liberal and imaginative treatment of sexuality. Germany, France, the United States, the
Scandinavian countries all had their *Cynosure* which shielded their loyal
subscribers from any whiff of grossness. James's narrator, a critic who
has sent an appreciation of the novelist John Delavoy to the *Cynosure*,
finds that its editors keeps delaying its appearance after praising it effu-
sively. Delavoy has recently died, and his sister, who has made a cult of
his memory and is steeped in his work, judges the narrator's essay to be
accurate, indeed impressive. But the editor finds it "indecent" and indelicate and finally drops all pretense: "You're not writing in *The
Cynosure* about the relation of the sexes. With those relations, with the
question of sex in any degree, I should suppose you would already have
seen that we have nothing whatever to do. If you want to know what
our public won't stand, there you have it." And he estimates in the many
thousands the subscribers he would lose if he printed the essay.[25]

As this and many other passages in Henry James's fiction suggest—for
he repeatedly returned to the fate of the serious writer in a vulgar and
repressive age—the antagonists did not engage on all fronts. Differences
in moral demands at least partly reflected differences in markets. Those
enormous, ever growing masses of readers who swallowed the serialized
entertainments in the *Gartenlaube* and family journals everywhere did
not object to the kind of censorship that *The Cynosure* imposed on
itself. They wanted the transgressions in love that reached tragic stature
in *Anna Karenina* or *Effi Briest* reduced to predictable simplicities and
reassuring lessons. Podsnap, that egregious hypocrite who deprecated
anything that might bring a blush to the cheek of the young person was,
to be sure, of Dickens's making, but Dickens did not need to strain his
imagination to invent him: the character had only too many counterparts
in real life. Gathering the family around the hearth or in the arbor on
fine evenings to have a reading of the latest installment was a very widespread middle-class custom across Europe and the United States. These
family audiences nearly always included growing daughters, that most

25. "John Delavoy" (1898), *The Complete Tales of Henry James*, ed. Leon Edel,
12 vols. (1962–1964), IX, *1892–1898*, 419, 420, 424.

fragile of beings, the slowest ships in the convoy of familial instruction to which all others must defer.

That is why Podsnappery could flourish. In 1887, the Norwegian-born writer Hjalmar Boyesen warned that the unwillingness of family periodicals to print anything unfit to be read to the family was threatening to ruin fiction in America. Even Trollope—who took pleasure, we remember, in leaving his audiences purer than they were—fell afoul of this cozy obstacle course: he recalled an English divine troubled by the way he had the heroine of *Can You Forgive Her?* exposed to sexual temptation. "It had been one of the innocent joys of his life, said the clergyman, to have my novels read to him by his daughters. But now I was writing a book which caused him to bid them close it!"[26] Trollope the amateur preacher caught up short by a professional for not sermonizing enough—and so the confusion continued.

One of the most authoritative middle-class voices betraying these uncertainties through reversals of course and unresolved inconsistencies was that extraordinarily successful English weekly, *The Saturday Review of Politics, Literature, Science, and Art*, launched in 1855, and edited by John Douglas Cook, irascible, demanding, a superb manager of men. The *Saturday Review* aimed not to be "bound to any party, and to be the mouthpiece of the middle moderate opinions of thoughtful and educated society."[27] To the end of Cook's reign, cut short by his death in 1868, the *Saturday Review* lived up to this program, speaking for moderate opinions, though often in immoderate tones. Its magisterial pronouncements, moral austerity, and intemperate reviews soon became its signature; its eviscerations of mediocre novels were so pitiless that readers wondered whether the *Saturday Review* did not select its pathetic targets just to exhibit its talent for literary assassination.

Cook assembled a troop of gifted publicists—Fitzjames Stephen, Henry Sumner Maine, George Henry Lewes, Philip G. Hamerton, Mark Pattison, Walter Bagehot. It was a brilliant and individualistic team, but Cook's policy of anonymity and skillful assignment of topics gave the *Saturday Review* an air of being written by a single person. For years it managed to present a united front in nearly all the domains that came under its stern observant eye: politics, foreign and domestic; science, aflame with

26. Boyesen: Henry Nash Smith, *Democracy and the Novel: Popular Resistance to Classic American Writers* (1978), 105, 186; Trollope: *Autobiography*, 157.

27. This was the formulation of its principal owner, the cultivated and opinionated Anglo-Catholic A. J. Beresford Hope. Merle Mowbray Bevington, *The Saturday Review, 1855–1868: Representative Educated Opinion in Victorian England* (1941), 16.

controversy in these days of Darwin; art, bursting with life in London and the main provincial towns; murder, to which it devoted extensive columns of legal and ethical reflection. Significantly, it was in literature that its uncertainty and anxiety emerged. The critics writing for the *Saturday Review* were not insensitive to purely aesthetic qualities, but the doctrine of art for art's sake worried them as a seductive invitation to moral laxity.

The intellectual home of the *Saturday Review* was the privileged and influential segment of the English middle classes that had enjoyed a classical education: a civilized minority interested in the latest developments in German universities and fascinated by theological disputations as much as by scientific discoveries; a minority that thought itself above bigotry though not above patriotism, did not need passages from the French translated, supported some political innovations yet preferred to deride nearly all of them as instances of foolish, impractical philanthropy, of democratic "Benevolism." In its indefatigable attacks on the modern woman, the *Saturday Review* did not disdain cheap jokes, ponderous sarcasms, and specious reasoning, all reflections of the anxieties hounding the substantial bourgeois of the day. It was no accident that it should be the *Saturday Review* that gave house room, in 1868, to Mrs. Linton's series of heavyhanded denunciations of "the girl of the period."

The educated bourgeoisie could feel safe with the *Saturday Review*. The two were in tune because they shared a profoundly skeptical view of human nature, which linked them to the anti-vice crusade, or at least made them find its panic-stricken campaigns appear comprehensible. It is interesting how earnestly those hunting out obscene publications invoked their duty to the rising generation: King George III's proclamation of 1787 had already announced the need to protect "the young and unwary"; after mid-nineteenth century, Lord Campbell and Anthony Comstock and René Bérenger appointed themselves protectors of the young, to make Great Britain, the United States, and France safe for morality. So did their allies everywhere. Their case seemed eminently reasonable: the young, not yet hardened by their encounters with harsh reality, were impressionable and hence susceptible to seducers. But this appeal drew on deeper sources than this; it assumed a fund of wickedness concealed in every child and adolescent, just waiting to be tapped. For it seemed to the moral school of the *Saturday Review* that in the contest between corruption and innocence, corruption almost invariably prevailed. In fact, this appeared true of everyone, young or not. Reviewing a cheerful novel by Mrs. Marsh, *The Rose of Ashurst*, the reviewer questioned her supposition that "all men are born good" and "all continue so for the rest

f their days, with very few exceptions"; after all, if she were right, "the
nly wonder is, that so many people are unhappy in the world." The
assions are "violent" and lie "fearfully near to heroic virtues." Again,
ommenting on the notorious trial of Madeleine Smith, tried for poisoning
er lover—the verdict came down as "Not Proven"—the *Saturday Re-
iew* argued that "the sexual passion" must "enter into the wildest forms
f crime" as long as "human nature is simply human."[28] It was sexual
assion, of course, that lascivious literature aroused and propelled into
ction.

This was the august vantage point from which the *Saturday Review*
urveyed the fiction of its day. But its incompatible ideals sent off its
ontributors into several directions at once. On the one hand, they took
are to distance themselves from what they liked to call "prudishness,"
nd to frown at the bloodlessness of English fiction. This criticism was not
riginal with the *Saturday Review*. At least half a dozen years before, in
851, an anonymous reviewer in *Fraser's Magazine*, brooding on English
ovels, had admitted, "Whatever sins against taste or morality may be
hargeable upon French novels, it cannot be denied that they possess in a
igh degree the power of fascinating the attention." Their style may be
reposterous and their characters absurd, they may be "extravagant, in-
lated, and demoralizing—but they are never dull." Readers of Balzac or
Alphonse Carr, George Sand or Sophie Gay will never drop their novels
'in a fit of *ennui*." To be sure, these French fictions are not healthy. Cer-
ainly, "if we are to make a choice between prosy decent books, and
vicious books that are written with sprightliness and skill, we are, of
:ourse, bound to prefer the former. There is no room or excuse for
hesitation." To deny room for hesitation so emphatically was to acknowledge its pressure. "But we cannot help regretting, at the same time, that
our English novelists, who, for the most part, write unexceptionable
morality, should not be able to make it a little more amusing. It is a pity
that morality should be rendered so excessively stupid on this side of the
Channel"—a cry from the heart of the decent, but bored, English reader
of novels. To judge from later outbursts, that cry was never stilled. As
late as the 1880s, Alexander Shand criticized the cheap popular novels that
untalented women writers were throwing onto the market for their
dullness—the price, he thought, of innocence: "The books may be pure,
but they are commonplace."[29] These writers would have been perfectly
at home in the *Saturday Review*.

28. "The Rose of Ashurst," *Saturday Review*, III (May 9, 1857), 437.
29. Anonymous: "English Novels," *Fraser's Magazine for Town and Country*, XX
(July-December 1851), 375; Shand: *Half a Century*, 241-42.

Throughout the decades, that review conducted comparative surveys o
its own, and the results were disheartening. The French were, and re
mained, a looming presence on the horizon of English literature; the
could be condemned but not ignored. While the English novel wa
blanketing its culture with an enervating pall, the French novel ha
corroded France's moral fiber. Nothing in fact gave the *Saturday Reviev*
greater pleasure, and placed it more securely within its reader's circl
of taste and feelings, than its derisive reviews of French novels and play
as schools for adultery, vice, and degradation—reviews always presentec
with a show of indignation but no show of astonishment. Again and agair
they would wonder out loud whether the French reading public recog
nized itself in such lurid tales and, if not, why it tolerated such slanders

Yet the French novel was not a wholly reliable scapegoat. On occasion
the *Saturday Review* would lapse into relativism: France and England are
after all, different societies and each may have exaggerated some partic
ular national traits in its literature. To write off France, one of the grea
nations in history—almost as great as England—as irredeemably vicious
is a libel. When, in 1857, Gustave Masson, a Frenchman long resident
and teaching in England, published an intemperate pamphlet attacking
recent French literature as a "moral wilderness" occupied by nothing
but "a dreary atheistic materialism," the *Saturday Review*, though with a
polite bow to Masson's scholarship, generously demurred. "It is true that
many French writers deserve the severest reprobation that can be applied
to them." Yet, surely, literary and cultural realities are more complicated
than this. "We cannot think, and do not believe, that France is utterly
corrupt and degraded; and it annoys us to see how frequently Frenchmen
of considerable talent and knowledge use language which implies that it
is." It was all a matter, fundamentally, of differing national styles. "We
firmly believe that the principal difference between the novelists of the
two countries is, that in France they address the most plain-spoken, and
in England the most reserved, of modern nations,"[30] a lame, if kindly,
conclusion, quite unwarranted by the savage reviews of French fiction
that had gone before.

While the *Saturday Review* was indecisive as to just how much impurity one should allow the writer of fiction, there were some authors
it judged to be plainly beyond the pale of decency. When Walt Whitman's *Leaves of Grass* came in for review, the magazine had some splendid
sport with it. It began by quoting, in full and with undisguised amusement,

30. "Light Literature in France," *Saturday Review*, IV (September 5, 1857), 219–20.

Ralph Waldo Emerson's delighted letter of acknowledgment to Whitman and other panegyrics the publisher had conveniently pasted into the volume. It then printed extensive excerpts from the poems only to conclude, bluntly: "After poetry like this, and criticism like this, it seems strange that we cannot recommend the book to our readers' perusal. But the truth is, that after every five or six pages of matter such as we have quoted, Mr. Whitman becomes exceedingly intelligible, but exceedingly obscene. If the *Leaves of Grass* should come into anybody's possession, our advice is to throw them instantly behind the fire."[31]

The reviewer's recommended mode of disposal is no less instructive than his judgment of Whitman's verses. He wants private action, not public intervention. Here, as often, the *Saturday Review* speaks in its liberal, sociological voice: laws do not change hearts and minds; they do not manufacture decency. "The loud indignation" of the English public against a filthy book "is our most effectual censor." The principle was clear: "We cannot suppress immorality by Acts of Parliament or police regulations." Consistent with this position, the *Saturday Review* had some harsh words for Lord Campbell, author of the Obscene Publications Act of 1857. Innocent that he was, he seemed just to have discovered pornography. There are indecent publications, just as there is wife-beating, but "we regret to say that, judging from the facts, the law appears utterly incapable of dealing with them."[32]

This seems straightforward enough. But once the Obscene Publications Act had become law, the *Saturday Review* complicated its stance. Continuing to argue that the laws act on the public only "by a very circuitous route," and that the "real deterring force" from immorality "is not fear, but conscience," it was ready, at the same time, to point out evasions of the Act to the authorities that they might deal severely with merchants in smut: "Without metaphor we should say, if one of the filthy brutes in question makes himself obnoxious, burn his stock, fine him, imprison him—if the public sentiment allows of it, flog him soundly —but avoid making laws which, whilst intended to repress his activity, practically tend only to divert it unto less conspicuous, but more injurious channels."[33] The issue had suddenly become, not law versus opinion, but effectual versus ineffectual law. A charitable way of describing this chaos of attitudes is to call it moderation or flexibility.

31. "Leaves of Grass," ibid., IX (March 15, 1856), 393–94.
32. "Wife-beating," ibid., III (May 16, 1857), 447.
33. "Holywell-Street Revived," ibid., VI (August 21, 1858), 180.

Another, probably deeper one, is visible confusion issuing from invisible conflict.

One classic instance of this conflict is the review of *Madame Bovary* in July 1857, certainly the work of Fitzjames Stephen who was practically never embarrassed for a firm opinion. Few texts document more eloquently than this essay nineteenth-century bourgeois uncertainty about erotic expression, the desperate yearning both for knowledge and for ignorance. Stephen begins with a flourish: "It was not without considerable hesitation that we determined to review *Madame Bovary*." This may be a rhetorical convention, but formula or confession, it admirably distills the reviewer's state of mind. Men have many good conscious reasons for hesitations, but since the *Saturday Review* reviewed French novels extensively and often, Stephen's reluctance declares his discomfort with a novel of undoubted power which he finds, at the same time, "offensive according to our views." It is "not a work," Stephen thought, "which we can recommend to any man, far less any woman, to read." Yet Flaubert's sheer stylistic bravura imposed itself to extract some grudging tributes: Flaubert describes the Bovarys' night at the marquis's party "with great spirit"; the scene bears "the mark of a good deal of patient and careful observation." So does Flaubert's account of "an agricultural show," that ominous prelude to Emma Bovary's first adultery; the amorous commonplaces uttered by Emma's future lover, Rodolphe, form an ironic counterpoint to the banalities issuing from the speakers' stand, but Fitzjames Stephen, in obtuseness or embarrassment, trivializes this brilliantly staged set piece as an instance of "several descriptions of local scenes." Yet for all these bright spots of innocence, Stephen finds *Madame Bovary* a cesspool of corruption, rotten and repellent. "There are probably half a dozen scenes in it which no English author of reputation would venture to insert in any of his publications." Worse, the novel as a whole is appalling: "Not merely the facts and the language, but the whole framework and tendency of the story, are symptoms of the most fatal kind." True, while "the character of Madame Bovary herself is one of the most essentially disgusting that we ever happened to meet with," the terrible punishment that the author metes out to her at the end, her hideous suicide, reads like an earnest warning against sin. Indeed that is perhaps the worst thing about *Madame Bovary*: Flaubert's "obvious intention" to "write a rather moral book." While this is not the only misperception that Fitzjames Stephen allowed himself, it is the most instructive. For if there is one thing that should have been obvious from Flaubert's text, it is that he did not intend his first novel to be a tract.

Stephen's buried conflict emerges all the more vividly in the gratuitous final paragraph in which he ruminates on the lessons of this novel for thoughtful English readers. Certainly English "light literature is pure enough," written "upon the principle that it is never to contain anything which a modest man might not, with satisfaction to himself, read aloud to a young lady." While, on Stephen's showing, this kind of self-censorship must be infinitely preferable to Flaubert's wallowing in adulterous affairs, he cannot help wondering: "Surely it is very questionable whether it is desirable that no novels should be written except those which are fit for young ladies to read." After all, such restrictions do not hold true for any other literature. "Theology, history, philosophy, morality, law, and physical science are all studied at the reader's peril," and he who professes to be offended by "indecent passages" in Herodotus's history or in Cook's Voyages, is simply "prudish." Stephen is moved to ask, provocatively, "Are works of the imagination, then, such mere toys that they ought always to be calculated for girlish ignorance?" It was a rhetorical question. "If Shakespeare had never written a line which women in the present day could not read, he would never have been the greatest of poets. If we had only expurgated copies of the classics, we should have a most inadequate conception of Greece and Rome." English authors seem to think "that the highest function of a poet is the amusement of children; but we are by no means prepared to say"—and here Stephen rears back for a characteristic *Saturday Review* epigram—"that, in literature, emasculation produces purity." Once again, Stephen reviews the painful evidence: most English writers are pure, but in their determined vacuous decency they flee the appalling but undeniable realities of the streets or the court rooms. This produces a final disturbing thought: "Whether a light literature entirely based upon love, and absolutely and systematically silent as to one most important side of it, may not have some tendency to stimulate passions to which it is far too proper ever to allude." But the *Saturday Review* will not get entangled with such treacherous matters. Perhaps erotic thoughts can arise from the most refined prose. That "is a question which is too wide for our limits on the present occasion."[34]

And there Stephen just about leaves it, but his discomfort leaps from the page. Had Stephen acknowledged to his readers, and to himself, that Flaubert had no objections to arousing his readers with his precise and suggestive notations of Emma's sensuality but still wanted to produce the most ambitious of literary masterpieces, his discomfort would have

34. "Madame Bovary," ibid., IV (July 11, 1857), 56–57.

been greater still. One wonders how he, or his colleagues on the *Saturday Review*, would have voted if they had been judges in the trial for obscenity to which *Madame Bovary* was subjected in France in 1857.

There was something to these troubled concerns. Fiction, after all, did more than invent or register lives and loves; it shaped both. Certainly reading, like writing, is an act of many dimensions. If making a novel is an intricate compromise between the author's instinctual and defensive needs, his craving for applause and his lust for experiment, reading it may gratify a desire for information about life, for relief from reality, for moments of erotic excitement, or for delight in wit and form. Author and reader reverberate to the same human passions and harbor the same human needs, but their particular experiences often differ markedly. A writer may not share the passions he excites. Much of the time, reading is playful regression—regression as it awakens and enlists memories, playful because the reader well knows, even as he is absorbed in his story, that it is not real somehow and that he can withdraw from its spell. But as long as the magic works, a fiction recalls (or poignantly invents) prized childhood recollections. The reader lives again among oedipal encounters and still earlier intimacies, experiencing, for blissful moments, the illusion of a happiness he may never have known. The work of reading calls upon all the principal institutions of the mind: it teases the id by counterfeiting instinctual satisfactions, flatters the ego with formal beauties, soothes the superego in enlisting the reader in an invisible moral community where the wicked and the innocent receive their due or (which should satisfy the most persecuting of consciences) where suffering comes to all as man's lot. The pleasures that reading gives stem from its being, in the psychoanalytic sense of the term, an economic activity: it rehearses, at a smaller expenditure of energy than action in reality would require, splendid adventures and forbidden pleasures, and all with little risk to the consumer.

Those anxious about novels in the nineteenth century, less representative than noisy but influential in part because they *were* so noisy, regarded the work of fiction in a more ominous light. Much of the self-conscious purity to which so many nineteenth-century novelists laid ostentatious claim was a deliberate, sometimes rather hysterical defense against the charge that the novel, any novel, served only to seduce the innocent and to confirm the wicked in his ways. To censors like Anthony Comstock and René Bérenger, two among the most active professional prudes of the late bourgeois century anywhere, the case allowed of no doubt whatever: fiction was an enticing guide to carnal knowledge and, with that, to romantic ruin. The prim and servile cleric Mr. Collins, in Jane Austen's *Pride and Prejudice*, who protests that he never reads novels, had much company in his time and many worried successors. They and their kind were sure that, had Emma Bovary not fed her parched imagination with novels, she would have become and remained a dutiful, if rather bored, wife. And they were afraid there were only too many potential Emma Bovarys in real life. Notoriously uneasy about their own hidden impulses, they could only conjecture that suggestive fiction must invite imitation—and most fiction struck them as suggestive. Their anxieties prevented them from seeing that reading might serve as a substitute for erotic gratification, might actually inhibit action by making it redundant. A work of fiction deserves to be called a work—an *oeuvre* or a *Werk*—not merely because it extracts a quantity of labor from the writer but also because it works in its readers. Yet the diversity of these workings was, until the advent of psychoanalysis, a closed book to the nervous protectors of bourgeois morality. Most were convinced that writers were, as the *Saturday Review* had put it firmly at mid-century, "the most influential of all teachers."[35]

We may take the measure and persistence of this anxiety by a glimpse at Louis Proal's substantial treatise, *Le crime et le suicide passionels*, published in 1900 and almost immediately translated into English. Proal, a presiding judge at the court of appeals at Riom, a criminologist, amateur statistician and agreeable, if rather emphatic writer, solemnly warned that "Love, which occupies so considerable a place in Life and Literature, claims ever more and more importance in the Annals of Crime and the Statistics of Suicide." He piles count after count of his indictment against modern love in exhaustive chapters on suicide, seduction, desertion, and adultery to buttress his diagnosis of their causes and proffer his hints for their amelioration. Crimes of passion, as he sees them, are a contemporary epidemic brought on by lenient juries, addiction to alcohol, precocity among the young, maternal indulgence, and, most portentously, by the literature of the day—by pornography, the trash that lending libraries distribute, the modern theatre, and the novel of passion. Proal never questioned the proposition that reading invites action; it never leads to catharsis. Hence he worried over the "immoderate reading of Novels depicting Love (for the delineation of Love awakens the corresponding feeling.)" Goethe had believed that the young can read without risk, but Goethe was wrong. "Parents cannot be too anxious as to the influence books have over their children." Perhaps mature readers "can defend

35. "Mr. Dickens as a Politician," *The Saturday Review*, III (January 3, 1857), 8.

themselves" against "literary sophistries and impure pictures." But "young
people, boys and girls, cannot. Vicious doctrines vitiate their mind, fou
pictures befoul their imagination, depraved books deprave their character."[36]

Proal's leading witnesses were criminals who had confessed, in the
dock or a suicide note, that they had been led astray by novels from
Werther on. Bad books liberate aggression; they clear the way to murder
and suicide. But, worse than that, they stimulate the libido. Witness
Mademoiselle Lemoine, who acquired national notoriety in the French
courts in 1859. She "became her coachman's mistress and subsequently
with her mother's assistance killed the child resulting from the illicit
connection"; beyond question she had been tempted into her horrifying
course by George Sand's fiction, "in which she found great ladies loving
inferiors, and wished to imitate them." It was certainly true that Angelina
Lemoine was acting out fantasies she had nourished during her reading;
at her trial she referred to her pregnancy as "the only way to complete
my novel"—the novel that she was living. No wonder Proal did not
think it an accident that seducers often lent "novels to girls they are
trying to lead astray," and cites in evidence for this vicious, almost infallible practice, Bourget's novel *Le Disciple*.[37] The novel, as it were,
condemned itself out of its own mouth.

There was need, Proal noted, to make distinctions. Some novels are
perfectly safe for married women but prove "perilous for young girls,
because they serve to overstimulate their romantic sentimentality." Once
again he called on a novel to make his case for him, the inescapable
Madame Bovary, which shows the young Emma Rouault led into temptation by such books as Bernardin de Saint-Pierre's *Paul et Virginie*. Such
an idyll might be more dangerous for a girl "than a modern naturalistic
novel." Girls in general, being more sentimental than boys, were in Proal's
judgment most susceptible to this fodder. Yet boys, too, were in danger:

36. Louis Proal, *Passion and Criminality in France: A Legal and Literary Study*
(1900; tr. A. R. Allison, 1901), v, 306–307.
37. Ibid., 421, 423. For Lemoine, see Mary S. Hartman, *Victorian Murderesses: A
True History of Thirteen Respectable French and English Women Accused of
Unspeakable Crimes* (1977), esp. 63, 277. In the 1920s, Jimmy Walker, mayor of
New York, was heard to say that no girl was ever seduced by a book, and the
evidence for the seductive power of fiction is indeed limited and scattered. One
instance that supports the censors' case comes from Theodore Dreiser's diary: he
records that "Lill" comes to visit; "I let her look at new dictionary of venery which
just came. She gets excited. Wants to copulate. We do, in back room. Lill leaves. I
go to bank, 2:45." June 6, 1917. Theodore Dreiser, *American Diaries, 1902–1926*, ed.
Thomas P. Riggio (1982), 165.

How powerful," he exclaims, "is the impulse to imitation found among
'oung men and women, particularly in France."[38] Had he been willing
o look beyond his national frontiers, he could have added, among others,
'ushkin's *Eugene Onegin*, whose innocent and sheltered heroine,
Tatyana, seduces herself into a near-fatal infatuation by swallowing
Rousseau's *La nouvelle Héloïse*, Goethe's *Werther*, and similar fare.

Some novelists, like George Sand, profess to believe that passion
'purifies Mankind," but, Proal argued, they are as far off the mark as
Goethe. The only passions that purify are patriotism, humanitarianism,
ity for the unfortunate, and respect for one's superiors. Probably even
more pernicious than Sand's misguided notions were the "Naturalistic
heories" of love advanced by Stendhal, Michelet, and Schopenhauer, to
ay nothing of romanticism, which, "notwithstanding all its lyrical aspira-
ions," only "ends by coming to the same conclusions as Naturalism. It
oo, with pathetic accents, glozing over a coarse sensuality, appeals to the
right of love, and even the *right of adultery*." It even enlists, as Sainte-
Beuve was driven to admit in his novel, *Volupté*, "the language of mystic
piety to express the sentiments of profane love." The Naturalists preach
he doctrine of "Fatalism," which holds that one's illicit passions are one's
fate and not one's fault, that love affairs or adultery are physiological
accidents, nothing more.[39]

After such panic-stricken analysis Proal's reform program, with which
he concludes his treatise, practically wrote itself. It calls for the reimposi-
tion of legal and social controls over the unruly passions that an obtuse
modern state has permitted to run wild. Proal calls for repeal of the
recent legislation leaving "drinking shops" unregulated, guaranteeing a
free press, and reestablishing divorce. "Poor humanity," Proal reminds
his readers in the last paragraph, is, after all, "largely composed of weak
and feeble creatures, slaves of mere passion and instinct." Uncontrolled
and unsupervised, it will "rapidly sink back toward sheer animality, if
Government, Legislation, Literature and Religion did not set before its
eyes an ideal of Justice and Morality, and help it on the upward path
towards the attainment of this ideal."[40] Proal's hysterical diagnoses and
repressive proposals found many readers to nod in agreement: it was not
yet the age of Freud. The arguments he proffers so earnestly and rehearses so relentlessly aptly sum up pervasive concerns. They were
symptoms of large anxieties that had manifested themselves throughout

38. Proal, *Passion and Criminality in France*, 425, 427–28.
39. Ibid., 438–40, 446.
40. Ibid., 679.

the nineteenth century in the crusades against masturbation, syphilis, contraception, and general immorality. Proal saw his world collapsing around him; his program of reform was a last effort to shore up what could still be saved. As we shall see, there were, by 1900, other ways of thinking about the work of fiction, but his warnings were, though a little extravagant and rather dogmatic, not yet eccentric for his age and his class.

3. Beyond Good and Evil

The conflicts disconcerting so self-assured a tribunal as the *Saturday Review* and so nervous a judge as Louis Proal had not begun with the moralistic campaigns of mid-century. They had an earlier source in the psychological novel, the subtle and persistent exploration of the protagonist's mind, which goes back at least to Benjamin Constant's *Adolphe* of 1816. These novels, which became something of a fashion in the nineteenth century, generally took the form of recollections recorded by articulate and unfortunate lovers—all naturally endowed with superb memories. In the very age of privacy, which raised to unprecedented heights the wall between what people discussed and what they felt, heroes and heroines grew positively garrulous under their authors' hands.[41] These imaginary men and women, supremely sensitive and susceptible to every whiff of amorous perfume, freely dwelt on passions that ordinary readers scarcely dared to admit to themselves. Their unbuttoned erotic revelations made the irrational fantasies and emotions of lovers the common coin of literature. Often—witness Sainte Beuve's *Volupté* of 1834, which draws heavily on his love affair with Victor Hugo's wife— the confessional mode produced novels of rather doubtful literary merits. But that scarcely inhibited their popularity.

The gradual proliferation of such novels signalizes, throughout the century, the existence of a vocal minority among writers, critics, and readers averse to moral uplift, at least of the conventional brand, and uneasy with the evasive treatment of erotic themes. By Victoria's last decades, this minority had grown confident and influential enough to do open combat with the didactic or prudent entertainers who had fairly dominated the first half of the century. The realists and their raucous successors, the naturalists, secured new territory for the objective and relatively uninhibited reporting on love and its roots in sensuality. In the

41. I intend to devote much of volume five in this series, tentatively entitled "Problematic Selves," to this increasing "psychologizing" of thought.

iid-1870s, in *Daniel Deronda*, George Eliot could still note: "it has long
een understood that the proprieties of literature are not those of prac-
cal life."[42] But by then, giving way to their curiosity though for the
1ost part still proceeding delicately, novelists had begun to tiptoe toward
he bedroom and to resist the pressure for dealing out poetic justice to
he characters they had imagined.

Realistic novelists aspired to more than the penetrating portrayal of
he social world; they sought at the same time to discover the psychologi-
al forces that pushed their animated puppets around the stage of life.
Theirs was an age that welcomed mechanistic theories of motivation and
he application of biological laws to public and private conduct, including
he urges and the pursuit of love. Zola's justly maligned determinism, an
vil-tasting compound of calamitous heredity and malign environment,
vas only an extreme version of common convictions borrowed from the
logmatic, insecure, and at times fantastic social sciences of the day.
ubtler hands refined these rather primitive efforts to subject fictional
characters to the scientific analysis of human nature, and launched discriminating investigations of the intricate workings, and clashes, of erotic
mpulses and cultural constraints. The psychological novel, whether
ervently confessional or coolly objective in tone, whether an exercise in
vistfulness or a diagram of amorous skirmishes, developed unexpected
ubtleties looking beyond the nineteenth century and issuing in Henry
James's brilliant closet dramas, Marcel Proust's brooding and exhaustive
philosophizing, James Joyce's experimental mimesis of kaleidoscopic
nental meanderings. These writers perfected literary techniques that
could do love the justice it deserved.

By their very nature, such maps to the travail of lovers from *Adolphe*
o *Ulysses* invited indifference to moral judgments. They made it difficult
o inject the author's omniscient and sententious voice. Rather they treated
ove as an experience beyond good and evil, not a policy or a sin but an
nfection, a contagion that the novelist can only record but neither praise
nor condemn. One does not argue with obsessions.

It is only natural that these novels should generally be cast in the first
person, though their authors liked to establish some distance from their
inventions by claiming to have been handed the manuscript by a stranger
or to have heard the tale from a friend in an expansive mood. This literary
device strictly circumscribed the narrator's horizon but at the same time,
and for that very reason, concentrated the reader's attention on the lover
and his fate. Lovers, we know, create exclusive small worlds that they

42. *Daniel Deronda* (1876; ed. Barbara Hardy, 1967), 288 [ch. 22].

alone inhabit; having invested most of their libido in the beloved, the
have little left over for others, let alone for public interests. The firs
person confession exemplifies this erotic isolationism.

In 1863, Eugène Fromentin attained a certain modest perfection in th
self-referential and self-lacerating genre with his only novel, *Dominiqu*
It remains the most rewarding fictional confession of the age, for it w:
once a famous novel and, well into the twentieth century, a rich subjec
for study. More insistently than other fictions of its kind, *Dominiqu*
documents the proposition that love feeds on memory, may, in fact, b
one of its forms. It does so in more ways than one: the middle-age
narrator recalls a love of his youth, still poignant but draped in the mis
of healing absence; Fromentin, himself middle-aged, drew the materi.
and, even more, the temper of his novel from a love affair that had con
sumed his youth and shaped his life. Fromentin's early passion, more tha
three years his senior and his childhood playmate—hence emotionall
always an "older woman" to him—had been called Jenny, and it wa
better than a convenient accident that this was his adored mother'
name as well. From the outset, Fromentin's love had been infected witl
recollections of infantile pleasures.

His *Dominique* does not replicate Fromentin's own experience at al
points, but its emotional accents—its muted tones, its charged encounters
its beautifully realized landscapes—cunningly convey the psychologica
significance of that experience for him. His Jenny had married, becom
his mistress for some time, and died young; Dominique's Madeleine als
marries someone else but then assumes the quixotic task of curing hi
infatuation by seeing him often, alone, under compromising circum
stances. The cure fails, as it must, largely because Madeleine, a loyal an
proper wife, loves Dominique in her turn. Her prescription is worse than
his disease and so the two part, poised near the abyss of adultery, neve
to meet again. But love survives, as memory.

Fromentin had undertaken to tell the story of his passion after Jenny
had died in 1844; fifteen years later, when he was nearly forty, a fashionable travel writer and a reputable Academic painter, he transformed hi:
passive suffering into the activity of making a novel. For Fromentin, hi:
nostalgic artistry with words was to heal the wounds of love. As Fromentin
told his friend George Sand, who was reading the manuscript for him and
scattering well-meant advice, he was writing to please himself, to "be
stirred once again by memories, to recapture my youth in the degree that
I grow away from it." The opening page of *Dominique* sets out his aim
even more accurately than this letter. Fromentin wanted not merely to
recapture memories but to overcome them. "I have found steadiness and

ranquility," the narrator says, alluding to his quiet life as an efficient
country squire complete with family and social obligations, "and that is
worth more than all hypotheses. I have reconciled myself to myself, which
s the greatest victory we can win over the impossible."[43] He insists that
the story he will so circumstantially tell and the wisdom he has so painfully acquired are by no means exceptional. The first has happened, and
the second applies, to many men. Resignation to duty and triumph over
memory are the best ways to the only kind of happiness that mortals have
a right to expect. Such insight has its moral dimension, but the gain—
like the essential energy of the novel—is psychological.

The slow retreat from conventional moralizing was not confined to
these internal analyses of one fictional lover's experiences. Even Thackeray,
always ready for a compromise with respectability but visibly chafing
under such constraints, at times shook off the requirement that schemers,
flirts, or adulterers be duly chastened at the end of a novel. In *Vanity
Fair*, while he awards the supreme prize, a loving and constant husband,
to Amelia—that whiny and obtuse heroine who gave goodness a bad
name—he took care to leave the wicked, irresistible Becky Sharp both
prosperous and unbowed. Other novelists soon followed Thackeray's
lead into unpleasantness.

To be sure, commonplace romantic fiction obeying the old sentimental prescriptions lost none of its appeal; what Grant Showerman
would call, in 1915, "just a nice story," remained the staple of best selling fiction. But serious novelists came to punish their creations less for
loving unwisely than for not loving at all: George Eliot did so with
Casaubon in *Middlemarch*, George Meredith with Sir Willoughby
Patterne in *The Egoist*, Theodor Fontane with the Baron von Instetten
in *Effi Briest*, Leo Tolstoy with Karenin in *Anna Karenina*, Thomas
Hardy with Jude Fawley and Sue Bridehead in *Jude the Obscure*. As the
great Brazilian critic and novelist, Machado de Assis, put it in his masterpiece, *Memórias Póstumas de Brás Cubas*, fiction was bidding fair to being
more than a pastime and less than a missionary activity—"mais do que
passa tempo e menos do que apostolado."[44]

This subversion of middle-class conventions began as a scandal and
ripened into a principle. Théophile Gautier's *Mademoiselle de Maupin*,
published during the self-satisfied early days of the July Monarchy,

43. Fromentin to George Sand, *Correspondance et fragments inédits*, ed. Pierre
Blanchon (Jacques-André Mérys) (1912), 139; *Dominique* (1863; ed. Daniel Leuwers,
1972), 3 [ch. 1].
44. (1880; ed. 1960), 116 [ch. 4]. (This novel is usually called *Epitaph of a Small
Winner* in American editions.)

paraded its offensiveness with a defiant fighting stance that later novelists
no longer needed. It was a calculated slap in the face of the bourgeoisie;
to enforce its aggressive point, Gautier armed the novel with a bellicose
preface in which he called respectability bad names and celebrated the
supremacy of beauty, by which he meant sensual enjoyment.

Gautier did not present himself as a mere sensualist. On the contrary,
he sternly—or, rather, gaily—assailed what he was pleased to call the
"great affectation of morality" which, he thought, was disgracing his
time and his culture—an affectation that would be ridiculous if it were
not so boring. "It is the fashion to be virtuous and Christian," he wrote;
people were now posing as St. Jerome the way they had once posed as
Don Juan. The only antidote is the untrammeled pursuit of erotic happiness. For Gautier, the supreme vice of the bourgeois world was its
unrelieved utilitarianism. "Nothing is truly beautiful unless it is useless,"
he argued; "everything that is useful is ugly, for it is the expression of
some need." Hence he praised the socialist projector Charles Fourier,
"the inventor of passionate attractions," as one of the few benefactors of
modern civilization; Fourier's idea of "using drives that one has so far
tried to curb" struck Gautier as nothing less than inspired.[45]

Faithfully carrying out his own program, Gautier tells the story of a
handsome and enterprising young woman intent on learning about life
by traveling dressed as a man: *Mademoiselle de Maupin* is, in its salacious
way, a *bildungsroman*. Gautier took the name of his heroine and significant details of her adventures from some well-known French anecdotes,
and borrowed heavily from Shakespeare's *As You Like It*, but these historical and literary echoes only make his sensuality all the more piquant.
Mademoiselle de Maupin's education culminates in her defloration described in luscious detail, and a few nocturnal hours in the arms of
Rosette, who has long adored Mademoiselle de Maupin in her masculine
guise. For, Gautier's heroine acts out the androgynous imagination: "My
fancy would be to have the two sexes in turn," to gratify her double
nature: "A man today, a woman tomorrow."[46]

Gautier's explicit, lovingly specific account of Mademoiselle de Maupin's initiation is essential to his polemic. This, he seems to be saying with
a sneer, is what bourgeois could never do and hardly even imagine.
D'Albert takes her hands, kisses each of her fingers in turn, "then very
delicately broke the ties of her dress, so that her bodice opened and the

45. *Mademoiselle de Maupin* (1835–36; ed. Geneviève van den Bogaert, 1966), 26–
27, 45, 50 [preface].
46. Ibid., 357 [ch. 15].

2

(1) Walter Bagehot, banker, economist, essayist, political thinker, wit, and touching lover. (2) Eliza Wilson Bagehot, no doubt a beauty in her own right, but somewhat idealized in this drawing done by her youngest sister Emilie.

(1) Dr. Otto Beneke, who spent his life in the Hamburg archives, and untold hours recording his love for "Mariettinola" Banks. (2) Moritz Retzsch, *The Chess Player*, etching. A once prominent German history and portrait painter, Retzsch (1779–1857) was a prolific illustrator. Goethe liked his illustrations for *Faust*; Heine called him a "master."

Emile-H. Meyer, untitled etching, serving as frontis
piece for Adolphe Retté, *Paradoxe sur l'Amour*
(1893). A fine specimen of the soft-core pornography
with a religious touch that was widely current in the
century.

Charles Kingsley, muscular Christian, novelist, author of children's books, inveterate polemicist against Roman Catholicism and "effeminate" Anglicanism.

Fanny Grenfell Kingsley in her ripe middle years.

I

(1) (2) (3) Charles Kingsley, drawings. Fanny Grenfell may have been somewhat troubled by these drawings, done by the man she loved, in which she
appears as a repentant, drably dressed Magdalen, or quite nude, either just
resting or exhausted from sexual intercourse. But she preserved them in her
journal.

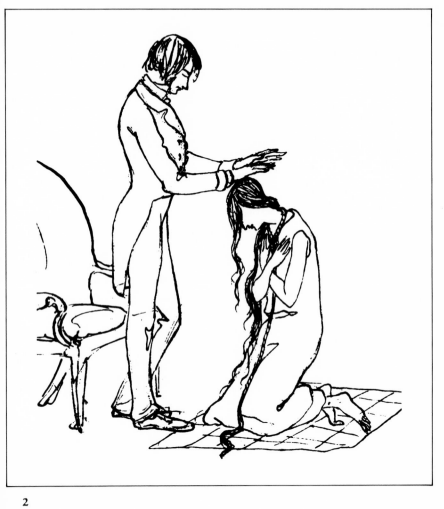

2

3

two white treasures appeared in all their splendor; on that breast gleaming and luminous as silver blossomed the two lovely roses of paradise. He gently squeezed the vermilion tips with his lips and then, in the same way, ran over them, all around." Inexperienced but unembarrassed and aroused, Mademoiselle de Maupin passionately responds to these caresses. D'Albert undresses her and she, cold as she is, poses for him in all her dazzling naked beauty until the two fall into bed for their consummatory embraces: "They no longer separated their kisses," and her 'fragrant lips made just one mouth with d'Albert's;—their chests swelled, their eyes were half closed;—their arms, limp with voluptuousness, no longer had the strength to squeeze the other's body.—The divine moment approached:—a last obstacle was overcome, a supreme spasm convulsively shook the two lovers," and the inquisitive traveler now, finally, had clarity on that "obscure point" which had made her so uneasy before. "However, since a single lesson, no matter how intelligent, cannot suffice, d'Albert gave her a second, then a third"—and here Gautier stops counting, professing respect for his readers' sensibilities and hinting that a complete count would only awaken their envy. Finally, gently kissing her sleeping lover for the last time, Mademoiselle de Maupin leaves him and goes to Rosette's room where she spends the night— though, the narrator blandly confesses, try as he did, he never discovered what she did there.[47]

Obviously, Gautier expected his readers to supply the missing erotic details, all the more suggestive for being unexpressed. Predictably, the slashing critical paganism of *Mademoiselle de Maupin* won resounding approval among the avant garde. Victor Hugo admired the novel, as did Balzac. Baudelaire, going to the essence of Gautier's message, thought it "a hymn to beauty"; his admirers called it original, audacious, vigorous, and magnificent, and saluted it as a pioneering foray in the noble cause of literature for literature's sake. Just as predictably, the respectable protested against its eroticism; some pronounced the novel charming but eccentric, imaginative but slippery, while others, less relaxed, warned against its seductive immorality. One reviewer, known to posterity only as B. Z., denounced it as the kind of book one cannot help but close after reading a single page "with disgust and indignation." And Eugène de Mirecourt, prolific biographer and journalistic historian, picturesquely accused Gautier of proffering, in *Mademoiselle de Maupin*, "poison in a diamond goblet." The author, he charged severely, "has made more than a bad book, he has committed a bad act," for "a young man just leaving

47. Ibid., 368–72 [ch. 16].

school, or a girl of fifteen, who happen to turn over one of these pages will be corrupted to the marrow of their bones."[48] A whiff of delicious impropriety clung to Gautier from them on, but all the virtuous indignation he provoked did not prevent him from carving out a career as a widely read poet and influential critic of the arts and literature; he became, as Henry James was to say gracefully after his death, "a sort of immeasurably lighter-handed Rabelais."[49]

The principal reason for Gautier's relative impunity was, no doubt, that the sensuality of his *Mademoiselle de Maupin* was blithe, unencumbered with solemnity, as it were, intransitive. The heroine's erotic enlightenment is, strictly speaking, not a lesson in love but an apprenticeship in sexual gratification; apart from soliciting pleasure in carnality and contempt for unimaginative bourgeois, nothing follows from it. Mademoiselle de Maupin comes, sees, is conquered—and disappears, knowing but unscathed. In somber contrast, the erotic adventures of Flaubert's Emma Bovary are laden with consequential pathos. Like Gautier, whom he rather admired, Flaubert dwells on the transience of sexual passion and analyzes its unhappy twists and turns when it is divorced from tenderness or disinterestedness; unlike Gautier, Flaubert, the technician at once skillful and pitiless, presents these ways of loving as so many invitations to disaster. Emma Rouault, before she becomes Emma Bovary, has been spoiled for real love by her luxuriant fantasies which, nourished by bad romantic novels, can only produce grievous disappointments in her drab provincial world. Emma emerges from Flaubert's first presentation as sensual as a kitten, with her darting little tongue, her erotic perception of religious ceremonial and sacred music, her narcissistic indulgence in fine stuffs, her self-intoxicated surrender to her mediocre and unfeeling lovers. Emma's fate is the price that her undisciplined heart exacts: sordid affairs, inexpungeable debts, suicide. To have prosecuted *Mademoiselle de Maupin*—and it was never prosecuted—would have been to break a butterfly upon a wheel; to recognize the devastating eroticism in *Madame Bovary* as a provocation to proper notions of love was an anxious but perceptive reading of its implications, clumsy and counterproductive though the campaign to suppress the book may have been.

More than twenty years later, the urbane and cosmopolitan Portuguese novelist Eça de Queiros published his own *Madame Bovary* without

48. B. Z.: *Revue de Paris, Bulletin Littéraire* (January 1836); Mirecourt: *Contemporains*, VI, "Théophile Gautier," both in René Jasinski, *Les Années romantiques de Théophile Gautier* (1929), 323–24.
49. James, "Théophile Gautier," *French Poets and Novelists* (1878; 2nd ed., 1884) 35.

arousing any disapproval at all. The passage of time, even more than the accident of place, made a difference. *O Primo Bazílio*, a tale of adultery in high Lisbon society, is a sardonic, sophisticated treatment of love among the prosperous; it is perfumed in carnality, and scatters reminiscences of Flaubert's first masterpiece: seductive novels, sordid love nests, repellent and effective blackmail, amorous carriage rides, a faithless woman's lingering death.

Queiros establishes the erotic climate of *O Primo Bazílio* on its opening pages. Luiza, attractive and susceptible, strokes her ear in a gesture as suggestive as the way her devoted and lively husband, Jorge, strokes his beard. The couple, young, spoiled, comfortably off, are both ardent sexual animals. Jorge, about to go off on an inspection trip for the Ministry of Mines—this will be his first extended absence from his wife— lets his mind play nostalgically over "the pleasures of the night" that he and his wife have enjoyed, and of their long, leisurely breakfasts "in such agreeable indolence."[50] Their love, so far untested and unchallenged, is comfortable, shallow. Jorge, who had always worshipped his mother, had married out of loneliness after her death; Luiza, fresh from a traumatic entanglement with her cousin Bazílio, for the sake of meeting half-unarticulated needs. But the two suit one another; their appetites—and this is a novel of appetites—seem to match. Going through their meals, taking off their clothes, soaking in their tubs are gratifications they like to luxuriate in. Their happiness together, Queiros notes in a pointed oral phrase, is delicious.

Adultery will prove more delicious still. Jorge is straitlaced: in some conversations on marital fidelity, he insists that a wronged husband has the moral obligation to kill his errant wife. Luiza is not so sure; she has been fed on literature like Dumas's *La dame aux camélias* and on the sexual caprices of her vapid, vicious, and promiscuous best friend. When cousin Bazílio returns to Lisbon, handsome and hungry, she is already half seduced, self-seduced, before he deploys the heavy artillery of deftly placed kisses, adroitly awakened memories, plausible invitations to forget her marriage vows. Jorge's absence is not just the occasion for Luiza's adultery—it virtually ensures its enactment.

From the beginning, Queiros, ready to trade suspense for erotic intimations, drops portentous hints of betrayals to come: the discussions on what the husband of a faithless wife should do to her are accompanied by Luiza's playful threats that she will get even with him if he stays away too long. Sensual enjoyment, spiced by forbidden actions, is *O Primo*

50. *O Primo Bazílio, Episodio Domestico* (1878; 3rd ed., 1887), 7.

Bazílio's principal theme. Bazílio, experienced and narcissistic, functions as Emma Bovary's two lovers in one: he has the cheap, plausible sentimentality of Léon and, even more, the self-absorbed, superficially attractive coarseness of Rodolphe. It is with almost sadistic glee that he exploits Luiza's compliant docility and uses her, Queiros notes emphatically, "*as if he paid her!*"[51] For a time, Luiza, vertiginous with a heady mixture of voluptuousness and curiosity, finds her sexual thralldom exciting.

In reporting the erotic encounters of *O Primo Bazílio*, Queiros lingers in a shadowy grey area between indiscretion and reticence, teasing and enabling the reader to fill in the outlines for himself. The first seduction—Queiros says no more—has Luiza murmuring feebly, "Jesus, No! No!" and "then her eyes closed."[52] This recalls Flaubert saying only that Emma Bovary "gave herself" to Rodolphe for the first time, weeping and hiding her face. Later, Queiros lifts the veil of his suggestive reticence a little: Luiza's slavish dependence firmly established, Bazílio ventures to vary his sexual routine to suit his tastes. One day, giddy on champagne, Luiza appears to her jaded lover, that blasé consumer of women, strangely irresistible, precisely as Rodolphe had been astonished at the hold that Emma, that avid provincial bourgeoise, had over him. Bazílio kneels down, kisses Luiza's feet, moves up to kiss her knees, "and then in a whisper asked her something. She blushed, smiled, said 'No! No!,' " the kind of refusal that Bazílio had long ago learned to interpret as assent. "When she came out of her delirium she hid her face in her hands, all scarlet, and murmured reproachfully, 'Oh, Bazílio!' " The episode gives Bazílio, twirling his mustaches, a great deal of satisfaction. He has taught his mistress "a new sensation," and that, he calculates, will make her more pliant to his wishes than ever.[53]

The rest of Queiros's novel is one long waiting for the prefigured end. Bazílio tires of his cousin and callously deserts her. A grasping, rancorous servant blackmails Luiza. Her husband returns. The servant conveniently drops dead, Bazílio leaves the country, and Jorge remains, though puzzled, unenlightened for some time about his wife's affair; but she sickens, and, almost in relief, expires. Bazílio returns to Lisbon; hearing of Luiza's death, his only regret is that he did not bring his mistress from Paris with him, a cynical conclusion appropriate to a tale singularly free of didactic intentions. Plainly, Queiros did not shrink from touchy subjects, though

51. Ibid., 280.
52. Ibid., 226.
53. Ibid., 303–304.

in *O Primo Bazílio* it is the treatment rather than the theme that carries his audacity. The tense triangle that adultery makes was, after all, no rarity in nineteenth-century fiction. There is a hint, though, no more, that Queiros was prepared to venture more deeply into the frightening and exciting domain of transgression. Luiza's lover is her cousin, close to, though not quite across, the boundary of forbidden attachments. Plainly, Bazílio takes pleasure from the doubly tabooed nature of his affair: for a time, he muses, beginning to get a little bored, "the romance had been delightful, quite exciting"; after all, it had been an interesting mixture of "adultery with a bit of incest."[54] In Queiros's greatest novel, *Os Maias*, of 1880, this bit of incest blossomed into a central and shocking theme.

Literary critics have said for generations that if *O primo Bazílio* was Queiros's *Madame Bovary*, the *Maias* was his *Education sentimentale*. It is true enough that in his later novel, Queiros borrows from Flaubert again, once more deliberately and unapologetically. But *Os Maias* is, though biting social satire, far more good-natured and amusing than *L'Education sentimentale*, which is steeped in frustration and bitterness. Queiros promenades his young protagonist, Carlos de Maia, through Lisbon's high society, with its abortive political intrigues and mechanical amorous sport, its professions and projects never carried through, its intense but largely pointless conversations about literature and the future of Portugal, its paralyzing boredom. But in Afonso de Maia, Carlos's beloved grand-father, Queiros created a memorable character, a dignified, civilized, and affectionate patriarch who finds no counterpart in Flaubert's blasted canvas. In the management of the incest theme, too, *Os Maias* and *L'Education sentimentale* diverge more than they meet. When, toward the end of Flaubert's novel, Frédéric Moreau once again encounters Madame Arnoux, whom he had loved two decades before, his memories momentarily defeat his perceptions. She is grey now—the sight of her hair hits him for a moment like a shock—but as his long, unconsummated love for her rises up before him, Frédéric's appetite for her revives. He had never forgotten her, and she had spoiled him for later affairs. "He frequented society and he had still other loves. But the perpetual memory of the first made them insipid." Flaubert sensed that men may love less what they see than what they remember, remember all the way back to the mother they knew—young, sustaining, fragrant. And Flaubert lends Frédéric Moreau a glimpse of that knowledge. As his anti-hero talks with his first love after all these years, she hints, broadly, that she had wanted to make him happy, and her confession frightens him. He "suspected

54. Ibid., 347.

Madame Arnoux of having come to offer herself to him, and he was seized once again with lust, stronger than ever, savage, rabid." Yet he is overcome by another, indefinable feeling, "an aversion like the dread of incest," and turns away with a gesture of fear that she interprets as considerateness. Moved, she kisses him goodbye, "on the forehead, like a mother."[55]

This utter futility is characteristic of Flaubert's temper: not even the incest, which would have been no incest, is allowed to succeed. Queiros, in *Os Maias*, is more audacious. Through all sorts of improbable melodramatic twists and turns worthy of lesser novels, Carlos de Maia finds himself passionately and seriously involved with a mysterious young beauty; Queiros sketches with evident and, it turns out, maliciously subversive enjoyment their days and nights together—harmonious, sensual, meant to last. Then the couple, preparing to marry, discover that they are brother and sister. In no mood to defy the incest prohibition they have unintentionally violated, they part, on good terms, forever.

Some critics have wanted to interpret Queiros's most ambitious novel as a symbolic lament for Portugal's inbred, claustrophobic, and unproductive culture in the late nineteenth century. But whatever the hidden agenda of Carlos de Maia's doomed love, the manifest story is plainly about a taboo set aside, unwittingly but decisively. Indeed, Queiros handles his story with a lightness of touch, almost a casualness, that seems inhospitable to such grave readings. The reader finds the sudden revelation sad, not revolting, and sad because it compels a charming, handsome, and devoted couple to separate. Queiros gives no room to the guilt which, the psychoanalysts tell us, attends even the wish for incest, let alone its realization.

Incest is, of course, an ancient theme. To judge from the permutations it undergoes in religious myth, folk tales, and polite literature all the way from the Old Testament to Thomas Mann's "Blood of the Walsungs," it is also a theme at once wholly irresistible and extremely delicate. It is certainly immortal, surviving the most drastic historical upheavals; there is something truly, singularly appropriate in Freud dramatizing that most prevalent of incest dreams, the oedipal triangle, by levying upon both Greek and Elizabethan tragedy. This ubiquity offers proof (if, after Freud, further proof is wanted) that love begins at home. What is more, the cloaks that incestuous desires assume graphically illustrate another fundamental Freudian proposition: supple and ingenious as the human

---

55. *L'Education sentimentale* (1869), Gustave Flaubert, *Oeuvres*, ed. Albert Thibaudet and René Dumesnil, 2 vols. (1951–1952), II, 448, 452, 453 [part III, ch. 6].

mind may be in pushing impermissible wishes out of sight, it cannot destroy them; they will reemerge heavily distorted, as neurotic symptoms, particular sexual tastes—or elaborate stories. Hence, since in most ages the incest taboo has extended beyond proscribing its violation to obstructing its discussion, the psychoanalytic perspective, uniquely equipped to decode men's involuntary confessions, acquires special pertinence for the historian of love.

There have been moments in the history of Western culture when inhibitions about delicate sexual issues break down long enough to permit their presentation in readable guises or with an almost brutal directness. Ancient Greek myths tell of sons castrating their fathers and brothers marrying their sisters. Sophocles's Oedipus, who kills his father and marries his mother, is told that in dreams, such prohibited gratifications are common; while Euripides, in his *Hippolytus*, devised a way around the blunt presentation of forbidden love by making Phaedra, who passionately loves the young Hippolytus, his stepmother rather than his mother—a mask that made literary history. Elizabethan drama, another repository of sexual candor, rehearsed the theme of incest either obliquely —witness the plays of Beaumont and Fletcher—or with no residue of reticence: John Ford's Giovanni, in *'Tis Pity she's a Whore*, is taken with his sister Annabella and consummates his criminal inclination. The English romantics were somewhat more discreet than this, but not much. Byron's characters hint broadly at incestuous involvements, while Shelley's closet drama, *The Cenci*, whose villainous protagonist works his perverse sexual will with his daughter, left even those granting Shelley great poetic gifts dismayed over the "unwholesome regions," the "common sewer," he had chosen to enter.[56] But for literatures more reticent, like that of Victoria's time, incest proved treacherous terrain, heavily defended, which the most uninhibited of novelists hesitated to enter. Affections skirting the incest taboo might seem disagreeably intense—witness the destructive love between brother and sister in George Eliot's *Mill on the Floss*—but novelists, under fire for suggestiveness, would generally flee to the high ground of safe innuendo. Queiros was a notable exception, but then even the incest he dared to portray as consummated was (at least in the manifest story) after all unintentional. For the most part, the perilous theme emerged, if

---

56. *Shelley: The Critical Heritage*, ed. James E. Barcus (1975), 163–64. Only a slightly disreputable artist like William Etty, widely censured for his enthusiastic preoccupation with naked female beauty, would have dared in the early nineteenth century to paint Venus, as he did more than once, seductively engaged in close converse with her son, Cupid, as though the two were an amorous couple on the edge of mutual seduction.

it emerged at all, as the unconscious disclosure of an author's fantasies that his public absorbed in the same unconscious way. Yet, whether return of a repressed fantasy or resort to a literary device, however powerful Victorian defenses might be, incestuous feelings were a persistent presence in nineteenth-century literature.

By far the most prominent among these feelings was the oedipal triangle. To be sure, the attractions of the triangular figure for the imaginative writer, whether overtly oedipal or not, are obvious and heavily overdetermined. Placing one man between two women he loves or who love him, moving a woman from a first love to a second, keeps uncertainty alive and provides opportunities for dramatic moments of noble resignation or of jealous rage. Novelists from Jane Austen to Emile Zola found such configurations and confrontations eminently serviceable. In *Wuthering Heights*, Emily Brontë pursued triangles through two generations. George Meredith briefly reenacted a familiar modern version of the myth in *The Ordeal of Richard Feverel*, in which he has Richard's cousin Clare marry a man her family had picked out for her; more than twice her age, he had been "an ancient admirer of his bride's mama." In *An Old Man's Love*, the last novel he published, Anthony Trollope placed a likeable orphan between the older man to whom she is bound in gratitude and the younger man she really loves. Theodor Fontane, in *Frau Jenny Treibel*, found a pleasing resolution for a determined young woman's very similar dilemma, as she maneuvers a well-situated gentleman into proposing to her: she repents of this mercenary arrangement and marries the young man who is her real, which is to say her emotional, choice. The once popular French novelist Barbey d'Aurevilley gave this fundamental intrigue a more scabrous turn in *Ce qui ne meurt pas*, in which the protagonist, married to an innocent and innocuous wife, starts an affair with her mother, whom he finds erotically more satisfying. Such twists never became tedious, for they awakened long-buried recollections in readers, and besides, writers could vary amorous triangles in astonishing ways. The Russian novelists specialized in them. In that splendid novel in verse, *Eugene Onegin*, Pushkin constructs a triangle consisting of the charming Tatiana, of Onegin, whom she never ceases to love, and of her mature husband to whom she remains faithful. Dostoevsky, for his part, has his novels swarm with dark, neurotic, often interlocking triangles: Prince Mishkin, in the *Idiot*, finds himself drawn to Aglaia and Nastasia Filippovna while Nastasia, in her turn, is involved at once with Mishkin and Rogozhin. Again in *The Brothers Karamazov*, one of the literary documents that Freud found an extremely telling instance of the Oedipus complex, the father, Fyodor Pavlovich Karamazov, and his lusty son, Dmitry, engage in bitter rivalry for the seductive Grushenka. Appropriately enough, Turgenev has his most famous hero, in *Fathers and Sons*, confound the generations in his sleep, as Bazarov exchanges, in a dream, Madame Odinstsova, whom he grudgingly loves, with his overly fond mother.

The sexual twists that nineteenth-century novelists could give to such troubling battles were sometimes highly unconventional. In *The Bostonians*, Henry James has the possessive, rather unfeminine reformer Olive Chancellor struggle with the reactionary, manly Southerner Basil Ransome over the lovely charismatic medium, Verena Tarrant. Fifteen years before, in 1871, Thomas Hardy had already toyed with this erotic variant in his first serious novel, *Desperate Remedies*: Miss Aldclyffe competes with Edward Springrove for the affections of her young dependent, Cytherea Graye; Hardy, indeed, imagines a rather steamy, often quoted intimate scene between the two women: " 'Cytherea,' " Miss Aldclyffe exclaims in a fit of jealousy, as the two lie in bed together, " 'try to love me more than you love him—do. I love you more sincerely than any man can do. Do. Cythie: don't let any man stand between us. O, I can't bear that!' She clasped Cytherea's neck again."[57] But Cytherea, who loves Edward steadfastly, resists the sensual lure thus offered and in the end Hardy resolves the triangle—just as Henry James would resolve it in *The Bostonians*—in favor of a heterosexual union. It would be too easy to call these the safe solutions; they were the solutions implicit in the push and pull of conflicting affections among the characters their authors had invented. But the blatant bisexual triangle that had, in 1835, let Mademoiselle de Maupin divide her erotic education between a man and a woman remained practically unique in nineteenth-century fiction outside pornography.

Triangles could be false trails ostentatiously staked out to intensify and to prolong suspense: George Eliot thus misled her readers in *Daniel Deronda*, whose eponymous hero seems to hesitate for several hundred pages between the self-centered, neurotic beauty, Gwendolen Harleth, and the unspoiled Jewish maiden, Mirah Cohen, when he is actually committed to Mirah all along. Or at times they were rather remote from the family drama: writers could devise triangles to dramatize ideas—ideas with erotic resonance—in combat. The protagonist of Eça de Queiros's *A Cidade e as serras*, as of Honoré de Balzac's *Illusions perdues*, finds the

---

57. Hardy, *Desperate Remedies: A Novel* (1871; ed. C. J. P. Beatty, 1975), 109.

attractions of the city and the countryside, the metropolis or the provinces, implacable rivals, allegorical representations of incompatible ways of living and of loving.

The least surprising, most popular triangle was the angry, sometimes deadly ballet of betrayal: in *Dom Casmurro*, as I have said, Machado de Assis traces the obsessions of a husband convinced that his wife has had a child by his best friend, while in *Memoriàs Posthumas de Braz Cubas*, he records the autobiography of a ghost in which the narrator's affair with a married woman figures prominently. The subject was evidently much on Machado's mind: his first story, which he wrote at eighteen, deals with a wife's adulterous love for her husband's closest friend.[58] For the other sophisticated writers of his age, infidelity proved a never failing resource. In *Spring Torrents*, Turgenev has the impressionable hero forget his exemplary affection for a charming and devoted Italian girl in the arms of a sensual, man-eating Russian tigress. Perez Galdós, for his part, proffered a rewarding modulation of adulterous warfare in *Fortunata y Jacinta*, his most sprawling and most impressive novel, grinding up the philandering Juanito between his barren middle-class wife Jacinta and his fertile working-class mistress Fortunata; the alliance the two women eventually conclude once again demonstrates the rich possibilities inherent in triangular relationships. Indeed, Theodor Fontane, Germany's most interesting novelist between Goethe and Mann, explicitly called one of his best-known novellas, *L'Adultera*. Nothing, after all, is duller (at least in fiction) than a love rapidly recognized and fully shared, shadowed by no hesitations, the partners keeping in step as their infatuation grows into lasting attachment. In 1881, after the Chamber of Deputies had rejected yet another bill proposing to restore divorce to France, Emile Zola wrote an amusing article in *Le Figaro*, in which he argued that legalizing divorce would be the ruin of literature: since divorce would make marital misery soluble—and, he implied, adultery more or less unnecessary—there would be nothing for novelists to write about.[59] He was only half jesting.

In short, the triangle is a figure at once tense and indispensable: it calls for a resolution that the skilled storyteller first withholds and at length grants. Like the writer who throws obstacles in the way of the lovers and makes them undergo the trial of conquering obstinate prejudgments or selfish conceit—witness Jane Austen in *Pride and Prejudice* and Charles Dickens in *Our Mutual Friend*—the inventor of fictional

58. Helen Caldwell, *Machado de Assis, The Brazilian Master and His Novels* (1970), 16.
59. "Le divorce et la littérature," *Le Figaro*, February 14, 1881, Zola, *Oeuvres complètes*, ed. Henri Mitterand, 15 vols. (1966–68), XIV (1966), 543–47.

triangles recognized that a happy ending, cleverly delayed, multiplied his readers' pleasure. Playfully compelling his characters—and hence his readers—to postpone the moment of final gratification, he followed the rhythms, almost imitated the techniques, of any but the most animalistic intercourse. The reader could revel not merely in the contemplation of erotic satisfaction but also in relief from perils braved and overcome. The expense of effort and anxiety make the final reward all the sweeter.

Practically all the novels I have adduced could document the sexual, normally oedipal elements in literary triangles. But Dickens's *David Copperfield* orchestrates Victorian Oedipus more consistently than any other novel in the bourgeois century, and hence deserves a more detailed exploration. In her charming narcissism and her girlish prettiness, Dora Spenlow, David Copperfield's first wife, is a stunning replica of his first love, his mother. As a little boy, he had lived with Clara Copperfield in a state of solitary bliss since his father, twice his mother's age, had died before he was born. Whatever caresses David Copperfield would bestow on Dora—significantly, we hear little about them—they seem like pale imitations of those he had lavished on his mother, caresses she had affectionately returned. When Clara Copperfield marries for a second time, succumbing to the dour courting of the self-righteous, rigid, and cruel Mr. Murdstone, her rash step revives the oedipal struggle in its most destructive form. David's marriage to Dora is not a resolution: she is simply his mother restored to life, with no sadistic Murdstone in the wings to contest possession.[60]

As if to reinforce his difficult, pervasive theme, Dickens made practically all the families in *David Copperfield* conveniently incomplete. Their domestic triangles have been shattered by death, providing the two surviving family members with ample opportunities for expressive, if controlled, togetherness—ample and undisturbed, since almost none of the many principals in the novel is burdened with a sibling. With a fine impartiality that runs counter to the actual incidence of incest—for in real life, carnal father-daughter affairs are far more common than their son-mother counterpart—Dickens has sons enjoying uninterrupted idylls with their mothers, daughters with their fathers. I have already spoken of Annie Strong and her husband-father; it is significant that in the climactic scene in which all suspicions of her misconduct are laid to rest, Annie first must silence her intrusive mother. But there are others. Mr. Peggotty, brother of David Copperfield's devoted nurse, loves his adopted "daughter," little Em'ly, above anyone in the world and she, ruined and

60. See above, pp. 148–49.

betrayed by her plausible seducer, David's schoolfriend Steerforth, turns to him for solace; Steerforth's mother, for her part, loves her son with a fiercely concentrated, exclusive passion—there is no intrusive Mr. Steerforth anywhere—which, in his own negligent way, young Steerforth reciprocates. Dora Spenlow's mother is dead, and when her adored father dies not long before Dora's marriage to David Copperfield, she flaunts her unresolved infantile ties by her hysterics, her noisy unwillingness to be consoled. Reversing generations, David's second wife, Agnes Wickfield, is loved by her father in a very similar, far more neurotic way; her mother had died, significantly at her daughter's birth, leaving a free field for Mr. Wickfield's consuming attachment to his only child. Fittingly, the principal villains of the novel, the Heeps, offer a caricature of such loves: Uriah Heep's father lives in his family's memory only as the coiner of humble aphorisms, allowing Uriah and his mother to form a repulsive but genuinely devoted pair. *David Copperfield* is the richest of fictions, but it is among other things a set of variations on love as transference. It is also, at the end, more than that. In marrying Agnes, who is in all respects except her beauty the opposite of Clara Copperfield and Dora Spenlow, David Copperfield has triumphantly transcended his Oedipus complex and found a new, worthy libidinal object for his life. Love, in *David Copperfield*, is not just transference, but also transference overcome, a truly happy ending of which Freud would have approved—if he could have believed in it.

Dickens never so much as hints at the regressive admixtures of the loves he explores in the novel he called his favorite child. This was his moral style at work, his intense preoccupation with decency in diction and conformity in message. It was also his willingness to trust his feeling for human passions for which he had no vocabulary and only an intuitive understanding. Agnes Wickfield's father acknowledges that his engrossing love for his daughter is diseased, but Dickens fails to diagnose his malady beyond noting that this love had warped Mr. Wickfield's judgment and driven him to drink. Freud once said that he envied poets and novelists because they managed through sheer empathy to stumble on psychological insights that it took psychoanalysts years to discover and substantiate. He might have added that novelists and poets often happened on such discoveries without precisely knowing what they saw so clearly. *David Copperfield* is a remarkable instance of such innocent, ignorant knowledge.

Dickens's canvass of the oedipal theme borrowed some distinct features from his own past, and other nineteenth-century novelists, too—Turgenev and Thackeray come quickly to mind—published literary versions of oedipal triangles as thinly disguised fragments of a great confession. *First Love*, one of Turgenev's most distinguished novellas, by his own admission autobiographical in inspiration and certainly autobiographical in sensibility, is the story of an adolescent boy's first fixation on a young woman—he is sixteen, she, twenty-one—who fascinates him from the moment he sees her. Vladimir, who has grown up in a repressed, tense, loveless household, is quite unprepared for Zinaida, a willful and sensual beauty, a magnet to men. A season of puppy love follows for Vladimir, marked by moments of delusive happiness, bouts of jealousy and despair. Then he discovers that Zinaida, with any number of men to choose from, is his father's mistress.

Worse is to come. Toward the end, Vladimir witnesses a sadistic imitation of the primal scene: he happens on his father and Zinaida talking earnestly together, probably about the other men in her life, when she suddenly holds out her hand and his father strikes her across her bare arm with his riding crop. Looking at her lover, saying not a word, she slowly raises her arm to her lips and kisses the crimson wound, while her father flings away the crop. That wound, that crop, that loving surrender to pain recall the child's parents entangled in sexual coupling, whether glimpsed in fantasy or surprised in reality. Turgenev has the narrator see it all once again that night in a dream, with his father holding the crop and the crimson mark not on Zinaida's arm but (through a second upward displacement) on her forehead, an erotic mark of Cain. In this terrible silent encounter, Turgenev has condensed the grimmer aspects of the oedipal conflict: the son, who loves and hates his powerful father, watching helplessly as that father attacks the object of the boy's adoration—an attack which, to compound his confusion and his misery, she seems to welcome. Yet Turgenev, ever the pessimist about the tender passion, shows love to be stronger than lovers. Not long before his premature, sudden death connected in some obscure way with Zinaida, Vladimir's father sends his son a message, at once cynical and depressed: "My son, beware of the love of women; beware of that great ecstasy—that slow poison."[61]

How unsettling the triangle Turgenev had devised in *First Love* was to his readers emerges somewhat obliquely from their responses; some found this tale of adultery, of a forty-year-old man carrying on with a seductress half his age, thoroughly sordid. Louis Viardot, for one, an intimate of Turgenev's and husband of Turgenev's great love, bluntly told his friend

61. Turgenev, *First Love* (1860; tr. Isaiah Berlin, 1950, ed. 1982), 119 [ch. 21].

that with this story he was descending into the sewer of the modern novel.[62] Preoccupied with this anal imagery—a great favorite with nineteenth-century purists—Viardot had little to say about the oedipal conflict that organizes the book. A more famous fiction than *First Love*, Thackeray's *Henry Esmond*, on the other hand, was openly criticized for precisely that strain.

Whatever his private reservations, Thackeray liked to describe *Henry Esmond* as his best novel. It was certainly his most carefully pondered and most deliberately composed: unlike his earlier *Vanity Fair* and *Pendennis*, it was published not serially but as a book. The reviews were enthusiastic, though not without some expressions of uneasiness. *Henry Esmond* had everything: precise historical detail, skillful imitations of the Queen Anne style, fatal duels, historic battles, forlorn political con spiracies, and, into the bargain, a winning young man's fascinating personal history complete with accusations of bastardy, closely guarded family secrets—and tortuous loves. Early in 1853, when Thackeray was on a lecture tour in the United States, *Harper's* spoke with appreciative wonder of "the Henry Esmond and Thackeray fever of the winter."[63]

Yet *Henry Esmond* paraded the oedipal theme with such bluntness that readers could not overlook it. Charlotte Brontë, who thought highly of Thackeray, tersely summed up what would become a prevalent view after she saw some of the novel in manuscript: "admirable and odious." George Eliot defined the odiousness: *Henry Esmond*, she wrote, is "the most uncomfortable book you can imagine." She recalled, not inaptly, one of George Sand's novels, *François le Champi*, in which a young man develops erotic feelings for a woman he has long regarded as his mother and eventually marries: "Well, the story of Esmond is just the same. The hero is in love with the daughter all through the book, and marries the mother in the end."[64] This synopsis accurately reflects Eliot's feelings, and those of a sizeable public, though (as careful students of Thackeray have not failed to point out) it oversimplifies Esmond's ambivalent feelings toward both mother and daughter and their equally ambivalent feelings toward him. But precisely this misreading is of interest: that so intelligent a reader as George Eliot overlooked the rather obvious bits of evidence

62. V. S. Pritchett, *The Gentle Barbarian: The Life and Work of Turgenev* (1977), 134–35.
63. Edward Douglas Branch, *The Sentimental Years, 1836–1860* (1934), 106.
64. Brontë: John Sutherland, "Introduction," William Makepeace Thackeray, *The History of Henry Esmond, Esq.* (1852; ed. John Sutherland and Michael Greenfield, 1970), 19; Eliot: to Mr. and Mrs. Charles Bray (November 13, 1852), George Eliot, *Letters*, ed. Gordon S. Haight, 9 vols. (1954–1978), II, 67.

Thackeray had thoughtfully planted along the way to justify the end-ing, suggests that his oedipal plot had touched on some intractable inner conflicts that interfered with accurate perception.

Other readers of *Henry Esmond* found its triangle no less disturbing. They enjoyed the story, admired the pastiche, and worried about the ending. Mary Chesnut who, as we know, thought *Esmond* his finest book, by the greatest of novelists, still rejected its resolution as "painfully re-volting"; it struck a "discordant note." Others were explicit about their discomfort in print. A reviewer in the *Athenaeum* suggested that Esmond's "sudden appearance . . . at the altar is somewhat like a marriage with his own mother. All the previous emotions of the piece return to haunt us." G. H. Lewes, more sophisticated than most readers—and most reviewers—balked at the ending as being less than "*vraisemblable.*" Similarly, Dickens's good friend and biographer, John Forster, while praising Thackeray's "skill and taste," thought "the thing is incredible, and there's an end on't." This refusal to believe was a polite form of denial, a deliberate failure to confront the oedipal implications of Thackeray's book. Mrs. Oliphant, a prolific and popular novelist in her own right and less refined in her literary palate than either Lewes or Forster, was uninhibited enough to be publicly appalled; using the strongest terms at her disposal, she denounced Henry Esmond's marriage as "monstrous," declaring that "our most sacred sentiments are outraged, and our best prejudices shocked by the leading feature of this tale"—all this in a highly admiring survey of Thackeray's work. Yet her indignation was uncommon in its severity. For most other critics, the brilliance of *Esmond* outshone its ending, and even that ending seemed to them unsettling rather than disgusting. Reviewing the book for the *Spectator* in an appreciation that Thackeray found most gratifying, George Brimley acknowledged that "nothing short of consummate skill could have saved" Esmond's love story "from becoming ridiculous or offensive, or both." But Thackeray had risen to the occasion, making Esmond's emotions credible as they grow "into a complex feeling, in which filial affection and an unconscious passion are curiously blended"—a felicitous and prescient formulation.[65]

The unconscious passion that Brimley shrewdly detected in *Esmond* also worked in its author. By tentatively laying bare the oedipal roots of love—he had done some of the digging in *Pendennis* before completing it to the best of his abilities in *Henry Esmond*—Thackeray was drawing

65. Chesnut: *Mary Chesnut's Civil War*, 279; *Athenaeum*: Gordon N. Ray, *Thackeray: The Age of Wisdom, 1847–1863* (1958), 192; Lewes: *Thackeray: The Critical Heritage*, ed. Geoffrey Tillotson and Donald Hawes (1968), 138; Forster: ibid., 145, 150; Oliphant: ibid., 209; Brimley: ibid., 142.

on the unfaltering mutual adoration that shadowed, and largely shaped his and his mother's life. He was to gain a certain distance from this over-powering attachment—doubtless the principal reason he could write so freely about a young man's love for an older woman. "It gives the keenest tortures of jealousy and disappointed yearning to my dearest old mother," he confessed to an old friend in 1852, the year that *Henry Esmond* was published, that "she can't be all in all to me, mother sister wife everything but it mayn't be." When he was a boy, "I thought her an Angel and worshipped her. I see but a woman now, O so tender so loving so cruel." Yet even this brave reaching for a measure of emotional objectivity to which he nerved himself in mid-life, smacks more of the melancholy of a disillusioned lover than the affectionate farewell of a mature son. But whatever this personal, half-understood source of Thackeray's percep-tion of the loves he felt and those he invented, what matters most are the reverberations he set up in his readers and his reviewers. They found his insights unpalatable but recognized their causes and accepted their consequences—reluctantly. In 1908, that authoritative and opinionated critic, George Saintsbury, displaying an unsuspected openness to complex erotic experience, concluded that *Henry Esmond* "is very shocking—and excessively human."[66] The book did not jeopardize Thackeray's place in the highly selective pantheon of great nineteenth-century novelists but, on the contrary, secured it.

Toward the last decades of the nineteenth century, this was the verdict of the civilized multitude. It did not blink at Baron von Instetten, who had first wooed Effi Briest's mother, later marrying Effi Briest herself. Similarly, every literate reader in the Spain of the 1870s found much to applaud and little to censure in Juan Valera's *Pepita Jiménez*, a classic that complicates its organizing triangle—a pious seminarian in turmoil as his religious vocation is subverted by an alluring young widow—with an oedipal theme that accompanies Luis's spiritual malaise like an obbligato. His father, a vigorous and still youthful widower, has his eye on that very widow, Pepita Jiménez, who is rich, devout, and enjoys an unblemished reputation. That she may be aware in her heart of hearts that she is a fine-looking, healthy young woman not made for perpetual mourning and conspicuous works of charity only enhances her attractions. Luis's rivalry with his father grows in tandem with his struggle between his religious commitments and amorous desires. The first small step he takes in freeing

66. Thackeray: Gordon N. Ray, *The Buried Life: A Study of the Relation Between Thackeray's Fiction and His Personal History* (1952), 51; Saintsbury: Geoffrey Tillotson, *A View of Victorian Literature* (1978), 181.

himself from the oedipal and the religious prohibitions that keep him from acknowledging his infatuation is a bit of self-deceptive self-analysis: wondering whether he resents his father's earlier mistreatment of his mother, he denies it vehemently, thus unconsciously acknowledging it. He is beginning to think about what had been unthinkable—his father's imperfections. The second step follows soon as Luis discovers a potent erotic element in his long-standing resolve to enter the priesthood. "Sometimes I imagine that there is in all this a touch of sensual pleasure."[67]

For a time all is well, or seems well, on both fronts. Luis is sure, very sure, that Pepita Jiménez will make a good stepmother for him, and equally sure that he does not love her. But the pressures of Eros are stronger than the defensive fortifications that his denials can construct. He refuses to castrate himself, even symbolically: "I am not about to tear out my eyes." And, just as he does not want to be Oedipus, he does not want to be Hippolytus either: Pepita is not yet his mother—or stepmother—not yet! But the struggle continues; this is a novel, after all, not a short story. Luis has anxiety dreams about Pepita—she kills him as Judith had killed Holofernes—revealing his deeply contradictory feelings, his yearning, and his fears. He meditates on love, finding "a thousand reasons for loving God and not loving her."

Pepita's conflicts match and mirror his own: when they kiss for the first time she faints. "But what good are the pleasures of the senses," Luis asks her in a last moment of casuistic hesitation, "what good all the glory and magnificence of the world, when a soul burns and pines for divine love?" It is a good speech, but not good enough. Pepita confesses her own sensuality: "I love in you, not the soul alone, but the body," and soon after, the two, overcome by their passion, consummate their affair. Yet all ends well: Luis and Pepita marry, with his father's blessing. Their love, for all its sensual impetuosity, carefully knits together, with a pious touch, the two strands of love that the nineteenth century did not like to see separated. The couple resolve, at the end, "to unite conjugal love with the love of God." The appearances have been preserved, and so *Pepita Jiménez* could slip into the camp of the moral novel; the lovers have sinned once, briefly, but made it good by marrying, and by sophistry. At moments when Luis finds his secular life vulgar and selfish, his wife hastens to dispel such "melancholy" notions and he "then recognizes and asserts that man may serve God in all states or conditions of life,"[68] and may—I should add—defeat the father, in both human and divine shape, with

67. Juan Valera, *Pepita Jiménez* (1874; ed. Carmen Martin Gaite, 1977), 54.
68. Ibid., 69, 98, 150, 155, 165, 187.

impunity. Juan Valera's most celebrated work is a pure instance of the novel as wish-fulfillment in action.

The innocence of *Pepita Jiménez* is as compromised as the innocence of its principal characters. Indeed, on some level, its readers must have been aware of its scandalous implications: neither Luis nor Pepita is punished for transgressions that a novelist only a quarter of a century earlier would have taken as the occasion for an elevating, suitable, delightfully pathetic ending. The same superb indifference to the moral profit one might wring from this kind of story informs *Fort comme la mort*, in which Guy de Maupassant gives the erotic triangle yet another twist—just what his public would have expected of him. The successful society painter Olivier Bertin, urbane, athletic, handsome, and aging—he is in his early fifties—has enjoyed for a dozen years the tender and protective love of Anne de Guilleroy, a rich bourgeoise who had made a pleasant and sensible marriage with an aristocrat in politics. Her affair with Bertin is downright domestic: her lover is an intimate of her household. But it must, even in the worldly circles in which the lovers move, remain clandestine, achingly intermittent. She is consumed with jealousy over the fashionable women he paints, the casual female acquaintances he cultivates; solicitously watching over Bertin, she is sadly aware that, though still fresh and immensely desirable, she is no longer in her first youth. But the nemesis of her love takes the most unexpected shape—her lovely young daughter, Annette. Bertin has known the girl ever since she was little, just old enough to accompany her mother to the sittings that led to the affair in which he is still placidly, a little passively, entangled. Now Nanette has returned to Paris to prepare for an advantageous marriage that her parents have arranged and Bertin, seeing her grown up, falls in love with her.

Actually, as Maupassant takes rather too much trouble to impress on his readers, Bertin's fantasized infidelity is by no means so unequivocal. The crisis, which his mistress sees looming on the horizon before he does, breaks upon Bertin and Anne de Guilleroy as her mother dies and she collapses in shock and sudden mourning, doing much damage to her appearance. Alone a good deal, Bertin lives most intensely through reminiscences; practicing a kind of mental masturbation, he enjoys recalling moments of bliss with Anne. Hence, while the contrast between the fading woman and the blossoming girl is poignant, what really animates Bertin is that he loves the mother once again through her daughter. Nanette has become what Anne once was. Just as Bertin had come to love Anne de Guilleroy when he painted her, looking charming in mourning for her father, he relives that infatuation as he now paints her daughter, just as charming in mourning for her grandmother. "Another love was entering, in spite of himself," or, rather, "the same love rewarmed by a new face."[69]

Somewhat monotonously, as though he could not bring himself to trust his readers, Maupassant reiterates that the two women look like sisters: the daughter is the mother reborn in looks, gestures, ways of carrying herself. Her very name makes the girl into a walking memory. Dutifully, Maupassant the novelist takes care to introduce complications, hesitations, and reversals to delay the denouement. Bertin attempts to repress his carnal interest in Nanette by insisting that he really likes older women best. At the same time, his mistress tries to keep him for herself by playing at mother before him; this converts Nanette into their daughter, and degrades Bertin's passion for the girl into a species of incest. His evasions fail, as do her schemes. The girl becomes an intrusive presence for Bertin and, increasingly convinced that she will never see him as anything but a likeable older man, as a paternal figure met across the years on occasions innocently enjoyed and fondly remembered, he lets himself be run over by a bus. Bertin's half-willed suicide masquerading as an accident makes him a victim neither of retributive justice nor of unappeasable guilt but of his inability to live with his aging body that can no longer fully serve his desires.

When *Fort comme la mort* appeared in 1889, Maupassant's old adversary, Firmin Boissin, who had dogged his steps before, was almost alone to wax indignant: "Adultery consummated," he snarled, "desire for incest, suicide—this is the work that a certain reviewer has saluted as a conversion!"[70] But in general the reception was appreciative and uncensorious. Indeed, this sort of disenchanted openness about the vicissitudes of love, which had seemed so threatening only three decades before at the time of *Madame Bovary*, had become, if far from commonplace or wholly proper, both plausible and not very objectionable. The sporadic, somewhat juvenile assaults on bourgeois respectability of a *Mademoiselle de Maupin* had graduated to matter-of-fact autopsies of adultery and delicate play with unorthodox sexual pleasures; the largely unconscious, inadvertent erotic disclosures of mid-nineteenth-century novels, to the studied disregard of the most sacrosanct of deadly bourgeois virtues.

Discretion about carnal love was on the defensive. Queiros's *Os Maias* had come out in 1880. Three years later, Edmond de Goncourt, com-

---

69. *Fort comme la mort* (1889; ed. 1908, in *Oeuvres complétes* de Guy de Maupassant, 29 vols. [1908–1910]), XXII, 293.

70. Artine Artinian, *Maupassant Criticism in France, 1880–1940* (1941), 102.

pleting a short tale, *Chérie*, angrily charged Emile Zola with stealing hi
revolutionary idea of introducing a young woman's first menstruatior
into the novel. While this minor and diverting literary tempest ovei
Goncourt's *Chérie* and Zola's *La joie de vivre* was raging in Paris, the
young Dutch writer Lodewijk van Deyssel was writing his impressionistic
novel, *Een Liefde*, published in 1887, in which he dwelled with circumstantial detail on a woman masturbating. By the early 1890s, after novelists
had been hinting at it for some time, Oscar Wilde and his friends, observing
only a minimum of restraint, tried to insert homosexual passions into the
canon. At first retrospect, the 1880s appear as a dramatic decade marking the transition between the age of reticence and the age of candor in
literary culture.

Appearances approximate realities, but the history of love in nineteenth-
century fiction was more involuted, more paradoxical than this. Practically every generalization in that history founders in exceptions. The
novel, that undependable mirror moving along the highway of culture,
was anything but indifferent to larger concerns. In some measure, it
reflected the political struggles of the time, its social aspirations, medical
knowledge, and passion for purity. But in the liberties it took and the
precautions it observed, it went its own way much of the time. Even
the division of the nineteenth century into early and late, a rather gross
division that has served me well so far, requires elaboration: the age does
not neatly divide into decades of mindless repression followed by decades
of unbuttoned tolerance. In short, the social fortunes of the middle classes
did not generate predictable styles of reading. Some middle-class consumers of fiction in the 1890s as in the 1830s ventured to follow their
erotic fantasies along the trail the novel was blazing for them; more of
them, more often, could not trust themselves to have their libidinal
imagination stimulated by tales of illicit affairs or suspect attachments.
One might have expected progress and security to breed a certain capacity
for tolerating excursions from propriety and unsettling psychological
revelations. In fact, around the middle of the nineteenth century, when
bourgeois nearly everywhere were extending and consolidating their
social influence, economic sway, and political power, the fiction they
read was commonly inhibited by an earnest, sometimes downright vindictive respect for decorum. There is scattered evidence, in fact, that the
pressures for restraint were intensifying in those years: in 1841, in his
introduction to *Oliver Twist*, Dickens had bluntly called Nancy a
prostitute, but in the edition of 1867, he omitted this suggestive epithet.
In France, meanwhile, in the mid-1850s, the Imperial government initiated

number of prosecutions, much applauded by respectable bourgeois, of
which the trial of Flaubert is only the most famous. In 1856, Xavier de
Montépin's risqué *Les Filles de Plâtre*, "an infamous book in every respect,"
he *Saturday Review* righteously called it, "infamous in shamelessness,
infamous in cynicism, infamous in the total absence of any gleam of good
feeling or right thinking," brought prison sentences for the author, his
publisher, and his printer. The *Saturday Review*, treating *Les Filles de
Plâtre* as one in a flourishing genre that included Gautier's *Mademoiselle
de Maupin*, applauded the severe verdict and called for more.[71]

The fate of Montépin is a necessary reminder that in the surprising
nineteenth century the stereotyped national variations in literary permissiveness, on which travelers and editorial writers liked to depend, were
far from wholly reliable. In 1889, when Mary J. Serrano translated Eça de
Queiros's *O Primo Bazílio* from the Portuguese for the American public,
she bowdlerized this "graphic picture of Lisbon life." She was happy to
place Queiros "at the head of the list of Portuguese novelists," but found
him unbearably explicit. So she "assumed the responsibility of softening
here and there, and even at times effacing, a line too sharply drawn, a
light or a shadow too strongly marked to please a taste that has been
largely formed on Puritan models." To her mind, the educated Portuguese
reading public, weaned on French literature, could stand accounts of
sensual baths, furtive assignations, and slavering sexual assaults; while
Americans, belated Puritans still, must be spared such incidents. The
oblique scene in which Bazílio thrills Luiza beyond bearing with cunnilingus is not to be found in her version. Serrano suggested, resorting a
little helplessly to a tired apology, that the cuts she had ventured to make
would not only keep "the interest of the story" quite "undiminished"
but also give "the ethical purposes" of the book "wider scope."[72]

This was as blatant a piece of denial as Fitzjames Stephen's imputation
of moral intentions to Flaubert, and interesting evidence for the tenacity
of moralistic fervor in literature. Serrano's comparative vista on contemporary fiction is even more interesting. Her rather severe view of
the French novel—and the Portuguese novel, she thought, simply swam
in the French wake—was, of course, generally shared and not wholly
unjust. But it was simply not true that in Paris, everything was permitted.
Perhaps no regimes prosecuted more works of fiction, certainly none more

71. Dickens: Kathleen Tillotson, *Novels of the Eighteen-Forties* (1955; ed. 1961),
67; Montépin: "A Forbidden Novel," *Saturday Review*, I (April 5, 1856), 461. For
this, the previous two and the following three paragraphs, see *Education of the
Senses*, 358–68, esp. 363.
72. *Dragon's Teeth: A Novel from the Portuguese* (1889), translator's preface.

vigorously, than Napoleon III's Empire or the early Third Republic
while French novelists were granted far freer access to regions of sensuality from which English or German writers continued to shrink, or
handled with their fingertips, the image of French bourgeois culture as
unequivocally liberal in matters of sex or drowning in immoral fiction is
the reverse of the rather more cheerless reality.

Nor did France give novelists unlimited license in the depiction of
love after the liberating 1880s. Even later, frightened publishers and
other public authorities sent capricious signals hard to read and madden-
ingly confusing to writers. In 1906, the erotic novelist Paul Léautaud, who
did not scruple to exploit his experiences for his "fictions," noted in his
journal that his editor, Alfred Vallette of the *Mercure de France*, was
replacing the most explicit passages in his novel *Amours* by dots; yet this
was the editor who had for years published the suggestive, often salacious
novels of his wife, Marguerite, who had achieved widespread notoriety
under her pen name Rachilde. Vallette's reasoning was of the sort Henry
James's politic editor of *The Cynosure* would have understood: "For
the sake of subscribers, readers, the *Mercure* goes practically everywhere. . . ."[73] Public officials and vigilantes everywhere acted to inhibit the
spread of what they diagnosed as poisonous propaganda for perverse loves.
Zola's English publisher, Henry Vizetelly, went to prison in 1889 for not
expurgating his translation of *La Terre* enough; van Deyssel, under attack
for being too faithful a disciple of his filthy French models, censored
himself in the second edition of *Een Liefde* and retreated from his provocative naturalism altogether; Oscar Wilde, as everyone knows, fell afoul
in 1895 of the English laws for flaunting the particular sexual appetites
at which his fiction had so smoothly hinted; the German authorities
prosecuted poets of passionate love like Richard Dehmel for taking unacceptable liberties in their sensual lyrics. The threat to books, authors,
and publishers—banning, fines, prison, bankruptcy—continued to hang
over the literature of love.

Yet, the embattled years after the 1880s, when the middle classes were
under increasing pressure from radical political and cultural adversaries,
from socialists, New Unionists, and derisive bohemians, did not propel
them into a crusade to restore the reign of sentimental tones and anodyne
evasions in fiction. When they had far better reasons to be nervous than
before, bourgeois showed themselves more prepared than ever to acknowledge the share of the body in love and to allow that wicked seducers

73. September 24, 1906, *Journal littéraire de Paul Léautaud*, vol. I, *1893–1906* (1954),
301.

prospered as often as virtuous maidens went unrewarded. Precisely at
the time that legal defenses against the realistic exploration of the erotic
in fiction might well have been strengthened, they were eroding at point
after point.

Some of these assaults on decorum were, to be sure, so provocative as
to arouse almost unanimous condemnation. Bourgeois flexibility had its
limits, even among the flexible. In Norway, that professional rebel Hans
Henrik Jaeger, blasphemer and anarchist, had his erotic novel, *Fra
Kristiania-Bohêmen*, confiscated by the police in the 1880s and was sent
briefly to prison; his last novel, *Syk Kjaerlighed*, over which Jaeger
labored for years around the turn of the century, could only be printed
privately and was not published until 1920, ten years after Jaeger's death,
and then in a German translation. The title of the book, *Sick Love*, is apt
enough; its designation as a novel less so. With its hero yearning tearfully
to melt into the lap of his mistress, its self-indulgent word-painting and
stammering expressionistic speeches, it is autobiography in the perfunctory
drape of fiction. Characteristically, *Sick Love*, faithful reflection of its
neurotic, alcoholic author, oscillates between sexual lust and lachrymose
guilt. The narrator has an insatiable appetite for cunnilingus, most avid
when his compliant mistress gives him access to her genitals while she is
menstruating. But once she has yielded with a smile to his importunities,
he besieges her with febrile demands for reassurance, begging her to tell
him that she still loves him. *Sick Love* is not obscene by calculation. It
does not describe sexual parts or record sexual intercourse with the
obligatory close-ups of pornography; the narrator's sexual program is
the physical counterpart of his regressive need for union with the
mother and his self-reproaches after orgasm are the pitiful appeals of a
nervous Lothario. Such intimate confessions parading as literature were
defensible principally on civil-libertarian grounds, and many bourgeois
confronted with such texts fled to the reticence in which they had
been schooled and chose order, however boring, over liberty, however
titillating.

The novelists setting off explosions in respectable middle-class culture
were not surprised at these retreats. They would have had a ready explanation for the paradoxes I have canvassed. The importunates, indeed
stupid interventions of legislators, divines, or pious distributors of books
struck them as simply another convincing, and depressing, instance of
bourgeois prudery. What else could one expect of crass materialists, of
unashamed philistines in power? In one way or another, avant garde
novelists asked this rhetorical question over and over again. Almost to his
last lucid day, Flaubert continued to assert that the bourgeoisie literally

made him sick, and his jaundiced views secured a wider hearing after his
death in 1880 than they had in his lifetime.

Van Deyssel was therefore far from original when he exclaimed that
"the bourgeois" is "that vile abscess in the lovely body of humanity!"
Looking back, he acknowledged that some of his bellicosity had been
sheer high spirits, a needle to prick the balloon of bourgeois complacency:
"We were eccentric and indecent," he wrote, "not because we took the
eccentric and the indecent for truth, but because eccentricity and indecency seemed to us the finest possible affirmation of our desire to have
everything permitted to us." But, however overstated, the charge against
the bourgeois as the enemy of literature was serious and seemed plausible
enough. Theodor Fontane, no fanatic, bluntly told his son that he had
intended *Frau Jenny Treibel*, his satirical novel about the Berlin parvenu
Bürgertum, "to show up the hollowness, the phrase-making (*Phrasen-
hafte*), the mendacity, the arrogance, the hard-heartedness of the bourgeois point of view."[74]

What Fontane and his fellow-critics, engaged in combat and steadily
under fire, could not see was that the bourgeois enemy was not mendacious or hard-hearted so much as anxious. Nor could they be expected
to be grateful for whatever liberality and tolerance many bourgeois
readers had been able to summon up in the most prudish days and were
increasingly displaying with the years. As the literary education of the
middle classes proceeded, it equipped them to accept, and even to enjoy,
the spaciousness of Tolstoy's universe of the senses and George's Eliot's
brilliant handling of mixed motives in love. Conventions about the treatment of love in fiction were shifting, and, like all change, this too awakened resistances that the embattled avant garde, understandably but
mistakenly, took to be the bourgeois consensus.

Not all readers shared in this shift; what I have called the community
of bourgeois fantasies, never robust, was shattered into segments of reading publics well before the nineteenth century was over. Influential and
outspoken setters of opinion kept Podsnap alive long after Dickens had
created him. Yet more and more middle-class readers were learning to
laugh at Podsnap—Dickens, after all, had made him to be laughed at—
and to resist him, in society and in themselves. While the crusaders'
appetites for prosecuting suggestive fiction never dried up, a substantial

74. Van Deyssel: Jacob de Graaf, *Le réveil littéraire en Hollande et le Naturalisme
Français, 1880–1900* (1937), 72, 63–64; Fontane: to his son Theo, May 9, 1888, Charlotte
Jolles, *Theodor Fontane* (1972), 77. It is worth adding that Fontane, never a pure
satirist, drew half-affectionate portraits of bourgeois social climbers in this novel,
and in others.

reservoir of good will for candor and complexity in literature had survived through the worst of times, and by the 1880s, the islands of
reticence were visibly shrinking. The fiction of Victoria's time, then,
was a literature of implications, of delicacy. Down to the end of the
century, not even the writers uncomfortable with common constraints,
including Meredith, Hardy, and Fontane, would provide physical details
of love-making or adultery; the aggressive physicality of Zola or
Goncourt was always crowding the edges of the permissible, even in
France. Yet the lovers of Trollope's *Framley Parsonage*, its author insisted, "longed for the other," and "were not ashamed to say so." Nor
were the novelists, if for the most part decorously. Even at its most
discreet, Victorian fiction amounts to a body of work that took a certain
delight in the erotic, suggesting civilized ways of coming to terms with
desire. By the time the nineteenth century gave way to the twentieth,
substantial numbers of cultivated middle-class readers were ready for the
wayward loves thrust upon them by Marcel Proust.

❧ FOUR ❧

Problematic Attachments

THE SETTING is an isolated country house at Montjouvain, late on a sultry afternoon. It is so hot that Mademoiselle Vinteuil, who lives there in solitude with her lover, has kept the windows open. Marcel, resting after one of his habitual walks along the Méséglise way, has fallen asleep in the sheltering shade within sight of the house. Like all narrators in first-person novels, he is a singularly lucky voyeur, Marcel more so than most—the world seems intent on pressing its disheartening pedagogic scenarios on him. When he wakes, trapped in his natural hiding place, he becomes involuntary spectator to a repulsive episode, a corrupt little ritual dance. Choreographed well in advance and permitting only minute improvisations, it is evidently essential to the lovers' sad and hostile erotic performances. Mademoiselle Vinteuil is alone, in deep mourning for her father, an obscure local musician—he will later prove to have been a composer of genius—who had died not long before, largely of grief over his beloved daughter's conduct. She is apparently expecting her paramour and arranges herself in anticipation, carefully placing a photograph of her father near the sofa on which she then fetchingly reclines. Soon after, her friend arrives and the predictable mutual seduction begins, with coy questions and rehearsed gestures; then, with sudden vehemence, her lover kisses Mademoiselle Vinteuil provocatively between her breasts and the two young women chase one another around the room, "clucking and screeching like amorous birds," falling at length onto the sofa. Playing out her assigned role, Mademoiselle Vinteuil calls her father's photograph, a fetish for their amorous play obviously in daily use, to the attention of her lover, who insults it until, raising the level of xcitement, she brutally offers to spit on it. The rest is lost, requiring maginative work from the reader, as Mademoiselle Vinteuil gets up nd closes the window, leaving Marcel to his reflections.[1]

It is a shocking scene, and Proust knew it to be shocking. Yet he insted, rightly, that it was indispensable to his design; it is the first adumration of a fundamental theme in his symphonic cycle of novels that ould swell to monstrous proportions once the narrator has gathered orldly experience and come to recognize an astonishing array of acuaintances, friends, and lovers to be inhabitants of Sodom and Gomorrah. roust was sensitive to the treacherous ground he was treading. Early n May 1908, as he was still groping his way toward *A la recherche du emps perdu*, he told his confidant Louis d'Albufera that he had more han half a dozen things "in the works," both fiction and essays on miscellaneous topics, including one on "Pederasty (not easy to publish)." This was more than the author's anxiety. Francis Jammes, a pious Symbolist whom Proust professed to admire, implored him to take out that offensive scene. Had Jammes known what Proust planned to make out of he baron de Charlus, outsized Dickensian social lion, opinionated aesthete nd—it would turn out in later volumes—confirmed homosexual, he would ave been more troubled still. But Proust intended to keep his text intact nd, not without a shiver of pride in his probity and his courage, he lescribed the novel to which he was dedicating his life, as improper, in act "extremely lewd in some parts."[2]

Yet in the smattering of reviews, articles, and interviews that greeted *Du côté de chez Swann* in 1913, its brief lesbian episode aroused no particular remark—not, apparently, because it was too delicate to touch, out because it was too familiar to deserve notice. To be sure, Proust had orchestrated much of the comment that his debut as a serious novelist provoked, pressing his friends to review *Swann* or to find sympathetic reviewers for it. But even those writing independently of Proust's suave importunities did not object to his introducing lesbians into his immortal exploration of involuntary memory. If they had reservations, it was about his style, not his indecency.

This interesting indifference had several causes. The year, after all, was 1913, and the reading public had been exposed for some decades to intimate erotic revelations, including sexual irregularities, in the press.

1. *Du côté de chez Swann* (1913), *A la recherche du temps perdu*, ed. Pierre Clarac and André Ferré, 3 vols. (1959–1966), I, 160–63.
2. Proust to Albufera (May 5 or 6, 1908), to Alfred Vallette (mid-August, 1909), *Correspondance de Marcel Proust*, ed. Philip Kolb, 9 vols. so far (1970–   ), VIII, 112–13; IX, 155.

During the very years that Proust had begun to brood on *Du côté d* *chez Swann*, the French had been deluged with circumstantial reports o improprieties reaching into the most exalted circles of Germany, includ ing Wilhelm II's court camarilla. The most spectacular victim was Princ Philipp zu Eulenburg, possibly the Emperor's closest friend, whose cas Proust found fascinating and followed closely. He was only one of man delighted Frenchmen who deluded themselves that homosexuality was German disease assuming epidemic proportions in imperial Berlin, tha "Sodom-on-the-Spree," and promptly dubbed Kaiser Wilhelm's intimat "Eulenbougre." The series of sensational newspaper stories and no les sensational trials in which Eulenburg, with his associates, figured afte 1906 made the journalistic canvassing of sexual aberrations almost obliga tory. One could ridicule or condemn, but one could not fail to discus them. Moreover, as an inveterate reader, Proust was thoroughly familia with his most influential forerunners, novelists who, as we know, hac deposited a choice and rather varied collection of homoerotic character in the minds of their public. George Sand and Honoré de Balzac, whos work was, of course, in Proust's bones, and which, whatever his cavils, h could never wholly escape, made literary history with their vivid homo sexual characters. There are some heated effusions of lesbian arousa between Pulchérie and her sister in Sand's *Lélia*, while Balzac's powerfu homosexual Vautrin looms over several of his major novels. If thes characters rarely reached the stature of protagonist, they prepared ar atmosphere of tentative tolerance for the portrayal of problematic lovers But there is another, more important, reason why Proust could safely show Mademoiselle Vinteuil and her coarse lesbian gallant preparing tc make love. Quite unlike Walt Whitman, or the lesser poets in the fugitive journals of the 1880s or 1890s, who had chanted the delights of such experiences and had been made to suffer for it, Proust made his homo sexuals, male or female, singularly joyless. The erotic episode forced on Marcel that afternoon on the Méséglise way is saddening with its stereo typed gestures, its routine viciousness, its total absence of spontaneous play; the sensual gratification the two women wring from one another has the compulsive urgency of the drug addict's search for his daily dose. The actors disporting themselves in this scene were members of a doomed race coupling in misery and helpless despair.

Proust's attitude toward his homosexual and bisexual characters pre cisely matched his attitude toward his own sexuality. Proust consciously treated homosexual urges as a curse, invincible and ineradicable, imposed by a blighted heredity and a poisonous environment. Authentic as it was, Proust's perspective on love as embodied in *A la recherche du temps erdu*, proved prudent as well. It was least dangerous in those years to speak about sexual aberrations as a physician, a moralist, or a patriot, to analyze them in technical terms, preferably in Latin, to expose them as an excrescence of modern civilization, or to find them rampant in other countries. "If there is one vice or malady repugnant to the French mentality, French morality, and French health," the French journalist J. Ernest-Charles wrote in *La Grande Revue* in 1910, "it is certainly to call things by their right names, pederasty." His formulation, repeated twice more, is as remarkable as its substance: Ernest-Charles left the essential nature of "pederasty" unsettled.[3] But, whether vice or malady, the one issue beyond debate among the respectable was that it did not deserve to be called love.

Proust's unsparing, depressed parading of men and women condemned to live as secret citizens of Sodom and Gomorrah offered palpable returns to the homosexuals of Proust's time. It was not the unequivocal approval they desired, but, then, if their erotic needs were a lot they could not escape, that absolved them of moral responsibility; a fate is not a vice. This unhappy perspective offered a measure of protection against the prosecuting itch of heterosexual purists or the indiscreet self-exposure of homoerotic propagandists. It was, in short, easier to publish an account of homosexuals if it conveyed pain rather than pleasure. Should they feel compelled to make an open avowal of their inclinations and practices, it was best if they came before the public weeping and rending their garments.

1. Dividends of Denial

The qualities distinguishing innocent from vicious love in the nineteenth century seemed virtually self-evident. Sophisticated cynics and somber moralists might agree that human nature had its passionate imperfections and that the official bourgeois ideal of love was excessively demanding. In consequence, many men—but few women—were forgiven for displaying these imperfections too blatantly. But while lapses from the ideal were inescapable, its principal articles of faith scarcely required discussion; everyone knew that they included virginity before marriage, unbroken monogamy, sexual intercourse moderate in quantity and procreative in intent, total abstention from masturbation, and the most scrupulous adherence to the taboos against incest and other sexual abominations.

Yet, since these matters went literally without saying, whole stretches between the domains of erotic probity and sinfulness were left vague, los in obscurity. When the moral guardians of the age, intent on protecting the innocent and rescuing the guilty, compiled their catalogue of wicked sexual offenses, they would thunder against incontinence, self-abuse, and fornication. The vices they did not mention were vices they could not, or did not want to imagine; the fairly explicit Proust was the beneficiary of a cultural revolution that had been decades in the making.

This gradually fading reticence about homosexuality was not hypocrisy. It was one way of attempting to resolve a familiar bourgeois dilemma in the face of untractable realities. The middle classes could never quite decide whether denial was a sounder cultural defense than candor. Late in the century, investigators into sexual conduct justified their intrusive prying into private lives on the general principle that lack of information is always damaging, an aid to passivity before presumably insoluble problems. But there was no blinking the fact that their inquiries were sure to touch on closely guarded, often embarrassing matters. Hence until the 1880s, and even later, most bourgeois chose the spurious safety of ignorance over the risky benefits of knowledge.

This choice had the paradoxical consequence that homosexual lovers, men and women alike, were safer in the earlier days of tight-lipped equivocations than in the later days of clinical inquisitiveness. As long as they preserved the appearances, bachelors were above suspicion and women sharing quiet establishments gathered only praise for their devoted friendship. The best way to disarm rumors was to act as though they were untrue: the principal reason why Tchaikovsky decided, in the mid-1870s, to get married was to give the lie to whispered (and accurate) insinuations that he was homosexual. It was only when they flaunted their disdain for reigning moral rules, only when the public could no longer ignore their conduct, that homosexuals found themselves under fire as respectable society struck back. What made George Sand a notorious figure in her day, for all the immense popularity of her fiction, was less the succession of her lovers, at least one of them a woman, than the publicity that attended her affairs, her parading in male attire, and her invasions of heavily defended masculine preserves by donning trousers and demonstratively smoking cigars. This sort of thing made the proper angry because it made them anxious.

It was precisely this anxiety that lay behind the vindictive glee that Oscar Wilde had to endure during his trials in the spring of 1895. It also informed the "bovine rage," as the brilliant music critic Ernest Newman called it, "of the Philistine." Wilde aroused offended prudery, stern pharisaism, and lip-licking prurience but, as well, baffled irritation s an exhibitionist who would not pursue his sordid sexual adventures iscreetly. His disdainful performance on the stand only exacerbated the rge for retribution. Let him claim that books are neither good not bad, nly well or badly written: the reading public took this aestheticism for mmorality. Let him present his attachments as pure, beautiful, supremely piritual successors to the loves of David and Jonathan or Plato and his able companions, and as enactments of Michelangelo's and Shakespeare's onnets: the evidence before the court was rather less elevating. To his evered denigrators, Wilde was the defiant and disdainful pervert who aad violated the supreme social rule of reticence. The sly or savage ommentary of the popular press, admittedly in search of cheap effects out not unrepresentative for all that, emphatically underscores this general ense of betrayal.

Some of the better newspapers, to be sure, barely mentioned the case; he *Manchester Guardian*, for one, almost ostentatiously confined itself o the salient facts and buried even these in scattered, unemphatic two- or three-line items. Others, like *The Times* or the *Pall Mall Gazette*, covered the trials in most satisfying detail, lavishly summarizing the testi- mony of the accused, the pleas of the attorneys, and the interventions of he judge; as they liked to do in sensational trials, they evoked the heated atmosphere of the court room by reporting the occasional outbursts of he audience—which the presiding judge promptly and sternly repressed. Implicitly, their work of descriptive reportage invited their readers to draw their own moralistic conclusions. But some daily and weekly papers could not resist the Wilde case as an opportunity to lecture the public, telling it what it wanted to hear. The *Westminster Gazette* thought the conviction "salutary," which "will undoubtedly do much good, not only in punishing actual criminals and putting the fear of the law into others, but also in checking unwholesome tendencies in art and literature." Most prominent among these tendencies, the editorialist argued, was "the at- tempt to separate 'art' from all relation to morality," a stance that was "at best a sophism, and at worst—what we have seen it in this case to be." Wilde's homosexual exploits, in short, were not his principal offense; that was, rather, his parading an amoralism bound to affront a culture dedicated to the ideal of not going too far.

In its curious editorial, published the Monday after Wilde's conviction, the *St. James's Gazette* exhibited this hunger for reticence to perfection. The writer argued that while "tolerance is one of the distinctive virtues of the modern world," it is a virtue that had been allowed to ripen into a vice. Cruelty, crime, skepticism, immorality—authors felt free to advocate all of these without raising an eyebrow. "This is the age of the

New Tolerance; and the first principle of the New Tolerance is that everything is an open question." The trials of Wilde had demonstrated what this "too-liberal" mental attitude could produce. The "perverted criminal" had received "a heavy but well-deserved sentence." This "person" will now enter "into the subterrene world of shade and obscurity," but he was leaving with the respectable public "a little sting of self reproach." The *St. James's Gazette* reminded its readers that five years earlier, it had "pointed out that a book of this writer's," obviously *The Picture of Dorian Gray*, "seemed less worthy the attention of the critic than the policeman," and aroused some opposition to its warning. Now the time for recognition had come. The *St. James's Gazette*, in short, had been right all along. "The painful and scandalous exposure of these weeks may do something to bring back a dash of wholesome bigotry into our art, our literature, our society, our view of things in general." The Wilde case would generate a necessary intolerance, "the intolerance without which a nation goes to collapse." The paper thus joined a wider yearning in hoping for a time of quiet, even if that entailed repression socially or if necessary, legally imposed. "The man," wrote the *Daily Telegraph* in full agreement, "has now suffered the penalties of his career, and may well be allowed to pass from the platform of publicity which he loved into that limbo of disrepute and forgetfulness which is his due."

A few editorial writers might profess to welcome the probing light of day that had finally laid bare the hidden decadence of which Wilde was the high priest. But their rejoicing in exposure was uncharacteristic. When, in December 1900, *The Times* noticed Wilde's death, the obituarist, after reviewing Wilde's witty, enormously successful comedies, added: "The revelations of the criminal trial in 1895 naturally made them impossible for some years." That adverb, *naturally*, is telling: the prevailing sentiment after Wilde's imprisonment was a wish for forgetfulness, for a return, however temporary, to the old days of protective ignorance.[4]

Sociologists from Emile Durkheim on have argued that society manufactures its deviates by defining normality and thus ascribing abnormality to the minorities who act out what more inhibited individuals only sublimate, dream about, or wholly repress. But the bourgeois style, a

4. Newman: "Oscar Wilde: A Literary Appreciation," *Oscar Wilde: The Critical Heritage*, ed. Karl Beckson (1970), 204; *Manchester Guardian*, May 24, 1895, p. 8, May 27, p. 8; *The Times* of London, May 2 ff, esp. May 27, 1895, p. 4; *Pall Mall Gazette*, esp. May 24, 1895; *Westminster Gazette*, "The End of the Wilde Case. Some Incidents and Morals," May 27, 1897, pp. 1–2, and see its issues of May 21, 22, and 25; *St. James's Gazette*, "Over-Tolerance," May 27, 1895, p. 3; London *Telegraph*, May 1895, passim; *London Evening News*, May 1895, passim; *The Times*, December 1, 1900: *Wilde: Critical Heritage*, 228.

mixture of delicate euphemisms and wide-eyed candor, complicates this generalization. After all, behind the sheltering facade of discretion, many nineteenth-century male and female homosexuals, defining their own forbidden ways of loving, enjoyed a privileged space of impunity for their unorthodox amorous arrangements. "A truly refined mind," says Mrs. General in Dickens's Little Dorrit, "will seem to be ignorant of the existence of anything that is not perfectly proper, placid, and pleasant." This sounds too much like conscious policy to capture the unconscious energies activating these bourgeois stratagems; Mrs. General is a caricature, and drawn as a caricature, even though she doubtless embodies an extreme style of defense in nineteenth-century middle-class culture. But more interesting and certainly more important was the bourgeois way of discussing, quite openly and with engaging innocence, characters and situations that modern, more sophisticated readers would call suspect. In 1811, the House of Lords found for two school mistresses who had sued the grandmother of one of their pupils for asserting that they were guilty of "improper and criminal conduct." Despite circumstantial and picturesque testimony about the way the two ladies carried on in bed together, the Law Lords vindicated their purity from a sheer failure of sexual imagination. "I do believe," Lord Gillies said, "that the crime here alleged has no existence"—certainly not in Great Britain.[5] After all, if one does not know what a lesbian is, or if she can only be found in the Orient, there is little point in expending indignation or visiting punishment closer to home on women who love women. That, too, is why in Little Dorrit Charles Dickens could develop the character of Miss Wade, that strange "self-tormentor" whom twentieth-century readers would unhesitatingly identify as a lesbian, without fear of reprisal—or, for that matter, without a very precise sense of how much he was saying. This was the paradoxical way in which respectable culture made much of the nineteenth century surprisingly permissive.

Yet the very reticence that served its sexual heretics so well has long obscured the historian's researches into the varities of loving in that age. Spectacular instances make anecdotal history; instructive as they are, the provocative pursuits of an iconoclast like Oscar Wilde, the orgies of a wealthy pederast like Friedrich Krupp, the chaste photographic debaucheries of an inhibited don like Lewis Carroll, the mannish ways of the much admired painter Rosa Bonheur, the lesbian circle presided over by Natalie Barney in Paris, or the flamboyant love affairs of bisexual

5. Dickens: Little Dorrit (1857; ed. John Holloway, 1967), 530 [Book II, ch. 5]; Lord Gillies: Lillian Faderman, Surpassing the Love of Men: Romantic Friendship and Love Between Women from the Renaissance to the Present (1981), 147–49.

performers like Paul Verlaine—"alcoholic, syphilitic, pederast, poet," as
he called himself[6]—are in the long run less valuable to the cultural historian than the jottings, joyous or tormented, of obscure men and women
seeking to sort out, to justify, or simply to recall, their heterodox sexual
appetites.

These jottings are rare, but they exist. On July 29, 1836, Albert Dodd,
then a student at Washington College in Hartford, Connecticut, started a
journal in the recommended way. Since 1833, he had been writing poetry
and legibly transcribing it into a bound volume that had printed, on its
title page, the portentous warning "PRIVATE." But this was different. One
of Dodd's professors had invited his students to improve their "pro-
ficiency in composition" by keeping a diary and, obedient and suggestible,
Dodd undertook to do some free associating on paper, "writing down my
thoughts, currente calamo, freely and at random, on any subject which
may arise in my mind." He invoked, with mock solemnity, the "Virgin
Goddess Minerva," to aid him in his design, lest he be defeated by
"negligence," which, he rightly sensed, has been the diary's most implacable adversary since time immemorial.

A fair classicist who enjoyed translating, and quoting, Greek and
Latin poetry, Dodd had every right to his invocation. But his conventional beginnings are not very promising; and indeed, at first, Dodd
confined himself to innocuous events and unexceptionable thoughts, in
the somewhat stilted way of someone following formulas and timidly
venturing to get acquainted with himself. On July 31, he mused on what
he called, a little obliquely, "my indefiniteness," the first, and for some
months, the only hint at introspection in his fragmentary autobiography.
He would note trips to New York and his indulgence in a favorite
pastime, going to the theatre, some disagreeable imbroglios with college
authorities, and preparations for transferring to Yale. As he put it severely
on February 2, 1837, "laziness on my part" had made his journal a skimpy,
episodic record.

But laziness alone was not responsible for his negligence. Beginning in
February 1837, in frantic compensation for his long silence, he now
confessed, with daily bursts of retrospective self-examination, that he had
left his journal untouched for months because he had feared to revive
"feelings of a sad and painful nature." He was, though, in conflict; his
fear was balanced by a wish: he regretted that he had not "faithfully

6. Alistair Elliot [reviewing Pierre Petitfils, *Verlaine*], "Alcoolique, syphilitique,
pédéraste, poète," *TLS* (April 10, 1981), 395.

portrayed all those scenes and thoughts" which, as he put it with engaging inconsistency, he would remember all his life yet stood in danger
of forgetting. The racing pulse of his entries, after blank months, attests
to floods of unmastered emotions swamping the dikes of his discretion.
His first year in college had been tranquil, all sunshine, filled with "many
pleasant, very many happy, hours." Then the second year had burst upon
him, and, with that, the heart-breaking disappointments of youthful love.
Albert Dodd was not quite nineteen, apparently unprepared for the
turmoil of his awakening, ambiguous sensuality. "After the sunshine
comes the storm," he wrote, ever ready to employ hackneyed phrases for
real feelings, "and the last year has mostly been cloudy and gloomy
enough."

Fortunately, Dodd was prepared to be more specific than this. "The
friend I loved, the first one whom I had ever truly loved in this wide
world, became estranged from me, as I indeed did from him also, and for
a time after I thought I had been a fool for wasting my affections on
one who had so repaid them." Prompted by inexpressible feelings, swallowing his pride, he had offered to "renew our friendship, and he was
glad to do so, and now I again have my friend." Then, without transition, moving without apparent strain from male to female loves, Dodd
records "another affliction in my list of woes for the past year." It was
the discovery "that *she* whom I loved had proved fickle and deceitful."
He labored to be fair to Julia, the girl to whom he had addressed an
impassioned sonnet two years earlier as his "first and only love." Now
she had let him down. "To be sure, she never in so many words said 'I
love you,' but her actions, and her treatment of me for a long time led
me to the conclusion that the affection which she well knew I had for
her was on her part returned." Sadly, "from that fond dream I have
awoke." His oscillations, between infatuated illusions and sober disenchantment, between beloved boy and beloved girl, mark the rest of
his artless record.

Two days after his reserve had given way, on February 4, 1837, Dodd
poignantly asked himself why he should have been so sensitive to John's
coldness. "Because," he replies, "I regard, I esteem, I *love* him more than
all the rest." He wonders, in the manner of countless lovers through the
ages, "does he care in particular for me?" and responds with the expected
denial: "I fear not." Yet his own feelings are beyond doubt. " 'John,
dear John,' " he wrote, enclosing his apostrophe in quotation marks as
though he were addressing his beloved friend in his mind, " 'I love you,
indeed I love you. But you are not here, you cannot hear me confess

this to you, a confession which perhaps you would care not for.' " Then
he defined his feelings, for himself, once again: "It is not friendship
merely which I feel for him, or it is friendship of the strongest kind. It
is a heart-felt, a manly, a pure, deep, and fervent love." It might in fact
be manly and pure, but it was heavily invested with libido, a "flame," as
Albert Dodd pictured it to himself, "that was burning" in his heart.

For reasons that the historian of love will recognize, Dodd had failed
to open himself to his friend. He was afraid of rejection. John "has a
heart," he reassured himself. "O yes he has an affectionate, a noble heart."
But he, Albert Dodd, trampling as a true lover on his self-esteem, was,
after all, "destitute of those qualities which are calculated to win the
friendship, the loving friendship of any." One quality he was confident
he possessed: "But I can love, God knows I can love." Yet matters other
than feelings of unworthiness and fear of rejection made him unhappy;
he was suffering with unspecified evils so intimate, perhaps so wicked,
that he could not fully entrust them even to his journal: "that ——
which has long troubled me; and also —— which has ditto. Besides there
is M. O. —— I dare not write even here these things —— which it is my
prayer may soon be settled." Plainly, he had some baffling and disconcerting erotic business on his mind. He wished to forget, thought of
death, called upon the "fiend" to be gone, defied the "blue devils" that
beset him.

Then, after a long dash, Dodd moves, in the free associative process
that an informal journal encourages, to "John Heath," upon whom his
thoughts dwell most affectionately. And he adds, immediately, as his
sexual choices once again vacillate between women and men, "I wonder
if I really loved Julia." He thinks he must have, though his "passion" for
her "is now nearly forgotten." Yet it seemed to him, as he pursued his
train of thought, "that the nature of my affection for A. H. and J. F. H.,"
for Anthony Halsey and John Heath, "was nearly the same as that
which I had for Julia. Yet one," he comments, as if in mild astonishment,
"was for a female, the other for"—and at this intriguing point someone,
probably the diarist himself, cut out the next page, leaving this effort at
self-analysis incomplete.

Incomplete but not incomprehensible: there is much more to the same
purpose in the entries that follow, right into the next academic year.
For all his infatuations with male friends, Dodd does not drop his masculine identifications. The poems he writes mainly address Julia or, later,
Elizabeth and her "loved form"; it would take humorless interpretations
to read perverted fervor into some bland verses "Ad Amicum" and into

his jocular account of Zeus's preference for homosexual over hetero-sexual love in his "The Disgrace of Hebe & Preferment of Ganymede." Similarly, the dreams that Dodd records are about women, and so are his associations. In one such dream, he sees his Julia in company with another girl, becoming enraged, "attacking her tooth and nail, real vixen like," quite out of character. In her uncontrollable passion she throws herself at him, sobbing. "We were standing up in the middle of the floor, and there the dear, beloved girl was in my arms, crying away with very rage, her little heart beating violently against mine; and her whole frame trembling and convulsed." Half aware of his orgasmic wish, Dodd comments: "O, what a sweet and thrilling embrace it was!"

The dream, he thought, was "curious," especially since an unexpected friend appeared in it, and since Julia never displayed such temper in real life. Yet it vividly reminded Dodd of a Christmas vacation he had spent, more than a year before, in Julia's home—"dear girl!"—where a kissing game ended in his kissing her for the first time, a kiss "sweet and delicious"—and returned. "Heavens!" he recalled in innocent remorse at an opportunity missed, "I did not take half the advantage that I might have done, for I was so astonished, and fluttered, and confused." But now, in his dream, with the trembling and convulsed girl in his arms, busy (as the dream work reverses the direction of his desires) trying to "soothe her passion," Dodd made up for what he had failed to extort a year before.

Some months later, in early June 1837, he dreamt of a girl again, this time of Elizabeth. "I thought I held you in my arms and you smiled upon me with a benignant look and that look said you loved. Dearest *best* Elizabeth." The poem he wrote "To Elizabeth" that very month pictures him as thinking of her all the time. Girls engrossed his fond attention during his waking hours; he liked to take walks that he might look at them, and proved exceedingly susceptible to their erotic charms. He much admired "Old Webb's daughter," a "lovely, perfectly beautiful girl, of handsome form, good size, beautiful complexion, the most rosy, luscious lips I ever beheld and such eyes," such eyes, "large and dark, perhaps dark blue, and melting."

But, while girls aroused him, boys aroused him even more. The "be-loved form" of John Heath remained with Dodd in John's absence; he could never stop reproaching himself for not telling John of his "deep and burning affection." Ambivalent as usual, Dodd commented that perhaps his reticence had been for the best; but in his journal, "in my private volume, whose pages shall be surveyed by no eyes," he could

safely "repeat" his "secret avowal" of his attachment, and confess that he
was thinking of his friend, his companion, his fraternity brother, "sole
inhabitant of my heart."

This avowal was sheer self-deception. Dodd had earlier declared his
warm feelings for "A. H.," and in March, he could no longer repress his
yearning for Anthony Halsey, for his Tony: "I do long to hear from him
again. How I love him! He lately seems to have occupied my thoughts
more than J. H. and I feel as if I loved him more ardently than John."
Dear Tony, Dodd was happy to record, returned his love. It was all very
complicated, but Alfred Dodd was sorting it out in his journal. "L-o-v-e,
love; what is love?" he asked and confessed himself unable to describe it.
"All I know is that there are three persons in this world whom I have
loved, and those are, Julia, John, & Anthony. Dear, beloved trio."

But it was an unequal trio, for it was with his *"Dearest Anthony"* that
Dodd seems to have come closest to physical consummation. He had
known Tony for years, even before college, and had always thought him
"so handsome." The two had become very intimate, even though they
did not room together. "How completely I loved him, how I doated on
him!" They would take long walks, and talk together for hours. And at
night, "Often too he shared my pillow—or I his, and then how sweet to
sleep with him, to hold his beloved form in my embrace, to have his arms
about my neck, to imprint upon his face sweet kisses! It was happiness
complete." Dodd did not think any of this questionable, let alone perverted behavior; he yearned for those days to return, to see Tony again,
to "behold his youth, beauty and innocence of ought of evil, how sweet
it would be! Dear, dearest Anthony!" Forgetting his tribute to John as
the "sole inhabitant" of his heart, Dodd now addressed his "adored
Anthony" as "mine own friend, my most beloved of all!" Yet even
this attachment was not wholly stable: in October 1837, near the end of
his journal, Dodd records that he has fallen in love with a freshman, an
infatuation which he, as a senior, finds at once wholly unsuitable and
perfectly proper: "I am conscious that I love him very much and more
perhaps than I do any other one."

Albert Dodd's complex loyalties aroused no perceptible conflicts in
him. In the presence of young men he did not forget his girls, in company with favorite girls, he thought of his men. One evening, listening
to Elizabeth singing his "special favorite" song, "Low wav'd the summer
wood and green," Dodd recalled that this was John Heath's favorite song
as well, wished for his presence at the recital, and recalled that he had
just received a letter from him. "Very welcome," it showed "that he
has not forgotten me." Oh, if John "would only go to Yale now, and I

too, how I should like it! ———." The long dash ends his yearning paragraph like an expectant sigh.[7]

Albert Dodd graduated from Yale with the class of 1838, having been elected to Skull and Bones and apparently escaping all those adolescent scrapes that had compromised his years at Washington College. He went on to study law and to practice it on the frontier, first in St. Louis and then in Bloomington, Illinois. The three letters to his mother and to one of his brothers that have survived date from this period, and show a man who had achieved self-mastery after tempestuous years. Writing to his mother late in 1843, he is dutiful and not very personal, except for some mild nostalgia about Connecticut Thanksgiving, with its delightful foods. A letter to his younger brother, of early 1844, has him striking the posture of Polonius, overwhelming Edward Dodd with good advice, principally on securing good temper "not only in appearance but in reality, both outwardly & inwardly, towards others as with yourself." Happy moods are a matter for the will: "The habit of cheerfulness is easily acquired by practice." It requires the ability to "look constantly on the bright side of things," without surrendering to deceptive dreams. Dodd confessed that he himself had not been so balanced and optimistic when he still lived at home, but would "fret and be sullen & cross about little matters."[8] Now, though, he was applying what he preached and the better for it. Here was a man who had wrestled with his adolescent impulses and won.

We shall never know how expensive this victory must have been to him. Dodd's promising career, which included a future in politics, was cruelly cut short only four months after he had philosophized for his brother Edward's benefit. In June 1844, riding home from a political meeting, he drowned in the swollen Mackinaw river. He was only twenty-six. Dodd had not married, but the biographical record of his class at Yale notes with becoming terseness that he had "contemplated marriage."[9] It seems probable, then—we cannot be sure—that his masculinity triumphed over his homosexual appetites, strong as these were, just as his programmatic even temper overcame his intermittent depressions. What is beyond doubt is that Albert Dodd, discovering his capacious gift for erotic

7. July 29, 31, 1836, February 2, 1837, Journal; "Julia" April 1835, album of poetry; February 4, 5, 7, 1837, Journal; "To Elizabeth" June 1838, "Ad Amicum" December 1838, "The Disgrace of Hebe & Preferment of Ganymede" December 1837, album of poetry; June 2, March 4, February 19, March 21, 24, 27, October 10, February 26, 1837, Journal. Albert Dodd Papers, Y-MA.
8. Albert Dodd to his mother, November 30, 1843; to his brother Edward, March 13, 1844, Albert Dodd Papers.
9. *Biographical Records of the Class of 1838, Yale College* (1879), 53.

investment in the first days of Queen Victoria's reign, loved men and women indiscriminately without undue self-laceration, without visible private guilt or degrading public shame. His bisexual inclinations seemed innocent to Dodd, and apparently to others, because his bearing and behavior, including his emotional attachments to others of his sex, did not affront current codes of conduct. Thus Dodd's impunity is a tribute to the unsuspected openness of his culture. He preserved the appearances; it never occurred to him, in fact, to do anything else. In a culture in which appearances thoughtfully preserved meant denials successfully sustained, Dodd was allowed to pursue his women—and his men—in peace.

Others, too, saw their crushes on school fellows or soldiers as quite innocent—at least in their conscious minds. They would brood, if they were inclined to brood at all, not over whether they were being wicked, but whether their infatuation was returned. Quite a few among them cultivated and discussed their passion, without a hint of embarrassment, let alone a sense of sin. Henri-Frédéric Amiel filled his voluble introspective journal with jottings about his passionate friendships, normally with one fellow student or another, praising their charms and lamenting their lapses. When, in the early summer of 1839, a beloved comrade seems angry with him and pointedly prefers the company of other young men, Amiel is disconsolate: "I have never told him how much pain this estrangement costs me. How I would love him if he fathomed it!" This was no passing flame. More than a year later, when the same friend failed to keep an appointment, "for the hundredth time," Amiel thought it right, and doubtless soothing, to entrust his dismay to his one faithful companion, his private journal.[10]

Like many of his contemporaries, Amiel did not need to invent some elaborate philosophical justification to justify his homoerotic attachments. He was no Walt Whitman. But Amiel emphatically argued that his passion for male company was essential to the pursuit of manliness. More than once he would reproach himself for being too much with women. "*Search out men more,*" he apostrophized himself after his adolescent infatuations were a dozen years behind him. "In talking, corresponding, communicating practically with women alone, you are making yourself effeminate." Ardent male friendships, then, far from irregular, let alone evil, seemed to him natural, downright necessary. In the late 1840s, the young English painters Holman Hunt and John Everett Millais formed an alliance that Hunt was to call, in retrospect, a "sacred friendship." The

10. June 28, 1839, October 14, 1840, Amiel, *Journal intime*, ed. Bernard Gagnebin and Philippe M. Monnier, 6 vols. so far (1976–   ), I, 117–18, 161.

two worked in the same studio whenever they could, collaborating on their paintings; they spent endless hours talking over coffee, wrote affectionate letters when they were apart, and wept at long separations. Hunt was led to ask whether "other men" had ever enjoyed such closeness.[11]

They had, and so had women. While passionate female intimacy was by no means reserved to puberty, it generally began in puberty, that time buffeted by physiological and psychological changes. Girls from prosperous families went away to school, took lessons or trips together, and faced the alien world of young men in tightly knit alliances for mutual support. In 1885 and 1886, in the "Private Record" that Mary I. Barrows, not yet sixteen, kept while she was at St. Margaret's School in Waterbury, Connecticut, she would faithfully recall her little daily triumphs and defeats as she negotiated her way around the erotic traps of a girls' private boarding school. The principal object of her affections was Mary Dennison, whom "Mabel" Barrows much loved and greatly missed. "Mary is *not back*," she noted on September 25, 1885, the first day of school, "and though her room, seat at table and at school are reserved for her, there is some doubt of it. I want her so—am very tired." Her fatigue could have been the natural consequence of her recent move back to school, or, just as naturally, of conflicts and anxieties about her love. The next day, she was elated to find herself placed, in the dining hall, at the headmaster's left, but depressed without her special friend: "I do miss Mary so." Some weeks after, when it seemed less likely than ever that her cherished friend would return, Mabel Barrows poured out her impotent rebelliousness against her fate, and her world: "Oh! If Mary Dennison were *only* here, this horrid place would be heaven again! How I *long* to have her back." Much like Albert Dodd, Mabel Barrows could muster only conventional language for very powerful feelings.

Other girls, meanwhile, beleaguered Mabel with passionate declarations. "Carrie said tonight she really believed she loved me," and on that same October evening her fellow student "Frank" told her that she loved Mabel "millions better" than she did another girl. Only three days after, Mabel Barrows seems to have forgotten her imperishable love for Mary Dennison: "Carrie and I lay on my bed all afternoon and either fought or spooned." But then, a week later, a "very affectionate letter from Mary," announcing her arrival, restored Mary's earlier ascendancy. "The dear girl!" Mabel exclaimed in delight. "I wish it was to stay." Mabel's wish was not to be realized, and visits from Mary would be all she would get.

11. Amiel: September 4, 1851, ibid., I, 1062; Hunt: Mary Lutyens, *Millais and the Ruskins* (1967), 131.

But Frank provided some welcome diversion. In early November, one morning, "Frank told me she didn't love me 'no more,' that I was not nice to anybody but Carrie." Later that day, the two girls returned to this engrossing theme, "& I said if she did not love me it was my misfortune— not my fault. I went up to her room, & was with her all evening, and guess she has concluded to love me some more after all." This scene obliquely hints at debauchery on Frank's bed, but, at least physically, it must have meant very little: by and large girls like Mabel Barrows were content with spooning, hugging, and arranging secret and delicious feasts—poor Mabel confessed to her diary in mid-winter that she weighed 150 pounds. It seems to have done her popularity among her classmates no harm.

For all her amorous experiments with Frank or Carrie, Mabel was never wholly disloyal to her beloved Mary. When in November the headmaster announced that Mary would finally arrive the next day, Mabel was "so excited and happy" that she slept little that night. Her welcome of Mary was ecstatic. There she was, with "her dear face," evidently happy to be back, "radiant." Almost the "first thing" that Mary whispered to Mabel was, " 'Sit with me?' " And so, Mabel's diary discloses, "sit with her I did, & she informed me that she was going to sleep with me. I pretended to be surprised," immensely pleased that the dear visitor should single her out for particular preference. So the innocent games quietly went on, until a letter from Mary in late January 1886 once more roused Mabel to eloquent words of longing: "I am *so lonely* without Mary & don't know what to do sometimes;" how much happier it would make her, she was certain, "to have her here to love and sympathize with me." Mary would write rarely, but her letters made up in bulk what they lacked in frequency: a nine-page outpouring arrived on January 26; another, twelve pages long, on March 8. Near the end of the school year, late in April, Mabel noted down one more declaration of her "strong love for Mary," testifying to a constancy that most other girls' crushes could not muster.

Almost inevitably, boys play subordinate parts in Mabel Barrows's entries, and those among her classmates who had discovered masculine charms aroused her strongly worded contempt. Hattie and Frank, she noted in mid-February, had attended a church supper the night before, "saw 3 fellows, and are consequently about daft. It makes me *sick* to hear them talk." She wondered "if those girls ever think how they live & breathe & have their being in the favor of men, while the latter never think of them except when they talk to them." It might be, she conceded, that "this is slightly overdrawn but I don't believe that the men make such geese of themselves."[12] Perhaps she was paraphrasing Byron's well-known lines about men finding love a thing apart, while it is women's whole existence. But whether borrowed or her own, her comparison of men to women shows Mabel Barrows to have been anything but a militant feminist; her open affection for other girls was not an impassioned rejection of men, but a natural phase in her young life.

The loves of Mabel Barrows, like those of Albert Dodd, then, were neither rare nor in themselves scandalous. Rather, they were indulgently smiled upon, fully expected. Occasionally, voices could be heard worrying over the long-range damage that such adolescent attachments, especially as fostered in boys' boarding schools, might do. In 1834, an anonymous writer in the respected English *Quarterly Journal of Education* asked, "Might not the want of character, the immorality of so many young men, particularly at college, be attributed in a great measure, to their earlier life at school?"[13] He was a fairly lonely and very temperate Cassandra; as late as 1906, Robert Musil's *Die Verwirrungen des Zöglings Törless*, a short novel detailing explicit homosexual and sadistic doings at a cadet school in the Austrian Empire, was greeted as a horrifying exposé. It should have surprised no one. After all, the Victorian decades fostered, even institutionalized, the segregation of young men and women in dress, in general appearance, in clubs, in sports, at work and play— and idealized the differences. The two sexes lived distinct lives, occupied distinct spheres, seemed to have distinct natures. But the power of denial was not to be underestimated; it did impressive work in the face of disagreeable evidence. The homoerotic aura of the nineteenth-century English public school, for one, its pretensions to discipline, purity, and decorum periodically tainted by scandal, became something of an open secret, the subject of gossip, inquiries—and fiction. Bourgeois culture found it possible both to worry about ardent adolescent friendships and to treat them as familiar and innocuous.

At times such attachments made their way into print, without deviousness or apology. In 1843, when the German actor and playwright Karl von Holtei published his expansive autobiography, he did not hesitate to invite his readers into his personal world of youthful homoerotic infatuation. Thirty years before, when he was fifteen, he had to say farewell to his intimate friend Karl, serving in the army. The moment moved

12. September 25, 26, October 13, 18, 21, 29, November 10, December 29, November 14, 1885, January 26, April 28, February 11, 1886, Mary I. Barrows, *Private Record*, 1885–1886, courtesy Susanna Barrows.
13. "English Boarding-Schools," *The Quarterly Journal of Education*, under the superintendence of the Society for the Diffusion of Useful Knowledge, VII (1834), 43.

him, and Karl, so profoundly "that we found neither words nor gestures
to express our feelings." This reticence, he confesses, was characteristic
of him. "The more goes on inside me, the more embarrassed I am to show
it." Only after Karl was gone, "when I heard the music of his regiment
resounding through the streets, when I said to myself, 'perhaps you will
never see him again,' then, only then, the bark of silent embarrassment
that had so far enclosed me, broke apart; a stream of tears broke forth,"
and he ran after the troops until at last he reached Karl and could press
his hand once more. Then Holtei sat down by the road "and wept most
pitiably," wholly unable to calm himself. As long as his friend had lived
in his family's house, as long as the two had seen each other every day,
every hour, Holtei had not noticed how much he had loved him—*wie
lieb ich ihn hatte*. But now that Karl had left, he wanted to "die of longing
for him."

From the distant, safe perspective of three decades, Holtei was ready
to recall this love of his adolescence and to anatomize it in detail. "This,"
he insisted, "was no longer the feeling of friendship" that he had harbored for "other boys of my age and my world." The melancholy that
had seized him on his farewell to Karl reminded him of "the inclination"
which, when he felt it for his Albertine, he had "called love." Thus,
precisely like Albert Dodd, Holtei could, without any sense of shame or
fear of ostracism, identify his love for a young man with his love for a
young woman. He quoted Bulwer Lytton to the effect that in the years
of adolescence, "before sexual love awakens," the "feeling of friendship
is almost a passion." Boys and girls at school, Bulwer Lytton had observed,
often show this kind of tempestuous affection, that "first indeterminate
longing of the heart for the principal food of human life—love." There
was evidently some advantage to denying the existence of infantile sexuality and placing the emergence of sexual love after puberty. But Holtei,
always self-analytical, asked himself whether he had been exceptionally
susceptible to this kind of amorous attachment in which the boundaries
between friendship and love were blurred. "My feeling for Karl was of
this sort." He left the question unanswered. But he recalled, matter-of-
factly, that as he came to travel about with his own regiment and made
interesting acquaintances, "I managed to get over the separation from my
friend only too soon."[14] Propagandists for the superiority of "Greek" over
other loves might say what they liked, but in real life homosexual affection
proved, for many others quite as much as for Holtei, no more durable
than its more conventional counterpart.

14. *Vierzig Jahre*, 8 vols. (1843–1850), I, 282–84.

The notion that youthful crushes or flames neither aimed at, or ever reached, sexual consummation, that their kisses, caresses, embraces, were not perilous steps down the path to vice but a touching rite of passage was complacent and self-serving. Passionate friendships begun in adolescence often survived the passing of years, the strain of physical separation, even the trauma of the partners' marriage. But these enduring attachments were generally discreet and, in any event, the nineteenth century mustered singular sympathy for warm language between friends. The cult of friendship, originating in the latter half of the eighteenth century but flourishing unabated through much of the nineteenth, permitted men to declare their love for other men—or women for other women—with impunity. Generally, of course, the embraces and kisses one friend bestowed on the other remained mere epistolary effusions. Hence the self-protective ideology asserting the innocence of friendship, no matter how heated, remained largely intact for decades.

There were those, to be sure, who felt their clandestine attachments as a kind of doom. Cowed by religious prohibitions, driven by the desire for social conformity, or bewildered by warm competing sentiments for the opposite sex, they would struggle, deny their tastes, and strenuously construct defensive ramparts. One of these miserable visitors to the realm of the Sodomites was Nicolai Gogol, desperately afraid of sexual expression, at ease with women only when they were visibly unthreatening, pious companions. Gogol clothed the love of his life for the intelligent, young, tubercular aristocrat Iosif Vielhorsky in the mantle of elevated friendship. Not long after Vielhorsky's early death in May 1839, mourning, distraught, but politic to the last, he recalled: "We had been long attached to each other, had long respected one another, but we became united intimately, indissolubly, and utterly fraternally only during his illness, alas." This fraternal union between the two young men included, as passages in Gogol's diaries disclose, lengthy vigils by Vielhorsky's bedside and explicit physical intimacy: " 'My savior,' he said to me. They still sound in my ears, those words. 'My angel! Did you miss me?' 'O, how I missed you,' he replied. I kissed him on the shoulder. He offered his cheek. We kissed; he was still pressing my hand."[15]

But decorous society, before proceeding to gossip or denunciation, would mobilize its ample resources for denial when someone of decent bearing and in a responsible position proved to have violated the rules of the game. Sinners must be punished, but scandal must be contained. Dr. C. J. Vaughan, a reforming and efficient headmaster of Harrow

15. From Simon Karlinsky, *The Sexual Labyrinth of Nicolai Gogol* (1976), 195–96.

between 1844 and 1859, a respected figure in the English educational establishment and a married man, was, in early 1858, surprised in a love affair with one of his pupils. It is safe to say that the great Dr. Arnold of Rugby, whose admiring disciple Vaughan proclaimed himself to be, would have been horrified. The other Harrovian to whom this sordid amour was discovered was, of all people, the young John Addington Symonds, later to acquire a considerable reputation as a cultivated travel writer, biographer, and cultural historian. At the time of this episode, he had not yet reconciled himself to his own homosexuality. Innocently, he confided the crushing news to his father, an eminent physician. Dr. Symonds promptly constituted himself, as it were, a vigilance committee of one; he induced Vaughan to resign his headmastership but permitted him to find refuge in honorable appointments in the Church of England. Shortly after, Lord Palmerston offered Vaughan the bishopric of Rochester and Vaughan, greatly flattered, accepted, only to be warned off by a threatening telegram from Dr. Symonds. As the entry in the *Dictionary of National Biography* later put it, protected by ignorance or guided by discretion, "probably after a severe struggle with his ambition," Vaughan changed his mind about Palmerston's invitation. A few, first startled by Vaughan's resignation of a headmaster's post in which he had distinguished himself and then amazed by his rejection of a clerical post he obviously coveted, came to suspect his real reasons. But to his death in 1897, they, and Vaughan, observed an utter silence, and he retained his place in the Church. When, late in his life, long after Dr. Symonds had died, Queen Victoria offered Vaughan the Deanery of Westminister, he declined once more. To the public at large, he always remained a great headmaster, voluminous author, and distinguished churchman. He made no secret of his affection for the boys he taught, and was celebrated for it in testimonial dinners and fond reminiscences.[16]

16. Phyllis Grosskurth, *John Addington Symonds: A Biography* (1964), 25–40; "Vaughan, C. J.," *Dictionary of National Biography*, ed. Sir Leslie Stephen and Sir Sidney Lee, 21 vols. (1885–1900), XX, 160. A rather similar case is that of William Johnson Cory, celebrated Eton master, composer of the Eton boat song, and an almost uninhibited lover of boys. His cycle of poems, *Ionica*, singing his affection for one of his pupils, first published anonymously in 1858, enjoyed a wide, and not merely underground, circulation. In 1872, the headmaster of Eton felt compelled to dismiss this immensely popular teacher, "not," as one recent student of the period rather innocently puts it, "for any very good reason save that it was dangerous for a school-master to allow his emotions to carry him so far that they were capable of being misunderstood." David Newsome, *Godliness and Good Learning: Four Studies on a Victorian Ideal* (1961), 87. On the contrary, one should say: it was dangerous once they were capable of being understood.

In his twisted and tormented career, Vaughan had lived out the compromise that the bourgeois century imposed on sexual heretics. He was fenced in but not exposed; his supreme punishment was being checked in his fondest ambitions. He could even indulge his sexual tastes as long as he chose his objects circumspectly and observed the rule of discretion. Then, toward the end of the nineteenth century, as the matter of homosexuality hesitantly came out into the open, principally for men, the fate of deviates only became more poignant. Far from easing their lives, the tentative new freedom only complicated them. The new attention generated hostility, fostered scandals, invited blackmail, ruined careers, drove some into suicide. This is the irony: the shift away from the delicacy that had governed the discussions, and even the thoughts, about erotic aberrations before the 1880s only increased public censure, not public approbation. The defensive stratagem of repression had had its virtues. What most of the nineteenth century had liked to call "vices which have no names," now became, in Lord Alfred Douglas's pathetic formula, the "love that dare not speak its name."[17] Many, heterosexuals and homosexuals alike, did not think this an improvement.

2. The Return of the Repressed

It was symptomatic of the general uncertainty surrounding the nature of sexual deviance and the proper role of the state in regulating intimate relations that the legislation which came to govern them in the nineteenth century moved in contradictory directions and sent out conflicting signals. France, always under the impress of the French Revolution, never touched the decision of the Constituent Assembly in 1791 to free homosexual contact between consenting adults from the stigma of criminality; the Code Napoléon had given that enactment authority and permanence. The Netherlands joined France in 1886, as did Italy in 1889, when they repealed all laws against male homosexual acts that did not outrage public decency, issue in violence, or victimize children. Before unification in 1871 imposed uniformity, the German states had treated these matters very variously, reflecting their own political fortunes rather than some distinctive Teutonic attitude: Bavaria and Hanover were only two states in which male homosexual acts did not invite the attention of

17. "A Forbidden Novel," *Saturday Review*, I (April 5, 1856), 461; Lord Alfred Douglas, "Two Loves" (1892; published in 1896, then suppressed by the author and republished in *Lyrics* [1935], 56–58.)

the prosecutor and to which homosexuals in trouble with the law would turn for shelter. The Prussian code of 1851, on the other hand, with its highly controversial Paragraph 143, annexed to homosexuality harsh penalties ranging up to prison sentences of four years—something of an improvement in a state that had, until 1794, treated homosexuals as felons exposed to burning at the stake. Despite the occasional earnest plea by jurists, physicians, and far from disinterested sexual reformers, it was this Prussian law, rather than Hanoverian tolerance, that the North German Federation adopted in 1869 and the German Empire took over two years later as the notorious Paragraph 175. It was to become a rallying cry for advocates of repeal everywhere. Punitive laws of this stripe, to be sure, were often enough counterproductive—they were hard to enforce. In Germany before 1900, on the average around 500 individuals were convicted each year under Paragraph 175—surely capturing no more than a vanishing fraction of homosexual acts consummated in the Empire. Indeed, lessening the stringency of penalties against sodomy and related offenses only increased the inclination of authorities to prosecute and of juries to convict. In Denmark, which abolished the death penalty for sexual offenses in 1866, this is precisely what happened.[18]

This involuted ballet of social anxieties and unintended consequences had its most spectacular incarnation in England in 1895, when, with Oscar Wilde's trials, many a newspaper reader became something of an expert on the scale of sexual offenses among which the law insisted on discriminating. While the death penalty for sodomy remained on the books until 1861, no one had been executed for such a crime for three decades. But then in 1885 the Labouchere Amendment to the Criminal Law Amendment Act struck directly at male homosexuals in their personal lives. Though originally designed to protect minors from being dragged into brothels or sold in the white slave trade, the Act specifically made "gross indecency" a felony. As John Addington Symonds, with a strong personal interest in the law, neatly epitomized its provisions, "(1) Sodomy is a felony, defined as the carnal knowledge (per anum) of any man or of any woman by a male person; punishable with penal servitude for life as a maximum. (2) The attempt to commit sodomy is punishable with ten

18. I am in this paragraph indebted to Vern L. Bullough, *Sexual Variance in Society and History* (1976), 565–86; James D. Steakley, *The Homosexual Emancipation Movement in Germany* (1975), ch. I; Jürgen Baumann, *Paragraph 175. Über die Möglichkeit, die einfache, nichtjugendgefährliche und nichtöffentliche Homosexualität unter Erwachsenen straffrei zu lassen* (1968); Grosskurth, *Symonds*, 283–84; Jeffrey Weeks, *Coming Out: Homosexual Politics in Britain, From the Nineteenth Century to the Present* (1977), ch. I, and p. 248.

years' penal servitude as a maximum. (3) The commission, in public or in private, by a male person with another male person, of 'any act of gross indecency,' is punishable with two years' imprisonment and hard labour."[19] Analyzing the failure of defensive mechanisms to keep unwelcome feelings and memories permanently from rising to awareness, Freud noted that when the repressed returns to consciousness, it does so in a distorted way, enforcing a compromise between the need for knowledge and the need to persist in ignorance. The late nineteenth-century legislation against sexual offenses and its capricious application demonstrates the return of the repressed in culture.

This failure of defensive mechanisms generated much vigorous, but for many readers highly confusing, literature. Germany alone produced something like a thousand pamphlets in the decade between 1898 and 1908 debating homosexuality and the law. A new and characteristic periodical, *Archiv für Kriminal-Anthropologie und Kriminalistik*, edited by Professor Hanns Gross and principally addressed to physicians, psychiatrists, and jurists, soberly discussed theories of homosexuality and criminal cases in which sexual motives appeared to be prominent. The most resounding salvos in this accelerating cannonade of confession, celebration, medical and legal inquiry were Oscar Wilde's *Picture of Dorian Gray*, which first appeared serially in 1890 and then as a book, considerably enlarged, the following year, and Richard von Krafft-Ebing's *Psychopathia Sexualis*, published in 1886. *Dorian Gray* was a homosexual tale by suggestion only, but with its lush coloring, its theatrical male friendships, and its polemics against social repression, it provided a model for the emerging candor about deviate love, and deceived no one. One reviewer bluntly said that its "dulness and incompetence" were "not redeemed because it constantly hints, not obscurely, at disgusting sins and abominable crimes." Another, no less blunt, thought it "undeniably amusing" but instinct with "dullness and dirt." A third, allowing the cleverness and ingenuity of *Dorian Gray*, regretted that its author seemed to be writing mainly for "outlawed noblemen and perverted telegraph boys." Presciently, John Addington Symonds told a friend, disapproving of *Dorian Gray* as "audacious" and "unwholesome in tone," that if "the British public will stand this, they can stand anything." Soon enough, that public made the limits of its tolerance all too plain.[20]

19. [Symonds], *A Problem in Modern Ethics. Being an Inquiry into the Phenomenon of Sexual Inversion Addressed Especially to Medical Psychologists and Jurists* (privately published in 1891; 1896), 135. Female homosexuals, being beyond most legislators' imagination, largely escaped their solicitude—a characteristic paradox.

20. Baumann, *Paragraph 175*, 84; *Wilde, Critical Heritage*, 68, 73, 75, 78.

Wilde's *Picture of Dorian Gray* did not make a revolution in awareness; a shift away from silence about homoeroticism in fiction had been
in the air for some time, heralded by a handful of novels. It is worth
reiterating that these heralds often portrayed and normally aroused
conflicting emotions. If Gautier's *Mademoiselle de Maupin* provided
ammunition for the avant garde's guerrilla warfare against the frightened
philistine in search of safety in love, Balzac's *La fille aux yeux d'or*,
though no less erotic, spoke for the other side in this moral debate.
Published in the year of *Mademoiselle de Maupin*, 1835, Balzac had
written the story not to shock bourgeois prudes but to warn against prevalent sexual corruption. Its protagonist, the uninhibited and amoral lesbian
marquise de St. Réal first buys the beautiful Paquita from her mother to
serve her insatiable lust and then murders her slave in a fit of insane
jealousy. As if these contrasting fictions did not introduce enough
ambiguous materials, readers could respond to such tales as Sheridan
Le Fanu's *Carmilla*, a ghost story on a theme very popular in the nineteenth century, in conflicting ways. In *Carmilla*, Le Fanu sublimates
homoerotic emotions into the chilling story of a vampire who, in the
guise of a lovely young woman, insinuates herself into the affections of
another lovely young woman to suck her blood. Few then read this sort
of familiar tale as a lesbian love story, but at some level of awareness the
appetite of one female beauty for another female beauty must have
registered as a hint at forbidden passions.

It was far easier to place Baudelaire's memorable poems about sapphists
and Courbet's canvas of two lush naked young women, entwined in
sleep. Baudelaire, after all, was an outsider, a scandalous figure, a blasphemer, better acquainted than any respectable poet should be with the
night side of Parisian life, with drugs and prostitutes. Courbet for his
part was scandalous in his own right, an artistic and political radical, who
had, moreover, painted this affectionate lesbian scene on commission from
Khalil Bey, a rich Turkish diplomat, who liked to look at such things.
Others were more casual about homoerotic moments; I have already
mentioned Théophile Gautier's bisexual Mademoiselle de Maupin, Thomas
Hardy's maternal and amorous Miss Aldclyffe, Henry James's intensely
competitive Olive Chancellor. I could have added, among others, characters in George Moore's *A Drama in Muslin*, J. P. Jacobsen's *Niels
Lyhne*, Eça de Queiros's *Os Maias*. In some of these tales, writers would
briefly introduce the homoerotic theme showing their hero in his youth,
and then drop the matter as of no particular consequence: for one in
A Relíquia, his novel about a supreme religious hypocrite, his schemes
and his downfall, Queiros has his protagonist, Theodorico, develop at

chool an intimate friendship with Chrispim, a boy as fair as an angel who
ikes to kiss Theodorico eagerly. Again in *Dom Casmurro*, Machado de
Assis has *his* protagonist, the narrator, admire the mathematical genius of
iis closest school friend so extravagantly that he hugs him, much to the
lismay of the padre who surprises the two in this tender scene.[21]
Bombarded with such images, whether fleeting or enduring, intended as
nirrors or as distortions of reality, the bourgeois public was being trained
o grasp the point of Wilde's *Picture of Dorian Gray*, if not necessarily
o like it.

Like Wilde, Krafft-Ebing was a culmination rather than a beginning.
His *Psychopathia Sexualis* brought him fame, controversy, and con-
:inuous demands for revised editions, but what was new in it was mainly
ts calm manner of presentation, its detailed, orderly, even stylish way
with sexual abnormalities. Eighteenth-century philosophes, Montesquieu,
Diderot, and Hemsterhuys, had already rather casually touched on what
Voltaire called "*l'amour socratique.*" Goethe had described the love of
boys, *Knabenliebe*, without apparent anxiety as being "as old as mankind; one could therefore say that it is in nature, even though it is against
nature." Early in the nineteenth century, a handful of publicists, savants,
and impassioned amateurs took up the issue. In 1829, in his *Die Bäder von
Lucca*, Heine savaged Graf von Platen, a maker of fastidious verses
equipped with impressive technical facility and burdened by all-too-
blatant homosexual longings, by quoting some of Platen's most damaging
lines and making free—all presumably in the service of his polemic—
with his painfully confessional poetic productions. Heine was not censored, but he was criticized for his lack of taste, of tact, and moderation,
by his friends and his enemies alike; his style of conducting debates did
not win wide support, even if it proved that one might exploit the tender
subject without fear of reprisals. Then, in 1836 and 1838, the Swiss auto-
didact Heinrich Hössli published a two-volume study, *Eros*, in which he
explored the love of men in ancient Greece, paying particular attention
to "Platonic love." Havelock Ellis, who read everything, thought the
book "a rather diffuse and tedious work," but its leading theme was to
become a commonplace in the literature. With better academic creden-
tials, in 1852, the eminent German forensic psychiatrist Johann Ludwig
Casper essayed to distinguish among several types of male loves—an
attempt to draw distinctions which is so often a sign of scientific progress.

21. Eça de Queiros: *A Relíquia* (1887; 2nd. ed., 1891), 14, 18–19; Machado de
Assis: *Dom Casmurro* (1899; ed. Maximiano de Carvalho e Silva, 1965, 3rd ed., 1975),
171–72.

But progress was slow, for its makers were visibly reluctant, though forcefully impelled, to soil their hands: in 1857, the French physician Auguste Tardieu, proclaiming the disgust that the subject of perversion inspired in him, forced himself to publish an outspoken "medical-legal study of assaults on morals," in which he collected an array of imaginative perversions he had encountered in his practice and his reading.[22]

It was not until the next decade that the subject found its language and its governing interpretation. In 1869, the Hungarian physician Dr. Karoly Maria Benkert produced that linguistic hybrid, "homosexuality," half Greek and half Latin, another, rather dubious, step toward a science of sexual aberrations. And in the same year, a recognized authority, the psychiatrist Dr. Carl Friedrich Otto Westphal, introduced an explanatory term that rapidly came to dominate the technical discussion of homosexuality: "contrary sexual feeling," he called it, *Die Conträre Sexualempfindung*. The term captured the imagination of professional students and passionate partisans alike. In 1882, the celebrated French neurologist, Jean-Martin Charcot, and a fellow expert, Valentin Magnan, published a study of the "Inversion of the genital sense," and a decade later, in 1891, the prolific German specialist on perversions, Dr. Albert Moll, brought out a book bearing precisely the title that Westphal had given his path-breaking work of 1869. When, five years after that, Dr. Hans Kurella translated what was to become the first volume in Havelock Ellis's monumental *Studies in the Psychology of Sex*, he chose for its title *Das konträre Geschlechtsgefühl*, and Ellis himself, when he could finally produce the book in English, called it *Sexual Inversion*. With its unmistakable insinuation that homosexual feelings are (as Goethe had already put it) at once natural and unnatural, the epithet retained enough vitality to survive into the twentieth century and into psychoanalytic literature: as late as 1908 and 1909, Dr. Isidor Sadger, an analyst specializing in the perversions, published articles on "*konträre Sexualempfindung*," and asked, in accord with the psychoanalyst's therapeutic ideal, whether the condition was curable. Even homosexuals found the name inescapable and professed to find it "neutral": John Addington Symonds observed in his posthumous *Problem in Modern Ethics* that since the "perversion of appetite," which only the ancient Greeks had valued, condemned their votaries to "pariahdom," only one modern scientific term was at least free of "male-

22. Goethe: conversation with Friedrich von Müller, April 7, 1830, *Gedenkausgabe der Werke, Briefe und Gespräche*, ed. Ernst Beutler, 24 vols. (1948–53), XXIII, 686; Heine: Jeffrey L. Sammons, *Heinrich Heine: A Modern Biography* (1979), 140–147; Ellis: *Sexual Inversion, Studies in the Psychology of Sex*, vol. I. (1897; 2nd. ed. 1900), 26; Tardieu: *Etude médico-légale sur les attentats aux moeurs* (1857).

dictions," namely " 'inverted sexual instinct.' "[23] This was a characteristic attitude among those aching to revise the prevailing view of sexual aberrations: half defiant and half conformist, homosexual publicists would wrily adopt the vocabulary of their culture and call their appetites perverted. Identifying with the aggressor and, at the same time, intent on disarming him, some of them even came to speak in mock derision of their loves: one of Lord Alfred Douglas's poems was entitled "In Praise of Shame."

Yet, as Proust discovered, one possible reading of "inversion" was welcome to homosexuals: the proposition that the love of man for man, or woman for woman, was not a matter of choice. On this point, the polemical writings of Carl Heinrich Ulrichs proved to be pioneering. A Hanoverian court official, Ulrichs was no scientist of inversion but an enthusiast; between 1863 and 1875 he poured out a round dozen of volumes elaborating his thesis that "uranism" is a congenital defect, the soul of a woman imprisoned in the body of a man. This meant that what Ulrichs called, a little clumsily, man-male sexual love, *mannmännliche Geschlechtsliebe*, was a sport of nature and removed all moral stigma from those condemned to enjoy it. By 1896, when Marc-André Raffalovich, well-known in his circles for his fluent and fairly explicit homoerotic verse, published a study on "uranism," Ulrichs's ideas appeared simplistic, even if his campaign had been epoch-making: "All that has been written," Raffalovich said, since it was discovered that "many men are born inverted," owes much "to the impulsion given by the famous invert, Ulrichs, who, proclaiming his own inversion, claimed justice and liberty for his brethren." But, he objected, "Ulrichs pleaded at once with too much enthusiasm and too much ignorance."[24] In reality, the term homosexuality is a single umbrella for a most diverse set of practices. For one thing, Raffalovich insisted reasonably enough, by no means all homosexuals are effeminate. The scientific community—like homosexual readers—could only agree with him: but Ulrichs's central, often reiterated idea, that to love one's own sex is not crime but fate, found sympathetic echoes among writers who felt unapologetic about their own sexual habits.

By the mid-1890s, writings on homoerotic sexuality became widely accessible. Ideologues like Edward Carpenter chanted the Whitmanesque love of comrades; versifiers like Lord Alfred Douglas, found, or founded, little journals to print their invocations to Greek love; venturesome physi-

---

23. Symonds, *Problem in Modern Ethics*, 1–3.
24. Raffalovich, *Uranisme et Unisexualité. Etude sur différentes manifestations de l'instinct sexuel* (1896), 26.

cians like Dr. "Laupts," an acquaintance of Zola's, published the life history of an "inverti-né," complete with commentary. In 1907, the pseudonymous "Max Kaufmann," retelling once again the familiar story of Heinrich Heine's scurrilous polemic against Graf von Platen, noted not without gratification: "Thanks to the scientific researches of the last few years in the area of sexual life, we have finally got to the point when we can 'call the child by its right name,' " and expect to be understood, "at least by the majority of the intellectual elite." Freud had written frankly about lesbian attachments as early as 1895; gradually, the educated reading public, the "intellectual elite," could turn to more and more explicit discussions of perversions—for knowledge or titillation.[25]

Doubtless, Krafft-Ebing's enormous prestige and Wilde's sleek story-telling had encouraged others, both to write and to read freely. Oscar Wilde's spectacular fall from grace had generated an impassioned international debate, all the more lively in that party lines did not all correspond to sexual tastes. Raffalovich was only the most articulate and most pitiless adversary that Wilde was to find among homosexuals. Wilde, Raffalovich told Dr. Laupts, had been "encouraged, tolerated by English society. He was called an institution." No wonder that his vanity grew out of all bounds, that he came to think of himself immune from the law. "He is victim of himself, of society and of his friends."[26] But more was at play in producing the new candor than one authoritative medical treatise and one resounding sexual scandal. The secularization of science, especially Darwin's fundamental and controversial propositions, had brought sexuality into the domain of the discussable: normal and abnormal sexual conduct alike were part of the evolutionary struggle by which nature selected the fit and rejected the unfit. The emerging discipline of sociology, searching for unemotional definitions of conformity and nonconformity, further contributed to the debate, just as Darwin and his followers had done: by making sexuality, including homosexuality, a candidate for dispassionate investigation. Involuntarily the purity crusaders, in the United States as in Europe, acted a little perversely to liberalize disclosure; with their irritating interventions into private opinions and tastes in reading or in art, they stimulated liberal minds to

25. Dr. Laupts, pseud. for Saint-Paul: *Tares et poisons. Perversions et Perversité sexuelles* (1896), preface by Emile Zola; Max Kaufmann: pseud. for Oskar Panizza (?), *Heinrich Heine contra Graf August von Platen und die Homoerotik* (1907), 7; Freud and Josef Breuer: *Studien über Hysterie* (1895), *G.W.*, I, 276, *Studies on Hysteria*, *S.E.*, II, 275.

26. Laupts, *Tares et poisons*, 127; see also Raffalovich's "report," ibid., 125–60, and Raffalovich's *Uranisme et unisexualité*, 24–81.

unaccustomed flights of candor and, simply by their strenuous work, called attention to subjects hitherto forbidden. What is more, the medical profession, which took deviance to be its proper province, accumulated both prestige and power in the last years of the nineteenth century, and its engrossing of the sexual domain meant that it came to propose all forms of homosexuality to be diseases. It is too much to say, but not by a great deal, that the 1870s and 1880s and 1890s invented homosexuality. Certainly, the new frankness about sexual life, whether acceptable or unacceptable, amply supports the notion, widespread among historians, that Victorian reticence began to lift two decades before the death of Queen Victoria. Well before 1900, homosexual feelings and actions, it seemed, deserved discussion, belonged to science, and should be removed from moralizing.

But the discussion remained shame-faced, the science uncertain, and the moralizing tenacious. This is not surprising. For some decades, after all, homosexuality had been a subject far less of serious investigation than of cautious defense or disparaging comment. From its beginnings, we know, the modern feminist movement had been the target of insults among which sexual innuendo would prove eminently serviceable—even before that decisive conclave at Seneca Falls in 1848, which produced the first comprehensive manifesto of necessary reforms in the relations between men and women. In vehement, muscular editorials and scarcely more temperate sermons, female feminists were denigrated as failed women, half-men, hens that crow. The sexual rhetoric of the anti-feminists did not simply keep pace with the woman's movement as it made its slow, obstructed way with its petitions and public pleas; rather, it reached hysterical intensity almost immediately. The protests of the early 1850s had already adopted a tone of terror insinuating nothing less than an imminent sexual catastrophe. Humor magazines and hostile legislators everywhere broadcast frightening pictures of appalling masculine harridans haranguing the House of Commons or the Chamber of Deputies, mustachioed women offending public decency by parading in trousers and waving about phallic cigars, freaks of nature invading men's most sacred precincts—clubs, sports, the professions. Male supporters of the movement were not forgotten: simpering mother's boys or soft aesthetes they seemed to be, with regular features, limp wrists, and submissive ways as they gladly watched the baby or did the shopping.[27] The ponderous sarcasm and unbridled ferocity—which is to say, the unmastered anxiety —with which many greeted the prospect of a redistribution of sexual

27. See *Education of the Senses*, ch. II.

roles, no matter how moderate, did something to accustom the public to the idea of sexual inversion, but it did nothing to foster its general acceptance, let alone its scientific study.

The small, far less aggressive movement on behalf of homosexual rights did little better. Dr. Benkert, the Hungarian physician who had coined the word, defended homosexuality in an open letter to the Prussian minister of justice, in which he rehearsed most of the arguments that the defenders of sexual permissiveness would employ in his time and long after: most states have legalized homosexuality without evident damage to their social fabric; "normal" persons, always the vast majority, have nothing to fear from inverts; great princes, statesmen, poets, playwrights, painters, and scientists have been homosexual, and to condemn them to prison (which, we know, the Prussian code prescribed) would have been absurd, cruel, damaging to culture; finally, sexual conduct is a private affair. Such special pleading, however reasonable, had no particular impact on public opinion except to raise the level of awareness a little; Ulrichs's rather pathetic propaganda for the beauties of "Uranian" love did not do much more. It was not until 1897, when a handful of German publishers, officials, and physicians, Dr. Magnus Hirschfeld most prominent among them, set up the Scientific Humanitarian Committee, that a formal campaign for homosexual rights was launched anywhere, deftly combined with the scientific investigation of sexual varieties. The *Komitee* got some unexpected support from leading German Social Democrats, August Bebel in Berlin and Eduard Bernstein in London, who saw, almost welcomed, homosexual scandals as a reflection on decadent bourgeois society.[28]

But these were minority opinions, and they did not hearten homosexuals enough to let them forego discretion. The much-quoted correspondence between John Addington Symonds and Walt Whitman suggests how nervous the most pressing advocates of male companionship still were even before the disgrace of Oscar Wilde, and how little of the unvarnished truth it seemed prudent to commit to paper. Symonds, one of Whitman's most fervent acolytes, had carried on a desultory, mutually congratulatory correspondence with the prophet of "adhesiveness" since 1871 and had sought, delicately, to make Whitman commit himself on the precise meaning of his more passionate lines, especially in the "Calamus" poems in *Leaves of Grass*. It was as if Symonds needed for

---

28. See the articles that Bernstein published in the theoretical organ of German Social Democracy in 1895, esp. "Aus Anlass eines Sensationsprozesses," *Die Neue Zeit*, XIII and XIV (1894–96), 171–76.

his own peace of mind to have Whitman formally on record. "In your conception of Comradeship," he inquired of Whitman on August 3, 1890, discarding most of his accustomed indirection at last, "do you contemplate the possible intrusion of those semi-sexual emotions and actions which no doubt do occur between men?" It seemed to Symonds that "the enthusiasm" of Whitman's Calamus poems was "calculated to encourage ardent and *physical* intimacies." The bait he dangled before the aging Whitman was a study which, he said, he could not write unless he had Whitman's views clearly before him. Whitman, carefully drafting his reply, denied everything with manufactured energetic indignation. He assured Symonds that he had had six children—"two are dead," he noted, masking his lie in false specificity—that his long life had been "jolly," and that, in any event, Symonds's implicit interpretation of those controversial passages in *Leaves of Grass* was nothing less than shocking: "Ab't the questions on Calamus pieces &c: they quite daze me. L. of G. is only to be rightly construed by and within its own atmosphere and essential character," and he added, to reinforce his denial, "that the Calamus part has even allow'd the possibility of such construction as mention'd is terrible." Disillusioned, Symonds chose to believe Whitman, and to write him off as one who "entertains feelings at least as hostile to sexual inversion as any law-abiding humdrum Anglo-Saxon could desire."[29]

That, in view of the prevailing temper, was obtuse. After all, Krafft-Ebing's *Psychopathia Sexualis*, with its parade of unsavory case histories and its very title, consigned sexual heresies to the domain of mental pathology. Value-charged adjectives like "revolting," which occasionally figure even in Freud's early papers, document the eagerness of medical specialists to put some disdainful distance between themselves and their interesting patients. When they wrote about these matters at all, they would normally begin with a defensive paragraph, draw on Krafft-Ebing's resounding reputation, or quote one another to encourage themselves. "The *physician*," Dr. Hermann Rohleder noted at the conclusion of his voluminous, wholly uninhibited series of lectures on sexuality normal and abnormal, "may shrink back with a shudder from all the abominations, but *it is part of his medical vocation if he wishes to judge his object, the living human being, his patient, truly and justly*." At the same time, though willing to catalogue, and meticulously describe, everything that one human being can perform sexually on the body of another—to say nothing of animals—these physicians, with the conspicuous exception

29. Grosskurth, *Symonds*, 272–74; Justin Kaplan, *Walt Whitman: A Life* (1980), 46–48.

of Freud and a handful of others, would resort to Latin, to keep the unauthorized from wading in these cesspools.[30]

While some good sense and humanity are by no means absent from these medical texts, homosexual tastes remained an uncomfortable theme, even for those who specialized in them and who, often quite unconsciously, derived some hidden pleasure from their work. The more a patient departed from straightforward, conventional heterosexual intercourse, preferably with a minimum of imaginative foreplay, the more censorious the physicians' prose became. While these nerve specialists pronounced homosexuals to be sick, they were reluctant to extend these sufferers the full measure of professional sympathy. They liked to speak, in their case histories, of possible rehabilitation, but the details of deviant sexual behavior struck them as repellent, barely mentionable, even in the obscurity of a learned tongue. Presenting *"le roman d'un inverti-né,"* Dr. Laupts noted, "I have felt obliged to put certain passages into Latin"; and he had chosen to do so thinking of "those persons, not used to medical studies, into whose hands this document might fall." In the preface to the first edition of his most famous book, Krafft-Ebing, claiming the "sad prerogative" of the physician to "view the shadow side of life, of human weakness and wretchedness," sternly noted that he was addressing "serious researchers in the domains of natural science and jurisprudence." In order to prevent the book from serving intruders as reading matter, he wrote, he had chosen a title that only the educated could understand and would employ "terminis technicis" wherever possible. This produced curious, and easily penetrable, mixed sentences, particularly in the case histories. Thus in "Observation No. 124," a thirty-year-old physician, a practicing homosexual, recounts his history which Krafft-Ebing renders, in part, as follows: "One evening I was seated at the opera next to an elderly gentleman. He courted me. I laughed heartily at the foolish old man and entered into his sport. Exinopinato genitalia mea prehendit, quo facto

30. Rohleder, *Vorlesungen über Geschlechtstrieb und gesamtes Geschlechtsleben des Menschen,* 2 vols. (1901; 2nd ed., 1907), II, 543. Note the interesting appeal by the Dutch physician S. A. M. von Römer, in his statistical study, *Die Uranische Familie. Untersuchungen über die Ascendenz der Uranier* (1906), which concludes with a heartfelt invocation to "Our Father," who will judge the "actions of his ignorant children" not by what they did, but whether their acts "came from love and were done with love" (p. 106). Henry Gibbons (private communication, December 15, 1983) has suggested, interestingly enough, that "keeping salacious material out of the hands of the unlettered is only one motivation [for the use of Latin]. Another, more subtle one is that Latin allows the researcher himself to distance himself from the material, to say without saying; for, as Hans Castorp told Clawdia (in Thomas Mann's *Zauberberg*), 'parler français, c'est parler sans parler.' "

tatim penis meus se erexit." In some alarm, the physician demanded to know what his neighbor had in mind. "He told me that he was in love with me. Since I had heard of hermaphrodites in the hospital, I thought had to do with one of them here, curiosus factus genitalia eius videre volui. Sicuti penem maximum eius erectus adspexi, perterritus effugi."[31] Whether this sort of prose encouraged the study of Latin is not on record.

In this select gallery of specialists, Havelock Ellis was practically unique: he visibly enjoyed his work. His sense of pleasure in sexuality, combined with his obsessive collecting of the many and varied gratifications that sexual inclinations can devise, gave Ellis a virtual monopoly on popularization in this still somewhat disreputable field around 1900. His was hard-won knowledge; with erotic peculiarities of his own, Ellis found tantalizing and troubling materials for his life's work in his own appetites and at his own hearth. The most arousing sight, to him, was a woman urinating. His wife turned out to be a lesbian. What is more, some who later recorded their reminiscences of him slyly intimated that writing about sex was about as close to orgasmic gratification as he ever came. The world did not know this. But, publishing as he was in the mid-1890s, just after the Wilde trials, Ellis confronted an English public scarcely inclined to make fine distinctions between scientists and apologists. He could not secure a respectable English publisher for *Sexual Inversion*, and became entangled with a swindler and adventurer; in 1898, when one of his faithful admirers, George Bedborough, was tried for selling a copy of *Sexual Inversion*, the indictment denounced the book as "a certain lewd wicked bawdy scandalous and obscene libel."[32] It was only with the passage of time, the cooling of tempers, and the unstinted approval of foreign scholars that the sobriety and earnestness of Ellis's work began to be recognized even in England.

Havelock Ellis was not a homosexual; in the early 1890s he could collaborate with John Addington Symonds without feeling any particular nervousness about his own inclinations. He was a strenuous advocate, but for larger causes. Ellis wanted life to be informed by knowledge and governed by love; his prolific output across the decades attests to his single-mindedness. Ellis had a mission, early conceived and never aban-

---

31. Dr. Laupts: *Tares et poisons*, 47; Krafft-Ebing: "Vorwort zur ersten Auflage," *Psychopathia Sexualis* (11th ed., 1901), 218–19.

32. Grosskurth, *Ellis*, 194. When, in 1885, Sir Richard Burton published a "Terminal Essay" appended to his translation of the Thousand and One Nights and included a frank, discriminating, and sympathetic exploration of "pederasty," he was courting prosecution but only reaped critical acclaim and financial success. See Fawn M. Brodie, *The Devil Drives: A Life of Sir Richard Burton* (1967), 305–11.

doned. As a young man, he reports in the preface to *Sexual Inversion*
he had resolved that "one main part of my life-work should be to make
clear the problems of sex." He acknowledged that he was writing "not
without moral fervor" but defined his ardor to be, as it were, objective
sex was simply "the central problem of life." While he was an enthusiast
for progress, he made courageous lunges at science and, with all his
improving purposes, the most determined efforts at disinterested research
After all, he noted, with the engaging naiveté that never abandoned him
"the problem of religion has practically been settled," while "the problem
of labour has at least been placed on a practical foundation." That left
"the question of sex" as the principal matter for future generations to
address. "Sex lies at the root of life, and we can never learn to reverence
life until we know how to understand sex." He immediately added
modestly reducing sententiousness to the dimensions of mere personal
opinion: "—So, at least, it seems to me." But for Ellis, moral fervor, far
from precluding sobriety and accuracy, imperiously demanded both. He
sought "that cold and dry light through which alone the goals of knowledge may truly be seen."[33]

Havelock Ellis's work is a vast tribute to his generous and slightly
sentimental vision. He made himself into a connoisseur of medical treatises
polemical tracts, and personal communications; there is something touching about this perpetual adolescent, this bushy-bearded, lifelong student
with his penetrating eyes, his unflagging curiosity, his literal-mindedness
and his optimism. In *Sexual Inversion*, for many his most explosive book
he summarizes the scholarly literature of the nineteenth century on
homosexuality—Hoessli, Westphal, Krafft-Ebing and the others—and
offers vignettes or case histories drawn indiscriminately from confessions
he had solicited, letters he had received, obscure monographs he had
unearthed. Raffalovich, Symonds, and their self-referential fellows had
done much the same. Even Ellis's suggestions for legal and social improvement in the status of the deviate resemble the homosexual publicists'
barely controlled rage for reform. But there was a subtle difference between his organized curiosity and their wishful thinking. Ellis was a born
world improver, broad in his sympathies, determined to find nothing
human alien to him. But his empiricist's passions, his sublimated voyeurism, remained in control. "Pathology," he concluded, "is but physiology
working under new conditions. The stream of nature still flows into the
bent channel of sexual inversion, and still runs according to law." For
Ellis, Nature always remained a supreme, adorable principle deserving

33. Ellis, *Sexual Inversion*, ix–x.

pitalization. Hence this "toilsome excursion" into inversion had not en, he thought, a waste of time. "With the knowledge here gained we e the better equipped to enter upon the study of the wider questions of x." This was more than a perfunctory peroration; it shows Ellis under- king his humane study of "this perverted tendency" less for the sake of cial renewal than for the sake of cultural science.[34] But then, for this tter-day philosophe, this Voltaire of sex, knowledge was the indispen- ble ground for improvement.

It was far less his conclusions than his attitude, his all too visible sym- athy with often unpalatable materials and his patience in gathering oteric information, that made Havelock Ellis's work on sexual inversion fresh and, for some years, so uninfluential. He followed other in- estigators like Dr. Albert Moll in considering sexual inversion to be rgely congenital and acquired homosexuality rare; inherited predisposi- ons were brought into play, he thought, in the course of maturation r through such accidents as seduction, prolonged imprisonment, or disappointment in love." In his chapter on homosexuality in women he ccepted the verdict of recognized authorities that lesbianism was prob- bly "little, if at all, less common in woman than in man," but that, at the me time, students of sex had learned "comparatively little of sexual version in woman." The case material was skimpy, and researchers ould glean less dependable information from physicians or psychologists an from novelists and poets—from Diderot and Balzac, Gautier and ola, Maupassant and Bourget, Swinburne and Verlaine. Yet, with other vestigators of such matters, Ellis found women mysterious. Having sserted that probably as many women were homosexual as men, he ould also say, a few pages later, that "many observers who are able to peak with authority," were finding that "homosexuality is increasing mong women" in the United States, in France, in Germany, in England. or a psychologist committed to the view that the homosexual orientation early always has congenital roots, Havelock Ellis was remarkably ready o attribute seductive powers to environmental influences, including that wholesome and inevitable movement," the struggle for woman's emanci- ation.[35] Ellis's pages on lesbianism disclose how little researchers into exuality knew in his day, how much they still had to learn.

But Havelock Ellis, a fanatic about reasonableness, knew this much: he concrete manifestations of inversion, together with the feelings they xpress, vary impressively. The thirty-odd cases he presents show that

34. Ibid., 158.
35. Ibid., 139, 78, 79, 99, 100.

while some men had practiced "*paedicatio* or *immissio penis in anum*, many had found gratification in "spooning," embraces, and mutu: masturbation. Some male homosexuals are effeminate, others masculin some display themselves, others seek concealment; some patheticall lament their fate, others find nothing objectionable in their sexual taste None of this was particularly new. But Ellis stressed what others, lik Krafft-Ebing, had only intimated: the conclusions that the investigator c sexual inversion will reach must vary with his particular angle of visio "It is natural that the police official should find that his cases are largel mere examples of disgusting vice and crime. It is natural that the asylur superintendent should find that we are chiefly dealing with a form o insanity." He added, equally, it was "equally natural that the sexu invert himself should find that he and his friends are not so very unlik ordinary persons."[36]

What, then, Ellis asked, is inversion? An abominable vice deservin prison? A diseased condition calling for the lunatic asylum? A natur monstrosity, a "sport" crying out for regulation? Or perhaps "as a fev assert," nothing less than "a beneficial variety of human emotion" de serving to be "tolerated or even fostered?" Judicious and prudently non committal, Ellis allowed that "there is probably an element of truth i more than one of these views." Actually, his considered position wa less vacillating, less timid than this: homosexuality in men and wome alike is an abnormality, much like colorblindness. Ellis acknowledge that society could not reasonably be "expected to tolerate the invert who flaunts "his perversion in its face" and who claims to be "of fine clay than the vulgar herd" just because he likes to "take his pleasure witl a soldier or a policeman." At the same time—and this, of course, wa Ellis's principal point—society "might well refrain from crushing witl undiscerning ignorance beneath a burden of shame the subject of ar abnormality which, as we have seen, has not been found incapable of fin uses." Just as society is "bound to protect the helpless members of society against the invert," it must protect the hapless invert against society.[3] This may read today, a century later, like a stressful effort not to b excessively offensive. In the years before 1900, it was, especially for th average bourgeois, a subversive point of view, even a little obscene.

Yet Ellis's ingenuous candor and magpie diligence were prudishnes itself compared to the poetry and short stories that newly emboldene homosexual writers dared commit to print in the early 1890s. Few ordi

36. Ibid., 50–51, 128.
37. Ibid., 128, 157.

ary bourgeois ever saw these productions; it took an alert editor, or a
pectacular trial, to give them any kind of currency. In December 1894,
n Oxford undergraduate, John Francis Bloxam, brought out the first,
nd, it turned out, the last, number of a new periodical, *Chameleon*. It
ontained, among other salacious things, two poems by Lord Alfred
)ouglas, one of which, "Two Loves," would figure prominently in the
Vilde trials the following year. The editor himself contributed anony-
nously two items that were, if anything, more explicit than Douglas's
anguid verse: a story about a homosexual love, "The Priest and the
Acolyte," and a poem recounting an erotic dream in which the "sweet
)oy-king" appears, "kissing the tears of the night away," and the dreamer
evels in

> the moisture of warm wet lips
> Upon my lips.

This was too much for Jerome K. Jerome, humorist, playwright, essayist.
Commenting editorially on *Chameleon* in his own paper, *To-Day*, he
reaped energetic epithets on young Bloxam and his productions in verse
nd prose. Jerome wanted to make sure, he said, not to be "mistaken for
prude on the prowl," and acknowledged that "young men," especially
hose who had just gone through public school, "are here and there
:ursed with these unnatural cravings." But it was for them to "wrestle
with the devil within them," not to enjoy and to advertise him. A dozen
or so years later, Marcel Proust would take this point. *Chameleon* was,
:o Jerome's mind, probably "a case for the police," for it was an "insult to
animal creation" and an "outrage to literature." Worse, it was an abomi-
nation: "garbage and offal." Subscribing to the diagnosis of the physicians,
Jerome called the magazine an "advocacy for indulgence in the cravings
of an unnatural disease." That was its crime: it seduced the young.[38]

Most modern readers will find the materials that crowded Bloxam's
Chameleon and similar ephemeral publications neither disgusting nor
dangerous. While they understandably varied with the particular sexual
:astes of the author, they were, within their specialized genres, exceedingly monotonous. Men who loved boys hymned the charms of naked
youths on the beach, women who loved women apostrophized Sappho.
Again, men who, to become sexually aroused, craved lovers from the
lower orders, exclaimed over the brawn of sailors or the vigor of athletes:
Edward Cracroft Lefroy, a short-lived, invalid Oxonian whose homo-

38. Timothy d'Arch Smith, ed., *Love in Earnest: Notes on the Lives and Writings of
English 'Uranian' Poets from 1889 to 1930* (1970), 54–59.

sexuality was purely theoretical and whose verse was given some post
humous circulation by John Addington Symonds after Leroy's death in
1891, could pay his poetic addresses to a cricket bowler and a football
player in two faultless sonnets. Instructively, always excepting that un
buttoned genius Walt Whitman, this literature was disciplined, highly
formal. But its feelings were almost naked: these texts rehearse wishful
fantasies as fulfilled or recall glowing memories of blissful embraces
rather defensively, they proclaim the purity of such loves, and their moral
superiority to the lustful or utilitarian sensuality to which ordinary
heterosexual mortals stooped.

There is an exquisite snobbery about these productions, addressed as
they are to an exclusive coterie, to a quietly superior, largely secret clan.
They are perfumed with evocations of nature and, often, suffused with
pious allusions: the fraternity of religion and sexuality that characterized
the work of many heterosexual literati also marks these knowing, subver
sive poems and stories. It was no accident that many homosexual poet
should have been clergymen. The Anglo-Catholic persuasion in particular
with its seductive mixture of theological conservatism, elaborate ritual
emotional piety, and invitations to celibacy, appealed to those, like Hurrell
Froude, condemned to wrestle with "thoughts which sometimes come
into my head," too "shocking even to name." John Henry Newman's
affection for Froude, like the passionate male friendships that punctuated
the lives of Edward Pusey and John Keble, had little that was overtly
carnal about them, but an erotic ingredient, half joyful and half desperate,
is unmistakable.[39] It was only too obtrusive to their implacable detractors:
in 1898, John Kensit, founder of the Protestant Truth Society, reported
to a meeting in London of a "ritualist" Good Friday service conducted
by "a priest in petticoats," and attended by "very poor specimens of
men . . . a peculiar sort of people, very peculiar indeed." Kensit was a
demagogue, his Society a gang of bullies who enjoyed nothing so much
as breaking up Anglo-Catholic services, and his audience already per-

39. "Only a year before his death, after nearly twenty years of misunderstandings
and estrangement, W. G. Ward (English Roman Catholic convert and controversialist) told the present biographer (Wilfrid Ward) of a dream he had had—how
he found himself at a dinner party next to a veiled lady, who charmed him more
and more as they talked. At last he exclaimed, 'I have never felt such charm in any
conversation since I used to talk with John Henry Newman, at Oxford.' 'I am John
Henry Newman,' the lady replied, and raising her veil showed the well-known face."
Geoffrey Faber, Oxford Apostles: A Character Study of the Oxford Movement (1933;
rev. ed. 1954), 46. Whatever the ideas latent in this beautiful vignette, the manifest
dream says much about Newman's impact on those who knew him and about his
associates.

uaded of, and theatrically revolted by, the "effeminacy" of all Anglo-
Catholics and their perverted flirtation with Rome. His proceedings were
the intermittent, never wholly dormant anti-Popery campaigns of Protestant extremists driven to the highest pitch of hysteria, as unscrupulous in
their tactics as they were intemperate in their rhetoric. The innuendos
that had already been tried on active feminists were transferred to those
whose religious observances appeared suspiciously lacking in manliness.

The transparently sexual insults that the likes of John Kensit did not
scruple to broadcast were often mere slander, and at all times betrayed a
febrile anxiety over the threat that sexual heretics, in thought or action,
imagined or real, appeared to pose. But it is true that the spirituality of the
victims, though normally sincere, even fervent, is not free from an admixture of apologetic evasiveness, a veil unconsciously thrown over
physical desire. Yet intense Christianity was not the only refuge to which
the troubled and the effete might repair in the nineteenth century; in that
civilized world, classical Greece was no less available as an ideal and a
seduction.

3. An Antique Persuasion

The attractions of the classical world for homosexual writers and readers
are too obvious to need detailed analysis. Many homosexuals, to be sure,
in many countries, gratified their inclinations, whether in stable domestic
arrangements or with prostitutes, without venturing to elevate them into
imitations of ancient Greek ideals—that sort of refined apologia was
reserved to those educated to write poetry or translate the classics. But
even those who did not flatter themselves as modern Greeks profited
from this distinguished ancestry: ancient myths and poems, words, and
ideas were woven into the texture of nineteenth-century civilization.

Greek culture, sovereign and superb, floated above criticism for the
most devout of cultivated Christians as for the most skeptical of modern
pagans. The Greeks' joy of life, their mental balance, their unashamed
exhibition of the body in gymnastics and sculpture—all unshadowed by
those darker realities to which nineteenth-century worshipers were conveniently blind—could serve as correctives to the ascetic severities of the
Christian dispensation. Classical culture was remote enough to be the
special province of those who could master difficult dead languages, yet
close enough to give pleasure and supply models. Now, beyond doubt,
the ancients had countenanced pederasty, all the more freely in that they
had surrounded it with elaborate rules. Their gods, with Zeus in the van-
guard, were libertines, often bisexual in their choice of erotic objects:

Ganymede, Zeus's beloved handsome cup-bearer, became a prized totem for men praising all-male love, prized and conventional, as much as Hadrian's beautiful catamite Antinoüs. Achilles had loved Patroclus beyond all women. Sappho had sung the beauties who had captivated her. And Plato, as every educated person knew, had dramatized the fervent feeling of man for man in his dialogues.

What made some of these antique instances particularly enticing was that one could point to their spirituality: there is no overt homosexual conduct in Homer, and Plato's scale of erotic preferences leads away from physical consummations to the contemplation of ideal beauty. To assimilate modern homosexual affairs to the exalted classical heritage was to borrow from its dignity, to claim a kind of historic rightness. The device was transparent, but no less popular for all that. Many saw through it, and some were willing to say so in print. Thus, the eminent Bostonian writer, editor, and liberal reformer Thomas Wentworth Higginson, reviewing Oscar Wilde's early poems in 1882, explicitly questioned their manliness: "Mr. Wilde may talk of Greece; but there is nothing Greek about his poems; his nudities do not suggest the sacred whiteness of an antique statue, but rather the forcible unveiling of some insulted innocence."[40] In these observations, the young Wilde appears as a literary rapist, probably homosexual.

Most scholars, more nervous than Higginson, did their best to evade the plain implications of their texts, ancient no less than modern. Through the first half of the nineteenth century, with an energy worthy of more pressing causes, German and English classicists debated whether Sappho's passionate "intercourse with her female friends" was innocent or otherwise, with the majority opting for "virginal purity." In his highly praised, widely used translations of Plato, Benjamin Jowett, acknowledging that the dialogues seemed to endorse male erotic attachments, proposed that modern readers transfer what Plato teaches about love "to the love of women before we can attach any serious meaning to his words." He professed to believe, embarrassment triumphing over evidence, that "had he lived in our times, he would have made the transposition himself."[41] Students of the classics covered their analyses of ancient texts with woolly imprecision, or read homosexual advocacy as irony, bowdlerized earthy epithets, changed the gender of pronouns, and explained away sensual festivals as innocuous social gatherings.

40. *Wilde, Critical Heritage*, 51.
41. Sappho: William Mure, "Sappho, and the Ideal Love of the Greeks," *Rheinisches Museum für Philologie*, ed. F. W. Welcker and F. Ritschl, XII (1857), 564, 568; Jowett: Frank M. Turner, *The Greek Heritage in Victorian Britain* (1981), 425.

Lord Alfred Douglas, John Addington Symonds, and others of their persuasion, whether in England or elsewhere, naturally disdained, while they often employed, such defensive devices. When they wrote about antique beauty or antique freedom with fastidious euphemisms, they did so not from prudishness but from policy. To be sure, Symonds, whose latent homosexual inclinations had been stimulated and licensed by his reading of Plato's *Phaedrus*, was ambivalent about the classics: he warned his friend Oscar Browning, a homosexual school master on the pattern of C. J. Vaughan, against the effect that homoerotic Greek literature might have on the young. But he was, in this gesture, either impishly playful or obeying a confessional compulsion and, at all events, highly unusual.[42] Others found ancient culture only too useful; it permitted them to dwell on what obsessed them, and to be understood mainly by those equipped to understand.

Walter Pater, influential Oxford don, suggestive and subjective essayist, master of paradoxes before Wilde, was adept in this kind of dealing. A discreet aesthete, he enjoyed the company of handsome young men but never compromised himself; he expressed himself more fully, if always obliquely, in his allusive writings, suffused with the classical spirit as then current in English public schools and the ancient universities. It was Pater who gave impressionable young men the vocabulary and the alibi to cultivate their sensations, reject Christian asceticism, live for the moment, and burn with a hard, gem-like flame.

The most consequential among Pater's declarations of adherence to the Greek ideal was probably his famous essay on the eighteenth-century German founder of art history, Johann Joachim Winckelmann. First published in the *Westminster Review* in 1867 and then incorporated, six years later, into his *Studies in the History of the Renaissance*, it is a masterpiece of indirection, no less extraordinary for being in part unconscious. Pater's "Winckelmann: Et Ego in Arcadia Fui," begins with a heartfelt sketch of Winckelmann's life. Born in poverty, yearning for the sunlight of the Mediterranean world, he laboriously educated himself in Germany and cynically converted to Roman Catholicism to find patrons who would subsidize his life's mission. Winckelmann was what Freud would later call an exception: deprived and destitute, he felt entitled to extract from the world whatever rewards it held for him, by whatever means he could devise. Looking "over the beautiful Roman prospect" in 1763, finally having reached one of his destinations, Winckelmann wrote, as Pater quotes him: "One gets spoiled here; but God owed me this; in my youth

42. Grosskurth, *Symonds*, 76, 268.

I suffered too much." His object, lucidly perceived and fanatically pursued, was beauty. And this beauty, as Pater could not deny, meant the male body. Art is frozen life, supremely worthy of study because it reflects and, to the sensitive student discloses, the breathing human form. Pater calls Winckelmann "wholly Greek" in that he had found what he sought in "the continual stir and motion of a comely human life," a phrase composed of some fairly obvious code words.[43]

In his early German phase, studying and begging, Winckelmann had at first "handled the words only of Greek poetry, stirred indeed and roused by them, yet divining beyond the words some unexpressed pulsation of sensuous life. Suddenly," as he visits Dresden, and comes upon antiquities for the first time—not the originals, by the way, but gypsum copies—"he is in contact with that life, still fervent in the relics of plastic art." Pater, as always, has chosen his words for their evocative value; they permit an innocent reading but invite a sexual interpretation: Winckelmann had only "handled" words, and been "stirred" and "roused" by them; as he comes to handle ancient art, the "unexpressed pulsation of sensuous life" struggles for expression, and he finally, literally, makes "contact" with that sensuality. Winckelmann is, from the beginning, purposeful; the "protracted longing" of his apprentice days is not "vague, romantic," but quite precise: "within its severe limits," Pater writes, once again resorting to meaningful metaphors, "his enthusiasm burns like lava."[44]

Pater does not quite say that Winckelmann burns, enthusiastically, for male lovers, but it is not eccentric for his time that he could, with impunity, almost say so: "That his affinity with Hellenism was not merely intellectual, that the subtler threads of temperament were inwoven in it, is proved by his romantic, fervent friendships with young men. He had known, he says, many young men more beautiful than Guido's archangel." If, as Pater argues, Winckelmann's ambition was not romantic, his appetite for beautiful young men was precisely that. Pater quotes what he calls, in his genial manner, a "characteristic" passage: "As it is confessedly the beauty of man which is to be conceived under one general idea, so I have noticed that those who are observant of beauty only in women, and are moved little or not at all by the beauty of men, seldom have an impartial, vital, inborn instinct for beauty in art. To such persons the beauty of Greek art will ever seem wanting, because its supreme beauty is rather male than female." Pater's only comment on this blatant de-

43. Pater, *Studies in the History of the Renaissance* (1873; 1877, ed. Modern Library, n.d.), 148, 151.
44. Ibid., 152, 154.

claration, which he goes on quoting for some sentences more, is a sympathetic biographical gloss: Winckelmann's search for male beauty often caused him pain. Pater then proceeds to contrast, tendentiously, antique Greek culture, its serenity, its wholeness, with his own philistine and nervous time: "What modern art has to do in the service of culture is so to rearrange the details of modern life, so to reflect it, that it may satisfy the spirit. And what does the spirit need in the face of modern life? The sense of freedom."[45] This is not a full-fledged brief for changing social attitudes about homosexual affairs, but Pater's essay remains a distinguished performance in the covert theatrics of homoerotic propaganda for which such texts had their uses and their receptive readers. It was the kind of performance that nineteenth-century bourgeois culture was preparing to absorb.

In 1873, the year that the first edition of Pater's essays on the Renaissance came out, John Addington Symonds wrote, but did not publish, *A Problem in Greek Ethics*, a skillful apologia for homosexuality, a plea in the guise of an exploration, restrained in tone and reasonable in argument. Its very title and its opening sentence adopt Westphal's vocabulary in designating homosexual love as a "sexual inversion."[46] And Symonds further covers his tracks by calling "boy-love," with apparent sincerity, a "vice." But there can be no doubt: he had designed these stratagems and the whole of his text to make his readers think better of "inverts" and of their "vice." That he chose to have, at first, no readers for this tract and later only a very few was a symptom of his conflict no less than of his fear. "You see," he wrote a friend much later, in 1889, "I have 'never spoken out.' " The reader he wanted most to reassure as he wrestled with his "strangely constituted" character was himself.[47]

Whoever his audience, *A Problem in Greek Ethics* is a sustained presentation buttressed with commendable scholarship: the institution of "paederastia, or boy-love" had been "a phenomenon of one of the most

45. Ibid., 159, 192. Pater's intimate friend, Richard Charles Jackson, a lay Anglo-Catholic brother of the order of St. Augustine (brother à Becket), wrote Pater a birthday poem that included this quatrain: "Your darling soul I say is inflamed with love for me;/ Your very eyes do move I cry with sympathy:/ Your darling feet and hands are blessings ruled by love,/ As forth was sent from out the Ark a turtle dove." David Hilliard, "Unenglish and Unmanly; Anglo-Catholicism and Homosexuality," *Victorian Studies*, xxv (1982), 193. Pater may have enjoyed the tribute, but he would have been too fastidious to write such embarrassing lines himself.
46. *A Problem in Greek Ethics, Being an Inquiry into the Phenomenon of Sexual Inversion Addressed to Medical Psychologists and Jurists*, 5. Printed privately in ten copies in 1883, it was published posthumously in 1901, but then only in 100 copies [preface].
47. Symonds to Henry Graham Dakyns, March 27, 1889, Grosskurth, *Symonds*, 277.

brilliant periods of human culture." This, Symonds implies, was surely no accident, though he does not draw the obvious inference. Indeed, his was a book in which a "Sodomite" could have taken little comfort. Symonds firmly argues that antique friendships between men were a form of "manly love," a "powerful and masculine emotion in which effeminacy had no part, and which by no means excluded the ordinary sexual feelings." He makes, once again, the familiar point that Achilles and Patroclus, who loved one another, were not pederasts. This was a safe position to which many advocates of fervent male attachments were glad to retreat. In fact, Symonds argues with a show of severity that "the legend of the rape of Ganymede was invented," to judge from a passage in Plato, "by the Cretans with the express purpose of investing their pleasures with a show of piety." Just as severely, he judged homosexuality in Rome to have been of a far lower order than Greek pederasty: Rome, corrupt and debased, Symonds charged, "never truly caught the Hellenic spirit." Sounding much like Heine half a century before him, Symonds saw Christianity as a necessary response to Roman sensuality, ending "logically" with "the cloister and the hermitage." But fortunately Christian culture had not rested content with this extreme "separation from nature"; instead it had developed a "nobler synthesis" with the cult of Mary, the rules of chivalry, in short, the elevation of woman.[48] Like many other homosexuals, Symonds professed sincere respect for the female of the species.

Some of Symonds's study is self-protective and some of it self-indulgent. To yield to his preoccupation with the history of homosexuality gave Symonds ample opportunity to dwell, in elevated language, on the superior beauty of the male over the female body and to quote freely from homoerotic poets. But later Symonds, especially in his Italian years, began not so much to speak as to act out his tastes with a kind of aggressive abandon, as if he needed to confess, over and over, the passion that had molded his life. He paraded his principal Venetian paramour, the handsome young gondolier Angelo Fusato, with little shame, and apparently no anxiety: in 1890, three years before his death, he invited himself and Angelo to a friend's house by describing Angelo as "an old peasant" who had been with him "for ten years, & is a very good fellow." A good fellow Fusato may have been, in his exploitative way, but, as Symonds's friends soon discovered, he was neither old nor a peasant. In 1892, when Symonds briefly returned to England, he insisted on bringing

48. *Problem in Greek Ethics,* 1, 3, 5–6, 72, 73.

Angelo with him.[49] His friends were hardly average bourgeois, but their acceptance of Symonds's arrangements throws some unsuspected light on the patience and flexibility, the sheer capacity to accept the unacceptable, of at least some among the late Victorians.

Symonds, the pagan lover of male beauty, was a complex and inconsistent being. After his death, Swinburne, who had little cause to condescend to devotees of unconventional practices, wickedly dismissed him as a "Platonic amorist of blue-breeched gondoliers." But Symonds was, if an errant husband, an affectionate father, who took pleasure in his advanced domestic pedagogy. "I am glad," he wrote to his daughter Madge in the late 1880s, "that you have discovered that your family is liberal in soul beyond most people. I think that we are." After all, "There is nothing middle class or *bourgeois* here." It was plain to him that "a large part of human life, the largest part, is involved in not being bourgeois." Symonds earnestly attempted all his life not to be bourgeois and vehemently denounced his compatriots: "A bourgeois Anglo-Saxon pack of Jesuits!"[50] But had he succeeded in stripping off his own bourgeois conscience, his inner life would have been more tranquil than it was.

Such tranquility, at least outward tranquility, was not beyond the reach of nineteenth-century homosexuals. It was precisely the quality that Edward Carpenter's fervent admirer, Edith Ellis—"Mrs. Havelock Ellis" on the title pages of her books—singled out for particular praise in her idol: "In these days of storm and stress," she wrote in 1910, "not only in politics, but in morals and personal faith, it is refreshing to study the works of a man who is at peace with himself." But Carpenter was impressive only in his acquaintances and far-ranging only in his influence; he seems to have specialized in knowing everyone on the edge of respectable bourgeois society, homosexual and otherwise: Walt Whitman, John Addington Symonds, Havelock Ellis, Olive Schreiner, George Bernard Shaw. An indefatigable scribbler of well-meaning and flabby libertarian essays, a tedious poet in the Whitmanesque manner without the Whitmanesque fire, he was a vegetarian, a teetotaller, a wearer of sandals and prophet of the simple life, a socialist, a democratic mystic, and something of an anti-Semite. Born in 1844, Carpenter took holy orders but stumbled on his true pagan mission (as the *Dictionary of National Biography* in-

49. Grosskurth, *Symonds*, 271.

50. Swinburne: Richard Jenkyns, *The Victorians and Ancient Greece* (1980), 283; "I am glad:" Symonds to his daughter Margaret, December 6, 1889; "A bourgeois pack:" Symonds to Edmund Gosse, December 23, 1885, Grosskurth, *Symonds*, 299, 283.

nocently put it) on an Italian trip in 1873, when he discovered "a new enthusiasm for Greek sculpture."[51] His very entry into the homoerotic ambiance was conventional.

But his way of life, an ostentatiously simple existence with chosen companions in the countryside punctuated by trips abroad and prolific writings on politics, literature, and sexuality, was anything but conventional and he knew it. "I see the heavens laughing," he wrote in his early prose poem, *Towards Democracy*, "I discern the half-hidden faces of the gods wherever I go, I see the transparent-opaque veil in which they hide themselves, yet I dare not say what I see, lest I should be locked up!" While he dared not say what he saw, never rending the transparent-opaque veil, he spent years retraversing ground that earlier students of homosexuality, like Ulrichs and Westphal, had made fairly familiar, and published books fetchingly titled *Love's Coming of Age* or, more to the point, *Intermediate Types Among Primitive Folk* or *The Intermediate Sex*. As his publications abundantly demonstrate, the homosexual habits of the ancient Greeks served Carpenter as they had served others: in chapters on what he calls "the Dorian solution," antique "boy-love or comrade love," he smoothly outlined its growth as a "positive institution" springing "quite naturally from the temperament of the people." He was, of course, a historian of sex with a purpose: "Any one nowadays may see" this Dorian temperament, he noted, "springing spontaneously, though obscurely, in all classes of modern society."[52] Carpenter was visibly pleased to welcome this development.

Although a striking number of English clerics and former public school boys would study and sing homoerotic love, they did not, of course, enjoy a monopoly on it. Some English practitioners exported this love to the Continent: Wilde may have initiated the young André Gide into homosexuality.[53] But, then, if it had not been that persuasive English siren, it would have been another, French or Arab. Certainly Marcel Proust and his cultivated circle, including the composer Reynaldo Hahn, needed no

51. Mrs. Havelock Ellis, *Three Modern Seers* (1910), 193; "Edward Carpenter," *Dictionary of National Biography, Supplement, 1922–1930*, ed. J. R. H. Weaver (1937), 159.

52. Carpenter, *Towards Democracy* (1883; complete ed. 1905), 65; *Intermediate Types Among Primitive Folk: A Study in Social Evolution* (1911; 2nd ed., 1919), 115. Carpenter was persuasive and hospitable. One of his many visitors and enthusiastic disciples was E. M. Forster, who went to see the prophet of rustic living and erotic freedom in the fall of 1913, when Forster was 34, and discreetly at work on a passionately felt, heavily autobiographical homosexual novel, *Maurice*, which was not published until 1971, the year after his death. See P. N. Furbank, *E. M. Forster: A Life*, 2 vols. (1977–78), I, 256–58.

53. George Painter, *André Gide* (1968), 25.

impulsions from Great Britain; they experimented amorously with one another or with their chauffeurs. The male brothel that Proust has the baron de Charlus visit late in *A la recherche du temps perdu* had its counterpart in all the capitals of Europe, and in lesser cities as well. Certainly, John Addington Symonds said a little melodramatically, the passion that had made its votaries into pariahs was everywhere: "The pulse of it can be felt in London, Paris, Berlin, Vienna, no less than in Constantinople, Naples, Teheran, and Moscow."[54]

Germans, too, derived much pleasing instruction from their traffic with the classics. Among the most interesting of them was Johann Baptist von Schweitzer, the radical attorney and novelist who was to achieve prominence and power in the young Social Democratic movement of the 1860s and the early 1870s, as agitator, editor, and party leader. In a light-hearted comedy of 1858, *Alkibiades oder Bilder aus Althellas*, he had already made a lawless and ambitious ancient pederast into a hero; four years later, he was convicted for soliciting an adolescent in a public park. Schweitzer strenuously denied the accusation, but his reputation was compromised, and his shocked working-class followers tried to exclude him from their meetings. But Ferdinand Lassalle, then undisputed dictator of the nascent German workers' party—himself a scandalous lover, though of women—firmly rejected their request as "philistine"; he cleanly separated Schweitzer's political work from his personal vagaries and pointedly reminded his comrades that, after all, the ancient Greeks, including statesmen and poets, had indulged in the love of boys. This rare plea for tolerance—it was not to grow conventional until half a century later—carried the day.[55] Clearly, Schweitzer did not need to study the Greek classics to feel homosexual urges, nor did Lassalle need to cite them in defense of Schweitzer, but it is a tribute to their authority to have them invoked to good effect more than two millennia after they had first been written.

For all his fleeting notoriety, Schweitzer was anything but a proselytizer for the revival of ancient persuasions. His erotic activities were, as Lassalle had decreed, a strictly private affair. The German hothouse coterie that came to be known before World War I as the George *Kreis*, an exclusive circle of poets and translators of poets, was, on the other hand, a veritable national phenomenon. Stefan George and his handsome acolytes

54. Symonds, *Problem in Modern Ethics*, 2.

55. Gustav Mayer, *Johann Baptist von Schweitzer und die Sozialdemokratie. Ein Beitrag zur Geschichte der deutschen Arbeiterbewegung* (1909), 9–15, 71–72, 91–92, 432–33; James D. Steakley, *The Homosexual Emancipation Movement in Germany* (1975), 1; August Bebel, *Aus meinem Leben*, 3 vols. (1911–14), II, 9–10.

distilled a subtle and, for many, irresistible brew of antiquarian scholarship, literary aestheticism, idiosyncratic spelling, cultural criticism, and homoerotic bonding. There were to be no women in the imagined and imaginative new Reich that Stefan George projected in his poetry and his manifestos. The publications of George and his most productive disciples worked as a salutary antidote to the academic stuffiness prevailing in Wilhelmine Germany. But George himself, with his stunning profile, hieratic verse, and demanding ways, barely avoided blasphemous identifications with sanctified figures of the past. Canonizing Vergil and Dante, organizing public readings and solemn, rather absurd festivals in which classical togas were prescribed, George held court for his gifted young men who all served their master and obeyed him in all things including, much of the time, remaining single on his command. One did not have to be a homosexual, or homoerotically inclined, to be admitted to the exclusive George Circle, but it helped.

The George Circle, which assisted restless, poetic, educated young German bourgeois to escape from what they despised as the boredom, the triviality, the materialism of their middle-class world, drew its saints from Christian and antique culture with unabashed eclecticism. With their vision of a new realm, they were modern pagans. In other countries, sexual outsiders made the classical model their sole resource. Thus it appears, like an oppressive leitmotiv, in Mikhail Alekseyevich Kuzmin's startling novella, *Wings*, first published in a Moscow Symbolist periodical in 1906, proving that Russia, too, had its modern Greeks. Kuzmin, an original, if resolutely minor writer dissatisfied with the tradition-bound Russian poets and the Russian Symbolists alike, advocated clarity and economy, and sought to wrench Russian poetry back to the precise rendering of worldly experience. In *Wings* he advertised that for him this distinctly included homosexual experience.

Though far from esoteric, Kuzmin's *Wings* is allusive rather than blunt, a mosaic of thoughts, intimations, fragmentary conversations that yields its pattern slowly. The novella traces the sexual awakening of its young protagonist, Vanya, in a series of impressionistic, often static episodes. At school in St. Petersburg, Vanya becomes aware of Stroop, rich, cultivated, somewhat eccentric, significantly half-English, who exercises considerable attractions on both men and women. Vanya's interest in Stroop is sincere but for a long time indeterminate, though one of Vanya's uncles, a grasping and experienced man of the world, broadly hints that Stroop's attentions to Vanya are improper. And one of his jealous girl cousins, in malicious banter, suggests he go and kiss his "precious Stroop." Erotic hints like this pervade *Wings*: when Vanya suggests that Stroop may be in love with a certain girl, another cousin finds this improbable: "He's a horse of a different color"—without specifying, or perhaps knowing, what that color may be.[56] The texture of homosexual seduction in *Wings* is made up of such tantalizing fragments.

The one dramatic event in Kuzmin's novella is the impulsive suicide of a girl in love with Stroop. She shoots herself in his apartment as she becomes desperately aware of Stroop's sexual entanglement with the handsome peasant, Fyodor: his face, just moments before she puts the revolver to her temple, "had a hectic flush, as if he had been either at the bottle or the rouge jar; his blouse was unbelted, his hair carefully combed, and, by the look of it, slightly curled, and he smelt strongly of Stroop's cologne." The catastrophe tears the slender threads that tie Vanya to Stroop, and their paths diverge. They meet again in Italy, the land of sexual liberation for inhibited Northerners, and it emerges that it had not been the girl's suicide that had alienated Vanya, but Stroop's homosexual love affair. Now Stroop places his former friend before the choice of remaining aloof or joining forces with him. Again the exchange is a frail tissue of intimations. "Would you like me to spell it out for you?" Stroop asks, and Vanya, whom life has by then taught much, replies, "No, don't, I understand."[57] That night, he decides to go away with Stroop, to consummate their homosexual union.

Much of the action in *Wings*, if action is the right word, takes place off stage. Detached bits of talk add erotic flavor to the pervading mood. Marya Dmitrievna, a young widow who is interested in Vanya, pours out to him the remembered transports of her married love-making—"flesh cleaves to flesh"—and then veers off, with piquant irrelevance, to muse about homosexuality: "Well, of course men love women and women love men; but sometimes, they say, it can happen that a woman loves a woman and a man a man." This, she adds, may be God's gift: "It's hard, Vanya, to deny the heart's longings—and sinful too maybe." In summer, as Vanya undresses to go swimming, his friend Sasha exclaims, "How well-formed you are, Vanechka!" Vanya himself becomes aware, as he frankly puts it, that he is beautiful.[58]

Greece plays its seductive supporting part in this homoerotic tragicomedy. Early in the novella, Stroop happens on Vanya sitting on a park bench, studying Homer. Vanya detests his assignment: "Greek is the worst!" But Stroop, almost with pity, defends the study of the ancient

56. Kuzmin, *Wings: Prose and Poetry*, tr. Neil Granoien and Michael Green (1972), 29, 21.
57. Ibid., 44, 108, 110.
58. Ibid., 48–49, 78.

languages. "What a child you are, Vanya. A whole world, whole worlds lie beyond your ken; a world of beauty, too." Without knowing and loving that world, he adds, a little sententiously, "no man can call himself educated." When Vanya demurs that one can always read the classics in translation, Stroop becomes almost contemptuous. Sounding much like Pater on Winckelmann, he tells Vanya that translation is a "soulless doll," while the original is "a flesh-and-blood being who laughs and frowns, a being you can love, kiss or hate, a being with blood flowing in his veins, instinct with the natural grace of the naked body."[59]

These metaphors, in themselves, seem harmless enough. But voices in Kuzmin's novella, that of Stroop and others, underscore the sexual meaning of literature as a sentient being one can kiss and whose nakedness one can admire. "We are Hellenes," someone is heard to say in Stroop's apartment. "Those who would bind the idea of beauty to the beauty of a woman seen through the eyes of a man—they reveal only vulgar lust and are furthest of all from the true idea of beauty. We are Hellenes, lovers of the beautiful, the bacchants of the coming day." Later, in Italy, a playwright tells Vanya of a drama he is developing, bold and original, retelling some Greek myths, complete with Ganymede and visions of sexual ecstasy: "Through a palpitating rosy mist we see the forty-eight positions of human coupling from the Indian *manuels érotiques.*" When Vanya, troubled by his conversation with Stroop about the study of Greek, consults his Greek teacher in his apartment, predictably decorated with a bust of Antinoüs, the teacher brings their talk around to the friendships of Achilles for Patroclus and of Orestes for Pylades. The Italians of the Renaissance, he tells Vanya, thought these attachments no better "than the love of Sodom," but for his own part, he is confident that "what matters is that love, whatever its nature, can never be depraved except in the eyes of a cynic." When, at the end of their inconclusive, disquieting, vaguely suggestive chat, Vanya discovers that his teacher knows Stroop very well indeed, the reader becomes uncomfortably conscious of a network of feelings and relationships that must insensibly, slowly capture Vanya and prepare him for Stroop's arms.[60]

Kuzmin went far beyond Symonds in his affirmation of Greek love. Symonds, too, had sought refuge in the writings of Plato, but, we know, he had found his own sexual needs shameful, requiring the apologia of a fateful inheritance. Kuzmin, though, insists, as others had before him, that the love of men for men is superior to heterosexual lust, and that, at

59. Ibid., 14.
60. Ibid., 32–33, 109, 26.

all events, modern Hellenes are only acting in accord with nature. The old reproaches against homosexuality fall away in this unapologetic ideology. Heartfelt advocacy of this sort might relieve the pent-up feelings of homosexuals in search of self-respect and, however pathetically solicited, of public approval. But it only exacerbated the dilemma that sexual heterodoxy presented to the nineteenth century. It called attention to a plight that most bourgeois wanted to evade, or hear about only in the belittling, distancing atmosphere of gossip about decadent aristocrats or careless bohemians. But as soon as the matter began to claim public attention, it became undeniable that homosexuality was not a vice that passed the bourgeoisie by without touching it. Early estimates of its incidence were extraordinarily modest: Ulrichs had offered the manifestly self-protective figure of .002% of the German population as a whole, while Benkert had conjectured that the homosexual population of Berlin might run as high as 1.4%, which amounted to about 10,000, both male and female, in that worldly city.[61] Others were willing to raise that estimate to four or even five percent. During the Victorian century, higher figures were mainly confined to the intimate correspondence of aficionados and the occasional compulsive boasting of the kind that Proust lent to his Baron de Charlus in his late, indiscreet phase. Whatever the figures, even muted, timid revelations appeared to bring not peace but further misery.

The most dignified, perhaps the only possible escape from this dilemma might have been an unblinking public airing of sexual variations in impulse and act, designed neither to apologize for deviations from the middle-class norm nor to suppress anxiety-provoking erotic ideas or conduct. But, with all its nods to candor, bourgeois culture could never quite adopt this sort of resolution. Both prohibitions and fears of sexual irregularities were too strongly entrenched. The fate of Havelock Ellis's first books sufficiently demonstrates this failure; Ellis was the proverbial prophet, mainly honored, as he was mainly printed, abroad. And the career, before World War I, of one among Ellis's first appreciative readers, Sigmund Freud, adds weight to this demonstration. Touched by Ellis's printed tribute to his own work on "the connection between hysteria and sexual life," Freud in return called Ellis intelligent and sensible. Three decades later, reading a biography of Havelock Ellis, Freud confessed to Ellis that he "could not omit looking for resemblances" and was happy

61. Steakley, *Homosexual Emancipation in Germany*, 14; Judd Marmor, "Overview," in Marmor, ed., *Homosexual Behavior: A Modern Reappraisal* (1980), 7.

to find them.⁶² They were there, but what divided these two researchers
into sexuality was quite as important and rather more interesting. Freud
was, like Ellis, a prince of candor. Like Ellis, too, Freud treated the sexual
drive as critically important in the economy of mental life, long grossly
neglected by timid, prejudiced and ignorant investigators. And, like
Ellis, Freud was an attentive student of the technical literature, ever ready
to give credit to his precursors where he thought credit was due.⁶³ But,
then, we know, Ellis was a collector and connoisseur; for all his aspirations, the scientist's gift for synthesis in which Freud displayed his
mastery, eluded him.

Freud's heroic enterprise of integrating the most diverse psychological
phenomena into a comprehensive theory of mind makes his contributions
to the understanding of sexual heterodoxy different in kind from the
work of his predecessors. Freud was not, as he was the first to acknowledge, a voice crying in the desert of denial; he cited Krafft-Ebing as well
as Ellis with respect. But what makes his views on homosexuality unique
is that he related it to human development in general and to the fundamental tenets of his thought—the unconscious, shifting erotic zones,
infantile sexuality, and the bisexual endowment of all humans. Together,
they put accepted interpretations of human sexual experience into question. If much, and the more powerful part, of mental activity is unconscious, the sexual impulses to which men and women testify can never
exhaust their fund of erotic feelings and conflicts. It is not the person who
displays some of the characteristics usually associated with the other sex,
but precisely the one who displays none of these who becomes interesting.
"From the perspective of psychoanalysis," Freud wrote in 1915, "the
exclusive sexual interest of man for woman is a problem requiring
elucidation, and not a foregone conclusion." The Don Juan who must
boastfully catalogue his innumerable seductions and the beauty who must
enslave every man she meets are more likely than less single-minded
mortals to suffer conflicts about their sexual nature; both may be closet
homosexuals so secretive that they themselves have no inkling how unsettled their erotic orientations really are. Cultural ideals, enshrined in
such deceptively perspicuous terms as "manliness" or "femininity," thus
became, on Freud's showing, terms rife with unsuspected ambiguities.

62. Freud to Fliess, January 3, 1899, *Aus den Anfängen der Psychoanalyse. Briefe
an Wilhelm Fliess, Abhandlungen und Notizen aus den Jahren 1887–1902*, ed. Ernst
Kris et al. (1950), 290; *The Complete Letters of Sigmund Freud to Wilhelm Fliess,
1887–1904*, ed. Jeffrey Moussaieff Masson (1985), 338. Freud to Ellis, September 12,
1926, *Briefe 1873–1939*, ed. Ernst L. Freud (1960), 367–68.
63. See above, pp. 88–89.

This was true all the more since the unconscious conceals unacknowledged admixtures of bisexuality, an element in human nature on which Freud came to insist. "Normally, in all of us, our life long, our libido oscillates between male and female objects; the bachelor gives up his friendships when he marries, and returns to the *Stammtisch* when his married life has grown stale."⁶⁴ Freud liked August Moebius's aphorism that we are all to some extent hysterics; his work leaves little doubt that we are all to some extent homosexuals.

The prominence of that homosexuality varies quite predictably from stage to stage of life. Children, in Freud's unattractive but instructive phrase, are polymorphously perverse. They can love things, animals, sounds, foods, experiences, and certainly humans of the same sex; their fantasies of impregnating and being impregnated by a parent, soon repressed, resemble nothing so much as the florid imaginings that stir up consumers of outlandish pornography. Then adolescents, having traversed the years of latency, once again battle with homoerotic desires, whether raw or sublimated, desires that compete with, and complicate, their burgeoning heterosexual maturity; they have amassed, and now revive, a diversified menu of urges and aversions from which they will take their favorite sexual pleasures. The records that Ralph Waldo Emerson and numerous other nineteenth-century young men and women left for posterity amply support the psychoanalytic view that this phase in life is a decisive moment in sexual history. But Freud went further. Adult sexuality, he argued, never wholly jettisons all its polymorphous past; the foreplay that introduces the most conventional love-making, the looking, pinching, licking, biting are reminders of the child's indiscriminate erotic tastes, subdued and pressed into the service of respectable intercourse. The very love that makes sexual congress something better than the abrupt, self-absorbed satisfaction of an insatiable appetite and respects the partner's erotic requirements draws on survivals from the sensual enjoyments of early years, scarcely remembered but still working in silence. For Freud, heterosexual genital love-making was not a matter of course, but an achievement, the culmination of a long, never painless, and never quite complete evolution.

64. *Drei Abhandlungen zur Sexualtheorie* (1905; note added 1915), *St.A.*, V, 56n, *Three Essays On the Theory of Sexuality*, S.E., VII, 146n; "Über die Psychogenese eines Falles von weiblicher Homosexualität (1920), *St.A.*, VII, 267, "The Psychogenesis of a Case of Homosexuality in a Woman," S.E., XVIII, 158. Freud's own handling of the adjectives "masculine" and "feminine" was quite inconsistent; he veered between their conventional employment and warning that they beg all the interesting questions.

Freud's biographical perception of sexual unfolding retained the norma-
tive hierarchy that had gone barely challenged through most of the
Christian centuries. But he proposed to reduce, perhaps wholly remove,
the ethical opprobrium that had for so long attached to the idea of
perversion; beyond that, he encouraged his readers to wonder whether
homosexuality, latent or manifest, is a perversion at all. Rather, it seemed
logical from Freud's perspective to see the homosexual, male or female,
as an instance of localized developmental arrest—arrest, because the homosexual remained fixated on erotic stages that more fortunate humans had
largely outgrown or successfully integrated; localized, because psychoanalysis found no reason to assume that this fixation handicapped the
homosexual as a moral, intellectual, political, or artistic animal.

This posture had important implications, and Freud ventured to explore
most of them. To begin with, "homosexuality" is an all too simple name
for a complicated phenomenon: some are temporary, others permanent
homosexuals; while some exclusively prefer their own sex, others on
occasion, or frequently, experiment with heterosexual coupling; some
homosexual men cannot bear women, others adore them; some imitate the
other sex in gait and speech, others are indistinguishable from their conventional counterparts. On these points, Freud found himself in accord
with such special pleaders as Raffalovich. Besides, the etiology of homosexualities was no less varied than their expressions. In his explanations,
Freud was a pluralist, not from scientific agnosticism but from clinical
experience. He had little patience with the prevalent theory that considered homosexual desires as an inherited form of degeneracy, though
he included biological predispositions in the possible amalgam. Nor were
the psychological hypotheses that Freud offered in any way reductive:
the most celebrated and most controversial of them—a domestic constellation of seductive mother and weak or absent father—was only one
among several. An inability to master bisexual traits, an adaptation to such
favoring situations as an untimely seduction, an extended sea voyage, or
a long prison sentence, a persistent narcissistic investment in one's own
body, even (in some cases) a loving father and cold mother, or, normally,
a combinations of these, could be grounds for adult homoerotic choices.

These complex origins made psychoanalytic therapy for homosexuals
relatively unpromising—to say nothing of analysands' resistance to
abandoning an erotic activity that gives them pleasure. Consistent with
his honesty and his theories, Freud thought that what psychoanalysis was
most likely to accomplish was not changing homosexual patients into
heterosexuals but allowing them to accept themselves, to take pleasure in
their pleasures. Freud's sometimes rather somber therapeutic pessimism

would not easily permit any other prognosis. But then, such an outcome might be perfectly satisfactory to these highly resistant analysands. After all, much of the travail besetting homosexuals in Freud's day stemmed less from their tastes than from their sense of shame and their fear of ostracism. Freud expected that psychoanalysis might partially relieve the first and hoped that it might gradually reduce the second.

For, when it came to sexual mores, Freud did not neglect the cultural implications of his theories. It was the one domain in which he liked to regard himself as a radical reformer. He thought it stupid and brutal, in some peculiar way defensive, to treat homosexuals as criminals or madmen. In his *Three Essays on the Theory of Sexuality*, first published in 1905 and repeatedly revised, he analyzed what he called the "sexual aberrations" with a calm sympathy and listed their varieties with a clinical candor that left no room for censoriousness. Later, in a footnote he added to the *Essays* in 1915, he made his position unequivocally explicit: "Psychoanalytic research most decisively opposes the attempt to segregate homosexuals from other human beings as a group with a peculiar nature. In studying sexual excitations other than those manifestly displayed, it has noted that all humans are capable of making a homosexual choice of object and have indeed done so in their unconscious." Freud was not unmindful that some of the men he most admired, Leonardo da Vinci and Michelangelo among them, had loved men and not women.[65]

Both radical and traditionalist, Freud eventually pleased nobody: not polemical homosexuals nor moralistic heterosexuals fighting to keep the old stigmas intact and prosecutions alive. The father of that "beautiful and clever" young lesbian whose case Freud published in 1920 may stand as a characteristic bourgeois confronted with an abnormality he cannot handle: that father, embittered by his daughter's homosexual inclinations and determined to combat them with all the means at his command in-

65. *Drei Abhandlungen zur Sexualtheorie*, St.A., V, 56n; *Three Essays on Sexuality*, S.E., 145n. Late in life, April 9, 1935, in a moving letter (written in English to an unidentified mother distressed at her son's choice of sexual objects), Freud reiterated his position with his resolute, tough-minded humaneness: "I gather from your letter," he wrote, "that your son is a homosexual" and he noted, ever attentive to the slightest of clues, that his correspondent had avoided that dread name. "May I question why you avoid it? Homosexuality is assuredly no advantage, but it is nothing to be ashamed of, no vice, no degradation, it cannot be classified as an illness; we consider it to be a variation of the sexual function, produced by a certain arrest of sexual development." And he reminded her that "many highly respectable individuals of ancient and modern times have been homosexuals, several of the greatest men among them." Then, having listed some of the usual names, including Plato, he told her: "It is a great injustice to persecute homosexuality as a crime—and a cruelty, too." *Briefe*, 416.

cluding despised psychoanalysis, must have vacillated, Freud tells his readers, between seeing her as "a vicious, a degenerate, or an insane being."[66] For Freud, plainly, as for Ellis, an intelligent, affectionate girl infatuated with an older woman was none of these.

In his views on homosexuality as on other sensitive issues, Freud affronted too many cherished notions, assailed too many useful cultural defenses, to gain a ready hearing. Certainly among the most scandalous of his proposals was to plot homoerotic desires onto the general scheme of human maturation: homosexual experiences may graduate to lasting attachment, thus joining what heterosexual love also joins—the sensual and the affectionate currents of libido. The psychoanalytic dispensation opened a perspective that, when Freud first advanced it, only passionate, deeply committed partisans were ready to endorse: it offered homosexuals the stature they had been so strenuously denied and, with that, access to the prized domain of love.

66. "Psychogenese eines Falles von weiblicher Homosexualität," St.A., VIII, 259; "Psychogenesis of a Case of Homosexuality in a Woman," S.E., XVIII, 149.

❧ FIVE ❧

Stratagems of Sensuality

THE REPERTORY of love, proverbially imprecise and elastic, can embrace any passionate and sustained movements of desire toward children or animals, things or works of art, ideals sacred or profane. No one would contradict Joseph Conrad, who said in 1904, in his *Nostromo*, that "The sentiment of love can enter into any subject and live ardently in remote phrases." Diderot, we know, had said it less elegantly, bluntly suggesting that all forms of love, including the most exalted, ultimately draw their strength from physical, carnal impulses.[1] Under persistent attack from anxieties or guilt feelings and from the stern organizing pressures of culture, erotic energies, at once insatiable and resourceful, deploy whatever stratagems human ingenuity can devise to serve their survival and gratification. Man's love of music, love of nature, love of God and other spiritual attachments, in short, draw on many and concealed springs. They may be firm and intelligently defended convictions, mechanical reenactments of fashionable postures or cherished possessions acquired after years of study, they may serve to separate the snobbish aesthete from the common herd or unite the individual to his group—or something of all these. What matters most here is that much of the time they prove to be displacements of erotic desire for which there is no conventional mode of expression.

Humanity has persistently employed these stratagems and just as persistently resented them. It has cherished the fantasy of a love permanently

---

1. Conrad: *Nostromo: A Tale of the Seaboard* (1904; ed. 1963), 62 [ch. 6]; Diderot: see above, p. 47.

255

untrammeled and undisciplined; and this daydream rose to the surfa
once again among anti-bourgeois Utopian reformers in the nineteen
century, a survival of imagined omnipotence that practically all childr
harbor but most adults abandon. In real life, instinctual demands w
turn into their opposite by the mechanism of reaction formation: lust ma
reappear as prudishness, anal eroticism as disgust, sexual curiosity as pu
poseful scientific research. Or, retaining all their charge, these deman
are displaced onto new objects, onto poems or symphonies or theologic
tracts. This, simply—too simply—put, is sublimation. "Sexual drives,"
once highly developed and extremely mobile, Freud argued, can plac
"extraordinarily large amounts of force" at the disposal of culture b
exchanging "their original aim" for another, "no longer sexual, b
psychically related" to them and "without significantly diminishing i
intensity."[2] Such transformations are essential to the human experienc
and, at their best, culturally adaptive. It is from their work that respec
able and respect-worthy loves are born.

Exercises in delicate, necessary, but unwelcome self-restraint are ofte
bound to fail. In the nineteenth century, as before, curbs on sexualit
proved to be obstacles, rather than aids, to adaptation. The classic neuroti
disorders of the time were modes of emotional control gone wrong: thos
ceremonies and prohibitions of obsessional neurotics and those distressin
conversion symptoms of hysterics were, Freud insisted, caricatures o
normality; they were intensified, sometimes bizarrely distorted com
promises between the ubiquitous drives or urgent affects and the defense
against them. What critics of the nineteenth-century bourgeoisie like
to stigmatize as its peculiar hypocrisy and emotional self-starvation wer
not unique failures of character. They were, rather, time-bound an
culture-bound ways of coping with universal human situations. It is only
poetic justice that Victoria's age should have been the one to identify, an
most conspicuously to suffer, the neuroses, undesirable commentaries o
the defects of bourgeois stratagems to contain sensuality, the shadow sid
of their successes.

Freud was the first to naturalize sublimation, that indispensable piece of
psychological work, in the mental sciences. But he did not sort out all its
intricacies, did not even fathom them. Sublimation is desexualization, the
withdrawal of erotic energies for other purposes, their employment in
other forms. But it is often accompanied by projection, the unconscious
act of endowing external objects—a work of art, nature, anything—with

---

2. Freud, "Die 'kulturelle' Sexualmoral und die moderne Nervosität" (1908), *St.A.*,
IX, 18; " 'Civilized' Sexual Morality and Modern Nervous Illness," *S.E.*, IX, 187.

xual qualities they do not really possess. To write an affectionate poem
out a landscape is sublimation; to invest a landscape with the ability to
ceive, give, or withhold love is projection. What is more, these two
ocedures may meet and merge. To compound complexities further,
blimation at once exhibits and contradicts what psychoanalysts call an
onomic process, in which the loss to sexuality reappears as a gain to
lture. Thus, a "young scholar" may, through practicing sexual self-
nial, "liberate energies for his studies." But it does not follow, either
theory or in practice, that the more rigorous the sexual abstention,
e more fruitful the cultural work; as Freud was intent on showing
the very paper in which he developed the idea of sublimation, excessive
lf-restraint only produces neurotic suffering. Total celibacy, he said,
ually makes "well-mannered weaklings," not "energetic thinkers, bold
mancipators or reformers." He thought "an abstinent artist barely pos-
ble"; it is far more probable that "his artistic achievement is powerfully
imulated by his sexual experience." Freud concluded, reasonably enough,
ways as willing to differentiate as he was to unify psychological
henomena, that "the relationship between possible sublimation and
ecessary sexual activity naturally fluctuates sharply among individuals
d even among different professions."[3]

Migrations of erotic desires were thus not always simple transfers of
nergy. The unconscious deploying its defenses resembles either a traveler
uying foreign currency to have a ready means for paying his way, or a
rader speculating in these currencies at favorable rates to wind up with
ividends on them all. There were many in the bourgeois century, notably
he notorious, much-ridiculed spinster attempting to impose her un-
vanted chastity on all, who imitated the traveler in exchanging the
ensuality they found too threatening for a censoriousness they found
ossible to manage. But many others profited from their maneuvers in
pectacular ways. Rather than merely warding off pain and thus realizing
ome pleasure, they would enlarge the range and improve the yield of
heir sensual satisfactions.

Less subtle and more credulous than Freud, there were those in the
ineteenth century who took a simple quantitative view of sublimation
nd credited the superstition that an artist should be sexually abstinent in
imes of intense creation. Zola gave this notion support in *L'Oeuvre*, his
ovel about a gifted, neurotic, doomed painter who, for some desperate
ime, refuses to touch his sensual and beautiful wife that he might re-
kindle his fading enthusiasm for the masterpiece that obsesses him. There

3. Ibid., 197.

is, too, a story about Balzac which, though probably apocryphal, sugges
that the myth enjoyed a certain currency: eager to conserve his resource
so the anecdote runs, Balzac would generally practice coitus reservati
with his mistresses. But once, carried away by the ardor of his sexu
partner, he allowed himself to reach orgasm, only to comment afterward
ruefully: "Well, there goes another book!"

This is scarcely convincing as evidence, but it discloses an undercurrei
in nineteenth-century thought ready to ground cultural work in sexu
energies. Whether he made that remark or not, Balzac certainly did sa}
uncharitably, that women who are bored and unattractive will pour ou
their frustrated longing for love into "devotion, cats, and little dogs.
Half a century later, by the 1880s, this kind of comment had gained th
status of a scientific truism and found wide application: the influentia
and eccentric Italian criminologist Cesare Lombroso argued that ther
is an admixture of sensuality in all crime. Hence, in the same decade, D
Benjamin Ball, professor of medicine at the University of Paris, did no
startle professional researchers or informed lay readers when he note
that virgins are often obsessed with the idea of sex and that many of then
are confirmed erotomaniacs. Freud was building on an emerging con
sensus when, in 1894, working out his early psychoanalytic ideas, h
derived "anxiety in deliberately abstinent persons, prudes" from a defens
against sexual arousal.[4]

Increasingly, researchers converged on the conviction that sexuality i
the most potent ingredient in the human makeup, more potent than
(perhaps the cause of) pride, greed, and fear. Schopenhauer, more than
half a century after his first discoveries, was gaining a hearing ever
among those who did not follow the rest of his philosophy. "Among the
regular and normal instincts with which nature has endowed us," Dr. Bal
wrote, "there is surely none that exercises so powerful an influence ovei
our sentiments and our character as does the genital instinct." Around
the same time, the Swedish physician Seved Ribbing grew lyrical about
the ubiquity of that instinct, that splendid urge to procreate. "A glance a
nature will show us immediately," he wrote, "how infinitely far the
significance and the effects of sexual life extend. The lilies of the field
bloom and the roses in the grove spread out their fragrance for that
reason and through its agency alone; blackbird and nightingale sing, the

4. Balzac: *Physiologie de mariage* (1829; ed. 1968), 56; Lombroso: *Delitti di libidine* (1882; 2nd enl. ed., 1886), 19; Freud: "Manuskript E" (? June 1894), see *Freud-Fliess Letters*, 78–83.

world of plants and animals clothes itself in lovely colors for that reason alone." Surely human life is unthinkable without sexuality. "Man and woman" he wrote, underscoring his assertion with his majestic reiterations, "develop to physical and spiritual perfection for that reason alone." If human sexuality were to disappear, "life would be reduced to a dismal desert; the arts, the sciences, the life of the state and of culture, indeed, a considerable part of religion, could no longer exist." Ribbing's fellow-Swede, August Strindberg, could only agree. "What haven't I shaken out of my pants!" he exclaimed with his customary carnal directness. "Novels and poems, plays good and bad, little Swedish and Chinese tales, four children, the fifth is on the way, and two wives."[5] Love, as Joseph Conrad put it, can live in the remotest phrases—ardently.

1. The Food of Love

Shortly after 1900, the German sexologist Dr. Friedrich Siebert of Munich discovered erotic sentiments reverberating in fantasies of cruelty and the consciousness of one's powers—*Kraftbewusstsein*—and in listening to opera: "I am certain that many a young lady, who has enjoyed Offenbach's music to *La belle Hélène*, would be quite offended if I tried to prove to her, by employing psychology, that she has provided herself, in addition to an aesthetic, with a little sexual pleasure as well." But even if she had not, he for his part certainly had. The enthusiasms—*Schwärmereien*—Siebert added, that are lavished on adored personages "living or dead," on "teachers of literature or religion, or stars from the sky of poetry," contain the same sort of erotic residues. Siebert was perceptive and frank enough to discover sexual impulses even in his political chauvinism: "Much in the sentiments I feel at the thought of Pan-German ideas and their realization strikes me like a sexual feeling of power."[6]

Siebert's rather patronizing allusion to young ladies giving themselves to Offenbach points to one of the favorite refuges to which sensuality could repair in the bourgeois century. The recognition that music, with its pulsating beat and baths of sound, its tantalizing delays, thrilling climaxes, and exhausted decrescendos has its roots in man's fundamental erotic drives is as old as Plato's *Symposium* and as modern as Thomas

---

5. Ball: *La folie érotique* (1888), 6; Ribbing: *Die sexuelle Hygiene und ihre ethischen Konsequenzen* (1888; tr. Dr. Oscar Ryher, 2nd ed., 1892), 7–8; Strindberg: [note January 26, 1904], *Ein Lesebuch für die niederen Stände*, ed. Jan Myrdal (1968; tr. Paul Baudisch, 1970, ed. 1977), 7.

6. *Sexuelle Moral und sexuelle Hygiene* (1901), 30.

Mann. In Mann's first masterpiece, *Buddenbrooks*, a professedly realistic and exhaustive family chronicle, the only overt orgasmic moments come as Hanno Buddenbrook is at the piano. A ruminative, self-sufficient boy fated to die young and to be the last of his clan, he is, in his shy way far closer to the sexual sources of art than his inhibited, driven, business-haunted father. It is Hanno's eighth birthday. Thomas Mann, who sturdily refuses to idealize any of his characters, has endowed the boy with strictly limited pianistic talents; Hanno's patience with practicing is unimpressive and his progress laborious. He likes to score effects, prolonging and intensifying tense pleasures, and to dream hovering over the keyboard, improvising and composing little pieces. One of these, with a highly unorthodox ending, he refuses to revise despite the protests of his sympathetic piano teacher, for passionate reasons of his own. Playing this favorite piece for his family, he is pale with a kind of intoxication. "And now came the finale, Hanno's beloved finale, which crowned the whole, with its primitive elevation. Softly and pure as a bell, tremolo, sounds the e-minor chord, pianissimo," caressed, enveloped, by his mother's violin accompaniment. "It grew, it rose, it swelled slowly, slowly; Hanno introduced, forte, the discordant c-sharp, leading back to the original key, and while the Stradivarius, surging and resonant, rustles about this c-sharp too, he raised the dissonance with all his might up to fortissimo." But Hanno was not ready for the denouement, not quite yet. "He denied himself the resolution, he kept it from himself and his listeners. What would it be, this resolution, this enchanting and liberated absorption in b-major? Happiness beyond compare, a satisfaction of superabundant sweetness. Peace! Bliss! The kingdom of heaven!— Not yet—! Just one more moment of delay, of hesitation, of tension, which must become intolerable so that the gratification may be all the more delicious.—Yet a last, a very last tasting of this pressing and driving yearning, this appetite of the whole being, this extreme and convulsive tension of the will which yet denied itself satisfaction and deliverance, because he knew: happiness is only a moment." Then, burdened with premature wisdom, he permits himself consummation. "The upper part of Hanno's body slowly straightened itself up, his eyes grew very big, his closed lips trembled, with a spasmodic tremor he drew in the air through his nostrils—and then bliss could no longer be held back. It came, it came over him, and he did not resist it any longer. His muscles relaxed, exhausted and overwhelmed his head sank onto his shoulders, his eyes closed, and a melancholy, almost anguished smile of inexpressible rapture played about his mouth," while the Stradivarius keeps him company right to the end, the son playing with his mother to climax to enjoy the after-low, happy and drained, entering privileged realms of intimacy that she had denied her husband.[7]

Throughout history, centuries before Thomas Mann would so blatantly exhibit the debt of music to libido, philosophers, writers and musicians had professed similar beliefs. Music was a resounding resource for poets in search of audible metaphors for amorous entanglements; music, they would say, can rouse and feed all the passions; lovers' declarations are, as Hamlet's to Ophelia's, "music vows." Composers, too, made great claims for the expressive powers of their creations. "I completely disagree with you," Tchaikovsky wrote to his patroness, Nadezhda von Meck, "when you say that music *cannot convey the all-embracing characteristics of the feeling of love.* I believe quite the contrary, that *music alone* can do this." He vigorously disputed her contention that with love, "*words* are necessary. O no! It is precisely here that words are not necessary—and where they are ineffectual, the more eloquent language, i.e. music, appears in all its power." For composers as for poets, music could become, under their pens, more than the food of love to embody its very essence, the fragile little barque of love diverted into ostensibly safe channels and floating above the undertow of heedless passion. The late Tolstoy, brimming over with revulsion at sexuality, forced the danger inherent in love out into the open in his *Kreutzer Sonata,* that terrifying story of music-making, jealousy, and murder; it is one long demonstration of how music incites to lustful indulgence, to flirtation and adultery. At its most innocuous, the lovely, ambiguous eloquence of its speech made music into the privileged messenger of Eros; Samuel Johnson, shrewd as usual, had long before recognized its value as a displacement when he called it "the only sensual pleasure without vice."[8] That, in a phrase, was its secret.

In the nineteenth century, the erotic work of music was, as it were, democratized. In fact, derisive contemporary observers had good sport coupling music with love in the crassest possible way. They unmasked it as a deadly efficient element in the social machinery of seduction: young women ensnaring eligible bachelors with their singing and piano playing. This was largely a malicious caricature, but, beyond question, this was an age when competent performances and musical education, often of a high caliber, became a staple in many middle-class households. It was an

7. Mann, *Buddenbrooks. Der Verfall einer Familie* (1901; ed. n.d.), 484–86 [Part VIII, ch. 6].

8. Tchaikovsky: February 21, 1878, David Brown, *Tchaikovsky: The Crisis Years, 1874–1878* (1982), 231; Johnson: "Anecdotes by William Seward," in *Johnsonian Miscellanies,* ed. G. B. Hill, vol. II (1897), 301.

age, too, that saw the founding of orchestras, conservatories, chamber groups, self-possessed, self-conscious bourgeois institutions. Listening acquired the stature of an art. The elect developed sitting silently, breathing in melodies and vibrating to harmonies, into a carefully cultivated posture, into an experience they were only too inclined to describe as sacred in nature. To absorb what gifted amateurs or professional performers dispensed in the drawing room or in the concert hall was more than a sheer passive undergoing; consumption of music could become an intense act of devotion. Henri-Frédéric Amiel, as susceptible to fine music as he was to emotional friendships, was only one of the untold thousands among civilized bourgeois to listen with his eyes tightly closed, as if to ward off mundane intrusions, to be "truly moved" and put in mind of "delightful sensations."[9] The cult of the virtuoso—Paganini, Liszt, Jenny Lind—made the erotic quality of these delightful sensations almost palpable.

If Amiel did not venture to analyze or even to decribe the delicious emotions that listening to music roused in him, others tried to do both— often eloquently in vain. Near the end of the nineteenth century, with Darwinian ideas of natural selection floating freely among the educated to be used, and abused, at will, researchers liked to associate musical activity —composing, playing, listening, singing, dancing—to sexual arousal; they were sure that it significantly aided the sexual selection of animals, including that supremely responsive animal, man. Biologists and anthropologists, lacking both precise information and a dependable vocabulary to capture these secular ecstasies, almost invariably borrowed their terminology from religion. Yet sensuality was never far to seek. Listening to Beethoven's Ninth Symphony, Havelock Ellis, who had surveyed the literature on this subject, found himself uplifted, especially by the "solemn hymn to Joy," his eyes shining. "I have heard the Ninth Symphony since, but I never again recaptured the rapture of that moment."[10] It was surely not an accident that he should have experienced this memorable performance in the company of his wife, just after he had been married.

Havelock Ellis was a musical amateur, speaking for literally millions of amateurs and using the vocabulary, at once vivid and exhausted, of his culture. For his part, Walt Whitman, who felt keenly what others often dimly surmised and who enjoyed trumpeting what others might only think, openly claimed orgasmic powers for music. Hearing the

9. March 28, 1850, *Journal intime*, ed. Bernard Gagnebin and Philippe M. Monnier, 6 vols. so far (1976–   ), I, 680.

10. *My Life* (1940), 242; see Ellis, *Analysis of the Sexual Impulse. Love and Pain. Analysis of the Sexual Impulse in Women* (1903; rev. ed., 1913), 29, 113–35.

trained soprano," he wrote in *Leaves of Grass*, "she convulses me like the climax of my love-grip." The pianist and conductor Carl Halle, still some decades from becoming Sir Charles Hallé, felt himself translated into celestial realms: "He is no man," Halle wrote his parents after listening to Chopin, "he is an angel, a god"; there was nothing to remind one "that it is a human who produces this music." Halle, working musician though he was, could be touched to tears while conducting opera, moved by affecting scenes" or "the beauty of the music." Ingres, too, who was, of course, a far more accomplished painter than he was violinist, would weep freely as he played Mozart violin sonatas with Halle at the piano.[11] To hear great music, then, especially when it was worthily performed, was, for many nineteenth-century bourgeois, to traffic with divinity. Writing to his mother in 1850 after hearing Jenny Lind, the young German surgeon Theodor Billroth, himself exquisitely musical, found her singing "heavenly"; he depicted himself staggering home more dreaming than awake, more insane than sober. He, too, much like Amiel, thought his language inadequate: "I must confess that I can find no words to express what I felt that morning." He concluded his letter, helplessly: "These days will be unforgettable all my life long. O! Could I only tell you, dear Mama, how elevated one feels amidst the general enthusiasm. Words are too feeble and too dead, to express this living sentiment. I can say no more! For *She* is indescribable."[12] His infatuation was beyond carnality—and beyond words.

The emotions for which some observers did find language were not always quite so disguised. In 1826, at La Scala in Milan, Mrs. Anna Jameson, a prolific author, watched in some dismay a beautiful English girl "apparently not fifteen, with laughing lips and dimpled cheeks, the very personification of blooming, innocent *English* loveliness," being captivated by the sensual miming in Vigano's ballet, *Didone Abbandonata*: "I watched her (I could not help it, when my interest was once awakened,) through the whole scene. I marked her increased agitation: I saw her cheeks flush, her eyes glisten, her bosom flutter, as if with sighs I could not overhear, till at length overpowered with emotion, she turned away her head, and covered her eyes with her hand." The girl was responding to "the celebrated cavern scene," drawn from the fourth book of Vergil which, Mrs. Jameson thought, was "rather too closely copied," if "inimitable"; the pas de deux had given this virginal adolescent

11. Whitman: "Song of Myself," *Leaves of Grass* (in this explicit form only in the first edition of 1855), *Poetry and Prose*, ed. Justin Kaplan (1982), 54; Hallé: Michael Kennedy, *The Hallé Tradition: A Century of Music* (1960), 8–9.
12. February 1850. *Briefe von Theodor Billroth* (1895; 8th ed., 1910), 8, 9, 13.

a glimpse of sexual fulfillment and aroused her slumbering sexual need
"Mothers!—" the woman who watched her appealed to her reader
"English mothers! who bring your daughters abroad to finish the
education—do ye well to expose them to scenes like these, and *force* th
young bud of early feeling into such a precious hot-bed as this?"[13] H
question, thoroughly conventional, condensed what troubled prope
bourgeois all across the century about the pressing of carnal knowledg
on the innocent, even in the guise of an enchanting performance. Balle
of course, especially Italian ballet, was frankly suggestive; far fro
prudently draping, it advertised and elaborated the erotic allegiances
music. More often, though, such eroticism, in the nineteenth century
masqueraded in higher pretensions; the more sensual the work, in fac
the more exalted the rhetoric accompanying it. Wagnerians, especiall
the most assiduous devotees, treated Wagner's music as revelation, as th
climax of German culture, as an unprecedented political and religiou
message. Wagner himself was the object of blasphemous worship. "W
recently had a very serious conversation on the subject of Richar
Wagner," Pierre Louÿs reported to Debussy. "I merely stated tha
Wagner was the greatest man who had ever existed, and I went no furthe
I didn't say that he was God himself, though indeed I may have though
something of the sort."[14] Debussy must have been appalled to receive thi
abject confession, but there were many lovers of music, even Frenchmer
who thought Louÿs's attitude the sober truth of the matter. The fashion
able audiences that thronged to the Bayreuth festivals from 1876 o
solemnly understood that they were attending a sacred rite.

Richard Wagner himself did much to foster and nothing to discourag
this sort of thing. It was no accident that he should explicitly reject th
name "opera" for his mature compositions. The merest hint that the
might inhabit the same vulgar world as that sort of entertainment wa
painful to him. In company with his worshipers, Wagner was ambivalen
about acknowledging that his music dramas manifestly embodied, an
boldly staged, sexual longings and fulfillments that ordinary mortals kee
to themselves, if they consciously experienced them at all. He acknowl
edged that some of his compositions were poems about love—*Tristan und
Isolde*, indeed, was a "monument" to it.[15] And his *Walküre*, as everybody
knows, glorifies incest between brother and sister. It is arguable (and ha

13. Mrs. Jameson, *Diary of an Ennuyée* (1826; new ed., 1885), 47–48.
14. Bryan Magee, *Aspects of Wagner* (1968), 47.
15. Richard Wagner, *Das Braune Buch. Tagebuchaufzeichnungen 1865 bis 1882*, ed
Joachim Bergfeld (1975), 166–67; Robert Gutman, *Richard Wagner: The Man, Hi
Mind, and His Music* (1968), 163.

en argued) that *Tristan* is far more than a love story, but it made agner's munificent patron, King Ludwig II of Bavaria, literally swoon, d the impression it leaves on its audiences remains that of a long drawn t and reiterated representation of sexual congress. Its music heavily derscores its story, especially in the love scenes with its luxuriant themes d flowing rhythms rising, rising, and those final satiated moments with istan breathing his last in Isolde's arms; it evokes the thrilling journey to at the French call the little death, which seals sexual intercourse hap- y completed. In such representations, the regressive pull toward primi- e feelings is almost irresistible, sublimation far from complete, with e erotic sources of the composition unmistakable, consciously exploited. Yet the same doctrine of distance permitting an academic nineteenth- ntury painter or sculptor to exhibit luscious bodies and suggestive scenes long as he draped them in exotic, religious, or mythological garb, also rmitted Wagnerians to elevate the Master's explorations of sensual ap- tites into the sphere of the sublime.[16] It is true that Thomas Mann uld, in "The Blood of the Walsungs," present a pair of young, rich, cadent twins who, after attending a performance of the *Walküre*, go me and imitate Siegmund and Sieglinde in a half-worshipful, half- nical parody of the opera they have just seen. But, then, after all, that as fiction, and wicked fiction at that. By and large, Wagner's audiences Bayreuth and elsewhere seem to have kept their sensual arousal under ntrol and enjoyed what they interpreted as a spiritual experience to be lowed not by incest, or a love death, but by supper.

Still, the overheated, heavily perfumed eroticism pervading Wagner's orks was there for all to experience, even outside Bayreuth. The English usic critic, H. Heathcote Statham, no Wagnerian, reported that at his st hearing of the "*Tannhäuser* Overture, at a very crowded concert," e audience was so carried away by "the reiterated scale passages for e violins at the climax" that they could not contain their feelings—the st part of the overture "was played amidst a crescendo of hand-clapping!" ore portentous than this irresistible rhythmic mimesis was the "power- l" impression that the German musicologist Ferdinand Pfohl, far more mpathetic than Statham, reported from Bayreuth after the first act of e "Tristan tragedy." "On all countenances," he recalled, one could "see e expression of the greatest emotion." Many were "weeping passion- ely"; not just "nervous ladies," overly sensitive and lyrical, but "serious en had tears in their eyes." A "young American was trembling so con- lsively that he had to be removed to get some fresh air." Pfohl found

16. For an analysis of the doctrine of distance, see *Education of the Senses*, 379–402.

(THE TENDER PASSIO

this effect astonishing and conceded that it hinted at "a pathologic
symptom." Yet, while "the Tristan music is indeed pathological throug
out," and "dangerous to those people who cannot muster the necessa
resistance to the Wagnerian bacillus," this "did not alter its greatness
any way." Certainly for all listeners, highly susceptible or not, Wagne
Tristan, he thought, was overwhelming and called for some defensi
measures. One could absorb this "continuing assault of passion, this i
cessant dithyramb of the highest delight and deepest pain" only "halfwa
as in a dream." The well-known theatre and music critic Theod
Goering, active for decades in Munich's cultural life and a somewh
reluctant convert to Wagner, thought the music of Tristan, though
part "ravishing" and in part "almost unendurably" boring, anything b
healthy; seeking for a descriptive equivalent, he hit upon "opium i
toxication": hashish, he imagined, worked that way.[17]

If this was the rather mixed verdict of admirers, Wagner's detracto
were far more outspoken, far more censorious about his corrupt an
seductive carnality. His "frequent use of the band to produce a tumu
tuous *crescendo*," Statham wrote in flat disapproval, was little bett
"than an appeal to the nervous excitability of the audience," designed t
"work up the listener's feelings to a climax." In sum, Statham not
severely, "that is what a great deal of Wagner's music really comes t
it is addressed, not to the intellect, but to the nervous system," and th
"unfortunately" holds even "in passages where, from the poetic situatio
we have every right to expect something higher." Statham regretted th
Wagner should separate the two currents of love and cultivate one at th
expense of the other: "Wagner's musical portrayal of love scenes co
tains far more of passion than of affection." He offered in evidenc
predictably enough, the "long duet between the two lovers in the secon
act of *Tristan*." While it contains, "no doubt, a certain wild pathos,"
appeared to Statham "only caterwauling translated into musical e
pression"—imitating the kind of noise that cats make when they are
heat. One might argue that Wagner is musically representing "an amoro
passion kindled unawares by an unholy magic," and therefore compelle
to be crass, but he has no such excuse for the first act of the *Walküre*,
which Siegmund hails Sieglinde "ecstatically as 'bride and sister,'"
kind of relationship which, Statham thought, "however in place in
mythological dictionary, is not a very pleasing idea to thrust forward be

17. Statham: *My Thoughts on Music and Musicians* (1892), 391n; Pfohl: "Bay
reuther Fanfaren (1891)," in *Die Nibelungen in Bayreuth* (1897), 46; Goering: *De
Messias von Bayreuth. Feuilletonistische Briefe an einen Freund in der Provinz* (1881
46n.

ore a civilized audience, and which, taken in conjunction with the
demonstrations of the orchestra, simply portrays the excitement of
sexual passion." What is worse, Wagner, Statham adds, growing ever
sterner, underscores the sexual meaning of this incestuous encounter with
his stage directions, which call for Siegmund to draw his sister to him
with furious ardor. The curtain falls rapidly"—leaving the audience,
Statham is moved to comment drily, "under the distinct impression that
it was quite time it did fall." Surely, he concludes, there is in the setting
not a hint" of "the nobility and the chivalry of love." In amorous
matters Wagner "seems to rise no higher than the idea of animal passion;
at all events, his music suggests nothing higher."[18]

Musical amateurs who had chosen Brahms over Wagner, preferring
music rooted in tradition to the Music of the Future, experienced the
Bayreuth occasions as obscene spectacles, as lush affairs. Wagnerians
strenuously denied the very thing they so oppressively displayed. But
the Brahmsians echoed, and sometimes anticipated, Nietzsche's famous denunciations of Wagner as a symptom, a sickness, a neurosis. That is how
Elizabet von Herzogenberg, a talented musician in her own right and a
close friend of Brahms, characterized her sense of the Bayreuth festival
of 1889, in a long letter to her friends, Adolf Hildebrand, Germany's
best -known sculptor, and his wife, Irene. Hers is a splendid epistle,
analysis as diatribe. She and her husband, she wrote, were very pleased
to have attended the festival at long last. "It has strengthened us mar-
velously"; the two had "never felt more clearly than we do now *why* we
resist this art." Their mutual friend Hermann Levi, the distinguished
conductor who was a passionate and submissive Wagnerian and who had,
for all that he was a Jew, conducted the première of *Parsifal*, "keeps
on hoping that we will be reborn once we have enjoyed salvation at the
source, but thank God we are too old to be caught in this way, and
privately I am sorry that he should expect such power of seduction from
external accessories— the *essence* of the matter, after all, remains the same
whether one experiences it in Bayreuth or in Munich."

It is with a fine sense of fitness that the writer of this intemperate but
telling report should use the sexual term "seduction" in close propinquity
to the religious term "salvation": she found the erotic elements in
Wagner's work, especially as enacted in his shrine, all too obvious and
wholly repulsive. But, once again, Elizabet von Herzogenberg was glad
she had gone: "We can now say what the Master had in mind, nothing
has remained concealed from us, and now more than ever we turn away

18. Statham, *My Thoughts on Music*, 409–10.

and solemnly proclaim that this table has not been set for us." Her culinary
metaphor is no less apt than the sexual one that had preceded it: the
regressions that music can induce may lead back to the very earliest, the
oral phase of development. Sardonically characterizing three furious
Wagnerians—Conrad Fiedler, the brilliant art critic and aesthetician, his
forceful wife Mary, and their intimate, Hermann Levi—a trio she knew
well and found pathetic, almost beyond comprehension, Elizabet von
Herzogenberg stayed with her oral vocabulary for some sentences: "Let
those who lie to themselves, like Fiedler, or those, like Mary and Levi
to whom this has indeed become a sacred thing, and who have long
ceased to be able to distinguish gluttony from aesthetic enjoyment—let
them sit down at the table and carouse." Such abject Wagnerians "attend
'Parsifal' the way Catholics on Good Friday attend holy graves; for
them it has become a divine service, and I should not like to peer into the
confusion of feelings with which Mary sits in her princely box, at 40
Marks per person, every night!" As for "Levi," Elizabet von Herzogenberg went on, without pity, he "felt better than expected; a kind of
weakness that again overcame him at a rehearsal had its origins not in
his nervous condition but in that nameless emotion that overcomes him
in view of the sacred task." Levi, a classic "neurasthenic" who suffered
from intermittent bouts of nervous collapse, was only too representative
in his worshipful and overwrought state. "The whole gang is in an unnaturally elevated, hysterically rapturous condition, like Ribera's saints
with their uplifted eyes, of which you see only the whites." Yet she was
not impressed and certainly not taken in: "Secretly, under his shirt, each
of them has a carefully cultivated stigma. O, I tell you," she went on
getting angrier by the minute and reaching for more and more redolent
physical metaphors, "the whole business smells really very bad, like a
church that has never been aired, or a butcher's stall in summer; there is
a bloodthirstiness and incense-snuffling, a sultry sensuality with holy and
solemn gestures, a heaviness and bombast unknown to all other art."

This erotic religiosity did not leave Elizabet von Herzogenberg untouched. She found it "brooding and looming," taking her breath away.
The only excuse she could find for a trained musician like Herman Levi,
sitting there without smiling, was "the sickly air in which everything
moves." But how a thoughtful, sound and sober judge of art like Conrad
Fiedler could find the Grail scene in *Parsifal* irresistible was beyond
her powers of explanation. Some Wagnerian pleasures were patent enough:
"Mary sits enthroned in Bayreuth as high priestess; she visibly enjoys
her exceptional position as an initiate, as a friend, as one also admitted to
the council of the gods, for the new cloak that Parsifal wears had

ctually been ordered on her advice and behold, it was good." While iedler, pale, "more Prince Consort than ever," had been cordial to the Ierzogenbergs, Mary was clearly irritated "at the heretics, appearing ninvited." But heretic Elizabet von Herzogenberg remained, uncon- erted and infuriated: the "spiritual hocuspocus" of *Parsifal*, she con- luded, was "nothing but sensuality, the sloppiest emotional debauchery nd unhealthiest stigmata-ecstasy. For a stomach accustomed to a diet f Bach it is almost an emetic."[19] Then, the tempest over, she laid down er pen.

This is an extraordinary document, proof that there were some at east in the bourgeois century—not all of them bourgeois—who were ree to recognize a sensual orgy when they saw one, and not too genteel o call it by its right name. Psychoanalysis has taught us to suspect the ehemence of Elizabet von Herzogenberg's dissection; it suggests some epressed desire for the eroticism that she so perceptively noted and so uriously rejected. Certainly, the power of Wagner's music even over its letractors is beyond question; it stems from its capacity to mobilize eelings that even Brahmsians, being only human, must share. But her ndignation was as unequivocal, destined as everyone is to ambivalence, as uch an emotion can be; the nauseating element in the Wagner cult, for er, was not its glorification of love, but precisely its perverse—she was onvinced, its insincere and histrionic—manifestations. She was no prude. Vhat she found most pernicious about Wagner's work and Wagner's nfluence, she had told Brahms a year before she had suffered her ex- osure to Bayreuth, is "that he has done away with delightful, fresh, naive ensuality and replaced it with a sultry, oppressive, melancholy, fatal one, sensuality that perpetually smells of a yearning for death and always ives the audience a kind of bad conscience, as though it were com- nitting an indiscretion to be in its presence."[20] Wagnerian eroticism, hen, was in her eyes a debased romanticism, food not for the true lover of nusic but for the philistine.[21] And this, whether one accepts her verdict n Wagner or not, remains as the solid residue of Elizabet von Herzogen- erg's partisan anatomy of Bayreuth and of Wagnerian celebrants:

19. Elizabet von Herzogenberg to Adolf and Irene Hildebrand, August 7, 1889, *Adolf von Hildebrand und seine Welt. Briefe und Erinnerungen,* ed. Bernhard Sattler 1962), 326–29.
20. Elizabet von Herzogenberg to Johannes Brahms, February 16, 1888. *Johannes Brahms im Briefwechsel mit Heinrich und Elisabet von Herzogenberg,* ed. Max Kalbeck, 2 vols. (1907), II, 177.
21. "All philistines here [in Leipzig] are jubilant about 'Siegfried' and 'Götter- ämmerung.'" Elizabet von Herzogenberg to Johannes Brahms, October 4, 1878. bid., I, 77.

Wagner's compositions were a powerful, often nakedly aggressive batter
of aesthetic devices permitting virtuous and cultivated bourgeois to in
dulge their erotic dreams and delude themselves with the comfortin
belief that they were doing something elevated.

2. A Budget of Displacements

To judge from the reception of Wagner, the sexual admixture in musi
was, to the initiated in the Victorian decades, no mystery. The eroti
reverberations in other human pursuits, especially those related to th
body, were if anything more obvious; intimate entanglements of the ac
of love with the act of eating had long been fairly plain to the most in
nocent soul. For many centuries, feasts have served as prelude an
inducement to sexual carousal; the erotic dimensions in Plato's account
of philosophic suppers or, in a coarser vein, Petronius's description o
Trimalchio's dinner, are wholly undisguised. In the nineteenth century
society novelists and librettists for operettas liked to show seducer
taking their complaisant and knowing victims to certain restaurant:
having reserved *chambres separées*, as the first act in a night of carna
debauchery. Even more than music, food is the food of love.

This conjunction of oral and genital gratifications was incorporate
in common speech centuries before the nineteenth, and in revealing way:
Culinary metaphors for the beloved, like "honey" and dozens of other:
in as many languages, only confirm this solid association between eatin
and love. The lover's offer to eat the beloved sufficiently hints at th
nostalgic elements in sexual pleasure; in German, "*Ich könnt' dich fressen,*
even descends to the level of animal feeding. To issue such a jocular in
vitation or to act it out playfully is to link the mutual exploration o
adult lovers to the demonstrative love of parents for their children. T
incorporate one's lover, if only in fantasy, is a regressive amorous assault
looking back to that infantile stage when the libidinal and the aggressiv
drives have not yet been clearly separated. The love bite which, we know
is such a familiar emblem of sexual intercourse that has not been reduce
to lazy routine is the most visible sign of the place that memories, un
conscious for the most part, claim in the love-making of adults.

The psychological element in eating is, to be sure, overdetermine
Gluttony is likely to be a symptom, not of love but of its absence, of
mental hunger delusively satisfied by physical means. Moreover, muc
ceremonial bourgeois eating in the nineteenth century—those grea
banquets with their crowded menus and abundant quantities—was no
an incitement to sexual activity but a substitute for it. All one could d

after such meals was to sleep, and sleep alone. Yet, whether a sublimation of amorous appetites or their fuel, the erotic roots of gourmandiz-
ing were always substantial and often quite obvious.

But sensuality also deployed stratagems that were masterpieces of indirection, expressions of feelings that seemed to have nothing in common
with sexual love at all. Perhaps the most successful representative of such
stratagems was the enthusiastic love of nature, which came to enjoy
unrivalled popularity, principally among the young and well-bred, in the
nineteenth century. Like other loves, this, too, had a long history, dating
back to ancient personifications of natural forces and primitive projec-
tions of human sentiments, through the scattered descriptions in the
Middle Ages and the Renaissance to the more direct and self-conscious
valuation of natural objects, of mountains and meadows and trees, in the
travel writings, the verse, and the philosophy of horticulture in the age
of the Enlightenment. But in the Victorian century that love became a
conspicuous tactic, both for escaping the implications of sensuality and
for intensifying its delights. "For some time now," a writer in the *Revue
des deux Mondes* observed in 1866, "a veritable fervor in the sentiment
of love" has "attached men of the arts and the sciences to nature." In the
nineteenth century, he noted, men no longer worship the mountains as
divinities, "but those who have traveled over them often love them with
a profound love." This attachment, at once deep and secular, had, he
thought, been prominent for some decades. When Gustave Flaubert's
intimate friend, Alfred Le Poittevin, told him that he was falling more
and more in love with nature, Flaubert responded that his own feelings
were more excited still, reaching toward frenzy. "Sometimes I look at
animals and even at trees with a tenderness that amounts to fellow-feeling," and, beyond that, he would experience, with nature, "sensations
that are almost voluptuous." Some found such sensations not almost but
wholly voluptuous. Amiel, recording in his diary his feelings about an
"admirable" November day, praised its "limpid mildness," its "penetrating
and suave charm," its "peaceful and caressing beauty." Nature seemed to
him like a loving mistress—*"une amante"*—at the "hour of farewell,
seeming to endow her last smile and her last look with all the power of
her magnetism," and to mingle "the vivacity of her tenderness" with
some indefinable "insinuating languor." As for himself, Amiel could only
contemplate and savor these riches.[22]

22. Elisée Rechus: "Du Sentiment de la Nature dans les sociétés modernes," *Revue
des deux Mondes*, LXIII (1866), 352, 354; Flaubert: May 26 (1845), *Correspondance*,
ed. Jean Bruneau, 2 vols. so far (1973–   ), I, *1830–1851*, 233–34; Amiel: November 3,
1850, *Journal intime*, I, 811.

It is no accident, then, that Ralph Waldo Emerson, the philosopher of Nature, should also be its poet. He endowed it with speech, with feelings, with profound meanings, with woman's power.

> Oh, call not nature dumb;
> These trees and stones are audible to me,
> These idle flowers, that tremble in the
> wind,
> I understand their faery syllables,
> And all their sad significance.

Nature was not always depressed; at times, when it spoke through spring flowers, Emerson found it cheerfully seductive:

> O come, then, quickly come!
> We are budding, we are blowing;
> And the wind that we perfume
> Sings a tune that's worth the knowing.

Nature is the cherished woman, the mother regained: crossing a common in the snow, at twilight, under cloudy skies, Emerson wrote in his first essay on Nature, he had found true exhilaration. "In the woods, too, a man casts off his years, as the snake his slough, and at what period soever of life, is always a child. In the woods, is perpetual youth." Indeed, he wrote in the second essay, "we nestle in nature." It is our first and unforgettable abode. "We never can part with it; the mind loves its old home: as water to our thirst, so is the rock, the ground, to our eyes and hands and feet." Nature, in all her forms, incarnates the beloved. Many other bourgeois, had they been equally able to recognize, and adept at recording, their feelings would have reported the same sensual commerce with nature.[23]

The educated came by these erotic perceptions quite naturally: they were bred to it. As small children, they had listened to, and later read for themselves, sentimental anthropomorphic poems about lambs and

---

23. Gay Wilson Allen, *Waldo Emerson* (1981), 104, 156; Emerson, "Nature" (1836), *The Selected Writings of Ralph Waldo Emerson*, ed. Brooks Atkinson (1940), 6; "Nature" (1844), ibid., 411. Keith Thomas has brilliantly demonstrated in *Man and the Natural World: Changing Attitudes in England, 1500–1800* (1983) that, in England at least, there was a drastic shift in the feeling for nature between the sixteenth and eighteenth, even more the nineteenth, centuries, from exploitation to conservation, from man the arbitrary lord of all he surveys to man the faithful steward of his patrimony. Reasons were commercial, scientific, aesthetic as much as amorous, perhaps even more—by no means all friends of trees and streams and lakes were necessarily lovers.

gardens. Beyond that, whatever sex education their parents or nurses thought proper to impart would draw liberally on broad analogies between the sexual history of birds or flowers and their own. The animism of exotic tribes that anthropologists were discovering on their field trips in the late nineteenth century, a projective perception of nature endowing plants and rocks with human emotions and human powers, was, suitably refined, a commonplace sentiment for the nineteenth-century youngster. In 1894, some years before Freud would make arresting, sweeping comparisons between children, neurotics, and "savages," the American educator William A. Hoyt speculated about "The Love of Nature as the Root of Teaching and Learning the Sciences." Significantly, Hoyt praised the child's identification with animate and inanimate nature as a valuable survival from less sophisticated ways of seeing the world. Primitive superstitions, he argued, embody "man's pristine closeness to nature," and the child's life begins, happily enough, with such superstitions; this healthy relation to the great outdoors will be sadly dissipated by its later experiences under the pressures of modern urban life. In her sensitive autobiography, the Norwegian novelist Sigrid Undset confirms this primitive eroticism as her earliest childhood memory: "The first thing Ingvild remembered was having just crawled from the lawn away to a strip of bare ground that lay in front of a hedge of green bushes." The time is the mid-1880s. "The mold is brown and loose and warmed by the sun, lovely to fill your hands with. The child lets it run through her fingers on to her bare calves and white socks, making them grey. Wild with delight she pours and pours, as fast as she can." This, and the swaying, glistening grass, the calm air and the warm wind the autobiographer recalled as a "kind of orgiastic joy." Hers was an innocent enough orgy: the young Zola, writing to his school friend Paul Cézanne, was in honorable company suggesting that he strongly preferred "virgin nature" to "nature that has been tormented and dressed."[24]

The nineteenth-century adult could not easily escape this sort of primitivism; many of the writers on sexuality ransacked the plant and animal worlds as a rich resource for artful introductions to a survey of human generative organs and processes. The celebrated Dr. John Harvey Kellogg of Battle Creek, Michigan, he of the health foods, moved in his immensely successful *Plain Facts for Old and Young* from sex in plants to sex in animals to sex in human beings, and coyly entertained his readers

---

24. Hoyt: *Pedagogical Seminary*, III (1894), 61–86; Undset: *The Longest Years* (1934; tr. Arthur G. Chater, 1935), 3–4; Zola: to Paul Cézanne, June 14, 1858, *Correspondance*, ed. B. H. Bakker, 4 vols. so far (1978–   ), I, 96.

with "vegetable husbands," and "polygamous flowers." Then, just as he assimilated the natural world to the human, he reversed the process: modern boys, who grow up too fast and adopt fashionable vices, looked to Dr. Kellogg like "human mushrooms"; addressing girls on the delicate subject of propagation, he likened fetuses to "human buds." For most literate persons, with the possible exception of natural scientists intent on separating themselves from the objects of their researches, this language betokened an appropriate, and was a cherished, habit of mind. Uncounted numbers of young bourgeois underwent an apprenticeship to Nature that spoke to them, as it spoke to the American temperance reformer Frances Willard, in a "constant, universal voice." That voice permitted Willard, as she records in her autobiography, to feel in closest unison with her adored father, a man who "had a heart that beat closer to Nature's own, than mother's even." It was to be expected. Frances Willard's mother had "felt the moral aspects of birds and woods and sky," but her father "loved them simply for themselves." A consummate gardener, he taught his children the "sweet, shy secrets" of the great outdoor world.[25] Nature could thus become a legitimate repository for the most unruly sensual demands. That it kept a girl close to the father she worshiped was a dividend gladly accepted and naively reported.

Conventional theological arguments, very ancient by the nineteenth century but still enjoying good repute, only served to confirm such ways of thinking and feeling. To take the continuing miracles of nature as one more, and persuasive, proof for the existence and benevolence of God was to license the most extravagant expressiveness. Writers on gardening, producing handbooks that could count on sizeable editions throughout the century, enlivened their chapters of sensible horticultural advice with rhapsodies about the emotional life of flowers and the human sentiments of plants. Little moralizing tales about the feelings of roses were common texts in family periodicals, catalogues meticulously interpreting the language of flowers an innocuous occupation and, incidentally, a boost for sales of bouquets to lovers. But that sort of thing worked in the same direction as the poets and the preachers. It eased the path of erotic displacement away from impermissible human targets.

That nineteenth-century bourgeois revelled sensually in their love for nature is more than an inference; it manifested itself in metaphors, analogies, verses. Robert Browning, who permitted sexuality to partici-

25. Kellogg: *Plain Facts for Old and Young* (1881; ed. 1886), 53, 329, 400–401; Willard: *Glimpses of Fifty Years. The Autobiography of an American Woman* (1889), 15–16.

late in the making of his poems rather more freely than did many other
poets, used the language of his fraternity when he evoked images of the
"western cloud/ All billowy bosomed," or saw "primal naked forms of
flowers."[26] Nineteenth-century poetry was everywhere flooded by such
provocations. So was its prose. With the natural sciences of the age
stepping from intellectual triumph to intellectual triumph, old anthropomorphic longings for nature, the great nourishing, embracing mother,
were beginning to lose some of their authority: nineteenth-century
physicists, chemists, astronomers, biologists took distance from such
seductive rhetoric to concentrate on describing natural phenomena and
seeking their laws. But emotional tributes to Nature, old and new, continued to influence the age. There was that "beautiful" hymn to nature
that, Freud said, had moved him to choose medicine as a career, and
Emerson's widely quoted essays on "Nature" in which he searched for "an
original relation to the universe."[27] Even Carlyle, who liked to think of
himself as a hard-headed scourge of sentimentalists, set the vicissitudes of
love in the theatre of nature. His Teufelsdröckh experiences "Blumine"—
meaningful girl's name!—as a force of nature: she, the flower, is a "Rose-
goddess," a "Queen of Hearts" in whose presence his heart swells "like
the Sea swelling when once near its Moon!" To love her, Teufelsdröckh
discovers, is not just like an erection; it is like hearing music, like wandering among the aerial light of the mountain tops. Her words to him "came
over him like dew on thirsty grass." This "Love-mania" cannot last;
Blumine dismisses him, but up to the orgasmic end the language of nature
aids Carlyle to express the inexpressible: " 'She put her hand in his, she
looked in his face, tears started to her eyes; in wild audacity he clasped
her to his bosom; their lips were joined, their two souls, like two dewdrops
rushed into one,—for the first time, and for the last!' Thus was Teufelsdröckh made immortal by a kiss. And then? Why, then—'thick curtains
of Night rushed over his soul, as rose the immeasurable Crash of Doom;
and through the ruins as of a shivered Universe was he falling, falling,
towards the Abyss.' " Their single, intense, crashing moment of bliss over,
his detumescence simultaneous and synonymous with farewell, the distraught Teufelsdröckh seeks symbolic solace in maternal nature: "into the
wilds of nature" he goes, "as if in her mother-bosom he would seek heal-

26. See, among others, such provocative Browning texts as "The Last Ride Together" or "Meeting at Night."
27. We now know that the essay that helped to inspire Freud and which he (like
everyone else then) attributed to Goethe, is really by Christoph Tobler. Peter Gay,
Freud, Jews, and Other Germans: Masters and Victims in Modernist Culture (1978),
52n.

ing."[28] That was as explicit as nineteenth-century writers were likely to become.

Such texts, and others like them, attest to an inexhaustible, unconscious need to find love in an oceanic regressive reunion with the first of all loved objects, and to drape erotic wishes in a decent, restrained vocabulary. Innumerable fictional nineteenth-century lovers, whether in rhymes or in story, rested their head on nature's breast, heard siren songs from the brooks, or read their amatory dejection in lowering thunder clouds. That is why writers of books on gardening felt free periodically to set aside their sturdy practicality to make liberal, though gentle, play with erotic metaphors. "The student of nature," Louisa Johnson wrote in her *Every Lady Her Own Flower Gardener*, in a splendid, by no means uncommon piece of projection, "is interested in all her manifold combinations: in her wildest attitudes, and her artful graces." Flower-gardening, she noted—the time was the late 1830s—"has become the dominant passion of the ladies of Great Britain." It forcibly brings reason and judgment into action; it fosters serious meditation and harmless, elegant fancy. "A flower-garden, to the young and single of my sex, acts upon the heart and affections as a nursery acts upon the matronly feelings.' Johnson had opened her book with the assertion that "a garden affords the purest of human pleasures."[29] That it afforded keen pleasure is well documented, activating the fancy and charming the affections, but that the pleasures were the purest of all is not so certain.

Gardening was in those years reserved for well-situated, sheltered young ladies who, in the opinion of most men, needed to exercise their imagination more than did worldly-wise males. This, at least, is the message of Thomas Bridgeman's successful *Florist's Guide*. Gardening Bridgeman holds, affords "substantial intellectual pleasure" and provides occupation that will keep people from vice. But the general tenor of his book, "chiefly designed for the use of the softer sex," is less virile than this. "While the hand is employed in cultivating the transient beauties of a garden," he writes, "the attentive mind will feast daintily on the study of nature." This delicate oral whisper is only a sample of what is to come. A labored allegory, "The Matrimonial Garden," which conclude

28. *Sartor Resartus* (1834; ed. 1908), 109, 113, 114, 116.
29. Louisa Johnson, *Every Lady Her Own Flower Gardener, Containing Simple and Practical Directions for Cultivating Plants and Flowers in the Northern and Southern States, Also Flora's Revealings, Hints for the Management of Flowers in Rooms,&c.*, *with Brief Botanical Descriptions of Plants and Flowers; the Whole in Plain and Simple Language, Expressly Calculated for Popular Use* (1st American ed., 1844), 2, 12, 2. First published in England in 1839, the book went through many editions under slightly different titles.

Bridgeman's book, is a riot of sensual images. Marriage is a kind of "seclusion," a "retired apartment," precisely like a garden. This "delightful enclosure," Bridgeman warns, must be approached 'prudently and cautiously." The female sexual organs, that retired apartment, seem here to be protected by a brimming moat of metaphor: they lie concealed behind the idea of marriage which, in turn, Bridgeman visualizes as a walled garden. If "its entrance is usually extremely gay and glittering," strewn "with flowers of every hue and every fragrance calculated to charm the eye and please the taste," some plants are injurious and must be rooted out. Permanent happiness in that garden may be only a dream, but, Bridgeman advises his reader, "if you are desirous that this garden shall yield you all the bliss of which it is capable, you must take with you that excellent flower called GOOD HUMOUR, which, of all the flowers of nature, is the most delicious and delicate." To drop or to lose it would be a calamity: "it is a treasure the loss of which, nothing can supply." Impotence or castration are irreparable. Many paths in this enclosed garden, notably some adjoining the first walk, "The Honey Moon Path," ought not to be entered; many shrubs are noxious. There is, to take but one, that "rough, sturdy plant, called OBSTINACY," which is indigestible and fatal if taken in large quantities. But, just opposite, the walker will find "that lovely and lively shrub called COMPLIANCE, which, though not always pleasant to the palate, is very salutary." It "leaves a sweetness in the mouth," and eventually "produces the most delicious fruit. Never be without a very large sprig in your hand."[30] And so forth, past several more bushes, into the consummations of homely philosophy.

It may seem heavy-handed to read this largely irrelevant postscript to a sensible guide as an extended metaphor for sexual intercourse or sexual panic. Surely it was not Bridgeman's intention to write polite pornography for young ladies. But "The Matrimonial Garden," precisely because it is so innocent, hints at the erotic investment that respectable, middle-class women regularly made through their genteel physical labors in the cultivated outdoors. They could enlist gardening as a substitute for less acceptable ventures, and as a way of taking the sting out of anxiety over love's pressing demands.

The love of nature thus held the most profitable possibilities for the sensual; it could make sex more delicious, reviving erotic memories and

---

30. Thomas Bridgeman, "Gardener, Seedsman, and Florist," *The Florist's Guide, Containing Practical Directions for the Cultivation of Annual, Biennial, and Perennial Flowering Plants, of Different Classes, Herbaceous and Shrubby, Bulbous, Fibrous and Tuberous Rooted, Including the Double Dahlia* (1844), iv–v, 160–64. This "article" is reprinted, in its entirety, in Doris L. Swartout, *An Age of Flowers* (1975), 15–19.

giving special poignancy to cherished anniversaries. In a normal life
history, sensual adolescents were likely to make nature the target of
boundless and risky longings; then, once happily married, they could
use nature to lend their satisfactions greater savor. The division was far
from absolute. When Charles Kingsley, precocious and from his earliest
years intensely interested in love, was only sixteen, he had grasped this
cheerful dialectic. "Teach her to love God," he wrote to a friend who had
evidently asked him for some advice, "teach her to love Nature. God is
love; and the more we love Him, the more we love all around us."[31]
Kingsley knew what he was talking about. His warm and atmospheric
evocations of nature, which many critics think the best things in his
novels, convey his excitement in its presence. "Once the love of nature
constituted my whole happiness," he wrote, recalling his Cambridge days,
"in the 'shadowy recollections' and vague emotions which were called up
by the inanimate creation, I found a mine of mysterious wealth, in which
I revelled while I knew not its value. The vast and the sublime, or the
excitement of violent motion, affected me almost to madness; I have shed
strange tears, I know not why, at the sight of the most luscious and
sunny prospects." It is mainly in Kingsley's adjectives—mysterious, luscious, delicious—that the explosive erotic charge is contained, and revealed. He can observe "the delicious shiver of those aspen leaves," and,
again, writing to the girl he loves, "Those delicious self-sown firs! Every
step I wander they whisper to me of you, the delicious past melting into
the more delicious future."[32]

Kingsley was fully aware that his love of nature was erotic in its
origins. Not long after he met the young woman he would marry, he
promised some day to tell her "of the dreamy days of boyhood, when I
knew and worshipped nothing but the physical"; of the days when he
drew enjoyment solely "from the semi-sensual delights of ear and eye,
from sun and stars, wood and wave, the *beautiful inanimate* in all its
forms." Nor did Kingsley feel in the least apologetic about his state:
"When I talk, then, of excitement," he wrote to her in the same year, "I
do not wish to destroy excitability, but to direct it into the proper
channel, and to bring it under subjection." He did not feel apologetic
because he could endow his sensual embrace of the outdoors with religious qualities: "I feel that sense of the mystery that is around me, I

---

31. Reminiscences by his friend Richard Cowley Powles, *Charles Kingsley: His
Letters and Memories of His Life*, ed. by his wife, 2 vols. (1876; ed. 1879), I, 16.
    32. Ibid., I, 18–19, 27; Kingsley to Fanny Grenfell, July 14, 1842; ibid., 54.

feel a gush of enthusiasm towards God, which seems its inseparable effect!" Far from Fanny Grenfell, uncertain whether he would ever be able to marry her, he consoled himself, and her, with a string of metaphors borrowed from generative nature: "Though there may be clouds between us now," he wrote to her in August 1842, "yet they are safe and dry, free from storm and rains—our parted state now is quiet grey weather, under which all tender things will spring up and grow, beneath the warm damp air, till they are ready for the next burst of sunshine to hurry them into blossom and fruit. Let us plant and rear all tender thoughts, knowing surely that those who sow in tears shall reap in joy." All of this enthusiasm did not cease with marriage: the more he loved his wife, the more he loved nature. Writing to her in 1849, from a solitary walking tour, he sent her a poem in which he wonders what the "green leaves," the "rosy rocks," and the "brown streams" are saying to him, and finds that their message is married and fertile love:

> O, rose is the colour of love and youth
> And green is the colour of faith and truth,
>   And brown of the fruitful clay.
> The earth is fruitful, and faithful, and
>   young,
> And her bridal morn shall rise ere long,
> And you shall know what the rocks and the
>   streams,
>   And the laughing green-woods say!

He had written the poem, he told his wife, "with many happy tears."[33] Nature, for Kingsley, was a defense against, and, far more, the source of added, erotic pleasure.

It was water even more than the woods or the hills, water yielding the most primitive of stimulation buoying up the body and caressing the skin, that Kingsley celebrated most rhapsodically: "the purple veil of water," to say nothing of the *"fiery sea."* Others, as disparate as Amiel and Whitman, found bathing, or just lolling in the wet element, a keenly sensual experience, at once refreshing and stirring. Indeed, Amiel could associate Venus Anadyomene, the goddess of love rising from the sea, with a cold bath he recorded in his private journal. Similarly, Flaubert has Emma Bovary, that doomed bourgeoise, "stretch her limbs lazily," as

33. Kingsley to Fanny Grenfell, January, February 1841; July 16, August 1842; September 4, 1849, ibid., I, 31, 33, 56, 60, 173. For more on this pair, see pp. 297–312.

she bathes in the amorous, hopelessly banal words of her lover Rodolphe.[34] The founding of hydropathic establishments in the United States of the 1840s, and later, institutionalized this water eroticism. Women who frequented them, like Catharine Beecher, found them places where they could freely discuss their bodies and, more or less artlessly, enjoy them. As the *Water Cure Journal* sketched the treatment in 1846: "A large coarse blanket is spread upon a mattress. The patient lies down upon it, as in the wet sheet, and is closely packed from neck to toe and covered with a number of other blankets." Then, "having duly sweated, the patient is unpacked, and steps into a shallow bath, preferably a plunge bath." Now, "this transition from copious perspiration to cold water is not only perfectly innocuous, but highly salutary. A powerful reaction, and a high degree of exhilaration and vigor are the result."[35] One might well believe it. This sort of a treatment provided some of the enjoyment of intercourse, and was much safer.

Still, the custom of the likes of Catharine Beecher ensured the respectability of such establishments and of such tactile experiences. In contrast, Natalie Barney, a programmatic and heterodox sensualist, recalled in her autobiography that a stream of water once served her as an imaginative instrument of masturbation: standing in her bathtub—she was about twelve —"the water that I made shoot up between my legs from the beak of a swan gave me the most intense sensation." It was as though she needed no one else to generate sexual pleasure: "I had become my own mistress-lover."[36] Most other lovers of watery nature were not quite so experimental as this, and experienced the bliss of the wet element in more discreet fashion.

Mabel Loomis Todd, that garrulous and uninhibited autobiographer, had a sense of smell no less keen, and no less erotic, than a tremulous sensivity to touch, especially to moisture on her skin. "There is a subtle odor about the Music Hall," she wrote after a trip to Boston. "Odors have always had this very great power over me," she commented. "They revive emotions and associations much more than anything else can do."

34. Charles Kingsley to Fanny Kingsley: mid-August 1849, *Letters*, I, 169–70; Amiel: June 19, 1851, *Journal intime*, I, 996; Whitman: Justin Kaplan, *Walt Whitman: A Life* (1980), 91; Flaubert: *Madame Bovary, Oeuvres*, ed. Albert Thibaudet and René Dumesnil, 2 vols. (1951–52), I, 433 [part II, ch. 9].

35. Kathryn Kish Sklar, *Catharine Beecher: A Study in American Domesticity* (1973), 206–209, 317. Spas, and indeed water cures, go back to the seventeenth, certainly to the eighteenth century, but it was in the nineteenth that they came into their own as the playgrounds of the bourgeoisie.

36. Jean Chalon, *Portrait of a Seductress: The World of Natalie Barney* (1976; tr. Carol Barko, 1979), 9.

This was not quite accurate, for Mabel Todd was just as sensual, possibly more so, in her descriptions of what she saw, heard, and touched: woods and trees, birds and insects, spray and sand, flowers studied on attentive walks or glimpsed on companionable drives. "Back again in one of the most beautiful spots in the world!" she wrote about Hampton, New Hampshire, in the summer of 1877. She was not yet twenty. "There is a happiness amounting to ecstasy in being on the long white beach, with lines of breakers rolling up in foam, the sun glittering on the little waves out to sea and the blessed east wind blowing health into one's face, an ecstasy which I have never experienced under any other circumstances but which is faintly suggested to me by seeing white steam come out of a pipe or chimney against the blue sky." All this worked to "send the blood dancing through my veins in exhilaration."[37] One must allow for prescribed adolescent formulas—how many beautiful spots in the world had she seen? What did she know of ecstasy?—she had not yet met her husband, David Peck Todd. But her precision in recording the tingle of foam-laden wind in her face, and her unconscious phallic fantasies breaking through with her association to pipes and chimneys emitting steam, hint at the sexual charge that participating in the world of nature and machines gave her.

In one sensitive rumination, Mabel Loomis, as she then still was, did justice to the fusion of feelings in her receptive mind, and the ease with which she could transfer emotions from one object of passionate interest to another: "I am writing now in a hammock, and it is just after sunset. The calmness of an evening after a perfect day is coming on. The birds are singing and twittering through the apple trees, & the western sky is full of burnished gold." She was glad she had "kept a journal all through my life, or the principal part of it, for it is pleasant to look back and see when and where I have had my pleasures, who I meet, and also to see my growth in various directions, as I always write about what interests me most at the time. At first it was school, little parties, then church and theology and boys, and after, music and writing, romance,—then nature and painting, the sea—many of these all together, until now—what shall I say of myself?" Here they were all together, the devices of her sensuality, in close, mutually reinforcing association. "Music, ever and always, romance? yes romance in a certain way, forever, hero-worship, passionate love of the sea and all nature, a desire for a perfect character, which I

37. July 27, 1883, Journal, III, MLT, box 46. June 29, 1877, Journal, II, MLT, box 45. For her "worship" of water, see July 15, Diary 1879, MLT, box 39; and June 3, 1880, Journal, III, box 46. Y-MA.

sometimes try to attain, sometimes forget, a great love for books and pictures, statues and all beautiful objects, and an intense love for personal ease and pleasure. 'Surely pleasure is the aim of life' or words to that effect, is the sentence of a philosopher."[38] As usual, her prose is somewhat suspect: the perfection of the day, the twittering of the birds, and the burnished gold of the evening sky sound a little mechanical; they suggest a self-conscious young lady watching herself writing in her journal. But the passage, like most of Mabel Todd's writing, breaks away from routine and ritual to tap deeper springs of feeling. Her exposition is engagingly free of cant about higher duties and moral obligations—even her attempt to perfect her character is an occasional effort only; she is drafting a menu of pleasures that she, a sensual adolescent, has enjoyed and expects to enjoy again.

This was in the summer of 1877. In the fall of the same year, she conducted an amusing little private quarrel with a young man of her acquaintance, "uncultivated in the finer points of life and society," for wanting to restrict the adjective *delicious*, a great favorite with her, to "eatables or drinkables." She had seen, she argues with one of those accesses of snobbery that makes a curious counterpoint to her self-proclaimed radicalism, "first class authors" apply the word more liberally in the *Atlantic*; "good usage" among cultivated people, she thought, rather than the dictionary, "is the highest possible authority." She could have added Charles Kingsley who, as we know, also thought firs and shivering aspen delicious, harbingers of a delicious future. The point of her outburst was that she wanted to apply the epithet to the maples and dogwood turning color in Wilmington, Massachusetts: "They are positively delicious." The "glory" of the autumn foliage she had glimpsed deserved nothing less than this oral accolade. "I am so glad I can get such intense happiness out of such simple things as a walk with my father and mother under a beautiful cloudy, grey sky, and stopping to see all the dear, growing things by the way." It was part of her somewhat grandiose self-image that she joined, in the most felicitous manner, natural simplicity with her cultivation.[39]

Later, after she was married, when she had come to relish explicit sexuality, she allowed herself to associate eroticism with nature far more openly. Not long after the birth of her daughter, she recalled the vacation trip she had taken with her husband during the first months of her

---

38. June 17, 1877. Ibid.
39. October 14, 1877. Ibid. The word "delicious," as I have shown (above, pp. 31–32), also figured prominently in the love letters of Walter Bagehot and Eliza Wilson.

pregnancy, and singled out the July day in Watkins, New York, when "my darling & I explored the Glen—which will never be thought of by me independently of the holy love which transfigured every rock & waterfall, every fern & dainty harebell, and which showed itself by tender words & still tenderer care in my climbing, & by sweetest caresses in every secluded nook." In her journal, surrendering to her associations as they paraded through her mind, she would talk of "all those delicate signs of summer's death which I so passionately loved, need, for my fullest happiness," and of "my ocean—the master of all nature to me,—life could hold nothing happier," only to move, without pause, to her "own precious husband, without whom I am thirsty indeed."[40] Marriage had added a new ingredient to her love of nature: memories.

This erotic mode of assimilating nature remained with Mabel Todd throughout her maturity; it explodes, with little rocket showers of joy and pathos, in the course of her long love affair with Austin Dickinson. One of his finest character traits, she observes in making a devoted catalogue of his incomparable assets, is that "he loves nature *exquisitely*." With the passage of years, as their sad ecstatic love went its way, nature increasingly acquired resonances of recollections and associations. "The drive from Northampton alone this sweet afternoon," she noted in her journal in the early fall of 1885, "brought you so vividly to my side. The clouds were the lightest and airiest—the shadows slanted down the side of Holyoke—the smell of clover was in the air, & of new-made hay. The roadsides were lined with big, purple-eyed daisies, wild roses," and all, all spoke to Mabel Todd of Austin Dickinson. As the couple played pathetically with thoughts of divorcing their respective spouses and, even more pathetically, with death wishes against the living obstacles to their marrying, they invested sights and sounds with meanings of stolen pleasures: partridges drumming in the spring woods, hot August days they had snatched for their excursions, chirping crickets became emblems of bliss remembered and hopes betrayed.[41]

In the anguished letter—one reiterated moan of pain interrupted by self-deceptive optimism—that Mabel Todd wrote to Austin Dickinson across several lovely August days in 1895 as he lay at home out of her reach, dying, she recalled the crickets once more: "Do you hear the crickets, *our* crickets, my beloved, at twilight? And when you hear them

40. "Millicent's Life," I [pp. 7–8], MLT, box 46; August 24, 1879, Journal, II. For a remarkable association of her feeling for nature and her sense of power, see "Millicent's Life," I [p. 15].

41. August 3, 1884, Journal, III; September 27, May 25, 1885, Journal, IV, MLT, box 46.

do you think of me? I sat on the east piazza last evening listening to them, and again in front of the house, until it seems to me you *must* be with me. Do you hear them sweetheart?" In her rebellious melancholy she evoked August, their August, just once more. "All these fair August days I can hardly breathe without you. *Our* month, and you so ill that you are shut away from me—but only for the time, dear. You are coming back, and then I shall tell you how lonesome the lights and shadows were on the far, dim hills"—the lights and shadows on the hills feeling as lonesome as she—"and how the blue haze choked me, and blinded my eyes"—the haze, not her tears, blinding her—"and how the rich odors of corn and tobacco suffocated me with recollection and anticipation." She would never tell him about the hills and the haze and the smell of corn, for Austin Dickinson died that week. On August 18, the day before his funeral, she made a forlorn little entry in her diary: "A still, utterly beautiful August day, insects chirping, and crickets, our crickets, at evening."[42] Disasters threaten, but they also mobilize defenses; they join undoing to other modes of coping with threatened irrevocable loss; what is happening cannot be happening. Thus the sufferer seeks to rescue from the shipwreck of hope the tattered remnants of gratifications remembered. In the midst of despair and defeat, sensuality will persist in its stratagems.

3. Glandular Christianity

Among the deviant paths that balked sexual impulses could take in their search for gratification, the one trespassing on the terrain of religion was, for the age of Victoria, by far the most interesting. It was, after all, for the middle classes, an age of faith under challenge—a faith normally inherited, but often enough thoughtful and troubled alike. There were believers who, especially by the end of the century, thought some forms that the love of God assumed rather suspect. By then, investigators had come to diagnose the religious fanaticism of adolescent boys and of middle-aged spinsters as maladies born of unsatisfied erotic desire. In 1895, Clara Barrus, devoted admirer and biographer of the "poet-naturalist" John Burroughs, stated flatly that women who think they are "the Virgin Mary, the bride of Christ, the Church, 'God's wife,' are sure, sooner or later, to disclose symptoms which show that they are in some way or other sexually depraved." Her tone may have been a little startling, her message was not. Long before, in 1817, Stendhal had already

42. August 10–14, 1895, MLT, box 101; August 18, 1895, Diary, MLT, box 41.

recorded, in Bologna: "Ave Maria (*twilight*), in Italy the hour for tenderness, for the pleasures of the soul and for melancholy: sensation intensified by the sound of those lovely bells." In the early 1840s, Amiel had credited Balzac, that "frightening" novelist, with understanding everything, including "the delights of faith" and "the mysteries of ecstasy." Then in 1850 he confessed, with his customary mixture of ingenuousness and penetration, that hearing religious music like Rossini's *Stabat Mater* and a trio from Haydn's *Creation*, had moved him deeply and "reawakened the delicious sensations I had experienced in earlier days."[43]

In his classic Gifford Lectures, *The Varieties of Religious Experience*, delivered in 1901 and 1902, William James would caution against the easy reduction of religion to sexuality which, he thought, had become only too fashionable. "We are surely all familiar in a general way," he said severely, "with this method of discrediting states of mind for which we have an antipathy."[44] The employment of psychology in the service of polemical aggression disturbed him, and not without justice. His strictures, though, eloquently exhibit the popularity of this reductionism. Still, it is worth noting that there were some in James's time who could recognize the sensual admixtures of religion perceptively, without animosity and wholly without condescension. In *Adam Bede*, George Eliot defined Seth Bede's first love as "hardly distinguishable from religious feeling. What deep and worthy love is so, whether of woman or child, or art or music. Our caresses, our tender words, our still raptures under the influence of autumn sunsets, or pillared vistas, or calm majestic statues, or Beethoven symphonies all bring with them the consciousness that they are mere waves and ripples in an unfathomable ocean of love and beauty." It is true that the detection of an intimate link between religious emotions and sensual needs, the persistence of what Freud was to call the "religious-libidinal cloud" into this scientific age, was particularly pleasing to unbelievers; it provided the exquisite pleasure of having one's cherished

---

43. Barrus: Ronald Pearsall, *Public Purity, Private Shame: Victorian Sexual Hypocrisy Exposed* (1976), 32; Stendhal: *De l'amour* (1822; ed. Henri Martineau, 1938), 282; Amiel: August 21, 1842, March 28, 1850, *Journal intime*, I, 201, 680.

44. *The Varieties of Religious Experience: A Study of Human Nature* (1902), 13–14. ". . . the fashion, quite common nowadays among certain writers, of criticizing the religious emotions by showing a connection between them and the sexual life. Conversion is a crisis of puberty and adolescence. The macerations of saints, and the devotion of missionaries, are instances of the parental instinct of self-sacrifice gone astray. For the hysterical nun, starving for the natural life, Christ is but an imaginary substitute for a more earthy object of affection. And the like." (11–12). Though not unfounded James's sturdy critique tends to overlook some telling psychological clues.

anticlericalism scientifically confirmed.[45] But the discovery of this link was not the prerogative of anticlerical polemicists retelling those old hostile jokes against amorous priests, prurient confessors, and complaisant penitents. Eliot's oceanic effusion, like Stendhal's and Amiel's somewhat less excited observations, demonstrates that one could be sympathetic to religion and still recognize its ties to erotic drives.

Hence by the late 1880s, Krafft-Ebing could calmly assert in his *Psycho-pathia Sexualis* that those "dark, incomprehensible urges," which explode in adolescence as sexuality, find many ways of expressing themselves, including religion and poetry, which, even after the turmoil of puberty has waned, "receive powerful assistance from the sexual realm." By 1900, in his essay on "The Auto-Erotic Factor in Religion," Havelock Ellis could say, with little fear of contradiction, that "the intimate association between the emotions of love and religion is well known to all those who are habitually brought into close contact with the phenomena of the religious life." He cited a number of modern studies, some rather theatrical, one dating back to 1832, all descrying the dynamic impact of sexual pathology on religious effervescence. In adducing lives of the Christian saints and martyrs, and attributing their courage at least in part to "an exaltation which they frankly drew from the sexual impulse," Ellis rightly suggested that the mechanism of displacement was far older than the bourgeois century. Certainly, the almost painfully obvious mingling of sacred and orgasmic ecstasy in the St. Theresa of Bernini's famous monument in Rome is a reminder that religiosity had its sensual side long before Havelock Ellis.[46] What gives displacement its particular interest for the student of the nineteenth-century middle class is that it was then generalized from saints to ordinary mortals, and that self-conscious and self-critical bourgeois undertook to study the phenomenon. This prominence of religion as both refuge and excuse for sensuality is another, highly persuasive instance of the pressures of reality: with religion so central to the nineteenth-century middle-class mind, it proved an inexhaustible resource for those seeking indirect, permissible modes of expression for their erotic needs.

45. Eliot: *Adam Bede* (1859; Pref. F. R. Leavis, 1961), 47 [ch. 3]; Freud: to Jung, February 18, 1912, *The Freud/Jung Letters: The Correspondence Between Sigmund Freud and C. G. Jung*, ed. William McGuire (tr. Ralph Manheim and R. F. C. Hull, 1974), 485.

46. Krafft-Ebing: *Psychopathia Sexualis* (1886; 11th ed., 1901), 7; Ellis: *Studies in the Psychology of Sex*, vol. II, *The Evolution of Modesty, The Phenomena of Sexual Periodicity, Auto-Eroticism* (1900), 267–68, 281.

For Ellis, as for his authorities, the dynamics of displacement were far from mysterious: "The suppression of the sexual emotions," he wrote, "often furnishes a powerful reservoir of energy to the religious emotions," and there are occasions, only too numerous, when "the suppressed sexual emotions break through all obstacles." Other authorities cited habitual self-pollution" as the source of hysteria which in turn generated the simulacrum of an unmeasured love for God. "Religious enthusiasm and excessive sexual excitability," the Catholic scholar Carl Capellmann observed in his treatise on pastoral medicine, "often accompany one another," particularly among inveterate masturbators.[47] This clinical, detached look was quite a comedown from the exalted vision of the German romantics praising love and religion as their twin deities.

In Havelock Ellis's view, the privileged moment when the pressure for sexual gratification became most imperious, and hence most unsettling, was the time of adolescence. Other specialists singled out other critical phases: in his book on the climacteric in women, the German physician Dr. E. Heinrich Kisch in 1874 pointed to the menopause as the time in which women's sexual sensibilities are particularly inclined to displacements: as they become convinced that their sexual charms are fading, women grow peevish and egotistical, and then manifest "that tendency toward *religious enthusiasm* which often degenerates into disease." Characteristically, it was in a book on women that Dr. Kisch made his observation; students of sexuality held women exceptionally vulnerable to that ludicrous, sentimental intoxication to which the Germans give the evocative, untranslatable name, *Schwärmerei*, and which generated, apart from scientific appraisals, irreverent lampoons and caricatures of simpering, irritating devout females. In the early 1850s, the Goncourt brothers, cynics and misogynists but, in this respect, in tune with the prejudices of their culture, had already sharply differentiated between the religious feelings of men and women, and diagnosed the latter as excuses for sensual self-indulgence. "For women," they wrote, "religion is not the discipline to which a man submits himself; it is an amorous effusion, an occasion for romantic devotion. In young girls it is a licensed outlet, a permission for exaltation, an authorization to have mystical adventures." If confessors should prove too kind, too humane, the Goncourts added, girls "will throw themselves at the severe ones, who will replace bourgeois life by a life of factitious emotions, by a martyrdom

---

47. Ellis: ibid., 282; Capellmann: *Pastoral Medicine* (1866; tr. Rev. William Dassel, 1879), 74.

that gives the martyrs, in their own eyes, something interesting an
superhuman."[48] Religious excitement, at least among women, containe
it seemed, an irreducible component of masochism.

This complacent view corresponded perfectly to men's derisive opinio
of women's intellectual powers. But some investigators frankly con
fessed that men were by no means exempt from these afflictions. In 190
Dr. Siebert, for one, acknowledged that he had in his youth displace
erotic wishes onto religious objects. He recognized that when he ha
suffered from a swooning religiosity, *einer schwärmerischen Religiositä*
his sentiments had had a distinct sexual resonance, and he recalled that th
slow waning of his mild religious mania had been accompanied by
recovery in his sexual life. Liberal bourgeois, as we know, fastened on th
unremitting interest in filthy pictures and salacious books of importunat
moral censors, and reproached the crusaders with an unacknowledge
but irrepressible lewdness of spirit. Ezra Heywood, the indefatigabl
assailant of Anthony Comstock and of his organized Christian allies
denounced him as a *"religio-maniac,"* supported by the "lasciviou
fanaticism of the Young Men's Christian Association." And Heywoo
professed to see this lascivious fanaticism—a telling phrase—in Comstock'
avid audiences, with "lust in every face." As the English publicist W. R
Greg formulated the matter in 1860: "Asceticism is the form which
religion takes in sensual minds," and there were many in his day whc
made his aphorism appear plausible.[49]

It was not the love of God that these critics wanted to assail so much
as its emotional perversion; Freud's identification of religion with neurosis
was still some years away, and by no means popular when he advanced
it. The holiness of matrimony was so triumphant a commonplace that
there seemed to be no other way of describing this best established of all
institutions. When, in the concluding section of *Les Misérables*, Victor
Hugo has Marius and Cosette marry, he could resort, in his delight at the
happy ending he had produced, only to this very cliché. On their wedding
night, the heavens open; there is an angel barring access to their room;

---

48. Kisch: *Das klimakterische Alter der Frauen in physiologischer und patho-
logischer Beziehung* (1874), 104; Goncourts: (1854), *Journal; mémoires de la vie
littéraire 1851–1896*, by Edmond and Jules de Goncourt, ed. Robert Ricatte, 22 vols.
(1956–58), I, 140. A writer in the English *Journal of Education* (November 1, 1881),
wrote: "There is, and always has been an undoubted coexistence of religiosity and
animalism." Brian Reade, ed., *Sexual Heretics: Male Homosexuality in English
Literature from 1850 to 1900* (1970), 4.

49. Siebert: *Sexuelle Moral* 30; Heywood: Heywood Broun and Margaret Leech,
Anthony Comstock: Roundsman of the Lord (1927), 172; Greg: "Kingsley and
Carlyle," *Literary and Social Judgments* (1873), 144.

and that night the house in which they sleep becomes a temple. In *What Women Should Know*, Mrs. Eliza B. Duffey thus spoke for a practically unbroken rhetorical consensus: "A pure marriage," she wrote, "in which affection is the ruling power and passion is curbed and held in control—in which the thought of self is kept secondary—is a true sacrament, blessing the participants. A marriage in which passion, unguided by reason, degenerates into lust, is a sacrament desecrated, a blessing turned into a curse." Even an "utter Radical" like Mabel Loomis Todd sounded much the same; she was far more inclined than the Mrs. Duffeys of her time to ascribe religious significance to sexual consummation, but marriage as such, to her mind, was something more elevated than a mere secular arrangement. Her religiosity was diffused, explicitly and emphatically divorced from all denominations, but her God, caring, benevolent, a celestial edition of her own father, threw a transfiguring light on the intimate relations between men and women.[50]

It took an authentic outsider like Annie Besant to recognize the self-deception that lies at the heart of such sentiments. Reflecting in 1893 on her calamitous marriage, she undertook what she called a "self-analysis," less epoch-making, surely, than the self-analysis that Freud was to begin shortly after, but impressive in its sensitivity, its wholehearted and courageous seriousness. As a young girl, Annie Besant had daydreamed "mystic fancies that twined themselves round the figure of Christ." The books of devotion she swallowed were "exceedingly glowing in their language," and she remembered that "the dawning feelings of womanhood unconsciously" lent them "a passionate fervor." She recognized, looking back on the 1860s, that she had been "absorbed in that passionate love of 'the Saviour' which, among emotional Catholics, really is the human passion of love transferred to an ideal—for women to Jesus, for men to the Virgin Mary." Listening only to her devotion to Christ, she permitted men to become her friends but not her lovers and, searching for a worthy sacrifice that she might make, she undertook to marry the Rev. Frank Besant. He was a logical choice. "One unlucky result" of the religion to which she was addicted, was "the idealization of the clergyman, the special messenger and chosen servant of the Lord." It "shed a glamour" over the part of the priest's wife, gave her a closeness to holy things "only second to that of the nun." So, her erotic path took a double turn,

50. Hugo: *Les Misérables* (1862), part V, book 6; Duffey: *What Women Should Know: A Woman's Book About Women* (1873), 113; Todd: Mabel to David Todd, March 12, 1898, commenting on her daughter's wish to be confirmed in the Episcopalian church. DPT, box 12, Y-MA.

veering from her adolescent sensuality to Jesus, and then to His repr
sentative, the irritable, domineering cleric who soon taught her who w
master in their house.[51] The lesson she learned was not the lesson he h
expected to teach; she came to see displacement for what it was.

While it is unconscious, and therefore really beyond the reach (
moral strictures, displacement is ultimately a self-serving mechanism th
cannot help inviting the charge of hypocrisy. It prevented many, to t
sure, from facing the demands of their sensuality, and distorted the
erotic experience by constricting their erotic opportunities. But it al
worked to license some forbidden longings by giving religious dignity t
earthy passions. Displacement is a dubious blessing, an attempt to escap
from repressions which for many neurotics only tightens their grip. But
is a generally efficacious mechanism of defense, doing what defenses ar
best equipped to do: reducing anxiety while, at the same time, permittin
some satisfaction to clamorous drives. In a time when much pleasure w;
under fire among the respectable of all denominations, and even som
unbelievers, displacement served the pleasure principle, at least some c
the time.

Havelock Ellis, like other students of sexuality in the late nineteent
century, defined displacement as a shift of mental qualities, as instinctu;
tensions secured discharge through indirect, socially acceptable path
The "auto-erotic impulse," as he put it, often passes "its unexpende
energy over to religious emotion, there to find the expansion hithert
denied it, the love of the human being becoming the love of the divine.
Freud, who had discovered "the mechanism of psychical *displacement*
in the making of dreams, traced its workings in the formation of religio
which, he bluntly asserted, "seems to be based on the suppression, th
renunciation of certain instinctual impulses."[52] It was becoming plain tha
religion, enjoying waves of revivals in the midst of subversive scientifi

51. Besant, *Autobiography* (1893), 82, 65–6, 68, 80–81.
52. Ellis: *Studies in the Psychology of Sex*, II, 267; Freud: "Zwangshandlunge
und Religionsübungen" (1907), *St.A.*, VII, 20, "Obsessive Actions and Religiou
Practices," *S.E.*, IX, 125. Freud, we know, had ruefully observed that imaginativ
writers often anticipated the most sober researcher. This held not only of possibly
linking sexual abstinence to creativity, in which Balzac and Zola evidently believe
(see above, pp. 256–57), but also of the contrary, that creativity may be a direct, no
always happy, outflowing of sexuality. Thus Byron derisively called Keats's work "the
Onanism of Poetry," and "a sort of mental masturbation—he is always f—gg——g hi
Imagination. I don't mean that he is *indecent*," he adds, "but viciously soliciting hi
own ideas into a state which is neither poetry nor any thing else but a Bedlam vision
produced by raw pork and opium." Byron to John Murray, November 4, 9, 1820,
Byron's Letters and Journals, ed. Leslie A. Marchand, 12 vols. (1973–1982), VII, 217,
225.

liscoveries, was a most appropriate compromise for the unconscious mind
o adopt in its flight from raw sexuality.

The writings of a once-famous Victorian poet, Coventry Patmore, and
he marriage of a once-famous Victorian couple, Charles and Fanny
Kingsley, document the ambiguous ways in which eroticism could be
transformed into religion in the bourgeois century. Coventry Patmore
njoys a curious, by no means flattering, posthumous fame. The title of
his best-known long poem, *The Angel in the House*, has been pressed
into service as a fitting epithet, usually applied in derision, for the Victor-
an housewife. The poem itself has been remorselessly scanned for its
exemplification of bourgeois sexual myths and their psychological roots:
male superiority shadowed by masculine uncertainty. Selling more than a
quarter million copies from the publication of its first part, *The Betrothal*,
in 1854, to the end of the century, it may claim the historian's attention
as the condensation of uncounted middle-class fantasies. It looks at first
glance like a representative specimen, an unimaginative anthology of
familiar prejudices. In a seemingly interminable parade of stanzas, *The
Angel in the House* rehearses predictable clichés about male mastery and
female surrender. The mastery is gentle, and the surrender slow, but in
elevated diction mirroring elevated thoughts less than the desperate
search for rhymes and for correct numbers, Patmore charts the young
years, the love and marriage, of a chivalrous man and a perfect woman.

To the twentieth-century sensibility, Patmore suffers from crippling
deficiencies as a poet: his ear and even more his taste are grievously untrustworthy. He alternates exalted musings on heavenly love with elaborately embroidered accounts of dress and meticulous transcriptions of
trivial conversations. His philosophizing now appears shallow and arch,
vitiated by intellectual confusion and an obsessive preoccupation: the
carnality of God. But his public, which rediscovered its wishes in his
verses, found his message sustaining, and thought rather well of him.
Writing to her fiancé William Graham Sumner in June 1870, Jeannie
Elliott expressed her pleasure in Patmore's poem. "It is very prettily
written." That was—then—the general opinion. *The Angel in the House*,
Edmund Gosse, who knew Patmore well, wrote in 1905, "pleased all
women and many men."[53] It was a time, after all, when angelic heroines
in novels still aroused approval rather than derision.

Patmore's passionate convictions are all the more instructive for that:
they were public property. In his most famous composition, man appears

53. Elliott: William Graham Sumner Papers, series I, box 25, Y-MA; Gosse:
Coventry Patmore (1905), 70.

as active, woman as passive. But his portrait barely conceals a strain of masculine envy: what man must struggle to conquer, woman naturally possesses; what man must painfully learn, woman simply knows. Wifely obedience, her sweet readiness to adapt herself to her husband's moods and anticipate his every wish, is less the tribute the weak pays to the strong than the gracious gift that a superior being bestows on a floundering mortal:

> Where she succeeds with cloudless brow,
> In common and in holy course,
> He fails, in spite of prayer and vow
> And agonies of faith and force.

This homage to woman could scarcely impress feminists, for it was, after all, compatible with denying her legal equality, or the vote, or the right to dispose of her own property. But it served as a hint, however slight, of perceptions somewhat more complex than the accepted truism of male supremacy.

Patmore in fact scattered more portentous hints than that; his manifest message conceals less anodyne, less derivative convictions. He supplied *The Angel in the House* with a framing story designed to lessen the impression that he had set his autobiography to verse. Yet his poem is, though not without invention, largely reportage; in an early letter to his first wife, his ideal and his inspiration, he assured her that "in all you do you are like an angel in heaven," and he delicately implied, in his correspondence and through carefully chosen euphemisms in his poem, that he thought sexual satisfaction the essential ingredient in a happy marriage. Patmore was didactic about the married state: he wanted it represented as a holy training ground for increasingly lofty felicities. Let other imaginative writers end their fictions with the wedding ceremony—Patmore treated this consummation as a mere prelude. "The vestal fire," he wrote in *The Pearl*,

> Is not, as some misread the Word,
> By marriage quenched, but flames the
> higher.

As he put it, succinctly, in prose: "All knowledge is nuptial knowledge."[54] While Patmore did not doubt that lasting legalized happiness is superior

---

54. Patmore to his wife: Derek Patmore, *The Life and Times of Coventry Patmore* (1949), 79; "nuptial knowledge": J. C. Reid, *The Mind and Art of Coventry Patmore* (1957), 76.

o the evanescent joys of carnal pleasures, his hymn to married bliss
ntimates that without those thoroughly erotic pleasures, marriage is but
traw and ashes. As long as it is performed within the hallowed terrain
hat religious doctrine and secular authority have mapped out for it,
exual activity is sacred activity. Or, as Patmore on occasion confesses,
he lover ascribes sanctity to his excitement, that he may satisfy his
ensual needs without guilt:

> He worships her, the more to exalt
> The profanation of a kiss.

t is actually impossible to separate, in *The Angel in the House*, the
acred from the profane, and this intermingling of the two spheres con-
titutes Patmore's latent message in the poem—its strength because he
put it there, its weakness because he never freed it from its vague and
uggestive aura. "The 'reconcilement of the highest with the lowest,'"
he wrote in a late collection of aphorisms and observations, "though an
infinite felicity, is an infinite sacrifice. Hence the mysterious and apparently unreasonable pathos in the highest and most perfect satisfactions
of love. The real and innermost bride is always 'Amoris Victima.'"
Indeed, elaborating his image, "the real and innermost sacrifice of the
Cross was the consummation of the descent of Divinity into the flesh and
its identification therewith; and the sigh which all creation heaved in that
moment has its echo in that of mortal love in the like descent. That sigh,"
Patmore concludes, joining one sensual stratagem to another, "is the
inmost heart of all music."[55]

In the poetry and prose that followed *The Angel in the House*, Patmore continued to spell out his eroticized religious ruminations. His
angel turns out to be the most carnal of creatures. We know the angels
of Scriptures and art as neutral beings; they are beyond desire. This
indeed is how many of Patmore's readers took his major poetic work,
whether they liked it or detested it. As critics have not failed to point
out, the couple whose ripening into married felicity *The Angel in the
House* rehearses at pitiless length have names symbolizing happiness and
honor linked forever: he is called Felix, she, Honoria. Yet even in his
early work, Patmore's angel is far from angelic. His very language
intimates intercourse:

---

55. "Magna Moralia, XLVIII," in *The Rod, The Root, And The Flower* (1895;
2nd ed., 1914), 200.

> benevolence, desire,
> Elsewhere ill-join'd or found apart,
> Become the pulses of one heart,
> Which now contracts and now dilates,
> And, both to the height exalting, mates
> Self-seeking to self-sacrifice.

It would take a powerful gift for denial, a gift that many of Patmore's proper readers cultivated, to overlook the sexual message of these lines the "heart" in marriage dilating and contracting and lifting the lovers to exalted heights.

It is tempting to attribute Patmore's late sensual work to his conversion in 1864. But while he wrote his most suggestive verse and prose in the 1870s, the elements of his erotic Christianity were fully assembled, and easily legible, well before then. He had, after all, published the concluding part of his *Angel in the House*, which adumbrates his erotic theology, the year before he joined the Roman Catholic Church. He did not convert to liberate his sensuality; his pressing sensuality eased him into conversion. Catholicism gave him some new elevated words, and new sacred pictures, to celebrate what he had always worshiped. Patmore's insinuating Catholic mysticism has been piously read as a commentary on the words of St. John, "God is Love."[56] They can be read more legitimately to suggest that Love is God.

This is more than a play on words. Whether Patmore is rewriting classical legends or meditating on melancholy, he returns and returns to moments of penetration. God's love for man is, to Patmore, a thrilling affair. "The soul becomes mystically united with God," as he sums up the matter in an aphorism, "and impregnated by him the instant she perfectly submits and says, 'Behold the handmaid of the Lord: be it done to me according to Thy word.'"[57] His poem *King Cophetua the First* tells the story of Jove who, discontented with the "Too Godlike" qualities of his companions, decides to make himself "a mistress out of clay!" As so often, Patmore praises the marriage of heaven and earth:

> The gust of love is mystery,
> Which poorly yet the heavens supply.
> Now where may God for mystery seek
> Save in the earthly, small, and weak?

56. Joachim V. Benson, in Terence L. Connolly, ed., *Coventry Patmore: Mystical Poems of Nuptial Love* (1938), xiv.
57. Connolly, ibid., 258.

and so, leaving his Juno with her "almost equal mind" to find love on earth, he encounters "A pretty, foolish, pensive maid"; trusting she tells him that she should like to be married, but rejects all the heroes, kings, and even gods that Jove proposes to secure for her, to insist on love himself. He grants her what he himself had sought, a "deep pagan night," and leaves her forever:

> Thenceforth the maiden sang and shone,
> Admired by all and woo'd by none,
> For, though she said she was a sinner,
> 'Twas clear to all that Jove was in her.

An exceptionally explicit variation on this theme is Patmore's *Eros and Psyche*, in which he inhabits, with ease, the mind of the woman apostrophizing her lover:

> O, heavenly Lover true,
> Is this thy mouth upon my forehead press'd?
> Are these thine arms about my bosom link'd?
> Are these thy hands that tremble near my heart,
> Where join two hearts, for juncture more distinct?
> By thee and by my maiden zone caress'd
>   . . .
> Ah, stir not to depart!
> Kiss me again, thy Wife and Virgin too!
> O Love, that, like a rose,
> Deckest my breast with beautiful repose,
> Kiss me again, and clasp me round the heart,
> Till fill'd with thee am I
> As the cocoon is with the butterfly!

The Christian God, whom Patmore worships as the male principle, was in the human soul as Jove was in his human mistress or Eros in Psyche, joining two hearts "for juncture more distinct." And this juncture had more than a touch of sado-masochism in it; Psyche declares herself ready to perform all sorts of masochistic acts to prove her love:

> Should'st thou me tell
> Out of thy warm caress to go
> And roll my body in the biting snow,
> My very body's joy were but increased;
> More pleasant 'tis to please thee than be
>   pleased.

Thy love has conquered me! do with me as thou
   wilt,
And use me as a chattel that is thine!
Kiss, tread me under foot, cherish or beat,
Sheathe in my heart sharp pain up to the hilt,
Invent what else were most perversely sweet.

Plainly, the sacred marriage between the divine and the human was, fo
Patmore, the continuation of highly physical, sometimes cruelly inven
tive, sexual intercourse in a higher realm. Reviving scriptural and apoc
ryphal prophecies as interpreted by Christian mystics across the centuries
Patmore returned to the potent old image of Christ, the bridegroom
making his beloved, the Church, his bride. He took the doctrine of th
Incarnation seriously.

The late embodiment of Patmore's erotic Christianity, an essay signifi
cantly entitled *Sponsa Dei*, is lost; burned, Edmund Gosse reports, at th
insistence of Gerard Manley Hopkins. Gosse, who had read the essay
more than once, describes it as "audacious"; this "vanished masterpiece"
was, he recalled, "not more or less than an interpretation of the lov
between the soul and God by an analogy of the love between a woman
and a man; it was, indeed, a transcendental treatise on Divine desire seen
through the veil of human desire." The loss of that masterpiece doe.
not make Patmore opaque; his views are quite unmistakable from th
apophthegms he allowed to survive. "He who does the will of God i
Christ's 'Mother, Sister, Brother,' and all other relations, Son, Daughter
Bride, and Bridegroom," and "those who indeed know Him, possess th
wishing rod." Thus Patmore linked his perverse pan-sexualism to th
marriage of the higher and the lower realms. His deity was capable o
the most human erotic longings: "God," he wrote, is "infatuated with
the beauty of the Soul." The passions are therefore not man's enemies
but his most trustworthy allies: "Happy he who has conquered his
passions, but far happier he whose servants and friends they have become."
If, "in vulgar minds the idea of passion is inseparable from that of dis
order," elevated minds understand that the matter is more complicated:
"virtues are nothing but ordered passions, and vices nothing but passions
in disorder." And Patmore never left the slightest doubt that he had the
amorous passions in mind. It is this libidinal view of religion that rescues
Patmore's writings from the reassertion of trite domestic themes. No
doubt, it had some morbid roots in fantasies weighed down with regret
and in erotic experiences recollected in depression. "My first nuptial
joy," Patmore wrote to a friend in June 1863, a year after his first wife

ad died, "was a poor thing compared with the infinite satisfaction I can now feel in the assurance, which time has brought, that my relation with her is as eternal as it is happy."[58] But the melancholy reverberating in his declaration is not typical of him; his persistent teaching is that the married state claims the exalted status of sanctity. Patmore's sexual apologetics are not sublimations or displacements so much as a way of having the best of two worlds—or, rather, of enjoying this world by invoking the authority of the other.

The sensual theology that Coventry Patmore lived and recorded for posterity, Charles Kingsley acted out in his private life. Kingsley's intimate passions did not escape public notice; he was, after all, a very well-known writer for adults and children, and an equally well-known political and religious polemicist. One sharp-eyed, malicious reviewer, alert to Kingsley's preoccupation with sex, accused his first novel, *Yeast*, of preaching indulgence in the passions and of "encouraging profligacy." The *Saturday Review*, in 1858, called him "the great Apostle of the Flesh," and characterized his poem, "Andromeda," as "a glowing titty-picture of the best kind," hardly an unequivocal compliment. Again the publicist W. R. Greg, an acute if opinionated reader of the signs of his times, complained in a general appreciation of 1860 that Kingsley was "not infrequently coarse." His victim was not surprised: Kingsley had long since dismissed Greg as a member of the heartless "Manchester School."[59] In his essay, Greg criticized Kingsley's "treatment of love and the relation between the sexes" as sometimes "needlessly venturesome and grating." Kingsley, he wrote, "likes to call things by their plain names; a fancy with which, in moderation, we sympathize. He thinks, further, that in treating of the various questions arising out of the relations between the sexes, we lost much and risk much by a mischievous reticence and a false and excessive delicacy; and in this opinion also we agree with him." At the same time, Greg demurred, Kingsley "unpleasantly" overstates the *"physical"* side of love. "He proclaims—with a

58. "Vanished masterpiece": Gosse, *Patmore*, 143–44; apophthegms: "Magna Moralia" XXXV, XXV, XVII, II, *Rod, Root, and Flower*, 185, 175, 166, 146; "My first nuptial joy": Gosse, *Patmore*, 193. It is hard to regret this "vanished masterpiece." Readers of Christian mystics or, for that matter, of John Donne's devotional sonnets, will readily recognize that Patmore's nuptial metaphors really are quite unoriginal and relatively tepid. (See below, p. 303, n. 67).

59. "Encouraging profligacy": Kingsley, *Letters*, I, 224; "Apostle": "Kingsley's Andromeda and other Poems," *Saturday Review*, V (June 5, 1858), 594; "not infrequently coarse": Greg, *Literary and Social Judgments*, 142; "Manchester School": Kingsley, *Letters*, I, 253.

courage which, in a clergyman especially, is above all praise—the right
of nature, and the intrinsic purity of natural instincts," and is "resolutel
bent on showing that the most passionate love may also be the purest, i
only it be legitimate in its circumstances and worthy in its object. H
seems to have almost grasped the grand cardinal truth that the real guil
lies not in mingling the gratification of passion with the sentiment of love
but in even for one moment permitting the former save under th
guidance and sanction of the latter." The grand cardinal truth Greg i
here announcing restates the ideal of love as the marriage of desire to
affection. At all events, Greg goes on, Kingsley's literary judgment ofter
falters, as he stresses the "animal magnetism" of love at the expense o
the "finer sentiments." Greg objects to Kingsley's heroines, "too sensitiv
to the influence of look and touch," and to his heroes, who win th
heroines "rather by mesmerism than by courtship." These are matters o
fine degree, decisions of taste, that undependable regulator of passionate
expression. Greg thought himself of Kingsley's persuasion; he, too, be
longed to the party of frankness. But he found Kingsley "a dangerou
ally" to the cause of candor in an age of restraint, an age "of vehemen
desires and feeble wills, of so much conventionalism and so little courage,"
when all are "slaves to what others think, and wish, to do, slaves to pas
creeds in which we have no longer pleasure."[60]

Greg's indignant outburst against his hypocritical age is a fresh reminder that while it was a time of silences, evasions, and indirections
they were indirections sufficiently blunt to find directions out. The
memorial to the life of Charles Kingsley that his adoring widow published in 1876, the year after his death, is marred by discreet, wholesale
excisions and massive self-censorship. This was the statue that Fanny
Kingsley thought proper to expose to the world: a decent torso. It wa
less than polished, or even finished, consisting mainly of excerpts from
Charles Kingsley's correspondence and memoranda found at home or
begged from his friends. Yet, though fragmentary and flattering, it was
a public monument much visited and greatly treasured; the first edition
of her Letters and Memories of His Life was so popular that Fanny
Kingsley was persuaded to issue a new version, both abridged and enriched, as early as 1879, and that reached its sixteenth printing only nine
years later. Here was a splendid vehicle for a public airing of Charles
Kingsley's personal views.

Fanny Kingsley's ruthless gentility makes her memorial an unwitting
informant to respectable modes of thinking in the second half of the

60. "Kingsley and Carlyle," Literary and Social Judgments, 145.

ineteenth century, for it permits the historian to reconstruct her hus-
and's erotic religion from the passages that his widow did not find
bjectionable enough to excise. Kingsley was a political man, a radical,
nd a patriot; affected to tears by the sufferings of the poor, he was
uite as emotional about the "plight" of British colonial governors per-
ecuted by humanitarians at home, draconic officials whom somewhat
ss militant Englishmen execrated for their cruelty to the natives under
heir rule. His cult of muscular Christianity gave Kingsley's politics a
porting, veritably pugilistic cast that oddly consorted with his energetic
rotestantism. Kingsley took vehement exception to this epithet, "mus-
ular"; he denounced it as an "impertinent name." But it fits him well.
'or, Kingsley, irritated by the doctrinal squabbles within his Anglican
ommunion, frightened by the widespread defections to the Church of
Rome, and tormented by his theological and, less consciously, his sexual
onflicts, lived the religious life as an unrelenting struggle. He looked at
ll of existence through the lenses of his Protestantism, but his thinking
bout theology was pervaded by his musings about the flesh. Kingsley's
eligious thought, early and late, is a sermon on marriage, and most carnal
narriage, in which sexual union is the companion of spiritual sympathy
nd the emblem of heavenly love. His sermon is a sexualized compound
f personal passions and traditional themes, reverberating with the mystic
narriage of Christ and His church and with a familiar apologetic argu-
nent that Christian, pagan, and deist thinkers had deployed through the
enturies: God manifests His existence not through His words alone,
ut through His works, through nature—through its order, its beauty,
ts stunning copiousness. This was a point against atheists that Kingsley,
vho delighted in the glowing exercise of walks, the suggestive shapes of
ills and valleys, and the never wearisome passing of the seasons, was not
nclined to overlook. But, however antique Kingsley's mode of argu-
nentation, its force stemmed from his sensuality. Nature emphatically
ncluded the human body and its "thrilling writhings."[61]

Kingsley, in fact, worships the body in such a perpetual state of ex-
itement that his faith amounts to an erotic pantheism restrained by the
Thirty-nine Articles. We may surmise from the confessional pages in his
arly novel, Yeast, that Kingsley satisfied his adolescent sexual appetites in
vays he later found detestable, but he retreated from his occasional
scapades to less compromising satisfactions. In the summer of 1839, when

61. "Impertinent name": Kingsley to F. D. Maurice (1857), Letters, II, 47–48;
"thrilling writhings": Kingsley to Fanny Grenfell, 1843, Susan Chitty, The Beast and
he Monk: A Life of Charles Kingsley (1974), 81. See also above, pp. 278–79.

he was an undergraduate at Magdalene College, Cambridge, he met Fanny
Grenfell for the first time and she later recalled his face, "with its un
satisfied, hungering, and at times defiant look," a look that contemporary
physicians would have been quick, and perhaps justified, to ascribe to
"self-abuse." His early letters to Fanny Grenfell are punctuated with
abashed confessions of his "unworthiness," and earnest appeals to save
him from his "weakness" for alcohol and other unspecified transgressions
from "continual temptations to return to old courses, whose habit re
mained." *She* was not the cause of his unhappiness: "My heart was
previously corrupted or I should have been sobered and calmed by
knowing you—*I* alone am in fault."[62]

Such pleas were abject enough, but the ideal of marriage, the spiritual
carnal union of two souls in ecstatic, though legal bondage, was even
then firmly implanted in his mind. These were the early years of the
Oxford Movement, which was to divide the Anglican Church through
all of Kingsley's lifetime and beyond, and even then, as an undergraduate
he was persuaded that Newman, Pusey, and their allies were seducers
into asceticism. During a long and frustrating engagement he discovered
theological grounds for his desire to marry: "Every step in love and to
God, and devotion to Him is a duty!" he wrote to Fanny in 1842. "That
doctrine was invented to allow mankind to exist, while a few self
conceited shut themselves up in a state of unnatural celibacy and morbid
excitement, in order to avoid their duty, instead of doing it." Kingsley
meant to do his duty; that this was to be a supreme pleasure did not
make it any the less a divine command. Again, in late 1843, he told
Fanny in one of his long letters that read like private tracts, "Every man
should be honoured as God's image, in the sense in which Novalis says—
that we touch Heaven when we lay our hand on a human body! . . ."
The ellipses after this exclamation probably mark a passage in which
Kingsley specified which body he wanted to touch. The very Scriptures
as I have noted, allowed him to regard marital congress as holy. "There
may be other meanings in that book besides the plain one," he wrote to
Fanny. "But this I will believe, that whatever mysticism the mystic may
find there, the simple human being, the lover of his wife, the father of
children, the lover of God's earth, glorying in matter and humanity, not
for that which they are, but that which they ought to be and will be.

62. Kingsley, *Letters*, I, 26 (his wife-to-be attributed his look to his religious
doubts); Charles Kingsley to Fanny Grenfell, October 27, February [18]41, Kingsley
Papers, BL, Add. Mss. 62552.

will find in the Bible the whole mystery solved." This glorying in matter and humanity is what he called, in the same letter, "healthy materialism."[63]

His marriage gave Charles Kingsley unrestricted opportunities to exercise that healthy materialism, and to explore what he had called that teeming tropic sea of Eros!" Certainly his hunger for married bliss did not abate with his regular enjoyment of it. I have quoted his exclamation to a friend in the sixth year of marriage: "People talk of love ending at the altar. Fools!" Kingsley knew better. "Man," he told a correspondent in 1848, "is a sexual animal," but he wanted to assign that characterization the most dignified possible meaning. Contrary to other exegetes, he argued that Adam and Eve did not have to await expulsion from Paradise before they were married; the married state itself is, he said more than once, a paradisaical experience. Hence marriage deserves a "higher and spiritual view," one that many men, crippled by a "vulgar and carnal conception of it," can never attain. Kingsley interpreted the passages, "male and female created he them," and "be fruitful and multiply," as biblical sanctions for his affirmation of sexuality and his detestation of asceticism. It was theologically sound to argue that, to realize their finest human possibilities, man and woman need a "complementum, a 'help meet.' " Nor did he hesitate to invoke divine authority for the expression of all-too-human erotic activity: "Man is a spirit-animal, and in communion with God's spirit has a right to believe that his affections are under the spirit's guidance, and that when he finds in himself such an affection to any single woman as true married lovers describe theirs to be, he is bound (duty to parents and country allowing) to give himself up to his love in childlike simplicity and self-abandonment." Like other theologians, and for his own reasons, Kingsley liked to quote St. John's famous "God is Love";[64] it was yet another proof that human, married, sexual love had its divine dimension.

In 1851, in an enormous letter to a country parson whom he had not met, but with whom he canvassed pressing religious issues by mail, Kingsley elaborated the philosophy of marriage he had developed as an undergraduate and was practicing as a husband. He was convinced that "the whole question is an anthropological one." It involved "that

63. Kingsley to Fanny Grenfell, August, 1842; October 27, 1843, *Letters*, I, 61, 76, I, 83.
64. Kingsley to the Rev. R. C. Powles, December 11, 1845; to J. M. Ludlow, August 17, 1849; to —— (1848); to Fanny Grenfell, February 26, 1845, *Letters*, I, 104, 172, 149–52, 100. For Patmore and this saying, see above, p. 294.

terrible question of 'Celibacy versus Marriage' " which, he conceded, he
had wrestled with earlier in his life. There were, to his mind, "two great
views of man." The first sees him—and her—as "a spirit embodied in
flesh and blood, with certain relations, namely, those of father, child,
husband, wife, brother, as necessary properties of his existence." The
second, found "principally among the upper classes, both among Christian
and heathens," sees man as a "spirit accidentally connected with, and
burdened by an animal." Kingsley, of course, subscribed to the first, for
the second makes ascetics, "unsexed by celibacy." With anthropomorphic
language and a pictorial directness that suggest happy sensual memories,
Kingsley once again rehearses his perception of God as the father, Christ
as the bridegroom, and humanity as brothers and sisters in a vast family.
The relations of humans to one another "are symbols of relations to
God." The Old Testament guarantees, and the New Testament, read
aright, confirms the "absolute and everlasting humanity, and therefore
sanctity," of these human relations, particularly those between husband
and wife.[65]

This kind of argumentation may appear to be simply self-indulgent
and self-interested, a facile proffering of spiritual reasons for doing
fleshly things. But Kingsley does not slight the part that struggle and
suffering play in sanctified married sensuality. Marital felicity must be
earned by abstention and self-castigation. Before he was married, he
confessed to Fanny—and as a widow she did not scruple to print his
confession—that his horror of mysticism, and of the lures of celibacy,
was not a lifelong conviction but a youthful longing conquered in study
and in anguish. We would call it a reaction formation. Love requires the
ingredient of "wholesome fear." It is "through fear that love is made
perfect; fear which bridles and guides the lover with awe." More, love
exacts pain; there were times when Kingsley called for a Saint Francis
to scourge men toward perfection—and Fanny Kingsley transmitted the
message. Even manliness was, for Kingsley, less a character trait freely
enjoyed than a conflict to be resolved over and over again. Through the
screen of his assertive masculinity, we glimpse painful episodes of homosexual panic. "Foppery," that "fastidious, maundering, die-away effeminacy," which he diagnosed as a fatal flaw in his High Church adversaries, fascinated him; his pupil and friend, John Martineau, whose "tender
recollections" Fanny Kingsley gave to posterity, found in Kingsley
"with all his man's strength" a "deep vein of *woman*," a "nervous sensi-
tiveness, and intensity of sympathy," to say nothing of a "tender, delicate

65. February 5, 1851, ibid., I, 205–11.

soothing touch."[66] Charles Kingsley's muscular Christianity served as corrective and cloak.

However explicit Kingsley's sensual theology, spread on the record in his writings and in the documents his widow saw fit to publish, it was his unpublished life that fully enacted Coventry Patmore's and his own erotic vision. Kingsley celebrated sexual passion with an energy that makes Patmore's artfully wrought imaginings appear amateurish, almost tepid, in comparison. His private outpourings contain nothing new in principle, but they retain all their intensity. Even more intense, however— and nothing in the published memorial has prepared the historian for it —are Fanny Kingsley's own sexual appetites; her ready response to Charles Kingsley's impassioned invitations almost matched his urgency. His longing for his fiancée's body, in no way drowned in routine after she had become his wife, seemed almost beyond bearing to him, and, at least in the early years, her need for him was little short of frantic. In the tense time before their marriage, he scourged himself to check his sensual ardor, and told Fanny that he did, asking her to join him in ascetic mortifications. These exercises, intended to restrain erotic thoughts, were erotic in themselves.[67] "How I will kiss away every trace of those un-natural stripes," Fanny exclaimed in the privacy of her diary after brooding on his sanctified masochism. But her yearning to kiss away the evidence of it was far less an intoxicated participation in his self-inflicted self-torments than a protest against them. "*Mortifying*" the body, she noted, "has the stamp of the *Devil* on them." Familiar religious phrases like "crucifying the flesh," or "mortifying the body," or, even more carnally, "dying daily," had long had, she confessed, "an inexpressible beauty" for her. But now that she faced the reality of the whip, her healthier instincts took over: "Is not that flesh the work of God! That body his work?" Her memories of her earnest religious training confused her, but she had come to distrust all this self-abasement and self-punishment. "Darling! Darling! Your scourging! that *horrible* tho't!"

66. For the reaction formation, see ibid., I, 45; for "wholesome fear," a passage of 1872, ibid., 154–55; for the needed "scourge," Kingsley to Powles, December 11, 1845, ibid., 104; for Martineau's comment, ibid., 240.

67. This principled masochism is not without its irony, for it is a copy—and a relatively feeble one—of the kind of self-laceration to which celebrated late-medieval Roman Catholic mystics, the very "fanatics" whom Kingsley battled all his life, were prone. Heinrich Suso, Johannes Tauler, and Mechtild of Magdeburg, who could all have given Kingsley lessons in scourging, lying on beds of nails, observing vows of silence, and living on virtually nothing, were well-known figures in Kingsley's day. Suso's autobiography was given a modern English translation in 1865, and Kingsley wrote a Preface for *The Life and Sermons of Tauler* (ibid., II, 14–16).

She reasoned that "if Adam had scourged his body in Paradise, he wd have insulted God! How changed is all!" And she fervently hoped that her marriage, should it ever come to pass, would induce Charles Kingsley to abandon his self-laceration forever. It would be *then* that she could kiss away his stripes. "Precious, precious body!" she exclaimed. "Please God it will need no more scourging when we are One!" Was it not *"Satan"* who had brought tears and death, sickness and sorrow to the world, who had afflicted "women with the spirit of Infirmity," and Job with "loathsome disease"? Was it not Christ, in holy contrast, who had made our bodies into "Temples of the Holy Ghost?"

Fanny Grenfell asked these probing skeptical questions in an extraordinary journal she kept in 1842 and 1843, during a Continental sojourn forced on her by her family. Soon after meeting Charles Kingsley three years before, she had come to love him; he passionately responded to her buxom good looks, her unwavering seriousness, her willingness to listen to his confessions of devastating religious doubts, doubts she received serenely, with her calm, secure piety. But the match was in no way suitable: Kingsley was poor and had few prospects; Grenfell was rich and moved in high society. Moreover, Fanny, orphaned as a little girl, had grown up under the care of possessive older sisters who were reluctant to surrender their cherished youngest into the hands of a hungry young cleric, however promising. In 1842, the pair agreed they would cease to see or write to each other for a year; to cure her melancholy and arrest her ominous loss of weight, Fanny Grenfell was sent abroad, to France and Italy.

This gave her the opportunity for solitary, self-started musings. Opening her journal, she set the tone: " 'O Love! *blessed wise* Madness'!" Much of what followed, essentially a continuous letter to the man she loved, fastens on this blessed madness. On October 27, 1842, she begins: "Darling! My love! My husband! must I confess it! that 8 weeks have passed since our lips parted & I have not had energy to begin this book." But once she had managed, as she put it, "to break the ice," her thoughts, and her pen, flowed more freely. Much of the time, she brooded on her longing, at once carnal and spiritual, for her absent darling, and on the impiety of her potent desire. "Once with you," she wrote in Genoa, on March 3, 1843, "I will drop all false dignity, mock modesty, & I will entreat you to hurry our wedding day, that we die not in the interval— Darling!" Her frustration was mounting and seemed almost intolerable. "Oh! that God wd have pity on me, tormented in this flame!" Her vocabulary was extravagant, her feeling authentic. So was her remorse: "Pray for me! How can *I* pray, when every tho't of my heart, every

Aspiration of my Soul proclaims me an Idolator & *you* my God!" This was strong stuff from a sound and well-brought up Anglican.

Her anguish was severe enough to cause visible physical side effects. "I feel so ill fading away," she wrote two days after her idolatrous entry. "It is not my fault. It is so sad to think if we are ever married you will have a skeleton for your bride! bitter! bitter! My maid said today after dressing me, that the only flesh I had on my bones was in my face—& that too is fading! bitter! bitter!" Sinner though she was, she craved God's pity: "I *did* pray for patience today, & oh! darling! I prayed so much for you—." She was at once avid and afraid. In June, she recorded being plagued by fears, and confided to her diary: "My idea of *perfect bliss, perfect repose, perfect security* is *sleeping in your arms*—can I be *afraid* of you?" This fear brought another in its train: "Will you be angry? Will you think my *Love* Imperfect? that worries me so!" Knowing her Bible, she knew that perfect love casteth out fear. Was her love, then, imperfect? "Darling, Darling," her torment forced from her, in mid-June, "*I do love you perfectly*—but I am a woman & I don't know what it is yet!" Fanny Grenfell's lack of erotic experience, her acceptance of a submissive role, coupled with her inability to sort out the place of sensuality in her love and to establish her right to her passions, made her very miserable.

Yet hesitantly, not always consistently, steadily appealing to the Bible for authority, Fanny Grenfell struggled toward a positive valuation of the sexual passion. Not long after she had worried over the possible imperfections in her love, she composed a little disquisition entitled "The Disclosure of GOD's Mind on the subject The Marriage Union." Liberally quoting from both the Old and the New Testaments, she was satisfied to acknowledge that man is woman's superior, woman man's helpmeet. Fortunately, though, there is also equality between the two, especially after marital intimacy has been established, "when married Man & Woman are *one flesh* (admirable mystery!)" Her contemplation of this admirable mystery permitted her to reason herself into nothing less than a pious celebration of sensuality. Thinking of Eve in paradise, she called to her darling Charles once again: "Beloved! if she shrank not, why sh'd *I*? If Holy Eden was the Scene of Marriage & Married Love, why should I fear to leap into your arms to realize one of Eden's blessings or taste an Enjoyment wh: *must* be pure if it was *tasted there!* I will trust & not be afraid!!" Plainly, she was afraid, but she was determined to overcome her fear. Her innocent sophistry gave her a way of acknowledging the blessings of sexual passion, of developing her own Christian version of the old theme of love's two interwoven strands.

In the same disquisition, indeed, this young solitary sophist invoked divine participation in the act of defloration. "Beloved!" she proposed. "Let us be married on a Saturday, that like Adam & Eve the first day that dawns upon us in our Married state may be the Sabbath! Let us act out as much as possible that Scene of Eden! That w'd be so holy a beginning!" Soon after enjoying one another in their "newly found bliss," the Kingsleys, just married, would greet the dawn, all the more "delicious from the thought that that day is God's as well as ours! & that in a few hours that day will bring to our lips & souls the great blessing of the Holy Sacrament." It was not sensuality, she protested, but rather "that sacred source *GOD's word*," which had shown her "that to the Pure all things are Pure!" And, "oh!," she added, "how pure that Institution must be wh: He Himself gave the man whom He had just created in *His Own Image*! I thank GOD & take courage!"[68]

Fanny Grenfell's protestations declare her need for courage, rather than her secure possession of it, but she was, with no help beyond the promptings of her own needs and some convenient scriptural passages, step by step clearing the way for a career of married sensual enjoyment free of guilt. For all her programmatic timidity, all her docility toward the wise young curate who would lead her into the realm of happiness, she was in the end less hesitant, less conflict-ridden than the man she adored about the essential innocence of, in fact duty toward, bodily pleasures. Though she was far less sophisticated a theologian than Charles Kingsley, she exceeded him in her aptitude for discovering serviceable texts in Scriptures.

After the couple had broken down her family's resistance and become engaged in 1843, they took greater liberties with one another than before. Recollections of rare earlier kisses had been almost fatal to his self-control, and to hers; after they had exchanged a long kiss on one of her visits to him, she had found that "my blood boils and bounds as I recall it." For these two, as for other middle-class couples, betrothal was an informal permission for extensive mutual exploration, short only of sexual intercourse: we "did all we could," Kingsley later recalled for his wife, "*before* we were one!" His recollection became a rhapsody: "My hands

68. The journal is a single volume of about 130 unnumbered pages without a title page. Characteristically, Fanny Grenfell took trouble to protect her privacy. "To be given *unread*," she noted on the opening page, "to Charles K. at my Death, if I die before we are One, which God in His Mercy forbid!" This instruction is dated "Oct. 27, 1842/Paris." The journal contains some of Charles Kingsley's erotic drawings pasted into it (see below, p. 309). Journal in possession and quoted with permission of Mrs. Angela Covey-Crump, Ely, Cambridgeshire.

re perfumed with her delicious limbs, and I cannot wash off the scent, nd every moment the thought comes across me of those mysterious ecesses of beauty where my hands have been wandering, and my heart inks with a sweet faintness"—and more, in fevered memory.[69]

But Kingsley and Grenfell were conscientious, pious, guilt-ridden 'rotestants no less than ecstatic lovers, and their physical happiness, ctual and prospective, troubled them. Hence he proposed to his fiancée, n a long letter written a few months before the great event, that they ot consummate their marriage for a period of probation. His letter was ectoring: "I ought to have forbidden you, when we parted, to keep a ournal; *I forbid it henceforth!*" But it was pleading as well: "Darling ne resolution I made in my sorrow, that I would ask a boon of you.—I vish to shew you & my God that I have gained purity & self-control— hat intense as my love is for your body, I do not love it but as the xpression & type of your spirit—and therefore when we are married, vill you consent to remain for the first month in my arms a *virgin* bride, sister only," until she had thus "thoroughly tested me, & let me test nyself." He acknowledged that this would be far from easy. "If you knew man's constitution you would appreciate the tremendous sacrifice; but ve shall only gain in happiness, by rising *gradually* without shock or erturbation, to our perfect bliss!" He was mixing his strenuous piety with ear of failure: Kingsley admitted to his bride that he was afraid "the blaze f your naked beauty" might make him impotent.[70]

After all this, the couple did not go through with their austere program f self-denial wrapped around each other. "Oh! to be once again with ou—to lie once more naked in your arms," Kingsley wrote to his wife uring the first year of their marriage. He fantasized "that you will once nore unrobe with utter delight those lovely limbs, & come to me a bride gain!" He then asked her, provocatively, "Shall we the first night we neet re-enact our marriage night?" Still, as Fanny had sketched their rst night in advance, the two alone at last with only a voyeuristic God ooking down at them as they tightly embraced, abstention is what they eriously planned to practice. Both, though, suspected that their passions vould be too strong, their self-controls inadequate: "I fear," she wrote,

69. Fanny Grenfell to Charles Kingsley (July 1843), Chitty, *Beast and Monk*, 66; harles Kingsley to Fanny Kingsley (misdated April 1, 1844), BL, Kingsley Papers, dd. Mss. 62553; Charles Kingsley to Fanny Grenfell, October 24, 1843, Chitty, *east and Monk*, 66, 82. After her engagement to David Todd, Mabel Loomis ounded very much that way (see *Education of the Senses*, 78–79).

70. Charles Kingsley to Fanny Grenfell [October 1, 1843], Kingsley Papers, BL, dd. Mss. 62552; Kingsley to Grenfell, 1843, Chitty, *Beast and Monk*, 86.

"you will yearn so for *fuller* communion that you will not be so happy
as me. And I too perhaps shall yearn, frightened as I am!"⁷¹

Yearning overcame anxiety and gave Charles more material for his
erotic sermons. It was as a Christian that he rehearsed his doctrine of
"healthy materialism," lecturing his fiancée and, later, his wife. "Matter
is holy," he wrote to Fanny during their engagement, "awful glorious
matter." He added, beyond mistaking, "Our animal enjoyments must be
religious ceremonies." His intention was to purify his bride's imagination, but, unconsciously at least, he was corrupting it. He invited her to
celebrate a simultaneous "Thanksgiving" with him. Take off your clothes,
he instructed her, say a prayer, "Then lie down, nestle to me, clasp your
arms and every limb around me, & with me repeat the *Te Deum* aloud, for
you are all mine, at 11 ¼—And then kiss me, & sleep!"⁷²

As early as 1843, Kingsley had tantalized the young woman not yet his
with a "wanton" fantasy that could only serve to excite her: "This morning I woke at 5, & as I lay, white limbs gleamed before me, & soft touches
pressed me, & a wanton tongue—yet chaste & holy!, stole between my
lips! What were you doing?—You were secretly kissing me early this
Wednesday morn!" Yet, while painting this lascivious scene, he did not
overlook its theological justification: "What is sensuality! Not the
enjoyment of *holy glorious matter*, but blindness to its spiritual meaning!"
He concluded, as so often, by invoking their deity: "How much more
delicious when in each others' arms, the flesh & the spirit shall tend the
same way, increasing each other's delight! Bless God Bless God!" His
very suggestion that they postpone sexual intercourse after marriage
could only awaken her senses with the prospect of eternal orgasms: "Will
not these thoughts give us more perfect delight when we lie naked in
each other's arms, clasped together toying with each other's limbs, buried
in each other's bodies, struggling, panting, dying for a moment. Shall
we not feel then, even then, that there is more in store for us, that those
thrilling writhings are but dim shadows of a union which shall be perfect?" It was a heady vision, licensed by Kingsley's appeal to scriptural
texts, one he took quite literally. From the beginning, he had insisted that
he only wanted to be with her, close, intertwined, in heaven forever.
Their marital enjoyment, he told her piously, "will become more confirmed when we are one, & in Heaven, our love will be without oscilla-

71. Charles Kingsley to Fanny Grenfell [1844], Kingsley Papers, BL, Add. Mss
62552; Fanny Grenfell to Charles Kingsley, December 9, 1843, Chitty, *Beast and Monk*,
88.
72. Charles Kingsley to Fanny Grenfell, October 2, 4, 1843, ibid., 80; October [5],
1843, Kingsley Papers, BL, Add. Mss., 62552.

tion, even at the same glorious full tide of delight." This was a little oblique, but he continued to explicate his meaning, as he did late in 1843: "Do I expect to marry an *angel*, passionless, unsympathizing?—No! My wife must be a woman—subject to like passions with myself!" And these passions would only rise to unprecedented heights in eternity. "What would life be without you?" he asked her rhetorically and perhaps a little tactlessly after more than four years of marriage. "What it is with you—but a brief pain to make us long for ever-lasting bliss—*There* we shall be in each others' arm forever—without a sigh or a cross—." He could call their marriage bed an altar, with no sense of incongruity.[73]

Charles Kingsley gave literally graphic expression to this peculiar fusion in the sketches he enclosed in some of his letters to his wife, a habit he had formed before they were married. These drawings mix theology and eroticism so explicitly that they are almost naive. One of them shows the young Kingsley absolving the kneeling penitent, Fanny, from her sins; it is uncharacteristic for the series only because the protagonists are clothed. In other sketches they appear slender, handsome, and naked: in one, the couple lies in sexual embrace, lashed to one another and to a cross, floating on a gentle wave in a sunny sea. In another, he has endowed himself with eagle's and her with butterfly wings; they are during intercourse—probably, to judge from her lassitude, just after orgasm—rising above a sunlit sea, through the clouds, toward heaven, with the pious reminder in a scroll floating above them: "He is not dead but sleepeth!"

Uncommon as Kingsley's exhibitionistic, blasphemous icons may have been, they were far from unique. They make more than fleeting appearances in the impious, Satanic, or semi-pornographic art and literature of the age: after mid-century, the inventive, once famous Belgian Decadent Félicien Rops devised some provocative variations on the theme of erotic crucifixions, illustrators like Emile-H. Meyer parodied that climactic moment of the Christian mythology, and in *A Relíquia*, Eça de Queiros wove a startling erotic fantasy around a cross and its holy burden. The protagonist of that amusing jest of a novel, who shams conspicuous piety that he may inherit the fortune of his dour, fanatically devout aunt, gazes during one of his nightly devotions at a wooden crucifix with its gilded Christ. "Slowly the precious metal, brilliantly agleam, faded and took on the color of flesh, warm and soft; the meager bones of the sad Messiah

73. Kingsley to Fanny Grenfell, October 4, 1843; 1843, Chitty, *Beast and Monk*, 81; May 15, September 25, 1843, October 27, 1848, Kingsley Papers, BL, Add. Mss., 62552, 62553; December 1843, Chitty, *Beast and Monk*, 91.

arranged themselves in divinely round and lovely shapes; from between
His crown of thorns emerged lascivious rings of curly, black hair; and
on his chest, over the two wounds, there arost two splendid, firm breast
with rosy tips—and there she was, my Adelia, on the cross, naked
superb, smiling, triumphant, profaning the altar as she held out her arm
to me!" Queiros has his "hero" say, "I saw this not as a temptation of the
devil but as a grace from the Lord."[74] The convenient and passionat
marriage between the "highest" and the "lowest" in man, which pervade
Patmore's and Kingsley's thought, seemed to linger just beneath the
surface of the nineteenth-century consciousness. It was in 1891, when
the second edition of *A Relíquia* appeared, that Joris-Karl Huysman
dissected this kind of hard-working wickedness in *Là-Bas*, and exploite
it to the full.

Rops, of course, was a notorious explorer of the borderlands surround
ing obscene art, Meyer frankly occupied that unrespectable terrain
Queiros was a sophisticated scoffer who thought nothing of portrayin
the protagonist of *A Relíquia* on his pilgrimage to the Holy Land in ar
unbroken voluptuous trance; and even Huysmans, though before 189
on his way from showy impiety to God, continued to enjoy the sensa
tional and the unconventional. In contrast, Kingsley was a moralisti
cleric and prolific controversialist. Yet his erotic vision, to judge by hi
drawings, was if anything as carnal, as exigent, as that of Queiros or
Huysmans at their most sophisticated. Those drawings, indeed, supply
some uncomfortable hints of sadism: the girl in her coarse penitent's shir
complete with rope around her neck, the couple tied tightly to the cross
Kingsley liked to draw naked women being abused, by man or nature
the unpublished illustrations to his youthful drama about St. Elizabeth
of Hungary fasten on torture; and his depiction of the murder of Queer
Gertrude, the saint's mother, showing her—nude, of course—being dis
emboweled and bitten, and being burned in her genitals by a long, wicked
phallic torch, would be at home in pornographic publications. The issue
is not whether the Kingsleys' marriage was a sadomasochistic union
what matters is that Charles Kingsley, the reforming divine and author
of children's books, thought it right to send such sketches to his Fanny
and possible that she might even enjoy them. In her memorial, she re
ferred to them, delicately and disingenuously, as "exquisite drawings ir
pen and ink." Fanny did not quite match Charles Kingsley's desire for
self-exposure. In May 1850, he wrote to her: "These soft, hot damp day:

74. Queiros, *A Relíquia* (1887; 2nd ed., 1891), 72 [part I]. For Emile H. Meyer
see above, p. 79.

fill me with yearning love; your image haunts me day and night as it did
before we were married, and the thought of that delicious sanctuary"—
but at this point his wife reached for her pen and scratched out the compromising words that came next.[75] She would not go so far as her husband, but she went far enough. Doting wife, possessive mother, protective
widow, fervent Christian, she was no angel.

Charles Kingsley and Coventry Patmore exhibit the versatility of displacement in the bourgeois century. Superficially, no two men could have
been less alike, though there were, as has become apparent, hidden
affinities between them. Patmore was a submissive, somewhat defensive
Roman Catholic convert; Kingsley an idiosyncratic, controversial, but
never heretical adherent to the Church of England who spent much of his
life trying to dissuade potential recruits to Catholicism. Patmore was, in
his occasional forays into politics, an unregenerate reactionary, more Tory
than the Tories of his day; Kingsley a political man to his bones, a Christian socialist who, even after his radicalism faded, continued to display
an earnest, far from patronizing sympathy for the victims of the Industrial
Revolution. Patmore could in his poetic fantasies slip with ease into a
female role; Kingsley, with all the emphatic manliness of the delicate
child and vulnerable adult, preached and practiced the virile outdoor life.
Both Patmore and Kingsley confessed to certain mystic inclinations,
but while Patmore surrendered to mysticism as to an all–embracing,
oceanic force, Kingsley only acknowledged his inclinations to his wife,
and fought them with a tough-minded empiricism that led him to take a
continuing interest in the natural sciences and to read Darwin with approval. Yet, in their way of exploiting religion in the interest of their
sensuality, the two were at one; even their theological argumentations
bear striking family resemblances.

Patmore and Kingsley, with their loyal readerships, spoke for more
than just themselves. Beyond this, they found echoes among some of their
less pious contemporaries. "Reverence" for the body, with all its erotic
implications, need not assume clerical garb. "We should learn to take an
equal pleasure," the secularist George Drysdale, English sexual reformer
and advocate of birth control, wrote in 1854, "and to have an equal
reverence for the sensual as the intellectual enjoyments, and in every
thing to attain to an impartial and well-balanced sense of the equal
grandeur of the material and the moral universe." This, he taught, is the

"true Physical and Spiritual Religion."[76] The stratagems of sensuality
were not confined to a single personal style or denominational commitment. But their way of taking refuge in religion, in a century and for a
class for which religion remained important, is an impressive tribute to
their flexibility. W. R. Greg had laid it down that asceticism is the religion
of the sensual. That was true for some. But for the likes of Patmore and
Kingsley, the religion of the sensual was sensuality. Seeking to spiritualize
the erotic, they only succeeded in eroticizing spirituality.

4. Sexualizing Modernity

Since religion had provided opportunities for erotic investment through
the ages, nineteenth-century sensual theologies were merely revised editions of ancient texts. But the age of Victoria also constructed some
targets for love unmistakably modern, targets that earlier centuries could
not have known, or even imagined. Writers and artists put mundane innovations to libidinal uses that their inventors had not intended, more
proof of how the world invades the mind, how concrete, time-bound
external forces leave their imprint on universal psychological mechanisms. In his twenty-volume tour through mid-nineteenth-century French
society, Emile Zola pressed both the department store and the railroad
into service as implausible but irresistible objects for erotic urges, and
his readers found his unconventional heroes and heroines anything but
absurd or far-fetched. Features of modernity, however rational, readily
lent themselves to sexualization.

For Zola, that impassioned partisan of progress, the department store
was "the poem of modern activity."[77] His *Au Bonheur des dames*, published in 1883, is among the lesser known volumes of his Rougon-Macquart
cycle, but it was well received by readers and critics alike, and it remains
an instructive, though not wholly reliable witness to the far-reaching
transformations within nineteenth-century bourgeois culture. One-sided
and distinctly theatrical, *Au Bonheur des dames* is precisely a poem of
modern activity, emphatically including sexual activity. It is all there:
the arduous, often pathetic struggle of the petty bourgeoisie; the anxious

76. A Doctor of Medicine [G. R. Drysdale], *The Elements of Social Science; or
Physical, Sexual and Natural Religion. An Exposition of the True and Only Cure of
the Three Primary Social Evils: Poverty, Prostitution and Celibacy* (1854; 20th ed.,
1881), 50.
77. "Ebauche" for *Au Bonheur des dames* (1883), in Zola, *Les Rougon-Macquart.
Histoire naturelle et sociale d'une famille sous le second Empire*, ed. Armand Lanoux
and Henri Mitterand, 5 vols. (1960–1967), III, 1679.

search for status among their prosperous counterparts; the feverish amusements and social pretensions of parvenus and patricians. Zola's imaginary department store, Au Bonheur des dames, is a microcosm, skillfully blending the features of such real Parisian bazaars as the Bon Marché and the Louvre. It is a paradise for its customers (which is to say, the ladies), whether rich or pinched for money, with its seemingly inexhaustible supplies of dresses, gloves, bolts of silk—and its breathtaking sales. But it is no paradise for those who work in the store: the quasi-military hierarchy organizing each department, the savage Darwinian competition among the sales force, the minute bookkeeping on the employees' performance which stimulates their cupidity and arouses their anxiety— all this makes it something of an inferno. The new middle class, the world of the clerk, assumes growing importance in this rational madhouse: the mail order department, which has been increasing its business at a stunning rate, had needed a dozen clerks just two years before the novel begins, but now it is already staffed with thirty clerks to open the mail, sort it, and fill the orders accurately and promptly.

The high priest presiding over this meticulously organized temple of consumption is Octave Mouret, its principal owner and unquestioned ruler. A Hobbesian sovereign, he has imposed a civic order on his teeming little universe by manipulations, cajolery, and, if he thinks it necessary, the brute means of peremptory dismissal. The larger ambiance of the bourgeoisie with all its tensions, on which Mouret's imaginative merchandising plays as though it were a docile instrument, impinges on *Au Bonheur des dames* time after time. There is the prudent customer who, as *bourgeoise sage et pratique*, cruises through the great bazaars of Paris like a good housekeeper at work, saving substantial sums at sales. There is the long-lost school friend whom Mouret happens to encounter at a reception and who has ended up as a minor bureaucrat earning three thousand francs a year. It was a respectable salary, but his most ordinary clerks, Mouret tells him, take home as much as this, while more experienced and intelligent ones may draw as much as twelve thousand a year. There is Mouret's smiling declaration, at that reception, that stores like his exist to enhance the well-being of the "middling bourgeoisie"—a pronouncement that, made in perfect sincerity, earns him a look of murderous hatred from one such middling bourgeois cursed with a wife suffering from an unslakable thirst for bargains she does not need and cannot afford. There are intimations of social mobility: the dormitory rooms that the sales girls come to occupy in the new grandiose buildings of Au Bonheur des dames are vastly superior to the old; accompanied by substantial raises in salary, they give the girls a taste for good soap and expensive underwear, and with that, "a natural stairway toward the bourgeoisie."[78]

Mouret's world is a world in motion and Mouret himself a triumphant exemplar of the career open to talents. A provincial nobody with a lively intelligence and very few scruples, Octave Mouret had landed in Paris, graduated from bed to bed, made a fortunate marriage, and, after his wife's death, converted his inheritance, control over Au Bonheur des dames, into a voracious empire. Driving, suave yet explosive, unquestionably in charge, one of the new men with his abundant energy, his easy success with women, his untraditional ideas, his willingness to risk all on a great sale, Mouret is a bourgeois conquistador. He takes unashamed pleasure in his commercial activities, his unremitting warfare against competitors large and small. The decadent pessimism that dogs some among his associates arouses him to healthy derisive laughter. "All the joy of action," Zola writes, "all the gaiety of existence, resound in his words." He is the modern hero Baudelaire had sought and Manet had painted; comfortably lecturing that old school friend who seems only half alive in his lassitude and passivity, he insists that he himself "belongs to his epoch." One would have to be deformed, ill-favored by nature "to refuse oneself to the work in hand," when there is so much work to be done, "when the whole century is throwing itself at the future." Fantasies of triumph are always in his mind; Mouret visualizes himself in his new large quarters, when they are still a remote wish, "master of the conquered city"—modern Paris.[79]

Zola makes no secret of his infatuation with the hero he has created. Octave Mouret's very ruthlessness is redeemed by his virile pleasure in himself, his unapologetic narcissism. Sketching the excitement of modern merchandising to a skeptical elderly financier, that financier, cool, shrewd, hard to impress, finds himself lured by the prospect that Mouret unfolds. The idea of organizing the project of a vast store serving thousands of customers daily is simple: "to sell cheap for the sake of selling a great deal; to sell a great deal for the sake of selling cheap." The financier is won over, almost. He admires Mouret's "imagination" and demurs only slightly: " 'Doubtless, the idea is seductive,' he said. 'Only, it's the idea of a poet. . . .' " As early as 1868, when Zola was adumbrating the scheme that would eventually grow into a score of linked novels, he saw the clash and the jostling of ambitions everywhere about him and found the spectacle bracing. By 1872, he envisioned a novel that would embody

78. *Au Bonheur des dames*, 444–52, 646 [ch. 3, 10].
79. Ibid., 451–55 [ch. 3].

one of its manifestations, *"le haut commerce (nouveautés)."* Suffering episodes of depression, Zola could not escape satirizing "the miscarriages of existence," notably in their middle-class guise. By and large, his world is harsh and grim, a military bulletin, not a pastoral poem. But by 1882 he was ready, as he put it with renewed, if perhaps slightly forced optimism, to "go with the century, express the century," a century that was preeminently "a century of action and of conquests." He was determined to describe and anatomize "the joy of action and the pleasure of existence." Mouret was his vehicle. He formulates Zola's fantasies more than once: "Action," he says, "contains its own reward. To act, to create, to fight against the facts, to conquer or be conquered by them, all human joy and health are in that!"[80]

Zola's eroticism had a good deal of aggression in it. In fact, this delighted bellicose vision of combat and conquest in the bourgeois world tempted Zola so severely that, for once, he could muster little sympathy for the victims, whether the "badly nourished, badly treated" clerks in the department store itself, or the shopkeepers in its neighborhood. Zola informed himself as he usually did. He walked through some of the flourishing Parisian stores and took voluminous notes; he consulted managers, architects, lawyers about the diverse, often baffling aspects of modern merchandising; he asked clerks to supply him with details about their life on the floor, their cubicles under the roof, their sparse free hours. He learned that most saleswomen had to take lovers to help pay their bills, and that some old, interesting small shops were being driven to the wall. He saw all this, and described it with his usual verve. But, as he put it, rather insensitively, in one of those memoranda he wrote to himself, "I shall not weep for them. On the contrary: for I want to show the triumph of modern activity." It was, as he said, "too bad" for those little shops: "They are crushed by the colossus."[81] And that, he said in *Au Bonheur des dames*, was that.

The confrontations that supply Zola's romance of the department store with its quota of excitement are stark and a little obvious, typical of all his fiction. Once again love, as in many of his novels, is the catalytic agent that drives the action forward to an unexpected denouement. Only here it assumes a guise unusual for Zola's work. Normally, with him, the passion of love is the source of the problem; in *Au Bonheur des dames* it supplies the key to the solution. Denise Baudu, the heroine, is a

---

80. Ibid., 457 [ch. 3]; list of novels to be done, ibid., 1774; ibid., 451 [ch. 3]; "ébauche," ibid., 1679.
81. Ibid., 505 [ch. 5]; "ébauche," ibid., 1680.

penniless provincial who comes to Paris with her two younger brothers after the death of her parents, to live with her uncle, a small linen draper. As she searches for her uncle's shop, the sight that rivets her to the spot is Au Bonheur des dames, primping for another day's business. In pathetic contrast, the Baudu establishment is dim, ill–stocked, in disarray, threatened by the new colossus across the street. With fitting irony, Denise finds employment in that department store; young, slight but, as she says, sturdy and, as she might have added, energetic and self-respecting, she will also find love there. For, after some inauspicious beginnings, she grows into an obsession with Octave Mouret; that superb ladies' man with a rich, socially prominent mistress, and surfeited with casual sexual adventures, comes to covet what he cannot obtain. He finds Denise, so different from any woman he has known, wholly irresistible, the source of anxious, angry, infatuated fantasies.

Denise is one of Zola's less plausible heroines, though he endows her with a humor, a gaiety, an intuitive intelligence that make her, as her character emerges, a most engaging creature and Mouret's worthy sparring partner. In a society addicted to loose living, in which nearly everyone has illicit affairs whether for pleasure or profit, she keeps herself chaste, with a determination at once combative and serene. Invited by her employer to join him for dinner—which clearly implies bed afterwards—she refuses the privilege. She does not preach but simply follows her moral impulses: fornication is not her style and, as she proudly puts it, she does not wish to share. Her resolute virginity proves the best, indeed the only, possible strategy to secure her prize, the commercial magnate Octave Mouret, in marriage. But, as she indignantly tells a friend, while she had discovered that she loves Mouret, she is not baiting a trap for him. Such a "calculation has never entered my head, and you know my horror of lies!"[82] The psychoanalytically informed historian may take her vehement denial as a covert confession, but that was certainly not Zola's intention: her conscience, so far as she knew, was clear.

Yet the results are as gratifying as if Denise had cleverly tried to snare her man: "Marry me, or I leave" becomes the simple, single issue. For his part, Mouret, haunted by his unique, incredible failure, suffers unaccustomed fits of sobbing, moments of mental confusion, outbursts of uncontrolled and impolitic rages. But the couple find one another, as they must, on the very last page, in a passionate tearful scene in Mouret's office; the splendid, unprecedented take of the day, over a million francs,

82. Ibid., 732 [ch. 12].

spread on his desk behind the happy pair, mutely dramatizes at once the power and the impotence of money before love. Its power, for it speaks of the energy and imagination in Mouret that make him so attractive to Denise Baudu; its impotence, since it could not buy her but leaves her, in the end, free and supreme. Mouret, assured at last of Denise's affection, promises her that, once married to him, she will rule all-powerful: *toute-puissante* is the charged last word of the novel.

To dramatize may be, as Henry James was not alone in affirming, the novelist's most exacting assignment. While the two intertwined duels that organize *Au Bonheur des dames*—the loving combat between a man and a woman, and the mortal struggle between a giant and a midget of commerce—touch pervasive nineteenth-century realities, Zola's presentation is analysis colored, and often overwhelmed, by lyricism. Obeying his need to compress and simplify, Zola appropriated the new Parisian world of department stores, in themselves exciting enough, speeded up their expansion, and overstated their conquests. What took Le Bon Marché or Le Louvre several decades to accomplish, Zola's Au Bonheur des dames manages in half a dozen years. If some neighborhood stores were, as Zola pitilessly put it, "crushed by the colossus," many others survived. Surely some customers could attend sales without salivating, their pupils neither dilated not contracted, their purchases appropriate to their income. The pressures on Zola to paint with a broad brush and primary colors were not purely literary: he wrote as he did, extolling energy, combat, even ruthlessness, to deafen the whispers of his own severe anxieties and to find fictional representations for his intermittently frustrated sensual needs and fantasies. However, Zola's ability to draw so directly on his own conflicts sharpened his observation. What he saw and recorded were important but relatively inaccessible aspects of the bourgeois experience: its diffuse, potent sensuality, and its capacity to enlist aggressive drives in the search for mastery. *Au Bonheur des dames* is drenched in eroticism and, to only a lesser extent, in aggression. The very name that Zola has devised for this department store testifies to the sexual basis of what, on the surface, is a set of rational commercial transactions. It is only when Mouret explains his merchandising in this way that the skeptical financier he tries to enlist in his schemes recognizes the full measure of Mouret's toughminded and exploitative vision: "I have the woman," Mouret tells him bluntly, "I don't give a damn about the rest!"[83] The rest, he knew, would follow.

83. Ibid., 460 [ch. 3].

Zola explicates this remark in some detail. Mouret's sole passion is "to
conquer woman." He wants her to be "queen in his house; he had built
her this temple, to have her at his mercy." And he does have her: with
barely concealed voluptuous excitement, Zola describes shopping at Au
Bonheur des dames as an erotic experience. The merchandise in the windows breathes, emits a suggestive tremor; throbbing warmly, it hints at,
yet hides, the treasures within. In the store itself, the atmosphere is, if
anything, more caressing, more seductive still. Customers enter a little
alcove in which lace is on display, with pale face, shining eyes, and a
drunken tremor; it is like a specially devised torture chamber for sinners,
a "corner of perdition where the strongest would succumb."[84] The dry
lips, the glittering eyes, the little beads of sweat on neck and forehead,
the rage to touch that mark customers closing in on a lovely shawl, a
tempting bolt of cotton, a stylish dress, all offered at irresistible prices,
are intimations of the passions, modeled on sexual excitement. They are
much like Hanno Buddenbrook's piano playing.

Talk of seduction swirls through the pages of *Au Bonheur des dames*:
ideas are seductive, and so, even more, are sales prices, advertisements and
displays, at which Mouret is, significantly, an acknowledged master.
"Everybody admitted it, the boss was the first window-dresser in Paris, a
revolutionary window-dresser in truth, who has founded the school of
the brutal and the colossal in the science of display." He had invented
shocking juxtapositions, wanting the stuffs "aflame in the most ardent
colors, taking life from one another." Denise herself, as Zola explicitly
says more than once, is "seduced" by the windows of Au Bonheur des
dames into the irresistible wish to work there, even as she refuses the
seductions of men. Zola takes care to introduce sexuality into pursuits
seemingly most remote from it: a cashier, Lhomme, whom Mouret at
times supplies with expensive tickets to concerts, loves music as a masturbator loves his fantasies: "he had only that one vice, music, a secret vice
that he satisfied in solitude." For the rest, though, the pleasures of Au Bonheur des dames resemble not solitary but shared vice. Explaining to conservative subordinates the utility of selling at least some attractive items at
a loss, Mouret drops into sensual talk quite naturally: these loss leaders will
"attract all the women," and, "seduced, infatuated with the mass of our
merchandise, they will empty their purses without counting!" Madame
Marty, that middling bourgeoise whose addiction to bargains drives her
sober husband to despair, is the exemplary victim of this calculating erotic

84. Ibid., 612 [ch. 8].

strategy: she wanders through the department store, or displays her purchases to her women friends, in a tremor of excitement, satisfying "a kind of sensual need." While she explores the counters at Au Bonheur des Dames she unwittingly trains her daughter Valentine, whom she often takes along on her shopping sprees, as her worthy successor in this materialistic debauchery; Valentine, "a tall girl of fourteen, thin and bold, already cast at the merchandise the guilty glances of a woman."[85] Mouret wanted and often got them early.

The atmosphere he creates for his customers is at once soothing and exciting; it lures shoppers from their ordinary existence into a warm, exotic environment of flowing abundance, inviting them to wander from floor to floor, greedily looking, greedily touching. These women, Zola tells his readers more than once, are pale with desire. Some, in fact, whether too poor to pay, too avid to wait, or too timid to tell their husbands, are inveigled, in this castle of seduction, into stealing. Such is the joy of possession, such are the orgies of consumption. Indeed, in Zola's paradise for women, consumption itself takes on erotic form. The word *manger* is as prominent in *Au Bonheur des dames* as *séduire*, possibly more so. Competitors devour one another with their sales, established sales women devour the recently hired with their persecutions, department stores devour old-fashioned shops with their capital, customers devour the merchandise with their eyes; ambitions, whether they inhabit lowly clerks or high-placed managers, proletarian girls or high-born ladies, are all appetites. At this point, sexuality blends into aggression; the two basic passions are, as always, intertwined and hard to disentangle. The scheme that Octave Mouret unfolds before the financier is, in the latter's silent commentary, a machine designed "to eat women." Indeed, the combative Social Darwinism that animates Octave Mouret is, once again, an exhilarating means of satisfying hunger: "he dreamt of organizing the house so as to exploit the appetites of others, for the tranquil and complete gratification of his own appetites." Success itself takes a sensual form for Mouret; he thinks of it, as Mabel Todd or Emma Bovary might have thought of it, as a bath.[86] His response to victory, to combat itself, is anything but abstract; it is physical, sexual.

While Zola expertly converted the modern department store into a steamy sanctuary of appetites, he projected still more potent sexual excite-

85. Ibid., 434, 391, 430, 425, 466, 486 [ch. 2, 1, 2, 2, 3, 4].
86. Ibid., 461, 422, 492 [ch. 3, 2, 4].

ment into another modern invention, the railroad. Here he was following
not creating, a fashion. Almost since its first spectacular runs in the mid
1820s, poets and novelists had employed the railroad as a symbol fo
power and for revenge. Especially the locomotive, which often prove
a killer in sober reality, seemed suitable as an engine of retribution, a soci:
superego punishing offenses against man and the gods. In a strange poer
of early 1880, "Die Brück am Tay," Theodor Fontane visualized the mos
destructive railroad disaster of his century as a demonic vengeance o
human presumption. On December 28, 1879, the railroad bridge ove
the river Tay near Dundee had collapsed during a storm, taking with
the train passing over, with its crew and all its hapless passengers. Fontan
sees the three witches of *Macbeth* lying in wait for the engineer who wit
his blind confidence in human contrivance pushes his train forwar
through the howling winds, trusting that his engine and the great—badl
engineered—bridge will defeat the hostile elements. But hubris ends
literally, in a fall, and the witches proclaim the moral that all man-mad
things are mere rubbish, mere vanity:

Tand, Tand,
Ist das Gebilde von Menschenhand.

In Fontane's lurid fable, the railroad is the victim making more victims
In other imaginative productions of the century, it becomes the instru
ment of punishment in a more active way. Dickens chose to dispose o:
John Carker, the villain of *Dombey and Son*, under an express train, usin
excited, disjointed phrases to imitate the thundering, unstoppable ap
proach of the deadly engine. Surprised at a station by the man he ha
betrayed, Carker steps back onto the tracks. "He heard a shout—anothe1
—saw the face change from its vindictive passion to a faint sickness and
terror—felt the earth tremble—knew in a moment that the rush wa:
come—uttered a shriek—looked round—saw the red eyes, bleared and
dim, in the daylight, close upon him—was beaten down, caught up, and
whirled away upon a jagged mill, that spun him round and round, and
struck him limb from limb and licked his stream of life up with its fiery
heat, and cast his mutilated fragments in the air." In the same manner,
though with more muted rhetoric, Trollope has the adventurer Lopez,
in *The Prime Minister*, commit suicide under a train. And, as we all know,
Tolstoy does away with the adulterous Anna Karenina in the same manner,
after a fatal railway accident early in the novel has forecast her tragic fate:
"Suddenly, remembering the man who had been run over the day she
first met Vronsky, she realized what she had to do." Her lover cooling,
her reputation ruined, her child lost to her, she realizes that she has to

throw herself under a train: " 'There, into the very middle, and I shall
punish him and escape from everybody and from myself!' "[87]

Anna Karenina's suicide, a pathetic mixture of despair and revenge, of
obedience to a punitive superego and rebellion against intolerable narcissistic injuries, was the final act of a transgression in the realm, and under
the impulsion, of Eros. In general, the railroad became, for the nineteenth-
century bourgeois imagination, a favorite actor in the theatre of libido. In
some fictions it figures as the loved object; in others, its part was supporting, merely instrumental: the train speeds the lover on his way to his
mistress. Thus in Friedrich Theodor Vischer's novel, *Auch Einer*, a
traveling lover apostrophizes panting steam and rolling wheels to speed
him home, home:

> Jetzt schnaube nur, Dampf, und brause!
> Jetzt rolle nur, Rad, und sause!
> Es geht nach Hause, nach Hause!

The car cannot tell how his pulses race; neither telegraph poles nor
vanishing miles can say how he longs to be with his beloved. Other passengers gossip and yawn, wishing for nothing while he only wants to go
faster and faster, to leave the babbling crowds behind and gain her warm
breast and her loving arms:

> Hinweg aus dem plappernden Schwarme,
> O, hin an die Brust, an die warme
> in die offnen, die liebenden Arme!

Vischer's repetitive, reiterative verses, which at once celebrate and mimic
the thrust of the engine and the clacking of wheels on the rails, pull the
reader along to experience some of the excitement of travel itself. They
hint, ever so subtly, at the rhythmic, accelerating activity the lovers will
enjoy once the traveler has reached those loving arms. In prose, too, such
mimesis became eminently popular. Dickens portrays Mr. Dombey on a
train, tormented by memories of his young son's death, carried along
mercilessly: "Away, with a shriek, and a roar, and a rattle, from the town,
burrowing among the dwellings of men and making the streets hum,
flashing out into the meadows for a moment, mining in through the
damp earth, booming on in darkness and heavy air, bursting out again

87. Fontane: "Die Brück am Tay (28. Dezember 1879)" (1880), *Theodor Fontane
Jubiläumsausgabe*, ed. Kurt Schreinert, 3 vols. (1968), III, 747-49; Dickens: *Dealings
with the Firm of Dombey and Son, Wholesale, Retail, and for Exportation* (1848;
ed. H. W. Garrod, 1950), 799; Trollope: *The Prime Minister* (1878; 3 vols. ed. 1922),
III, 85-86; Tolstoy: *Anna Karenina* (1875-77; tr. Louise and Aylmer Maude, 1918, ed.
1949, 2 vols. in 1), II, 380 [part VII, ch. 31].

into the sunny days so bright and wide; away, with a shriek and a roa
and a rattle, through the fields, through the woods, through the cor
through the hay, through the chalk, through the mould, through the cla
through the rock, among objects close at hand and almost in the gras
ever flying from the traveller, and a deceitful distance ever moving slow
within him; like as in the track of the remorseless monster, Death!"—an
so on, for paragraphs more.[88]

Though Mr. Dombey's thoughts are on death, Dickens's prose h
something erotic about it, with its evocation of power, speed, and ac
celeration. In such writing, railroad locomotion stands as an emblem c
libidinal energies as it charts their rising curve of engagement. The imita
tion is deliberate; the eroticism in the main unconscious: in her poem, "Au
der Eisenbahn," dating from 1844, Luise von Plönnies utters the rhyme
wish that the speed and freedom of railway travel may become a mode
for the rapid diffusion of free speech. But sexual emotions cluster beneatl
the surface of her political message; Plönnies's train is a "quick lightning,
which rushes through the glorious day, blusters through dark night
thunders over foaming waters, flashes past the edge of the abyss, an agile
bold, rousing thing of power:

> Rascher Blitz, der hin mich trägt,
> Pfeilschnell von der Gluth bewegt,
> Sausend durch des Tages Pracht,
> Brausend durch die dunkle Nacht,
> Donnernd über Stromesschäumen,
> Blitzend an des Abgrunds Säumen. . . .

All is agitation in this vision, and heat, and daring, as the train skirt
precipices and penetrates tunnels. The French, too, after liberating
themselves from linguistic importations like *le railway*, *le tunnel*, *le ballast*
le tender, to say nothing of *express*, *trucks*, and *wagons*, produced rail
road poetry in their own vocabulary, in which they delighted in the
sensuality of *vitesse*. Their poems, strictly minor but sufficiently rousing
make the engine a panting centaur impatient to shed his bridle, or a
vertiginous stallion.[89]

---

88. Vischer: *Auch Einer: Eine Reisebekanntschaft* (1878; ed. n.d.), 357; Dickens:
Dombey and Son, 280–81.

89. Plönnies: *Gesammelte Gedichte* (1844), 182; for some specimens of French
railroad poetry, see Jean-Pons Viennet, *Epitre à Despréaux* (1855), Paul Bourget,
Edel, un départ (1878) and others, in Marc Baroli, *Le train dans la littérature française*
(1963), 117, 153 and *passim*.

However limited the success of versifiers trying to wrest memorable poetry from a nineteenth-century invention, their poems attempt to convey its hidden sensual reverberations. Railway travel, with its regular, audible pulse, its impressive capacity to accelerate motion and its veiled threats to life and limb, awakened infantile memories, memories of being tossed up into the air, or rocked asleep, as a child. Such travel was at once exciting and soporific, productive of tensions both anticipated and feared. In his *Three Essays on the Theory of Sexuality*, Freud specially notes "the shaking of carriage drives and, later, of railroad travel," which "has such a fascinating effect upon older children, so that every boy, at least, has at some time in his life wanted to be an engine driver or a coachman." He added, a little puzzled by the phenomenon, but nonetheless certain of its existence, that there is an "exquisite sexual symbolism" in railroad travel and a "compulsive link" between it and sexuality, which "clearly stems from the pleasurable character of the sensations of movement."[90] Trains were erotic causes and could become erotic objects.

Not all the translations of the steam engine into an animated being or all the imitations of the train's rhythms were, to be sure, deeply felt. Such devices quickly established themselves as favorites, and became a hackneyed literary convention. By the 1850s, it was commonplace to lend the train, especially the locomotive, human, or at least living, qualities, to visualize it as a galloping horse, as a demon who carries passengers in its mighty arms, as a monster coughing out its black lungs, as a beast that taps its way through the darkness, rushes in elation through smiling landscapes, and roars with pain and pleasure. But Walt Whitman's hymn "To a Locomotive in Winter" is more than mechanical poetic license; with unconcealed erotic anthropomorphism, Whitman adores the engine's "measured dual throbbing" and its "beat convulsive," its "black cylindrical body," its "swelling pant and roar," its "great protruding head-light" and its "knitted frame." The locomotive is, to Whitman,

> Type of the modern—emblem of motion and
>   power—
>   pulse of the continent.

Keenly aware of its prosaic nature, he calls on it "for once" to "come serve the Muse and merge in verse":

90. *Drei Abhandlungen zur Sexualtheorie* (1905), *St.A.*, V, 107; *Three Essays on the Theory of Sexuality*, S.E., VII, 202.

Fierce-throated beauty!
Roll through my chant with all thy lawless
    music, thy swinging lamps at night,
Thy madly-whistled laughter, echoing,
    rumbling like
    an earthquake, rousing all—
Rousing all with its virility and its autonomy:

Law of thyself complete, thine own track
    firmly holding,
(No sweetness debonair of tearful harp or
    glib piano thine.)

Whitman's wishful erotic vision—the locomotive as the throbbing, swelling, convulsively beating emblem of motion and power—is wholly unapologetic. There were other writers (or at least characters that writers
found it possible to imagine) in love with locomotives. One of these is
Martial Hébert, the hero of Jules Claretie's novel *Le train 17*: Hébert, a
young laborer, finds bliss as stoker on an engine. He fondly regards locomotives as human: "Railroads, he declared, engines, all these beings of
iron and cast iron, which seem to be alive, and which, with their muscles
of copper or steel, take the place of human muscles—they tempt me." In
the presence of his engine, Hébert allows himself to experience a "strange
and magnetic sensation" as he listens to its strident whistle, feels its
internal palpitations, watches its jets of vapor; when the locomotive heats
up for travel, he stands as close to it as he can, to bathe in its warmth and,
all surrounded by its steam, to be covered by "a humid kiss."[91] In the end,
Hébert commits suicide by throwing himself under his locomotive, but
Claretie did not intend this ending as an exhibition of the railroad's
demonic power; Hébert had been driven to despondency by the death of
his child and the infidelity of his wife. *Le train 17* remains, for all its
technological decor, a relatively conventional love story.

  In forceful contrast, Zola's *La bête humaine* is a brooding, terrifying
tale of modern ambivalence: of fierce love and fiercer hate, enacted on and
through the railroad. Although the book stands as the most sustained
imaginative exploration of the railroad to appear in the nineteenth century,
it is not a pure railroad novel. Nearing the end of his Rougon-Macquart
cycle, and committed to two themes—crime and the railroad—neither

  91. Whitman: "To a Locomotive in Winter," *Leaves of Grass* (1891–92), Walt
Whitman, *Complete Poetry and Collected Prose*, ed. Justin Kaplan (1982), 583;
Claretie: *Le train 17* (1877; ed. ca. 1905), 114–15.

f which he had the heart to give up, Zola took the simplest way out: he
vrote a novel that amalgamated them. This means that the scenery in *La
bête humaine*—stations, engines, compartments, tracks, level crossings—is
more than a set of passive backdrops before which the real action takes
place. They saturate the atmosphere, and more: trains and locomotives
are principal actors in Zola's melodrama. They are living beings loved and
feared, endowed by infatuated operators and even by objective observers
with human emotions like affection, loyalty, and murderous rage. In the
actions of these iron giants, as in those of the human protagonists, love
and hate, life and death, are inextricably intertwined; the locomotives
exhibit and reinforce Zola's gloomy vision of the horror at the heart of
erotic experience. *La bête humaine* is a melancholy meditation on two
double, internally divided natures: the savage animal inhabiting every
human being, and the souls that animate privileged machines like locomotives. One of its most pathetic characters, Phasie, who has watched thousands of trains rushing past her house fronting a level crossing, yokes
these two ungainly and dangerous centaurs together in a single philosophical reflection: "Oh!" she says, speaking of the railroad, "it's a fine invention, no denying that. People travel fast, they know more." But, she
adds, "wild beasts remain wild beasts, and they can go on inventing ever
better machines, there will be wild beasts beneath all the same."[92] *La bête
humaine* exhibits these beasts unleashed; animal men and human machines
fated to live and die together.

On the opening page, there is a moment of deceptive peace, almost of
serenity, as Zola sketches the prospect of the Gare Saint-Lazare, the
Parisian station to which Monet had devoted a series of canvases in the
mid-1870s. But sexual passions, their derivatives and pathologies, soon
invade this modern idyll of tranquil bustle and busy anticipation. Roubaud,
the provincial station master through whose eyes Zola had visualized the
Gare Saint-Lazare, discovers that his wife had once had an elderly lover
and forces her to join him in killing the aged lecher. They commit their
act of jealous revenge on a train, in a brightly lit compartment, and are
observed by Jacques Lantier, a luckless heir of the Rougon-Macquart
curse, doomed by his appalling hereditary taint to suffer recurrent, inexplicable, overpowering urges to murder a woman in a moment of erotic
excitement. He almost kills Flore, a girl who has long loved him, and
later Flore, driven to distraction by her unrequited passion for Jacques,
commits suicide under a train. Jacques himself will die by a train at the
very end of the novel, locked in a fatal embrace with the stoker Pecqueux,

92. *La bête humaine* (1890), in Zola, *Les Rougon-Macquart*, IV, 1032 [ch. 2].

whose girl Jacques had seduced, and who attacks him as the two drive their train through the night. "Pecqueux," so Zola describes the combat, with the voluptuous explicitness that was his signature, "with a final rush, hurled Jacques off; and Jacques, frantic, sensing the void behind him, grimly clung to his neck so tightly that he dragged him along. There were two terrible screams, which mingled, which faded. The two men fell together, dragged under the wheels by the action of the speed, and cut to pieces, hacked, still in their embrace, in this terrible hug—they who had so long lived like brothers. They were found headless, without feet, two bloody trunks still clasped as it to stifle each other."[93] The hug that is the posture of love has become the device of death.

The heartless engine that mortally mutilates Jacques and his rival and then, "like an animal seized by madness," goes roaring through the night, was not the locomotive that Jacques had loved. It was new and did not even have a name but a number: 608. It could not compare to the old engine, Lison. Yet 608, too, was somehow human: Jacques, as he liked to say, had had her maidenhead, and he found her "restive, capricious, like those young fillies who have to be mastered through wear and tear before they resign themselves to the harness." Even Pecqueux, the stoker, would swear at this locomotive as though she were a recalcitrant, tantalizing woman, a disgraceful slut. The other one, Lison, had been so docile! Jacques could only agree; the moods of No. 608 made him miss Lison all the more. But Lison was dead. Earlier, when he had still been driving Lison, Flore had gently teased Jacques about his infatuation: observing that he seemed to have no use for girls, she asked, "Are you then in love with your locomotive alone? People joke about it, you know. They say that you're always polishing her, to make her shine, as if you had caresses only for her."[94]

It was true. With Lison, whom he had driven, and loved, for more than four years, Jacques never felt any perverse urges to kill. This locomotive, so submissive, so reliable, had, for him, "the rare qualities of a good woman." So he kept her shiny and in the best of trim. But, "wounded" in a damaging snow storm, she had lost some of her responsiveness and her accustomed vigor, and Jacques's tender feelings took a sad, almost desperate turn, aware as he was that she was marked by mortal illness. Then she died, in an accident in which Jacques, too, was almost killed. The gentle, lovable Lison breathed her last and Jacques, gravely in-

93. Ibid., 1330–31 [ch. 12].
94. Ibid., 1330, 1301, 1040 [ch. 12, 12, 2].

ired, watched her die and, weeping, wished to die with her. No woman
in Jacques's life had ever enlisted so pure a passion as this.

One of Zola's most perceptive reviewers, Jules Lemaître, noted that the
novel was a study of "the most fearful and most mysterious" among man's
primordial instincts: the instinct of destruction and murder and its
obscure correlation with the amorous instinct."[95] *La bête humaine* is not a
romance by an infatuated modern who loved machines with human attributes more than men with animal proclivities. Zola, though a partisan
of science, still implicated the living, palpitating engine that was the
emblem of the nineteenth century, in the "obscure correlation" of love and
hate. No. 608, his invention, after all, as much as Lison, was proof that a
locomotive could be as sadistic as any man, as malicious, and, worse, as
castrating, as any woman.

La bête humaine is a nightmare subjected to the secondary revision of
literary discipline. Its somewhat obtrusive, somewhat predictable symbolism—progress rushing from station to station, France out of control,
the cave man immured within civilized man—thinly veils Zola's obsessive
and frightened fantasies. He himself was haunted by the spectre of being
buried alive in a tunnel, and that is a far cry from Freud's manageable
travel anxiety, as far as Jacques's passion for Lison is from the tame
titimulation that titillated the average traveler. Zola's—or Whitman's—
highly charged expressive manifestations are far from representative.
Few travelers, whether in commerce or for pleasure, were after all
likely to commit murder on a train, or to avow their love for a locomotive. They might dream of such things, nothing more. But, just as the
neurotic analysand exhibits, in striking form and uncommon intensity, the
conflicts working in less troubled individuals, so these extremists of the
pen, precisely because they are so extravagant, give access to the concealed
tensions and desires that visited more ordinary middle-class minds in the
machine age. Most, even those not given to writing novels or painting
pictures, found the steadily increasing power of the machine at once
exhilarating and frightening; its potential for construction and destruction,
for the production of wealth or the dealing of death, seemed perhaps
equal—at all events, equally unpredictable.

At first, the imagination of writers, and of painters in their company,
seems to have lost heart, almost failed, before the industrial experience.
Literary historians have noted that the quaint, sometimes tortured efforts
to assimilate steam engines or railroad trains to accepted rhetorical con-

95. Ibid., 1128, 1266–67 [ch. 5, 10]; Review, in ibid., 1747.

ventions only document a certain helplessness. Just as, in the dawn o
printing, designers carefully cut typefaces that would imitate the letter
characteristic of manuscripts, so anxious artists of the nineteenth centur
appropriated time-worn metaphors and tropes and decorative devices t
disguise rather than exhibit the machine. Thus in 1811, Robert Southe
could describe the Black Country, that "hell above ground," with its hill
of slag, its stifling smoke, its "huge black piles, consisting chiefly o
chimneys and furnaces," as a fine instance of "the *damnable picturesque*."[9]
It was damnable perhaps, but it was certainly picturesque: merely
variation on a known genre, which is always a reassuring thing. Other
would invoke aesthetic categories like the sublime to tame the imposing
often depressing structures and the massive moving vehicles increasingl
dominating the landscape. Such borrowings were ways of binding th
unease, that mixture of excitement and fear, that at first characterize
middle-class responses to the factory, the machine—and the railroad
Then, perhaps by mid-century, certainly by the 1870s, calmer, less anxiou
perceptions began to compete with the more febrile imaginings of earlie
decades. A certain sense of confident mastery, of control accompanied b
manageable anxiety—or by no anxiety whatever—spread among middle
class minds. Phobias were challenged by what the psychoanalyst Ott
Fenichel has called the counter-phobic attitude, by demonstrations o
daring and nonchalance, or were, in some instances, actually overcome

In the art of the age, beginning with Turner's atmospheric, supremel
charged *Rain, Steam and Speed: The Great Western Railway*, of 1844
and culminating three decades later in Manet's and Monet's tranqui
renditions of the Gare Saint-Lazare, the railroad was gradually assimilate
into the bourgeois consciousness. This did not put an end to its mystery
or its troubling erotic implications; Walt Whitman's hymn to a locomo
tive dates, after all, from 1876; Zola imagined his lovable Lison as lat
as 1890. The railroad joined the love of music, of nature, of God, in th
arsenal of expressive erotic vehicles to expand—and at the same time t
police—the terrain of modern middle-class sensual love. All together, thi
family of stratagems enriched bourgeois erotic life, lent it a certair
piquancy, and helped to contain the tensions under which their de
manding culture compelled the middle classes to live. But, as will becom
apparent, it could not discharge or resolve these tensions.

96. Mario Praz, *The Hero in Eclipse in Victorian Fiction* (1952; tr. Angu
Davidson, 1956), 180. I should note that I could have included other types of eroti
displacement, such as sports and competitions, in this chapter. But since in these th
aggressive component has the upper hand, I am saving them for consideration in th
next volume, provisionally titled "The Cultivation of Hatred."

≥ SIX ≤

The Price of Repression

AROUND THE middle of the nineteenth century, physicians and social observers discovered that simply being a bourgeois imposed a formidable strain on that species. Familiar distressing manifestations of private vice and social decay—"self-abuse," birth control, and general immorality—were embedded in more sweeping anxiety-producing worries. The perpetual need of the middle classes to redefine and defend the domain of the private, to flaunt the emblems of respectability, to deserve and cope with success, and to regulate their commerce with deep, often unconscious feelings of love and hate, appeared to be extracting an extortionate psychological tribute, embodied in two quite diverse phenomena: nervousness and prostitution.

There were moments when these cultural symptoms established an destructive personal union. In a characteristically inconclusive story of 1888, "An Attack of Nerves," Anton Chekhov has a morbidly sensitive law student, Vasiliev, suffer a neurotic breakdown after a dismaying excursion through a fleet of Moscow whorehouses with two fellow students. Exceedingly vulnerable, with his overdeveloped gift for empathy, Vasiliev interprets the pathos and vulgarity of the scenes he has witnessed as an imperious call to duty. He is horrified by the callousness of his friends and grows obsessed by the need to remedy the ills suddenly revealed to him; seeking a way of rescuing all fallen women and overpowered by the magnitude of his perplexities, he suffers "an attack of nerves" requiring the attention of a psychiatrist, who proves to be as insensitive as his drinking companions.

Chekhov's story is fiction, though it draws on reality: it was written

as a memorial to the writer Garsin, who had been active in rehabilitatin
prostitutes and made tragic stories out of his experiences.[1] Real life, to
without admixtures of the imagination, could bring nervousness an
prostitution together. In a tract of 1912, Jane Addams noted that th
"distaste and distress" many feel at the sight of prostitutes "sometime
leads to actual nervous collapse." She quotes a "distinguished Englishman,
perhaps Gladstone, to the effect that soberminded people who hav
" 'looked the hideous evil full in the face, have often asserted that nothin
in their experience has seemed to threaten them so nearly with a loss c
reason.' "[2] Most of her contemporaries, ordinary bourgeois no less tha
physicians or satirists, were prepared to regard nervousness and prostitu
tion as florid symptoms of a malaise inherent in the very nature of middle
class culture. To them, it was the heavy price that this culture had to pa
for its sadly repressed ways of loving. They were wrong.

1. The Modern Malady of Love

Nervousness is a modern disease—or, at least, a modern diagnosis—wit
ancient roots. Plato's engaging tale about the origins of amorous attrac
tion, one half of the once-united bisexual creature desperately desirin
the other half from which it had been torn, survived into the nineteent
century as an enduring metaphor for lonely, fragmented human being
in search of love's healing power. St. Augustine, too, and after hir
medieval mystics, had seen culture, the source of gratifications, as als
a prominent cause of mental malaise: they mourned humanity's estrange
ment from God once it had deserted His embracing paradise to live i
cities, and become slaves to the passions, thus losing its primal innocenc
and, with that, its hold on the universal ground of being.

These philosophical fancies or theological jeremiads represented, wit
almost no concealment, wishes for regression from adult individuality t
infantile union. Late-eighteenth- and nineteenth-century cultural critic
and social scientists translated these collective longings into technica
terminology or into radical strategies designed to remedy human isola
tion through political action, social policy, or moral reform. The resonan
names they invented or popularized—alienation, demoralization, rootless
ness, anomie, or, in Carlyle's vivid phrase, the "huge demon of Mechan

---

1. George Siegel, "The Fallen Woman in Nineteenth Century Russian Literature,
Harvard Slavic Studies, V (1970), 102–106.
2. Addams, *A New Conscience and an Ancient Evil* (1912), 141–44.

ism"—overlapped in meaning and came to be almost identical in usage.[3] However diverse their original intentions, these epithets were all implicitly about love or, rather, its deplorable absence. In 1776, in his epoch-making *Wealth of Nations*, Adam Smith had presciently forecast the contradictory, often baleful impact of the division of labor on the cogs in the industrial machine deprived of essential human contacts and activities. Then in the early 1790s, in his *Briefe über die aesthetische Erziehung des Menschen*, Friedrich Schiller had written some influential pages on the fragmentation of modern man, the specialized animal. It was culture itself, he said somberly, that had dealt humans their near-fatal wound, degrading them into rootless beings who concentrate on some single pursuit at the expense of all else, thus sacrificing the sense of versatility and the ability to play. Later, in the early nineteenth century, Hegel introduced the category of alienation into philosophic discourse; and, pushing Hegel's observations into the subversive study of class conflict and personal deprivation, Marx stigmatized the condition of man in modern capitalist society, a hostile stranger alike to his work, to his fellows, and to himself. Finally, Emile Durkheim took "anomie," that old reproachful synonym for the absence of divine regulation, and supplied it with formidable quantitative sociological underpinnings; he saw disorienting phenomena besetting modern society—a sense of uncertainty and unpredictability, the child of an overweening, socially fostered egotism.

This was highly charged language. But even terms not intended to be critical were conscripted in the service of the great anti-bourgeois campaign mounted by social critics from various, often conflicting directions. Ferdinand Tönnies, that unconventional and versatile German sociologist, had employed his famous pair, *Gemeinschaft* and *Gesellschaft*, community and society, to sum up the course of modern social evolution from one to the other. He was far from proposing a retreat from the flawed society of his own day to some idealized past community. But the inference that most of his readers felt impelled to draw was that mechanical loveless *Gesellschaft* had destroyed the organic, emotional bonds that *Gemeinschaft* had so long cherished.

In this domain of invidious translations from technical terminology to words of abuse, the history of "nervousness" is particularly interesting since, far more than "alienation" or "anomie," the term entered common

3. Carlyle, "Chartism" (1839), *Selected Writings*, ed. Alan Shelston (1971), 174 [ch. 4].

parlance and shaped bourgeois self-perceptions in the mid- and late-nineteenth century. To make it more interesting still, nervousness, almost as much as religious mania, came to be perceived as somehow, subtly or grossly, involved with erotic life. "The modern malady of love," Arthur Symons intoned in a poem of 1897, "is nerves."[4] Most others did not see—took care not to see—this connection.

Until 1800, and continuing in active usage until the late nineteenth century and beyond, "nervous" or "nerveux" meant vigorous, forcible, sinewy, free from debility of any sort; one spoke, in praise, of a drafts-man's nervous line or of a nervous racehorse. But by 1783, sensitively descrying a new signification hovering in the wings, Samuel Johnson wrote to his friend, Mrs. Thrale, about "a tender, irritable, and *as it is not very properly called*, a nervous constitution." The old meaning, to be sure, long coexisted with the new. As late as 1868, Charles C. Eastlake, denigrating the Italian style of architecture, suggested that what England wanted was "a less refined and more nervous expression of architectural beauty," which he defined as possessing "bold and sturdy features."[5] For Eastlake, "nervous" still was practically synonymous with "virile." But the new meaning, as is the way with telling linguistic innovations, moved with fair efficiency to crowd out the old and eventually monopolize the field of discourse. When a character in Dickens's novels is nervous, he is fearful and upset, perspiring or biting his lips. Nervous characters in Fontane or Zola betray precisely the same disconsolate state of mind.

By mid-nineteenth century, the modern meaning was firmly in place, on the Continent as much as in Britain. A pervasive refrain in the letters of the eminent German pianist and conductor, Hans von Bülow, a walking anthology of tremulous responses, lamented that noise, boredom, interruptions, excessive work, the English language, or lack of sleep, all made him "frightfully nervous."[6] Ordinary Germans were no strangers to such expressions. A soldier in camp during the Franco-Prussian War diagnosed the "atrocious headaches" that his "Jeannettchen" was suffering at home as a consequence of the summer heat which had "attacked her nerves." Another German, the journalist and editor Otto von Leixner, significantly

---

4. Symons, "Nerves," *Poetry of the 'Nineties*, ed. R. K. R. Thornton (1970), 137.

5. Johnson: to Mrs. Thrale, November 24, [17]83, *The Letters of Samuel Johnson*, ed. R. W. Chapman, 3 vols. (1952), III, 106, italics mine; Eastlake: *Hints on Household Taste* (1868), 17. I have selected the instances in the text to illustrate the shifts and varieties of meaning and their diagnostic uses only.

6. Bülow to Jessie Laussot, May 4, 1874, *Briefe und Schriften*, ed. Marie von Bülow, 8 vols. (1895–96; 2nd ed., 1896–1908), V, 178.

Mabel Barrows, not quite sixteen.

THE LINE OF BEAUTY

Athletic: "Don't *you* bicycle?"

Esthetic: "Er—no. It develops the c of the legs so! Makes 'em stick out, know! So coarse! Positive deformit

I

(1) *The Great Social Evil.* A much-reproduced mid-nineteenth-century cartoon, it draws a rather obvious but still poignant contrast between the miserable street walkers standing in the rain, "not a hundred miles" from London's theatre district, and the glorified, pampered, if tubercular courtesan of Giuseppe Verdi's *La Traviata.* (2) *The Line of Beauty, Punch,* 1879. The candor that a respectable, self-censoring, "genteel" nineteenth century could afford: *Punch* lampooned effeminate aesthetes to general amusement for decades.

H. Lüder, *Vor der Polizei-Wache*. A Berlin prostitute being handed into a police wagon. The action takes place around 1880.

Dante Gabriel Rossetti, *Found*. Pathos: the country boy and his lost love.

Abraham Solomon, *The Lion in Love*. One among a number of versions exploring this fertile theme.

Guillaume Geefs, *The Lion in Love*. Geefs (1805–1883) was a prominent, highly regarded Belgian sculptor in his time, although by the turn of the century his reputation had dropped disastrously.

John Bell, *Una and the Lion*, in Parian ware made after the model Bell designed in 1847; one version was exhibited at the Crystal Palace in 1851.

I

(1) Guillaume Geefs, *Geneviève of Brabant*, shown at the Crystal Palace exhibition in 1851. (2) Guillaume Geefs, *The Faithful Messenger*, another contribution to the Great Exhibition.

moved from physical to psychological causes in confiding his state to his
diary: "The nervous excitement in which I have been living for some
weeks has depressed me considerably," and he included among the sources
of his depression doubts about his friends, the illness of his mother, and "a
new love which can only end in renunciation."[7] His enumeration and,
even more significantly, his association of these grounds for nervousness
—his friends, his mother, his love—strongly hint at an inchoate awareness
that his malaise was the somatic equivalent of erotic conflicts. Texts from
other countries tell the same story: difficult and uncertain loves got on
nineteenth-century nerves; a quavering voice, a trembling hand, a twitch-
ing face betrayed the anxious, often sexual, turmoil within.

By the 1860s and 1870s, physicians and popular journalists had promoted
the idea of nervousness into a widely discussed phenomenon, and cultural
critics began to link it to the stresses they thought typical of, in fact,
virtually unique to, the society of their time. Zola called Hippolyte
Taine a "sick and restless spirit" filled with "passionate aspirations toward strength and the free life," a product of "our century of nerves."
That was in 1866; more than two decades later, Vincent Van Gogh
tentatively predicted that "perhaps some day everyone will be neurotic."
Almost everyone, it would seem, already was. In 1887, an anonymous
German journalist reported to his readers, a little sententiously, that "the
modern disease" was making "rapid progress" among city dwellers:
"everyone is nervous." The bearing of these observations was plain:
nervousness was very widespread, on the increase, and characteristic.
Even children could not escape: in 1895, the *New Haven Leader* carried
a prominent two-column advertisement for "Paine's Celery Compound,"
a natural medicine designed to "strengthen" youngsters displaying the
dread symptoms haunting this century of nerves. "Nervous exhaustion in
children," the copy writer asserted, "is worrying a great many fathers and
mothers these days," and its cause was "the hurry and bustle of modern
life," which produces "a constantly increasing strain upon grown men
and women," and brings "nervousness" in its train.[8]

By the 1890s, the arguments adduced in the advertisement for Paine's
Celery Compound—if not for the compound itself—appeared compelling.

---

7. Heinrich Sahler to Jeannettchen: July 12, 1870, Köln, Historisches Archiv;
Leixner: December 9, 1874, Journal IV, Berlin Stabi.
8. Zola: *Mes Haines, Oeuvres*, ed. Eugène Fasquelle, 50 vols. (1927–29), XL, 158–
9; Van Gogh: Meyer Schapiro, *Vincent Van Gogh* (1952), 33; "Everyone is
nervous": *Der Sammler* [Augsburg], May 10, 1887, p. 6; *New Haven Leader*: April
, 1895.

Observations detailing the modern malaise often did not mention nervousness in so many words, but described its workings: in his *Scholar Gipsy*
Matthew Arnold had already gloomily surveyed

> this strange disease of modern life,
> With its sick hurry, its divided aims.

In the 1860s, psychiatrists like Henry Maudsley confidently asserted that
modern civilization is pathogenic. These diagnosticians in poetry and prose
would find, in the following decades, impressive evidence to corroborate
their educated guesses, little to induce them to modify, let alone discard
them. In fact, the intimate continuous interplay of modern love and
modern nervousness did not remain wholly repressed. I have already
quoted a line from Arthur Symons: "The modern malady of love is
nerves." His poem goes on to define that malady as a paralyzing, unconquerable erotic self-consciousness:

> Love, once a simple madness, now observes
> The stages of his passionate disease,
> And is twice sorrowful because he sees,
> Inch by inch entering, the fatal knife.

Such tainted, sickly love was psychological in its effects but social in its
origins.

Yet it was not necessarily everyone's lot; while Symons did not explicitly say so, his readers easily understood him to portray, not without
some self-satisfaction, the sensitive outsider ill at ease in bluff, hearty
sports-loving England. Symons's nervous lover was the devotee of refinement and experimentation in poetry and the arts, a member of the select
somewhat effete coterie of "intense" aesthetes whom that gifted philistine
George du Maurier, had been cruelly lampooning in the pages of *Punch*
for two decades. Nervousness was, on Symons's showing, the splendid
defect of the happy few, a stigma of high civilization devoutly cultivated
and proudly displayed. Others in the moralistic Anglo-Saxon societies
deplored this sort of nervous self-consciousness as an ominous decline from
manliness. In the much-quoted diatribe that Henry James lends Basil
Ransom, his engaging, reactionary Southern male in *The Bostonians*
nervous disorders and sexual impotence are linked, and frightening
phenomena. Displaying some hysterical touches of his own, Ransom rants
against his time, that "feminine, nervous, hysterical, chattering, canting

ge."[9] Complacent or appalled, nineteenth-century students of their culture agreed that nervousness was a pervasive symptom.

While a few, like Symons, singled out the exquisite and the cultivated as conspicuous nervous types, far more observers thought women the most likely victims. As early as the 1840s, when the discussion of contemporary nervousness was just getting under way, two Americans, Catharine Beecher and Dr. William Alcott, suggested that women's susceptibility to nervous strain was no accident. Alcott largely contented himself with citing "those indefinable and indescribable feelings of ennui" that trouble women and which, "for want of a better name, are called, in their various forms, 'nervousness.' " Once prey to such feelings, female sufferers would seek relief in compulsively consuming excessive amounts of sweets and coffee or tea, become addicted to ammonia, camphor, and cologne, or, in extreme cases, to laudanum and antimony. Beecher, more rewarding, proceeded to a political diagnosis: American women, especially those of the "middle ranks," were nervous because they were idle, kept from deploying their natural gifts.[10] Thus the general preoccupation with nervousness impinged on the burgeoning mid-nineteenth-century woman's movement: anti-feminists argued that women must remain at home and devote themselves exclusively to housekeeping and motherhood because they are too fragile, too nervous, to enter the world; feminists, drawing on the same material, countered that women needed unobstructed access to higher education, the professions, and the vote because it was their very vegetating in abject, stultifying domesticity that made them nervous. The feminists read nervousness not as a cause but as an effect. The passage of time would prove them right.

But men, too, were nervous. That is why students of the phenomenon began to hunt for an explanation that would account for more than women's striking vulnerability to attacks of nerves. That advertisement in the *New Haven Leader* had accused what it had called "the hurry and bustle of modern life." But the discovery that the cause of modern nervousness was modern civilization itself was, though resounding, not very informative. Slowly, slightly less vague, slightly less rhetorical explanations

9. Arnold: *The Scholar Gipsy* (1852–53), *The Poems of Matthew Arnold*, ed. Kenneth Allott (1965; 2nd ed. Miriam Allott, 1979), 366; Maudsley: *The Physiology and Pathology of the Mind* (1867), Part 2, ch. 1; Symons: see note 4 above; James: *The Bostonians* (1886; Introd. Lionel Trilling, 1952), 289 [ch. 34].

10. William Alcott: *The Young Woman's Guide to Excellence* (1840; 13th ed., 1847), 295–99; Catharine Beecher: *Treatise on Domestic Economy* (1842), Kathryn Kish Sklar, *Catharine Beecher: A Study in American Domesticity* (1973), 306.

became available. As far back as the early 1850s, Elizabeth Gaskell had
supplied her heroine in *North and South*, Margaret Hale, with a reflective
speech in which she attributes industrial unrest to the unassimilable impulses swamping nineteenth-century urban existence: " 'It is the town
life,' said she. 'Their nerves are quickened by the haste and bustle and
speed of everything around them.' " The countryside, with its outdoor
pursuits, seemed far healthier to her.[11]

Gaskell was speaking of the industrial working class. But her view was
even more forcibly applied to the middle classes as the discussion of
nervousness grew more anxious, the coverage more abundant. By 1879,
Frederic Harrison, the distinguished English positivist, could deplore
"that rattle and restlessness of life which belongs to the industrial maelstrom wherein we ever revolve." Possibly the most appalling detritus that
this maelstrom left in its wake, he thought, was the massive quantity of
trash that the printing presses were pouring out, trash which, Harrison
almost helplessly proposed, should all be thrown into the dust bin.[12] It
was hardly a sophisticated response. In the next decade and after, this
sort of aristocratic despair was thoroughly democratized, reaching those
efficient transmission belts of learned attitudes to a half-learned public,
the popular weeklies. Before 1900, almost everyone knew all about
nervousness.

The Germans in particular made *Nervosität* their own. By 1900, the
once famous cultural historian Karl Lamprecht saw it as the defining
characteristic of the modern German mind. A decade before, in 1890, the
Gartenlaube, always keen on keeping its readership up to date on new
developments in medicine and hygiene, printed two articles on the subject.
The first, on the games of the young, by C. Falkenhorst, advocated vigorous outdoor sports as a sure antidote to the prevailing unhealthly emphasis
on mental training, with its attendant depressing effects. "Our youth,"
Falkenhorst thought, has become "blasé"; it "lacks the cheerful disposition
that used to distinguish earlier generations." While he did not spell it out,
Falkenhorst was joining the camp of the anxiety-ridden eugenicists and
populationists, who were noisily deploring the shortage of virile young
men to serve in the wars of the future, what with *Gymnasiasten* wearing
glasses, flexing feeble muscles, ruining their health with masturbation,
and sealing their doom by contracting venereal diseases. The sexual implications of nervousness, if not its roots, were obvious to Falkenhorst.

11. Gaskell, *North and South* (1855; ed. Dorothy Collin, 1970), 376 [ch. 37].
12. John Gross: *The Rise and Fall of the Man of Letters: A Study of the Idiosyncratic and the Humane in Modern Literature* (1969; ed. 1970), 115–16.

and, he feared, highly visible in his country. His article opens with a generalization that neither he nor his readers thought needed proof: "Our age suffers from nervous weakness; it is the malady of the nineteenth century," the "consequence of a way of life altered with the progress of our civilization, which strains the mind and neglects the body."[13]

Professor Dr. E. Heinrich Kisch, that fashionable resort physician who specialized in female disorders and who addressed the troubling matter of painful nerves in the next number of the Gartenlaube, did not materially dissent from Falkenhorst. His advice, indeed, encapsulated the current wisdom: "The best protection against nervous pains always consists of carefully managing one's nervous energies" by avoiding excessive mental and physical strain, by taking systematic physical exercise, observing a "rational rhythm of work and recreation," and, finally, "toughening up one's body and steeling one's psychological powers of resistance, doing everything to prevent our sensitivity from degenerating into weak sensibility, our emotions into delicacy."[14] Sexual innuendo was rarely absent from learned discussion on this topic. In the Germany of the 1880s and 1890s, as in Germany's much-admired England, nervousness appeared as a failure of nerve, a menacing effeminacy that could be alleviated, or wholly cured, by strenuous sports, cold showers, and the vigorous reassertion of male superiority.

The appearance of Professor Dr. Kisch in the pages of the Gartenlaube —by no means the only time a distinguished authority deigned to address the general reader there—hints at the intensity of professional concern, coupled with the appetite of a wide public for information about the latest researches in the matter of nerves. Indeed, physicians earnestly pursued this modern uneasiness in their own technical journals and in lectures to their colleagues. In 1893, Dr. Wilhelm Erb, an eminent nerve specialist with an extensive bibliography on syphilis and an impressive reputation, published an essay characteristic of this professional worry, "On the Growing Nervousness of Our Time." Its title states Erb's conviction that nervousness was indubitably on the rise. "Political, social, and cultural conditions," he argued, have "an immense influence on man's nervous system," and that system had in the past century experienced "frightful convulsions" beginning with the French Revolution and continuing with the uninterrupted "excitement" of the Napoleonic wars, the rise of nationalism, the revolutions of 1848. To this formidable list, Erb added "the rapid growth of large cities with all its unfortunate con-

13. Falkenhorst, "Jugendspiel," Gartenlaube, XXXVIII (1890), 219–20.
14. Kirsch, "Nervenschmerzen," ibid., 236–36.

sequences: the creation of mighty industrial centers filled with proletarians." Not all of these shocks had been caused by misfortunes: much like Durkheim, Erb took progress itself, the very achievements of the age, to be a prominent cause of nervous disorders. Again, much like Durkheim, he argued that increasing luxury had created unprecedented opportunities, stimulated new needs, and thus fed discontent. The age had fostered mental overburdening in the universities and the professions alike and, with that, a damaging reliance on such stimulants as alcohol, coffee, late nights, pulsating music, and suggestive plays. The multiplication of traffic, the invention of the telegraph and telephone, the conversion of night into day had further exacerbated the "haste and agitation." The very search for relaxation only aggravated already barely tolerable tensions and pushed nerves over the edge. Modern culture stirs up sensuality, heats up the lust for pleasure. No wonder, Erb concludes, that "nervous illnesses," notably hysteria, hypochondria and, above all, "neurasthenia," have increased dramatically. It was all, Erb thought, very worrisome.[15]

Other Germans thought so too. Some, who did not initiate their own research, imported it: after the prolific Italian sexologist Paolo Mantegazza brought out his *Il secolo nevrosico* in 1886, a German version, *Das nervöse Jahrhundert*, was promptly prepared and followed two years later. The great Krafft-Ebing soon joined in. In a study of 1895, he insisted that "nervousness is rising fatally," spurred on by "antihygienic elements" like rapid and abrupt changes in the "mercantile, industrial, agrarian," to say nothing of the "political and social" conditions of civilized countries.[16] He was saying nothing new: in 1893, a group of ten specialists from German-speaking countries had published a handbook on neurasthenia complete with a bibliography of more than a hundred titles that had appeared since 1881 in the German language alone.[17] They made their compilation in the midst of a vigorous and inconclusive debate in Germany over the question of overburdening students in *Gymnasium* and university alike. Emperor Wilhelm II intervened in his impulsive and intrusive way, but the experts reached no final agreement: while sympathetic pedagogues cautioned against excessive intellectual burdens as the agents of nervous collapse and, all too often, of suicide, some moralists found the modern

15. Erb, "Über die wachsende Nervosität unserer Zeit" (1893), *Gesammelte Abhandlungen*, 2 vols. (1910), II, 279–99 passim.
16. Krafft-Ebing, *Nervosität und neurasthenische Zustände* (1895).
17. *Handbuch der Neurasthenie* (1893). Andreas Steiner, "*Das nervöse Zeitalter.*" *Der Begriff der Nervosität bei Laien und Ärzten in Deutschland und Österreich um 1900* (1964), 36.

youngster only too spoiled and unhappily spared the hardships essential
for proper character formation. "In addition to our rushed existence," the
minor philosopher Bartholomäus von Carneri concluded, "modern education is one of the principal causes of that nervousness that is growing more
and more common."[18] If the compilers of the *Handbuch der Neurasthenie*
had proceeded to a second edition after 1893, they would have made it
far more voluminous.

For all this massive outpouring, the descriptions and diagnoses of nervousness offered during these decades varied little; they remained mired
in imprecise generalities, colorful laments, and facile slogans. How slowly
clinical understanding had advanced even after 1900 emerges from one
of the most perceptive and engaging representatives in the literature,
J. A. Hobson's *Psychology of Jingoism*, published under the impress of
English bellicosity during the Boer War. Though observant and fiercely
independent, Hobson speaks with the voice of earlier explorers. Sounding
much like Elizabeth Gaskell half a century before him, he found that "the
bad conditions of town life in our great industrial centres, lowering the
vitality of the inhabitants, operate with peculiar force upon their nervous
organization." The "nervous wear and tear" that "the constant struggle
for a livelihood" imposes is "so grave" that it becomes "quite apparent in
the features of a town population," which "marks them out with tolerable
distinctness from country folk. In every nation, which has proceeded far
in modern industrialism," Hobson added, here echoing the Frederic
Harrison of 1879, "the prevalence of neurotic diseases attests the general
nervous strain to which the population is subjected."[19] Nor was Hobson
particularly innovative in his view that modern urban civilization floods
individuals with streams of hectic impressions, drowns them in emotions
they cannot absorb or even sort out, let alone master. His exposition invites, as it implies, not merely the aquatic, but also the electric metaphors
to which late-nineteenth-century writers were addicted: the mind of
modern town dwellers is like a vulnerable, heavily used power plant
repeatedly put out of commission by unmanageable drains on its resources.

This favorite, unmistakably modern metaphor ranged nervousness
among other mental ailments generally thought to be somatic both in
symptoms and origins. It illustrates the widespread ambivalence over the
place of mind in human experience. Right through the nineteenth century, specialists in nervous diseases carried on an impassioned controversy
over whether neuroses and psychoses are congenital and physiological, or

18. Carneri, *Der moderne Mensch*, 26.
19. Hobson, *The Psychology of Jingoism* (1901), 7-8.

acquired and psychological in nature. By and large, the theorists defending
their mental origins were in a minority. The famous English neurologist
Henry Maudsley spoke for a solid majority when he laid it down in 1874,
that "it is not our business, it is not in our power, to explain *psychologically*
the origin and nature" of insanity; indeed, "the explanation, when it
comes, will come not from the mental, but from the physical side."[20]
Moreover, it would come, most of his fellow investigators thought, from
the genetic side; Emile Zola's doomed mad characters following out their
assigned destiny were astonishing only in being so emphatically indebted
to their malign inheritance. There was some informed and powerful
dissent: the great Philippe Pinel had introduced what came to be called
"medical psychology" around 1800, and some of his radical ideas had
radiated out from France. Specialists in hysteria, notably Robert Brudenell
Carter in mid-century England and Jean-Martin Charcot in Paris a decade
or two later, established an influential countercurrent that kept the debate
alive and, in the long run, made it scientifically productive. It is poignant
to see Freud around 1890 and after feeling his way toward his discoveries, manfully wrestling with the reigning physiological persuasion
and employing, ever more confidently, psychological explanations for
psychological ailments. He had strong resistance to overcome, including
his own.

Until psychoanalysis gave the study of nervousness a new direction, the
massive literature growing up around it came to be highly predictable
and long remained strikingly inconclusive. But the oppressive generalizations dominating that literature were at least partially subverted, even
before Freud, by those who refused to treat nervousness as an unequivocal calamity. The pioneering American neurologist Dr. George Beard,
in fact, made his reputation by showing how to extract rewards from
misery. He was not alone. Witness Arthur Symons's half alarmed, half
complacent anatomy of "nerves," and Dr. Wilhelm Erb, who had made
progress a cause of nervousness, though not nervousness a cause of progress. Earlier, Edmond de Goncourt had been prepared to underscore the
cultural benefits of nerves: "Remember," he wrote, "that our work rests
on nervous malady; that is perhaps its originality." The German poet
Richard Dehmel agreed. "To open all the senses, *that* frees the soul. We
cannot get excited enough!" he wrote in 1894. "Our nervousness is a true
blessing, which our fools deplore. It is nothing less than an instinctual aid

20. Michael J. Clark, "The Rejection of Psychological Approaches to Mental Disorder in Late-Nineteenth-Century British Psychiatry," Andrew Scull, ed., *Madhouses
Mad-Doctors, and Madmen: The Social History of Psychiatry in the Victorian Era*
(1981), 271.

rom nature, to bring a bit of fresh pulse into our dulled cultural blood.
How nervous the Renaissance was!"[21] These assertions were variants on
the avant-garde theme of the damned artist, the inspired madman, the
chosen spirit who translates the traumas of his culture into imperishable
creations. But Beard boldly extended this paradox to businessmen and
housewives, good bourgeois all, who in their own mundane way demonstrated that nervousness had its uses. It seemed, to Beard, the necessary
defect of some noteworthy achievements.

Dr. George M. Beard was a power to reckon with in his time and
beyond, abroad still more than in the United States. His books were
seriously discussed and quickly translated, and his controversial ideas
faithfully quoted in Europe. When, in 1885, the readers of the *Gartenlaube*
were made acquainted with the great mental healer, German physicians
had long known about him.[22] Thomas Alva Edison, with whom Beard
had worked on some electrical experiments in the mid-1870s, continued to
profess his respect for him as a "logical and conservative" scientific
worker; the German sex specialist, Dr. Albert Moll, declared himself
happy as late as 1910, almost three decades after Beard's death, to write
an introduction to his selected papers. Born in 1839, in Connecticut, the
son of a relatively impecunious and conspicuously devout Congrega-
tionalist minister, he attended boarding school at Andover and graduated
from Yale in 1862, determined to become a physician, and a distinguished
one. "An enthusiastic disciple of Hippocrates," he called himself in 1863
in a letter to his fiancée, and his career, enlivened by disputes and crowned
with triumphs, bears him out. It was concentrated and intense, cut short
by pneumonia in 1883. A restless experimenter and accomplished debater,
a prolific popularizer, Beard courted controversy and, rather given to
self-exploration, knew it: "Several courses I have taken have made me
enemies," he wrote when he was in his third year at Yale. "I am willing,
I desire to have opposition, if it comes legitimately. In fact, I covet it."[23]
One of the activities that brought him the opposition he craved was
exposing charlatans claiming mediumistic powers.

It was as an experimental scientist lusting for the posture of gladiator
that Beard early began to play with "electrotherapy," to the amusement
of his family and the dismay of his fellow physicians. While he was still

21. Goncourt: Paul Bourget, *Essais de psychologie contemporaine*, 2 vols. (1883–85),
II, 162; Dehmel: to Hedwig Lachmann, August 16, 1894, *Ausgewählte Briefe aus den
Jahren 1883 bis 1902*, ed. Isi Dehmel (1922), 169.
22. A. Lammers, "Trinkgewohnheiten der Völker," *Gartenlaube*, XXXII (1885), 60.
23. Beard: to Elizabeth Alden, August 21, 1863; Edison: to Grace Beard, October
15, 1908; Moll: to the same, January 13, 1910; February 3, 1861, "Journal of George
Miller Beard," p. 157, series I and II, box 1, George M. Beard Papers, Y-MA.

at Andover, he had gone to "see a lady who cures diseases by electricity," and had become converted to the treatment. "Electricity helps me very much," he noted; at Yale, he bought himself a battery that he kept in his room for further experimentation.[24] Beard's first publication, in 1866, the year he graduated from medical school, was a paper on "Electricity as a Tonic," and, after his death in 1883, a classmate recalled that Beard had become passionately engaged with electricity precisely because medical circles thought so little of it.[25] He was, as his friends could not help observing, a man of original powers never content with his gifts. All his life, Beard was fighting more battles than he knew.

Like most of his contemporaries, Beard, too, was intermittently afflicted by ill health. His mother had died when he was three; most of his family, as his correspondence attests, suffered from one disorder after another, often tenacious and sometimes threatening. His sister Susan reported, among other ailments, "nervousness—headaches—weariness.' Beard came by his obsessions honestly. The journal he kept during his youth exhibits his preoccupations with the minutiae of his physical and mental condition: he is beset with ringing in his ears, he is depressed, he needs to gain weight, he has hurt his knee. Nervousness entered this clinical picture early and prophetically: in March 1858, he consulted "an Eclectic physician" only to be told "there was little vitality in me—was very nervous—must avoid mental application." When he came to Yale, in "the City of Elms, surrounded by convenience and luxury," his weight went up and his general condition much improved, but he continued to monitor his body with a kind of compulsive tenderness, an anxious narcissistic dwelling on his weight, his stamina, his fat cheeks.[26]

Beard's chosen adversary was his appetite. The need to control his craving for food and worldly pleasure punctuates his thinking like so many sobering reminders. In his young years, before he discreetly discarded the conventional pieties he had absorbed at home and among his friends, he was something of a prig; not content with faithfully attending divine services and running Sunday school classes, he took frequent occasion to deplore the low moral standards of his schoolmates: "*Drink, ride, carouse—swear*—is this enlightened New England? A pious young man is like a lamb among wolves." To wrestle down the wolf-like ravening desires lurking in his own mind, he adopted stern resolutions to work harder, eat less, help others, think better thoughts; he tried to steady his

24. August 8, 30, 1858, Journal, pp. 107, 112, ibid.
25. *Class of 1862 Yale. Portraits and Sketches* (1899), 241, 246–47.
26. October 1861 (?), March, September 28 (?), 1858, Journal, pp. 181, 73, 113, Beard Papers.

character by constructing a cage of proverbs within which he might safely live. " 'Order is Heaven's first law,' " he wrote, quoting some unnamed moralist, and added: "System is essential to success—something determined, set, fixed upon is necessary." Pretentious as these youthful formulations may be, they point toward the equipment essential to the effective mental healer: "I have learned to read men," he wrote in 1858, just before entering Yale, mingled with all conditions of men, "sounded the great fundamental principles of human Nature," and, disclosing the relevance of such abstract attainments to himself, studied "the laws of my physical constitution. I have regained my health." A few days later he quoted the inescapable "Know Thyself" in Greek, and commented, "How important!"[27]

Self-knowledge was important for George Beard principally to help him attack, if never wholly resolve, the conflict between his wish to conform and his need to rebel. His hectic professional life provided a viable, somewhat unstable compromise; in 1856, his father had, rather dourly, warned him against the perils of success—"immoderate elation of too great self dependence or of an over estimate of our powers, attainments and goodness"—but Beard could never resist the temptations of popularity, even notoriety.[28] In a medical career spanning only seventeen years, Beard gave uncounted lectures and demonstrations, ran a busy practice, traveled widely, published scores of articles and ten books, pioneered the study of such puzzling ailments as seasickness, at once somatic and psychological, and coined the term "neurasthenia." He was a physician who never wearied of warning the world against the perils of overdrawing one's bank account of nervous energy, and his life stands as a refutation of his theories.

His most influential book was doubtless *A Practical Treatise on Nervous Exhaustion (Neurasthenia), Its Symptoms, Nature, Sequences, Treatment,* published in 1880, and almost immediately translated into German. Its sequel, on *American Nervousness, Its Causes and Consequences,* which followed the next year, also aroused intense international discussion. The German response was warm appreciation not unmixed with *Schadenfreude*: it seemed appropriate somehow that an American physician should have isolated the syndrome of neurasthenia. As the Swiss neurologist Otto Ludwig Binswanger put it in 1896, Beard's claim that neurasthenia had first emerged in the United States was "of course" erroneous; still, the nationality of its "discoverer" vividly demonstrates the "inti-

27. Ca. June 11, March, August, August 29, 1858, pp. 93, 75, 104, 108, ibid.
28. Spencer F. Beard to George M. Beard, December 1, 1856, ibid.

mate connections" between the ailment and "modern life," with its "unbridled hurrying and hunting after money and property, the immense
progress in the technological arena."[29] The United States, after all, was
rapidly becoming the most advanced of all industrial nations and must
therefore display the most flamboyant symptoms of nervousness.

Dr. Beard gladly admitted—practically boasted—that the United States
led the world in neurasthenia; other countries, like Great Britain, were
making impressive strides in catching up, but so far to no avail. In his
own country, as Beard documented with numerous, often curious examples, almost everyone was neurasthenic; indeed, American blacks had
grown more nervous since their emancipation from slavery. Nervousness,
Beard wrote, at one with specialists everywhere, was on the rise across
the cultivated world. But this was not wholly a bad thing: Beard's
American Nervousness, relatively optimistic in tone, is his richest, in a
special way his most deeply felt book, an exercise in patriotism almost as
much as a contribution to classifying diseases.

America's special place among nervous nations, and the increasing
nervousness of its citizens, black and white alike, was in Beard's view
perfectly natural: "Modern nervousness is the cry of the system struggling with its environment." As always, civilization is exacting its pound
of flesh. Beard postulated that the nervous races and classes are more
civilized and that "brain workers," the most nervous of all, live longest.
Yet the price is admittedly high. Nervousness manifests itself in an
assortment of disagreeable symptoms: "Insomnia, flushing, drowsiness,
bad dreams, cerebral irritation, dilated pupils, pain, pressure and heaviness in the head . . . noises in the ears . . . mental irritability, tenderness
of the teeth and gums . . . sweating hands and feet with redness, fear of
lightning, or fear of responsibility, of open places or of closed places, fear
of society, fear of being alone, fear of fears, fear of contamination, fear
of everything . . ."—all of these indications that the reserves of mental
strength have been exhausted.[30]

Certain general symptoms of nervousness are most noticeable in "the
higher orders" of America. They show an increased sensitivity and susceptibility to stimulants and narcotics; Americans, as Europeans always
note with astonishment, cannot hold their liquor; many of them do not
drink at all, and few of them can really stand smoking. "To see how an

29. Sigmund Freud, "Die 'kulturelle' Sexualmoral und die moderne Nervosität"
(1908), *St.A.*, IX, 15–16; " 'Civilized' Sexual Morality and Modern Nervous Illness," *S.E.*, IX, 184.
30. Beard, *American Nervousness, Its Causes and Consequences. A Supplement to
Nervous Exhaustion (Neurasthenia)* (1881), 138, 7.

Englishman can drink is alone worth the ocean voyage." As for the Germans: "Gallons upon gallons of their summer beer" they "will drink day after day or in a single evening, a quantity of fluid, considered merely as water, that would suffice a brain-working, indoor-living American for a week or month." Beard finds it equally remarkable how sensitive Americans have become to medication; they require smaller doses than anyone else in other countries. Their labile state is evidenced by indigestion, loss of appetite, the spread of nearsightedness, the early, rapid decay of teeth: "Dr. J. N. Farrar, of New York, estimates that $500,000 in pure gold is each year put into the mouths of Americans." Baldness, too, is becoming more visible in the United States, as is susceptibility to heat or cold. Ominously but predictably, Americans have taken to dosing themselves freely: "America is a nation of drug takers."[31]

When Beard moves from symptoms to causes, he is, if anything, even freer of nagging doubts. He emphatically does not rule out climate or race from the etiology of nervousness, but insists that the "chief and primary cause" of the "very rapid increase of nervousness," is *modern civilization*, which is distinguished from the ancient by these five characteristics: steam power, the periodical press, the telegraph, the sciences, and the mental activity of women." To this terse catalogue he adds political machines, "the religious excitements that are the sequels of Protestantism," the intricacies of education, and the "evil" of "specialization." Beard is prepared to offer details: he cites the rigidity of modern schedules, the omnipresence of demanding clocks and enforced punctuality, the ill effects of noise, the increased vogue for travel, the accelerating circulation of new ideas, the systematic and exacerbated form of gambling known as stock speculation, the accumulated capacity for such feelings as sorrow—witness philanthropy—and the conventional "repression of emotion" that keeps people from laughing and crying freely.[32]

Even freedom makes Americans nervous, especially when it lures them into the political game. "Before the late election," Beard recalls, in one of the most astonishing paragraphs in this astonishing book, "one of my patients informed me, to my alarm, that he was getting interested in politics. He had been treated most successfully for nerve troubles, two years ago, and had been put into working order, and had been able to work hard; but I knew that, like most of his class, he was living on a small reserve of nerve force." Apparently Beard's patient could not resist the pernicious, glittering bait of national affairs. "He said that great issues

31. Ibid., 34, 32, 48, 64.
32. Ibid., vi, 99, 58.

were before us, and the neglect of politics on the part of intelligent men was the ruin of their nation." Beard vigorously remonstrated: " 'My friend,' " he told him, " 'presidents and politicians are chips and foam on the surface of the sea; they are not the sea; tossed up by the tide and left on the shore, but they are not the tide; fold your arms and go to bed and most of the evils of this world will correct themselves, and, of those that remain, few will be modified by anything that you or I can do.' " As Beard had anticipated, his patient paid no attention to this advice, and "A day or two before the election," he "came to my office, entirely prostrated, and confessed a most interesting fact—that five minutes conversation on politics had taken all his nerve from him, doing more to exhaust him than months of steady work."[33]

But Beard, as I have noted, finds compensations. One, on which he dwells with evident relish and which has particular resonance for the historian of love, is "the phenomenal beauty of the American girl," a lovely sight he considers "of the greatest interest both to the physiologist and the sociologist, since it has no precedent, in recorded history, at least." He explains it partly by climate, which makes for "fineness of organization," partly by the way that American girls are "pushed forward," and "rapidly," into school, into society, hence into conversation and entertainment. For Beard, as for other neurologists of his century the physical and the mental continuously interact—here, for the American girl, with the happiest possible result. As her "mental faculties" are quickly developed, her cerebral beauty grows and is joined to fineness of organization; "by the union of those two, human beauty reaches its highest." Beard was willing to concede that "handsome women are found here and there in Great Britain, and rarely in Germany; more frequently in France and Austria, in Italy and Spain; and in all these countries one may find individuals that approximate the highest type of American beauty." But they cannot measure up. "In America, it is the extent—the commonness of this beauty, which is so remarkably, unprecedentedly, and scientifically interesting. It is not possible to go to an opera in any of our large cities without seeing more of the representatives of the highest type of female beauty than can be found in months of travel in any part of Europe." Hence Beard attributes the "almost universal homeliness of female faces among European works of art" to the fact that "the best of the masters never saw a handsome woman. One can scarcely believe that Rubens, had he lived in America, or even in England, at the present time, would have given us such imposing and terrible types of female countenances.

33. Ibid., 124–25.

If Raphael had been wont to see every day in Rome or Naples what he would now see every day in New York, Baltimore, or Chicago, it would seem probable that, in his Sistine Madonna he would have preferred a face of, at least, moderate beauty, to the neurasthenic and anemic type that is there represented."[34]

It is fitting that Beard intended the book on which he was working when death silenced him as an extension of his great discovery, neurasthenia, into the realm of sexual malfunctioning; he saw the phenomenal beauty of the American girl, and the susceptibility of the American male to that beauty, as the ambiguous achievements of high civilization. "Sexual neurasthenia" was, for Beard, a "special variety" of the general syndrome. The symptoms were the usual ones: impotence, spermatorrhea, depression, "morbid fears of morbid impulses." Its causes, though, were fairly complex; they included "evil habits," the excessive use of tobacco and alcohol, even (once again) the climate, but all these were "secondary to the one great predisposing cause—civilization." And, just as Americans were, for well known reasons, the most nervous people in the world, so sexual neurasthenia was "more common in America than in any other country"; the harsh climate and the "opportunities and necessities of a rising civilization in a new and immense continent" made this dubious preeminence inescapable.[35]

At the same time, these were only the gloomy shadows in a nuanced picture. "The Indian squaw," Beard noted, "keeps almost all of her force in reserve," for she is, as he nicely put it, "unblessed and uncursed by the exhausting sentiment of love." Yet consider, in contrast, "the sensitive white woman—preeminently the American woman, with small inherited endowment of force; living in-doors; torn and crossed by happy or unhappy love; subsisting on fiction, journals, receptions; way-laid at all hours by the cruellest of robbers, worry and ambition." She can "never hold a powerful reserve, but must live and does live, in a physical sense, from hand to mouth, giving out quite as fast as she takes in—much faster often times—and needing long periods of rest before and after any important campaign." Yet she lives "as long as her Indian sister—much longer, it may be," bearing "age far better, and carrying the affections and the feelings of youth into the decline of life." Unlike the Indian squaw, in short, the sensitive American woman is both blessed and cursed by love. Beard proposes to resolve this curious conundrum

34. Ibid., 65–67.
35. Beard, *Sexual Neurasthenia (Nervous Exhaustion). Its Hygiene, Causes, Symptoms, and Treatment, With a Chapter on Diet for the Nervous* (ed. A. D. Rockwell from the posthumous manuscript, 1884), 14–16.

by means of what he calls "physical analyses," which turn out to be the old mechanical hydraulic and electrical metaphors: the mind is like a clock or a furnace or a power plant which, however vulnerable to shock or over-use, functions well if it is continuously wound up or replenished.[36] The lesson is plain to Beard, who never lacked in self-confidence, at least in print: industrial bourgeois civilization is tiring, overpowering, the source of strain. The sentiment of love characteristic of it is nothing less than exhausting. But, having listed in the finest detail the sufferings to which cultivated modern urban men and women are condemned, Beard finds it possible to conclude that he would not have it otherwise.

The involuntary humor of Dr. Beard's chain of reasoning and parade of witnesses, like the incurable imprecision of other students of modern nervousness, only consolidates their utility as clues to their culture. Responsible physicians and philosophers agreed, without audible dissent, dependable evidence, or precise definitions, that the incidence of nervousness had markedly accelerated in the late nineteenth century. They had no way of measuring its incidence in their own time, no rational comparisons with earlier ages, no statistics of any kind. They made do with anecdotal case reports, casual observations, seductive metaphors, literary fancies. Nor did it occur to them that the new alertness to neurasthenia across Western civilization—that alertness, at all events, was beyond doubt—might simply reflect an unprecedented sensitivity to an old ailment known under other names. Besides, the symptoms of contemporary culture they liked to adduce in proof were, though plausible enough villains, not really demonstrated agents of nervousness. Modern urban life, one might argue—as some did—was a stimulating, exhilarating brew: its anonymity offering welcome escape from the prying of small-town neighbors, its bustle thrilling experiences to the energetic, its diversity an informal tuition in worldliness. After all, the modern city, to paraphrase Marx and Engels in the Communist Manifesto, had freed millions from the idiocy of rural life. The unequivocal assertions of Erb or Hobson were not statements of fact so much as manifestations of anxiety—shot through with hope in Beard's writings, but quite unrelieved in those of others. In large measure, the diagnosis of nervousness was a form of auto-intoxication on the part of the diagnosticians.

The inclination of learned men in the late nineteenth century to frighten themselves and their audiences is impressive. They dreaded spectres that they themselves had painted on the wall. For an age that prided itself

36. Ibid., 60–62.

on its science both pure and applied, the decades from the 1860s and 1870s onward swallowed more pernicious half-truths and sheer nonsense than its presumably less knowledgeable predecessors, nonsense about racial characteristics, the sway of inherited qualities, the decay of culture, and the dangers of sexual experimentation. Men of science could always mask their anxiety behind high-flown verbiage and imposing sounding theories, but it was there. Nervousness, in short, was less a pervasive symptom of bourgeois society than of those who detected it. Maladaptation to drastic social change was not the prerogative of the poor, the disinherited, the displaced.

The discovery and promotion of nervousness in the nineteenth century therefore turns out to be largely another eloquent witness to the anxiety that innovation generates. The learned and the articulate were sensitive instruments vibrating to personal, professional, and social tensions; all were reading their own temperature as the climate of opinion. Freud would later give this defensive strategy the name of projection. And there was one particular ingredient in the anxiety-making changes characterizing the century that molded the myth of neurasthenia more significantly than any other: the changing role of sexuality and the equivocal situation of love. For decades in the mid- and late nineteenth century, the sexual implications of the nervous panic over nervousness remained relatively quiescent, victimized by repression. They would not emerge into full view until Freud's brilliant paper on " 'Civilized' Sexual Morality and Modern Nervous Illness." But they had left more or less noticeable deposits in earlier texts: Mr. Wilfer, in Charles Dickens's *Our Mutual Friend*, becomes nervous in a kind of sexual panic as he thinks of confronting his formidable wife; Elizabeth Gaskell, writing to her sister-in-law, describes the bride's anticipation of the married state, and with that, of sexual initiation, as a nervous time. Otto von Leixner suffered from nervous depression as he reflected on his various travails in love. Arthur Symons virtually equated modern love with modern nerves. Dr. Beard treated sexual neurasthenia as a particularly vivid instance of general nervousness. What Freud did in his paper of 1908 was to make this erotic component of "neurasthenia" wholly explicit and elevate it into the principal cause of the phenomenon. He replaced the commonplace and indeterminate appraisal of nervousness as the price of culture with the far more precise, far more startling diagnosis of nervousness as the price of repression.

Freud opens his paper conventionally enough: he does not take issue with the accepted view that nervousness is on the rise, and quotes at some length, without demurrers, several representative authorities, including

Erb and Krafft-Ebing. He objects to their verdicts only because he thinks
them superficial, not because he thinks them wrong. But this objection
points to his analytical contribution: "The damaging influence of culture
essentially reduces itself to the harmful suppression of sexual life among
civilized nations (or strata) by means of the 'civilized' sexual morality
that prevails among them." In general, he notes, "our culture is constructed on the suppression of drives."[37] That some such suppression is
necessary is, as we know, a cardinal element in his theory of culture. But
modern middle-class civilization, Freud rather grimly insisted, exacts
excessive renunciation. It stands at the extreme end of self-denial.

Civilization, in Freud's schematic overview, goes through three stages
of acceptable sexual conduct: in the first, all sexual activity is free,
whether it aims at reproduction or not; in the second, only sexual activity
serving the purposes of reproduction is permitted; in the third, this restric-
tion becomes even more exquisite in that it officially allows only "legitimate reproduction." But many humans are so constituted that they
cannot meet the demands of the second stage, let alone those of the third.
After all, what this highest flowering of civilization "asks of the individual
is that both sexes practice abstinence until they are married."[38] Only a
select minority can remain securely perched on this level by means of
successful sublimation; others become neurotic or suffer related psychic
damage. Having educated the young to deny their most exigent drives,
culture suddenly thrusts them into a situation where satisfaction is permitted—but only within unconscionably repressive limits. Contemporary
pressures to restrict the size of families compel contraception, and all
devices known in Freud's day, in his judgment, compromised sexual
pleasure. The demand for lifelong fidelity is even more productive of
intolerable frustrations in many minds. Modern marriage, one might
epitomize Freud's bleak appraisal, is not the cure for sexual unease, but
its continuation by other means. Freud said more than once that in his
world, men's conduct in love generally bore the stamp of psychological
impotence, and that only a very few among the educated showed a proper
fusion of the tender and the sensual currents of the libidinal drive.[39] The
sacrifices that modern "civilized" sexual morality exacts, then, must make
many nervous: Freud's quotation marks around "civilized" were aggres-

37. Freud, " 'Kulturelle' Sexualmoral," *St.A.*, IX, 16–18; " 'Civilized' Sexual Morality," *S.E.*, IX, 185–86.
38. Ibid., *St.A.*, IX, 23; *S.E.*, IX, 193.
39. "Über die allgemeinste Erniedrigung des Liebeslebens" (1912), *St.A.*, V, 204;
"On the Universal Tendency to Debasement in the Sphere of Love," *S.E.*, IX, 185.

ively ironic. Modern nervousness, to state Freud's conclusion more precisely than before, is the price of *bourgeois* sexual repression.

Freud frequently returned to this bourgeois repression in his diagnosis of contemporary culture. The poor, after all, whether urban or rural, did not find it necessary, or possible, to adhere to such unrealistic moral standards. Writing to the influential American psychiatrist James J. Putnam in 1915, he said: "Sexual morality, as society—and at its most extreme, American society—defines it, seems very despicable to me. I stand for a much freer sexual life," if not for his own sake so much as for the sake of middle-class society.[40]

Freud's linking of nervousness to socially imposed sexual frustrations, reversing the accepted view that nervousness is the fruit of sexual debauchery, is the first original idea for some decades in a vast literature, and an impressive instance of his readiness to recognize cultural components in individual psychology. But, however imaginative and innovative, Freud's theory of modern nervousness did not escape the entrenched prejudices of his time. No doubt, in tracing its manifestations back to some sexual malaise, Freud perceived the genesis of "nerves" more acutely than anyone had before him. But in uncritically accepting current estimates worrying over an accelerating incidence of nervous disorders, he joined psychiatrists and journalists on rather untrustworthy and, for him, rather unfamiliar ground. Freud was, after all, a professional skeptic who rarely accepted anything on faith. His grim assessment of bourgeois sexual life underestimates the capacity of suffering young men and women to overcome, in their adult lives, the silences, evasions, and prohibitions with which they had grown up. It underestimates the erotic knowledge that respectable bourgeois could amass in their reticent, circumspect, often priggish environment. And it underestimates the openness and directness of many bourgeois confronting their erotic needs and their fulfillment in legitimate love. In company with other cultural critics, in short, Freud misread the evidence about the prudery of bourgeois culture and its baneful consequences. In many years of busy practice, Freud amassed varied and persuasive clinical material to support his conviction that those whom society condemned to years of sexual abstinence, inadequate sexual information, and lifelong sexual loyalties often developed crippling psychological maladjustments. But then, the patients Freud saw in his con-

40. Freud to Putnam (July 8, 1915), *James Jackson Putnam and Psychoanalysis. Letters between Putnam and Sigmund Freud, Ernest Jones, William James, Sandor Ferenczi, and Morton Prince, 1877–1917,* ed. Nathan G. Hale, Jr. (1971), 189. For Freud on the psychology of the poor, see below, p. 391.

sulting room were the casualties of their culture, and his habit of drawing
on them for social-psychological generalizations entangled him in some
rather dubious judgments. In general, Freud's psychoanalytic practice
and psychological theories fertilized one another. His superb gift for
detecting essential resemblances among the most diverse mental phenomena, and his assumption that neurotics are much like other people
generally served him well. But on the theme of modern nervousness—
which was, in Freud's mind, only a special aspect of the larger theme of
love—he permitted his clinical experience to throw his diagnosis of culture off course. His analysis of the untoward effects that sexual frustration
imposes on psychological well-being joined his discovery of the concealed
power of the unconscious and the phenomenon of transference to shed
desperately needed light on modern, nervous, middle-class love. But it
also partially obscured some important realities about middle-class culture
in Victoria's and Freud's decades. The casualties he treated were not
quite typical bourgeois, certainly not in their erotic lives. Freud's rather
mechanical anti-Americanism in his remarks to Putnam should have
warned us: he did not always rise above his time and class. In ways that
neither Freud—nor, for that matter, his critics—would have appreciated,
he was a representative as much as a critic of his time.[41] That nervousness
was the price of repression thus remains an unsubstantiated claim, at best
a specialized discovery.

2. From Hysteria to Remorse

Nervousness was a fantasy encapsulating a tiny core of reality; prostitution a reality enveloped in a dense fog of fantasy. Throughout the nineteenth century, venal sex was doubtless a conspicuous and distressing
presence. One could hardly evade it in the streets or certain cafés, near
railroad terminals or theaters. It fueled a thriving local and international
trade, employing women who supplemented their meager wages by
occasional street-walking or who made the "gay life" their living; it
supported pimps and white slave traders and provided supplementary
revenues to waiters and hotel keepers, to physicians, blackmailers, and

---

41. None of these cavils, I should note, in any way invalidates Freud's central
psychoanalytic propositions. They only raise questions about his cultural criticism.
See also *Education of the Senses*, 264–65, 417–18, 459–60. The most sensible dissent
from the prevailing view on nervousness that I have found is in a letter of Anton
Chekhov to Yelena Shavrova: "I can't accept the idea of 'our nervous age,' because
people have been nervous in all ages." *Letters of Anton Chekhov*, tr. Michael Henry
Heim in collaboration with Simon Karlinsky, ed. Karlinsky (1973), 270.

orrupt public officials. The business, vicious and profitable, claimed ountless victims and caused untold misery: degradation, squalor, rampant alcoholism, bouts of venereal disease, repeated prison sentences, nd, often, untimely death. Those dazzling careers enjoyed by the *randes horizontales* who slept with millionaires and princes, and who were reputed to invest the money they made with their bodies, were ntypical, the stuff of legend in more ways than one; the spectacular eports about their way of living only served to obscure the sordid fates f their far less fortunate and far more numerous colleagues in the trade. The settings in which all these mercenaries of love worked were so many vorlds: pathetic and unsanitary shacks where clients stood in line for heir quick turn, repellent rented rooms off some back alley in the rabbit varrens of nineteenth-century slums, solid middle-class houses frequented lmost as much for their music and their relaxing atmosphere in the ublic lounge as for the purchased orgasm upstairs, luxurious establishnents providing choice suppers, leisurely encounters, and an imaginative nenu of sexual services. Taken together, nineteenth-century prostitution vas the marketplace of sex, catering to every possible taste at every ossible price.

This diversity characterizing these centers of gratification mirrored, f course, that of their clients. Prostitutes, as the indignant American physician George H. Napheys complained in 1871, entertained "the gambler, the thief, the policy dealer, the ruffian; and with these, the college student, the bank clerk, the member of the fashionable club; ye, and also the father of the family, the husband of a pure wife, the nead of the firm, the member of the church; all these, every night, in ll our great cities." To hear the reformers, the modern city was nothing better than one vast, pullulating brothel. "We are all horror stricken," exclaimed an anonymous English pamphleteer in 1858, "at the extent to which prostitution is carried, throughout every rank of society."[42]

The urges that financed nineteenth-century commercial sex add up to a comprehensive catalogue of needs driving the starved sailor on shore leave, the traveling salesman briefly off the domestic leash, the tremulous school boy pushed into initiation by a genial father or shameless classmate, the boastful Don Juan wrestling with unconscious homoerotic panic, to say nothing of the surfeited sophisticate in search of a new experience, the homosexual afraid to cruise in bath houses or public urinals, and the

42. Napheys: *The Transmission of Life. Counsels on the Nature and Hygiene of the Masculine Function* (1871; new ed., 1889), 117; Anon.: *Marriage and Prostitution* (1858) [a 5-page pamphlet published at Oxford], 3.

unsatisfied husband rooting around for an erotic pleasure that he was to
maladroit to elicit or his wife too prim to supply at home. And brothe
were, of course, not the only way of selling sex in the nineteenth century
They competed with prostitutes registered with the police plying the
trade in unsavory little hotels, ragged clandestine street walkers wh
satisfied their clients for a miserable pittance in abandoned store hous
or pressed against some filthy city wall, expensive courtesans who ente
tained a select list of lovers in their own quarters, and kept wome
whether casual mistresses or substitute wives.

It was all a question of income, appetites, and erotic habits. When th
American classicist Thomas Anthony Thacher was a theology student i
Berlin in the early 1840s, he was told that most of his German fello
students "spent the night in houses of ill-fame in the Mauer Strasse," an
at times, in the public baths: "There, too you can have a girl." Fou
decades later, in his famous story about the Tellier establishment, Guy d
Maupassant captured, and somewhat glamorized, the cozy domesticit
that middle-class brothels could offer; much to the dismay of its faithfu
clients, the house temporarily closes its doors as the whores, madam an
all, take time off to attend a first communion service. When, in 1888
seven years after its publication, Joris-Karl Huysmans traveled throug
Hamburg's famed bordellos, he had Maupassant's story very much i
mind as he reported on the local "brothels for seamen, infinitely superio
to the Maisons Tellier of the Latin Quarter" and those "for bankers
where the girls are young Hungarians of 15 or 16, and the bedrooms ar
filled with orchids."[43] In France, after mid-century such houses lost muc
custom to clandestine prostitutes and to illicit fronts such as shop
ostensibly selling gloves or tobacco. Many established places only staye
in business by diversifying their offerings and equipping themselves t
gratify specialized tastes: voyeurism, homosexuality, sadism, masochism
oral or anal intercourse, group sex, or erotic theatricals that would sampl
every conceivable variety of sexual pleasure including bestiality wit
Great Danes.[44]

Some collectors of experience thought they could detect national style
in commercial sex: Huysmans reported to a friend, perhaps rather to
infatuated with his story, that the prostitutes he had encountered ir
Hamburg were so patriotic that "before performing the sensual rites

43. Thacher: June 10 (1844), Diary, Day Family Papers, Y-MA; Huysmans
Robert Baldick, *The Life of J.-K. Huysmans* (1955), 123.
44. Alain Corbin, *Les Filles de noce. Misère sexuelle et prostitution aux 19e et 20e
siècles* (1978), 182–89.

they insist on saluting the portrait of their Emperor which hangs over every bed." This rather implausible Teutonic obeisance was matched by more plausible idolatry in Catholic countries. The Goncourts recorded an anecdote told them by a young man from the Foreign Ministry, presumably drawing on his own experience: in Spain, it seemed, a statue of Saint Anthony was on display in every brothel; when business was lively, the resident whores would kneel to him in prayer; when it was slack, they would break one of his fingers or his arms; when the run of slow trade continued, they would throw him down the well and buy another. And Hippolyte Taine, summing up his impressions of the English character, took care to distinguish it from the French, especially when confronted with the joys of illicit love: "An Englishman in the condition of adultery is unhappy; his conscience torments him at the finest moment." In fact, Englishmen going to a brothel or to a sleazy hotel for an assignation retain their characteristic bearing and gravity. "Whether mature man or respectable young man, on that evening the stroller is supposed to be travelling or at his club. He does not make himself conspicuous, does not offer his arm; his expedition is secret and anonymous; it is nothing more than an irruption of the beast that everyone of us carries within himself." Lasting liaisons, Taine thought, were more frequent and less clandestine: "English shop keepers' wives take rich gentlemen as lovers, bourgeois and gentry like to keep the farmers' daughters they have seduced."[45] Different as they might be, proper bourgeois Englishmen and Frenchmen—at least in Taine's mordant comparative portrait—liked domestic comfort and stability even on their flights from home.

As these observations suggest, by no means all bourgeois were reformers. Many of them, especially down to the 1850s but even after that, thought of prostitution with equanimity or resignation, as a resource for the perverted, comfort for the displaced, or school for the inexperienced. To stamp out prostitution, they liked to say, would require a fundamental and hence almost unthinkable change in human nature. For many, it was an evil that defied cure; for others, one that should be allowed to fester. Dr. William Acton, whose smoothly written but tendentious and unreliable book on prostitution did much, in 1857 and after, to prompt public discussion, spoke for this influential gloomy party when he described

<hr/>

45. Huysmans: Baldick, *Life*, 123; Goncourts: January 1862, *Journal, Mémoires de la vie littéraire 1851–1896*, ed. Robert Ricatte, 22 vols. (1956–58), V, 49–50; Taine: *Notes sur l'Angleterre* (1872; 9th ed., 1890), 129, 132. Significantly (which is to say, a little helplessly), Taine turns to fiction, George Eliot's *Adam Bede*, to document his last point. Ibid., 130n.

commercial sex as "an inevitable attendant upon civilized, and especially closely-packed, population," in short, now and forever "ineradicable."[46] Insouciant memoirs or sprightly fictions only encouraged this complacency masquerading as pessimism. The impulse for improvement could find little nourishment here.

Nor, as the journals of the Goncourts amply reveal, did world-weary disillusionment offer much material for reformist intentions. No one has canvassed the ashen taste of purchased pleasure more brutally than these brothers, who frequented fashionable establishments in Paris, collected salacious stories from their friends, and invited choice professionals to spend the night with them. The Goncourts' view of life was admittedly sour; both took a certain pleasure in decay and reveled in the shabbiness of their time which they made it their sad and fascinating business to record for posterity. Their picture of the monotonous vulgarity of even the "better" prostitute, her loss of stable identity, her underlying despair, her invincible stupidity, is cruel and intolerably condescending: "These women are pretty little animals who sometimes raise themselves to the intelligence of a monkey." They did not trouble to anatomize the men who, like themselves, felt the need to traffic with such animals. Supposedly elegant houses did not impress them; they saw the tawdriness that hungrier clients, intent only on their appetites, took care to overlook: "So this is the little paradise of which attachés speak as a dream from THE THOUSAND AND ONE NIGHTS!" they wrote of one such establishment. "The salon is the salon of a dentist," with pretentious furniture, faded curtains, cheap engravings. Truly, "men are not very demanding in the setting of their pleasures."[47] They recognized the grip of passion on perception; they knew that fantasy often invents what reality cannot supply.

The Goncourts watched, sampled, and turned away with the shrug of the connoisseur who finds the world less enticing than he had once dreamed: the dreary question, "Is that all?" is written over all their accounts of the prostitution they helped support. But their cynicism, whether convenient pose or authentic feeling, was a posture that most bourgeois thought they could not afford in the face of the "social evil," which seemed to be inundating their cities and infecting their young. The facts that made them anxious were bad enough, but widespread intimations of impending catastrophe and universal corruption, and the

46. Acton, *Prostitution: Considered in its Moral, Social, and Sanitary Aspects, in London and Other Large Cities and Garrison Towns: With Proposals for the Control and Prevention of Its Attendant Evils* (1857; 2nd. ed., 1870), 3.

47. March 10, 1862; December 13, 1857; February 16, 1862, *Journal*, V, 69; II, 188–89; V, 55.

sheer rage of many reformers, shows something more at work than rational concern over real evils, realistically perceived. "It is a singular characteristic of our time," the anonymous author of *Prostitution in Berlin* wrote in 1846, doubtless unaware that he was resorting to a sexual metaphor, "*to penetrate into the deepest and most mysterious folds of our social conditions.*" Earlier times, he continued, had scarcely pronounced such words as "bordello," but now there were serious attempts to understand the prostitute; the press was devoting space to her almost daily. This trait of the age, the author thought, was most commendable. It stemmed from the modern urge to grant dignity to the most wretched of fellow beings, from the thirst for knowledge, but also "from a powerful, unmistakable *fear*," a fear of "the waves of the proletariat, poverty, and particularly immorality" making ready to engulf "the fruits of our highly developed civilization."[48] This was comprehensive and perceptive, and was to hold true for decades after it was written: somewhat like the high-pitched literature worrying over nervousness, campaigns to protect society from the pollution of commercial vice (or the gloomy conclusion that such labors were futile) served self-control as much as social purification. Both were compromised by touches of hysteria.

One striking symptom of that hysteria was bloated estimates of whores infesting the great cities of the Western world. Samuel Bracebridge, who worked with Henry Mayhew in his compilation of interviews and vignettes, *London Labour and the London Poor*, claimed in 1862 that there were at least 80,000 prostitutes in London, while ten years later Maxime du Camp, in his sprawling panorama of Paris, put the number of prostitutes there at 120,000. This was not a new game. William Acton had noted in 1857, sensibly enough, that estimates tended to vary "according to the opportunities, credulity, or religious fervor of observers." He cited Patrick Colquhoun, "a magistrate at the Thames Police Court," who around 1800 had given the figure for London as 50,000, while some decades later Henry Phillpotts, Bishop of Exeter, "spoke of them as reaching 80,000," a figure that James Beard Talbot, "secretary of a society for the protection of young females," and, obviously, Bracebridge, had accepted without quibbling. In the same year that Acton published his book, *Lancet*, the respected English medical journal, estimated that one out of every sixteen women in London was a whore, which added up to the same magical figure—80,000. Some three decades later, James B. Wookey, who had left the Salvation Army to join the more strenuous Gospel Purity Association, claimed that there were in England "nearly

48. [W. Stieber], *Die Prostitution in Berlin und ihre Opfer* (1846), 1–2.

150,000 fallen girls who gain their daily bread by leading a life of sin
and shame." In his exhaustive compendium on Berlin prostitution, Hans
Ostwald ridiculed those who "in the old days steadily wailed about the
large number of prostitutes"; experts used to assert that in the 1840s,
"one Berlin woman out of eight was a whore," an estimate he obviously
thought absurdly inflated.[49] Indeed, these confident but ill-grounded
speculations were in large measure self-serving; they satisfied the demand
for scandal and lent anti-vice crusaders, like James Wookey, an importance that the true figures, though dismaying enough, could not have
sustained. The public that chose to accept these figures and transformed
the nuisances parading the streets into veritable armies of the evening
thus put their fears on record. Their fears and their buried wishes, for
there can be little doubt: a good measure of fascination that the plague of
prostitution exercised on the virtuous stemmed from unsatisfied erotic
needs. The whole debate points to primitive ambivalences, to paralyzing
self-doubts, in the camp of critics and crusaders alike. This preoccupation
with the invasion of loose women was so intense, the estimates of their
strength so obviously the offspring of emotion rather than of counting,
that we are plainly watching the defensive maneuver of reaction formation in play. Prostitution was frightening not simply because it awakened
the spectres of venereal disease and of blossoming immorality among
susceptible adolescents, but also, and significantly, because it called up
deeply repressed desires for the kind of sensual adventurism that the
respectable had been taught to despise and had learned to censor.

From the 1830s on, students of the trade in sex weighed down their
treatises with carefully drawn classifications and meticulous tables or
charts. Some of them, like the great Dr. Alexandre Parent-Duchâtelet—
"the Newton of harlotry," an English journal graciously called him—did
extensive research in the field, which is to say, Paris. But their discoveries
and recommendations, like those of more casual observers, mingled fact
and fiction, guess-work and desire, in undetermined proportions. What
they have mainly left behind is a flavor of the lasting and anxiety-
provoking fascination that prostitution exercised on their century. Metaphors of darkness and horror burden their expositions right to the end

---

49. Acton, *Prostitution*, 3–8; Michael Pearson, *The Age of Consent: Victorian
Prostitution and its Enemies* (1972), 25, 113; Ostwald, *Das Berliner Dirnentum* (1907),
2 vols. in 6 separately paginated sections, I, section 2, 71. Acton, though skeptical of
much wild guessing, indulged in it himself: he thought that many estimates were low
and that 210,000 unmarried English women, or one in twelve, "have strayed from the
path of virtue." *Prostitution*, 7.

of Victoria's reign. Dr. Acton evoked some of this atmosphere when he noted in 1870, looking back to the first edition of his *Prostitution* on the occasion of publishing the second, "during the intervening period prostitution, with its attendant evils, has been the subject of anxious inquiry."[50]

This anxiety, now more or less in the open, was compounded of diverse ingredients, of which ignorance was only the most prominent— an ignorance not relieved by a certain measure of self-interest. For every police commissioner who, nervously anticipating criticisms of his professional performance, intentionally underreported the number of street walkers working his jurisdiction, there must have been a dozen reformers of whom I have spoken, nervous men and women who, alarmed at the spread of clandestine prostitution, fastened onto the most improbable guesses. Nor was the gingerly manner with which publicists walked around this delicate subject calculated to correct widespread, panic-stricken preconceptions even after it had been ventilated in legislatures and periodicals. As late as 1884, a German expert on prostitution, Hermann Dalton, prefaced his lecture to an evangelical mission society in St. Petersburg by evoking his unwillingness to "undertake the work," which required "with every step" a new effort to overcome his "unspeakable reluctance to take cognizance of this darkest night side of the life of sin." He vividly called up the "dread" which these "uncanny abysses" awakened in him, as he had entered the dens of vice in Europe's great cities, tempted to pass them by "with hastening step, with bated breath, with closed eyes."[51]

His was a pervasive sentiment. In 1846, an anonymous German author described prostitution as *"the most frightful fetter under which mankind has ever languished,"* and *"the most dreadful weapon of hell being flourished over our heads more and more threateningly."* In the preceding decades, some troubled reformers in New York spoke of the "thrill of horror" that "every virtuous man and woman" must feel at the spectacle; and they resorted to *Hamlet* to convey the depth of their dismay. "Did not prudence and delicacy forbid the disgusting detail of what has been brought to our knowledge," they "could a tale disclose which would cause the blood to 'chill within the veins, and each particular hair to stand erect, like quills upon the fretted porcupine.'" In 1886, reporting to the directors of the Prison Society of Rhineland-Westphalia, the German pastor H. Stursberg confessed, "At times, I should have liked to

50. "Newton of Harlotry": Brian Harrison, "Underneath the Victorians," *Victorian Studies*, X (March 1967), 242; Acton: *Prostitution*, v.
51. Dalton, *Der soziale Aussatz. Ein Wort über Prostitution und Magdalenenasyle* 1884), 4-5.

put down my pen, because it resisted drawing such dark pictures, though a great deal had already been eliminated." Prostitution was, after all, "a dreadful enemy, a horrifying destroyer of the moral and physical vitality of our nation," doing its "work of destruction first in darkness with great power and much cunning, deceptively restrained here, with unheard-of impudence there." Not even the French, notorious abroad for their cool tolerance of immorality, were immune to such feelings and such rhetoric. "I could have gone further," the prolific chronicler of Paris, Charles Virmaitre, told his readers on introducing his little book, *Trottoirs et lupanars.* "For, alas!, I have not said everything: the tide of 'girls' and their pimps is rising ceaselessly. The day is near when, if we continue the policy of laissez faire, legislators will be powerless."[52]

Still, this omnipresent and distasteful spectre of vice did not inhibit inquiry or the search for remedies. In 1850, after completing *David Copperfield,* in which fallen women had assumed a certain prominence, Charles Dickens told the philanthropist Angela Burdett-Coutts that "the sad subject" of prostitution was "difficult to approach," especially in a book "intended for readers of all classes and all ages of life." But he professed "not the least misgivings about being able to bring people gently to its consideration." Such circumspection consisted, in the many volumes devoted to the sad subject, of the largely unplanned convention of protesting that nothing could safely be said about prostitution and little had yet been said, and then proceeding to say it. This literary formula gave the Victorian century space for an impressive measure of frankness while hinting that frankness was out of reach. In 1858, in his voluminous survey of the history of prostitution in all lands, Dr. William Sanger viewed himself as the brave, isolated explorer whom a prudish and complacent society might well scorn, but who felt obliged to press on: "An unseen evil, of which only the effects are visible, is more frightful than one whose dimensions are apparent." In the same year, writing to the *British Medical Journal,* not very subtly puffing his own contribution, Dr. Acton suggested that "but a few weeks ago," prostitution "did not admit of discussion"; now, presumably with his book before the public, it suddenly did.[53]

52. Anon.: [Stieber], *Prostitution in Berlin,* 210; "horror": *First Annual Report of the Executive Committee of the New York Magdalen Society* (1831), 8; Stursberg: *Die Prostitution in Deutschland und ihre Bekämpfung* (1886; 2nd ed., 1887), 3; Virmaitre: *Trottoirs et lupanars* (1897), 5.

53. Dickens: to Burdett-Coutts, February 4, 1850, *Letters from Charles Dickens to Angela Burdett-Coutts 1841–1865,* ed. Edgar Johnson (1953), 165; Sanger: Dr. William W. Sanger, *The History of Prostitution: Its Extent, Causes, and Effects Throughout the World* (1858) 17–18; Acton: *Prostitution,* ed. and abr. Peter Fryer (1968), 7

But Acton praised himself beyond his merits: reticence had been far
:ss extreme than he intimated. Eight years before, assuming the mantle
f the explorer, W. R. Greg had published an important unsigned article
n prostitution in the *Westminster Review*; while touched by compassion
or the victims of vice, its prevalent tone is a kind of awe that the author
eels at his daring in venturing to discuss this matter at all. Reviewing
nd, following the custom of the time, extensively quoting from four
ublications on prostitution, Greg thought it necessary to prepare the
round before he could combat the "false and mischievous delicacy"
nd the "culpable moral cowardice" that had so far shrunk from "the
onsideration of the great social vice of Prostitution," and to persuade
oth himself and his readers that to confront this "loathsome" matter
vas to effect good and to mitigate suffering. He was fully aware, he wrote,
hat "mischief is risked by bringing the subject prominently before the
ublic eye," and that it is "a matter on which it is not easy to speak
penly." But men's awareness of the limits to their information, their
ear of being scoffed at by "the vulgar and lightminded," and a false
efinement had "already too long withheld serious and benevolent men
rom facing one of the sorest evils that the English sun now shines upon."
)nly after this, after mobilizing his massive defensive artillery, and after
arefully discriminating "fornication" (the "unnatural" gratification of
ust with paid victims) from "sexual indulgence" (which, however tragic,
vas at least natural), that Greg felt free to address the "painful and
erplexing question" which "statesmen, moralists, and philanthropists"
ad so far avoided.[54]

Greg had his counterparts on the Continent: there, too, writers on
rostitution spoke of the unspeakable in a slightly tremulous tone and
vith an air of brave discovery. In 1848, Dr. Heinrich Lippert prefaced
iis survey of that "cancerous growth" in Hamburg with the observation
hat prostitution has only very recently entered the "literary market-
lace" as a "special topic," and he singled out writers in Paris and
ondon—whose very books Greg would review in 1850—for pioneering
n its scientific discussion. Berlin, too, he was pleased to note, had just
ontributed a well-informed volume on prostitution; the time was now
ipe to follow the "excellent" Parent-Duchâtelet, the French investigator
vhose exhaustive canvass of prostitution in Paris had become an instant
lassic upon its appearance in 1836. "I am by no means unaware," Lippert
sserted, "that the wider public accepts such studies with a certain shy

54. Greg, "Art. VII—I. De la Prostitution dans la Ville de Paris, Par Parent-
)uchâtelet . . . ," *Westminster Review*, LIII (June 1850), 448–49.

reticence." Yet "it is not the topic that is decisive, but the mode and manner of its treatment alone." Lippert was confident that "Parent-Duchâtelet could look the keenest moralist, the most severe ascetic freely and frankly in the eyes." He recalled what he had said two years earlier, in the preface to his book on venereal diseases: "It is ridiculous in our enlightened age," to "offer excuses concerning the indecency of a topic. The physician," he argued, reasonably enough, "is not created for an ideal world; he is supposed to help abate the real evils in the world, and devote himself to their study all the more thoroughly, the more wide-spread they are."[55] It was only after he had offered this conventional apologia for unconventionality that Lippert proceeded to an analysis of prostitution in Hamburg. His indirections reflect a wider reticence on this sensitive theme, a reticence most suitably displayed in decent novels and family magazines. Gradually, physicians, and, following them their respectable public, found it possible, indeed felt compelled, to talk about prostitution.

But, as they spoke, they could hardly repress their anxiety. Nor was this anxiety allayed by an intriguing paradox to which the tribe of experts on mercantile sex, and after them the general public, rapidly became much attached. More than a hundred years after the brilliant cynic, Bernard Mandeville, had first advanced his wicked proposition that private vices produce public benefits, his notorious aphorism seemed borne out by prostitution. In the 1830s, the Saint-Simonians accused good bourgeois of securing their daughters' virginity "by levying a tribute upon the daughters of the poor who walk the streets." Saint-Simon and his disciples were, to be sure, dedicated students—both prophets and critics—of modern commercial society and just as dedicated advocates of equality for women; their charges were therefore likely to be dismissed as tendentious. But Parent-Duchâtelet took the same view: prostitutes, he wrote, keep lustful men "from perverting your daughters and your servants," and thus "contribute to the maintenance of order and tranquility in society."[56]

Dr. Parent-Duchâtelet secured imposing authority for his views, and his idea that prostitution is the safety valve of respectability carried the day. This, then, was the price that bourgeois society was willing to pay for its repressions! His admiring followers echoed him without cavils or

55. Dr. H[einrich] Lippert, Die Prostitution in Hamburg in ihren eigenthümlichen Verhältnissen (1848), ii–iii.
56. Frank E. Manuel, The Prophets of Paris: Turgot, Condorcet, Saint-Simon, Fourier, Comte (1962), 156; Parent-Duchâtelet, De la prostitution dans la ville de Paris, 2 vols. (1836), II, 41, 512; Corbin, Les filles de noce, 15–16.

amendments, and so did others elsewhere. In the early 1860s, in his widely
read *History of European Morals*, W. E. H. Lecky again argued that
the whore "is ultimately the most efficient guardian of virtue. But for her,
the unchallenged purity of countless happy homes would be polluted,
and not a few who, in the pride of their untempted chastity, think of her
with an indignant shudder would have known the agony of remorse and
despair." In 1866, Fjodor Dostoevsky imported this critique of middle-
class pieties into his novel *Crime and Punishment;* thinking of the young
women who end up as prostitutes, he comments: "That's as it should be,
they tell us. A certain percentage, they tell us, must every year go . . .
that way . . . to the devil, I suppose, so that the rest may remain chaste,
and not be interfered with." Naturally, this accusation particularly suited
the scourges of bourgeois hypocrisy: in his immensely popular *Woman
under Socialism*, first published in 1883, often reprinted and translated,
August Bebel devoted a whole chapter to proving that prostitution was
"a necessary social institution of the capitalist world." Then, in 1890,
Grant Allen, scientist, satirist, and feminist reformer, made the charge
again: "Our existing system is really a joint system of marriage and
prostitution in which the second element is a necessary corollary and
safeguard of the first."[57] It was an unpleasant paradox, counterpart to the
paradox of modern nervousness: the bourgeois anxiously biting his lip
in the midst of his social, economic, and political triumphs was also the
bourgeois preserving the chastity of his women by corrupting the
chastity of others.

By the time that Grant Allen was bringing Mandeville up to date,
though, there were those disposed to see the paradox not as an irony of
bourgeois culture but as a defense against reform: in 1882, Yves Guyot,
the leading advocate of abolishing all brothels in France, had devised a
little dialogue between himself and "Joseph Prudhomme," the quintessential French bourgeois, in which Prudhomme mouths the clichés,
"Prostitution is a necessary evil," and "Prostitution is the safeguard of
families," only to have Guyot decisively refute him. Even before Guyot,
Gustave Flaubert had enshrined the paradox in his malicious dictionary
of stupid commonplaces which, according to him, governed and dis-
figured his culture: "The courtesan," he intoned, "is a necessary evil.—

57. Lecky: *History of European Morals*, in Glen Petrie, *A Singular Iniquity: The
Campaigns of Josephine Butler* (1971), 85; Dostoevsky: *Crime and Punishment* (1866;
tr. Constance Garnett, n.d.), 52 [Part One, ch. 4]; Bebel: *Woman under Socialism*
(1883; tr. Daniel De Leon, 1904, ed. 1971), 144–66; Allen: Susan B. Casteras, *The
Substance or the Shadow: Images of Victorian Womanhood* (1982), 53.

Safeguard for our daughters and our sisters (as long as there are bach
elors.)"[58] Flaubert, of course, in no way committed himself to the accu
racy of this assertion; on the contrary, to record that bourgeois believed
it meant that it was probably nonsense.

Such spirited wrangles should not obscure the serious and essentially
responsible quality of the decades-long and painfully inconclusive controversy pitting the proponents of licensed brothels against the advocates
of their abolition. Partisans of one position could not see the virtues of
its converse, but both were mobilized to defend the same ideals: personal
purity and public health. It was the question of means, not of ends, that
caused all the controversy, for these means reflected incompatible preferences grounded in conflicting religious convictions, practical considerations, even national styles. The American scholar Charles K. Needham, who collected and translated Continental books on sex and vice
debated these conflicts in his commentary on a Dr. Louis Martineau's
polemic against clandestine prostitution. "To what extent ought the
State to interfere in regard to prostitution? Shall it suppress, tolerate, or
license it?" This, of course, was the critical question. Martineau favored
licensing, and Needham had appreciative words for his "excellent treatise"
and its "broad-minded" author "who has had much experience in the
care and treatment of venereal women." Yet, for all the merits of Martineau's presentation, it left Needham unpersuaded. "He cannot get away
from the idea of paternalism—so dear to every French reformer—
whereby the government can aid or force men to be better than they
want to be." Significantly, he attributed Martineau's pessimism, his readiness to settle for an assault on syphilis, to his nationality: given his
experience of his fellow-Frenchmen, Martineau simply could not bring
himself to believe that they are ready for the ideal of a society free from
"fornication and adultery." And Needham injected a feminist view by
noting that clients are far more likely to engender infected children
than are their whores, who are practically sterile. "If restrictive measures
are necessary," Needham pointedly asked, "why not attack the men more
than the women, since they are the more to blame, so far as bad results
to posterity are concerned?"[59] His somewhat irritated nationalistic self-
satisfaction apart, Needham's comments, read in conjunction with the
book that prompted them, provide a useful conspectus of the debate that

58. Guyot: La Prostitution (1882), 460; Flaubert: "Le dictionnaire des Idées
reçues," Oeuvres, ed. Albert Thibaudet and René Dumesnil, 2 vols. (1951–1952), II,
1005.
59. Needham's (undated) commentary is bound into Martineau, La prostitution
clandestine (1885; 2nd ed., n.d.).

ivided so many sober Victorians throughout their century, in country
fter country.

The alliances formed by all this controversy were curiously ill-assorted:
he case for legal, inspected houses of prostitution enlisted *roués* who
hought them splendid agencies singularly equipped to train the young
r entertain the bored, and devout purifiers intent on quarantining the
arriers of venereal disease. On the other side, the opposition to legal
rostitution mobilized feminists outraged at the double standard that
xposed suspected "loose women" to humiliating medical inspection and
etention while leaving their male customers alone, and social conserva-
ives who had no use for feminism but found the very idea of officially
anctioned vice an offensive contradiction in terms and, worse, a disgrace
o civilized society. But controversial ideas in search of public policy
ormally produce such incongruous alignments; they did not diminish or
ecessarily discredit the general alarm over prostitution as such. Certainly
ineteenth-century investigations into commercial vice, from the sensa-
ional, impressionistic accounts by Henry Mayhew and his associates to
he sober, quantitative studies of countless local committess across the
Western world, discovered shameful patterns of exploitation and dismay-
ng networks of vice, crime, and officialdom. In the English city of York,
or one, about one out of every six clients of local prostitutes was a
oliceman.[60]

Plainly, it was easier to lament the vice than to prescribe an effective
emedy for it. But the laments were a necessary starting point. They
onveyed at least some information, habituated the public to a measure of
andor, and prepared the way for a shift in attitudes—beyond com-
lacency. That is why Greg's article in the *Westminster Review* is some-
hing of a historic document. After his extended, somewhat misleading
rologue, Greg draws the profile of the wretched prostitute, the induce-
nents pushing her into the paths of vice, the numbers of prostitutes in
ngland, the means of reducing "this hideous gangrene of English
ociety," and of rehabilitating the fallen girls. While not wholly free
rom credulity, Greg's good sense and sympathy control his moral out-
age; he rejects the celebrated estimates of Patrick Colquhoun as a
monstrous exaggeration" and offers, as the principal impulse for a young
voman's "choice" of the prostitute's life, the extreme poverty at the
ower rungs of the English working classes. They live, he notes, in in-
ected hovels, sleeping together in a single miserable room, a very

60. Frances Finnegan, *Poverty and Prostitution: A Study of Victorian Prostitution
York* (1979), 122.

rehearsal for corruption, and they earn, mainly as seamstresses, far too
little, and that far too sporadically, to remain chaste and survive.[61] Greg'
adjectives are inflamed, his nouns heated, but his anger serves his announced practical intentions: to promote rational discussion and move
toward sensible remedies.

Greg's leisurely essay, long enough to make a pamphlet, is instructive
both for its human and scientific attitudes, its pressure for accurate information and clear thinking, and for its rhetorical strategies. Whatever
its limitations, the essay enriched the texture of carnal knowledge among
the educated bourgeoisie. But Greg had ancestors in his enterprise; one of
the four works he was reviewing, Parent-Duchâtelet's *De la prostitution
dans la ville de Paris*, had come out fourteen years earlier; another, Henry
Mayhew's series of "letters" to the *Morning Chronicle*, from which Greg
quoted some of the most "heart-rending statements"[62] for several page
on end, were available to the general reading public and used the infallible
method of the affecting anecdotal interview; the other two, James Beard
Talbot's *Miseries of Prostitution*, and Dr. Michael Ryan's *Prostitution in
London*, each far stronger in assertion than in facts and both noisy exemplars of the alarmist school, were, respectively, six and eleven years old.
He could have added Dr. William Tait's *Magdalenism, an Inquiry into the
Extent, Causes and Consequences of Prostitution in Edinburgh*, firs
published in 1840, or Ralph Wardlaw's rather more entertaining *Lecture
on Female Prostitution* of 1842, which was rich in vignettes about respectable bordellos, mainly in Edinburgh, frequented by local worthies
Moreover, researchers in other countries had subjected commercial vice
to quantitative investigations some years before Greg decided to tackle
this "loathsome" matter. Parent-Duchâtelet had generated a small derivative literature, most notably F. F. A. Béraud's substantial *Les filles publiques de Paris, et la police qui les régit* of 1839, and several monographs
that exported Parent-Duchâtelet's positivist, obsessive reaching for precision to the French provinces.[63] In the German states, too, inquiries into
the legal and moral aspects of prostitution and the private life of the prostitute enjoyed a certain efflorescence in the mid- and late 1840s; it would
have flourished more luxuriantly still if the censor had not partially

61. Greg, "De la prostitution . . . ," 449–50, 474–75. One cannot wholly acquit Greg
of credulity for, on the same page that he rejects Colquhoun's estimates as
monstrous exaggeration, he asks his readers to trust Ryan and Talbot who, though
they are more moderate, largely follow in Colquhoun's footsteps.
62. Ibid., 467.
63. Alain Corbin speaks of Parent-Duchâtelet's "obsession with the quantitative."
Les filles de noce, 34.

inhibited the flow of publications. If prostitution was a secret in Europe before 1848, it was an open secret. After all, as Dr. William Sanger noted a decade later near the conclusion of his great history, prostitution was "a problem the solution of which has for centuries interested philanthropists and statesmen in different countries."[64]

Amid the massive literature pouring out in France, Sweden, everywhere, from the 1840s on, the controversial pamphlets published in northern Germany are of particular interest, for they reveal the honest doubts of the reformers and the ambivalence of the public officials they were seeking to influence. For the most part, they are sober enough, reciting the prehistory of the problem, quoting extracts from local legislation, offering tables detailing the ages and origins and prices of prostitutes, descriptions of selected bordellos, and classifications of types of whores and their customers. Yet some authors, like Dr. Heinrich Lippert, splash some colors over their drab recitals with a moralizing sentence here and a physical description there; Lippert's prostitutes are servants of Venus and nymphs of the alleys—euphemisms that serve gentility far less than his need for elegant variations.

But the energy animating this German literature is less literary or erotic than political: the conflicting ways of controlling the social evil stimulated sudden twists and turns of argumentation and policy alike. After some tentative efforts to restrict them, King Frederick William IV had, by royal edict, ordered all Prussian bordellos closed on December 31, 1845, thus reversing his country's long-standing practice of tolerating controlled prostitution. In 1845, in fact, just anticipating the edict, Dr. Adolf Patze, a small-town physician, had eloquently defended brothels as the only reliable mode of keeping the pest of syphilis in check.[65] A year later, an anonymous writer who claimed to have access to police records, took the other side, with much subtlety, arguing for the closing of bordellos in Berlin. He justified his position with the obligatory, immensely

64. Sanger, *History of Prostitution*, 627. In 1845, Dr. Adolf Patze noted in the preface to his little book on bordellos that he had written a paper on syphilis at the beginning of that year; it had "found a welcome reception" with "the editors of the periodical," but its publication was "frustrated by the severity of the censor." *Ueber Bordelle und die Sittenverderbniss unserer Zeit* (1845), iii.

65. This polemical literature served the modern urge to know in more ways than one. That provincial doctor from the Pomeranian town of Grabow, Dr. Adolf Patze, whom I have just quoted, was something of a pioneer in the study of sexuality. He notes, in passing and without any pride of discovery—speaking psychoanalysis, as it were, without knowing it—that the suppression of the sexual drives produces "hypochondriacal depressions" especially among unmarried teachers and students of theology; and in a casual footnote he observes that this drive makes its appearance among small children, as early as the age of three. Ibid., 58, 48n.

elaborated survey of the legislative history of Berlin prostitution, continued with some brief but telling chapters discriminating different classes of prostitutes, described their bodies, analyzed their origins, and speculated on their pathetic fates. His book provoked a reply in the following year by Dr. Carl Röhrmann, like his unknown adversary not a physician but a lawyer. Röhrmann pointed proudly to his unofficial status and accused his anonymous adversary of writing at the behest, and probably in the pay, of the police, to rationalize the new Prussian edict. While claiming to be hostile to prostitution, Röhrmann thought the banning of bordellos a mistake: "The ideas that stimulated the Prussian administration as it suppressed the institution of tolerated prostitution are in their nature praiseworthy, and in accord with the principles of morality. But that they will or can have the hoped-for *practical results* I doubt."[66] Hole-and-corner prostitution had markedly increased, and the risk of venereal infection had increased with it.

Most articulate public opinion ranged itself in Dr. Röhrmann's camp; a series of articles published in 1847 in the *Vossische Zeitung* drew the balance after two years of experience with the new policy and concluded that it was the offspring of the "well-meaning" but "wholly mistaken" notion that a highly civilized and enlightened country could dispense with whorehouses. What had happened, the newspaper suggested, was that the social evil, far from diminishing, had simply spread across the city. In 1850, Dr. Franz Josef Behrend published a "memorandum" at the instance of the government that came to the same conclusion: prostitution, the source of syphilis, must be carefully watched by the police, and this task is best accomplished in tolerated brothels where medical examinations can be properly performed three times a week.[67] Indeed, the government, largely persuaded though vacillating, returned to the old ways for a time: it reopened the Berlin bordellos in 1851, only to reverse itself again and close them once more five years later. These continual mid-course corrections eloquently attest that no policy was without its drawbacks. In some measure, the Prussian authorities, officials and physicians alike, seemed to be saying that sensuality is always out of

66. [Stieber], *Die Prostitution in Berlin, Passim;* Röhrmann, *Der sittliche Zustand von Berlin nach Aufhebung der geduldeten Prostitution des weiblichen Geschlechts. Ein Beitrag zur Geschichte der Gegenwart unterstützt durch die vollständigen und freimüthigen Biographieen der bekanntesten prostituirten Frauenzimmer in Berlin* (1847), 54–55.
67. *Vossische:* Dr. Philipp Loewe, *Die Prostitution aller Zeiten und Völker mit besonderer Berücksichtigung von Berlin. Ein Beitrag zu der obschwebenden Bordellfrage* (1852) 43; Dr. Behrend: *Die Prostitution in Berlin und die gegen sie und die Syphilis zu nehmenden Massregeln* (1850), 291–94.

control. The reformers, growing more aggressive though no less nervous decade by decade, would take a far less fatalistic line.

As candid interest in prostitution and the prostitute markedly intensified from mid-century on, the partisans of tolerated brothels, whether panic-stricken over the "ineradicable evil" or arming themselves to battle it, began to lose ground. The shift away from cynicism or hysteria was not clear-cut and never complete, but it was unmistakable. As so often, we may read the fiction of the day as a suggestive, though far from reliable, barometer of public attitudes, varying across time and space, as a measure of what proper readers wanted to hear, or could tolerate.

French novels, as expected, long took a rather relaxed view of brothels or of "loose" women, exploiting them as sources of entertaining plots or poignant characters. The sentimental pathos of Murger's flighty and impecunious bohemians and, even more, of Dumas fils' *Dame aux camélias*, idealized the *lorette* and the *cocotte* out of all recognition: much, we are told, is forgiven Dumas's Marguerite Gautier because she has loved much.[68] Late in the Second Empire, a whole sub-literature grew up around these modern Magdalens, these "lovely sinners" and "little ladies of the theatre"; these fictions (in their way, grossly distorted reportage) helped to establish the myth of the courtesan with a heart of gold, untainted by her shameful trade.[69] They suggest how persistently "wicked," or, rather, sexually promiscuous, women haunted the fantasies of conventional and inhibited burghers. That is why the *Dame aux camélias* was such a master stroke: the consumptive kept woman, at once seductive and doomed, condensed pressing and improper desires into a single theatrical character, even providing for her redemption through suffering and a heart-rending death. On the lighter side, but inviting the same gush of unpolitical sympathy, Maupassant produced his poignant tale of a patriotic prostitute, *Boule de suif*, and, we recall, of the good-hearted and pious whores working at the *Maison* Tellier: the most solemn of readers could not mistake this amusing story as a critique of bourgeois hypocrisy or a call to action.

Nor was Zola's sensational and somber *Nana* calculated to rip the false face of glamour from the sickly grimace of commercial sex. While Zola has his young and voluptuous heroine die a hideous, disfiguring death,

68. Dumas's dramatic version of his novel *La dame aux camélias* (1852) explicitly ends with this apostrophe.
69. See Henri Mitterand, "Etude," to *Nana*, in Emile Zola, *Les Rougon-Macquart, Histoire Naturelle et sociale d'une Famille sous le Second Empire*, ed. Armand Lanoux and Henri Mitterand, 5 vols. (1960–1967), II, 1655.

her irresistible erotic perfume luring all manner of men (and some women), to say nothing of her improbable sexual athleticism, lent the courtesan a vitality and a naive, earthy charm she rarely possessed in real life. Zola, in any event, was not concerned in this novel with the realistic, critical examination of prostitution as such; for all his meticulous investigations and customary documentation, he intended a moral tract offering a wry tribute to raw, overpowering, destructive sexual power. Philosophizing, as was his way, with a bludgeon, he wrote in his preliminary sketch, "The philosophical subject is this: a whole society throwing itself at ass. A whole pack of hounds after a bitch, who is not in heat and makes fun of the dogs who chase her. *The poem of male desires*, the great lever that moves the world. There is only ass and religion."[70] This, far from a benign portrait of the *demi-monde*, constitutes an all-out assault on uninhibited devouring lust that turns all pleasures into pock-marked decay. Yet, however severe Zola's purpose, this was not the tone the reformers wanted, or could use. They saw nothing poetic in male desires.

But *Nana*, which came out in 1880, had some interesting and more usable competitors; for some time, novelists in France had been telling a less strident, less mock-heroic tale than this. Joris-Karl Huysmans's *Marthe* of 1876, and Edmond de Goncourt's *La fille Eliza*, published the following year, are clinical, almost documentary novellas that brought unsparing realism to bear on a titillating and, for all the exposés, still rather mysterious profession. Then, in 1881, the great Spanish novelist Benito Pérez Galdós imported the lessons and techniques of these French realists to a shocked Spain with his *La desheredada*, whose hapless and unglamorized heroine ends up as a prostitute.

Elsewhere, the stance of tough-minded resignation or facile amusement had long been under fire. Russian writers from Gogol to Dostoevsky, Chernishevsky to Chekhov, portrayed the prostitute as a human being; sentimentally at times, but more often realistically, they had their heroes, whether innocent dupes or guileless saints, labor to rehabilitate the fallen woman—not always in vain. Similarly, in England, the few writers who touched on "the subject" found both sentimentality and levity out of place. In *Mary Barton*, her first novel, Elizabeth Gaskell eschewed all false pathos or bourgeois condescension; she shows Esther, the street walker, her predictable misery and her drunken fate, with sympathetic seriousness and a reporter's regard for social realities. She followed this up five years later, in 1853, with *Ruth*, a rather more schematic novel about a fallen girl who retains her virginal innocence throughout. The

70. See ibid., 1665.

book was severely criticized and, by some venturesome spirits, warmly praised, but whatever its complex fate among its readers, Gaskell's *Ruth* was yet another sign that the old attitudes toward prostitution were under pressure.[71]

The most telling deposits marking this erosion of complacency were left on the novels of Dickens. Some of his perceptive readers have justly complained that Dickens the writer treating whores was rather more mawkish and far more self-censoring than Dickens the social reformer. In his preface to the first edition of *Oliver Twist*, he bluntly called Nancy "a prostitute," a plain epithet he dropped later, but even in that edition he left her way of life decently veiled and gave her demise a pathos worthy of less compromised heroines. Again, the lines that Dickens gives Martha Endell, the prostitute in *David Copperfield*, display a purity of diction and a wealth of metaphor more appropriate to a second-rate melodrama on the London stage than to a miserable whore in the London slums.[72] Yet, this very unwillingness to deploy in his fiction the sensible attitude toward "fallen women" that distinguished his efforts to rehabilitate them makes *Oliver Twist* and *David Copperfield* representative of the conflicts clouding contemporary English opinion. Besides, they gently nudge the reader toward a new compassion on which humane philanthropic actions could build: David Copperfield's friends who begin by despising Martha the sinner in pharisaic speeches come to accept her essential humanity, her right to pity, and set to the work of rescue—Martha ends up finding a husband in the Australian bush.

This was the attitude that encouraged Dickens's good friend, Wilkie Collins, to depict, in *The New Magdalen*, the heart-rending struggles of a reformed prostitute to regain her footing in respectable society; his generally objective treatment punctuated the complacent claim, advanced by Dr. Acton among others, that if they so chose, whores could make a new life for themselves with some ease. Suffering moments of confusion and backsliding that reflected and in turn aroused keenly felt long-

71. "I am told, to my great astonishment," Charles Kingsley wrote to Mrs. Gaskell on July 25, 1853, "that you have heard painful speeches on account of 'Ruth'; what was told me raised all my indignation and disgust. . . . But this I can tell you, that among all my large acquaintance I never heard [complaints] or have heard . . . one unanimous opinion of the beauty and righteousness of the book. . . . English people, in general, have but one opinion of 'Ruth', and that is, one of utter satisfaction." *Charles Kingsley: His Letters and Memories of His Life*, edited by his wife, 2 vols. (1876; 16th ed., 1888), I, 294–95.
72. See Philip Collins, *Dickens and Crime* (1962; 2nd ed., 1964), ch. IV; K. J. Fielding, *Charles Dickens: A Critical Introduction* (1958), 104. As is well known, the sympathetic portrayal of the fallen woman was a familiar theme in painting; Dante Gabriel Rossetti's "Found" is only the most famous of these.

suppressed anxieties about illicit love, bourgeois began to move from
denial or hysteria about prostitution to a measure of understanding and
attempts at reparation.

Superficially, the change seemed to be mainly one in the quantity of
publications; in important features, the reports and polemics of 1900 and
after resemble their distinguished ancestors, Parent-Duchâtelet's comprehensive treatise or the pointed pamphlets of his followers. But the later
literature generally avoided the lapses into naiveté and myth-making
that had compromised many earlier writings on sexuality, proper or
improper: its tone became a little cooler, its statistical apparatus a little
more copious, the official status of its authors a little more obtrusive, and
its anxious tone, though no less urgent, a little more controlled. But
what distinguished the work of 1900 from that of 1840 was its readiness
to hold society responsible for the scourge of prostitution, and its attendant stress on reform, particularly on the rehabilitation of the prostitute. The themes dominating the reports that municipalities commissioned
in the latter half of the century show bourgeois remorse in action.

While civic investigations into the "social evil" go back to the 1860s,
after 1900 literally dozens of cities—Newark, Toronto, Stuttgart—tum-
bled over one another to appoint citizens' committees or invite social
scientists to discriminate fact from romance about the social evil, to lay
bare the unpalatable truths about infection and corruption, and to
recommend legislative action. Those notable inquiries into commercial
vice that are such a characteristic feature of the American Progressive
era had their worthy counterparts in England and on the Continent. The
family resemblance of these reports is striking in their reasoning and the
very rhythms of their prose. They are normally headed by a list of the
Committee (or Commission) of Twelve (or Fifteen, or Twenty), as a
badge guaranteeing the sense of purpose and serious responsibility. And
the local worthies appointed to enlighten and advise their fellow citizens
are almost invariably drawn from the same population: there is a minister, a priest, and a rabbi, occasionally a labor leader, there are physicians,
lawyers, philanthropists, educators, social workers, some of these always
women. The report itself charts local conditions, street by street, often
house by house, estimates the social cost of vice, discloses the ties between prostitution and crime, investigates the reasons why young women
enter the life, gives harrowing facts on the incidence of venereal disease,
and then offers specific recommendations, looking both to education and
to the law for remedies. Nearly all of them, in fact, devote as much
space—often more—to the uses of sex education and the need to improve
the economic lot of the population from which prostitutes are largely

drawn, as they do to proposed legislation. Greg's collective book review of 1850 is the grandparent of all these reports in its mixture of scientific probity, moral outrage, and social engineering, only less precise, less official, and less remorseful.

The name "social evil" has been ridiculed as a genteel euphemism, but these reports speak out without evasiveness or false modesty; the term is, in fact, both accurate and revealing, for it places the campaigns against prostitution into a larger cultural frame. This outpouring of municipal inquiries—in the United States, at least six cities chartered Vice Commissions in the year 1911 alone—bespeaks a far more general concern; they formed a division in the army combating immorality. They intersect, especially in their urgent proposals for sex education in the home and in the schools, with the conclusions that regional and international congresses on social hygiene were reaching in the same years. Morality was in mortal danger, and so was health, from the same polluted sources: poverty and ignorance. The intentions of these commissions and congresses were in a strict sense conservative, but the implications of their proposals were often radically subversive: these pillars of the bourgeois community were suggesting with one voice that if one could only abolish poverty and disseminate the facts of life, vice and misery would disappear forever.

Meanwhile, there were the victims, most conspicuously the prostitute herself. She began to elicit sympathy as her "protector" never could. "The 'pimp,'" exclaimed Olive Christian Malvery, who ran the humane Mackirdy Home in London, "is, without any exception, a cur. The one thing he would dread would be a horse-whipping." But some authorities remained tough-minded and hard-hearted. For municipal councillors of port cities or commanders of army posts—usually the most emphatic advocates of legalized and controlled bordellos—the victim who mattered was the soldier, the sailor, or the casual visitor. Self-proclaimed realists were in fact disposed to find reformers sentimental, downright comical: "Let writers, novelists, dramatize 'the fallen woman,'" Dr. A. Corlieu wrote in 1887 in his book on prostitution in Paris. "Let them construct, if they want, an argument against society as it is; let them set themselves up as philanthropists and thus seek a fleeting fame—we have no truck with this sort of thing. Moved by praise-worthy feelings, they would like, if not to dry up, at least to stop this current which swells every year whatever one does, whatever one writes." Many administrators and at least some physicians, untouched by the humanitarian agitation swirling about them, continued to argue that prostitutes should be efficiently segregated and harshly punished. But increasingly, social scientists, moral reformers, civil servants, and medical specialists found the lot of the prostitute her-

self an absorbing and unresolved moral task. They had a keenly attentive
bourgeois audience with them. All of them together presided over a
somewhat reluctant but ultimately rather impressive outburst of humanity
toward the fallen woman, a dawning awareness of her as a sufferer as
much as a cause of suffering. In her tract of 1912, *A New Conscience and
an Ancient Evil*, Jane Addams found this development as noteworthy as
its halting pace. Prostitution had "received less philanthropic effort than
any other well-recognized menace to the community, largely because
there is something peculiarly distasteful and distressing in personal acquaintance with its victims." Yet (as Addams modestly did not say) at
long last, partly reflecting the work of intrepid publicists like herself,
this imbalance, which had its roots in the emotional resistances of bourgeois culture, was being corrected. "Philanthropy" had gradually been
"impelled to a consideration of prostitution in relation to the welfare and
the orderly existence of society itself."[73] The whore had come to insinuate herself into the agenda of the bourgeois superego.

   There were those for whom she had been there all along; late-nineteenth-
century reformers found welcome models in the strenuous activities of
their predecessors—religious orders, public officials, and private philanthropists. Beginning two or three decades before Victoria's accession
to the throne in 1837, "penitentiaries" and shelters for "Magdalens" had
begun to dot most great cities, and some small ones. They were the
philanthropic nineteenth-century heirs of eighteenth-century lock hos-
pitals, established in London and elsewhere to segregate those afflicted
with venereal disease. The Home for Fallen Women, Urania Cottage,
that the enormously wealthy English heiress Angela Burdett-Coutts
established in 1846 with the humane counsel and energetic support of
Charles Dickens, was a fairly characteristic exercise of the benevolent
imagination: in 1856, there had been sixty Magdalen homes in England,
a number that had leaped more than five-fold, to 308, half a century
later. By then, these had cared for about 12,500 prostitutes. Refuges,
often sadly inadequate, long on earnest good will and short on funds, did
their best to provide temporary homes for ignorant and impecunious
country girls highly vulnerable to the seductions of the streets, or for
young prostitutes, weary and ashamed.

   Other reformers, in other countries, were far from idle. The New
York Magdalen Society was founded in 1830 to provide an *"Asylum for*

73. Mackirdy: Mrs. Archibald Mackirdy and W. N. Willis, *The White Slave Trade*
(1909; 2nd ed., 1912), 108; Corlieu: *La prostitution à Paris* (1887), 9; Addams: *New
Conscience and Ancient Evil*, 141–44.

females who have deviated from the paths of virtue, and are desirous of being restored to a respectable station in society, by religious instruction and the formation of moral and industrial habits." In Berlin, a society devoted to raising public morality sponsored a "Mägdehaus" to which young women arriving in the capital could repair to find protection against "crime and shame." Berlin, too, had the largest *Magdalenenstift* in Germany; in 1885–86 it accepted 120 "pupils." Other Magdalen shelters had been active in the German states for years; the oldest, in the small Rhenish town of Kaiserswerth, had in the half century since its opening in 1833 accepted 880 young women. It offered, like the others, shelter, nourishment, religious instruction, some rudimentary training in domestic skills, and counseling to place their charges—all with limited resources and against formidable odds.[74]

They were formidable indeed. Most of the young women induced to enter such shelters were very young, hopelessly ignorant, lacking all salable commodities except their bodies, usually fleeing or driven from brutal, indifferent or torn families; if they had broken away from prostitution, they were coarsened, defiant, often desperately ill. Many girls did not leave these shelters alive. "It is a sphere of activity cluttered with thorns," the German pastor H. Stursberg sighed, only to rally: "All the more splendid the victory, when love, which believes all and hopes all, which gives up on no one, succeeds in rescuing someone from these depths." Analyzing the work done by the Rhineland shelters he had studied in the mid-1880s, Stursberg estimated that they had "really rescued" a third of the pathetic floating population they were devoted to serving.

No one, not even the most self-deluded, ever thought that the Magdalen shelters permanently rehabilitated more than half of their "pupils": in 1831, the Executive Committee of the young New York Magdalen Society, looking about them for encouragement, found grounds for hope in reports from similar institutions elsewhere. The "Bristol Penitentiary," they reported, "has been favored with signal success"; for the last thirty years, "*two-fifths* of all the inmates have become known as restored to virtue and society," while the Liverpool Magdalen Society, after thirteen

---

74. Magdalen Homes: F. K. Prochaska, *Women and Philanthropy in Nineteenth-Century England* (1980), 188–89; "Mägdehaus": *Daheim*, XXI (1885), 654–55. There had been sporadic efforts to rehabilitate the most promising, least "hardened" of prostitutes long before; a division in that sprawling Parisian complex, the *Salpêtrière*, was by the 1680s devoted to housing prostitutes who might be led back to decent ways. Marc Micale, "A Critical Study of Jean Martin Charcot" (Yale dissertation in progress), ch. 2.

years, "report that out of the 213 admissions, *one-third* had been restored
to their friends, or placed in service after being radically reformed."
Elsewhere, in Bath or in Philadelphia, the figures were less cheering or
less conclusive, but the directors of the New York Magdalen Society
professed delight with even these far from dazzling results. Yet, if anything, these figures were excessively optimistic: they notoriously sub-
sumed, under their "successes," young women's fates which, more closely
examined, would look rather dismal. The writers of these reports were
intent on painting the brightest possible picture to attract potential donors;
men and women of good will, incredulous at the resistant materials
refusing to be malleable to their pious hands, they were inclined to
encourage themselves by encouraging the others in their annual accounting.[75]

The homes of mercy they superintended were often strict, punitive, and
vengeful, enforcing the most rigid middle-class standards and piety with
a pitiless hand. Toward the end of the bourgeois century, Olive Christian
Malvery recalled once visiting a depressing "Magdalene's Home," in
which "women with close-cropped hair were at work over wash-tubs in
a semi-underground place," wearing "hideous little caps" and "stiff
straight gowns of a very ugly material. They were, in fact, branded."[76]
Burdett-Coutts's Urania Cottage was, though in its own way censorious,
far nearer the agreeable end of the scale. The house gave shelter to
thirteen young prostitutes willing to be reclaimed, and regulated their
days with rigorous benevolence, forcefully directing them to mend their
ways and to emigrate. It was a highly troublesome venture, though
Charles Dickens himself, in his thoughtful, immensely detailed letters to
his rich philanthropic friend, and his direct interventions in the management of the Cottage, proved himself sturdy in his good sense and good
will, wholly free from cant. A prostitute entering Urania Cottage, he
suggested, should be told that "she has come there for *useful* repentance
and reform, and because her past life has been dreadful in its nature and
consequences, and full of affliction, misery, and despair *to herself*."
Dickens thought of such young women as victims: "Never mind society
while she is at that pass. Society has used her ill and turned away from
her, and she cannot be expected to take much heed of its rights and
wrongs." Nor did he think that drabness in the Cottage had anything to
commend it for those to be reclaimed: "Color these people always want,

75. Stursberg: *Prostitution in Deutschland*, 84; New-York Magdalen Society: *First
Annual Report*, 18–20.
76. Mackirdy and Willis, *White Slave Trade*, 110.

and color (as allied to fancy), I would always give them."[77] This was the voice of the pioneer, filled not with self-satisfied compassion but, rather, a genuine, unequivocal empathy for these girls' needs. Reporting in an anonymous article in his periodical, *Household Words*, Dickens took pleasure in an interim balance sheet: Urania Cottage had provided a temporary refuge for fifty-seven girls by 1853; seven of these had left on their own, seven had run away, ten unregenerates had been expelled, three, in a way the most pathetic of the lot, had "relapsed" on the long passage to Australia. But, then, thirty had made new lives in several colonial outposts, and seven of these had actually found husbands.[78] The reclaimed whore of fiction who turns her back on vice in remorse to establish her own respectable family rested, at least in some measure, on fact.

The well-intentioned projects to wean the prostitute from her life often appeared condescending and maladroit. Even when they were in sensitive and skillful hands, the temptation of the streets, the habits of gratification, the ravages of disease, the sheer differences in vocabularies and values made rehabilitation a painful, sometimes a faintly comical affair. At best, the no-man's land between the charitable bourgeois and the corrupted proletarian was mined with mutual incomprehension and barely concealed mutual suspicion; at worst, the middle-class sense of guilt appeared, to the half-reluctant recipients of philanthropic attentions, little more than a rehearsal of self-indulgence. But, whatever the mixture of motives and the high probability of failure, publications on the social evil rarely failed to explore the rehabilitation of the prostitute, either making proposals for healthful entertainment and shelters supervised by pious guardians, or reporting on what had already been done in the community, with the purpose of having it done still better. "To the average individual, it is true," the economist E. R. A. Seligman, Secretary to the New York Committee of Fifteen, reasoned in 1902, "there is something exceedingly repulsive in the idea of the restoration to decent society of women who have lived a vicious life." Yet, he sternly reminded his readers, "these women are members of society and can hardly be refused by Government the right to reform."[79]

Had Seligman written a few years later, he could have been far less

77. Dickens to Burdett-Coutts, May 26, 1846, *The Letters of Charles Dickens*, vol. IV, *1844–1846*, ed. Kathleen Tillotson (1977), 553; *Letters to Burdett-Coutts*, 328–29.
78. *Household Words*, April 23, 1853.
79. *The Social Evil With Special Reference to Conditions Existing in the City of New York, A Report prepared under the Direction of the Committee of Fifteen*, E. R. A. Seligman, Secretary (1902), 81.

pessimistic about the "average individual," for charitable individuals and institutions, both sectarian and secular, were continuing to join the already flourishing enterprise of reforming prostitutes in a fairly ambitious way. From about 1903 on, a number of European cities, including Breslau, Leipzig, Zurich, Vienna, and Stockholm, appointed policewomen to seek out prostitutes susceptible of moral reform, and these cities, like others, established asylums that would reeducate fallen women, heal their bodies, teach them skills, find them jobs. Municipalities could, by then, draw on the accumulated experience of institutions active for half a century or more. The Vice Commission of Minneapolis reported in 1911 that "persons who have lapsed from virtue, but who have not yet wholly abandoned themselves to an evil life," could find shelter, among several places, in a Norwegian Home and at the House of the Good Shepherd, and its report to the mayor detailed local efforts with unconcealed satisfaction: "While your Honor's Commission, in many of these recommendations, have laid the emphasis on Prevention, they would not ignore or lightly esteem the noble institutions that gather up the wreckage and seek to repair and reform. A great work is being done by devoted and heroic souls, in this direction, and the community should understand what they are trying to accomplish." A little later, in 1913, the Vice Commission of Philadelphia was somewhat less sanguine: "It must be remembered that rescue homes and kindred institutions are primarily intended only for those who *desire* to reform, and this number is unhappily not large." Still, the Commission did not advise abandoning the good work; it recommended the establishment of special centers for feeble-minded prostitutes—a large number, it would seem—and of a permanent Night Court, and urged more effective supervision of "places of amusement, especially dance halls, frequented by minors" through policewomen who could gather "some kind of information" and "exercise control" more easily than men.[80] This defiant hope against the odds is fairly characteristic; the labor of draining the cesspool of vice loomed as an assignment at once herculean and interminable, since its supplies never seemed to dry up and its ingenious, unscrupulous profiteers never seemed at a loss how to evade new legal restrictions or improved police surveillance. Yet it was necessary and, fortunately, at times visibly rewarding. Some of the writers, indeed, give the appearance of viewing with alarm that they might, all the more, point with pride. But all had

80. *Report of the Vice Commission of Minneapolis to His Honor, James C. Haynes, Mayor* (1911), 117; *The Vice Commission of Philadelphia. A Report on Existing Conditions with Recommendations to the Honorable Rudolph Blankenburg, Mayor of Philadelphia* (1913), 36–37.

come to agree that, whatever their prognoses, the work belonged prominently among the social duties that vigilant bourgeois had learned to
impose on themselves. It is this principled, undaunted aspiration to effect
the rehabilitation of fallen women, far more than the bourgeois' much-
ridiculed craving for degraded love objects, that gives the worldwide
campaign against prostitution and for the prostitute its secure place in
the erotic economy of the late-nineteenth-century middle classes.

That campaign drew on diverse motives for action: concern for the
public health, moral outrage at sexual exploitation and political corruption, a sense of obligation to the unfortunate both religious and secular in
origin. Much of the debate had skirted the realm of fantasy. As we have
seen, prostitution was just exotic, alarming, and exciting enough to elicit
uncontrolled overstatement and fanciful generalizations, tales about epidemics of syphilis sweeping the world of the respectable, or about a vast
mafia of white slavers dragging innocent maidens into commercial vice.
Yet there was some substance to these anxious forecasts and urgent
appeals for remedies: one did not need to be a determined Evangelical
to deplore the white slave trade or suffer from syphilidophobia to feel
real concern at the risks of venereal infection. The white slaver was not
an imaginary bugbear. There was, we must remember, for nearly all the
nineteenth century, no reliable cure for syphilis and, for that matter,
much diagnostic confusion about venereal disorders. Yet when all is
said, the unceasing production of literature, the intense labors of committees, the irresolute postures of legislators betray the presence of a
nonrational, partly repressed dimension in the nineteenth-century treatment of prostitution: collective fantasies of rescue and reparation.

Such fantasies, principally accessible through their more spectacular
derivatives, are ways of facing the urgent, often conflicting pressures of
sexuality and aggression and, more than that, of forestalling the unbear-
able feelings of guilt they can impose. They can be enacted in the world
or in the mind: the conscientious philanthropist repairing the social
ravages for which he feels somehow responsible is a common instance
of the first; the adolescent lover imagining himself rescuing his beloved
from mortal enemies or burning buildings a no less common instance of
the second. Charles Dickens, we know, lived out fantasies by acting as
Angela Burdett-Coutts's advisor, and he recorded them by exposing his
favorite fictional hero, David Copperfield, to adolescent, dreamy moments of heroism as he loves Miss Larkins, in vain, "wishing that a fire
would burst out; that the assembled crowd would stand appalled; that I,
dashing through them with a ladder, might rear it against her window,

save her in my arms, go back for something she had left behind, and perish in the flames."[81] In an exigent culture like that of the nineteenth-century bourgeoisie, penetrated and refined by demanding religious convictions and exquisite ethical standards, both will reach for exceptionally intense expression. When the object of rescue and remorse is a fallen woman, these fantasies gain particular poignancy, for they draw crucial childhood experiences into their orbit. They revive and enlist early memories.

As children learn the facts of sexual intercourse, they must absorb the knowledge that one's parents, too, do this sort of thing—that they, the children, indeed, are its products. Boys and girls alike must suffer this disillusionment, and they will respond with a variety of defensive tactics. They will repress the information, vehemently deny it—or playfully elaborate it into a grandiose fantasy of degradation and rescue, with the parents in the role of culprit and the child as the doughty St. George. Psychoanalysts have generally discovered this fantasy assuming particular prominence in the boy.[82] In helpless rage and balked desire, they argue, he will degrade his mother into the simulacrum of the available female, a scenario that makes the second act essential: that in which he rescues the mother, in whatever form he may encounter her likeness in later years. Thus he undoes carnal reality and restores the first love of his life to her immaculate status: the angel in the house. Significantly, while there were rescuers rather grudging on this point, prevailing opinion held that rehabilitated whores should be allowed to marry. Erotic pleasures were not to be permanently denied but thoughtfully policed. The fully developed and socially adaptive rescue fantasy, in short, in concert with other motives, sought an ethically and emotionally acceptable place for sensuality itself, complete with happy ending. The great nineteenth-century

---

81. *David Copperfield* (1850; ed. Nina Burgis, 1983), 221 [ch. 18]. Here is an irresistible instance from real life: "I could die happy doing something for you. (Just imagine a guy with spectacles and a girl mouth doing the Sir Lancelot.) Since I can't rescue you from any monster or carry you from a sinking ship—simply because I'd be afraid of the monsters, couldn't carry you, and can't swim—I'll have to go to work and make money enough to pay my debts and then get you to take me for what I am: just a common everyday man whose instincts are to be ornery, who's anxious to be right." Harry Truman to Bess Wallace, November 19, 1913, *Dear Bess: The Letters from Harry to Bess Truman, 1910–1959*, ed. Robert H. Ferrell (1983), 145.

82. The psychoanalytic literature on the rescue fantasy, initiated by Freud, concentrates on the largely unconscious drama as it unfolds in the male of the species. There are complex technical issues here; suffice it to say that I am generalizing the fantasy to the female as well—the cultural evidence calls for nothing less.

bourgeois crusade to reclaim prostitutes was not a hypocritical search for a moral holiday in the pious guise of performing an onerous duty. It drew strength from related crusades to rehabilitate the criminal and reeducate the misfit, all heritages of the disinterested social engineering proposed by the men of the Enlightenment. In 1904, Professor Alfred Fournier of the French Academy of Medicine summed up a century of humane efforts in a report to the Commission Extra-parlementaire du Régime des Moeurs: whatever medical treatment, even hospitalization, the prostitute required for her own and her society's health, the treatment must be "humanitarian," if possible "moralizing," and "tolerant, enlightened, charitable."[83]

It must be apparent that the rescue fantasy these campaigns enacted was a special case of the more elusive but doubtless even more pervasive repressed fantasy of reparation. Both were antidotes to ambivalence. Now ambivalence needs managing almost from the beginning of life, for children experience neither love nor hate as a pure culture. Nor is it a very stable one: mothers, fathers, siblings, nurses, all cherished persons in their young life awaken rage, draw upon themselves potent destructive impulses that are frightening to experience and seem difficult to master. They threaten children far more than they can realistically threaten the adults who have incurred the displeasure of their offspring. Awkwardly, clumsily, yet with a desperate sincerity, children work to bring their undesired fury under control; later, as their superego forms, they seek to propitiate those powerful, looming figures, to anticipate and thus to avert their retaliation. The offer of reparation, to make good voluntarily, unasked, the grave offense of having harbored wicked thoughts against good people, appears the most promising way of appeasing one's guilt feelings. "You have to forgive us," Arnold Toynbee told a working-class audience in 1883, "for we have wronged you."[84] This was the conscience with which nineteenth-century bourgeois felt they had to wrestle as they saw, studied, and hoped to repair the social wreckage around them. What could be more soothing to their exigent superego, a purer, more conspicuous instance of reparation, than to bring hardened prostitutes once again under the sway of moral life?

83. Fournier: *Défense de la santé et de la morale publiques* (1904), 65, 71. "In the beginning was the Enlightenment," as Gordon Wright has put it. "Rehabilitation, except in the restricted form of expiation through suffering, remained an almost unknown concept until the nineteenth century." *Between the Guillotine and Liberty: Two Centuries of the Crime Problem in France* (1983), 110.

84. Peter d'Alroy Jones, *The Christian Socialist Revival, 1877–1914: Religion, Class, and Social Conscience in Late-Victorian England* (1968), 85n; see *Education of the Senses*, 43.

But that escape route from guilt was available to everyone. The rescue fantasy was not a male monopoly; in the nineteenth century, women, in fact, played a substantial, increasingly prominent role in reclaiming prostitutes. In 1890, visiting Mrs. Chant's Refuge for Erring Women in Chicago, Mabel Todd was moved to tears of sympathy and could not bring herself to disapprove of these fallen girls, whether they had sinned from love or lust.[85] And Angela Burdett-Coutts did not confine her charitable interests to throwing discreet checks at favorite causes; she kept close watch over her Urania Cottage and over its graduates even after they had left the home country for distant colonies. There was no one like her anywhere: none had her money or, for that matter, quite her style in philanthropy. But other women brought to bear uncommon energies and intelligence to translate both rescue and reparation fantasies into reality by participating prominently in voluntary organizations or the struggle for remedial legislation.

Everyone knew the names of Josephine Butler and Jane Addams, the first the most tenacious lobbyist against the double standard that the nineteenth century was to know, the second the famous founder of Hull House in Chicago. These were the woman generals in the twin armies of rehabilitation. But literally thousands of women everywhere, mainly prosperous and educated bourgeoises, served them in lesser, though still highly visible ranks. As I have noted, virtually every local committee inquiring into the social evil took on women members, not as ballast or decoration but as working partners in a difficult, far from grateful enterprise; they proved themselves indispensable in raising money, founding shelters, alerting public opinion, bullying politicians, and, nothing daunted, going into the field at considerable risk to their sensibilities and their physical safety. With a bravery that complacent males had thought reserved to themselves, female activists would hold evening meetings in sordid parts of town, accost swarms of street walkers, and go so far as to invade bordellos on the track of potential recruits for purification.

These confrontations no doubt had their ludicrous moments, as tenderly raised, well-spoken rescue workers piously labored to persuade the tough, painted women of the streets to abandon their life, but the courage of these philanthropists remains impressive. For it was dangerous work they were doing; they were subjected to abuse, obscenities, sometimes showers of rotten tomatoes and vicious bodily assault.[86] Yet they

85. See *Education of the Senses*, 98.
86. Prochaska, *Women and Philanthropy in England*, 191–202.

ever for a moment doubted the need for their work and the value of
heir sacrifice, for they were wholly unpersuaded by the plausible
sociological speculations of Lecky and his allies: they did not see prostitution as a safety valve but as a deeply distressing and possibly remediable
evil; they were moved by the plight of the fallen girl rather than comforted
by her presumed social utility. Besides, the rescue work certainly proved
of inestimable psychological import for the rescuers. "I have seen young
girls suffer and grow sensibly lowered in vitality in the first year after
they leave school," Jane Addams said in a famous lecture of 1892. "The
desire for action, the wish to right wrong and alleviate suffering, haunts
them daily." She noted that "we have in America a fast-growing number
of cultivated young people who have no recognized outlet for their
active faculties." They hear of social misery; society smiles on them but
does not prepare them to act. She quoted Huxley to the effect that "the
sense of uselessness is the severest shock which the human system can sustain, and that, if persistently sustained, it results in atrophy of function."[87]
If the educated woman of the late nineteenth century yearned to apply
her book learning and social good will in the real world, the crusade to
rehabilitate prostitutes provided one longed-for, gratifying—and permissible—opportunity.

For, despite all its lame and cruel jokes at the expense of intrusive busy-
bodies, bourgeois society gladly tolerated this kind of feminine activity.
With its long and honorable history, it perfectly suited the traditional
picture of woman's exalted mission in the world. "If to men have been
given the bodily strength and the intellectual preeminence," the prolific,
devout English author and activist Ellice Hopkins wrote in 1877, "it is
the woman who is the conscience of the world." She thought this to be a
truth "too long forgotten," but in fact it did not run counter to men's
accustomed perception of the female sex and her destiny.[88] Only Hopkins's
stress on action might jar a little. Just as conventional nineteenth-century
men found it far easier to visualize women as teachers or nurses than as
lawyers or architects, so they could, without unduly straining their imagination, see women taking a sympathetic interest in the squalid world
of prostitution. After all (as the self-serving and defensive truism had it),
women are more pure-minded, more considerate, more tender and affectionate than men—and less busy. Roman Catholics invoked the Virgin
Mary as the incarnation of charity, and those professing other faiths had

87. Addams, "The Subjective Necessity for Social Settlements," in *Philanthropy
and Social Progress*, seven essays by Jane Addams et al. (1893), 12–15.
88. Prochaska, *Women and Philanthropy in England*, 204.

other ego ideals, quite as feminine, right at hand: the legends that rapidl
formed around Florence Nightingale, the Lady with the Lamp who ha
saved the lives or soothed the last hours of countless British lads servir
in the Crimea, were only the most famous of these. Normally, to be sur
women exercised all these lovable traits at home, but the wider worl
seemed only an extension of the househould. In fact, many educate
women adopted this condescending male view that they might pursu
their social purposes enveloped in general approval. As early as 1839, a
anonymous woman writer provided a rationale that others would echc
woman's sense of mission to do good in society is simply "the flow c
maternal love."[89] Only churlish and reactionary satirists would try to dar
that flow rather than harness it.

The unprecedented concentration of philanthropic attention on th
fallen woman and her possible rehabilitation is a dramatic instance o
how particular social circumstances shape universal human traits, how th
world invades the mind. The nineteenth century imposed on its middl
classes a unique constellation of economic, political, and cultural realitie
that directed their attempts to cope with sexuality and guilt towar
strenuous activity; they cultivated their conscience, whether devout o
irreverent, with a peculiar ferocity neither dimmed nor seriously com
promised by the convenient moments of amnesia or self-serving con
tradictions that their critics professed to find characteristic of their mora
style. The spread of prosperity generated abundant surplus funds beggin
to be invested not just in shares of stock but also in doing good. Th
growing assertiveness of burghers in the political sphere, generating vista
of emancipation from aristocratic tutelage, found rewarding targets fo
the exercise of energy and decisiveness in social investigation and rescu
work. The exemption of most middle-class women from economic activity
pushed them, eager for work, into philanthropy. There had, of course
been Magdalens before; charity was an ancient idea; even the rehabilitation of miserable sinners was not an invention of the bourgeois century
But the mixture of psychological pressures, economic opportunities, and
political space for maneuver had never been as favorable for the activation
of remorseful fantasies, and their translation into reality, as it was to be
from the 1840s and 1850s on.

The principal aims, inherent strains, and uncertain rewards of these
fantasies at work made themselves most conspicuous in the conscientious
diaries of William Ewart Gladstone. Beginning in the early 1840s, Glad-

89. Ibid., 7.

tone, already a prominent politician, developed an intense interest in the reclamation of prostitutes. His contemporaries knew it: reticent as he was, Gladstone made no secret of his missionary ministrations and defied attempts at blackmail with a calm courage that testifies, not to the ease of his conscience—Gladstone's conscience was never easy—but to the probity of his conscious intentions. He did not conceal his expeditions from his beloved wife Catherine: on August 2, 1850, the day after Gladstone had, he hoped, persuaded a prostitute to enter a rehabilitation home, he told his dearest "C.," and she, as he noted in his diary, "approved & with much interest." At times, indeed, he would bring his disreputable acquaintances home to her. If Catherine Gladstone was not privy to all of her husband's latent wishes, she was well-informed of his manifest actions.[90]

Gladstone's translation of his fantasies into a philanthropic mission had begun as a relatively routine practice and grew into an obsession. In February 1845, he had joined a small secret lay brotherhood that exacted acts of charity from its members. Gradually, he came to specialize in prostitutes: on August 19, 1845, the day that his fourth child was baptized, he found time to visit with one of his new charges. It was not until May 1849 that he began to take his nocturnal walks through the streets of London after the House of Commons rose, to seek out fallen women and persuade them to subject themselves to the discipline of a House of Mercy. Gladstone, who read everything, had read Parent-Duchâtelet by the early summer of 1845 and, of course, five years later, W. R. Greg's article on prostitution in the *Westminster Review*.[91] But he needed them only for the statistics; he had defined his moral assignment long before. Christian charity was, for him, a matter of work, not of words.

It proved bitter, unrewarding work. On January 20, 1854, after he had been engaged in it for a decade, Gladstone drew up a balance sheet far less satisfactory than the one Charles Dickens had published the year before: "This morning," he wrote, "I lay awake till four with a sad & perplexing subject: it was reflecting on & counting up the numbers of

90. August 2, 1850, *The Gladstone Diaries*, ed. M. R. D. Foot and H. C. G. Matthew, 8 vols. so far (1968–   ), IV, 231. On July 26, 1851, he wrote to his wife: "When you say I do not know half the evil of your life, you say that which I believe in almost every case is true between one human being and another; but it sets me thinking how little you know the evil of mine of which at the last day I shall have a strange tale to tell." Quoted by Matthew, "Introduction," ibid., III, xlviii.
91. See August 19, July 9, 1845; July 8, 1850; ibid., III, 477, 467; IV, 224. One "partially rescued prostitute" wrote him after she had spent some time in a House of Mercy: "I have no doubt that you wished to do me some service, but I did not fancy being shut up in such a place as that for perhaps twelve months. I should have committed suicide." Quoted by Matthew, ibid., III, xlv. The path of the rescuer is stony.

unhappy beings, now present to my memory with whom during now s
many years I have conversed indoors and out. I reckoned from 80 to 9c
Among these there is but one of whom I know that the miserable life ha
been abandoned *and* that I can fairly join that fact with influence o
mine." It was an appalling record. "Yet this were much more than enougl
for all the labour & the time, had it been purely spent on my part." But—
and this was the true ground of his distress—the time had been impurely
spent. "The case is far otherwise: & tho' probably in none of these instance
have I not spoken good words, yet so bewildered have I been that they
constitute the chief burden of my soul."[92] The burden was that he enjoyee
his work all too much; the girls of the streets aroused him sexually.

Erotic fantasies had been troubling this great self-examiner for som
years. At times, as he confessed in his diary with heart-rending remorse
he could not resist the temptation to read what he called pornography
so deep was his shame at his appetite for these sinful and criminal im
purities—the words are his—that he could record it only in Italian.[9]
His cherished Catherine was often unavailable to him, with her monoton
ous rhythm of pregnancies and her frequent long visits to friends anc
relatives. His repeated frustrations, coupled with the incessant pressure
of his political career and his family obligations, sometimes seem to have
set up in him the wish for a reward, for the untrammeled gratification of
his erotic needs. These needs were exigent, which is to say, normal. Eros
troubled his calm in his most exalted moments, when he suspected it least
"The mind while engaged in prayer," Gladstone once noted, unconsciously
applying a telling metaphor, "should be like the bow at the moment before
the arrow leaves the string: and should discharge itself, should project its
whole force into every petition—How arduous a work!"[94] Loyally
though he loved his wife, there was in his ruminations and his activities a
certain pressure toward revenge for her repeated inaccessibility to him—
an inaccessibility doubtless all the more maddening for being largely his
doing. At all events, Gladstone's fantasies of rescue and reparation uncom
fortably concentrated his erotic excitability on some dangerous beings, on
young, often attractive prostitutes whom he saw in provocative places,
under provocative circumstances. His efforts, as he himself recognized,
were at once tests and temptations, and tests all the more worthy as he
found the temptations practically irresistible.

92. Ibid., IV, 586.
93. For instances, see May 15, 18, 1848, ibid., IV, 36–37.
94. February 29, 1844, ibid., III, 351.

In later life he struck up a friendship with Catherine Walters, "Skittles," one of the most appealing and intelligent of England's high-priced courtesans, and was slandered for that, too. "He manages to combine his missionary meddling with a keen appreciation of a pretty face," Henry Labouchere, Gladstone's follower in the House of Commons and a wicked wit, said of him. "He has never been known to rescue any of our East End whores, nor for that matter is it easy to contemplate his rescuing any ugly women, and I am quite sure his conception of the Magdalen is of an incomparable example of pulchritude with a superb figure and carriage." Reading such contemporary verdicts, later writers assailing what they were pleased to call Victorian hypocrisy needed only to copy. But while Labouchere was right about Gladstone's clandestine sexual arousal, he wholly missed his anguish. Miserably, Gladstone even doubted the purity of his intentions in confessing his horrendous lapses to his diary: "Even in making this record," he noted, "I know not whether it be for evil or for good: it is however, with pain & this is my hope, but Oh! not enough pain, a weak ineffectual pain whereas it should be one piercing the inmost soul. O that I may attain to such a pain."[95] There were times when he did; his moral masochism was powerful and sensitive.

One resolution Gladstone discovered for these erotic conflicts was, literally, self-flagellation: when he found himself unable to resist sensual literature, or his potential charges became too exciting, he would scourge himself. It was, for this most self-probing of bourgeois diarists, a doubtful resolution, for he suspected that he took some pleasure in the stripes he inflicted on himself.[96] After all, punishment that brings even a hint of gratification negates its very purpose. Gladstone found his defenses as perplexing as his drives, and little less shameful.

How seriously he took his sinful appetites emerges from a canvass he made in late 1845, in which he listed the "channels," the "incentives," and the "chief actual dangers" leading to "impurity," as well as his "remedies." The channels included, significantly, beyond conversation, seeing and hearing, also touch and thought: both in his most public and most secluded moments, his sensual nature rose up to plague him. These incentives for impurity show his need for structure, the regularity of habit;

95. Henry Blyth, *Skittles, The Last Victorian Courtesan. The Life and Times of Catherine Walters* (1970), 187; July 19, 1848, *Gladstone Diaries*, IV, 55.
96. "Has it been sufficiently considered, how far pain may become the ground of enjoyment. How far satisfaction and even an action delighting in pain may be a true experimental phenomenon of the human mind." January 4, 1843, ibid., III, 250; a passage to which Matthew, ever alert, calls attention, ibid., xlviin.

for he found himself endangered not merely by idleness and exhaustion but also by "absence from usual place," "interruptions of usual habits," and "curiosity of sympathy." His remedies included prayer, "realising the presence of the Lord crucified & Enthroned," and several specific, highly concrete prohibitions—"abstinence," "not to linger," not to "look over books in bookshops except known ones," and "D[itt]o as to looking in printshop windows"—as though he wanted, consciously, to convert his sexual longings into phobias. He appended a list, which he kept up until 1849, of the dates when he had indulged in pornography, and when he had flagellated himself.[97] All of this in the midst of teaching his children, walking with his wife, wasting trying hours on tangled family business affairs, attending the House of Commons, writing voluminous dispatches, and studying theological and political literature at a pace, and with a concentration, that would have been staggering in a man doing nothing but reading. The excitement of his family concerns and his public career, far from absorbing, only stimulated his sexual energies. Hence his mission to the prostitutes, a manifest expression of his fantasies, became, not part of his solution but part of his problem. Trying manfully to raise fallen women to his level, he felt himself in persistent peril of descending to theirs.

It is always risky to take so outsize a figure as Gladstone as representative of more ordinary mortals, yet what distinguished him from them was not his tormented conscience, but his troubled sensitivity to its punitive reproaches. His experience supplies material wholly congruent with the other evidence I have rehearsed in these pages. Certainly, some bachelors would resort to prostitutes to appease their clamorous senses, chafing as they did under the long engagements that respectable society inflicted on men not yet established enough to marry and unable to sustain celibacy until the wedding night. Just as certainly, a minority of restless, unsatisfied husbands would slake their thirst for sexual adventure by buying outside what they could not get within their home. To that extent, Mandeville's notorious paradox—private vices, public benefits—has some substance. But a miserable exclamation of Thackeray's illustrates the working of this way of feeling. Toward the end of his unrewarding, disillusioning love for Mrs. Brookfield, he caustically told his mother: "Very likely it's *a* woman I want more that any particular one: and some day may be investing a trull in the street with that priceless jewel my heart." For the time, at least, lust and affection emphatically ran, for Thackeray, in divergent directions. But it was precisely the purpose of the general

97. See October 26, 1845, ibid., III, 492–93.

crusade against prostitution to rejoin them, to heal their division in a love that was physical and spiritual together. "Say I got my desire," Thackeray went on, "I should despise a woman; and the very day of the sacrifice would be the end of the attachment."[98] This was the sort of desperate carnality to which prostitution pandered.

The lure of prostitution, then, only widened the split between the two currents of love that Freud took to be a symptom of unresolved neurotic business and which his culture condemned as degrading to its erotic ideal. The reformers were right on this crucial issue. If the claim that nervousness was the characteristic malaise of the bourgeois century has proved to be highly dubious, the assertion that prostitution was a welcome safeguard for the middle-class family, the necessary by-product of the repressions it imposed, has turned out to have even less merit. Prostitution was far less the price of repression than a sign of its failure.

Fortunately, it is not necessary—nor, indeed, possible—to reduce middle-class ways of loving to a formula. Bourgeois in love could be very different from one another. Nor was their fate free of paradoxes: there were untold instances where love followed, not romance but rational arrangements; and French bourgeois—even more, bourgeoises—living in a cultural climate foreigners liked to describe as awash with open lasciviousness, had relatively modest expectations of lasting amorous delights. Moreover, nineteenth-century bourgeois proved very much like persons of other classes and other ages. Idiosyncratic intimate histories and the divergent pressures exerted by religious allegiances, social distinctions, and national habits must make any description of characteristic middle-class styles in love and sex richly polychromatic, any definition extremely flexible and accommodating. This is why I have repeatedly felt impelled to caution that the middling orders living in the decades of Victoria and Freud had not invented their ideals of love or their dominant attitudes toward sexuality. Lust, anxiety, defense mechanisms, after all, are neither local nor evanescent affairs; they made nineteenth-century bourgeois brothers to ancient Greeks or contemporary laborers.

Still, bourgeois in their century set certain unmistakable emotional accents, loved and hated in ways that were very much their own. I recall only their rage for privacy, their impassioned rehabilitation of prostitutes, their consequential rediscovery of sexual perversions, their mobilizing imaginative disguises for sensuality, their strident slanders of woman oddly combined with a new respect for her capacities. Even the

98. Humphry House, "Thackeray's Letters," in All in Due Time: Collected Essays and Broadcast Talks (1955), 108.

most general attitudes identifying middle-class culture—its responses to drastic transformations in political, economic, and medical conditions, and its commitment to confidence shadowed by intrusive anxieties—borrowed from, and in turn reveal much about, that bourgeois style of loving. In middle-class hands, the definition of love as a happy conjunction of excitement and tenderness, though wholly derivative, took on distinctive shape. The dimensions of history, both vertical and horizontal, are, as every historian has good reason to know, arenas for the tense coexistence of the momentary, the transient, and the persistent, of the individual, the class-bound, and the universal. Drives and defenses may endure, but they are malleable, plastic, impressively mobile. I said, introducing *Education of the Senses*, that nineteenth-century middle-class culture had not lost its capacity to astound. But there is nothing so astonishing after all about the proposition that in that age, the bourgeoisie set up as its idol a black-coated Eros, celebrated, and for the most part obeyed him.

≥ EPILOGUE ≤

Black-Coated Eros

1. Between Condescension and Envy

THOSE LIVING in the decades of Victoria believed that there was a
bourgeois way with love. "There is a psychology of the common man,"
Sigmund Freud wrote to his fiancée in 1883, "that is rather different from
ours." Articulate working men had long taken the same view. "I have
found," the self-educated trade union radical James Dawson Burn wrote
in 1855, "that nearly every class of people in the kingdom have a moral
code of their own, and every body of men has its own standards of
perfection."[1]

These differences made themselves particularly conspicuous in the
sphere of erotic feeling and conduct. The psychology of the aristocrat
seemed, to bourgeois moralists and satirists, no less different from theirs
than that of the lower orders. But it was far more unequivocal; the literature of middle-class writers on the erotic pursuits of the nobility was
dominated by sensational recitals of licentious doings: it liked to treat the
aristocrat as a debauched sophisticate, as a vigorous or languid connoisseur
of vice, the provider of appalling—which is to say, entertaining—scandal.
"We know," one German critic exclaimed in the 1890s, "in what a
swamp of profligacy the upper and uppermost 10,000 wade about!" Another, analyzing modern immorality, agreed: "Neither the aristocracy of
blood," Dr. Theodor Kornig wrote in some heat, "nor the aristocracy of

1. "Psychology of the common man": Sigmund Freud to Martha Bernays, August
29, 1883, *Freud, Briefe 1873–1939*, ed. Ernst L. Freud (1960), 49; Burn: *The Autobiography of A Beggar Boy*, in David Vincent, *Bread, Knowledge and Freedom: A
Study of Nineteenth-Century Working Class Autobiography* (1981), 24.

money claim to provide a moral model. The reports on the immoral goings-on among many military circles are not mere fables"; on the contrary, "immorality is fostered even more by the scions of the rich parvenu families in our large cities, whose heroic deeds on this field bring blushes of shame to our face."[2] Following suit, much fiction of the century depicted nobles as effete or unscrupulous lovers, as heartless seducers sowing their wild oats among their inferiors.

Aristocrats were the easy butts of satire in feuilletons, popular stories, and private diaries. It was satire not untouched by the wish to emulate: those rich, aspiring bourgeois who aped the nobility generally did so in their sexual conduct no less than in their furniture or their entertainments. The journals of the Goncourt brothers are filled with telling, wicked instances of such social mimicry. They record a tale of Emile de Girardin, the powerful founder of the French popular press, who was married to a lively playwright and novelist. One day, a friend of his "said to him: 'Introduce me to your wife.' 'Gladly.' He takes him to his wife's room, opens the door, closes it again and tells him: 'Impossible! She is in bed with Monsieur M——, and he's horribly jealous.' "[3] Such anecdotes hopelessly trivialized the nineteenth-century upper classes and nobility in love, but they were the staple of common and frivolous conviction.

In contrast, bourgeois appraisals of the erotic life among the lower orders were earnest and emotionally charged. Many bourgeois obliquely confessed that they found working-class or peasant love life exciting; the strange secretive pursuits of A. J. Munby, that discreet and fashionable English barrister who enjoyed a lifelong infatuation with brawny working-class women and secretly married one of them, was only the most extravagant expression of a more general subterranean middle-class sensibility. Not surprisingly, then, given this interest, bourgeois appraisals were also flatly contradictory, in the lessons they implied and the very facts they found worth recording. All they agreed on was that the difference between the psychologies of the middle and the lower classes is fundamental. Cynical as ever, the Goncourt brothers provided an economic rationale for that difference, most marked in the lower classes' love life: "There are very few natural virtues. Many virtues are impossible to the common people. Below two thousand *livres* annual income, a

2. An unidentified Protestant pastor in a communication to Carl Julius Immanuel Wagner: in Wagner, ed., *Die geschlechtlich-sittlichen Verhältnisse der evangelischen Landbewohner im deutschen Reiche*, 2 vols. (1895–96), II, 28; "Aristocracy of blood": Dr. Theodor G. Kornig, *Die Hygiene der Keuschheit* (1890; 2nd ed. 1891), 57.

3. Edmond and Jules de Goncourt, January 1852, *Journal; mémoires de la vie littéraire, 1851–1896*, ed. Robert Ricatte, 22 vols. (1956–58), I, 53.

rtain moral sense does not exist. One needs leisure to love one's chil-
en. There are only very few mothers in the working class. A thousand
ntiments are acquired" and, significantly, the Goncourts list first among
.ose, unavailable to the poor, "platonic love."⁴ Long before, romantic
itics of industrialism like William Wordsworth had lamented that
>verty and squalor were forcing laborers into criminal loves.

This was, and remained, the prevailing view. But it did not drown
.t a vocal few who insisted, rather, that the lower orders were modest
.d chaste. Not all of the poor, to be sure, basked in this charitable
:visionism: it was the women who were presumed to stand as the
.ardians of chastity, and the rural population was thought to be far
.ore disciplined in its sexual mores than the denizens of foul, over-
:owded urban slums. This well-meaning minority woud cite quaint
:asant customs that brought the young of both sexes together with no
.oral risk. On a trip to the Loire Inférieure in the early 1830s, Abel
.ugo, playwright, literary historian, dilettante, and much-quoted folk-
.rist, observed with astonishment that in the large farms of the region,
.oung men and women slept in the same large dormitory. "This ming-
.ng of the sexes," he was told, "produced none of the vices so common
. our own towns. The young girls sleep tranquilly, in safety, separated
:om the young men solely by a light cloth, and there are never any
:asons for employing greater constraints than that. At bed time, each
.limbs into his bed, drawing the curtains, shutting himself in as into a
.om, without any pleasantries disturbing this regular custom. Mores in
.e environs of Châteaubriant are so pure that if a young girl has the
.isfortune of falling (which is quite rare in this region), the memory of
:r transgression lives from generation to generation."⁵ This charming,
.aive primitivist account was intended, and taken, as a reproach to those
.egenerate bourgeois who imitated aristocratic debauchery.

Twentieth-century folklorists, less credulous, better informed, and
.ore tentative than their nineteenth-century precursors, have discovered
.arked regional, even local variations in rural morality; they see divergent
.herited customs and utilitarian motives dictating chastity in one village
.nd promiscuity in another. But in the age of Victoria, students of those
.emote beings, peasants and laborers, were likely to ignore such fine
.hadings and offer categorical verdicts. Perhaps the most single-minded

---

4. February 19, 1857, ibid., II, 79.
5. Hugo, *La France pittoresque, ou Description pittoresque, topographique et
.tatistique des départements et colonies de la France,* 3 vols. (1835), II, 154. It is only
.air to note that this exhaustive compendium sometimes records less pleasant habits
.mong the French peasantry.

among the champions of the lower orders and assailants of their "better:
was, not surprisingly, Charles Dickens. Alluding, in *David Copperfiel*
to young David's nurse, Peggotty, and to her nautical family, David
adored school friend Steerforth pronounces "that sort of people" to b
quite another order of being from themselves. " 'They are not to b
expected to be as sensitive as we are. Their delicacy is not to be shocke
or hurt easily. They are wonderfully virtuous, I dare say,' " he goes o
in his suave, derisive little speech, but " 'they have not very fine natures.' '
Dickens, of course, though thoroughly aware of the yawning gulf separat
ing the classes in his time, lends Steerforth, that charismatic snob, suc
superb views only to invite dissent from them: the decency, humanit)
and indeed the fine, sensitive nature of the honest poor was, for hin
beyond question. In their later fateful encounter, it would be the spoile
Steerforth who would corrupt the virtue of little Em'ly and elicit th
capacity of her family, "that sort of people," for vulnerability and del
cacy. In his last great novel, *Our Mutual Friend*, Dickens reinforces th
critical stance; he has the polished young lawyer Eugene Wrayburn marr
Lizzie Hexam, daughter of a disreputable water scavenger, thus scanda]
izing Society—and Dickens leaves no doubt that he finds the coup]
admirable, and Society contemptible.

Some of these conflicting interpretations had their origins in the dis
tinct realities to which they appealed. Uniform as the poor might loo
from the distances of wealth and station, they were no less finely cali
brated than their more fortunate contemporaries. Drifters, migrator
laborers, the unskilled, and the unlucky were, in their sexual conduct a
in much else, a far remove from sober artisans and farmers. The "deserv
ing poor," whether serious chapel goers or no less serious socialists, wer
as intent on respectability as the most proper bourgeois.

Informed students of the lower social ranks understood this wel]
Lamenting what he called "the reign of the flesh" among German yout]
in the 1890s, an anonymous Thuringian pastor noted that "in this respect
the purest are still the daughters (hardly the sons) of the lower middlin;
orders (*Mittelstand*), the daughters of prosperous artisans, and in som
regions, too, the daughters of the richer peasants."[7] This was a necessar)
effort at precision, far from unknown to others: social investigators lik
Le Play in France, Booth in England, Riehl in Germany, made such dis
criminations as a matter of course. Even Dickens who, more than most
liked to imagine the lovely flower of chastity growing in the dankes

6. Dickens, *David Copperfield* (1850; ed. Trevor Blount, 1966), 352 [ch. 20].
7. In Wagner, *Die geschlechtlich-sittlichen Verhältnisse*, II, 787.

eaches of slum land, could not overlook the vicious consequences of destitution and overcrowding. But neglecting these refinements, the vague awareness of lower-class mores entered as an indispensable ingredient into the making of bourgeois erotic self-definitions; indeed, the preoccupation with these mores assumed increasing prominence as the age of Victoria wore on and bourgeois came to inspect their innermost feelings with a new, uneasy self-consciousness.[8] By the end of the century, anthropological, sociological, and psychological investigations of peasants and laborers added up to a substantial scientific corpus, but they were also unwitting exercises in cultural autobiography. These reports, poised as they were between condescension and envy, often rather resemble responses to projective tests, disclosing bourgeois satisfied with their own sexual performance—or anxious about it.

For the middle-class majority, peasants and laborers encapsulated in their sexual conduct survivals of freer, almost savage modes of appeasing erotic appetites. Freud thought it instructive that while middle-class men stop telling dirty jokes when a woman joins them, "Among country people and in inns frequented by common folk, one may observe that the obscene story makes its appearance only as the waitress or the innkeeper's wife comes in." Again George Meredith, in his disenchanted cycle of sonnets about modern bourgeois love, apostrophized rustics by patronizing them:

> You burly lovers on the village green,
> Yours is a lower, and a happier star!

The poor of city and country appeared, in this collective portrait, as if drawn by Breughel with corrections by Bosch: untamed, brimming with animal vitality, taking their pleasures where they found them.[9]

Far too often, the worried observer feared, they found those pleasures at home, disregarding the sacred incest barrier as a mere formal obstacle, to be breached at will. This was not a whispered secret: before mid-century, medical investigators, government reports, and polite periodicals canvassed with some freedom what they thought egregious violations of middle-class moral and general religious restraint. In 1835, the Académie des Sciences Morales et Politiques asked Dr. Louis Villermé to look into the "physical and moral conditions of the working classes." What he

---

8. I plan to devote a volume, the fifth, provisionally entitled "Problematic Selves," to this striking phenomenon.

9. Freud: *Der Witz und seine Beziehung zum Unbewussten* (1905), *St.A.*, IV, 94, *Jokes and Their Relation to the Unconscious*, S.E., VIII, 99; Meredith: *Modern Love*, XXII, *The Poems of George Meredith*, ed. Phyllis B. Bartlett, 2 vols. (1978), I, 129.

396

THE TENDER PASSION

found horrified him: hideous poverty, casual mixing of the sexes in the workplace and in miserable hovels, and "impure beds" polluted by promiscuity and incest. A decade and a half later, in 1850, reporting to the city of London on its appalling sanitary conditions, the great reformer John Simon bluntly warned that "side by side with pestilence there stalks a deadlier presence blighting the moral existence of a rising population rendering their hearts hopeless, their acts ruffianly and incestuous." The *Saturday Review* soon struck the same chord. "Crowded and inefficient accommodations of too many," it thought, "—the great majority, we fear—of the labourers' and artisans' cottages in our rural districts and our towns," must inevitably produce the "great social evil" of sexual immorality. Sentimental cant about "thatched roofs golden with the stonecrop or green with velvet moss" as "abodes of health and innocence, of primitive manners, and Saxon purity," was, in its view, a most damaging self-deception. The laborer's daughter, "too old for school (if she has been there), and too young for service," loiters about among idle young men who, like her, "have grown up more quickly in frame than in reason." In their coarse sensual sport, they fail to acquire the "nobler restraints of principle" that have become second nature to conventional men and women. The very vocabulary of sexual self-control is alien to them. Preachers might thunder against incest, but the young would not know the word and (the *Saturday Review* darkly hinted) scarcely mind practicing it. The sermon *they* knew and "would have no difficulty in conning and digesting," was "the devil's sermon which was dinned into them, evening after evening, by the small, low, reeking, pitch-dark chamber into which they found themselves, boys and girls, huddled and cribbed together through the live-long night, with nothing to amuse and nothing to instruct them."[10] The notorious erotic freedom of the lower orders proved, once honestly studied, a kind of slavery.

Nor was it a slavery redeemed by pleasure. Some students of contemporary love conjectured that the overflowing, uninhibited lusts of the poor rarely generated exquisite sexual gratification. "In villages and in the countryside, where men and women are given over to physical labor," the French physician, Auguste Debay, argued in his authoritative book on the hygiene and physiology of marriage, "and where the imagi-

---

10. Villermé: William H. Sewell, Jr., *Work and Revolution in France: The Language of Labor from the Old Regime to 1848* (1980), 223–32, 312–13; Simon: Geoffrey Best, *Mid-Victorian Britain 1851–75* (1971), 60; "sexual immorality": *Saturday Review*, "Another Great Social Evil," V (April 3, 1858), 239. To underscore the urgency of the problem, the journal deliberately used, in the title and the body of the essay, the term usually reserved for prostitution.

nation is little or not at all developed, desires are not so frequent, and pleasure does not reach the same degree" that it does in cities, among the prosperous and idle. "The men make love brutally to satisfy a need,—the women in general experience only a sensation of friction, more or less vivid according to their temperament. Most of them remain indifferent or show no sign of pleasure at all."[11] These natural creatures of middle-class perception, then, hastily copulated like two animals in the rutting season, or performed institutionalized rapes. Zola's brutish rustics and proletarians, as he sketches them in his *La Terre* or *L'Assommoir*, coarse, unceremonious, pulsating with unbridled passion, seemed only too true to life. That is why they were so offensive—or so refreshing. For, while many derided this savage love-making as a primitive urge that the better sort had happily refined, others regretted it as an ideal that the bourgeoisie had cravenly deserted. The very erotic license that many bourgeois deplored as low and bestial, others celebrated for being close to nature. Whether the lower orders were sensual and happy, sensual and unhappy, or chaste and happy—to list only the three leading views—their attitudes toward love and lust could serve as a commentary, perhaps as a corrective, for the middle classes.

These confusions did little to clarify matters for good bourgeois as they maneuvered their way through a moral maze constructed of traditional ethics, harsh cultural demands on their self-discipline, heady and troubling biological theories, and the new opportunities presented by nineteenth-century technological civilization—including unprecedentedly safe, and easy, means of birth control. Libido has been difficult as long as humans have lived in complex civilizations, probably even before that; the sexual urge, indiscriminate and heedless, has always battled cultural prohibitions of one sort or another. One culture's unnameable vice may be another culture's cherished duty. But all cultures have designated some sexual conduct as unacceptable and some sexual wishes as beyond the bounds of legitimate fulfillment. The tension is always there, but in the nineteenth century many bourgeois obscurely felt, and some discontented spirits openly charged, that the level of tension was too high, especially among their own numbers. The censorious reaction of articulate elements within respectable society seemed disproportionate to the action of the sexual drive; by the 1890s, psychologists and sex-ologists were, as we know, beginning to plead that the strength of repression far exceeded the immoral propensities inherent in an instinct that had already been thoroughly subdued. If, as they agreed, the sexual

---

11. Debay, *Hygiène et physiologie du mariage* (1848), 102.

urge could be awakened or reined in, trained to lust or asceticism, bourgeois nineteenth-century society appeared to be very much in the camp
of self-denial, of what Bertrand Russell was to call "black-coated Respectability, the living God."[12]

Two little fables, one written near the beginning of Victoria's reign,
the other more than a decade after her death, stake out the limits and
confirm the self-referential role of these bourgeois explorations of lower-
class sexuality. In 1846, Jules Michelet, of all nineteenth-century French
historians the most passionate and most unapologetic of preachers, published a hymn to his nation, Le peuple, at once paean and lament. There
was much in his time that made him indignant, but what roused him to
heights of eloquence was what he perceived to be the moral decay of the
bourgeoisie. Especially the upper middle class, he thought, was debasing
the sacred institution of marriage into a calculating financial transaction.
The young man making his way, Michelet argued, would do well to
choose a woman of the people, hard though it might be to raise her to
his cultural level. She will work for him, admire him, give him love—in
short, true happiness. That young bourgeois should emulate working
men, who normally have just such wives. But, though he has likely known
this kind of love, he will probably reject it for what he fancies as a
"brilliant" alliance: "Sad victim of greed, you might have had that
happiness. But you sacrificed it. The humble girl you loved, who loved
you, but whom you have forsaken—well may you regret her!" Plainly,
if the bourgeoisie wishes to "recover from its premature exhaustion" and
take, once again, "the path to strength, beauty, and a bright future," it
must unite its young men with women of the lower orders. In actuality,
hélas, ambitious bourgeois of the 1840s were doing just the opposite:
they "marry late, already worn out, and generally take a sickly young
lady." The dreadful results were, for Michelet, spread across the social
landscape of France: incapable of great endeavors, the minds of the
bourgeoisie were atrophying; their children, if they survive at all, are
sickly; the "governing classes" must therefore, sooner or later, "consume
themselves in vain words and empty agitation."[13] Michelet's bourgeois,
whether prudent rentiers or plunging speculators, turn all of life into
business. His stirring rhetoric hints at the pathetic sexual life of the
governing classes: moments of lust swamped by impotence in the husband,
frigidity in the wife, and yawning indifference in both.

12. Russell to Gilbert Murray, December 12, 1902, The Autobiography of Bertrand
Russell, 1872–1914 (1967), 244.
13. Michelet, The People (1846; tr. John P. McKay, 1973), 168.

The case history that Freud invented for his listeners at the University of Vienna in 1917 is far subtler than Michelet's in its psychological finesse and far less inclined to didactic self-indulgence. But what matters is that its portrayal of the lower-class girl is precisely the opposite of Michelet's lyrical evocation of her innocent and trusting nature. Yet Freud, much like Michelet, devised his fiction to convey his sense of alarm at contemporary bourgeois sexuality. He imagines two girls living in the same house, one the caretaker's, the other the landlord's little daughter. Bourgeois and proletarian girl play freely with one another, and their childish games soon take a sexual turn; in these games, the caretaker's daughter who, even at five or six, has witnessed much adult sexual conduct, usually takes the lead. The erotic excitement the two generate with their charged make-believe is bound to eventuate in masturbation for both. But after that the sexual histories of these girls will diverge. The little proletarian will continue to masturbate without guilt, then give it up as she begins to menstruate; whether she later goes on the stage to end up marrying an aristocrat or finds a less brilliant career, "in any case she will fulfill her life undamaged by the premature exercise of her sexuality, free from neurosis." In contrast her friend, the landlord's little daughter, will struggle guiltily with masturbation; not surprisingly, she will later turn from sexual information with real, if "unexplained" distaste, only to acquire, as a young adult, a neurosis, the consequence of repressing her sexual impulses. Freud concludes, "sexual activity appeared to the caretaker's daughter just as natural and unproblematic in later life as it had in childhood," yet the landlord's daughter "experienced the impact of education and acknowledged its claims."[14] The moral of Freud's parable is no less transparent than that of Michelet's sermon, though its accents are somewhat different. Freud agrees with Michelet that the middle-class mode of life generates sexual disorder, but rejects his notion that sensual corruption must follow; rather, neurosis is the offering that modern bourgeois civilization brings to atone for its delicacy and its restraint.

For all, it seems, was not pure loss, not even in Freud's pessimistic appraisal of middle-class love. Patience, self-sacrifice, sobriety produced their own gratifications. Writing to his fiancée in the summer of 1883, he sketched out the costs and rewards of bourgeois self-control. She had evidently described to him, with some revulsion, the noisy vulgarity of an open-air market, and he agreed with her that "it is not pretty or elevating to see how the common people amuse themselves." This prompted some

14. Freud, *Vorlesungen zur Einführung in die Psychoanalyse* (1916–17), *St.A.*, I, 346; *Introductory Lectures on Psycho-Analysis*, S.E., XVI, 353–54.

thoughts that had obtruded themselves during a performance of "Carmen":
The rabble lives without constraint, while we deprive ourselves—*Das
Gesindel lebt sich aus und Wir entbehren.* Why? "To maintain our
integrity." Cultivated bourgeois husband their health, their capacity for
pleasure, their excitement: "We keep ourselves for something, we know
not what, and this habit of constantly suppressing our natural drives gives
us the character of refinement." Far from lacking sensitivity, the educated
"feel more deeply" than the common people, who "cannot exist without
their thick skin and their irresponsibility—*leichten Sinn.*" It makes no
sense for them to postpone or carefully shape their pleasures; they are
"too powerless, too exposed, to be like us."[15]

Freud knew very little about the private lives of the lower orders; his
formulations are less a portrait of laborers and peasants than the self-
portrait of a young educated bourgeois in love, in all his pride, bitterness,
and frustration. That is precisely why they incarnate the paradox pervading the idea of black-coated Eros: postponing his sexual gratification, the
bourgeois risks neurotic suffering and, with that, marital misery. But,
since he has been schooled to greater sensitivity than the unpolished
majority of the population, his readiness for erotic variations, his capacity
for sexual play, should also be highly developed. The very training of
the nerves among the cultivated can become a source of pleasure and of
pain: it can make for either artificiality as well as a paralyzing distance
from natural impulses, or the kind of refinement which, as Freud saw it,
characterized bourgeois culture, including, I add, its erotic culture. Sex,
we know, demands a kind of knowledge, and, certainly many of the poor
had knowledge thrust on them, in fetid dwellings or among foul-mouthed
fellow laborers. But the young among the nineteenth-century middle
classes, too, even the girls, knew far more than their parents, they themselves, or, for that matter, their historians, suspected. In fact, the sort of
erotically stimulating knowledge that was available to them, whether
through books, or pictures, or foreign sights, was beyond the reach of the
poor. The middle classes, then, appeared at once more likely and less likely
than the lower classes to secure sexual gratification. In this manner, their
conflicting reports about lower-class sexual love mirror the complications
of their own.

Throughout most of the nineteenth century, middle-class prejudices
about lower-class erotic mores were fed, or at least not subverted, by
the ignorance I have just commented on. In 1838, William Makepeace

15. Freud to Martha Bernays, August 29, 1883, *Briefe*, 48–49.

Thackeray had admitted, reasonably enough, that "an English gentleman knows as much about the people of Lapland or California"—these were the days, one must remember, when very little was known about California—"as he does of the aborigines of The Seven Dials or the natives of Wapping."[16] In those years, one was largely dependent on sentimental novels by George Sand or the naive generalizations of Abel Hugo, who peppered dependable statistics on every *département* of France with credulous comments on local customs. The lower orders themselves offered meddlesome inquirers little help. Defying their reputation for the frank handling of essential bodily functions, including all possible acts of love, laborers and peasants often showed themselves fiercely reticent about their intimate lives; their distrust of intruding interrogators armed with questionnaires more than matched the bourgeoisie's celebrated passion for privacy.

Among the dubious, often arid sources of information about lower-class love, workers' autobiographies played a most ambiguous role. They were fairly rare, and rarely spontaneous; unlike their middle-class counterparts, few peasants or working men—or their wives—had the time, or cultivated the habit, of systematic introspection. A handful of them kept a diary, that indispensable middle-class repository of past experience. Some working-class autobiographies, notably in England, were modern secular versions of Puritan self-examination or drew on the oral tradition of story telling. Most of them, everywhere, needed to prove some cherished point with the history of an exemplary life: the abounding grace of God poured out to the least of sinners, the rewards awaiting prudence and hard work, or the brutal injustices inherent in capitalistic class society.[17] They exude the aroma of tracts. Sometimes it was the enforced idleness of exile that drove the worker to reminisce on paper. Often, an alert pedagogue or editor, or a pastor endowed with a stern social conscience, would prompt aged or invalided laborers to fix their memories for posterity. Probably the best known of these instigators was the German pastor and, later, Social Democratic deputy, Paul Göhre. As a young theology student, he had worked for three months in a machine-tool factory posing as an apprentice, and his graphic first-hand report, published in 1891, had caused a certain sensation. Göhre was steadily traveling toward the political left, toward socialism and anticlericalism; after 1900, with his experiences on the workshop floor and with Christian

16. *Fraser's Weekly*, March 1838, in Louis James, *Fiction for the Working Man 1830-50* (1963), 1.
17. Vincent, *Bread, Knowledge and Freedom*, chs. 1 and 2.

politicians much in mind, he provoked and edited the autobiographies of five working men. As we shall see, two of these, by Moritz Bromme and Wenzel Holek, yield uncommonly useful information about the erotic habits of the lower orders; artless and unpolished as they were, these painful self-portraits became models for other, often less revealing, memoirs.

The autobiographies of French workers were, especially compared to Bromme's and Holek's disclosures, exceptionally reticent about intimate matters; they were more decorous even than the English. Some of them, like Agricol Perdiguier's *Mémoires d'un compagnon*, have become indispensable sources for the historian seeking authoritative information about craftsmen's ritual-ridden organizations. But most of them, with Martin Nadaud's *Léonard, maçon de la Creuse*, the best-known example, were political testaments, taking the reader through the revolution of 1848, the emergence of, and splits among, radical ideologues in the Second Empire, the Commune of 1871. Characteristically, a good portion of these autobiographies were written in political exile: Perdiguier's, for one, in Antwerp and Switzerland in 1852 and 1853, others in London, in Lausanne, even in Paraguay. They are anything but impersonal presentations; on the contrary, they vibrate with commitment. But their passions are those of the militant, recording triumphs and disasters at the meeting hall, on the barricades, in the legislature. If they allude in passing to the misery of working-class women or canvass the author's childhood and early years, they do so mainly to enforce a moral (or, better, a political) lesson. The moments they touch on love are therefore all the more illuminating: Nadaud recounts meeting a pretty girl, "so reserved, so gracious, so radiant with youth and beauty" that he found her supremely desirable and courted her awkwardly until he eventually married her, after the drawn-out negotiations and formalities imperative in French country-life. Perdiguier departs from the recital of his *tour de France* and the elaborate ceremonies of the joiners just long enough to describe his state of mind at some country feasts: "I tasted happiness, such great happiness! extreme happiness! . . . and yet incomplete! . . . My heart yearned for more. . . . But I could not give myself over to lost women I did not love," or "seduce a young girl with fine promises, with endless oaths of attachment, make her a mother and then abandon her, bring trouble and despair to her family, break her heart, kill her." That was not "in accord with my principles, not in my character. I loved, I burned, I suffered, I was violent, shaken, pulled in opposite directions by my passion and my conscience; the one wanted it, the other told it: 'Stop,

that is wicked.' "[18] In these stiff, all too literary paragraphs, we sense the
earnest lover intent on sharing the pressures of his emotional life, however
uneasy he might be with the vocabulary appropriate to his passion.

By themselves, these testimonies offer only fragmentary, almost accidental insights into the love life of the lower orders. They need to be
supplemented by tough-minded, outspoken and tenacious investigations;
and, with the passing decades, an already keen appetite for social information intensified to generate an avalanche of inquiries—on the budgets of
peasants, on public health, on prostitution—that could only drag the
private lives of the poor into the light of sociological attention. Earlier on,
in his autobiography, Francis Place, the self-educated London master tailor
and political organizer, had complained that "the manners of the people,
have seldom been attended to by writers of any repute"—except to discredit them. "What is known of them can be gleaned only from a few
passing incidents."[19] By the 1880s and 1890s, this was no longer true, and
anyone interested in the topic could move beyond projection, or sentimental conjecture, to a more realistic, more differentiated portrait of love
among the poor, whether reputable or disreputable. These investigations
mainly fed the philanthropic imagination, or served legislators in search
of a policy, but incidentally they could also provide welcome material for
the middle-class reader intent on moral and erotic self-definition.

By 1898, such a reader could even call on a psychoanalytic profile of
the sexual malaise current among the Viennese working class. It is an
interesting survey, which throws a bridge between the theories that the
arch-bourgeois, Sigmund Freud, was then developing and the neurotic
symptoms of that class which, he believed, had a psychology very different from his own. In the spring of 1897, Dr. Felix Gattel went to Vienna
for half a year, apparently to become Freud's patient and pupil. While he
was there, he studied a hundred neurasthenics and anxiety neurotics drawn
from the population of Dr. Krafft-Ebing's psychiatric outpatient clinic,
the *Ambulatorium*. His case reports and his conclusions are rather crudely
formulated, but they amply confirmed Freud's confident and disturbing
proposition that all neuroses have a sexual etiology. Gattel's case histories
also persuasively demonstrated what many bourgeois of his time were
inclined to doubt: it might well be (as he circumspectly put it) that

18. Nadaud: *Léonard, maçon de la Creuse* (1895; ed. Jean-Pierre Rioux, 1976),
136–47; Perdiguier: *Mémoires d'un compagnon* (1854–55; pref. Jean Bernard, 1964),
211–12, . . . in original.
19. Samuel Pyeatt Menefee, *Wives for Sale: An Ethnographic Study of British
Popular Divorce* (1981), 4.

working-class patients "perhaps place somewhat less value on self-observation than people just intellectually active."[20] But they suffered anxiety attacks, found their behavior inhibited by phobias, experienced physical symptoms—aches, pains, tremors, sweating—that had unmistakable psychological origins. They masturbated, yielding to a variety of fantasies. Their sexual histories, in short, boxed the compass: some were thoughtful, others thoughtless of their partners; some performed as sexual athletes, others admitted to impotence; some found consistent and solid gratification in intercourse, others had never had an orgasm. Not even hysteria, which many observers thought the privileged malaise of the middle class, was absent from the clinicial picture. The Vienna poor were, in short, less brutish, less predictable, and more human than many their betters believed—they were almost, one might say, like bourgeois.

All together, at the end of the nineteenth century, the sexual information available for comparisons, whether invidious or envious, should have offered few surprises to the unprejudiced and the well-informed. While snobs might continue to sneer, the erotic life of the nineteenth-century peasant and working classes was as rich in amplitude, if not in refined gambits, as that of their employers and exploiters. If many peasants derided love as an undependable guide to marriage alliances, if many working men and women went through life with few kisses and few endearments, there were many others who loved and lost, loved and won, in the best middle-class style. It all depended. What had long been suspected turned out to be true: precisely like the amorous experience of the bourgeoisie, that of the lower orders did not evolve in splendid, or miserable, isolation from their social, economic, and religious environments. As the *Saturday Review* had boldly said half a century before, and as common sense had argued all along, level of income and steadiness of employment dictated the chances of privacy at home and the sort of companions one would find at work. The parental bedroom, the factory floor, the socialist assembly, the gospel meeting, the amusement park, or the dance hall, each contributed to erotic information and shaped erotic conduct; they were invitations to self-respect, opportunities for instruction or temptations to promiscuity. There is scattered but pervasive evidence that the poorer the poor, the less protected they were from sexual assault or, at the very least, from premature sexual knowledge. At the

20. Felix Gattel, *Über die sexuellen Ursachen der Neurasthenie und Angstneurose* (1898), 12; Frank J. Sulloway, *Freud, Biologist of the Mind: Beyond the Psychoanalytic Legend* (1979), 513–15.

same time, strict parents, religious inhibitions, or local traditions complicated the picture. Moreover, however marked a distinction there might be between the mentality of the lower and that of the middle classes, both were endowed with the same drives and the same strategies of defense, if deployed in characteristic ways. Like a young bourgeoise, a young working-class girl could repress intimate sights and sounds; the kind of learned ignorance, the systematic forgetting, prevalent among the one also helped to delimit the sexual awareness of the other. In the interviews with working-class and peasant women that became a staple for social investigators, the girl who entered marriage wholly ignorant of the facts of physiology and the processes of pregnancy quite outweighed the sophisticate of sex.

But, of necessity, the poor knew more, and repressed less, than their middle-class contemporaries. The *Saturday Review* was right to say flatly, in 1858, that "the best and most innocent-minded girl of the labouring class knows far more at fifteen than the high-born damsel of twenty-five." There was sexual instruction for the laboring classes that no amount of denial could push out of consciousness. Early traumas—fathers initiating their daughters or brothers their sisters—often succumbed to repression. But later incidents involving boarders or fellow workers remained etched in the memory. "I saw drunkenness and lust in appalling forms in the place where I worked," Charles Shaw, a potter, recalled late in life about the works where he had toiled as a boy. The shop floor and the midday break were settings for the grossest banter and the most explicit sexual byplay. Male workers would verbally and physically assault women workers, issue coarsely worded invitations, or throw themselves on a girl to mimic sexual intercourse, all to the applause of the bystanders. In the moral hierarchy of these feckless beings, the girl who talked back stood high. In 1877, the Czech-German Wenzel Holek worked for a brick factory in the nearby clay pit. Though only thirteen, he had heard and seen much, he recalled, and so was scarcely astonished at the language he now heard, "but some of it was too much for me." Especially on "sexual matters, the most disgusting expressions flew about. The fellows, half-naked, dirty, black, looking scrubby and besotted, wallowed in all this; the coarser and the more revolting it was, the better they found it, the more pleasure it gave them." One woman worker, Rosa, about forty, was particularly popular for giving as good as she got. One day, encountering a worker dressed in a torn shirt and concealing his bulk behind a crude apron he had fashioned from a sack, Rosa leaped at him, and shouted that it was time to ring the bell for noon. Then she shoved his apron aside and grabbed his member, singing out, "Bim, bam; bim, bam; bim, bam!" Everyone doubled over with laughter.[21] Holek took the trouble to record this incident not because it was rare, but because he thought it typical.

Moritz Bromme enlarges Holek's store of appalling anecdotes in his autobiography. He recalled that when he was about fourteen, working in a button-making factory, the women in his department embarrassed him by changing their clothes, taking off their corsets, right before his eyes, all the while "making immoral conversation." When a visibly pregnant worker repeatedly attempted to seduce him, "raising her skirt and fixing her garter," he could only respond with fear and disgust. Women, if anything, suffered from such barbarity even more. Around 1860, at thirteen and holding her first job as a seamstress, Ottilie Baader, later a leading Social Democrat, had unwelcome, often incomprehensible sexual knowledge thrust upon her by the woman who ran the shop: "Never again have I heard anyone talk as shamelessly as this woman did about the most intimate matters." Ignorant and innocent as she was, it took Baader some time to understand that, *Die Näherinnen gehen ja doch alle auf den Strich!* was nothing less than the slangy, confident prediction that all seamstresses end up as whores. But she found the ominous sexual meaning of the vulgar innuendos and dirty jokes she heard quite unmistakable.[22] The sheer joylessness of this practical sexual education is what these reminiscences, and many others, have in common. It was a school that bourgeois adolescents were generally fortunate enough to escape.

This, then, is the way that the poor—or, at least, the large unlucky mass among them—introduced one another to the pleasures of Eros. But they were exposed to another kind of education as well, by members of the middle classes, by those I have called their employers and exploiters. There was much muttering among the well-to-do that servants might seduce their children; whatever substance there was to the fear—and there was some—it was rather more likely for the head or the sons of the house to seduce servants, as it was for employers to take advantage of the economic dependency of their women workers to procure a little sexual amusement for themselves. In 1883, Harriet A. Kidd of Stafford-

21. *Saturday Review*: "Another Great Social Evil," V (April 3, 1858), 239; Shaw: Vincent, *Bread, Knowledge and Freedom*, 47n; Holek: *Lebensgang eines deutsch-tschechischen Handarbeiters* (1909), 117–18. For repression, see *Education of the Senses*, ch. IV.

22. Bromme: *Lebensgeschichte eines modernen Fabrikarbeiters* (1905), 110, 124; Baader: *Ein steiniger Weg, Lebenserinnerungen* (1921), 11.

shire was working in a silk mill for "a gentleman of good position and high standing in the town." She was seventeen. One evening, her employer sent her to his house, "ostensibly to take a parcel of books, but really with a very different object. When I arrived at the house all the family were away, and before he would allow me to leave he forced me to yield to him. At eighteen I was a mother." Mortally ashamed and afraid, she kept the secret, and with that her job, for years. While he was still a boy, Wenzel Holek had the unsought opportunity of witnessing a similar display of power. He happened upon a manager in a compromising situation in the storeroom of the sugar-beet factory where he was working: "the beautiful Marie," one of his few favorites among the working girls for her exceptional decency of speech, was "lying on a pile of empty sacks, half naked." Red-faced and yelling with rage, the manager jumped up as Holek innocently interrupted his pleasures. When, later, Holek recounted the incident to an intimate in the strictest confidence, his friend, more experienced and more cynical, told him calmly: "Oh, that's nothing new. And do you know why someone like her would do this sort of thing? She can do what she wants in the factory, the gentlemen won't torment her, curse her, or fine her." Girls like her made more money than those who refused to play such sordid games: "Where do you think some of them get their pretty dresses?" But ever after, whenever Holek met the beautiful Marie, who was anything but brazen, a victim rather than a schemer, she would avoid him or drop her eyes. "She was ashamed," Holek compassionately remembered. "But I felt sorry for her."[23]

A few years later, while working in another factory, Holek met Luise, his landlady's daughter, who paid the price for rejecting such importunities. One night an assistant manager had sent her to his house, near the factory, to make his bed for him. "And Luise," Holek reports, a little ingenuously, "thinking no evil in her virginal purity and honorableness, obeyed his orders and went." But the manager had followed her. "He locked the door and tried right off to make her yield to him. At first with honeyed words and cloying promises, then by force. In the end, there was a regular wrestling match between them, in total silence," until the girl threatened to scream for help. Fearful of the consequences, he let her go. But from then on, he subjected Luise to such chicanery that she was forced to leave town. "It is well known," as Moritz Bromme mused in his autobiography, "that there are those among manufacturers

23. Kidd: in a letter quoted by the editor in *Life as We Have Known It*, ed. Margaret Llewelyn Davies (1931), 76; Holek: *Lebensgang*, 81–83.

employing women workers, who should like to claim not merely their labor power but their bodies as well, and who look back enviously at the former privileges of feudal proprietors who could afford the *jus primae noctis.*" Many of them, he added, need no such legal permission, "since they do not, thanks to their authority, find much resistance." Still, often, "proletarian women" would "reject such offers decisively." Then they would suffer for it.[24] Bromme was active in the Social Democratic Party, but he did not make these observations because he was a socialist; rather, he was, or at least remained, a socialist because he made such observations.

Stories of this sort were staples of radical folklore, but one did not have to be a radical to credit and deplore them. As early as 1859, Dr. William Acton had sympathetically spoken of "the young housemaid or pretty parlour-maid in the same street in which the sickly lady has given birth to a sickly child, to whom healthy milk is life, and anything else death. With shame and horror the girl bears a child to the butler, or the policeman, or her master's son." The evidence was all around him, to be preserved in amber in working-class memoirs and the vital statistics on illegitimacy. Moritz Bromme records that the woman he married "had had a child before" by a bookkeeper in the store where his Emma had served as a maid. The American sociologist Lester Frank Ward had caught one of his tenants in Washington, a theology student, seducing his black domestic. And in England in 1863, Lucy Luck, just after her mother's death, went into service, fortunate in a kind mistress, but wary and frightened of her master, apparently a lustful and violent man: "That man, who had a wife and was a father to three little children, did all he could, time after time, to try and ruin me, a poor orphan of only fifteen years old. He would boast to me, and even tell me the names of other girls he had carried on with. God alone kept me from falling a victim to that wretched man, for I could not have been my own keeper." Her accents were purloined from melodrama, but her terror was authentic and her experience only too common.[25] In 1904, in a meticulous statistical survey of bastardy among German and Austrian working women, the sociologist Othmar Spann demonstrated beyond cavil that domestics were most at risk, far more than girls working in the factories: in Berlin, over a third of all illegitimate children were born to domestic servants, a

---

24. Holek: ibid., 171–73; Bromme: *Lebensgeschichte,* 216.
25. Acton: "Unmarried Wet-Nurses," *Lancet,* I (1859), 175; Bromme: *Lebensgeschichte,* 221; Ward: see *Education of the Senses,* 416–17; Luck: "A Little of My Life," *London Mercury* (November 1925–April 1926), in John Burnett, ed., *Useful Toil: Autobiographies of Working People from the 1820s to the 1920s* (1974), 72. Burnett comments (ibid., 68) on Luck's sub-literary borrowings.

figure that also held for Vienna; in Frankfurt, the rate almost reached fifty percent. While by no means all these bastards were visible testimony to seduction in the domestic's new "home," the contribution of master, or son, of the house seems to have been appreciable. The widespread claim that unscrupulous bourgeois seducers were responsible for driving thousands of young women into the life of prostitution was exaggerated. Still, there was no scarcity of those who, feeling the need and sensing their opportunity, treated domestic servants, in the blunt words of one English house maid, as "fair game."[26]

But whatever the nature of their sexual education, the amorous memories of these lower-class autobiographers are mantled in melancholy. There were, to be sure, those the English called the rough, male and female, who sought sexual satisfaction without hesitation and without blushing. Bromme was certainly not unique in preserving sharply etched vignettes of young girls impudently displaying their bodies in the hope of capturing the timid young man who had inflamed them. Moreover, there must have been uncounted ecstatic moments of sexual fulfillment, whether in casual encounters or in enduring affairs or, for that matter, in marriage. But again and again, lower-class love-making seems to have been more oppressive than enjoyable. This is quite understandable. After all, the environment for erotic pleasure that bourgeois had come to take for granted—privacy, cleanliness, and good health—remained only a wistful fantasy for most of the poor. What seems so uncommon among them, for all the passion that flashes fleetingly here and there, is the sheer sexual exuberance that colored the erotic experience of Charles Kingsley, or Jules Michelet, or thousands of less articulate bourgeois. The private sexual histories of the nineteenth-century poor are only too often studies in dismay, in a helpless yielding to impulses that would not be denied and could rarely be simply enjoyed.[27]

26. Spann: "Die geschlechtlich-sittlichen Verhältnisse im Dienstboten– und Arbeiterinnenstande, gemessen an der Erscheinung der unehelichen Geburten," *Zeitschrift für Sozialwissenschaft*, VII (1904), 287–303; "fair game": Lilian Westall, "The Good Old Days," unpublished autobiography excerpted in Burnett, *Useful Toil*, 217.

27. The evidence for this statement must remain impressionistic, but it seems to hold true especially for women. See the testimony of Dr. Debay, above, pp. 396–7, and Standish Meacham's well-informed observation about the English working classes as late as 1900: "An 'agreeable' husband might be one who could, in addition [to facing crises sensibly in his wife's company], offer his wife the pleasure of sexual fulfillment. Yet if we can believe the admittedly scanty evidence, few women expected that satisfaction or considered it important to their marriage. More frequently, 'agreeability' meant a husband's willingness to spare his wife as much as possible from the trials of a sex life which she conceived as a duty but could not enjoy." *A Life Apart: The English Working Class, 1890–1914* (1977), 66.

I have no intention of milking the pathos inherent in the erotic situation
of the poor. After all, "every body of men," as that Scottish working-class
autobiographer, James Burn, had so astutely put it, "has its own standards
of perfection." Many rural communities across Europe saw nothing
shameful about premarital pregnancy, let alone intercourse; some, in
fact, welcomed it as a necessary rehearsal for marriage, undeniable evidence of the young woman's capacity for motherhood. Again, footloose
journeymen picking up work here and there, trekking from place to
place, often had only the most casual conception of marriage and made
convenient, short-lived arrangements on the road. The evidence for such
morals is, for the time before 1900, very rich. In the mid-1890s, the
German pastor Carl Wagner mobilized scores of his fellow divines across
the country for a frank, comprehensive, and therefore rather controversial survey of the "sexual-moral" situation of the Protestant rural
population in the German Reich. The responses, arranged into two
substantial volumes, were with predictable regional variations almost
monotonously repetitive. Rural households, except for the influential but
numerically small minority of prosperous farmers, tolerated what, from
any respectable perspective, were indecently intimate conditions; children
would hear obscene sexual talk and often witness sexual intercourse, and
not, as many of the respondents intimated, just among animals. Adolescents of both sexes were even worse off: they lacked the most elementary
sense of self-control, pairing off after dances and similar seductive entertainments; their reading, cheap novels of love and adventure, only fed
their erotic imagination. Premarital pregnancies were the rule and a solid
proportion of unions—in some districts as many as three-quarters of them
—were solemnized after the bride was visibly pregnant. Easy promiscuity,
the seduction of young girls, even incest, were far from unknown.
Wagner and his fellow investigators were dismayed but scarcely astonished. Poverty, they knew, meant not just crowding and disease, but,
necessarily, the liberation of impulses, the absence of all restraining
influence—in short, the grossest disregard of Christian decency. Yet the
Wagner survey leaves the impression that the German peasantry was
scarcely disturbed by its sexual situation.[28] Freud was right: high civilization, refined culture, called for expensive sacrifices. Romance was a luxury
for those who could afford it.

Still, gauche and stereotyped as their comments on love normally were,
hard as it was for them to find the time or the energy to taste it to the
full, the poor could experience it as intensely and painfully as any settled

28. See Wagner, *Die geschlechtlich-sittlichen Verhältnisse, passim.*

bourgeois. In the early 1860s, one anonymous English navvy, dictating his reminiscences to a journalist, recalled that as a young man he had kept company with a muscular, hard-working, provident girl he had affectionately called his "little mouse." But she had died—killed herself with overwork, he thought—and then, "after I lost my poor 'little mouse,' I felt very uneasy in my mind, and I did not rightly get over it for about two years." His work of mourning took even longer; for several years he "had never seen any one I cared about." Finally he met Anne, whom he immediately fancied for a wife; the two "walked out" for some weeks and then got married. "Some people tell you it's unlucky to marry," the navvy commented, "but all I can say is that it's the luckiest day's work that ever I done in my life." It was love at first sight. His Anne brought steadiness into the navvy's life, and helped to cure him of his appetite for drink—the reasons that numerous working men gave for wanting to marry. In return, when she fell seriously ill and was unable to work for a year, he faithfully nursed her and did such "unmanly" chores as cooking, cleaning the house, and preparing her gruel.[29] "That sort of people," as Steerforth called them, were visibly capable of tenderness and enduring affection. The word "love" sat awkwardly under their pen as they apostrophized "my new passions of love," or "the Joy & Bliss of Loving," or the state of being "head over heels in love." Yet one laborer burst out with the declaration, "I was as fond of my wife Has a Cat is of New Milk"—a precious jewel of expressiveness in a shopful of literary tinsel.[30] The depth of working-class attachments is beyond question.

Whatever its expressions, lower-class love was enveloped in the pressure of unloving circumstances. Often, it was overwhelmed by them. Significantly, the navvy, praising his marriage, resorts to the metaphor of work—the luckiest day's work he ever done in his life. The Chartist John Bezer, a spirited writer, entitled a chapter of his autobiography, "Love, Marriage, and Beggary," concisely yoking together a conjunction only too familiar in working-class lives. Marriage offered the scantiest opportunities and the scarcest funds for relaxed loving. Dreaded spells of unemployment, even more dreaded bouts with illness, incapacitating accidents at work, the reiterated and cumulative burden of motherhood, to say nothing of the pitiful wages that only the most skilled of working men could hope to exceed, all made the founding of a family a risky, often highly improvident venture. Ignorance about contraceptive aids or

29. "Autobiography of a Navvy," *Macmillan's Magazine*, V (1861–62), in Burnett, *Useful Toil*, 58, 61, 63.
30. Vincent, *Bread, Knowledge and Freedom*, 46–47, 42.

THE TENDER PASSION

awkwardness in employing them put many a young couple before an accomplished fact they did not welcome. Often, a young lover callously demanded that his pregnant girl get an abortion; others, like Moritz Bromme, married her. But to give the child a name was one thing, to find happiness in the midst of privation was quite another. Bromme, in the circumstantial chapter he devotes to his married life in his memoirs, details the subversion of good feelings by grinding misery. A certain incompatibility of interests and tastes aroused intermittent irritation between husband and wife, and, as Bromme generously concedes, his wife was fundamentally good-natured, but driven to distraction by the lack of everything and the nerve-wracking uncertainty. Most of their quarrels would have been quickly resolved, or would never have erupted, if there had been more money in the house.[31]

The affair into which Wenzel Holek drifted with his Luise touchingly documents the sadness of which I speak. Luise, the virtuous virgin, so superior to her drab little world, and Holek, who admired her for disdaining the sexual aggressiveness of other working girls, were the most reluctant of lovers. Holek took an oath, "in God's name," that he would respect his girl's innocence. But, as months went by, his infatuation grew more avid, and Luise, too, began to respond to his evident arousal. The couple became, he later remembered, "more and more insatiable with one another! And ever freer and bolder!" They sought out solitude for their embraces. "Sometimes, when we sat together, uninterrupted, fondling each other, and had sufficiently protested our mutual fidelity," there would come, "suddenly, a deep silence: the drivers were stirring, vehemently, and could no longer be controlled." In the end, the two proved only human. "I violated my oath and Luise forgot her innocence." The pair lived together, in what the Germans picturesquely call a wild marriage, for seven years until they solemnized it "before God."[32]

There was much respectable indignation at this sort of behavior, at the reckless promiscuity of the lower classes, their immoral displays at dances, and the alarming number of illegitimate children they produced. These strictures had their basis in fact, but they reverberate with anxiety at bourgeois sexual performance; they read sometimes like sheer envy which is, after all, a form of anxiety, too. Yet this moralizing also harbors

31. John James Bezer: "The Autobiography of One of the Chartist Rebels of 1848" (1851), ed. David Vincent, *Testaments of Radicalism: Memoirs of Working Class Politicians 1790–1885* (1977), 177; Bromme: *Lebensgeschichte,* "Verheiratet," 219–42.

32. Holek, *Lebensgang,* 235. Bromme's courtship was just as hesitant and even more overpowering: he made his girl pregnant and then married her—for that reason. *Lebensgeschichte,* 216, 219.

a sense of pride. Few middle-class couples would, of course, have dreamt in those decades of entering an illicit union, even if there were those too impatient to wait who consummated their affair during their engagement. But what principally differentiates the love of Wenzel and Luise Holek from that of Charles and Fanny Kingsley is the essential ground tone of their amorous experience. Lower-class attachments were pervaded by stolid endurance, a heavy mood of resignation, which made sexual activity just another irresistible force in life. Middle-class lovers, too, had their quarrels, their setbacks, their frustrations. Still, it was largely reserved for good bourgeois to recall their sensual experiences with glowing metaphors, to call them delicious, remember a little heaven after dinner, enter paradise together, or to celebrate their love by vaulting over the sofa.

2. The Lion in Love: Last Thoughts

Among the sculptures scattered across the Great Crystal Palace Exhibition of 1851, there was a group by the Belgian sculptor Guillaume Geefs called *The Lion in Love*. Like other works of art gracing this meticulously organized jungle of machinery, furniture, and other assorted products of human ingenuity, it served as a reminder of nineteenth-century aspirations to higher things, as an emblem to modern cultivation. *The Lion in Love* depicts a sturdy undraped young woman seated on the back of a lion who simpers up to her while she is serenely clipping his claws. Geefs was in those years sufficiently known for the *Art-Journal*, in its lavishly illustrated special issue devoted to the Exhibition, to salute him as "eminent." In its informal catalogue, it reproduced two other pieces he had shown. One of these, *The Faithful Messenger*, was a rendering of "a young Greek girl separated from her lover, who is refreshing the carrier-pigeon, returned from conveying to him her missive of affection"; the story, the *Art-Journal* thought, was "told with graceful simplicity." As for the other, Geefs had drawn the theme "from the old and beautiful national legend of GENEVIEVE OF BRABANT; who, wrongfully accused of infidelity, is driven by her lord to the wilds of the forest, where she and her infant are succoured by a fawn until her innocence is established." As before, the commentary stressed the narrative element: "The story is simply and touchingly told, and the group well composed by the accomplished artist."[33]

33. *The Art-Journal Illustrated Catalogue: The Industry of All Nations* (1851), 234, 288.

414 THE TENDER PASSION

To judge by these three exemplars of Geefs's work, his taste ran to meaningful women, preferably active in intimate pairs—woman and lion, woman and pigeon, woman and child—with the woman, scantily clad, dominating the composition. The pieces on which his considerable contemporary reputation rested were, however, not allegories so much as monuments and portrait busts, all of them decently attired. Born at Antwerp in 1805, Geefs learned his craft through traditional channels, the studios of masters in Antwerp and Paris. Beginning in the 1820s, impressively facile and instantly popular, Geefs developed the art of public and private portraiture into a profitable domestic industry; at the height of his career, inundated with commissions, he had his five brothers, all sculptors, working for him. One distinguished historian of Belgian art, Paul Fierens, has described him as the artist proper for a bourgeois age; a thoroughly decent sort, he was a "good citizen, himself a bourgeois, rich and esteemed (he was the son of a baker at Borgerhout), excellent husband, great traveller, sculptor of kings, queens, ministers, generals, academicians, big manufacturers and beautiful society ladies." Geefs's technique was impeccable: he could render stuffs—uniforms, decorations, soft boots—with the best of them. But after a time, Fierens complains, Geefs declined into "mediocrity, into platitude," and he instances *The Lion in Love* as a depressing, "insufferable" product of Geefs's sentimental vein.[34] That may be; but Geefs's plaster group reaches deeper into his fantasies than his adroit, widely acclaimed standing monument to a contemporary Belgian statesman, General Belliard. Slightly embarrassing as art, perhaps, *The Lion in Love* opens enticing vistas to its culture as it plays ingenuously on the strings of unsophisticated sensibility.

The evidentiary value of Geefs's allegorical composition is only enhanced by its wide popularity; his subject made something of a career for itself. Abraham Solomon, an agreeable though distinctly minor narrative painter, exhibited a jocular *Lion in Love* at the Royal Academy in 1858; his conceit—the earnest, virile male roped in by the shrewdly modest, quietly exultant female as he holds her wool for her—was a theme in which the age delighted. Two lithographs published in Germany around 1850 belong to the same family; an anonymous lithographer called one of them, with engaging directness, *Captured and Tamed!* John Tenniel, who had illustrated Aesop's fables in 1848—including a charming representation of *The Lion in Love*—adapted it for a cartoon lampooning Napoleon III in thrall to his wife, Eugénie. Indeed, at the very Exhibition to which Geefs had sent his allegorical scene of domestication, the English

34. Fierens and others, *L'Art en Belgique du moyen age à nos jours* (1947), 423.

culptor John Bell showed *Una and the Lion*, taking his text from the *'aerie Queene*, in which Una personifies truth and is followed on her vanderings by a lion she had tamed with her gentle innocence. For the benefit of those who had never read, or could not recall, Spenser's masterpiece, Bell had named his sculpture *Purity*. The *Art-Journal* pronounced his rendering "a highly poetical work."[35] To emphasize the lesson in virginal inviolability, Bell decorated his lion with an improbable garland and a little dove, while Una herself holds a lily. Plainly, Geefs's contemporaries found something irresistible about the ascendancy of mild female strength over rude male power.

For nineteenth-century viewers, such groups formed benign tableaux, documenting serenity rather than conflict. *Punch*, with its ponderous jocularity, illustrated a poem directed against detractors of the Great Exhibition with a light-hearted parody of Geefs's sculpture. And at least one visitor to the Exhibition whose response has been preserved found *The Lion in Love* most edifying. "The monarch of the forest, unable to resist the seducing loveliness of a nude female who is seated on his back and fascinating him with her eyes, is quietly submitting to be deprived of his claws." It was a scene, he thought, that "allegorically represents the power of beauty over savage nature."[36] The manifest presentation, whatever its concealed meaning, supports this assessment: the monarch of the forest consents to have his nails clipped without a tremor and with what would appear to be a coy, infatuated smile.

This benignity is all the more remarkable in view of the Aesopian fable from which Geefs's sculpture is ultimately derived. A lion, the fable goes, falls heedlessly in love with the daughter of a woodsman who, afraid to rebuff the infatuated animal yet unwilling to hand over his child to him, agrees to the marriage on condition that the lion submit to having his claws pulled and his teeth plucked lest he hurt, or frighten, the tender maiden. Driven by his irrational passion, the lion foolishly accepts these conditions; no sooner is he toothless and declawed, than the woodsman kills him with a club—or, in the more tepid translation that Tenniel illustrated, drives him away. Those modern versions that find it necessary to explicate the meaning of Aesop's fables append a warning against blind infatuation, which propels the young into ill-considered marriages. Yet most in the nineteenth century liked to think of love as a beneficent force that united rather than divided individuals. For visitors to the Great

---

35. *Art-Journal Illustrated Catalogue*, 325.
36. See *Punch*: XXI (1851), 94; "power of beauty": C. H. Gibbs-Smith, *The Great Exhibition of 1851*, Victoria and Albert Museum (1950; rev. ed., 1964), 127.

Exhibition, Geefs's amorous lion, very much like those officers a
gentlemen tamed by well-bred girls in paintings and lithographs, invi
a pleasing, culturally useful application.

To take this mildly amusing, literally superficial interpretation
exhaustive is to give *The Lion in Love* an impoverished reading. It
more rewarding to treat the sculpture as a dream in plaster: like a drea
it conceals stormy conflicts behind a picturesque façade and conden
a rich array of meanings into one terse statement. It represents a wish a
fact. Geefs's group, heavily overdetermined, touches on the princi
themes of these first two volumes of *The Bourgeois Experience*: the p
vasive struggle in middle-class culture between candor and reticence; t
hunger for moralizing all aspects of life, including art; the inclination
defuse explosive erotic themes by molding them into acceptable for
In short, *The Lion in Love* has something to say about the ambiguo
relation, in its century of change, between freedom and control in t
domain of love.

Geefs's *Lion in Love*, to notice its most obvious quality first, is a wo
of art, and as such it embodies the doctrine of distance at work: it is
telling instance of how nineteenth-century artists would extort permissio
as it were, to show a naked body in all its seductive beauty. This, v
know, was one favorite, and highly effective, method for bourge
culture to convey the sort of sensual information hard to come by
"real" life. By clothing the charms of the human figure in the prop
formal garb of mythology, history, or allegory, art exhibited those charr
with impunity. This meant that it could be erotically expressive whi
protesting, in all sincerity, that it was pursuing elevated aims.[37] It
further worth noting that *The Lion in Love* provides carnal knowledg
not merely by presenting an attractive nude as a charming or pure
decorative object: the group conveys a lesson that may appear banal t
critical spirits, but was taken to be moral in its essence.

The implications of Geefs's sculpture, though, reach beyond its s
way of displaying firm breasts and rounded thighs before mixed con
pany. It seems only reasonable to wonder whether its action is quite s
innocuous as it is advertised to be: the woman's action uncomfortabl
hints at an astutely disguised castration. If so, this cannot have bee
Geefs's anxious response to the woman's movement: *The Lion in Lou*
was sculpted at mid-century, when feminism was in its very infancy an
had certainly not reached Belgium. What is more, that pervasive nine

37. For the doctrine, see *Education of the Senses*, 391–99.

eenth-century theme in art and literature, the devouring female—the
man-eating Sphinx of Gustave Moreau, the murderous Madonnas of
Edvard Munch, the half-masculine shrews of the humor magazines, the
crowing hens of American editorial writers—was only incidentally a
reaction to the campaign for women's rights. To be sure, the pastors and
journalists, sociologists and politicians who denounced the feminists
assembled at Seneca Falls in 1848, and their successors, perceived feminism
as a well-defined assault on their supremacy in the world, in the parlor,
and, doubtless, in bed. But the more celebrated depictions of woman as
monster had more widely ramified roots than this. In an age in which
avant-gardes in painting and poetry and philosophy were beginning to
lose touch with the bourgeois public nourished on academic ideals and
traditional subject matter, gifted rebels joined forces with other fearful
males largely by accident. The psychological universe that Munch in-
habited in common with Geefs was very large. This is not to deny
innovating artists and writers of the century a capacity for sounding the
depths of the human mind and its preoccupations. But it was far less the
time-bound problems of the nineteenth-century bourgeoisie that they
captured and portrayed, than universal, timeless masculine concerns. What
made the age distinctive in this respect was not that it made men fearful
of women, but that it permitted them to pour their sexual malaise into
their work and to use their art as an expressive vehicle as it had never been
used before.

The fashion of fatal woman in the nineteenth century reveals therefore
less the menace of feminism than the contours of liberal culture. Alike
the fashion and the feminism were consequences of conflicts besetting the
time in which both emerged. It was a culture rigid in defense of traditional positions—nineteenth-century bourgeois confirm Freud's dictum
that no one likes to give up a pleasure once enjoyed. But that culture
was also more flexible than its predecessors; the promise of new pleasures
invited the taking of chances. The tortuous course and ultimate triumph
of the woman's movement demonstrate the capacity of many bourgeois
to rethink their cultural defenses and revise their social ideals. Influential
men came to see that the angel in the house was no angel and need not
stay in the house. At the same time, the piling up of poems and paintings
and novels about predatory females testifies to the capacity of liberal
culture to probe delicate and difficult issues that, with a fair degree of
explicitness, touched on some of the most closely guarded secrets of male
sexuality. Few of those who agonized in public over dangerous women
were censured, let alone censored, for exposing their scars or their

wounds. Liberal nineteenth-century culture was rife with anxiety, b
it was at once mature and worried enough to permit its anxieties to rise
public awareness.[38]

Bourgeois, in short, were compelled to contend with that supreme a
familiar nineteenth-century reality, the demands of the new. My leadi
witnesses, from John Stuart Mill to Walter Bagehot, Alexis de Tocqu
ville to Emile Zola, Jacob Burckhardt to Hans von Bülow, agreed th
theirs was a nerve-wracking age of transition, an age in which the i
pulse for change and the need for control were impossible to overloc
And the more insistent the impulse, the more imperative the need. It
a commonplace to say that history is a record of change, but never tru
than in the nineteenth century. Transitions were exerting pressures
all fronts of feeling and activity, and love was not exempt. To ha
lived before the railroad came, Thackeray once observed, was to ha
lived before the Flood. To have lived before modern contraception, o
might add, or modern hygiene, was to have been quite as antediluvia
The fabled solidity of bourgeois life was therefore as much a defen
hastily erected as it was a goal happily reached. What the psychoanaly
Heinz Hartmann has called the average expectable environment w
built, for the nineteenth century, on the shifting sands of innovation.

While by no means all the innovations were unwelcome, one of th
most far-reaching discoveries of the nineteenth century was that goc
news produces anxiety quite as much as bad. Sudden prosperity is as ha
to assimilate emotionally as drastic economic decline. As students
psychology and sociology also discovered: at all times, even at the bes
humanity is permitted to enjoy its pleasures only through conflict, an
with severe limitations on its desires. The cost of survival is instinctu
sacrifice. Thus, the human is a paradoxical lot: men and women cann
live without civilization, but to live in civilization always leaves them i
painful ways unsatisfied. That is why the constraints it imposes are
once indispensable and unpopular.

These paradoxes pervaded bourgeois love no less than other aspects c
bourgeois existence. Love, we have seen, is the proverbial enemy o
order; it scorns long-established barriers, tramples on sacred rules. Bu
it also holds out the promise of security and permanence. Similarly, sexu
desire chafes at controls; it is impatient of delay, imperious with soci
fetters. Yet, as bourgeois well knew, though did not always say blunth
such desire is essential to love. If love without enduring affection is bar

38. For details on the castrating female in nineteenth-century art and literature, se
ibid., 197–213.

lust, love without erotic appetite is "mere" friendship. The point was to have them both in suitable proportion and decent guise. "WHAT IS LOVE?" Dr. George Napheys asked in the late 1860s; speaking, not for a venture-some minority but for the bulk of respectable opinion, he replied: "It has a divided nature. As we have an immortal soul, but a body of clay," so "love has a physiological and a moral nature." It embraces the senti-ment that makes adults look to marriage and offspring; but then "Nature, as beneficent to those who obey her precepts as she is merciless to those who disregard them, has added to this sentiment of love a physical pleasure in its gratification." Mankind is subject to a "passion which is the love of the body," and, in an emotional passage, Napheys defended that love, "THE DIGNITY AND PROPRIETY OF THE SEXUAL INSTINCT." But there is also, equally necessary, "another emotion," which might be defined as "exalted friendship." Only the combination of the two, con-summated in marriage, Napheys believed, is true love. Chastity, he noted severely, is not a synonym for celibacy; rather, it is found most often, most happily, under "the gentle yoke of matrimony."[39] Geefs's sculpture illustrates Napheys's definition of love to perfection. The monarch of the forest, the embodiment of raw sexual power, readily submits to beauty, which calls forth decorum, delicacy, and tenderness, to live on happily, the tamed cat of passion, presumably under the gentle yoke of matrimony. Thus interpreted, The Lion in Love stands for a cherished bourgeois ideal.

Ideals are wishes. They are desires purified, aims in view, statements of good intentions; they condense the cultural superego into exacting pre-cepts, exemplary stories, or moralistic works of art. The bourgeois erotic ideal was, in two words, married love; to frequent prostitutes or to discover one's potency only with sexual partners one cannot respect, or, for that matter, to flee into celibacy, is to betray it. George Bernard Shaw meant precisely that with his disrespectful witticism, which he puts into the mouth of his Don Juan, that marriage is the most licentious of institutions.

It also proved very demanding. Respectable lovers had to contend, not merely with their own desires, but with the reproachful presence of high-minded moral guardians. And the noise that the censorious made was admittedly resounding. It has left its impress on historians of the nine-teenth century, who are bound to recall (much to the middle classes' damage) George Moore's spirited and furious protest, significantly titled

39. The Physical Life of Woman: Advice to the Maiden, Wife and Mother (1869; 3rd ed. 1888), 56–58, 96.

Literature at Nurse; the reign of prudish editors and circulating libraries
the telling jokes at the expense of smug and uncultivated bourgeois in th
biting German humor magazine *Simplicissimus*; the trials of Henr
Vizetelly for his English version of Zola's *La Terre*, not quite decen
enough; and the articulate opposition, the angry anti-bourgeois crusader
hunting hypocrites in country after country. Scourges of the cantinç
middle class, from Lord Byron and Gustave Flaubert to Henrik Ibsen
Friedrich Nietzsche, and George Bernard Shaw were not just beinç
self-indulgent. There was much to lament and lampoon: the deadening
complacency that often routed liberal open-mindedness, the self-serving
denial of unsavory realities, the philistinism that allowed the half-educated
to bully talented, original painters and poets, and the teary sentimentality
that could choke off the honest exploration of mixed motives or flourishing vices, of the ravages of time or the corruptions of affluence. The
spread of prosperity among the middling orders was a danger no less than
a joy. As publishers, editors, and impresarios discovered to their cost, the
capacity of professional purifiers to shape their culture was too formidable
to be safely ignored; they managed to affect—and distort—the ways that
the nineteenth-century bourgeois wrote, talked, even thought about
sensual love.[40]

Still, the notoriety that the angry, self-selected censors of middle-class
morality enjoyed was out of proportion to their numbers and, in the end,
their influence. They could intimidate Thackeray, prosecute Baudelaire,
infuriate Fontane: they forced on popular periodicals a certain anodyne

40. Few nineteenth-century figures testify to the sheer complexity of their culture
more eloquently than William Makepeace Thackeray, with his gift for distance and
his compromises; physician to his society and, in almost equal measure, its profiteer,
he at once diagnosed and embodied his time, sometimes pilloried and sometimes
excused the sordid facts of life, and practiced what he satirized. He was not merely
a great critic of Vanity Fair, he kept a booth there. But at least he had few illusions
about the place. Men and women were, he believed, an alloy, whoring after incompatible gods; they called for a mixed verdict, severe but not uncharitable: "I often
think that in one's intercourse with others," he told his mother, whom he told everything, "the party who hates you, & he who loves you, are both right." (August 12–
14, 1842, *The Letters and Private Papers of William Makepeace Thackeray*, ed.
Gordon N. Ray, 4 vols. [1945–46], II, 72.) The contending voices attempting to explain the age to itself and calling one another names sometimes turned the bazaar that
is civilization into an undignified brawl; they were, to Thackeray's taste, too intense,
too sure of themselves, too disdainful of their rivals, and much too loud. He often
intimated, especially in his early years when the satirist had nearly driven out the
sentimentalist lurking within him, that what he called the sanctity of private life was
only a convenient slogan, serving to exempt from scrutiny scandalous truths badly
needing ventilation. But he also saw that reserved private domain as a signal
achievement of his century, too precious to be sacrificed to righteous fanatics of any
party. It gave bourgeois lovers room for play.

one. But their work does not stamp explicit middle-class lovers, the Roes or the Kingsleys as secret perverts or as Bohemians who had somehow strayed into bourgeois culture disguised as pious Christians. Such couples were unusual but not eccentric. Doubtless, the treasury of letters and diaries that chance or inattentive heirs permitted to survive leaves little doubt that their century in fact swarmed with exceptions. Merely to quote these couples is to subvert the Victorians' reputation for prissiness and prudery.

To say all this is simply to assert that nineteenth-century middle-class culture was electric with tensions and contradictory impulsions. Black-coated Eros was bursting with vitality, thoroughly aware of his sensual needs but, at the same time, frequently victimized by disagreeable inhibitions. The earthiness of the bourgeois explorers in the ill-charted domain of love defines the expressive limits of the gamut available to the respectable in their century. In the company of other mortals, nineteenth-century bourgeois were more inclined to flee reality than to stare it in the face; they were given, all too humanly, to the cant of idealization and sought the comforts of repression. But, then, their reality was oppressively with them, and impertinently invaded the most assiduously protected precincts of their love. Try as they might, they could not easily escape the sights of hunger and poverty and of the maimed, or the capricious aggressions of untimely death—recurrent epidemics, dangerous illnesses, and scarcely less dangerous physicians—or, even more to the point, the moral dilemmas and physical vagaries of contraception and the mortal risks of childbirth for mother and infant alike. The fatal association of love with death, which had become, by the 1880s, a facile metaphor for orgasm and a hackneyed operatic conceit, was only too obtrusive, too sobering a presence in the lives of bourgeois in their century. This was the world, often ugly and perilous, in which respectable lovers were compelled to move.

Their century was an earnest age, addicted to guilty rehearsals of its failings and earnest efforts at reforming them. But it also had its rather less solemn face; its hard-driving, vindictive superego was by no means in undisputed control. Self-scrutiny and self-deception were in uneasy balance, in the domain of love as much as anywhere else. This precariousness marks the work of nineteenth-century painters and novelists, composers and scholars, physicians and housewives. But the exceptionally determined bourgeois separation between private and public business significantly increases the need for interpreting the evidence. There is more of it, and much of it far more frankly erotic, than we have been instructed to believe. Yet—and both conclusions belong together—it

calls for a reading that will not remain satisfied with manifest surface
The middle classes resented the intrusions of the outside world; the
would write their love letters in learned languages at critical points, ar
lyrically celebrated their right to secrets. Theirs are the accents, r
strained and self-protective, that are far more familiar to the historia
of the nineteenth century than the sensual freedom of the Roes or tl
Kingsleys: middle-class men and women were generally ill at ease ne
so much with their amorous emotions as with giving them voice.

Nineteenth-century bourgeois, then, defying all the trespassers, bui
their emotional fortress and guarded it closely, and, with that, have mac
it hard for the historian to infiltrate it and to draw its outlines. But the
defensiveness was a tribute to passion, displaying a wry respect for i
powers. It invites the paradoxical speculation that the century of Victor
was at heart more profoundly erotic than ages more casual about the
carnal desires and consummations. This is the place to recall Eliza Wilson's
somewhat prayerful optimism in her letter to her fiancé, Walter Bageho*
"Happy marriages are not uncommon." Her hopes, we may now affirs
with some confidence, were well grounded. Bourgeois lovers had the
share of fatuity and failures. But for all the traumas that sexuality an
parenthood, inquisitive relatives, and subterranean survivals of early love
forced upon them, they also enjoyed their quiet triumphs. Marriage wa
not just the source of conflicts, but also a means for their resolution. Fo
the nineteenth-century bourgeoisie, Eros had often proved flirtatious o
difficult. Yet he was also very much present and supremely desirable. Th
smile of Geefs's lion is not forced. Necessarily, the Victorian middl
classes tamed that lion in their own way, in styles of thinking and behavin
that are no longer our own. We must therefore once again learn to rea
them, if we wish to recapture that particular mixture of sensuality an
shy reticence, and the subtle, poignant compromises between drives an
defenses with which they regulated their loves in imagination and in life

Bibliographical Essay

Following the lead of the bibliographical essay in the preceding volume, *Education of the Senses*, this essay makes no claim to completeness. In compiling it, I have concentrated on the books and articles and unpublished sources that have taught me the most, intrigued me and stimulated my thinking, and roused me to opposition. Anyone interested in my debts to the psychoanalytic literature—a debt that is not decreasing—should consult my bibliographical comments in *Education of the Senses*, esp. 463–66 and 469.

BOURGEOIS EXPERIENCES, II:
Counterpoint

The copious, immensely revealing materials left by Otto Beneke—his diaries and letters—are deposited in the archive he headed, the Staatsarchiv of the Freie und Hansestadt Hamburg. The brief biographies of Beneke in the *Allgemeine Deutsche Biographie*, XLVI (1902), 355–58, and that of his father Ferdinand, ibid., II (1875), 327, are adequate for their limited purposes. For the atmosphere surrounding Beneke's particularism, Olga Herschel, *Die öffentliche Meinung in Hamburg in ihrer Haltung zu Bismarck 1864–1866* (1916), a terse monograph, is most useful. See also the scholarly survey by Renate Hauschild-Thiessen, "Hamburg im Kriege 1870/71," *Zeitschrift des Vereins für Hamburgische Geschichte*, LVII (1971), 3–45. Her lapidary note on Beneke's ambition is in ibid., LX (1974), 239. See also her "Hamburg, Lübeck, Bremen und das Haus der Oesterlinge in Antwerpen nach dem Frieden von Campo Formio," ibid., 125–37, with details on Beneke's father. Hauschild-Thiessen has also published interesting letters by Beneke's brother, "Alfred Beneke, Ein junger Hamburger Kaufmann in New York. Briefe an seine Angehörigen aus den Jahren 1844 bis 1847," ibid., LI (1965), 49–100. The biography of Beneke's chief, Johann Martin Dappenberg, in the *Allgemeine Deutsche Biographie*, XVII (1883), 707–15, is full and instructive.

J. G. Gallois, *Geschichte der Stadt Hamburg*, vol. III, *Specielle Geschich.
der Stadt seit 1814* (1856), is a highly detailed and dependable contempora
account, including a careful description of the great fire of 1842 (pp. 612–45)
which Beneke so modestly distinguished himself. For that fire there is t
illustrated study by Ludlof Wienbarg, *Hamburg und seine Brandtage: ein h.
torisch-kritischer Beitrag* (1843). Ernst Baasch, *Geschichte Hamburgs 181
1918* (1924–25), 2 vols., is particularly informative, notably, for my purpos
vol. I, *1814–1867*. See also Baasch's essay, *Der Einfluss des Handels auf d
Geistesleben Hamburgs* (1909). Percy Ernst Schramm, *Hamburger Biede
meier* (1962), is popular, informal, and short. Mosche Zimmermann, *Ha
burgischer Patriotismus und deutscher Nationalismus: Die Emanzipation d
Juden in Hamburg 1830–1865* (1979), goes beyond its announced aim of d
tailing Jewish history; the pages on the fire (19–88) are excellent. I have a
profited from Helmut Böhme's comparative study, *Frankfurt und Hambur
Des deutschen Reiches Silber- und Goldloch und die allerenglischste Stadt d
Kontinents* (1968), with a comprehensive bibliography. Werner Jochmann a
Hans-Dieter Loose, eds., *Hamburg: Geschichte der Stadt und ihrer Bewohn
(1982), is a modern, very substantial, collective history. I also found helpf
Hans-Dieter Loose, ed., *Gelehrte in Hamburg im 18. und 19. Jahrhunde
(1976), a collection of biographies. For the significant powerful institution
the Oberalten, I have consulted the still useful old study of F. Georg Buek, *D
Hamburgischen Oberalten, ihre bürgerliche Wirksamkeit und ihre Famili
(1857). See also Hans-Dieter Loose, "Die Jastram-Snitgerschen Wirren in d
zeitgenössischen Geschichtsschreibung," *Zeitschrift des Vereins für Hamburg
sche Geschichte*, LIII (1967), 7–8; the monograph by Jürgen Bolland, *Senat un
Bürgerschaft: über das Verhältnis zwischen Bürger und Stadtregiment im alte
Hamburg* (1954), is an authoritative essay.

When Norman St. John-Stevas's edition of *The Collected Works of Walt
Bagehot* (9 vols., so far, 1965–   ) is completed, it will supersede the earli
editions of Bagehot's writings, of which that by Mrs. Russell Barrington, *Wor.
and Life of Walter Bagehot*, 10 vols. (1914–15), remains the one to be consulte
Eliza Wilson Bagehot's diaries, incompletely preserved, dry, factual, too bri
to be ever really satisfying, in Mr. St. John-Stevas's possession, to which I ha
access, retain a certain value. Among the attractive features of St. John-Stevas
edition, in addition to reliability of attribution and completeness of coverag
are the introductory essays, notably St. John-Stevas's own, "Walter Bagehot:
Short Biography," *Collected Works of Bagehot*, I, 29–83, as well as "The Pol
tical Genius of Walter Bagehot," in the fifth and Jacques Barzun's crisp essa
"Bagehot as Historian" in the third volume. Among biographies, Mrs. Barrin
ton's *Life of Walter Bagehot* (1914), also published the following year as th
concluding volume of her edition of Bagehot's writings, is rich in inside i
formation and now lost materials, but prudent. It must be supplemented wi
more modern lives, notably Alastair Buchan, *The Spare Chancellor: The Li
of Walter Bagehot* (1959), judicious and economical, to be read in conjunctio
with William Irvine, *Walter Bagehot* (1939). Mrs. Barrington's publicatio
*The Love-Letters of Walter Bagehot and Eliza Wilson written from 10 N
vember 1857 to 23 April 1858* (1933), has naturally proved indispensable to m
her bulky biography of her father and family, *The Servant of All*, 2 vol

927), is also a treasure trove of diaries and letters no longer extant. Sister artha Westwater's *The Wilson Sisters: A Biographical Study of Upper iddle-Class Victorian Life* (1984), securely based on an intimate knowledge ' Eliza Bagehot's diaries, is too censorious and condescending to be really re- aling. In sharp contrast, the memoir, "Walter Bagehot," that his closest friend, ichard Holt Hutton, published in the *Fortnightly Review* in 1877 (and then parately in the same year) retains all its freshness.

Among special essays on Bagehot, who has been much written about, I want • single out the brilliant brief essay by John W. Burrow, "Sense and Cir- imstances: Bagehot and the Nature of Political Understanding," in Stefan ollini, Donald Winch, and John Burrow, *That Noble Science of Politics: A :udy in Nineteenth-Century Intellectual History* (1983), 161–81; C. H. •river, "Walter Bagehot and the Social Psychologists," in F. J. C. Hearnshaw, l., *The Social and Political Ideas of Some Representative Thinkers of the 'ictorian Age* (1931), which is suggestive but leaves room for more work. See so the compact sensible pages in Crane Brinton, *English Political Thought in)e 19th Century* (1933; ed. 1962), esp. 87–115, in George Watson, *The English deology: Studies in the Language of Victorian Politics* (1973) passim; and iertrude Himmelfarb, "Walter Bagehot: A Common Man with Uncommon leas," in *Victorian Minds* (1968), 220–35. Sir Leslie Stephen's essay, "Walter agehot," printed in his *Studies of a Biographer*, 4 vols., III (1902), is inter- sting as the response of a near-contemporary to Bagehot's penchant for leorizing. G. M. Young's classic description of Bagehot as "The Greatest 'ictorian," published in *Today and Yesterday* (1948), is conveniently available ι W. D. Handcock, ed., G. M. Young, *Victorian Essays* (1962), 123–28. There ave been several reissues of Bagehot's most enduring work, *The English Con- :itution* (1867; with an added ch. 1872, rev. ed., 1873), most notably by R. H. . Crossman (1963).

ONE: Two Currents of Love

jeneral histories of love at their best are bound to be overwhelmed by their naterials, and present themselves as rapid romps. Morton M. Hunt, *The Natural Iistory of Love* (1959), though helpful, runs from the ancient Greeks to mid- wentieth century; the superficial, somewhat condescending quality of its :hapter on the Victorians is indicated by its title, "The Angel in the House." Ielmut Kuhn, *"Liebe": Geschichte eines Begriffes* (1975), is a compact)hilosophical conceptual survey. Sydney L. W. Mellen, *The Evolution of Love* . 1981), is an archeologist's informative contribution including "love" among)rimates and early humans; he finds (not wholly persuasively) what he dubs 'reud's "rococo edifice called the Oedipus complex" open to simpler explana- ions, with incest avoidance *"latent"* and normal in most humans "during nfancy and early childhood—along with the mating impulse," for evolutionary easons (p. 164). In contrast, Irving Singer's long, civilized essay, *The Nature •f Love*, vol. I, *Plato to Luther* (1966; 2nd ed. 1984), and II, *Courtly and Romantic* (1984), with the concluding volume yet to come, happily avoids such misreadings. I have learned from John Bayley, *The Character of Love: A

Study in the Literature of Personality (1960), which begins with gene
thoughts and then offers chapters on courtly love, Shakespeare, and Hei
James. Laurence Lerner, *Love and Marriage: Literature and its Social Cont*
(1979), is a stimulating essay but too much concentrated on Ruskin's rat
extreme views and still beholden to the traditional view of Victorian won
that I am committed to modifying (see "The Angel in the House," pp. 130-4
The same need for revision compromises Bernard I. Murstein's *Love, S*
Marriage Through the Ages (1974), bulky and typical: "Victorian love
tempted to fuse the spirit of romanticism with the traditional conservatism
a guilt-ridden theological concept of marriage. Women were elevated to
position of earthly angels—venerated but powerless. . . . Victorian love prov
a failure, as documented by the rise of prostitution and the resentment
women against this pale substitute for freedom" (p. 278). And see Suzar
Lilar, *Aspects of Love in Western Society* (1963; tr. Jonathan Griffin, 196
which has interesting comments on "androgyny" and the "resacralization"
love. Volumes II and III of Michel Foucault's projected six-volume histori
survey of love and sex, *Histoire de la sexualité*, appeared the week of his de
(1984), and take his enterprise through the ancient Greek and Latin "discours
Among collections of letters, Antonia Fraser, *Love Letters: An Antholo*
(1976), is most handy. Thomas Gould, *Platonic Love* (1963), takes E
through the centuries in his strikingly varied incarnations; it is far m
authoritative on Plato than on Freud. See also Fritz Möschler, *Platons Eroslel*
und Schopenhauers Willensphilosophie (1907), a short exposition. I should n
that much of the mischief about the bourgeois' "inability to love" and to f
high passions can be found in Werner Sombart, *Der Bourgeois: Zur Geist*
geschichte des modernen Wirtschaftsmenschen (1913; tr. Mr. Epstein as *T*
Quintessence of Capitalism, 1915), which has had undeserved influence.

Critical to an understanding of Christian love and its pagan counterpart
the distinction drawn sharply (too sharply) by Anders Nygren's learn
treatise *Agape and Eros* (1929; tr. P. S. Watson, 1953). The Jesuit M.
D'Arcy's *The Mind and Heart of Love* (1945; 2nd ed. 1956) is an attempt
revise Nygren. Just as suggestive and as open to debate is Denis de Rougemoi
Love in the Western World (1939; tr. Montgomery Belgion, rev. ed. 195*
which attempts to link courtly love with heresy. John C. Moore, *Love*
Twelfth-Century France (1972) is a historian's lucid, brief survey of what
reliably know of the varieties of medieval love; it has a helpful bibliographi
note. Sidney Painter, *French Chivalry: Chivalric Ideas and Practics in Mediev*
France (1940), remains indispensable. C. S. Lewis, *The Allegory of Love* (193*
is elegant, and rather opinionated, about medieval literature on this subje
See also Myrrha Lot-Borodine, *De l' amour profane à l'amour sacré: Etudes*
psychologie sentimentale au Moyen Age (1961). Recent scholarship
Christian love and sensuality during the Middle Ages and beyond is beautiful
summarized and further advanced in Jean-Louis Flandrin, *L'église et le co*
trôle des naissances (1970), and in his fine essays, *Le sexe et l'occident: Evol*
tion des attitudes et des comportements (1981). Emmanuel Le Roy Ladur
Montaillou: The Promised Land of Error (1975; abridged ed. tr. Barbara Bra
1978), has concrete and fascinating material on love and sexuality in an ear
fourteenth-century village.

I have used, for Andreas Capellanus, *The Art of Courtly Love*, the translation by John Jay Parry (1941). A new edition, by P. G. Walsh, *Andreas Capellanus on Love* (1982), sums up revisionist thought on courtly love, warning that marriage was prized in its time, and that the celebrated troubadour poems are literary works rather than social history.

The pages of Jacob Burckhardt's classic, *The Civilization of the Renaissance in Italy* (1860; tr. S. G. C. Middlemore, 1878), esp. parts V and VI, remain immensely worth perusing. See also Ruth Kelso, *Doctrine for the Lady of the Renaissance* (1956). For the Puritans, there is the brilliant corrective essay by Edmund S. Morgan, "The Puritans and Sex," *The New England Quarterly*, XV (1942), 591–607, and his authoritative analysis, *The Puritan Family: Religion and Domestic Relations in Seventeenth-Century New England* (1944; rev. ed., 1966), well known, though too often conveniently disregarded by historians of love. Once again, I have used Jean H. Hagstrum's illuminating *Sex And Sensibility: Ideal and Erotic Love from Milton To Mozart* (1980), despite a few perverse judgments (*"Don Giovanni* is a flawed work" [!]—p. 323.)

Love in the Enlightenment still needs a full-scale study; I have touched on it in *The Enlightenment: An Interpretation*, 2 vols. (1966, 1969), esp. vol. II, 187–207, on which I have drawn here. And see my essay, "Three Stages on Love's Way: Rousseau, Laclos, Diderot" (1957), in *The Party of Humanity: Essays in the French Enlightenment* (1964), 133–61. Diderot is the most radical among the philosophes, describing, in his *Supplément au Voyage de Bougainville* (1796; ed. Herbert Dieckmann, 1955), 16–17, largely imaginary Tahitians, maidens and young men, coupling without shame and introduced to guilt by the visiting French priests. Leo Spitzer's chapter in *Linguistics and Literary History* (1948), "The Style of Diderot," 135–91, is a sophisticated appreciation of the sensuality pervading Diderot's way with words.

Romanticism is notoriously hard to define. In 1923, in his celebrated devastation of the term and the concept, Arthur O. Lovejoy proposed that scholars either scrap it entirely (since, as he proved, it had lent itself to all possible definitions) or that they at least use "romanticism" in the plural: "On the Discrimination of Romanticisms," *PMLA*, XXIX (1924), 229–53, reprinted in *Essays in the History of Ideas* (1948), 228–53. It was not until literally a quarter of a century later that René Wellek rescued the name by discovering some common characteristics in all romanticisms: "The Concept of Romanticism in Literary History" (1949) and his postscript, "Romanticism Re-examined," both in *Concepts of Criticism* (1963), 128–98, 199–221. Another thoughtful effort at definition is Geoffrey Thurley, *The Romantic Predicament* (1984). In the scanty psychoanalytic literature on romanticism, William N. Evans's "Two Kinds of Romantic Love," *PQ*, XX (1953) is brief but helpful on the masochistic strain. I shall be listing titles specifically devoted to romantic literature below; here I will mention only that inescapable classic by Mario Praz, *The Romantic Agony* (1933; 2nd ed. tr. Angus Davidson, 1951). And see Pierre Moreau, *Amours romantiques* (1963), which concentrates on France, esp. Chateaubriand.

There is much of interest on thoughts about love in Germany (both on the *Aufklärung* and *Romantik*) in Paul Kluckhohn, *Die Auffassung der Liebe in der Literatur des 18. Jahrhunderts und in der deutschen Romantik* (1922; 2nd ed. 1931); in Julius Steinberg, *Liebe und Ehe in Schleiermachers Kreis* (1921 and in the collection of papers edited by Siegbert Prawer, *The Romant Period in Germany* (1970). See also Hans Steffen, ed. *Die deutsche Romanti Poetik, Formen und Motive* (1967; 2nd. ed. 1970), and Werner Kohlschmid *Geschichte der deutschen Literatur*, vol. III, *Von der Romantik bis zum späte Goethe* (1974). The literature on Friedrich Schlegel is large; Julien Roug *Erläuterungen zu Friedrich Schlegels Lucinde* (1904), competently deals wit his radical romantic novel. Ernst Behler, *Friedrich Schlegel in Selbstzeugnisse und Bilddokumenten* (1966), is short, meaty, with an excellent bibliograph The intelligent old book by Ricarda Huch, *Ausbreitung und Verfall de Romantik* (1902; new ed. 1951 under the title *Die Romantik: Blütezeit, Au breitung und Verfall*), is subjective, anecdotal, but still valuable. Amid th overpowering, never-ceasing stream of secondary literature on Goethe I reca only Barker Fairley's classic *A Study of Goethe* (1947), Georg Simmel's sug gestive old essay, *Goethe* (1913), two volumes by Karl Viëtor, *Goethe the Poe* (1949) and *Goethe the Thinker* (1950), and some fascinating close readings b Albrecht Schöne, *Götterzeichen, Liebeszauber, Satanskult: Neue Einblicke i alte Goethetexte* (1982).

Among the English romantics, Shelley and Byron continue to generate th largest number of monographs. I have learned from James O. Allsup, *Th Magic Circle: A Study of Shelley's Concept of Love* (1976), more fror Nathaniel Brown, *Sexuality and Feminism in Shelley* (1979), and from th annotated *Shelley on Love: An Anthology*, ed. Richard Holmes (1980). Sylv Norman, *Flight of the Skylark: The Development of Shelley's Reputatio* (1954), traces his influence. For Byron, Leslie A. Marchand, *Byron: / Biography*, 3 vols. (1958), sober and very detailed, is authoritative; and see th convenient anthology, *Byron: a Collection of Critical Essays*, ed. Paul Wes (1963). For his reputation the old book by Samuel C. Chew, *Byron in Englana His Fame and After-Fame* (1924), retains its uses. Christopher Ricks, *Keats an Embarrassment* (1974), comes upon the subject obliquely and suggestively. *Th Love Letters of William and Mary Wordsworth*, ed. Beth Darlington (1981) are moving, passionate, virtually exploding the traditional form. Among gen eral treatments, Anne K. Mellor, *English Romantic Irony* (1980), esp. 31–76 deals deftly with themes of romantic love. Frederick L. Beaty, *Light from Heaven: Love in British Romantic Literature* (1971), is an orderly and de pendable survey concentrating on the main figures. French Romanticism ha elicited ample commentary. *French Literature and Its Background*, ed. Joh Cruickshank, vol. IV, *The Early Nineteenth Century* (1969) has some ex cellent if spare essays. See also Paul Van Tieghem, *Le Romantisme Françai* (1951). Albert Joseph George, *The Development of French Romanticism: Th Impact of the Industrial Revolution on Literature* (1955) goes beyond it rather specialized argument. It should be supplemented with D. O. Evans *Social Romanticism in France, 1830–1848* (1951). For a rather miscellaneou gathering of papers, not without its interest, see *Aimer en France, 1760–1860* 2 vols., ed. Paul Viallaneix and Jean Ehrard (1977). Among French romantic I mention (apart from Stendhal), Alfred de Musset is most relevant; I hav depended on Yves Lainey, *Musset ou la difficulté d'aimer* (1978). George Sanc did not just write key texts, but *became* something of a key text on the theme of love lived and recorded. In a growing literature, see Joseph Barry, *Infamous Woman: The Life of George Sand* (1977), and Barry's generous collection of texts, *George Sand: In Her Own Words* (1979). A. W. Raitt, *Prosper Merimée* (1970), is full and informative. The important typology dividing mankind between Hebrews and Hellenes has been widely canvassed, notably by David J. DeLaura's informative *Hebrew and Hellene in Victorian England: Newman, Arnold, and Pater* (1969). The pertinent pages (214, 233–37) in Lionel Trilling's elegant and patrician *Matthew Arnold* (1939; 2nd. ed. 1949) are still unsurpassed despite active recent scholarship on Arnold. These studies need to be read in conjunction with two important, sensible critical studies by Henry Hatfield, *Aesthetic Paganism in German Literature from Winckelmann to the Death of Goethe* (1964) and *Clashing Myths in German Literature from Heine to Rilke* (1974); see also Frank M. Turner's authoritative *The Greek Heritage in Victorian Britain* (1981).

The most dependable studies of Stendhal remain those of Henri Martineau, notably *L'Oeuvre de Stendhal: histoire de ses livres et de sa pensée* (1951) and his brilliant *Le coeur de Stendhal*, 2 vols. (1952–53). Victor Brombert, *Stendhal et la voie oblique: l'auteur devant son monde romanesque* (1954), is urbane, stimulating. Gilbert D. Chaitin, *The Unhappy Few: A Psychological Study of the Novels of Stendhal* (1972), is a penetrating, often necessarily speculative psychoanalytic essay. There are useful psychological comments in Hans Boll Johansen, "Les paradigmes psychologiques dans l'amour Stendhalien," *Stendhal Club*, XIII, No. 51 (April 15, 1971), 183–200. Léon Blum, *Stendhal et le Beylisme* (1914; 3rd ed. 1947) remains indispensable on the Stendhalian stance in life. See in addition (among several good biographical studies) Robert M. Adams, *Stendhal: Notes on a Novelist* (1959), Geoffrey Strickland, *Stendhal: The Education of a Novelist* (1974), esp. (for purposes of this chapter), pp. 44–48, and Joanna Richardson, *Stendhal* (1974). Stendhal's claim to be a romantic is noted in several of these (and some other) works; witness esp. his letter to Adolphe de Mareste of April 14, 1818: "To distract yourself from politics, become a romantic." *Correspondance*, 3 vols., ed. Henri Martineau and V. del Litto (1962–68), vol. I, *1800–1821*, 1911. On his influence abroad, there is André Strauss, *La fortune de Stendhal en Angleterre* (1966). There are some striking psychoanalytic comments in Edmund Bergler, *Talleyrand, Napoleon, Stendhal, Grabbe; Psychoanalytisch-Biographische Essays* (1935).

Balzac has been well served. See Jean-Hervé Donnard, *Balzac, Les réalites économiques et sociales dans 'La comédie humaine'* (1961), informative about Balzac's views on women, education, and marriage, themes also explored in satisfying detail in Arlette Michel, *Le mariage chez Honoré de Balzac, Amour et féminisme* (1978). The modern edition of Balzac *Physiologie du mariage*, ed. Maurice Regard (1968), which I have used, is excellent. For Balzac's dependence on Stendhal's *De l'Amour*, F. W. J. Hemmings is conclusive: "Balzac's *Les chouans* and Stendhal's *De l'Amour*," in *Balzac and the Nineteenth Century, Studies in French Literature presented to Herbert J. Hunt* (1972), 99–110. The unpublished 1826 version of Balzac's physiology, an important text, was edited in 1940 by Maurice Bardèche, *La physiologie du mariage pré-originale*.

The authoritative study of Bourget's development is Michel Mansuy, *U* *Moderne. Paul Bourget de l'enfance au 'Disciple'* (1961). I add Albert Feuillera *Paul Bourget, Histoire d'un esprit sous la IIIe République* (1937). Emilie Carassus, *Le snobisme et les lettres françaises de Paul Bourget à Marcel Prou 1884-1914* (1966), is valuable for Bourget's snobbery, while Richard Griffith *The Reactionary Revolution: The Catholic Revival in French Literature 187‹ 1914* (1966), is equally valuable for Bourget's religiosity. Victor Brombert, *Tl Intellectual Hero: Studies in the French Novel, 1880-1955*, has a fine chapt‹ (iv) on Bourget's *Le disciple.*

Patrick Gardiner, *Schopenhauer* (1967), is remarkable and rare: at on‹ economical and penetrating. Father F. Copleston, *Arthur Schopenhaue‹ Philosopher of Pessimism* (1946), is scathing but worth pondering. The ne‹ rologist Paul Julius Moebius's *Über Schopenhauer* (1899) remains an inte esting document, as does the early life by Helen Zimmern, *Arthur Schope‹ hauer. His Life and His Philosophy* (1876). *Arthur Schopenhauer, Gesammel‹ Briefe,* ed. Arthur Hübscher (1978) is an excellent edition of rather disappoin ing letters. Since Schopenhauer's influence described such a strange cur‹ (from total and prolonged neglect to faddish admiration by the educate multitude), reception studies are particularly welcome. Bernhard Sorg, *Z‹ literarischen Schopenhauer-Rezeption im 19. Jahrhundert* (1975) usefully i‹ cludes Richard Wagner and Wilhelm Busch as rather willful followers of tl Great Pessimist. See also Ludwig von Golther, *Der moderne Pessimism‹* (1878). For Schopenhauer's influence on Thomas Mann, there are interestir comments in Erich Heller, *The Ironic German: A Study of Thomas Mar* (1958). Alexandre Baillot, *Influence de Schopenhauer en France* (1927), pe forms a similar service for France.

On the disagreeable subject of Schopenhauer's misogyny, see esp. the earl comments by Pierre Miramont, "La femme d'après Schopenhauer," *La nouvel Revue,* XXX (1884), 700-43; and André Fauconnet, "Essai sur la psycholog de la femme chez Schopenhauer" (1905) as well as Fauconnet's brief, inte esting "Schopenhauer précurseur de Freud" (1933), both in *Etudes sur l'All‹ magne* (1934), 28-72, 185-201.

Nietzsche's doughtiest modern champion (extremely necessary when he fir wrote, correcting horrendous misreadings and pillorying appalling mistransl tions) has been Walter A. Kaufmann. His *Nietzsche: Philosopher, Psychologi‹ Antichrist* (1950; 4th ed., 1974) was truly epoch making. But some correctio‹ of Kaufmann's enthusiastic apologies have commended themselves; see Hatfiel *Clashing Myths in German Literature,* ch. V. As for Nietzsche on wome Kaufmann always insisted that his "all-too-human judgments—especially abo‹ women," are "philosophically irrelevant." *Nietzsche* (ed. 1950), 63. Karl Jo‹ *Nietzsche und die Romantik* (1905; 2nd ed. 1923), contains an interestir essay on Nietzsche's intellectual forebears. And see Helmut Walter Bra‹ *Nietzsche und die Frauen* (1931). J. P. Stern's essays, *Nietzsche* (1978), ar *A Study of Nietzsche* (1979), are concise and, in the best sense, suggestive.

With all its obvious interest to psychoanalysis, the technical literature ‹ love is, considering its importance, relatively scanty—though much of what h appeared is of high caliber. The idea of love pervades Freud's work; the mo relevant titles are: *Drei Abhandlungen zur Sexualtheorie* (1905), *St. A.,* ‹

37–145, *Three Essays on the Theory of Sexuality*, *S.E.*, VII, 125–245; "Beiträge zur Psychologie des Liebeslebens" (1910, 1912, 1918), *St. A.*, V, 185–228, "Contributions to the Psychology of Love," I, II, III, *S.E.*, XI, 163–208; "Bemerkungen über die Übertragungsliebe" (1915), *St.A.*, XI, 217–30, "Observations on Transferenec-Love," *S.E.*, XII, 157–73. Eduard Hitchmann, "Freud's Conception of Love," *Int. J. Psycho-Anal.*, XXXIII (1952), 421–28, has no references and remains on the surface. Among recent titles, I am most indebted to three papers as well as a not-yet published book-length manuscript by Martin S. Bergmann, "Psychoanalytic Observations on the Capacity to Love," in *Separation-Individuation*, ed. J. B. McDevitt and C. F. Settlage (1971), 15–40, "On the Intrapsychic Function of Falling in Love," *PQ*, XLIX (1980), 56–76, and "Platonic Love, Transference Love, and Love in Real Life," *J. Amer. Psychoanal. Assn.*, XXX (1982), 87–111. Of Otto F. Kernberg's difficult but rewarding technical papers, I single out "Barriers to Falling and Remaining in Love," ibid., XXII (1974), 486–511; "Mature Love: Prerequisites and Characteristics," ibid., 743–68; and "Boundaries and Structure in Love Relations," ibid., XXV (1977), 81–114. Among Michael Balint's stimulating papers, the (justly) most cited is "On genital love," *Primary Love and Psychoanalytic Technique* (1959), 109–20. Other psychoanalytic presentations include Leon L. Altman, "Some Vicissitudes of Love," ibid., 35–52; Robert C. Bak, "Being in Love and Object Loss," *Int. J. Psycho-Anal.*, LIV (1973), 1–18; Jacob A. Arlow, "Object Concept and Object Choice," *PQ*, XLIX (1980), 109–33; Roy Schafer, "The Interpretation of Transference and the Conditions for Loving," *J. Amer. Psychoanal. Assn.*, XXV (1977), 335–62 and Therese Benedek, "Ambivalence, Passion, and Love," ibid., 35–52. The seminal writings by Margaret S. Mahler on early childhood are of cardinal importance in establishing a history of love. Most notable are (in collaboration with Manuel Furer) *On Human Symbiosis and the Vicissitudes of Individuation: Infantile Psychosis* (1968) and (with Fred Pine and Anni Bergman) *The Psychological Birth of the Human Infant: Symbiosis and Individuation* (1975). Serge Lebovici, "The Origins and Development of the Oedipus Complex," *Int. J. Psycho-Anal.*, LXIII (1982), 201–15, is a persuasive restatement and defense.

On Freud's influence, still an inadequately explored field, we have pioneering studies by Hannah S. Decker, *Freud in Germany: Revolution and Reaction in Science 1893–1907* (1977), sober, unpolemical, but revisionist; David Shakow and David Rapaport, *The Influence of Freud on American Psychology* (1964), a brief treatment; and Nathan G. Hale, Jr., *Freud and the Americans: The Beginnings of Psychoanalysis in the United States 1876–1917* (1971), a searching survey.

TWO: Experience: the Best Teacher

The original, well-informed, controversial study by Jack Goody, *The Development of the Family and Marriage in Europe* (1983), deals lucidly with the matter of dowries (and money in marriage generally) through history, esp. in Appendix 2, "From Brideprice to Dowry?" He draws on the compendious *A History of Matrimonial Institutions* by G. E. Howard, 2 vols. (1904) amid a large literature and, most effectively, on his own *Production and Reproduction: a Comparative Study of the Domestic Domain* (1976), as on Goody, Joan Thirsk, and E. P. Thompson, eds., *Family and Inheritance: Rural Society in Western Europe, 1200–1800* (1977). See also the highly interesting article by D. O. Hughes, "From Brideprice to Dowry in Mediterranean Europe," *Journal of Family History*, III (1978), 262–96. For nineteenth-century France, there are the pertinent pages in Theodore Zeldin, *France 1848–1945*, vol. I, *Ambition, Love and Politics* (1973), esp. in ch. 11, "Marriage and Morals." Important among his sources is Albert Eyquem, *Le Régime dotal. Son histoire, son évolution et ses transformations au 19e siècle sous l'influence de la jurisprudence et du notariat* (1903). Bonnie G. Smith touches on dowries and related practices in *Ladies of the Leisure Class: The Bourgeoises of Northern France in the Nineteenth Century* (1981). There are relevant comments too, in Richard Stites, *The Women's Liberation Movement in Russia: Feminism, Nihilism, and Bolshevism 1860–1930* (1978). I have, as the text reveals, learned much from the thorough, beautifully documented essay by Marion A. Kaplan, "For Love or Money: The Marriage Strategies of Jews in Imperial Germany," Leo Baeck Institute, *Year Book XXVIII* (1983), 263–300; it goes beyond its announced intentions. The autobiography by Rahel Straus, *Wir lebten in Deutschland: Erinnerungen einer deutschen Jüdin 1880–1933*, ed. Max Kreutzberger (1961), has immensely revealing material for this theme. There are some quotable texts for England in the anthology collected by Janet Murray, *Strong Minded Women and other Lost Voices from 19th Century England* (1982), esp. in Part II, "Woman's Sphere." For the United States, Carl N. Degler, *At Odds: Women and the Family in America from the Revolution to the Present* (1980), is required reading. Priscilla Robertson, *An Experience of Women: Patterns and Change in Nineteenth-Century Europe* (1982), offers valuable comparative observations. Four monographs dealing with earlier periods have assisted me to see nineteenth-century patterns of money in courtship and marriage in perspective: Steven Ozment, *When Fathers Ruled: Family Life in Reformation Europe* (1983), Hilda L. Smith, *Reason's Disciples: Seventeenth-Century English Feminists* (1982), Katharine M. Rogers, *Feminism in Eighteenth-Century England* (1982), and, though not on the bourgeoisie still illuminating, Robert Forster, *The Nobility of Toulouse in the Eighteenth Century: A Social and Economic Study* (1960).

Needless to say, the whole panoply of studies on the modern family (see my bibliographical essay, *Education of the Senses*, 501–5) is relevant to these pages. I list again only the compendious and reliable survey equipped with full bibliographies, Michael Mitterauer and Reinhard Sieder, *The European Family: Patriarchy to Partnership from the Middle Ages to the Present* (1977; tr. and rev. 1982). Michael Anderson's crisp survey, *Approaches to the History of the Western Family 1500–1914* (1980), is suggestive though necessarily very brief on "spouse selection" and "the functions of marriage."

Among the energetic contemporary polemics on the nature of marriage, and the relations of men to women in general, the most trenchant entry is doubtless the radical American feminist Charlotte Perkins Gilman's *Women and Economics: The Economic Factor between Men and Women as a Factor in Social Evolution* (1898; with introduction and notes by Carl N. Degler, 1966).

While Beatrice Webb drew generously on her vast diary in her first auto-biography, *My Apprenticeship*, first published in 1926 and reissued in 1971, the publication of that brilliant self-examination, edited by Norman and Jeanne MacKenzie, however incomplete, remains an event: 4 vols. (1982–85). The first, *The Diary of Beatrice Webb, 1873–1892, Glitter Around and Darkness Within* was decisive for me, though I also consulted the full transcription available in microfiche. The same editors have brought out *The Letters of Sidney and Beatrice Webb*, only marginally less revealing than her journals. Jeanne MacKenzie, *A Victorian Courtship: The Story of Beatrice Potter and Sidney Webb* (1979), is brisk and perceptive; it largely, but not wholly, supersedes Margaret Cole's admiring biography, *Beatrice Webb* (1946). The outpouring of monographs and studies on her later political opinions and in-fluence is not directly relevant to my theme.

The subliterature on the loves of great men and women that I briefly consider in the text was extremely bulky. Here are three further instances: Clara E. Laughlin, *Stories of Authors' Loves*, 2 vols. (1902), generously illustrated with photographs of its subjects, and proffering such chapters as "The Peace that Came to Tennyson," or "The Long, Long Faithfulness of Honoré de Balzac"; Myrtle Reed, *Love Affairs of Literary Men* (1907), with embossed cover, colored running heads, and long excerpts from the love letters of Swift and others; Ralph Nevill, *The Romantic Past* (1912), philosophizes on woman, "Nature's most charming blunder," and concentrates on the loves of artists and statesmen. For John Stuart Mill, F. A. von Hayek, ed., *John Stuart Mill and Harriet Taylor: Their Correspondence and Subsequent Marriage* (1951) is authoritative; Michael St. John Packe, *The Life of John Stuart Mill* (1954), relatively superficial. See also Bruce Mazlish, *James and John Stuart Mill: Father and Son in the Nineteenth Century* (1975), esp. chs. 12 and 13; Mazlish's interpretation of Mill's dream (pp. 302–3) is similar to, though not identical with, mine.

I must not neglect the sensitive (if ultimately not wholly satisfactory) chapter on love (XIII) in Walter E. Houghton, *The Victorian Frame of Mind, 1830–1870* (1957), which had already served me well in *Education of the Senses*.

The whole issue of engagements and courtship is, for the historian, more or less (so to speak) virgin territory. Ellen K. Rothman, *Hands and Hearts: A History of Courtship in America* (1984), resting on exhaustive archival re-search, should be a model to others.

THREE: The Work of Fiction

In light of the vast amplitude of nineteenth-century fiction, the historian of nineteenth-century bourgeois love must choose among his literary informants. It has long been an article of faith among sociologists of literature that second-rate, even third-rate, fictions provide superior access to their time than do its masterpieces. The point is not without merit. Popular novels, written for rapid, quite shallow consumption, are closer to naked wishes than the searching, discriminating, imaginative exploration that the serious writer tends to under-

434   BIBLIOGRAPHICAL ESSA

take. They are easy to read—by their later students little less than by thei intended public. Moreover, a mediocre fiction exhibits defenses no less brutall than wishes. Yet (as I have noted in the text) the first-rate fictions can b immensely rewarding (even to the historian) since they dig deep, see a grea deal, and do not evade complexities. Hence my concentration on masterpiece:

The literature on literature is even more exhaustive than that dealing wit my other themes; I have therefore been more ruthlessly selective here than i the other chapters. No critics, after all, dealing with the nineteenth-centur novel can avoid talking about love. The most instructive title, from which have learned much, is A. O. J. Cockshut, *Man and Woman: A Study of Lov and the Novel, 1740–1940* (1978). Russell M. Goldfarb, *Sexual Repression an Victorian Literature* (1970), is credulous but covers a wide field. Wendell Stac Johnson, *Sex and Marriage in Victorian Poetry* (1975), is far more sophis ticated. There are penetrating comments on love in important nineteenth century novels in Michael Black, *The Literature of Fidelity* (1975). John Bay ley, *The Characters of Love: A Study in the Literature of Personality* (1960, while (except for Henry James's *Golden Bowl*) mainly on earlier literatur« has a suggestive introduction. I found René Girard, *Deceit, Desire, and th Novel: Self and Other in Literary Structure* (1961; tr. Yvonne Freccero, 1965, less rewarding except for some stimulating comments on the triangle.

The psychoanalytic literature on writing is growing steadily. Freud himse. ventured into this area of applied psychoanalysis, with uneven results, an« scattered remarks on fiction through his voluminous writings. His discover that fantasies hold a commanding place in the life of the mind (and that, rightl read, one has much to learn from fiction) constitutes a very valuable but sadl neglected instrument for historical inquiry. Freud's decisive texts are: *De Wahn und die Träume in W. Jensens 'Gradiva,'* (1907), *St. A.*, X, 9–8 *Delusions and Dreams in Jensen's 'Gradiva,'* S.E., IX, 3–95, a fascinating psy choanalysis of a novella; "Der Dichter und das Phantasieren" (1908), *St. A.*, X 169–79, "Creative Writers and Day-Dreaming," *S.E.*, IX, 141–53, a brief, preg nant paper on the uses of memory and fantasy; "Eine Kindheitserinnerung au 'Dichtung und Wahrheit' " (1917), *St. A.*, X, 255–661, "A Childhood Recollec tion from 'Dichtung und Wahrheit,' " *S.E.*, XVII, 145–56; and "Dostojewsl und die Vatertötung" (1928), *St. A.*, X, 267–86, "Dostoevsky and Parricide, *S.E.*, XXI, 175–96. The Dostoevsky paper has been subjected to very sever (though not conclusive) scrutiny in Joseph Frank, *Dostoevsky: The Seeds c Revolt, 1821–1849* (1976), Appendix: "Freud's Case-History of Dostoevsky. Jack J. Spector, *The Aesthetics of Freud: A Study in Psychoanalysis and A* (1972), is a lucid introduction to this aspect of Freud's work though mainly o art; see also Peter Brückner, "Sigmund Freud's Privatlektüre," *Psyche*, X' (1961–62), 881–902, and ibid., XVI (1962), 881–95; and two illuminating essay by Sir Ernst Gombrich, "Freud's Aesthetics," *Encounter*, XXVI (Januar 1966), 30–40, and "Psychoanalysis and the History of Art" (1954), cor veniently accessible in *Meditations on a Hobby Horse and Other Essays on th Theory of Art* (1963), 30–44. The survey by Frederick J. Hoffman, *Freudian ism and the Literary Mind* (1945; 2nd ed. 1957), is informative on receptior William Empson's important and imaginative essay, *Seven Types of Ambiguit*

(1931), and the perceptive study by Walter Muschg, *Psychoanalyse und Literaturwissenschaft* (1930), retain much of their authority.

More psychoanalysts than I can possibly record here have followed the Master in applying insights from their discipline to novels, stories, and poems. The pages of *Imago* and the *American Imago* have been strewn with their contributions (as well as with papers by nonanalysts), and the section on "Applied Psychoanalysis" of the annual *Psychoanalytic Study of the Child* often has a paper on psychoanalysis and literature. Among the first and most prolific of the analysts was Otto Rank, with his essays on *The Double* (1914; tr. Harry Tucker, Jr., 1971), *The Don Juan Legend* (1922; tr. David G. Winter, 1975), and others. I found most helpful Rank's vast compendium, *Das Inzest-Motiv in Dichtung und Sage* (1912; 2nd ed., 1926). Ernest Jones's still controversial *Hamlet and Oedipus*, first adumbrated as a paper in 1901 and enlarged into a book in 1949 (it takes off from the famous passage on Hamlet in Freud's *Interpretation of Dreams* [*St. A.*, II, 268–70; *S.E.*, IV, 264–66]) has been criticized as literal-minded and unliterary, but as a modest psychoanalytic explanation of Hamlet's hesitation (and of nothing more) it seems persuasive. Ernst Kris's much quoted collection of essays, *Psychoanalytic Explorations in Art* (1952), has some important chapters on literature and brings psychoanalytic ego psychology into the picture. Kurt R. Eissler, *Goethe: A Psychoanalytic Study 1775–1786*, 2 vols. (1963), is an erudite and encyclopedic exploration of ten decisive years in Goethe's life. Eissler's *Leonardo da Vinci: Psychoanalytic Notes on the Enigma* (1962), though written as a polemical response to Meyer Schapiro's thoughtful article, "Leonardo and Freud: An Art-Historical Study," *Journal of the History of Ideas*, XVII (1956), 147–78, contains some important observations on psychoanalytic views of creativity. Marie Bonaparte, *The Life and Works of Edgar Allan Poe: A Psycho-Analytic Interpretation* (1933; tr. John Rodker, 1949), is fascinating if perhaps a trifle mechanical on the cathartic function of literary creation. The eminent English psychoanalyst Ella Freeman Sharpe, who came to the trade from literature, has some lovely short papers on Shakespeare and the religious poet Francis Thompson in *Collected Papers on Psycho-Analysis*, ed. Marjorie Brierley (1950), 183–265. Phyllis Greenacre has long made the writer her special province; see among her writings, *Swift and Carroll: A Psychoanalytic Study of Two Lives* (1955), "The Childhood of the Artist: Libidinal Phase Development and Giftedness" (1957), "The Family Romance of the Artist" (1958), "Play in Relation to Creative Imagination" (1959), "Woman as Artist" (1960), and "On Nonsense" (1966), all in *Emotional Growth: Psychoanalytic Studies of the Gifted and a Great Variety of Other Individuals*, 2 vols. continuously paginated (1971), II, 479–504, 505–32, 555–74, 575–91, 592–615. Bernard C. Meyer, *Joseph Conrad: A Psychoanalytic Biography* (1967), is among the most telling of the genre. John E. Gedo, *Portraits of the Artist: Creativity and Its Vicissitudes* (1983), has stimulating and original chapters. See also Lili Peller, "Daydreams and Children's Favorite Books: Psychoanalytic Comments," *PSC*, XIV (1959), 414–33; Francis D. Baudry, "Adolescent Love and Self-Analysis as Contributors to Flaubert's Creativity," ibid., XXXV (1980), 377–416, a most informative piece; and Iza S. Erlich, " 'The Peasant Marey': A Screen Memory," ibid., XXVI (1981),

381–89 on a story by Dostoevsky. I have also profited from Aaron A. Esma
"The Nature of the Artistic Gift," *American Imago*, XXVI (1979), 305–1
and Robert Waelder, *Psychoanalytic Avenues to Art* (1965), which scatte
immensely stimulating ideas. (There is a convenient anthology of long pape
in *Imago* from 1912 to 1937, including work by Rank, Hanns Sachs, Theod
Reik, and others, edited by Jens Malte Fischer, *Psychoanalytische Literatu
interpretation* [1980]).

Nonanalysts, too, have freely delved into psychoanalytic criticism. Analys
have mainly concentrated on the writer and his work, and somewhat (thoug
not wholly) neglected his audience. Norman H. Holland has made the ps
choanalysis of reading his specialty in a series of stimulating volumes: *Ps
choanalysis and Shakespeare* (1964), *The Dynamics of Literary Respon
(1968), which I have found particularly valuable, *Poems in Persons: An Intr
duction to the Psychoanalysis of Literature* (1973), and *5 Readers Readin
(1975). Meredith Anne Skura's informed and evocative *The Literary Use
the Psychoanalytic Process* (1981) proposes how to read texts as case historie
fantasies, dreams, and transference manifestations; its radically defended clai
that literary characters are not persons is (at least to me, in the form in whic
she states it) not convincing. Elizabeth Dalton, *Unconscious Structure
'The Idiot': A Study in Literature and Psychoanalysis* (1979) has precisel
tried to understand the protagonists of Dostoevsky's great novel by treatir
them as real, with brilliant results. The older anthology edited by Willia
Phillips, *Art and Psychoanalysis* (1957), remains handy but must be suppl
mented with more recent work, such as Arthur Mitzman, "The Unstrun
Orpheus: Flaubert's Youth and the Psycho-Social Origins of Art for Art
Sake," *The Psychohistory Review*, VI (1977), 27–42. See also the surveys b
Claudia C. Morrison, *Freud and the Critic: The Early Use of Depth Psycholog
in Literary Criticism* (1968), and Morton Kaplan and Robert Kloss, *The U
spoken Motive: A Guide to Psychoanalytic Literary Criticism* (1973). Simo
O. Lesser, *Fiction and the Unconscious* (1957), was something of a pione
and very much remains worth studying. His more recent essays have bee
edited under the title *The Whispered Meanings* by Robert Sprinch and Richa
W. Noland (1977). See also Frederick Crews, ed., *Psychoanalysis and Literar
Process* (1970). (It is only fair to note that Crews has since recanted and view
psychoanalysis with horror, but his earlier psychoanalytic criticism retai
some interest, notably *The Sins of the Fathers: Hawthorne's Psychologic
Themes* [1966].) There are some interesting treatments of dreams, es
Laurence M. Porter, *The Literary Dream in French Romanticism: A Psych
analytic Interpretation* (1979), and Alain Besançon, "Fonction du rêve dans
roman russe," in *Histoire et expérience du moi* (1971), 107–31. Leon Edel h
long ruminated over psychoanalysis and literature; see *The Modern Psycholog
cal Novel* (1955; 2nd ed. 1961). More recently, he has applied his ideas (n
always successfully) to individual modern novelists including James Joy
(whom he detests), and Willa Cather (whom he respects) in *Stuff of Slee
and Dreams: Experiments in Literary Psychology* (1982). Keith M. May, *O
of the Maelstrom: Psychology and the Novel in the Twentieth Century* (1977
is rather slapdash. Marthe Robert, *Origins of the Novel* (1972; tr. Sach

Rabinovitch, 1980) imaginatively links the rise of the novel to psychoanalysis and develops the Freudian category of the "family romance" at some length. Not all reading of reading has, of course, been psychoanalytic. Jane P. Tompkins's intelligently comprehensive anthology, *Reader-Response Criticism: From Formalism to Post-Structuralism* (1980), which includes pieces by Georges Poulet, Stanley Fish, and others, is helpful. Wolfgang Iser, *The Act of Reading: A Theory of Aesthetic Response* (1976), is difficult but rewarding.

On the troubling question of multiple reading publics in the bourgeois century, I have relied mainly on R. K. Webb, *The British Working Class Reader 1790–1848* (1955), which goes beyond its announced theme, and his brilliant essay, "The Victorian Reading Public," in Boris Ford, ed., *The Pelican Guide to English Literature*, vol. VI, *From Dickens to Hardy* (1958; rev. ed. 1982), 198–219. For France, there is James Smith Allen, *Popular French Romanticism: Authors, Readers and Books in the 19th Century* (1981), which does not neglect the marketplace. Klaus Heitmann, *Der Immoralismus-Prozess gegen die französische Literatur im 19. Jahrhundert* (1970) is a copiously documented study. Herbert Ross Brown, *The Sentimental Novel in America, 1789–1860* (1940), which has a chapter on "sex and sensibility," should be supplemented with Henry Nash Smith, *Democracy and the Novel: Popular Resistance to Classic American Writers* (1978), short and highly stimulating. Q. D. Leavis, *Fiction and the Reading Public* (1932), an exercise in outrage and nostalgia, is useful mainly as a symptom. For Germany, there are Ernest K. Bramsted, *Aristocracy and the Middle-Classes in Germany: Social Types in German Literature 1830–1900* (1937; 2nd ed., 1964), an influential sociological analysis; and Rudolf Schenda, *Volk ohne Buch: Studien zur Sozialgeschichte der populären Lesestoffe 1770–1910* (1970), which, though learned and wide-ranging, is too angry to be wholly dependable. Ronald Hingley, *Russian Writers and Society, 1825–1904* (1967), is illuminating.

I am much in debt to René Wellek's magisterial *A History of Modern Criticism, 1750–1950*, 4 vols. so far (1955–   ), esp. vols. III, *The Age of Transition*, and IV, *The Later Nineteenth Century* (both 1965), grounded in encyclopedic reading in all relevant languages and superb commonsensical judgment. George Watson, *The Literary Critics: A Study of English Descriptive Criticism* (1962: 2nd ed. 1973), is both brisk and enjoyable. M. H. Abrams, *The Mirror and the Lamp: Romantic Theory and the Critical Tradition* (1953), is deservedly a classic; to be read with his no less impressive *Natural Supernaturalism: Tradition and Revolution in Romantic Literature* (1971), which concentrates on secularization in England and Germany. C. M. Bowra, *The Romantic Imagination* (1950), is a stimulating set of lectures on the English romantics. Marilyn Butler, *Romantics, Rebels, and Reactionaries: English Literature 1760–1830* (1981), is a feisty study of the English arts "in an age of revolution." Barbara Fass, *La Belle Dame sans Merci and the Aesthetics of Romanticism* (1974), deals with a theme particularly relevant to my enterprise, the fatal woman, in several countries. John B. Halstead, ed., *Romanticism* (1969), is a wide-ranging anthology of short excerpts. There is much of interest in Donald D. Stone, *The Romantic Impulse in Victorian Fiction*, (1980) as in Anne Mellor, *English Romantic Irony* cited before.

For realism, see above all the masterly study by Erich Auerbach, *Mimesis: The Representation of Reality in Western Literature* (1946; tr. Willard R. Trask, 1953), deservedly influential for its penetrating treatment of the serious attitude in literature toward "ordinary" things. George J. Becker, ed., *Documents of Modern Literary Realism* (1963), is an intelligent and bulky collection of the main polemical texts with an excellent long introductory essay. Linda Nochlin deftly considers the movement in both literature and art in her attractive *Realism* (1971), perhaps a little too wedded to the proposition that the bourgeoisie triumphed in the nineteenth century. For French realist novelists, see Harry Levin, *The Gates of Horn: A Study of Five French Realists* (1963), on Stendhal, Balzac, Flaubert, Zola, and Proust. Damian Grant's little guide, *Realism* (1970), is surprisingly rich for its terseness. See its equally helpful sequel, Lilian R. Furst and Peter N. Skrine, *Naturalism* (1971). D. A. Williams, ed., *The Monster in the Mirror: Studies in Nineteenth-Century Realism* (1978), has some excellent essays by various hands on novels other than the English and French standbys, such as Strindberg's *The Red Room* and Galdós's *Fortunata y Jacinta*. And see the brisk essays in F. W. J. Hemmings, ed., *The Age of Realism* (1974), both general and particular, on Russia, France, Germany, Spain, Portugal, and Italy.

But Peter Brooks, *The Melodramatic Imagination: Balzac, Henry James, Melodrama, and the Mode of Excess* (1976), aptly shows the porousness of such categories. And Vladimir Nabokov, *Lectures on Literature* (1980), includes revisionist chapters on seven major nineteenth- and early twentieth-century writers from Jane Austen to James Joyce, in turn provocative, delightful, and irritating.

Among recent other treatments of English literature I have found useful, there are Geoffrey Tillotson, *A View of Victorian Literature* (1978), a posthumous collection of essays on individual novelists, eccentric with some remarkable insights; Kathleen Tillotson, *Novels of the Eighteen-Forties* (1954; 2nd impression 1956), which has become a minor classic I have depended on. Ian Watt, ed., *The Victorian Novel: Modern Essays in Criticism* (1971), gathers up some interesting shorter papers by leading literary historians. See also U. C. Knoepflmacher, *Laughter and Despair: Readings in Ten Novels of the Victorian Era* (1971). David Cecil, *Early Victorian Novelists: Essays in Revaluation* (1934), is pleasing but shallow. I found T. B. Tomlinson, *The English Middle-Class Novel* (1976) stimulating but a little slight. In contrast, Martin Price, *Forms of Life: Character and Moral Imagination in the Novel* (1983), is a serious exploration, particularly rewarding on the leading figures. And see Jefferson Hunter's lively survey, *Edwardian Fiction* (1982), to be read in conjunction with Samuel Hynes's magisterial *The Edwardian Turn of Mind* (1968). John Lucas, *The Literature of Change: Studies in the Nineteenth-Century Provincial Novel* (1977; 2nd ed., 1980), concentrates on Gaskell and Hardy, interesting but somewhat compromised by a rigid sociological stance. There are perceptive (if somewhat specialized) insights in J. Hillis Miller, *Fiction and Repetition: Seven English Novels* (1982). I enjoyed Roger B. Hankle, *Comedy and Culture: England 1820–1900* (1980), which places the comic English vision within a middle-class context, as well as Karen Chase, *Eros and Psyche: The Representation of Personality in Charlotte Brontë,*

Charles Dickens, and George Eliot (1984). David Grylls, *Guardians and Angels: Parents and Children in Nineteenth-Century Literature* (1978), has much interesting material on England. Winifred Hughes, *The Maniac in the Cellar: Sensation Novelists of the 1860s* (1980), concentrates enjoyably on M. E. Braddon and other best-sellers of her type. Recent years have seen an explosion of books on women writers and women characters, many of them marked by rage, but some of them highly illuminating. Mary Poovey, *The Proper Lady and the Woman Writer: Ideology as Style in the Works of Mary Wollstonecraft, Mary Shelley and Jane Austen* (1984), is a brilliant study of inner conflicts between domesticity and self-realization in pre-Victorian times; Merryn Williams, *Women in the English Novel: 1800–1900* (1984), is a neat, sensible survey of women from Austen to Hardy, both in English fiction and in English life. Patricia Beer, *Reader, I Married Him* (1974), agreeably discusses the women in the novels of Jane Austen, Charlotte Brontë, Elizabeth Gaskell, and George Eliot. Elaine Showalter, *A Literature of Their Own: British Women Novelists from Brontë to Lessing* (1977), is more polemical. So are Françoise Basch, *Relative Creatures: Victorian Women in Society and the Novel* (1972; tr. Anthony Rudolf, 1974), and Sandra M. Gilbert and Susan Gubar, *The Madwoman in the Attic: The Woman Writer and the Nineteenth-Century Literary Imagination* (1979), which moves, exhaustively, "toward a feminist poetic." Mirabel Cecil, *Heroines in Love, 1750–1974* (1974), offers interesting extracts from women's periodicals with full introductions.

The standard modern life of Dickens is Edgar Johnson, *Charles Dickens: His Tragedy and Triumph*, 2 vols. (1953; 2nd abridged ed., 1977), very full but compromised by a naive perception of Dickens the realistic and increasingly radical social critic; the best antidote is the splendid economical essay by Humphry House, *The Dickens World* (1941; 2nd ed., 1942), a classic treatment of his constructive imagination. John Butt and Kathleen Tillotson, *Dickens at Work* (1957), is a painstaking and important study of his habits. Philip Collins has done authoritative books on *Dickens and Crime* (1962; 2nd. ed., 1965), and *Dickens and Education* (1963). George H. Ford, *Dickens and His Readers: Aspects of Novel Criticism since 1836* (1955), illuminates the tides of taste and the shifting views; so does *Dickens: The Critical Heritage*, ed. Philip Collins (1971). See also the suggestive essays by J. Hillis Miller, *Charles Dickens: The World of His Novels* (1958), and A. O. J. Cockshut, *The Imagination of Charles Dickens* (1961).

Dickens (especially his "favourite child") seems to have invited psychoanalytic interpretations; I mention only Leonard Manheim, "The Personal History of David Copperfield," *American Imago*, IX (1952), 21–43, E. Pearlman, "David Copperfield Dreams of Drowning," ibid., XXVIII (1971), 391–403; and Gordon D. Hirsch, "A Psychoanalytic Rereading of *David Copperfield*," *The Victorian Newsletter*, No. 58 (Fall 1980), 1–5, accessible also in *Charles Dickens, New Perspectives*, ed. Wendell Stacy Johnson (1982), 83–93.

Gordon N. Ray's two-volume biography, *Thackeray: The Uses of Adversity, 1811–1836* (1955), and *Thackeray: The Age of Wisdom, 1847–1863* (1958) is authoritative; so is Ray's *The Buried Life: A Study of the Relation between Thackeray's Fiction and his Personal History* (1952), a beautifully informed exploration of the psychological background of *Vanity Fair, Henry*

Esmond, and the other novels which avoids reductionism. I am indebted to Ray's edition of Thackeray's *Letters and Private Papers*, 4 vols. (1945–46). John E Tilford, Jr., has dealt with the oedipal side of Esmond (as has J. Hillis Miller *Fiction and Repetition* [above, 438]): "The Love Theme of Henry Esmond," *PMLA*, LXVII (1952), 684–701, and " 'Unsavoury Plot' of *Henry Esmond*,' *Nineteenth Century Fiction*, VI (1951), 121–30. I have found John Carey's disturbing and controversial essay, *Thackeray: Prodigal Genius* (1977), which charts a marked decline in Thackeray's satirical energies from novel to novel only too persuasive.

Trollope, once somewhat neglected by the critics, is being better served year by year. Michael Sadleir, *Trollope, A Commentary* (1927; 3rd ed., 1945), and A. O. J. Cockshut, *Anthony Trollope: A Critical Study* (1955), are very helpful. Shirley Robin Letwin, *The Gentleman in Trollope: Individuality and Moral Conduct* (1982), has an excellent chapter (IX) on love that casts its net more widely than Trollope. It may be read with Robin Gilmour's sensible *The Idea of the Gentleman in the Victorian Novel* (1984). Donald Smalley, ed. *Anthony Trollope, The Critical Heritage* (1969) is very much worthwhile. Trollope's *Autobiography* (1883, and often reprinted) is essential, for it *is* the man, no style and all. N. John Hall's definitive edition of *The Letters of Anthony Trollope*, 2 vols. (1983), which supersedes earlier editions, confirms the evidence of the *Autobiography*; it shows, as Stephen Wall observed in the *TLS* (February 3, 1984), perhaps a bit harshly, "the artist as philistine."

Gordon S. Haight, *George Eliot: A Biography* (1968), is simply standard. Haight's edition of essays, *A Century of George Eliot Criticism* (1965), collects excellent papers. Barbara Hardy, *Particularities: Readings in George Eliot* (1982), has several perceptive pieces on themes relevant to my intentions. See also Hardy's impressive *The Novels of George Eliot: A Study in Form* (1959). Richard Ellmann, "Dorothea's Husbands," in *Golden Codgers: Biographical Speculations* (1973), 17–38, is stimulating, as expected. Juliet McMaster, "George Eliot's Language of the Sense" in Gordon S. Haight and Rosemary T. Van Arsdel, eds., *George Eliot: A Centenary Tribute* (1982), 11–27, analyzes Eliot's way with sex in her novels.

Hardy has been fortunate. There are two impressive recent biographies, by Robert Gittings, *Young Thomas Hardy* (1975) and *Thomas Hardy's Later Years* (1978); and by Michael Millgate, *Thomas Hardy: A Biography* (1982). On the sexuality of his female characters, see Penny Boumelha, *Thomas Hardy and Women: Sexual Ideology and Narrative Form* (1982), and Norman Page, ed., *Thomas Hardy: The Writer and His Background* (1980); it has, among other illuminating essays, a contribution by James Gibson, "Hardy and His Readers," which deals with the censorship Hardy had to endure (also, of course, a running theme in the biographies). I have profited from the psychoanalytic paper by Carol and Duane Edwards, "Jude the Obscure: A Psychoanalytic Study," *University of Hartford Studies in Literature*, XIII (1981), 78–90.

For other English novelists I have mentioned, see Kenneth Robinson, *Wilkie Collins: A Biography* (1951; 2nd ed., 1974), and Nuel Pharr Davis, *The Life of Wilkie Collins* (1956); Walter F. Wright, *Art and Substance in George Meredith* (1953); V. S. Pritchett, *George Meredith and English Comedy* (1969), a delightful set of lectures, and Sir Osbert Sitwell, *The Novels of Meredith and Some Notes on the English Novel* (1948). I found two interesting articles on Charlotte Brontë, both by Robert B. Heilman, particularly stimulating: "Charlotte Brontë's New Gothic," *From Jane Austen to Joseph Conrad*, ed. Robert C. Rathburn and Martin Steinmann, Jr. (1958), 118–32, and "Charlotte Brontë, Reason, and the Moon," *Nineteenth-Century Fiction* (1960), 283–302, in addition to the standard modern life by Winifred Gérin, *Charlotte Brontë* (1967). John Maynard, *Charlotte Brontë and Sexuality* (1984), an interesting exploration of subterranean erotic themes in her work, came too late to be considered in detail, but in no way contradicts my general view of Victorian fiction. For Elizabeth Gaskell, that most gratifying of writers, see W. A. Craik, *Elizabeth Gaskell and the English Provincial Novel* (1975), M. Granz, *Elizabeth Gaskell: the Artist in Conflict* (1968), and the edition of her delightful *Letters* by J. A. V. Chapple and Arthur Pollard (1966). Two recent studies are relevant to erotic themes in nineteenth-century English literature: Richard Barickman, Susan MacDonald, and Myra Stark, *Corrupt Relations: Dickens, Thackeray, Trollope, Collins, and the Victorian Sexual System* (1982), an interesting analysis of prevailing views about the nature of Victorian society and rather original readings of these novelists' treatment of women; and Dianne F. Sadoff, *Monsters of Affection: Dickens, Eliot and Brontë on Fatherhood* (1982), which analyzes these novelists from a psychoanalytic perspective.

Of the many histories of French literature, I have relied mainly on several volumes in the multi-volume collection *Littérature française*, ed. Claude Pichois, esp. Max Milner, *Le Romantisme*, vol. I (*1820–1843*) (1968), and Raymond Pouilliart, *Le Romantisme*, vol. III (*1869–1896*) (1968). The terse essays collected in John Cruickshank, *French Literature and its Background*, vol. IV, *The Early Nineteenth Century* (1969), and vol. V, *The Late Nineteenth Century* (1969), are highly informative. Martin Turnell, *The Novel in France* (1950), paints the background but concentrates on Constant, Stendhal, Balzac, and Flaubert. Victor Brombert, *The Romantic Prison: The French Tradition* (1978), pursues a startling theme through modern French fiction. Paul Bénichou, *Le sacre de l'écrivain, 1750–1830* (1973), an important book, discloses its point in its subtitle, "Essay on the advent of a laic spiritual power in modern France." F. W. J. Hemmings, *Culture and Society in France 1848–1898: Dissidents and Philistines* (1971) is a splendid introduction to the cultural history of literature. Henry James's reviews and essays on French writers, collected in *French Poets and Novelists* (1878; 2nd ed. 1884), is more than a document for their time; James's formulations are felicitous and extraordinarily just.

For Stendhal, see above, 429. The literature on Balzac I have listed (see above 429) should be supplemented with H. J. Hunt, *Honoré de Balzac: A Biography* (1957), and Hunt, *Balzac's 'Comédie Humaine'* (1959; 2nd. ed., 1964). See also F. W. J. Hemmings, *Balzac: an Interpretation of 'La Comédie humaine'* (1967), and Bernard Guyon, *La pensée politique et sociale de Balzac* (1947; 2nd. ed., 1967). V. S. Pritchett, *Balzac* (1973), is vigorous. And see the revealing article by Walter M. Kendrick, "Balzac and British Realism: Mid-Victorian Theories of the Novel," *Victorian Studies*, XX (Autumn 1976), 5–24. Philip Spencer, *Flaubert: A Biography* (1952), is fluent and informative and Benjamin F. Bart, *Flaubert* (1967), is very comprehensive. Victor Brombert's elegant *The Novels*

442   BIBLIOGRAPHICAL ESSAY

of Flaubert: A Study of Themes and Techniques (1966) has brilliant insights. For the early Flaubert, Jean Bruneau's fine *Les Débuts littéraires de Gustave Flaubert, 1831–1845* (1962) is indispensable. Bruneau's incomparable edition of Flaubert's letters, that treasure house of style and rage, *Correspondance*, 2 vols. so far (1973–   ) has reached the year 1858. Francis Steegmuller, *Flaubert and Madame Bovary: A Double Portrait* (1939; 2nd. ed., 1947) is informal and enjoyable. Benjamin Bart offers, in *Madame Bovary and the Critics* (1966) a helpful anthology; Maurice Nadeau, *Gustave Flaubert, écrivain. Essai* (1969; 2nd ed., 1980), is penetrating. Pierre Coguy, *L'Education sentimentale de Flaubert: Le monde en creux* (1975), has addressed the oedipal issue (pp. 177–87).

Eugène Fromentin, the novelist of memory, has been amply studied. Pierre Blanchon (Jacques-André Mérys), *Eugène Fromentin. Lettres de jeunesse. Biographie et notes* (1912), and *Eugène Fromentin, Correspondance et Fragments inédits. Biographie et notes* (1912), supply the documentation. Marie-Anne Eckstein, *Le rôle du souvenir dans l'oeuvre d'Eugène Fromentin* (1970), concentrates on his overriding passion; Camille Reynaud, *Le Genèse de 'Dominique'* (1937), is a detailed examination of how Fromentin came to write his most famous book. And see, in English, Arthur R. Evans, Jr., *The Literary Art of Eugène Fromentin: A Study in Style and Motif* (1964). Fromentin's travel report, *The Masters of Past Time: Dutch and Flemish Painting From Van Eyck to Rembrandt* (1876; tr. Andrew Boyle, 1913), can still be read with interest.

George Sand's English following has justly called for comment. Paul G. Blount, *George Sand and the Victorian World* (1979), neatly complements Patricia Thomson, *George Sand and the Victorians: Her Influence and Reputation in Nineteenth-Century England* (1977).

For Gautier, see Réne Jasinski's exhaustive *Les Années romantiques de Th. Gautier* (1929), P. E. Tennant's very short, biographically oriented *Théophile Gautier* (1975), and Joanna Richardson, *Théophile Gautier, his Life and Times* (1958). For his notorious novel, there is Bertrand de Gelannes, *La Maupin, l'étrange aventurière* (1955). Maupassant has been soundly treated by Francis Steegmuller, *Maupassant: A Lion in the Path* (1949), René Dumesnil, *Guy de Maupassant* (1933; 2nd ed., 1947), and the informal study by Paul Ignotus, *The Paradox of Maupassant* (1966). For Paul Léautaud, minor novelist and excessively frank diarist, see Marie Dormoy, *La vie secrète de Paul Léautaud* (1972), and James Harding, *Lost Illusions: Paul Léautaud and his World* (1974), rather overwrought.

German fiction has been thoroughly canvassed. Eric A. Blackall, *The Novels of the German Romantics* (1983) is authoritative. Claude David, *Geschichte der deutschen Literatur; Zwischen Romantik und Symbolismus 1820–85* (1966), is a masterly survey by a leading French Germanist. And see J. P. Stern, *Reinterpretations* (1964), a collection of penetrating essays, as are Friedrich Sengle's *Arbeiten zur deutschen Literatur 1750–1850* (1965), and Walter Höllerer's *Zwischen Klassik und Moderne. Lachen und Weinen in der Dichtung einer Übergangszeit* (1958), which deals principally with the 1830s and 1840s. E. K. Bennett, *A History of the German 'Novelle'* (1934; rev. and ed. H. M. Waidson, 1961), has long been a standard work. Michael Beddoes, *The Fiction of Humanity: Studies in the Bildungsroman from Wieland to Thomas Mann* (1983), ably surveys this genre; it should be read in conjunction with

W. H. Bruford's informative essay *The German Tradition of Self-Cultivation. 'Bildung' from Humboldt to Thomas Mann* (1975). And see Clifford Albrecht Bernd's short *German Poetic Realism* (1981).

The standard biography of Fontane is Hans-Heinrich Reuter, *Theodor Fontane*, 2 vols. (1968), well informed and immensely detailed, but compromised by his somewhat flat-footed Marxism. Charlotte Jolles, *Theodor Fontane* (1972), is a useful concise survey of the literature both by and on him. Peter Demetz, *Formen des Realismus: Theodor Fontane. Kritische Untersuchungen* (1964; 2nd ed., 1966), is a brilliant essay that places Fontane in the international literary context where he belongs. Helmuth Nürnberger, *Theodor Fontane in Selbstzeugnissen und Bilddokumenten* (1968), is brief and informative. And see Alan Bance, *Theodor Fontane: The Major Novels* (1982). Among the essays on various nineteenth-century novels that make up his *Romane des 19. Jahrhunderts. Wirklichkeit und Kunstcharakter* (1963), Walther Killy has an illuminating chapter (IX) on Fontane's *Irrungen, Wirrungen*. See also Erich Heller, "Fontane and the Novelist's Art," *TLS* (October 20, 1978), 1222–24.

Adolf Muschg, *Gottfried Keller* (1977), is an argumentative, sometimes profound essay with a long documentary section.

For the Spanish novel in general, there are D. L. Shaw's *The Nineteenth Century* (1972), in the general *Literary History of Spain*, ed. R. O. Jones, and S. H. Eoff, *The Modern Spanish Novel* (1962). For Valera, see, above all, Jean Krynen, *L'Esthétisme de Juan Valera* (1946), and Alberto Jiménez, *Juan Valera y la Generación de 1868* (1955). Galdós has been treated frequently and well. Among modern studies, see Stephen Gilman, *Galdós and the Art of the European Novel, 1867–1887* (1982), Diane F. Urey's specialized but suggestive *Galdós and the Irony of Language* (1982), and Peter A. Bly, *Galdós's Novel of the Historical Imagination* (1983). Joseph Schraibman, *Dreams in the Novels of Galdos* (1960) usefully surveys the literary function of dreams in general. Eça de Queirós has been principally appreciated by Portuguese and French critics; Alexander Coleman, *Eça de Queiros and European Realism* (1980), is the first comprehensive treatment in English. And see Jean Girodon, "Eça et Madame Bovary," *Biblios* (1949), 210–27. There is also Alvaro Lins, *História literária de Eça de Queirós* (1939; 3rd ed., 1960), and the distinguished Portuguese work by J. G. Simões, *Eça de Queirós* (1961). For Queirós's Brazilian counterpart, there is Helen Caldwell, *Machado de Assis: The Brazilian Master and His Novels* (1970). Machado de Assis, *The Devil's Church and Other Stories*, tr. Jack Schmitt and Lorie Ishimatsu (1977), is a good collection of Machado's vignettes and short short stories, to complement the major novels now available in English.

For Lodewijk van Deyssel, I have drawn on Jacob de Graff, *Le réveil littéraire en Hollande et le Naturalisme Français, 1880–1900* (1937).

I have had fairly little to say on the Scandinavians. I have used Harald Beyer, *A History of Norwegian Literature* (1952; tr. Einar Haugen, 1956). Brian W. Downs, *Modern Norwegian Literature 1860–1918* (1966) is vigorous and opinionated; and see Brita M. E. Mortensen and Brian W. Downs, *Strindberg: An Introduction to His Life and Work* (1965). Hans Henrik Jaeger's pathetic last novel was translated into German by Niels Hoyer, pseud., under the title *Kranke Liebe*, 3 vols. 1920.

Henry Gifford's set of essays, *The Novel in Russia* (1964), is balanced. So is
Richard Freeborn, *The Rise of the Russian Novel: Studies in the Russian
Novel from 'Eugene Onegin' to 'War and Peace'* (1973). A recent crop of
books on Tolstoy valiantly swells the flood of writings on the master: Boris
Eikhenbaum, *Tolstoi in the Sixties* (tr. Duffield White, 1982) and *Tolstoi in
the Seventies* (tr. Albert Kaspin, 1982), are absolutely authoritative; for a critical
appreciation see Simon Karlinsky, "Monstrous Masterpieces," *TLS* (February
18, 1983), 161. Henry Gifford, *Tolstoy* (1982) is a dependable, very brief
introduction. See also John Bayley, *Tolstoy and the Novel* (1966), and Isaiah
Berlin's little classic, *The Hedgehog and the Fox* (1953), which superbly
analyzes Tolstoy's view of history.

For Dostoevsky, see Donald Fanger, *Dostoevsky and Romantic Realism: A
Study of Dostoevsky in Relation to Balzac, Dickens, and Gogol* (1967), which
reasonably breaks through old classifications; and the introductory study by
Edward Wasiolek, *Dostoevsky: The Major Fiction* (1964); Robert Louis
Jackson, *The Art of Dostoevsky: Deliriums and Nocturnes* (1982), and his
earlier *Dostoevsky's Quest for Form* (1966) are both admiring but persuasive.
Joseph Frank's biography (two volumes so far, *Dostoevsky: The Seeds of
Revolt, 1821–1849* [1976], and *Dostoevsky: The Years of Ordeal, 1850–1859*
[1983]) is masterly, even though I do not accept his devastating verdict on
Freud. (I should note, in this connection, Vladimir Nabokov's *Lectures on
Russian Literature*, ed. Fredson Bowers [1981], which cover Chekhov, Dostoev-
sky, Gogol, Gorki, Tolstoy, and Turgenev; often hilarious, usually original,
Nabokov is so severely one-sided, as in his detestation of Dostoevsky, that he
sometimes becomes preposterous.)

In sharp contrast, Nabokov's essay, *Nikolai Gogol* (1947), is rational and
stimulating. Donald Fanger, *The Creation of Nicolai Gogol* (1979), is cautious
but generally convincing. See also Victor Erlich's engaging brief study, *Gogol*
(1969). Simon Karlinsky, *The Sexual Labyrinth of Nikolai Gogol* (1976), is
an important exploration of Gogol's painfully concealed homosexuality and its
impact on his writings (more significant for ch. IV). It should be supplemented
with Hugh McLean's subtle essay, "Gogol's Retreat from Love: Toward an
Interpretation of Mirgorod," *American Contributions to the Fourth International Congress of Slavists* (1958), 225–44. As for Turgenev, V. S. Pritchett,
The Gentle Barbarian: The Life and Work of Turgenev (1977), is agreeable;
it should be supplemented with Avrahm Yarmolinsky, *Turgenev: The Man,
His Art and His Age* (1926; 2nd ed., 1959), Richard Freeborn, *Turgenev: The
Novelist's Novelist* (1962), and April Fitzlyon's biography of Turgenev's great
love, *The Price of Genius: The Life of Pauline Viardot* (1964). Isaiah Berlin's
essay, *Fathers and Children*, The Romanes Lecture (1972), is splendid.

As for some special themes: James B. Twitchell, *The Living Dead: A Study
of the Vampire in Romantic Fiction* (1981), is both amusing and informative.
Judith Armstrong, *The Novel of Adultery* (1966), deals tersely with that
favorite of fictional themes; so does Tony Tanner, *Adultery in the Novel:
Contract and Transgression* (1979), an often suggestive, close, but highly willful
reading of Rousseau's *La nouvelle Héloïse*, Goethe's *Die Wahlverwandtschaften*,
and Flaubert's *Madame Bovary*; a second volume is promised. There is illuminating material on the artistic representation of this transgression in T. J. Edelstein,

"Augustus Egg's triptych: a narrative of Victorian adultery," *Burlington Magazine*, CXXV (April 1983), 202–210. On this, as on related issues, Nina Auerbach, *Woman and the Demon: The Life of A Victorian Myth* (1982), esp. chs. IV and V, is provocative. The growing literature on incest is reviewed in Robin Fox, *The Red Lamp of Incest* (1980), which adds a rich bibliography. Rank, *Das Inzest-Motiv*, is very useful here; Marc Lanval, *L'Etiologie de la Répression de l'Inceste* (1945), is a sociological study; Henry Mills, *Forbidden Fruit: A Study of the Incest Theme in Erotic Literature* (1973), is thin. Michel Fougères, *La Liebestod dans le Roman français, anglais et allemand au XVIIIᵉ Siècle* (1974), sets the stage for the nineteenth century. I am again indebted to Mary S. Hartman, *Victorian Murderesses: A True History of Thirteen Respectable French and English Women Accused of Unspeakable Crimes* (1977), a delightful book with penetrating comments on the impact of reading on the impressionable. Maurice Charney's essays on a clutch of novels, none of them nineteenth-century, *Sexual Fiction* (1981), is vigorous and amusing, though his bourgeoisie is not quite mine. Paul Englisch, *Geschichte der erotischen Literatur* (1932), includes pornography, as does my *Education of the Senses*, 358–79. There is much of interest in the psychologist Henry A. Murray's edition of Herman Melville's *Pierre* (1949), which candidly discusses its themes of incest and oedipal struggles. Elizabeth Stevens Prioleau detects erotic themes behind the calm surfaces of Howells's novels in *The Circle of Eros: Sexuality in the Work of William Dean Howells* (1983), showing once again that eroticism is a matter not just of finding what one is looking for, but of finding what has always been there.

FOUR: Problematic Attachments

The best treatment of the paradox of nineteenth-century homosexuality I have seen is in Lillian Faderman, *Surpassing the Love of Men: Romantic Friendship and Love Between Women from the Renaissance to the Present* (1981), extremely comprehensive in its coverage of fiction, diaries and other materials, a little too enthusiastic to be wholly objective, but stimulating. The celebrated case of slander against two affectionate young Scottish teachers, which Faderman touches on in this book, she has explored at length in *Scotch Verdict* (1983) in an extraordinary work of detection. The documents in the case, petitions, judgments—a very handy volume—have been made available: *Miss Marianne Woods and Miss Jane Pirie against Dame Helen Cumming Gordon* (1975). Two biographies shed interesting light on two very different women: Peter Gunn, *Vernon Lee: Violet Paget, 1856–1935* (1964), and Dore Ashton and Denise Browne Hare, *Rosa Bonheur: A Life and A Legend* (1981); both show how unconventional women could survive the Victorian era. But lesbians were not always safe from the law: see Louis Crompton, "The Myth of Lesbian Impunity: Capital Laws from 1270 to 1791," *Journal of Homosexuality*, VI (1980–81), 11–25. Of Carroll Smith-Rosenberg's path-breaking articles, the one most relevant to this chapter (and reaching beyond its announced area) is "The Female World of Love and Ritual: Relations Between Women in Nineteenth-Century America," *Signs: A Journal of Women in Culture and Society*,

I (1975), 1–29, conveniently reprinted in Smith-Rosenberg, *Disorderly Conduct: Visions of Gender in Victorian America* (1985), 53–76, an important gathering of her work.

General histories of homosexuality tend to suffer from sensationalism, special pleading, or shallowness. A typical instance of all three is A. L. Rowse, *Homosexuals in History: A Study of Ambivalence in Society, Literature, and the Arts* (1977), whose subtitle only underscores the author's confusion. Vern L. Bullough, *Sexual Variance in Society and History* (1976), has much material but is not profound. H. Montgomery Hyde, *The Other Love: An Historical and Contemporary Survey of Homosexuality in Britain* (1970), is judicious, comprehensive, and popular. Over against this, John Boswell, *Christianity, Social Tolerance, and Homosexuality: Gay People in Western Europe From the Beginning of the Christian Era to the Fourteenth Century* (1980), is learned and transcends its set limits to enter the thickets of linguistic usage. It should be read in conjunction with K. J. Dover, *Greek Homosexuality* (1978), another model of scholarship. Thomas Africa, "Homosexuals in Greek History," *The Journal of Psychohistory*, IX (Spring 1982), 401–20, helpfully canvasses the recent literature in the light of ancient texts. There is a still useful survey of the pioneering students of the subject in Havelock Ellis, *Studies in the Psychology of Sex*, vol. I, *Sexual Inversion* (1897; 2nd. ed., 1900). See also Ferdinand Karsch-Haack, *Der Putzmacher von Glarus: Heinrich Hössli* (1903) on one of the earliest.

The psychoanalytic discussion of the topic begins, of course, with Freud, who necessarily recurred to it over and over. The *locus classicus* is *Three Essays on Sexuality*; see also, from a large repertoire, his case histories, above all, "Bruchstück einer Hysterie-Analyse" (1905), *St. A.*, VI, 86–186, "Fragment of an Analysis of a Case of Hysteria," *S.E.*, VII, 3–122, the "Dora Case"; "Analyse der Phobie eines fünf-jährigen Knaben" (1909), *St. A.*, VIII, 9–123; "Analysis of a Phobia in a Five-Year-Old Boy," *S.E.*, x, 3–149, "Little Hans"; "Psychoanalytische Bemerkungen über einen autobiographisch beschriebenen Fall von Paranoia (Dementia Paranoides)" (1911), *St. A.*, VII, "Psychoanalytic Notes on an Autobiographical Account of a Case of Paranoia," *S.E.*, XII, 3–82, "the Schreber Case"; "Aus der Geschichte einer infantilen Neurose" (1918), *St. A.*, VIII, 125–232, "From the History of an Infantile Neurosis," *S.E.*, XVII, 3–122, "The Wolf Man"; "Über die Psychogenese eines Falles von weiblicher Homosexualität" (1920), *St. A.*, VII, 255–81, "The Psychogenesis of a Case of Homosexuality in a Woman," *S.E.*, XVIII, 145–72. In addition, see Freud's much maligned paper on Leonardo, "Eine Kindheitserinnerung des Leonardo da Vinci" (1910), *St. A.*, X, 87–150, "Leonardo da Vinci and a Memory of His Childhood," *S.E.*, XI, 59–137. And see Freud, "Über einige neurotische Mechanismen bei Eifersucht, Paranoia und Homosexualität" (1922), *St. A.*, VII, 217–28; "Some Neurotic Mechanisms in Jealousy, Paranoia and Homosexuality," *S.E.*, XVIII, 221–32.

There is a competent tracing of Freud's and Freudian views (on homosexuality in men) into the early 1960s in George H. Wiedeman, "Survey of Psychoanalytic Literature on Overt Male Homosexuality," *J. Amer. Psychoanal. Assn.*, X (1962), 386–409, carried forward by Wiedeman, "Homosexuality, A Survey," ibid., XXII (1974), 651–96. Ronald Bayer, *Homosexuality and*

merican Psychiatry: The Politics of Diagnosis (1981), also has a reasonable
istorical survey (ch. I). The contributions to the psychoanalytic symposium
eprinted in the *Int. J. Psycho-Anal.* under various titles, XLV (1964), by W.
I. Gillespie (203–09), Francis Pasche (210–13), George H. Wiedeman (214–
6), Ralph R. Greenson (217–19), and Robert J. Stoller (220–25) are an inter-
sting conspectus of psychoanalytic thinking on the subject.

Important recent psychoanalytic contributions include the collective study
which explicitly rejects Freud's doctrine of bisexuality) edited by Irving
Bieber, *Homosexuality: A Psychoanalytic Study of Male Homosexuals* (1962);
Charles Socarides, *Beyond Sexual Freedom* (1975), and his earlier statement,
The Overt Homosexual (1968); and the work of Robert J. Stoller, who has
made the distinction between sexual endowment (sex) and imposed identity
gender) his own, esp. in *Sex and Gender*, vol. I, *On the Development of
Masculinity and Femininity* (1968). And see Judd Marmor, ed., *Homosexual
Behavior: A Modern Reappraisal* (1980), collecting useful papers and with a
ensible introduction. Hendrik M. Ruitenbeek, ed., *Homosexuality and Creative
Genius* (1967), though it contains J. C. Lapp's informative essay, "The Watcher
Betrayed and the Fatal Woman: Some Recurring Patterns in Zola," is less
rewarding.

For nonpsychoanalytic studies, see esp. Alan P. Bell and Martin S. Weinberg,
Homosexualities: A Study of Diversity Among Men and Women (1978), a
product of the Kinsey Institute which, as the title makes clear, stresses the
varieties. Alfred C. Kinsey, Wardell B. Pomeroy, and Clyde E. Martin, *Sexual
Behavior in the Human Male* (1948), though methodologically far from persuasive, made revolutionary assertions about the frequency of homosexual
experiences, and attempted a quantitative classification of "the heterosexual-
homosexual balance." It was followed by Kinsey, Pomeroy, Martin, and P. H.
Gebhard, *Sexual Behavior in the Human Female* (1953). In this connection,
Paul Robinson, *The Modernization of Sex: Havelock Ellis, Alfred Kinsey,
William Masters and Virginia Johnson* (1976), a brief, intelligent essay, is
particularly worth reading. Lionel Trilling, "The Kinsey Report" (1948), *The
Liberal Imagination: Essays on Literature and Society* (1950), 223–42, has not
lost its sting. Wainwright Churchill, *Homosexual Behavior Among Males* is,
as the subtitle declares, *A Cross-Cultural and Cross-Species Investigation*
(1967). Important work has also been done by Evelyn Hooker, listed and
conveniently summed up in "Sexual Behavior: Homosexuality," *International
Encyclopedia of the Social Sciences*, ed. David L. Sills, 18 vols. (1968–79), XIV,
222–33, exceptional for its reasonableness. Erwin J. Haeberle has been editing
important documents illuminating the rise of sexology, esp. *Anfänge der
Sexualwissenschaft: Historische Dokumente* (1983); the English version, an
illustrated brochure, *The Birth of Sexology: A Brief History in Documents*
(1983), a catalogue; see also his two articles: "The Jewish Contribution to the
Development of Sexology," *The Journal of Sex Research*, XVIII (November
1982), 305–23, mainly on Magnus Hirschfeld and Max Marcuse, and "Human
Rights and Sexual Rights: The Legacy of René Guyon," *Medicine and Law*,
II (1983), 159–72. And see Joachim S. Hohmann, ed. and comp., *Der unter-
drückte Sexus: Historische Texte und Kommentare zur Homosexualität* (1977),
good early texts and modern pleas.

448

The standard biography of Marcel Proust is George D. Painter, *Proust: T Early Years* (1959), and *Proust: The Later Years* (1965); very detailed, it co scientiously identifies characters. Among a steadily blossoming critical literatu Roger Shattuck, *Proust* (1974), is outstanding for its economy and brillian Proust's revealing letters are being carefully edited by Philip Kolb; the *Co respondance de Marcel Proust* (1970–   ) has now reached volume IX a the year 1909. J. E. Rivers, *Proust and the Art of Love: The Aesthetics Sexuality in the Life, Times and Art of Marcel Proust* (1980), is very thoroug but marred by its strident defensive tone and appalling lack of familiarity wi Freud's ideas, which it ignorantly criticizes. Robert Alter, "Proust and t Ideological Reader," *Salmagundi*, Nos. 58–59 (Fall 1982–Winter 1983), 347–5 contains a telling critique of Rivers. I also found useful Léon Pierre-Quir *Proust et la stratégie littéraire* (1954), and Douglas W. Alden's pedestrian b compendious *Marcel Proust and his French Critics* (1940), according to whic Proust's reputation had rightfully [!] declined by the late 1930s. For Pa Verlaine, celebrated poet and pederast, there is now Pierre Petitfils, *Verlai* (1981).

With Oscar Wilde, about whom much has been written, we must wait fo the forthcoming biography by Richard Ellmann. Meanwhile there is his info mative published lecture, *Oscar Wilde at Oxford* (1984). See also *Oscar Wild The Critical Heritage*, ed. Karl Beckson (1970), a comprehensive compilatio of responses; *The Letters of Oscar Wilde*, ed. Rupert Hart-Davis (1962), model of editing and a feast for those eager to correct certain convention views; for the sad last years, H. Montgomery Hyde, *Oscar Wilde: The Afte math* (1963), and Hesketh Pearson's informal *The Life of Oscar Wilde* (1954 Among the revisionists is Ruper Croft-Cooke, *Feasting with Panthers: A Ne Consideration of Some Late Victorian Writers* (1967), which takes rece scholarship into account but is very hard on Wilde; the book also has livel appraisals of Swinburne and Symonds. On the latter, Phyllis Grosskurth, *Joh Addington Symonds: A Biography* (1964), is outspoken, dependable, indee definitive; I have leaned on it. Grosskurth's edition of Symonds's unpublishe *Memoirs* (1984) is excellent. Some interesting sidelights on the socialist atti tude toward Oscar Wilde in particular (and homosexuality in general) ar thrown by the Revisionist Socialist Eduard Bernstein in "Aus Anlass eine Sensationsprozesses," *Die Neue Zeit*, XIV (1895), 171–76. And see Franço Porché, *L'Amour qui n'ose pas dire son nom (Oscar Wilde)* (1927), a brie not very original survey. On the impress of Dorian Gray, see the early stud by R. H. Sherard, *Oscar Wilde* (1902). Michael Levey, *The Case of Walte Pater* (1978) is perceptive if short; and see the interesting monograph by Joh J. Conlon, *Walter Pater and the French Tradition* (1982). There are revealin glimpses of attitudes toward homosexuality, both secretly accepting and pub licly (with few exceptions) appalled, in the England of the 1860s and on, i Donald Thomas, *Swinburne, The Poet in His World* (1979), especially ch. III and in Fawn M. Brodie, *The Devil Drives: A Life of Sir Richard Burto* (1967), which has excellent pages on censorship. But Burton's own impunity despite his bold exposition of homosexuality in his essays on *A Thousand an One Nights*, or George Moore's novel, *A Drama in Muslin: A Realistic Nove* (1886; new ed. with introduction by A. Norman Jeffares, 1981), show tha the English cultural response to homoeroticism was complex. For Whitman, stronger on the man than on the poetry, there is Justin Kaplan's solid *Walt Whitman: A Life* (1980). For Edward Carpenter, see, in addition to Phyllis Grosskurth, *Havelock Ellis: A Biography* (1980), Sheila Rowbotham, "Edward Carpenter: Prophet of the New Life," in Rowbotham and Jeffrey Weeks, *Socialism and the New Life* (1977), 25–138, which goes to the sources; the appreciation by Mrs. Havelock Ellis, *Three Modern Seers* (1910), of whom Carpenter is one (pp. 193–227), Emile Delavaney's speculative *D. H. Lawrence and Edward Carpenter. A Study in Edwardian Transition* (1971), and Chushichi Tsuzuki, *Edward Carpenter, 1844–1929: Prophet of Human Fellowship* (1980), which is frank, and useful on the cultural environment. For Gogol, see Simon Karlinsky and Hugh McLean, above, 444. Kuzmin has been well, if briefly, treated in Renato Poggioli, *The Poets of Russia, 1890–1930* (1960), 216–23.

Hans Mayer, *Aussenseiter* (1975), collects passionate essays on such "outsiders" as women, Jews, and "Sodomites" with short biographies of a number of well-known homosexuals and some others, like Hans Christian Anderson, where the issue remains a little obscure. An earlier conspectus of "famous homosexuals" is Dr. Albert Moll, *Berühmte Homosexuelle*, in *Grenzfragen des Nerven- und Seelenlebens*, ed. Dr. L. Loewenfeld, No. 75 (1910). For *Tchaikovsky*, the second volume of David Brown's projected three-volume biography, *The Crisis Years, 1874–1878* (1983), is definitive.

On homosexuals, male and female, in literature, see once again, the informative pages of A. O. Cockshut, *Man and Woman* (above, 434). Jeffrey Meyers, *Homosexuality and Literature 1890–1930* (1977), briefly and sensibly looks at Wilde, Gide, Mann, and others. For France, the essays in George Stambolian and Elaine Marks, eds., *Homosexualities and French Literature: Cultural Contexts/Critical Texts* (1979), are of very unequal value. There are two excellent collections for England: *Sexual Heretics: Male Homosexuality in English Literature from 1850 to 1900*, ed. with a fine introduction by Brian Reade (1970) and *Love in Earnest: Notes on the Lives and Writings of English 'Uranian' Poets from 1889 to 1930* (1970), ed. Timothy d'Arch Smith. An anthology from the German periodical, *Jahrbuch für Sexuelle Zwischenstufen, Auswahl aus den Jahrgängen 1899–1923*, ed. Schmidt (1983), collects some important early papers including Eduard Bertz's essay on Whitman (1905), pp. 57–141.

Among pieces of legislation, the German paragraph 175 is most notorious. See James D. Steakley, *The Homosexual Emancipation Movement in Germany* (1975), very brief, to be supplemented with Jürgen Baumann's history and plea, *Paragraph 175* (1968). Rivers's account of the great German homosexual scandals (above, 448), in which Proust was interested, is too apologetic to be useful; far more scholarly and dependable is Isabel V. Hull, *The Entourage of Kaiser Wilhelm II, 1888–1918* (1982). And see John Lauritsen and David Thorstad, *The Early Homosexual Rights Movement (1864–1935)* (1974), short but goes beyond Germany. For England, there is Jeffrey Weeks, *Coming Out: Homosexual Politics in Britain from the Nineteenth Century to the Present* (1977), and the relevant chapters (esp. II and VI) in Weeks, *Sex, Politics and Society: The Regulation of Sexuality Since 1800* (1981). H. E. Wortham, *Oscar Browning* (1927), has been superseded by Ian Anstruther, *Oscar Brown-*

ing: A Biography (1983). Edward C. Mack, *Public Schools and British Opinion
1780 to 1860: The Relationship Between Contemporary Ideas and the Evolution
of an English Institution* (1939), is detailed and informative, but avoids sex
altogether. Far more candid are Jonathan Gathorne-Hardy, *The Old School
Tie: The Phenomenon of the English Public School* (1978; publ. in England
the year before as *The Public School Phenomenon, 597–1977*), and the clear-
headed study by John Chandos, *Boys Together: English Public Schools 1800–
1864* (1984), with a revealing chapter (XIV) and more on suppressed scandal
—material that Phyllis Grosskurth had already explored in her biography of
Symonds. David Newsome, *Godliness and Good Learning: Four Studies on a
Victorian Ideal* (1961), is rich on public schools, very moving, and strangely
innocent.

For Greece as apology for homosexuality in modern England, see esp. Frank
Turner's *Greek Heritage* (above, 429) and Richard Jenkyns, *The Victorians
and Ancient Greece* (1980). On Newman and the others, there is the classic by
Geoffrey Faber, *Oxford Apostles: A Character Study of the Oxford Movement* (1933; 2nd ed., 1936), and David Hilliard, "Unenglish and Unmanly:
Anglo-Catholicism and Homosexuality," *Victorian Studies*, XXV (1982), 181–
210, with reasonable comments on Faber's controversial study. On the fanatic
John Kensit, the pages in Owen Chadwick, *The Victorian Church*, Part II
(1970), 355–57, are penetrating.

For Germany, see the titles cited above, and the literature on the George
Circle, notably the compendious anthology, *Der George-Kreis*, ed. Georg
Peter Landmann (1965), with substantial excerpts from the writings of the
disciples, and the excellent biographical study by the French Germanist Claude
David, *Stefan George: Son Oeuvre poétique* (1952), also available in German:
Stefan George: Sein dichterisches Werk (tr. Alexa Remmen, 1967). Franz
Schonauer, *Stefan George in Selbstzeugnissen und Bilddokumenten* (1969), is a
fair summary with an excellent bibliography. And see Melitta Gerhard, *Stefan
George, Dichtung und Kündung* (1962), H. Stefan Schultz, *Studien zur
Dichtung Stefan Georges* (1967), Erich von Kahler, *Stefan George* (1964), a
civilized lecture; these titles mainly deal with George as poet and prophet.
Karlhans Kluncker, *Blätter für die Kunst. Zeitschrift der Dichterschule Stefan
Georges* (1974), studies the periodical of the Circle. A cultural (and sexual)
history of the group remains a desideratum. Meanwhile, there are some useful
comments in Walter Z. Laqueur, *Young Germany: A History of the German
Youth Movement* (1962), and *Kulturkritik und Jugendkult*, ed. Walter Rüegg
(1974). For Schweitzer, the homosexual German socialist, we have the thorough
life by Gustav Mayer, *Johann Baptist von Schweitzer und die Sozialdemokratie.
Ein Beitrag zur Geschichte der deutschen Arbeiterbewegung* (1909), as well
as the judicious pages in August Bebel's pedestrian but dependable autobiography, *Aus meinem Leben*, 3 vols. (1911–1914), esp. vol. II. The professional
journal, *Archiv für Kriminal-Anthropologie und Kriminalistik*, ed. Prof. Dr.
Hans Gross, made the legal issue of homosexual conduct very much its own;
from about 1900 on, each issue was likely to have an article on a legal case or
a report on a recent book on "contrary sexual feelings." Aimée Duc (pseud.),
Sind es Frauen? a novel of 1901, on what its subtitle calls "the third sex,"
repays reading. There are interesting observations in George L. Mosse, "Na-

tionalism and Respectability: Normal and Abnormal Sexuality in the Nineteenth Century," *Journal of Contemporary History*, XVII (1982), 221–46. For a sympathetic historical treatment of lesbians in Germany, see Gudrun Schwarz, "'Mannweiber' in Männertheorien," in Karin Hausen, ed., *Frauen Suchen Ihre Geschichte: Historische Studien zum 19. und 20. Jahrhundert* (1983), 62–80.

There is an excellent recent article by George Chauncey, Jr., "From Sexual Inversion to Homosexuality: Medicine and The Changing Conceptualization of Female Deviance," *Salmagundi*, Nos. 58–59 (1982–83), 114–46, which surveys the available (and controversial) material for the United States in the late nineteenth and early twentieth century and warns against an excessive stress on ideology. Guy Hocquenghem, *Homosexual Desire* (1972; tr. Daniella Dangoor, 1978), and the earlier Xavier Mayne, pseud., *The Intersexes* (1910), are comparative studies of legislation.

FIVE: Stratagems of Sensuality

The classic work on the defensive strategies with which humans get through life remains Anna Freud, *The Ego and the Mechanisms of Defence* (1936; tr. Cecil Baines, 1937). Freud himself never developed a full theory of that subtlest and "healthiest" of defenses, sublimation; we may draw on extensive passages in his papers, notably the classic "Die Verdrängung" (1915), *St.A.*, III, 103–18, "Repression," *S.E.*, XIV, 141–58; and see the famous case history of the Wolf Man, "Aus der Geschichte einer infantilen Neurose" (1918), *St.A.*, VIII, 125–232, "From the History of an Infantile Neurosis," *S.E.*, XVII, 1–122. Freud scattered some pregnant later hints in *Das Ich und das Es* (1923), *St.A.*, VIII, 273–330, *The Ego and the Id*, *S.E.*, XIX, 3–66. Among important early papers on sublimation, one by Siegfried Bernfeld "Zur Sublimierungstheorie," *Imago*, XVII (1931), 399–409 bears reading. Imre Hermann, "Die Regel der Gleichzeitigkeit in der Sublimierungsarbeit," ibid., X (1924), also deserves attention, as do two elegant papers by Ella F. Sharpe, "Certain Aspects of Sublimation and Delusion" (1930), and "Similar and Divergent Unconscious Determinants Underlying the Sublimations of Pure Art and Pure Science" (1935), both in *Collected Papers on Psycho-Analysis*, ed. Marjorie Brierley (1950), 125–36, 137–54. See also Edward Glover, "Sublimation, Substitution and Social Anxiety," *Int. J. Psycho-Anal.* (1931), abridged in *On the Early Development of Mind* (1956), 130–60. Hans W. Loewald has made sublimation the subject of some seminal lectures he is gathering into a book worth waiting for. Meanwhile, he has observations in his *Papers on Psychoanalysis* (1980), notably in "Comments on some Instinctual Manifestations of Superego Formation" (1973), 326–41. Mark Kanzer, "Acting Out, Sublimation and Reality Testing," *J. Amer. Psychoanal. Assn.*, V (1951), 663–84, is suggestive. So is George E. Gross and Isaiah A. Rubin, "Sublimation: The Study of an Instinctual Vicissitude," *PSC*, XXVII (1972), 354–59. Heinz Hartmann, "Notes on the Theory of Sublimation" (1955), in *Essays on Ego Psychology: Selected Problems in Psychoanalytic Theory* (1964), 215–240, ably sums up the debate.

For the related mechanism of reaction formation, we have Freud's diverse comments in his papers on metapsychology and, more densely clustered, in

Hemmung, Symptom und Angst (1926), *St.A.*, VI, 227–308, *Inhibitions, Symptoms and Anxiety, S.E.*, XX, 77–174. And see Otto Fenichel's landmark paper, "The Counter-Phobic Attitude" (1939), in *The Collected Papers of Otto Fenichel*, Second Series, ed. Hanna Fenichel and David Rapaport (1954), 163–73. On keeping reaction formation apart from sublimation (no easy task), see Fenichel, *The Psychoanalytic Theory of Neurosis* (1945), esp. 151–53, and the Hartmann paper cited above.

The psychoanalytic study of music is in its early phases, but the series of five articles, "The Psychodynamic Meaning of Music" by Pinchas Noy, in *Journal for Music Therapy*, III (1966), 126–34; IV (1967), 7–23, 45–51, 81–94, and 117–25 offers much food for thought. So do Heinz Kohut, "Observations on the Psychological Functions of Music," *J. Amer. Psychoanal. Assn.*, V (1957), 389–407; Otto Isakower, "On the Exceptional Position of the Auditory Sphere," *Int. J. Psycho-Anal.*, XX (1939) 340–48; and more far-reaching papers by Mark Kanzer, "Contemporary Psychoanalytic Views of Aesthetics," ibid., 514–24; Isidor H. Coriat, "Some Aspects of a Psychoanalytic Interpretation of Music," *Psychoanalytic Review*, XXXII (1945), 408–18; and Martin L. Nass, "Some Considerations of a Psychoanalytic Interpretation of Music," *PQ*, XL (1971), 303–16. There are helpful comments in Jack J. Spector, *The Aesthetics of Freud: A Study in Psychoanalysis and Art* (1972), which also has a most useful bibliography.

Treatments of musical theory, aesthetics, and psychology are, of course, legion. William Weber, *Music and the Middle Class: The Social Structure of Concert Life in London, Paris and Vienna* (1975), is a first sketch for a sociological history of music in the Victorian century. I add the theoretical presentation by Leonard B. Meyer, *Emotion and Meaning in Music* (1956), Gerald Abraham's set of lectures, *The Tradition of Western Music* (1974), which compresses much wisdom into an economical compass, and an illuminating, sensitive set of lectures by Roger Sessions, *The Musical Experience of Composer, Performer, Listener* (1950). Among Donald Francis Tovey's many fine short essays, "Words and Music: Some *Obiter Dicta*" (1938), in *The Main Stream of Music and Other Essays* (1949; ed. 1959), 202–19, is particularly relevant. I am also indebted to Deryck Cooke, *The Language of Music* (1959).

For Sir Charles Hallé, see, above all, Michael Kennedy, *The Hallé Tradition: A Century of Music* (1960), equally informative about the man and his orchestra. See C. E. Hallé, ed., *Life and Letters of Sir Charles Hallé* (1896), for solid biographical information. The Henry Watson Music Library in Manchester is a treasure house.

The literature on Wagner is almost boundless; I forebear citing more than a small fraction of it here. The (often unintentionally) most revealing documents are *Cosima Wagner's Diaries, 1869–1883*, ed. Martin Gregor-Dellin and Dietrich Mack, 2 vols. (1976–77; tr. Geoffrey Skelton, 1978–80). Richard Wagner, *My Life* (first complete ed. 1963; tr. Andrew Gray, ed. Mary Whittall, 1983), is voluminous, mendacious—and necessary. So is *The Diary of Richard Wagner: The Brown Book, 1865–1882*, ed. Joachim Bergfeld (1975; tr. George Bird, 1980). Among the many biographies, Robert Gutman, *Richard Wagner: The Man, The Mind, and His Music* (1968), is supreme among the hostile school; the most persuasive defense of Wagner I know, by no means ignoring his musical eroticism, is the terse essay by Bryan Magee, *Aspects of Wagner* (1968), which is almost persuasive. The mammoth biography by Ernest Newman, *The Life of Wagner*, 4 vols. (1933–47) retains much of its authority and continues to repay rereading; Newman's single-volume essay, *Wagner as Man and Artist* (1913; 2nd. ed. 1924), was a splendid anticipation of his later masterpiece. Among Carl Dahlhaus's several authoritative writings on Wagner, his *Wagner's Konzeption des musikalischen Dramas* (1971), though short, says the essential. Ronald Taylor, *Richard Wagner: His Life, Art and Thought* (1979) is a good modern instance of the apologetic school. Derek Watson, *Richard Wagner: A Biography* (1979), is more balanced. I have learned from the essays gathered by Peter Burbidge and Richard Sutton in *The Wagner Companion* (1979), esp. from Deryck Cooke, "Wagner's Musical Language," 225–68, and Lucy Beckett, "Wagner and His Critics," 365–99. I have tried to sketch the erotic atmosphere around Wagner and the dependence of his admirers on the Master in "Hermann Levi: A Study in Service and Self-Hatred," *Freud, Jews and Other Germans: Masters and Victims in Modernist Culture* (1978), 189–230. In the same volume (pp. 231–56), I have briefly accounted for the contemporary reception of Brahms's work. In this connection, I found particularly suggestive Imogen Fellinger, "Das Brahms-Bild der Allgemeinen Musikalischen Zeitung (1863 bis 1882)," in Heinz Becker, ed., *Beiträge zur Geschichte der Musikkritik* (1965), 27–54, an article that goes beyond its stated intention. For the anti-Wagnerian atmosphere around Brahms, see *Briefe von Theodor Billroth* (1895; 8th ed. 1910), and the exhaustive biography by Max Kalbeck, *Johannes Brahms*, 4 vols. in 8 (1904–14), adoring but scholarly. Hans Gal, *Johannes Brahms. Werk und Persönlichkeit* (1961), is a creditable modern biography. Among the articles in *Brahms-Studien*, vol. 1 (1974), the most rewarding are: Kurt Stephenson, "Der Komponist Brahms im eigenen Urteil," 7–24, Siegfried Kross, "Brahms—der unromantische Romantiker," 25–44, and Carl Dahlhaus, "Brahms und die Idee der Kammermusik," 45–58. Arnold Schoenberg's well-known essay, "Brahms the Progressive" (1933; rev. 1947), in *Style and Idea* (1950), 52–101, Proves that Brahms was not just an epigone. See in this context my "For Beckmesser: Eduard Hanslick, Victim and Prophet," *Freud, Jews and Other Germans*, 257–77. Hanslick's autobiography, *Aus meinem Leben*, 2 vols. (1894), is appealing and contentious without being angry.

The psychoanalytic literature on the eroticization of nature is most skimpy. Hanns Sachs, "Über Naturgefühl," *Imago*, I (1912), 119–31, remains suggestive; he sees it as a projection of repressed narcissism. The sociologist W. J. Thomas's short "Discussion: The Sexual Element in Sensibility," *Psychological Review*, XI (1904), 61–67, is an early effort, in the age of Havelock Ellis, to come to grips with the issue. (As for Ellis, Grosskurth's life, *Havelock Ellis: A Biography* [1980], clearly supersedes all others.) The comprehensive biography, *Waldo Emerson*, by Gay Wilson Allen (1981) is most serviceable; it says much about Nature. Among older studies (anything but Freudian), I found suggestions in Ferdinand Hoffmann, *Der Sinn für Naturschönheiten in alter und neuer Zeit* (1889), Sir Archibald Geikie, *The Love of Nature among the Romans during the Last Decades of the Republic and the First Century of the Empire* (1912), old-fashioned but comprehensive intellectual history, and Wilhelm Ganzenmüller, *Das Naturgefühl im Mittelalter* (1914). More recent, far more rewarding work includes Marjorie Hope Nicolson, *Mountain Gloom and Mountain Glory* (1959), a brilliant pioneering essay; U. C. Knoepflmacher and G. B Tennyson, eds., *Nature and the Victorian Imagination* (1977), full of interesting essays, notably Tennyson's "The Sacramental Imagination," 370–90, and George H. Ford, "Felicitous Space: The Cottage Controversy," 29–48; and, above all, Keith Thomas's lucid, scholarly, and authoritative Trevelyan Lectures, *Man and the Natural World: Changing Attitudes in England 1500–1800* (1983; unaccountably and pretentiously subtitled by the publisher *A History of the Modern Sensibility*, for the American edition), which chronicles the shift of attitudes toward animals, flora, and fauna in England across three hundred years—a model for other studies. M. H. Abrams's justly praised *Natural Supernaturalism: Tradition and Revolution in Romantic Literature* (1971) does not neglect the romantic worship of Nature. The seminal checklist by Arthur O. Lovejoy, "Nature as Aesthetic Norm" (1927), in *Essays in the History of Ideas* (1948), 69–78, opened up the theme for further research. There is much of interest about the German publicist, novelist, critic, and nature-mystic Wilhelm Bölsche (who brought out a three-volume work, *Das Liebesleben in der Natur*, between 1898 and 1902) in Alfred H. Kelly, "Darwinism and the Working Class in Wilhelmian Germany," Seymour Drescher et al. eds., *Political Symbolism in Modern Europe: Essays in Honor of George L. Mosse* (1982), and in Kelly, *The Descent of Darwin: The Popularization of Darwinism in Germany, 1860–1914* (1981).

In the prospering, but still fairly constricted field of the psychology of religion, Robert N. Bellah's essays have been particularly instructive for me. See *Beyond Belief: Essays on Religion in a Post-Traditional World* (1970); particularly relevant to my purposes in this volume is "Father and Son in Christianity and Confucianism," 76–99, which briefly comes to grips with the psychoanalytic view of religion. Bellah's article, "The Sociology of Religion," *International Encyclopedia of the Social Sciences*, XIII, 406–13, sums up the field without neglecting psychology. Among Freud's several papers on the subject, two are pertinent, "Zwangshandlungen und Religionsübungen" (1907), *St. A.*, VII, 11–21, "Obsessive Actions and Religious Practices," *S.E.*, IX, 115–27; and *Die Zukunft einer Illusion* (1927), *St. A.*, IX, 135–89, *The Future of an Illusion*, *S.E.*, XXI, 1–56. Other psychoanalytic approaches to religion include such stimulating essays as Erich Fromm, *The Dogma of Christ, and Other Essays on Religion, Psychology, and Culture* (1963), which brings together some of Fromm's earlier essays, still "orthodox." Mortimer Ostow and Ben-Ami Scharfstein, *The Need to Believe* (1954), is a handy compendium of psychoanalytic ideas on religious ritual and belief. For a less hostile psychoanalytic perception of religion, see Hans W. Loewald, *Psychoanalysis and the History of the Individual* (1978), esp. ch. III, "Comments on Religious Experience." The classics, Emile Durkheim's *The Elementary Forms of the Religious Life* (1912; tr. Joseph Ward Swain, 1915), and Max Weber's extremely controversial, *The Protestant Ethic and the Spirit of Capitalism* (1904–5; tr. Talcott Parsons, 1930), are only indirectly relevant here, but they significantly illustrate ways of thinking about the social function of religion which shed light on the displacements I analyze in the text. Charles Y. Glock and Philip E. Hammond, eds., *Beyond the Classics? Essays in the Scientific Study of Religion*

(1973), contains illuminating essays evaluating Durkheim, Weber, Freud, Malinowski, and William James in the light of modern research; I am particularly beholden to Paul W. Pruyser, "Sigmund Freud and His Legacy: Psychoanalytic Psychology of Religion," 243–90. Pruyser's *A Dynamic Psychology of Religion* (1968) is sound and interesting, esp. ch. VI, "Emotional Processes in Religion." In comparison, Walter Houston Clark, *The Psychology of Religion: An Introduction to Religious Experience and Behavior* (1958), is reductionist. Among Bryan R. Wilson's books on the theme, *Religion in Secular Society: A Sociological Comment* (1966) perhaps encapsulates his views best. Clifford Geertz's essay, "Religion as a Cultural System" (1966), conveniently available in his *The Interpretation of Cultures* (1973), 87–125, is powerfully argued. There are many usable, spirited comments on religion and sexual frustration in G. Rattray Taylor, *Sex in History* (1954). On religion and sex, a topic widely discussed, Havelock Ellis offers interesting details in "The Auto-Erotic Factor in Religion," *Studies in the Psychology of Sex*, vol. II (1900), 267–82. More recent work includes Louis J. Kern, *An Ordered Love: Sex Roles and Sexuality in Victorian Utopias—The Shakers, the Mormons, and the Oneida Community* (1981), and Lawrence Foster, *Religion and Sexuality: Three American Communal Experiments of the Nineteenth Century* (1981), which treats Kern's three Utopias somewhat differently. There is fascinating material in J. F. C. Harrison, *The Second Coming: Popular Millenarianism 1780–1850* (1979). And see again, with some illuminating pages, Abrams, *Natural Supernaturalism* (above, 454). The most aggressive and most exciting brief for treating religion as the great neurosis in human history is Weston La Barre's brilliant, uncompromising *The Ghost Dance: The Origins of Religion* (1970), from which I have taken both ideas and comfort.

For Patmore, see especially Derek Patmore, *The Life and Times of Coventry Patmore* (1949), and J. C. Reid, *The Mind and Art of Coventry Patmore* (1957). Edmund Gosse, *Coventry Patmore* (1905), is a pious celebration, not without its uses. See also Terence L. Connolly, ed., *Coventry Patmore: Mystical Poems of Nuptial Love* (1938), which gathers some inaccessible texts and has introductory comments by Joachim V. Benson. Carol Christ, "Victorian Masculinity and the Angel in the House," in Martha Vicinus, ed., *A Widening Sphere: Changing Roles of Victorian Women* (1977), 146–62, tries, somewhat tendentiously, to discuss that favorite Victorian cliché about the domestic angel. Most books on Victorian sexuality pay their tribute to Patmore's immortal title at least in passing; of the works I discuss in my bibliography to *Education of the Senses* on p. 466, the most pertinent is Fraser Harrison, *The Dark Angel: Aspects of Victorian Sexuality* (1977), 47–50. June Badeni's informative life of the friend of Patmore's old age, *The Slender Tree: A Life of Alice Maynell* (1981), has some excellent pages on him, notably 90–129. See also Wendell Stacy Johnson, *Sex and Marriage in Victorian Poetry* (1975).

The most sensitive and (in the good sense) imaginative, biography of Kingsley (it led me to his drawings and the "diary" of his fiancée, among other things), is doubtless Susan Chitty, *The Beast and the Monk: A Life of Charles Kingsley* (1975). In addition, R. B. Martin, *The Dust of Combat* (1959) eminently deserves reading. See also Brenda Colloms, *Charles Kingsley* (1974), which concentrates on his ideas on social reform. Walter E. Houghton, *The Victorian Frame of Mind, 1830-1870* (1957), discusses his "wild oats," and several related themes, 375-77. Allan John Hartley, *The Novels of Charles Kingsley: A Christian Social Interpretation* (1978) views the fiction from an unusual perspective. W. R. Greg, "Kingsley and Carlyle," in *Literary and Social Judgments* (1973), is a revealing contemporary verdict. His widow's much read and often reprinted collection, *Charles Kingsley: His Letters and Memories of His Life*, 2 vols. (best ed. 1879), discloses even more than Fanny Kingsley thought it prudent to disclose. For the great American anti-smut reformer, see Heywood Broun and Margaret Leech, *Anthony Comstock Roundsman of the Lord* (1927). David J. Pivar, *Purity Crusade, Sexual Morality and Social Control, 1868-1900* (1973), is illuminating; and see Paul S. Boyer *Purity in Print: The Vice-Society Movement and Book Censorship in America* (1968), as well as Joseph R. Gusfield, *Symbolic Crusade: Status Politics and the American Temperance Movement* (1963), which works with Richard Hofstadter's analytical category of status anxiety.

There is a small, respectable literature analyzing the impact of the modern commercial and industrial world on fiction, poetry, and art on which I have drawn. But none even touches on eroticization, a psychoanalytic theme calling out for much further work. On "libidinization" in general, see Edward Glover, "Unconscious Functions of Education" (1937), in *Early Development of Mind*, 283-89. The Marxist view is represented in the stimulating, much-cited book by Francis Klingender, *Art and the Industrial Revolution* (1947; 2nd ed., 1968). Sigfried Giedion, *Mechanization Takes Command* (1948), a classic in industrial history, has much interesting material. See also Herbert Read, *Art and Industry* (1961), which continues the thought of his "Machine Aesthetic" (1946), in *Coat of Many Colors* (1954). A most stimulating, beautifully illustrated "production" is K. G. Pontus Hultén, *The Machine as seen at the end of the mechanical age*, Exhibition Catalogue, Museum of Modern Art, New York (1968). For England there is preeminently the anthology compiled by Jeremy Warburg, *The Industrial Muse: The Industrial Revolution in English Poetry* (1958), to be used in conjunction with Warburg's essay, "Poetry and Industrialism: Some Refractory Material in Nineteenth Century and Later English Verse," *Modern Language Review*, LIII (1958), 161-70. Herbert L. Sussman, *Victorians and the Machine: The Literary Response to Technology* (1968), concentrates on the major English writers from Thomas Carlyle to Rudyard Kipling, with useful chapters on Charles Dickens, John Ruskin, William Morris, Samuel Butler, and H. G. Wells in between. See also Walter J. Hipple, *The Beautiful, the Sublime, and the Picturesque* (1957). John Baur, *Revolution and Tradition in American Art* (1951), is good on the machine aesthetic.

For France, see Marc Baroli, *Le train dans la littérature française* (1963), very useful and comprehensive. Elliott M. Grant, *French Poetry and Modern Industry 1830-1870* (1927), is informative. See also Paul Ginestier, *The Poet and the Machine* (1954; tr. Martin B. Friedman, 1961).

The anthology edited by Keith Bullivant and Hugh Ridley, *Industrie und deutsche Literatur, 1830-1914* (1976) is, though compact, thoughtfully selected and brings together some little-known material. The older study by Hans

Kistenmacher, *Maschine und Dichtung: Ein Beitrag zur Geschichte der deutschen Literatur im 19. Jahrhundert* (1914), and the dissertation by Felix Zimmermann, *Die Widerspiegelung der Technik in der deutschen Dichtung von Goethe bis zur Gegenwart* (1913), remain worth perusing.

Leo Marx, *The Machine in the Garden: Technology and the Pastoral Ideal in America* (1965), is a sensitive and stimulating essay not averse to citing Freud. Like most of the other later literature on this topic, it acknowledges the pioneering work of Henry Nash Smith, *Virgin Land: The American West as Myth and Symbol* (1950). See also Marvin Fisher, "The Iconology of Industrialism, 1830–60," *American Quarterly*, XIII (1961), 347–64. There is much pertinent thinking in Barbara Novak, *Nature and Culture: American Landscape and Painting, 1825–1875* (1980). And see Roderick Nash, *Wilderness and the American Mind* (1967; rev. ed. 1973), as well as the interesting study by John F. Kasson, *Civilizing the Machine: Technology and Republican Values in America, 1776–1900* (1976), which has chapters (3 and 4) on "Technology and Imaginative Freedom: R. W. Emerson," and "The Aesthetics of Machinery."

The two Zola novels from the Rougon-Macquart cycle I use as proof texts have had good editions and studies. Both are best read in the five-volume Pléiade edition (1960–1967): *Au bonheur des dames*, III (1964), 387–803, with the exhaustive apparatus at 1667–1734; *La bête humaine*, IV, (1966), 995–1331, with *its* apparatus, no less exhaustive, at 1705–91. I have also learned from Colette Becker's edition of *Au Bonheur des Dames* (1971). For that novel, the best study is an indirect one: Michael B. Miller, *The Bon Marché: Bourgeois Culture and the Department Store, 1869–1920* (1981), which alludes to Zola's imaginary department store often, and compares it with the reality. Most French publications on the great bazaars (as Miller points out, p. 7n) are uncritical celebrations or simply anecdotal. His bibliography is very full. Dr. Paul Dubuisson, *Les Voleuses des grands magasins* (1902), is a curious depiction of a curious phenomenon: the kleptomaniac. There is now a fascinating paper on that theme by Patricia O'Brien, "The Kleptomania Diagnosis: Bourgeois Women and Theft in Late Nineteenth-Century France," *Journal of Social History*, XVII (1984), 65–77. See also Aimé Dupuy, "Les Grands magasins et leur histoire littéraire," *L'Information Historique* (May–June 1958), 106–12; and Marcel Candille, "De la réalité au roman. Au Bon Marché de M. et Mme Boucicaut et Au Bonheur des Dames de Zola," *Revue de l'Assistance publique à Paris*, III (January–February 1953), 75–91.

Zola's railroad novel has been studied rather more fully. In addition to Baroli's book on the train in French literature (cited just above), there are Martin Kanes, *Zola's 'La Bête humaine,' A Study in Literary Creation* (1962), and J. H. Matthews, "The Railway in Zola's 'La bête humaine,'" *Symposium*, XIV (Spring 1960), 53–59. A. Bronson Feldman, "Zola and the Riddle of Sadism," *American Imago*, XIII (1956), 415–25, offers some psychoanalytic hints. John Addington Symonds's interpretation, "La bête humaine: A Study in Zola's Idealism," in *In the Key of Blue and Other Prose Essays* (1893), 111–31, is mainly of historical interest. Brian Nelson's analysis of Zola, the half-bourgeois anti-bourgeois, *Zola and the Bourgeoisie: A Study of Themes and Techniques in 'Les Rougon-Macquart'* (1983), beautifully places the novelist and his novels.

Monet's paintings of the Gare St. Lazare are discussed in all the studies of his work (see the attractive *Monet* by William C. Seitz [ca. 1960], esp. 106–7 or in general treatments like John Rewald, *The History of Impressionism* [1946; fourth ed. 1973], 379–80). Among the articles, see esp. Rodolphe Walter "Saint-Lazare l'impressioniste," *Oeil*, no. 292 (November 1979), 48–55. There are interesting comparisons with other Gare St.-Lazare paintings in J. Kirk T. Varnedoe and Thomas P. Lee, eds., *Gustave Caillebotte: A Retrospective Exhibition, 1976–1977* (1976). John Gage, *Turner: Rain, Steam and Speed* (1972), is a fine monograph devoted to Turner's famous railroad painting. C Hamilton Ellis, *Railway Art* (1977), is a well-illustrated picture book; it may be supplemented with the exhibition catalogue, *Art and the Industrial Revolution*, Manchester City Gallery (1968).

SIX: The Price of Repression

I have based this section on long-term, wide-ranging, though unsystematic reading in late-eighteenth-century and in nineteenth-century sources. There is need for some comprehensive studies of nervousness as a modern disease; Andreas Steiner, *"Das Nervöse Zeitalter." Der Begriff der Nervosität bei Laien und Ärzten in Deutschland und Österreich um 1900* (1964), is informative on Germany and Austria. Note its concise bibliography. James C. Albisetti, *Secondary School Reform in Imperial Germany* (1983), has a strong chapter (IV) on "The Overburdening of German Youth," which rehearses the late-nineteenth-century debate over what was presumably making German students nervous. Hysteria also deserves further exploration. Ilza Veith, *Hysteria: The History of a Disease* (1965), is a far from exhaustive survey; the historical section (ch. IV) in Alan Krohn, *Hysteria: The Elusive Neurosis* (1978), is relatively slight. To it should be added Harold Merskey, *The Analysis of Hysteria* (1979), which does not neglect the historical dimension. Edward Shorter's fully annotated article, "Les désordres psychosomatiques, sont ils 'hystériques'? Notes pour une recherche historique," *Cahiers internationaux de Sociologie*, LXXVI (1984), 201–24, seeks to reinterpret hysteria. See also Carroll Smith-Rosenberg, "The Hysterical Woman: Sex Roles and Role Conflict in 19th-century America," *Social Research*, XXXIX (1972), 652–78.

The large interpretative literature on Hegel and Marx necessarily touches on "alienation"; perhaps best are Jean Hyppolite, *Studies on Marx and Hegel* (1955; tr. John O'Neill, 1969), George Lichtheim, *Marxism: An Historical and Critical Study* (1961; 2nd. ed. 1965), Isaiah Berlin, *Karl Marx* (1939; 3rd. ed. 1973), distinguished by its lucidity. Heinrich Popitz, *Der entfremdete Mensch: Zeitkritik und Geschichtsphilosophie des jungen Marx* (1953), and far more sympathetically, Herbert Marcuse, *Reason and Revolution: Hegel and the Rise of Social Theory* (1941; 2nd. ed., 1955). For "anomie," see esp. Robert K. Merton, "Social Structure and Anomie," in Merton, *Social Theory and Social Structure* (1938; rev. ed., 1957), 131–60; Kurt H. Wolff, ed., *Emile Durkheim, 1858–1917: A Collection of Essays with Translations and Bibliography* (1960); and Steven Lukes, *Emile Durkheim. His Life and Work: A Historical and Critical Study* (1972), esp. pp. 207–25. Ferdinand Tönnies, the fascinating German sociologist, he of "Gemeinschaft und Gesellschaft," could profit from far more extensive study; meanwhile, there are Rudolf Heberle, "The Sociological System of Ferdinand Tönnies: 'Community' and 'Society,'" in Harry Barnes, ed., *An Introduction to the History of Sociology* (1948), 227–48; Louis Wirth, "The Sociology of Ferdinand Tönnies," *American Journal of Sociology*, XXXII (1926), 412–22; Anthony Oberschall, *Empirical Social Research in Germany 1848–1914* (1965); Albert Salomon, "In Memoriam Ferdinand Tönnies (1855–1936)," *Social Research*, III (1936), 384–63; and E. G. Jacoby, "Ferdinand Tönnies, Sociologist. A Centennial Tribute," *Kyklos*, VIII (1955), 144–59.

J. A. Hobson, too, especially his psychological aperçus, deserves fresh work. H. N. Brailsford, *The Life-work of J. A. Hobson* (1948), is a competent introduction; Hobson's autobiography, *Confessions of an Economic Heretic* (1938), is engaging. See also Paul T. Homan, *Contemporary Economic Thought* (1928), 281–374.

Dr. George M. Beard, the "inventor" of "neurasthenia," is best captured in the sensitive essay by Barbara Sicherman, "The Paradox of Prudence: Mental Health in the Gilded Age," *The Journal of American History*, LXII (March 1976), 890–912, esp. 892 and 902–5 (conveniently reprinted in the interesting anthology, ed. Andrew Scull, *Madhouses, Mad-Doctors, and Madmen: The Social History of Psychiatry in the Victorian Era* [1981], 218–40). And see Sicherman, *The Quest for Mental Health in America, 1880–1917* (1980). In addition, there are Eric T. Carlson, "George M. Beard and Neurasthenia," in E. R. Wallace and C. Pressley, eds., *Essays in the History of Psychiatry, Supplement to Psychiatric Forum* (1980), 50–57; and Charles E. Rosenberg, "The Place of George M. Beard in Nineteenth-Century Psychiatry," *Bulletin of the History of Medicine*, XXVI (1962), 245–59, now (under a different title) in Rosenberg, *No Other Gods: On Science and American Social Thought* (1976), 98–108, with valuable bibliographical information. See also the reminiscences of A. D. Rockwell (for years Beard's collaborator), *Rambling Recollections: An Autobiography* (1920). Nathan Hale, *Freud and the Americans* (above, 431), puts Beard into his context. So does Henri F. Ellenberger, *The Discovery of the Unconscious: The History and Evolution of Dynamic Psychiatry* (1970), bulky, useful, but (on Freud) unsympathetic. I have also learned from Michael J. Clark's brilliant "The Rejection of Psychological Approaches to Mental Disorder in Late-Nineteenth Century British Psychiatry," in Scull's anthology on *Madhouses*, cited just above (pp. 271–321.) Klaus Doerner, *Madmen and the Bourgeoisie* (1969; tr. Joachim Neugroschel and Jean Steinberg, 1981), is a tendentious historical treatment fastening on the "exploitation" of the insane in the nineteenth century.

Traditionally, the bulk of the literature on prostitution (apart from the polemics themselves and the "scientific" surveys, which are all tight-lipped enough) has been anecdotal, racy, amused, and intent on being amusing; it has largely focused on expensive and colorful courtesans. Typical of this superficial, though by no means useless if relentlessly cheerful sub-genre is Cyril Pearl, *The Girl With the Swansdown Seat: An Informal Report on Some Aspects of Mid-Victorian Morality* (1955); Henry Blyth, *Skittles, the Last Victorian Courtesan. The Life and Times of Catherine Walters* (1970), which

has material on Gladstone; and the heavily illustrated volume by Joann
Richardson, *The Courtesans: The Demi-monde in 19th Century France* (1967)
G. L. Simons, *A Place for Pleasure: The History of the Brothel* (1975), offer
a brisk gallop through the continents and the centuries; and see the highly
informal Martin Seymour-Smith, *Fallen Women. A skeptical enquiry into the
treatment of prostitutes, their clients and their pimps in literature* (1969). (That
sort of literature was, of course, not unknown to the nineteenth century; one
curious representative is the anonymous *Le putanisme d'Amsterdam*, a reprint
of 1883, complete with an appreciative introduction, of a book first published
in 1681).

There are numerous general histories, most of them necessarily rather sweeping: thus Fernando Henriques, *Prostitution and Society*, 3 vols. (1962–1968)
of which the last, *Modern Sexuality*, is relevant to this chapter; it is compendious, derivative, and not always dependable. See also Vern L. Bullough,
The History of Prostitution (1964), and Vern and Bonnie Bullough, *Prostitution: An Illustrated Social History* (1978), and George Scott, *Ladies of Vice: A
History of Prostitution from Antiquity to the Present Day* (1968). The classic
international survey of the early twentieth century, Abraham Flexner, *Prostitution in Europe* (1914), remains worth study. Robert Baldick's *The Life of
J.-K. Huysmans* (1955) thoroughly explores the expeditions of one eager
amateur among the bordellos of Western Europe.

Since World War II, social historians have taken the "social evil" seriously
and produced some impressive monographs. There is, for one, Frances Finnegan,
Poverty and Prostitution: A Study of Victorian Prostitution in York (1979),
a model monograph that incidentally debunks some favorite, self-satisfied
clichés about the "life." Judith R. and Daniel J. Walkowitz, " 'We are not
Beasts of the Field,' Prostitution and the Poor in Plymouth and Southampton
Under the Contagious Diseases Acts," *Feminist Studies*, I (Winter 1973), 73–
106, has become a minor classic; Judith Walkowitz, "The Making of an Outcast
Group: Prostitutes and Working Women in Nineteenth-Century Plymouth and
Southampton," in Martha Vicinus, ed., *A Widening Sphere*, 72–93, continued
this inquiry, while her *Prostitution and Victorian Society: Women, Class and
the State* (1980) considerably expanded the material and scope of the articles.
The Walkowitzs' principal interest is in the Contagious Diseases Acts and their
eventual repeal; more on that issue in Paul McHugh, *Prostitution and Victorian
Social Reform* (1980), which focuses on a close, unsentimental analysis of
pressure group tactics and raises some pointed psychological questions about
the crusaders. See in this connection the popular study by Michael Pearson, *The
Age of Consent: Victorian Prostitution and its Enemies* (1972). Brian Harrison's
review (and critique) of Steven Marcus, *The Other Victorians*, "Underneath
the Victorians," *Victorian Studies*, X (March 1967), 239–62, contains immensely valuable observations to serve as correctives for extravagant and
excited guessing. See also E. M. Sigsworth and T. J. Wyke, "A Study of
Victorian Prostitution and Venereal Disease," in Martha Vicinus, ed., *Suffer
and Be Still: Women in the Victorian Age* (1972), 77–99. Keith Thomas's important article, "The Double Standard," *Journal of the History of Ideas*, XX
(1959), 195–216 is most illuminating. Fraser Harrison, *The Dark Angel*, and
Jeffrey Weeks, *Sex, Politics and Society: The Regulation of Sexuality Since*

1800 (1981), have numerous pages on prostitutes. A look at the *Saturday Review* in its first years of existence (note, as some examples, the issues of January 23, February 27, and April 3, 1858) suggests that, by mid-century, Victorians were willing to talk about prostitution with a fair measure of seriousness and freedom. Josephine Butler has been much studied, both in the titles I have cited and in several biographies, perhaps best by Glen Petrie, *A Singular Iniquity: The Campaigns of Josephine Butler* (1971). Josephine E. Butler, *An Autobiographical Memoir*, ed. George W. and Lucy A. Johnson (1909), is worshipful but rich in material.

Ruth Rosen is sober and informative in her poignantly illustrated *The Lost Sisterhood: Prostitution in America, 1900–1918* (1982). Her edition (with Sue Davidson) of *The Maimie Papers* (1977), drawn from the collections at the Sophia Smith Library, Northampton, Massachusetts, is very revealing. See also Mark Thomas Connelly, *The Response to Prostitution in the Progressive Era* (1980), which goes beyond my summary treatment of anti-vice committees and commissions. Alain Corbin, *Les filles de noce. Misère sexuelle et prostitution aux 19e et 20e siècles* (1978), is a monumental work of scholarship beginning with the investigations of Parent-Duchâtelet in the 1830s and ending in our time; it is concerned with the epochal struggle between those who wanted to legalize and those who wanted to outlaw prostitution (in her perceptive review, "Artisans of the Sidewalk," *Radical History Review*, XXVI [1982], 88–101, Judith Coffin notes Corbin's engagement in current controversies; I also note his excessive dependence on Michel Foucault). Corbin supersedes most earlier studies. Among modern monographs and syntheses, though, there are valuable suggestions in James F. McMillan, *Housewife or Harlot: The Place of Women in French Society, 1870–1940* (1981), and in Robert Wheaton and Tamara K. Hareven, eds., *Family and Sexuality in French History* (1980). See also Jean Borie, *Le tyran timide. Le naturalisme de la femme au XIXe siècle* (1973). Corbin cites a wealth of earlier studies on which he has relied. Among these, the most interesting for my purposes proved to be Dr. L. Martineau, *La Prostitution clandestine* (1885); Charles Virmaître, author of scores of little books on Paris, *Trottoirs et lupanars* (1893); Professor Alfred Fournier, of the Academy of Medicine, *Défense de la santé et de la morale publiques*, Rapport fait à la Commission extra-parlementaire de Régime des moeurs (1904), which rehearses the various schools of thought, and Louis Fiaux, *La Prostitution "cloîtrée," Les maisons de femmes autorisées par la Police, devant la Médecine publique* (1902). See also Alexandre Dumas père, *Filles, lorettes et courtisanes* (1843), a mixture of statistics, anecdotes, and moralizing sententiousness. I add Dr. Sicard de Plauzoles, *La fonction sexuelle. Au point de vue de l'Ethique et de l'Hygiène sociales* (1908).

For Germany there is now Richard J. Evans, "Prostitution, State and Society in Imperial Germany," *Past and Present*, No. 70 (1976), 106–29 a pioneering essay rich with bibliographical indications. Among earlier studies, A. Neher, *Die Geheime und Öffentliche Prostitution in Stuttgart, Karlsruhe und München* (1912), is particularly well informed about three major cities. For a fine modern local study analyzing the vicissitudes of legislation in one German city, see Alfred Urban, *Staat und Prostitution in Hamburg vom Beginn der Reglementierung bis zur Aufhebung der Kasernierung (1807–1927)* (1972). Pastor

H. Stursberg's *Die Prostitution in Deutschland und ihre Bekämpfung* (1886; 2nd ed., 1887), is a touching plea but based on first-hand investigations. Camillo Karl Schneider, *Die Prostitutierte und die Gesellschaft. Eine soziologisch-ethische Studie* (1908), surveys in detail the social position of the whore and the causes of prostitution, summarizes the views of reglementists and abolitionists, and has a good section on the rescue of the prostitute (115–19). Hans Ostwald, *Das Berliner Dirnentum*, 2 vols. (1907), is a very detailed account that includes material on legislation. See also R. Hessen, *Die Prostitution in Deutschland* (1907). Dr. Fr. J. Bahrend, *Die Prostitution in Berlin und die gegen sie und die Syphilis zu nehmenden Massregeln* (1850), is characteristic of the controversial literature at mid-century. I comment on others in the text. There is a remarkable outside view of the German situation by that crusader against the double standard, Josephine Butler, *The New Era: Containing a Retrospect of the History of the Regulation System in Berlin, of the Repeated Opposition directed Against the System There, and the Causes of the Failure of that Opposition; With an Indication of the Lessons to be Learned from Past Failure, and of the Source whence Hope Arises For the Future* (1872). Two interesting contemporary treatments, both influenced by Schopenhauer's aphorism that prostitution is a human sacrifice on the altar of monogamy, are Hans Schneickert, "Zur Prostitutionsfrage," *Archiv für Kriminal-Anthropologie und Kriminalistik*, IIL (1912), 56–61, and Ed. v Grabe, "Prostitution, Kriminalität und Psychopathie," ibid., 135–81, very revealing.

For Austria, there is an experimental essay that goes beyond its title, Sander L. Gilman, "Freud and the Prostitute: Male Stereotypes of Female Sexuality in fin-de-siècle Vienna," *Journal of the American Academy of Psychoanalysis* IX (1981), 337–60. Among the most rewarding representatives of the early prescientific literature for Austria is Dr. Ant. J. Gross-Hoffinger, *Die Schicksale der Frauen und die Prostitution im Zusammenhange mit dem Prinzip der Unauflösbarkeit der katholischen Ehe und besonders der österreichischer Gesetzgebung* (1847), a potpourri of polemics, aphorisms, and statistics.

The philanthropic impulse is beginning to receive the attention it deserves mainly for and in Britain. Brian Harrison, "Philanthropy and the Victorians" in Harrison, *Peaceable Kingdoms: Stability and Change in Modern Britain* (1982), 217–59, is a much-revised version of a splendid article first published in *Victorian Studies* in 1966; his book as a whole, a series of linked essays on England's political culture, is pertinent to my concerns in this chapter. Without using such psychoanalytic terms as "guilt" or "rescue fantasy," Harrison has illustrated both in that article as well as in "The Rhetoric of Reform in Modern Britain: 1780–1918," in ibid., 399–402, and in "State Intervention and Moral Reform in Nineteenth-Century England," in Patricia Hollis, ed., *Pressure from Without in Early Victorian England* (1974), esp. 310–15. F. K. Prochaska offers, in *Women and Philanthropy in Nineteenth-Century England* (1980), an informative survey of women doing both private charity and public lobbying. F. B. Smith, *Florence Nightingale: Reputation and Power* (1982), is a tenaciously argued, thoroughly documented, more than a touch too destructive debunking of the Lady with the Lamp. For Burdett-Coutts, see esp. Edna Healey, *Lady Unknown: The Life of Angela Burdett-Coutts* (1978); Diana Orton, *Mad of Gold: A Biography of Angela Burdett Coutts* (1980); Philip Collins, *Dickens and Crime* (1962; 2nd ed., 1964), ch. 4; and *Letters from Charles Dickens to Angela Burdett-Coutts 1841–1865*, ed. Edgar Johnson (1953), gradually being superseded by the critical "Pilgrim" edition of Dickens's volume. Norris Pope, *Dickens and Charity* (1978), concentrates on Dickens's complex relations with the Evangelicals.

In addition to the committee reports of New York, Philadelphia, and Minneapolis that I cite in the text, I have used reports from New Orleans (1855), Tokyo (1905), Lima (1909), Cleveland (1913), Honolulu, St. Louis, Newark (all 1914), as well as Dr. Isadore Dyer, *The Municipal Control of Prostitution* (1900). There are countless more, inviting analysis.

The psychoanalytic literature on the rescue fantasy is not large. A pioneer was Karl Abraham: "Manifestations of the Female Castration Complex" (1921), in *Selected Papers*, and "The Rescue and Murder of the Father in Neurotic Phantasy-Formation" (1922), *Clinical Papers and Essays on Psycho-Analysis* (1955), 68–75. There is also Edward Glover, "The Psychopathology of Prostitution," in *The Roots of Crime: Selected Papers on Psycho-Analysis* (1960), 244–67. Otto Rank has scattered and interesting hints in *Das Inzest-Motiv* (above, 435). Harold Greenwald, *The Elegant Prostitute: A Social and Psychoanalytic Study* (1970; the 1st ed. [1958] was titled *The Call Girl*), contains strenuously informal case reports and some speculation. See Freud's seminal comments in "Über einen besonderen Typus der Objektwahl beim Manne" (1910), *St.A.*, V, 185–95, esp. 192–93; "A Special Type of Choice of Object Made by Men," *S.E.*, XI, 163–75, esp. 170–72. Bernard C. Meyer's lecture, "Some Observations on the Rescue of Fallen Women," *PQ*, LIII (1984), 208–38, is interesting but focuses, in the orthodox psychoanalytic way, on men alone. These are, as I said in the text, technical issues, involving differential superego formation between the sexes on which the late Freud insisted, but I believe the evidence, especially from nineteenth-century philanthropy, is persuasive that the rescue fantasy haunts women quite as much as men. Some tentative steps toward a psychoanalytic reappraisal of women were taken in a Special Issue of *The Psychoanalytic Review*, LXIX (Spring 1982), ed. Leila Lerner, "Women and Individuation: Emerging Views," including a solid survey by Zenia Odes Fliegel, "Half A Century Later: Current Status of Freud's Controversial Views on Women," 7–28. And see Harold P. Blum, ed., *Female Psychology* (1977).

The rescue fantasy is integrally related to the no less widespread fantasy known as the family romance—the belief, often reaching consciousness, that one is not the son, or daughter, of one's parents but boasts a more exalted heritage. Freud's classic presentation is "Der Familienroman der Neurotiker," *St.A.*, IV, 221–26; "Family Romances," *S.E.*, IX, 237–41. The best summary of, and commentary on, the literature is Linda Joan Kaplan, "The Concept of the Family Romance," *Psychoanalytic Review*, LXI (1974), 169–202. Among psychoanalysts, Phyllis Greenacre has concentrated on the theme; note particularly her "The Family Romance of the Artist" (1958), reprinted in *Emotional Growth*, II, 505–32. For heartening corroboration from a nonanalyst, see Edmund S. Conklin, "The Foster-Child Fantasy," *American Journal of Psychology*, XXXI (1920), 59–76.

The fallen woman is, as everyone knows, a rich theme for literature—and only less so for painting. I have drawn on George Siegel's meaty essay, "The Fallen Woman in Nineteenth Century Russian Literature," *Harvard Slavic Studies*, V (1970), 81–107. It may be supplemented with comments by Simon Karlinsky, *The Sexual Labyrinth of Gogol* (1976), esp. 116–17; and Elizabeth Dalton, *Unconscious Structure in 'The Idiot,'* (1979), 90. For the Fallen Woman in painting note esp. Susan P. Casteras, *The Substance or the Shadow* (1982), 36–38. Linda Nochlin, "Lost and *Found*: Once More the Fallen Woman," *Art Bulletin*, LX (1978), 139–53, returns to Dante Gabriel Rossetti's famous canvas, profitably. Cockshut, *Man and Woman*, again has sensible observations, this time on prostitutes in literature, esp. 20–23, and 86–92 (on Gaskell's *Ruth*.) And see the survey by George Watt, *The Fallen Woman in the Nineteenth-Century English Novel* (1984). Dumas *fils' La Dame aux camélias* can be studied in a fine modern edition that includes the novel, the play, and the libretto for Verdi's *La Traviata*, ed. Hans-Jorg Neuschafer and Gilbert Sigaux (1981). Christiane Issartel, *Les Dames aux Camélias: De l'histoire à la légende* (1982), ably connects facts and fictions. Robert Ricatte, *La Genèse de 'La Fille Elisa,' d'après des notes inédits d'Edmond et Jules de Goncourt* (1960) carefully traces the making of Goncourt's novel about the prostitute Eliza.

EPILOGUE: Black-Coated Eros

A full historical treatment of the invidious comparisons that nineteenth-century bourgeois liked to draw at the expense of their neighbors, the aristocracy and the "lower orders," remains a desideratum. My quotations in the text from Michelet and Freud are only a beginning. There are helpful comments on Abel Hugo in Jean-Louis Flandrin, *Families in Former Times: Kinship, Household and Sexuality* (1976; tr. Richard Southern, 1970), 112–18. Equally helpful is Peter Keating, *The Working Classes in Victorian Fiction* (1971). Richard Faber, *Proper Stations: Class in Victorian Fiction* (1971), though suggestive, is slight. Sheila M. Smith, *The Other Nation: The Poor in English Novels of the 1840s and 1850s* (1980), is far more substantial. Amid the growing literature on the depiction of the poor in art, one outstanding essay is T. J. Edelstein's "They Sang 'The Song of the Shirt': The Visual Iconology of the Seamstress," *Victorian Studies*, XXIII (Winter 1980), 183–210.

The rediscovery, reediting, and republication of working-class autobiographies from the nineteenth and early twentieth century has in recent decades become a productive (though sometimes ideologically freighted) cottage industry. To begin with Britain: I have found the material gathered in John Burnett, ed., *Useful Toil: Autobiographies of Working People from the 1820s to the 1920s* (1974), particularly informative; it includes satisfying extracts from inaccessible and from some unpublished memoirs, and surrounds the primary material with thoughtful comments. David Vincent has edited, in full, five autobiographies, *Testaments of Radicalism: Memoirs of Working Class Politicians 1790–1885* (1977), and provided them with illuminating introductions. Vincent's *Bread, Knowledge and Freedom: A Study of Nineteenth-Century Working Class Autobiography* (1981) explores this and other material he has gathered in a judicious survey complete with an extensive bibliography;

see also his fine article, "Love and Death and the Nineteenth-Century Working Class," *Social History*, V (May 1980), 223–47. I have learned much from him. Brian Harrison's *Peaceable Kingdom* is immensely instructive, as always, notably "Traditions of Respectability in British Labour History," esp. 174–76. The two slim and moving volumes edited by Margaret Llewellyn Davies, *Maternity: Letters from Working Women* (1915; introduction by Linda Gordon, 1978), and *Life as We Have Known It, By Co-operative Working Women* (1931) are only too rich in troubling true stories. A sweeping compilation, William Matthews, *British Autobiographies* (1955), though helpful, is woefully incomplete. For the Puritan heritage in British autobiography, see in addition to Vincent, Owen C. Watkins, *The Puritan Experience* (1972), and John C. Morris, *Versions of the Self* (1966).

Moving beyond versions of the self, I found an ample literature (though by no means ample enough on questions of working-class and rural sexuality and love) on which to draw. Samuel Pyeatt Menefee, *Wives for Sale: An Ethnographic Study of British Popular Divorce* (1981), documents the survival of a "quaint," really cruel, lower-class custom into the nineteenth century; it provides the factual backdrop for the famous opening of Hardy's *Mayor of Casterbridge*. Anthony S. Wohl's conjectures on the impact of squalor and ill-health on the erotic relations of the working classes in *Endangered Lives: Public Health in Victorian Britain* (1983) are well-informed. See also his "Sex and the Single Room: Incest among the Victorian Working Classes," in Wohl, ed., *The Victorian Family: Structure and Stresses* (1978), 197–216. Robert Roberts, *The Classic Slum: Salford Life in the First Quarter of the Century* (1971) is itself a minor classic; candid and unsentimental and affectionate. It has been put to good use in Standish Meacham, *A Life Apart: The English Working Class 1890–1914* (1977), a dependable study that does not neglect working men's (and women's) erotic life.

The publications of England's great social investigators are simply indispensable. Charles Booth's *Life and Labour of the People in London* first appeared in one volume in 1889, eventually (1902–3) to grow to seventeen volumes; for an intelligent if concise gathering of excerpts, see Albert Fried and Richard Elman, eds., *Charles Booth's London* (1969), and Peter Keating, ed., *Into Unknown England, 1866–1913, Selections from the Social Explorers* (1976), which casts its net more widely. B. S. Rowntree, *Poverty: A Study of Town Life* (1901), is an important text. See Asa Briggs's instructive *Social Thought and Social Action: A Study of the Work of Seebohm Rowntree* (1961). See again Brian Harrison, "Finding Out How the Other Half Live: Social Research and British Government Since 1780," *Peaceable Kingdom*, 260–308.

For the historical background to nineteenth-century lower class sexuality, see some of the contributions to Paul-Gabriel Boucé, ed., *Sexuality in Eighteenth-Century Britain* (1982), and the most unfortunately titled, but exceedingly sober and informative study of the sex lives of ordinary Englishmen and women in one county between 1603 and 1660, G. R. Quaife's *Wanton Wenches and Wayward Wives: Peasants and Illicit Sex in Early Seventeenth Century England* (1979). Lawrence Stone's controversial *The Family, Sex and Marriage in England, 1500–1800* (1977) (see *Education of the Senses*, 503) is not reliable on the "lower orders"; significantly, he has eliminated this material from his abridged edition (1979). There is much material in Arthur N. Gilbert, "Buggery and the British Navy, 1700–1861," *Journal of Social History*, X (1976), 72–98.

The lives of servants are, of course, only too relevant here. See Pamela Horn, *The Rise and Fall of the Victorian Servant* (1975), and the terse comparative study by Theresa M. McBride, *The Domestic Revolution: The Modernisation of Household Service in England and France 1820–1920* (1976), which has two or three pages (not enough) on sexual exploitation. For another comparative glance, see Faye E. Dudden, *Serving Women: Household Service in Nineteenth-Century America* (1983), with precise statements on servants' (and employers') sexual conduct. See also, for historical comparisons, Cissie C. Fairchilds, *Domestic Enemies: Servants and their Masters in Old Regime France* (1984).

For that lover (and photographer) of the English working-class woman, A. J. Munby, incidentally revealing in his eccentric way about more widespread and less extravagant attitudes, there is Derek Hudson, *Munby, Man of Two Worlds: The Life and Diaries of Arthur J. Munby 1828–1910* (1972), which draws liberally on Munby's private records; and the felicitous mixture of photographs and comments, both largely taken from Munby's collections, Michael Hiley, *Victorian Working Women: Portraits from Life* (1979).

French working-class memoirs are illuminating paradoxically because they are so reticent about private life. Principal among these autobiographies are Agricol Perdiguier, *Mémoires d'un compagnon* (1914; pref. Jean Bernard, 1964); Martin Nadaud, *Léonard, maçon de la Creuse* (1895; ed. Jean-Pierre Rioux, 1976); Victorine B . . . , *Souvenirs d'une morte vivante* (1909; pref. Lucien Descaves, 1976); Norbert Truquin, *Mémoires et aventures d'un prolétaire à travers la révolution* (n.d.; intro. Paule Lejeune, 1977); Louise Michel, *Mémoires* (1886; ed. 1975). Pierre-Jakez Helias, *The Horse of Pride: Life in a Breton Village* (1975; tr. and abr. June Guicharnaud, 1978), is a moving atmospheric retrospect. Eugen Weber, *Peasants into Frenchmen: The Modernization of Rural France, 1870–1914* (1976) is an exhaustive, learned survey of rural habits; its periodization remains somewhat controversial (see Michael Burns, *Rural Society and French Politics: Boulangism and the Dreyfus Affair 1886–1900* [1984]). There are also Martine Segalen, *Love and Power in the Peasant Family: Rural France in the Nineteenth Century* (1980; tr. Sarah Matthews, 1983), which levies on folklore and takes account of regional variations; and a skillful collection of texts by Jean-Louis Flandrin, *Les Amours Paysannes (XVIe–XIXe siècle)* (1975). See also Michel Frey, "Du mariage et du concubinage dans les classes populaires à Paris (1846–1847)," *Annales*, XXXIII (July–August 1978), 803–29, a careful revisionist article. Denis Poulot, *Question Sociale. Le sublime, ou le travailleur comme it est en 1870, et ce qu'il peut être* (1870; introd. study by Alain Cottereau, 1980) has long been used as a source of working-class culture as seen by an articulate and opinionated employer. There is comparative material in Theodore Zeldin, "The Conflict of Moralities: Confession, Sin and Pleasure in the Nineteenth Century," in Zeldin, ed., *Conflicts in French Society: Anticlericalism, Education and Morals in the*

19th Century (1970), 13–50. Maurice Agulhon, *La république au village: Les populations du Var de la Révolution à la Seconde République* (1970), is a classic study of sociability.

There is an interesting nineteenth-century attempt to lend the study of comparative morality the authority of statistics: E. Bertrand, "Essai sur la moralité comparative des diverses classes de la population et principalement des classes ouvrières," *Journal de la Société de Statistique de Paris*, XIII, 10 (October 1872), 253–71, and ibid., 11 (November 1872), 281–88.

In addition to the work of Flandrin on middle-class views of the lower orders, see the informative paper by Lucien W. White, "Moral Aspects of Zola's Naturalism Judged by His Contemporaries and by Himself," *Modern Language Quarterly*, XXIII (1962), 360–72; and Guy Robert, *"La Terre" d'Emile Zola. Etude historique et critique* (1952). (I am indebted to an unpublished paper by Janet R. Potash on "Naturalism and the Morality of Literature" [1973] for both these titles). Zola's fiction is, of course, a treasure trove of information and prejudices, esp. *L'Assommoir* (1877), *Germinal* (1884), and *La Terre* (1887).

Of German autobiographies stimulated by Paul Göhre, the one now available is that by Moritz Th. W. Bromme, *Lebensgeschichte eines modernen Fabrikarbeiters* (1905; afterword by Bernd Neumann, 1971). Others (all of them revealing) include Karl Fischer, *Denkwürdigkeiten und Erinnerungen eines Arbeiters*, 2 vols. (1903–4); Wenzel Holek, *Lebensgang eines deutsch-tschechischen Handarbeiters* (1909), and Franz Rehbein, *Das Leben eines Landarbeiters* (1911). August Bebel's famous autobiography, *Aus meinem Leben*, remains very much worth reading. Important also are the *Lebenserinnerungen, 1848–1930* (1922) by the pioneering educator Helene Lange; Anon., *Aus der Gedankenwelt einer Arbeiterfrau. Von ihr selbst erzählt*, ed. C. Moszeit (1909); Adelheid Popp, *Jugendgeschichte einer Arbeiterin* (1909; 3rd. ed. 1927); and Ottilie Baader, *Ein steiniger Weg. Lebenserinnerungen* (1921). And the volumes edited by Adolf Levenstein, gathering poems, letters, essays, self-revealing comments by workers, all in 1909, are rich: *Arbeiter-Philosophen und Dichter*, and *Aus der Tiefe. Arbeiterbriefe. Beiträge zur Seelen-Analyse moderner Arbeiter* reach deep. *Proletarische Lebensläufe. Autobiographische Dokumente zur Entstehung der zweiten Kultur in Deutschland*, vol. I, *Anfänge bis 1914*, ed. Wolfgang Emmerich (1974) is a diligent and useful compilation somewhat compromised by the editor's extreme Marxist bias.

For Paul Göhre himself, see his *Drei Monate Fabrikarbeiter und Handwerksbursche* (1891), and the relevant pages in Anthony Oberschall, *Empirical Social Research in Germany, 1848–1914* (1965), esp. 28–30, 80–82. The bulky compilation by the Protestant pastor Carl Julius Immanuel Wagner, *Die geschlechtlich-sittlichen Verhältnisse der evangelischen Landbewohner im deutschen Reiche*, 2 vols. (1895–96), remains a gold mine. Cecilia A. Trunz, *Die Autobiographien von deutschen Industriearbeitern* (1934), briefly surveys the available memoir literature, terribly marred by a Nazi perspective. In a different world altogether is the brief but meaty essay by Wolfram Fischer, "Arbeitermemoiren als Quellen für Geschichte und Volkskunde der industriellen

Gesellschaft" (1958), in Fischer, *Wirtschaft und Gesellschaft im Zeitalter der Industrialisierung* (1972), 214–23. R. P. Neuman, "Industrialization and Sexual Behavior: Some Aspects of Working-Class Life in Imperial Germany," in Robert J. Bezucha, ed., *Modern European Social History* (1972), 270–98, uses the autobiographies to excellent purpose. I found Neuman's concise essay, "Working Class Birth Control in Wilhelmian Germany," *Comparative Studies in Society and History*, XX (July 1978), 408–28, equally impressive. For general studies of German memoirs, see Theodor Klaiber, *Die deutsche Selbstbiographie* (1921). For an earlier time, there is the fine social-historical work by Helmut Möller, *Die kleinbürgerliche Familie im 18. Jahrhundert. Verhalten und Gruppenkultur* (1969), a model that has unfortunately had no successors.

Statistical surveys, both old and new, have yielded eloquent illegitimacy rates. I have used in the text Othmar Spann, "Die geschlechtlich-sittlichen Verhältnisse im Dienstboten- und Arbeiterinnenstande, gemessen an der Erscheinung der unehelichen Geburten," *Zeitschrift für Sozialwissenschaft*, VII (1904), 287–303; and see Spann, *Untersuchungen über die uneheliche Bevölkerung in Frankfurt am Main* (1905), with a helpful earlier survey by Friedrich Lindner, *Die unehelichen Geburten als Sozialphänomen. Ein Beitrag zur Statistik der Bevölkerungsbewegung im Königreiche Bayern* (1900). More recently, there is John Knodel, "Law, Marriage, and Illegitimacy in Nineteenth Century Germany," *Population Studies*, XX (March 1967), 279–94. J. Michael Phayer, *Sexual Liberation and Religion in Nineteenth Century Europe* (1977), ch. 2, "Proletarian Sexuality," examines illegitimacy figures for Bavaria.

Since the aristocracy enters my text only marginally, I shall mention only a handful of titles that contributed most: Ernest K. Bramsted, *Aristocracy and the Middle-Classes in Germany: Social Types in German Literature 1830–1900* (1937; rev. ed., 1964), a pioneering attempt to apply sociological categories to literary texts, and with much to say about middle-class attitudes toward their "betters." Heinz Gollwitzer, *Die Standesherren, Die politische und gesellschaftliche Stellung der Mediatisierten, 1815–1918. Ein Beitrag zur deutschen Sozialgeschichte* (1957), is an excellent study of a much neglected segment of the German aristocracy. For England, see for the background, Randolph Trumbach, *The Rise of the Egalitarian Family: Aristocratic Kinship and Domestic Relations in 18th Century England* (1978), an intelligent essay somewhat undermined by an ill-informed critique of Freud. Among Mark Girouard's writings, *The Return to Camelot: Chivalry and the English Gentleman* (1981), has material on attitudes. See also Stella Margetson, *Victorian High Society* (1980). There are fascinating details in Kenneth Ballhatchet, *Race, Sex and Class under the Raj: Imperial Attitudes and Policies and their Critics 1793–1905* (1979).

For Guillaume Geefs, see Paul Fierens, in Paul Fierens, ed., *L'Art en Belgique du moyen age à nos jours* (1947), 420–23. In addition to Geefs's sculptures shown in *The Art-Journal Illustrated Catalogue: The Industry of All Nations* (1851), pp. 234, 288, *The Lion in Love* can be seen in *Great Exhibition of the Works of Industry of All Nations. Official Descriptive Catalogue. By Authority of the Royal Commission*, 3 vols. (1851), II, pl. 234, before p. 1167.

Finally, on bourgeois marriages happy and otherwise, see Polly Longsworth, *Austin and Mabel: The Amherst Affair and Love Letters of Austin Dickinson and Mabel Loomis Todd* (1984), an admirably annotated collection of letters that expands points I made in the introductory chapter about Mabel Todd in *Education of the Senses*. Phyllis Rose, *Parallel Lives: Five Victorian Marriages* (1984), on the Carlyles, Ruskins, Mills, Dickenses, George Eliot and George Henry Lewes is useful mainly for those who do not know these rather pathetic stories.

Illustrations and Sources

Measurements in inches, width preceding height

Norman Hirst, *Walter Bagehot*, mezzotint. From Mrs. Russell Barrington, *Life of Walter Bagehot* (1914), frontispiece.

Emilie Isabel Wilson, *Elizabeth Wilson*, sketch. From ibid., between pp. 238–39.

Dr. Otto Beneke, oil portrait. Courtesy of the Staatsarchiv der Freien und Hansestadt Hamburg.

Moritz Retzsch, *The Chess Player*, etching. Courtesy of the Staatsarchiv der Freien und Hansestadt Hamburg.

Emile-H. Meyer, untitled etching. Frontispiece for Adolphe Retté, *Paradoxe sur l'Amour* (1893).

Charles Kingsley. Courtesy of the Bettman Archive.

Fanny Grenfell Kingsley. Courtesy of Mrs. Angela Covey-Crump, Ely, England.

Charles Kingsley, drawing. Courtesy of Mrs. Angela Covey-Crump.

Charles Kingsley, drawing. Courtesy of Mrs. Angela Covey-Crump.

Charles Kingsley, drawing. Courtesy of Mrs. Angela Covey-Crump.

Mabel Barrows. Courtesy of Susanna Barrows.

The Great Social Evil. From Edna Healey, *Lady Unknown: The Life of Angela Burdett-Coutts* (1978), 81.

The Line of Beauty, in *Punch*, LXXVII (December 6, 1879), 262.

H. Lüder, *Vor der Polizei-Wache*. From Max Ring, *Die deutsche Kaiserstadt Berlin und ihre Umgebung*, 2 vols. (1883–84), II, 44.

Dante Gabriel Rossetti, *Found*, oil on canvas (36 × 31½ inches). Delaware Art Museum, Samuel and Mary R. Bancroft Collection.

Abraham Solomon, *The Lion in Love*, oil on canvas (28 × 35 inches). Exhibited 1858. From *Apollo Magazine*, IIIC (January–June 1973), 21. Courtesy Christie's.

Guillaume Geefs, *The Lion in Love*, sculpture. Exhibited 1851. From C. H. Gibbs Smith, *The Great Exhibition of 1851. A Commemorative Album* (1950; ed. 1964), 127.

ILLUSTRATIONS AND SOURCES

John Bell, *Una and the Lion*, Parian Ware (1861), from the design of 1847.
    Courtesy of the Board of Trustees of the Victoria and Albert Museum.
Guillaume Geefs, *Geneviève of Brabant*, sculpture. From *The Crystal Palace
    Exhibition: Illustrated Catalogue*, Special Issue of *The Art-Journal* (1851),
    288.
Guillaume Geefs, *The Faithful Messenger*. From ibid., 234.

Acknowledgments

This volume, like its predecessor, has depended heavily on the kindness of strangers—and on that of friends, colleagues, and students. These paragraphs are my attempt to recall them all, in gratitude.

Some of the lectureships I had acknowledged in *Education of the Senses* must be mentioned again here, since they permitted me to adumbrate ideas and try out formulations central to this volume: the Martin Rist Lectures at the Iliff School of Theology in Denver of 1977; the Christian Gauss Lectures in Criticism at Princeton University in the spring of 1979; the Ena H. Thompson Lectureship at Pomona College, which I had the honor to inaugurate in the spring of 1980; and the four Freud Lectures I gave at Yale in the fall of 1980 under the sponsorship of the Western New England Institute of Psychoanalysis and the Humanities Center of my university. To these I should add the John Teall Memorial Lecture in April 1980 at Mount Holyoke College on "Strategies of Sensuality: Aspects of Bourgeois Sexuality in the Nineteenth Century," and my lecture on Patmore and Kingsley delivered at the British Art Center at Yale later that year. More recently, in 1984, I was delighted to be the Merle Curti Lecturer at the University of Wisconsin at Madison, which gave me a rich opportunity to try out some key propositions of Chapter Three on fiction; in December 1984, I offered a compressed version of these lectures at the Humanities Center at Yale. And the month before, as the Ida Beam Lecturer at the University of Iowa, Iowa City, I summarized the thesis of this volume in a public performance. I want to note, filled with pleasant memories, that I was superbly (which is to say, hospitably, patiently, and constructively) received everywhere, and the opportunity of seeing old friends and making new ones—friends and critics!—was a more than incidental bonus of all this verbal activity. Nor can I forget that I owe a real debt (which I want particularly to record now that I have retired this course) to my Yale undergraduate students in History 229a, a course that changed with the years as my own work progressed. They were attentive, generous with their interest, and, in their own way, very helpful to me.

473

The foundations that have supported my large-scale enterprise, which I gratefully mentioned in *Education of the Senses*, played a no less conspicuous role in the making of the present book. The Research Division of the National Endowment for the Humanities bought me time, travel, and books with two immensely welcome grants stretching from 1973 to 1975, and from 1981 to 1984. The Humanities Division of the Rockefeller Foundation and the John Simon Guggenheim Memorial Foundation substantially aided my search for time and resources with their fellowship support—further enhanced by the Rockefeller Foundation's unbureaucratic readiness to match N.E.H. funds, a readiness equally displayed by the Fund for Research of the American Psychoanalytic Association, which went out on a limb to foster my historical research, really quite remote from the purely technical investigations that are its regular concern. The A. Whitney Griswold Fund at Yale helped me defray costs of typing and making Xerox copies. My thanks to all of these are anything but perfunctory; I am delighted that I can herewith discharge some of the debts I have incurred in the only way a scholar can—by producing what he had promised to produce.

I also want to acknowledge, once again, with real pleasure, the help of Yale administrators for smoothing my way. Joseph Warner and Linda Downey at the Grants and Contracts Administration took much time to guide me through the mazes of applications and budgets; as did Loueva Pflueger, cheerfully, of my own department. Howard Lamar, fellow historian and Dean of Yale College, inventively worked out a schedule that permitted me to combine teaching with research. My gratitude to Robert Balay and his talented, much harassed, under-appreciated staff of reference librarians, is unstinted. Betty Paine took a professional interest in my work, lending me books and finding quotations in addition to patiently typing my often rather illegible manuscripts; Mary Kuntz, and her predecessor Janet Gertz, both adepts in the way of the modern world, put these chapters onto the word processor with dispatch and elegance. Other local experts to whom I am indebted include Suzanna Lengyel, who volunteered important advice; Susanne Roberts of the Bibliography Department in the Sterling Library, who was supportive about what I insisted were necessary acquisitions; Teri Edelstein, then at the British Art Center, who gave much needed counsel on nineteenth-century English art; Judith Schiff, Chief Research Archivist at our Department of Manuscripts and Archives, who supplied valuable information about collections and pictures; Diane Kaplan and Bruce Stark, who discovered some wonderful diaries and letters for me; Diane Ducharme, who took time to discuss the Roe Papers with me. Gloria Locke, too, was most helpful.

It is not necessary for me to list, once again, all the archives and archivists from Oslo to Cologne, Berlin to Stanford, Munich to Oxford and Cambridge (see *Education of the Senses*, 515) who answered my letters in copious detail or guided me through their collections. I must single out, though, for the invaluable Beneke Papers, Dr. Eckardt at the Staatsarchiv of the Freie und Hansestadt Hamburg, and the librarians (especially Dr. C. J. Wright) at the British Library in London for both the Kingsley and the Wilson Papers. The Right Honourable Norman St. John-Stevas and Miss Nina Burgis (with whom I had a memorable conversation in London) were exceptionally forthcoming with the papers of Eliza Wilson Bagehot; Mrs. Angela Covey-Crump no less so with the fascinating diaries of Fanny Grenfell Kingsley, as with Charles Kingsley's drawings. The day I spent in Mrs. Covey-Crump's dining room at the cathedral town of Ely, reading, looking, and transcribing, remains in my mind as an ideal occasion—the kind of day a scholar fantasizes about and is sometimes allowed to enjoy.

When I wrote the acknowledgments for *Education of the Senses* late in 1983, I had just completed my candidacy at the Western New England Institute for Psychoanalysis; now that I have officially graduated, with my shingle as "Graduate in Research" hanging in my office, I find myself a member of the Institute. The chore of training over, my sense of obligation continues. I have expressed my gratitude on the dedication page of my *Freud for Historians* (1985) to both Drs. Richard Newman and Ernst Prelinger (who also read the manuscript). But I do not want to omit my thanks to my other instructors and fellow candidates here—they, in a very real sense, made this book possible.

It is far better than a polite commonplace to say that a book—and especially such a large one—is a conversation and a collaboration. To me, one of the pleasures of researching, thinking through, and writing books like this is the amiable and prolonged debates it generates between the author and his first audience. I am thinking particularly of friends like the psychoanalyst Martin Bergmann, who not only perused (and discussed with me) the early chapters, but also let me see his large and ambitious, not yet published, manuscript, at once history and analysis, "The Anatomy of Love"; Stefan Collini, who patiently listened to expositions of my general thesis and outlines and made candid if kindly comments on both; Richard Ellmann, who helped out both in general and in particular—notably with Oscar Wilde; Dick and Peggy Kuhns, philosopher and psychologist respectively, who gave lovingly of their time and their wisdom in innumerable discussions about fundamentals in Vermont, in New York City, and in Hamden; Jerry Meyer, with whom I naturally talked extensively about the psychoanalytic theories underlying my work; Quentin Skinner, with whom I have had the pleasure of talking serious shop for nearly twenty years, held still—but fortunately not too still—for my ideas; Wim Smit, my former colleague at Columbia University, who sent me a revealing, detailed memorandum on Lodewijk van Deyssel; Gladys Topkis of Yale University Press, who was generous with assistance in many ways; and Vann Woodward, who was, as always, there when I needed him.

Others, too, joined in this professional conversation. My former student James Albisetti, now teaching history at the University of Kentucky, supplied me with some welcome quotations; Madelon Bedell generously tried to resolve a puzzle about a poem by Louisa May Alcott; my colleague Paul Bushkovitch gave me valuable clues to Russian homosexual literature; Caroline Bynum of the University of Washington helpfully copied some hard-to-come-by material by Freud; Lady Chitty was most generous about my inquiries about her sources for her accurate and entertaining biography of Charles Kingsley; Sophie Glazer sent tidbits I could invariably use; Liliane Greene, of Yale's French department, talked about nineteenth-century French literature with me; another colleague, Bob Herbert, was just as helpful about French art;

Isabel Hull of Cornell, a fine German historian, corresponded with me about love and sexuality in nineteenth-century Germany; Jane Isay, once of the Yale University Press, saw to it that I could get, in a hurry, books I desperately needed; the psychoanalyst Dr. Mark Kanzer kindly sent me an offprint I felt under pressure to see promptly; Dr. Bernard C. Meyer, another psychoanalyst, shared an important article with me; Stephen Kern, a historian who works in areas very similar to mine, subjected my ideas to a scrutiny as searching as it was supportive; Carl Landauer, my former student, found the time, in the midst of completing his dissertation, to think, and think well, about my work; John Lauritsen clarified some obscurities in German homosexuality; Mark Micale, now working on Charcot, has been an intellectual resource in more ways than he knows; I found use in some research notes, compiled some years ago, by Debra Perry; Harry Payne shared with me a fascinating manuscript on some (just as fascinating) modern English figures; Dean Michael S. Pincus of Fairleigh Dickinson University gave me the benefit of his knowledge of modern Spanish literature; Barbara Corrado Pope generously supplied information about a French correspondence on which she is working; a paper by Janet Potash, a graduate of my department (acknowledged in the Bibliography) provided information; my colleagues George Schoolfield and Jeffrey Sammons gave expert counsel with Scandinavian and German novels; Alan Spitzer, at the University of Iowa, proved not only a splendid host, but also a fine partner in shop talk; I am grateful to James Steakley of Wisconsin for help with German homosexuality; Mary Lee Townsend was splendid on German censorship; Paul B. Wehn of Cambridge University Press supplied me with some much-needed literature; Carl D. Weiner gave information about a letter; Sister Martha Westwater wrote to me about the Wilson sisters; Sean Wilentz of Princeton University discussed *Uncle Tom's Cabin* with me when I needed it; and Anthony S. Wohl of Vassar proved not merely a most indulgent reviewer but also an informative correspondent. My research assistants Karen Bradley, Georges Magaud, Jeffrey Sturges, and Sally Tittman dug up some interesting articles.

The support of Oxford University Press continues unabated. I particularly thank Nancy Lane—more than an editor—and Rosemary Wellner, for seeing this bulky manuscript through the press with a maximum of good advice and a minimum of friction. Nor do I want to forget Sheldon Meyer, the editor who launched this whole enterprise with me, or my copy editor for the first volume, Stephanie Golden, who did far more than her share to secure the continuity of a project for which she did so much valuable work.

As with *Education of the Senses*, so now, my readers deserve particular acknowledgment. Peter Demetz (and Julie Iovine) proffered valued detailed criticisms especially on literature; John Merriman, my colleague and intimate friend (ably assisted by Carol Payne, with a good eye for nuances), went over the whole manuscript and his vigorous, always good-tempered comments, especially on social history, proved of remarkable benefit to me. My debt to Henry Gibbons and Susanna Barrows, once my students and now, I am glad to say, my friends, is enormous; he weighed every word of this manuscript, gave it the most searching reading, compelled me, fortunately, to rethink some troubling questions of psychoanalytic theory, especially, but not only, on female sexuality. Susanna supplied me with some splendid unpublished materials and illustrations. And once again I find myself Bob Webb's debtor: he took immense care with this manuscript, both as the experienced editor and superb historian he is, and made numerous suggestions from which I profited very much indeed.

And, as before, I want to give a separate paragraph to Ruth Gay, whose dislike for "and" at the beginning of a sentence is uncompromising. Her thoughtfulness and precision in the midst of pressing work of her own, often involving two or more readings of each chapter, considerably improved this book in matters of tone and substance alike. Alert as always to my need for material that is obscure and usually overlooked, she found some magnificent documents in the Yale Archives. I called her, in my earlier acknowledgment, critic, editor, researcher, and enthusiast all in one. Since I cannot improve on this formulation and since it still holds valid, I can do no better than to repeat it here.

PETER GAY

Index

482

INDEX

Duffey, Eliza B.: *What Women Should Know*, 289
Duhring, Julia, 120, 138
Dumas, Alexandre (fils), 78; on marriage, 104n; *Dame aux camélias*, 369
Durkheim, Emile, 204, 331, 338

Eastlake, Charles C., 332
Eating: eroticism, 270–71
The Economist, 19
Edison, Thomas Alva, 341
Ego: in love, 66, 93
Einheirat, 102
Electrotherapy, 341–42
Eliot, George, 196, 440; *Middlemarch*, 136, 151, 171; *Adam Bede*, 143–44, 147, 150, 285, 355n; *Daniel Deronda*, 169, 181; *The Mill on the Floss*, 179; on *Henry Esmond*, 186
Elliott, Jeannie, 291
Ellis, Edith, 243
Ellis, Havelock, 223, 243, 249–50, 262; *Studies in the Psychology of Sex*, 224; mission, 231–33; *Sexual Inversion*, 231–34; position on homosexuality, 234; on the auto-erotic in religion, 286; on religion, 287
Emerson, Ralph Waldo, 45, 152, 251, 272, 275
Engagement. 433; sexual experimentation during, 12, 306
Engels, Friedrich. *See* Marx, Karl
English fiction, 163; bloodlessness of, 159–60
Enlightenment: challenge to accept views on love, 50–52; anti-religious crusade, 51–52; work on love, 53; love in, 427
Ennui, 62
Erb, William, 337–38, 340, 348, 350
Ernest-Charles, J., 201
Eros, 56
Erotic idealization, 93–94
Eroticization, 456
Erotic residues, 259
Esquirol, Etienne, 18

Eternal love, 54, 58
Etty, William, 179n
Eulenberg, Philipp zu, 200
Euripides, 179
Experience, 96–97
Eyre, Edward, 39n

Falkenhorst, C., 336–37
Fallen woman: in literature, 463–64. *See also* Prostitutes
Family periodicals, 156–57
Family romance, 49, 463
Fantasies, 139–40; Freud on, 139, 434. *See also* Rescue fantasy
Fantasy of reparation, 380–81
Fatalism, 167
Fatal woman, 417–18, 437
Fawcett, Millicent Garrett, 107
Feminism, 417
Feminists, 107, 335; denigration of, 227; opposition to legalized prostitution, 365
Femme honnête, 69
La Femme jugée par l'Homme, 78
Fenichel, Otto, 328
Fiasco. *See* Impotence
Fiction: *Saturday Review*'s view of, 158–59. *See also* Novel
Fiedler, Conrad, 268–69
Fiedler, Mary, 268–69
Fierens, Paul: on Geefs, 414
Fischer, Kuno, 88n
Flaubert, Gustave, 142, 195–96, 271, 279–80, 363–64, 441; *Education sentimentale*, 138, 177–78; *Madame Bovary*, 162–64, 166, 174, 191; trial of, 193
Fontane, Theodor, 141, 153–54; *Effi Briest*, 143–44, 147, 156, 171, 188; *Frau Jenny Treibel*, 180, 196; *L'Adultera*, 182; "Die Brück am Tay," 320
Food: as food of love, 270
Ford, John: *'Tis Pity she's a Whore*, 179
Forster, E. M.: *Maurice*, 244n

Forster, John, 142, 187
Fourier, Charles, 96, 172
Fournier, Alfred, 381
France: marital choices in, 99–100
Fraser's Magazine, 159
Frederick III, 38
Frederick William IV, 367
French: as experts on love, 78–79
French novel, 135–36, 159–60, 193–94, 369–70, 441
Freud, Sigmund, 50, 53, 60, 89, 226, 275, 340, 444, 446–47; on sexual frustration, 11; on finding of love object, 21–22, 67; on dreams, 29; on love, 45, 90; theory of libido, 46, 54, 87, 90, 92–95; on sublimation, 52, 256–57; theories about love, 87–88, 90, 430; *Interpretation of Dreams*, 88n, 139; on Nietzsche, 88; giving credit to others, 88–89; theory of neuroses, 89n, 256, 399, 403; theory of development, 90–93; on role of memory in love, 91–92; on sexual drives, 256; on fantasies, 139, 434; on Oedipus complex, 139; on writer, 139; on oedipal triangle, 178; on poets' and novelists' empathy, 184; on repression, 221; on Ellis, 249–50; on masculine and feminine, 250–51; on sexual impulses, 250–51; on homosexuality, 250 52; bisexuality theory, 251, 447; *Three Essays on the Theory of Sexuality*, 253, 323; on treatment of homosexuals as criminals or madmen, 253; on abstinence, 258; on railroad travel, 323; " 'Civilized' Sexual Morality and Modern Nervous Illness," 349–50; on civilized sexual morality, 350–52; linkage of nervousness and sexual frustration, 350–